# MANAGEMENT ACCOUNTING

### R.C. SEKHAR

*Former Professor Emeritus*
*T A Pai Management Institute (TAPMI)*
*Manipal*

### A.V. RAJAGOPALAN

*Adjunct Professor (Research)*
*T A Pai Management Institute (TAPMI)*
*Manipal*

# OXFORD

## UNIVERSITY PRESS

**OXFORD**
UNIVERSITY PRESS

Oxford University Press is a department of the University of Oxford.
It furthers the University's objective of excellence in research, scholarship,
and education by publishing worldwide. Oxford is a registered trademark of
Oxford University Press in the UK and in certain other countries.

Published in India by
Oxford University Press
YMCA Library Building, 1 Jai Singh Road, New Delhi 110001, India

First published in 2013
Second impression 2015

ISBN-13: 978-0-19-568360-8
ISBN-10: 0-19-568360-9

Typeset in Baskerville
by Innovative Processors, New Delhi 110 002
Printed in India by Manipal Technologies Ltd., Karnataka 576104

# Preface

Globalization has opened up a number of avenues and opportunities for business communities the world over. They have progressed both in terms of size and complexity in the last two decades. This transformation has placed a premium on the competencies of management at all levels. In this context, management accounting has become a strategic tool to enable managers to address the core functions of organizations, namely planning, decision-making, and control.

This field of study is built upon the basic edifice of financial accounting. It also includes the discipline of cost accounting. Further, it draws on inputs from the technical and other activities of business organizations and has over the years assumed a multi-disciplinary flavour. Engineering and commercial divisions of organizations are increasingly engaged in managerial accounting exercises alongside the finance wing.

Cost and managerial accounting principles find wide application in the manufacturing and service sectors as well as not-for-profit and government entities. Its need is felt in a wide range of organizations—big and small—and is extensively used in non-governemnt organizations (NGOs), project management teams, consultancies, defence establishments, and other diverse sectors, such as education, health, and agriculture. The growth of multinational companies (MNCs) has given rise to the need for uniform methods of cost presentation and controls. The strides made by the profession gave birth to a plethora of newer methods, such as activity-based costing (ABC), target costing, and balanced scorecard.

Acknowledging the role of cost and management accounting in the commercial and non-commercial sectors, various countries—both in the developed and developing worlds—have established dedicated institutions, often supported by a separate legislation to nurture the managerial accounting profession. Two of these institutions are the Chartered Institute of Management Accountants (CIMA), UK, and the Institute of Management Accountants (IMA), USA. In India, the Institute of Cost and Works Accountants of India (ICWAI) was established in 1959 by an Act of Parliament with a network of Regional Councils and Chapters.

These institutions are professional bodies undertaking specific research in this topic, networking with similar bodies both nationally and internationally, and also conducting regular courses to train people in this field. These institutions have also come out with cost accounting standards. Besides, researches in these areas are regularly conducted by universities and business schools; and important articles come out at regular intervals. This has become, in short, a significant field for both active field research and professional development.

## About the Book

The utility of the knowledge of management accounting has become so widely acknowledged, that it has been prescribed as a separate topic in the curricula of several universities as also business schools. Besides, all executive management courses have incorporated it as a prescribed course in their syllabi. The readers are required to understand the basics of the subject as well as its applications. In order to facilitate this process, this book contains detailed discussions of concepts supported by chapter-end exercises. In addition, suitable real-life examples are given at appropriate places to highlight the relevance of the concepts discussed. The book includes unique concepts, such as balanced scorecards, e-budgeting, cost audit, and cost accounting standards. Another value addition is the discussion on the statistical tools to capture costs. These are topics of considerable relevance to both students and practitioners. An additional feature of this book is the introduction of mathematical approaches in appropriate chapters.

The case-study method as a part of the pedagogy has gained momentum in recent years. This approach has the advantage of providing situations for the readers to recall the various concepts learnt and apply them in demanding real-life situations. Keeping this in view, the book contains case studies with discussion questions at the end of the chapters. Readers may have to apply more than one tool or technique to solve these cases, which often do not have one single right answer. Students will find this approach quite helpful in imbibing the concepts discussed in the book.

## Content and Structure

The book is divided into five parts comprising 16 chapters and 4 appendices.

The contributions of Prof. Sekhar are responsible for the first three parts. His active interest in mathematics and quantitative techniques has given a new dimension to this volume. Prof. Rajagopalan's contribution is mainly the last part and addition of chapter-end questions for some of the initial chapters.

Part I deals with *Management Accounting Fundamentals*. It consists of Chapters 1, 2, and 3. Chapter 1 provides an introduction to management accounting. The various roles of accountants are explained vis-à-vis the accounting systems. This chapter also discusses management accounting in developing countries, and the moral and ethical imperatives of accountants along with the applicable statutory controls.

Chapter 2 provides a broad view of financial accounting, the accounting conventions, and the financial statements. This chapter also covers the books of accounts, preparation of financial statements using ratio analysis, and the accounting standards. The concepts of internal audit and internal control are also explained. Chapter 3 describes various cost-related topics, such as cost objects, responsibility centres, cost behaviour, and the role of cost drivers. This chapter introduces direct and indirect costs, unit cost, and other types of costs.

Part II discusses the *Tools for Management Accounting* in Chapters 4–10. Chapter 4 deals with cost-volume-profit (CVP) analysis and highlights the concept of contribution. This chapter explains the various types of break-even analysis and the related principles of operating leverage, margin of safety, and the roles of fixed costs and variable costs. Chapter 5 deals with the various types of costing systems, namely job, process, unit, and hybrid.

Chapter 6 deals with the emerging concept of activity-based costing (ABC). This system provides for better allocation of the overheads and is acknowledged as an efficient tool for cost control and cost reduction. Chapter 7 focuses on responsibility accounting and budgeting and explains it in the context of behaviour and strategy.

Chapter 8 discusses standard costing and the related variances. Chapter 9 is devoted to competitive benchmarking. Chapter 10 deals with the different costs for inventory valuation, and also explains various tools and enhancements, such as EOQ, JIT, and back flush costing.

The managerial applications find place in Part III titled *Management Accounting for Decision-making*, which contains Chapters 11–14. Chapter 11 travels into the realms of decision-making and discusses the costs that are relevant for different situations.

Chapter 12 captures the complex behaviour of costs and the use of statistical tools to predict costs. Chapter 13 discusses the important area of pricing under complex situations. Chapter 14 is devoted to the more esoteric arena of managerial ethics and the behavioural issues closely associated with conflict management and employee morale.

Part IV titled *Management Control Systems* comprises Chapters 15 and 16. This part deals with certain emerging areas that enhance the value of this textbook. Chapter 15 takes a holistic look into the management control systems practised in organizations. It touches upon the levers of controls and the impact of various types of control measures. Chapter 16 discusses the relatively modern concept of balanced scorecard and its role as an effective tool for performance measurement.

Appendices 1–4 in Part V provide a brief overview of certain issues in management accounting, which have become important in the current context, such as e-budgeting, cost audit, cost accounting standards (CAS), and costing in government and not-for-profit organizations (NPOs).

Readers are welcome to send feedback and suggestions for further improvement.

**R.C. Sekhar**

**A.V. Rajagopalan**

# Acknowledgements

The book was commenced by Prof. R.C. Sekhar, who was an esteemed faculty of the TA Pai Management Institute (TAPMI). Halfway through the writing of this book, Prof. Sekhar met with an unfortunate accident, which reduced his ability to carry on with his work. On the advice of well-wishers and fellow faculty members of TAPMI, I took over the completion of the balance work. The academic world owes a great deal to Prof. Sekhar, who was an erudite scholar, a prolific reader, and a multi-faceted personality with a great sense of humour. This book is a tribute to that great man. Thanks are also due to his wife Mrs Bhavani Sekhar and son Dr Raghuram Sekhar, who graciously consented to the continuation of the book. Unfortunately, Prof. Sekhar passed away sometime back.

My association with this book is due to the opportunity given to me by the faculty members of TAPMI, Manipal. I owe a deep sense of gratitude to all my colleagues. My love for the profession was ignited through my association with the organizations I served in India and abroad, such as Coal India Ltd, Maruti Udyog Ltd, National Dairy Development Board (NDDB), Gujarat Cooperative Milk Marketing Federation Ltd (GCMMF), Kaduna State Agricultural Development Project (KADP), Nigeria, Tanzania Distilleries Ltd (TDL), Tanzania, and the Ministry of Finance and Economic Planning, Botswana.

I learnt a lot about the subject and my own limitations through teaching in various institutions, such as TAPMI, Bharathidasan Institute of Management (BIM), ICWAI, Institute of Rural Management Anand (IRMA), Sri Chandrasekharendra Saraswathi Viswa Mahavidyalaya University (SCSVMV), Kancheepuram, TS Narayanaswami College of Arts and Sciences, Institute of Finance Management (Dar-Es-Salaam), and Oakland University, Michigan State, USA.

With much pleasure I recollect the support given by esteemed Prof. Jaisankaran of BIM, Bengaluru, who introduced me into the field of academia. I owe special thanks to Mr Balakrishnan, President and Company Secretary of India Cements Ltd, who is a remarkable catalyst for all my efforts.

I owe a great deal to the inspiration given by the members and staff of ICWAI. I recollect with pleasure my association with Mr M. Gopalakrishnan, currently the President of ICWAI, who has contributed a great deal to the profession. I also developed a great rapport with Mr A.N. Raman, Chairman of the Research and Journal Committee of ICWAI. He is a highly respected name in the accounting world for his pioneering contributions in the fields of ABC analysis and balanced scorecard techniques.

I would like to gratefully acknowledge the inspiration that I got from my family, where writing is an inborn trait. My eldest brother Mr Sugavaneswaran has authored several books on Indian philosophy. The next in order, Mr Subramanian's forte is literature and he has contributed several original works for which he was awarded the Sahitya Academy Award in 2009. My sisters Gowri and Lakshmi have been prolific writers and translators. My distinguished family has produced more than two hundred books and the count is still going on .... It is my proud privilege to bow to them with respect and awe. They provoked me to write and write and never give up writing. (Apparently I have a distinct genetic advantage!)

The one person whom I should thank with utmost sincerity is my wife Padmalatha, who had put up with my idiosyncrasies and unpredictable moods, and stood by my side during really difficult periods of my life. Her assistance in writing this book is invaluable. My children Aravind and Aparna, in a sharp reversal of roles, supported and applauded my academic adventures, much more than what I ever did to them. In simple terms, this book is here because of them.

I gratefully acknowledge the secretarial help provided by Ms Shantha Nayak and Ms Shruthi. My research assistant Ms Swapna Hegde was of invaluable help in completing the book. The entire staff of TAPMI with their willing cooperation need special mention. I also want to thank former Directors of TAPMI, Dr Nagabhramam, Dr Saji Gopinath, and Dr A.S. Vasudev Rao, for their profound commitment to research and publication. The current Director, Dr R.C. Natarajan, needs special mention for his encouragement.

I would also like to thank Ms Kamaldeep Kaur, who provided some additional examples to bring out the practical aspects of the subject.

My sincere thanks are due to the editors of Oxford University Press for their active support and perseverance.

There is an intellectual aura about Manipal—reasonably remote, yet not cut off from normal amenities. It has a poetic atmosphere, which promotes the deeper urge for self-actualization. I humbly bow to the eternal nature that embraces this modest seat of learning, with serenity and whispered rhapsodies.

Finally, I bow to the Almighty for converting this dream into reality.

**A.V. Rajagopalan**

# Features of the Book

**Tensions of accountants**

Accountants report to accountees on the transactions of accounters, which may cause tension. Professional councils help to lay down codes which reduce tension.

accounting would cove and benefits.

In all these roles, of privacy and loyalty public good on the othe contemplate on reveali beleaguer accountants. support of their profess

**Sidebars**

Every chapter contains several sidebars that summarize the key concepts, which will help you in recapitulating the ideas.

**Solved Examples**

Numerous solved examples provided in every chapter will help you understand the applications of various accounting concepts.

**Example 4.3** BEP of the Fruit Stall

Let us calculate the break-even point both in quantity ($Q_{bep}$) and sale value (Sales$_{bep}$) for the data given in Example 4.1 and 4.2.

$Q_{bep}$ for a month $= 1000 \div 5 = 200$
Sales$_{bep}$ for a month $= 1000 \div (5 \div 20) = ₹4000$

$$\underset{\text{cost}}{\text{Fixed}} \quad \underset{\text{margin}}{\text{Contribution}}$$

We can check that Sales$_{bep}$=$Q_{bep} \times$ Price (20)

**Exhibit 2.1** The myth of cash accounting

Darbara Singh felt that he could try nothing more sophisticated than keeping a cash book faithfully. He bought goods worth ₹2,00,000 on credit but sold the entire goods on a cash basis for ₹1,80,000. At the end of this period he had in hand ₹1,80,000 and was quite happy with his performance. If he had followed accrual accounting, he would have known that he had actually lost ₹20,000 as sales would show ₹1,80,000 and purchases ₹2,00,000.

**Exhibits**

Several interesting mini-cases are provided throughout the book, which will help to illustrate important concepts discussed in the chapter.

## Concept Review Questions

Review questions are provided at the end of every chapter to gauge your understanding of the concepts.

## Numerical Problems

A number of numerical problems are provided in the chapters to aid managerial decision-making.

## Projects

Every chapter contains student activities which will give you a hands-on experience of how management accounting works in the real world.

## Case Studies

Several case studies with discussion questions are provided in every chapter to understand managerial decision-making under various circumstances.

# Brief Contents

# Detailed Contents

## PART I: MANAGEMENT ACCOUNTING FUNDAMENTALS

## PART II: Tools for Management Accounting

## PART IV: MANAGEMENT CONTROL SYSTEMS

# PART I

## Management Accounting Fundamentals

1. Introduction to Managerial Accounting
2. Financial Accounting and Financial Statement Analysis
3. Terminology of Costing

# Introduction to Managerial Accounting

## INTRODUCTION

In this chapter we shall explore the broad concepts of managerial accounting. The chapter is aimed at enabling persons from a non-financial background to look at accountants as their friends and helpers in achieving the strategic goals of the organization with the least cost and effort. The tag of 'management' is added on to 'accounting' in order to emphasize the role of accountants in the current times of being handmaids to managers.

Notwithstanding the rich spectrum of information which accounting systems have to offer to management, the extent of alienation of accounting from management in some quarters became starkly evident when Bernie Ebbers, the Chairman of WorldCom, one of the biggest companies of the world, pleaded ignorance of the mystique of accounting when accused of signing a blatantly fraudulent balance sheet, which brought on him a savage punishment of twenty five years of imprisonment.

Accounting can help in a wide range of activities—in micro-level management, providing signals in the marketplace for those who have to choose a place for their funds, and in public policy decision-making. There is an inadequate understanding of the potential of accounting in many parts of the world, including the United States of America where massive investments in maintaining accounting systems have co-existed with a poor use of the information available in these systems (Krumviede 2005). This chapter is an attempt to improve matters. In this chapter we shall also discuss how both financial and cost accounting are increasingly being used in managerial decisions, and the need for managers and accountants to work together in a relationship of mutual trust. Because of the extent of trust bestowed on accountants for managerial decisions, they need to strive to improve their competence, techniques, and professional ethical standards.

## USERS OF ACCOUNTING SYSTEMS AND ACCOUNTING INFORMATION

The power of management accounting lies in its usefulness for a wide spectrum of stakeholders, as follows:

1. Owners, be they sole proprietors, partners, shareholders in private limited companies or public limited companies, can evaluate their managers. In public limited companies, they have the option of selling off their shares if they feel that things are going the wrong way.
2. Owners as the primary stakeholders get the information to improve corporate governance.
3. Managers make use of accounting information, which keeps them forewarned about their performance and enables them to take mid-course corrective measures and answer the owners.
4. Creditors get information which acts as a window to enable them to regulate their relationship with the organization. The law has gone to great lengths to prescribe the type of accounting information which would help them.
5. Potential investors have no means to take an a priori decision about an organization without the aid of credible information provided by the accounting system. Accounting standards developed all over the world, often supported by law, have held that the survival of capitalism is critically dependent upon trustworthy accounting systems.

The credibility of any information provided by a management accountant is dependent not only on the honesty and integrity of the accountant who is giving it, but also the accounting system that is in his/her command. These systems could be described as institutions that go towards building the social capital of a nation.

## ROLES OF AN ACCOUNTANT

An accountant has several roles in an organization. Let us discuss some of these roles in detail.

### Accountants as Attention Directors, Problem Solvers, and Scorekeepers

**Three roles of accountants**
Problem-solving, scorekeeping, and attention drawing are the three roles of accountants.

The work of accountants is beset with inherent tensions and conflicts because of the several roles played by them. There could be high stakes for a breach of trust. According to Horngren et al. (2003), organizations expect an accountant to be a problem solver, scorekeeper, and attention director.

Problem-solving skills would involve the framing of models for capturing the relevant issues and the use of accounting data analysis to help the management to solve the problems. Typically, if one had to choose between A and B—alternative investments—an accountant would estimate the related alternative streams of cash flows along with their probability of variations, and suggest which would be better for a given level of risk. To be a scorekeeper is to be the custodian of numbers indicating performance levels against benchmarks available in targeted plans. Thus, an accountant may draw up a variance analysis between budgeted profits and actual profits, analysing the reason for the variance, be it sales price, sales quantity, raw material usage and raw material prices, machine availability, or labour productivity. The attention director's role is to draw the attention of the management to the emerging trends in data, which may need attention for mid-term correction if the strategies have to be achieved. Thus, an accountant may point out that the sales returns are increasing and may affect future sales and profitability, or that delays in designing a new product could affect its markets and costs.

These three roles are inherent in staff functions in several functional disciplines, but they assume more importance in the case of accountants as they have reliable independent data with them that, in one way or the other, are usually also checked and authenticated by external authorities. These well-known functions of accountants have been fitted into a sophisticated sociological framework by Yuri Ijiri (Horngren et al. 2003). His framework also shows the sources of tension for accountants in the real world of organizations.

## Ijiri's Accountee–Accounter–Accountant Model

The accountant, according to Ijiri, has two types of roles in organizations, one as the supplier of information for decision-making and a second for performance evaluation and accountability. He/she gives information to the manager within the organization, as also do different stakeholders, such as employees, shareholders, and creditors. Based on this information they have to take their own decisions. Ethical equity and fairness can be ensured in only that there is no asymmetry of information, and the same information is available to everyone correctly and fully. The accountant's role in this is critical and ethically invaluable.

In the accountability model, which is distinctly different from the information supplier model, the accountant's role is to provide information on the working of the accounter, who is accountable to the accountee. The terms *accounter* and *accountee* were coined by Ijiri. The accounter is the agent of the accountee, who is the principal. If we reflect on the basic concepts of the law of contract, the accountee may want information even if it is uncomfortable for the accounter. The accountant should function as a scorekeeper for the accountee. The accounter, on the other hand, would want to reveal as little information as possible that may reflect poorly on him/her. Control theory would show that such consequent tension can be ameliorated by trust and could be optimally balanced if some privacy and autonomy is given to the accounter, but not such total autonomy that the system may spin out of control due to what is known as 'opportunistic behaviour' on the part of the accounter.

The role of an accountant does not end with this negative connotation. He/she can also be a problem-solver for the accounter rather than being just a scorekeeper for the accountee. When the accountee is society at large and the accounter is the organization as a whole, the scope of accounting would cover social accounting, including environmental costs and benefits.

In all these roles, there could arise a conflict of interests between ethics of privacy and loyalty on the one hand and ethics of public disclosure and public good on the other. Caught in the crossfire, accountants may have to contemplate on revealing the whole truth. Power struggles could sometimes beleaguer accountants. In this difficult task, accountants have the peer support of their professional councils.

**Tensions of accountants**
Accountants report to accountees on the transactions of accounters, which may cause tension. Professional councils help to lay down codes which reduce tension.

In India, we have councils like the Institute of Chartered Accountants of India (ICAI) and the Institute of Cost and Works Accountants of India (ICWAI). Similar professional councils exist in other countries of the world. Due to historical reasons, Indian institutions have greater fraternal association with the Anglo-Saxon institutions, namely those in the British Commonwealth and the United States of America. These councils have built codes of conduct which attempt to protect accountants, accounters, and accountees from the adverse effects of the conflict of ethics.

A brief description of the codes is given in Annexure 1.1. The case studies at the end of the chapter have some examples of ethical dilemmas of accountants. We shall deal with these issues in greater detail later in the chapter.

## PACIOLI'S DOUBLE-ENTRY BOOKKEEPING AND ACCOUNTING SYSTEMS

**Pacioli's double entry bookkeeping**
It is one of the greatest inventions of mankind—what we owe will always be equal to what we own and every change in what we owe or own will have a dual effect of changing what we owe and own.

The skills and techniques possessed by present-day accountants are the proud heritage of over three thousand years. Indian practices were ingenious and were often regulated by the state (Sekhar 2002). One of the most brilliant inventions of the world was the system of double-entry bookkeeping described by Luca Pacioli, a product of the Renaissance in 15$^{th}$ century Italy (Tinius and White 1990). Computerization has not rendered this basic system suggested by Pacioli obsolete, as it is ideally fitted to the managerial needs of business units involved in economic activity.

We shall now describe the essence of this system and discuss how it supports the entire gamut of financial accounting, cost accounting, and management accounting. We shall deal with the detailed documentation required for this and the important signals available from one of the standard outputs of accounting systems, namely, the balance sheet, in Chapter 2.

Double-entry booking is built on the conception that every transaction in an organization would result in the increase or decrease in what it owns or what it owes, with an equivalent and corresponding increase or decrease in what it owes or what it owns. This duality will ensure that what is owed is equal to what it owns. The reader may note that we have not used the words 'debit' or 'credit', which are, to many, the soul of accounting. They are not. The words 'debit' and 'credit' are, at best, shorthand descriptions that, for the present, we are relegating to technical texts to keep our minds clear of jargon.

The essence of double-entry bookkeeping could be illustrated as follows:

The owner brings in cash of ₹1000 to the organization. What it owes to the owner is increased by ₹1000 and what it owns in cash is increased by ₹1000. Note that in this process we have established what is known as the 'entity' concept in accounting. The entity is different from the owner. The organization buys in cash material worth ₹500 and uses it in production. What it owns in cash is reduced by ₹500 and what it owns in terms of product value increases by ₹500. The organization employs labour and pays ₹500 in cash. What it owns in cash is further reduced by ₹500 and what the organization owns in terms of the value of the cost of production increases by ₹500. The value stands now at a figure of ₹1000 (material consumed ₹500 + labour ₹500). This underlines the money and cost concept of valuation in the balance sheet. The organization sells the product for cash of ₹1500. What it owns in value of product decreases by ₹1000 but what it owns in cash increases by ₹1500. At this stage what it owns (₹1500) in cash is more than what it owes to the owner (₹1000). This is profit which the organization owes as dividend to the owner. This again re-emphasizes the property rights and legal relationship between the owner and the entity.

Thus, when the balance sheet is made on that day of what the organization owns and owes, it will show cash of ₹1500 as 'owned', ₹1000 as 'owed' to the owner as the initial investment, and ₹500 as 'owed' to the owner as dividend. The organization is obliged by the structure of property rights in that it will have to pay the profits to the owner or re-invest it in business as if it has been paid by the owner again.

The cash owned is known as an asset and what the organization owes is known as liability. It may be summarized that in a balance sheet, assets always equal liability, and therefore, a balance sheet balances.

**Why balance sheet balances**
Since every transaction of increase or decrease of what we own and owe reduces or increases what we own or owe correspondingly, and if in the net what we own is more than what we owe, the difference is profit and is owed to the owner. Reverse is the case if what we owe is more than what we own.

It may be noted that the accounts aggregate only transactions which change what we own and what we owe under different categories. Thus, Pacioli's great invention has enabled the easy emergence of the balance sheet at the end of a series of transactions. This method is also used by modern computers to aggregate the consequences of a series of discrete transactions. We have also found that the cost of production is also a byproduct of the process.

If, at an intermediary stage, the cost of production is too high with respect to quantities produced or if the total production is good but the percentage of good quality units is questionable, the organization will typically get a signal from the management accountant. This process may require edifice documentation and procedures, which is cost-effective and avoids drudgery. These will be described in Chapter 2.

## ESSENCE OF FINANCIAL ACCOUNTING

In the previous section we discussed how Pacioli's double-entry bookkeeping is the fountainhead of all accounting. Let us now understand that part of accounting which is labelled as *financial accounting*. The most important output of the system of financial accounting is the *balance sheet* and *profit and loss account* to be made available to the stakeholders, the main ones being the owners and shareholders.

In a somewhat simplified understanding, financial accounting deals with all the processes which enable the organization to present to external stakeholders of an organization, the balance sheet on specified dates and an exploratory statement of changes in the balance sheet from the previous date to the next. The latter is basically the profit and loss account, which shows the profit or loss generated in the intermediate period; as explained earlier, this shows the accretion or decrement of what the organization owes to the owner.

**True and fair balance sheet**
The primary concern of financial accounting is making sure the balance sheet is true and fair.

How much detail should be provided in the balance sheet and the profit and loss account and what is the criterion for a true and fair view of the organization? In deciding this, the law takes into account a balance between privacy and autonomy of the organization and the need for public disclosures in sufficient detail so that stakeholders would be enabled to make their choices; vendors, to sell goods to them; shareholders, to invest or divest; and depositors and lenders, to give deposits or lend to the organization. These are governed by various enactments. The primary law is the Companies Acts of different countries. In addition to the company law, councils of professional accountants have evolved a set of norms which balance the need for privacy and public disclosure. These laws may generally follow a similar pattern, but could be different in significant ways. Thus, the generally accepted accounting principles (GAAP) of the US requires segment profits to be disclosed, whereas the Indian accounting standards (AS) till recently did not require this (http://www.icai.org). Even now only companies listed in the stock exchange, banks, financial institutions, insurance companies, industrial concerns whose turnover is over ₹50 crore, and commercial concerns with more than ₹10 crore have to show the segment information.

**Judgement estimates**
Financial accounts are not only factual but also use judgemental estimates, the basis for which must be disclosed. These could turn out to be cover-ups for frauds as in the cases of Enron and WorldCom.

The true and fair view of the balance sheet is not merely an accurate aggregation of the transactions of the organization. It also involves considerable exercise in judgement, which goes much beyond a mere observation of facts. How much of the monies that the organization owns in the form of dues from others is truly recoverable? When do we recognize a sale? Should it be only after cash is received for the sale or when the goods are handed over to the purchaser, as required in the contract? How to value the closing stocks? Are they saleable, and, if so, at what prices? Is our estimation of what we owe correct? Are the claims of others on you justified? When does an amount become payable to the outside claimant? These involve some judgement on the part of the accountant as well as the accounter (these terms have been defined earlier in the chapter). In all these issues, explicit disclosure is an important consideration. The legal pronouncements and norms of professional bodies also provide guidelines on how to take a fair decision. However, because of the existence of many subjective features and grey areas in accounting, great scams and frauds were perpetrated by global giants such as Enron and WorldCom, in which big audit firms such as Arthur Anderson were also said to be involved.

Financial accounts are audited by accountants whose qualifications are prescribed in law. In India, they are usually chartered accountants who are qualified under the certifying procedure of the Institute of Chartered Accountants of India (ICAI)—a body constituted under an Act of the parliament. Every country has similar arrangements. This entire scheme of making a balance sheet and profit and loss account to provide a true and fair picture of an organization is often considered, rightly or wrongly, as the crucial engine of the capitalist system of free markets, and a primary prerequisite for development (May and Sundem 1995).

## COST ACCOUNTING

**Use of resource in process and products**
The main focus in cost accounting is the measurement of used resources in products and services. It is a handmaid to financial accounts in inventory valuation.

If financial accounting is focused on the production of a true and fair balance sheet, *cost accounting* focuses on the use of resources of an organization in its products and services. Its strength is enhanced in its being reconcilable with the financial accounts. Its credibility is established in this process. Since no balance sheet can be prepared without valuing inventories, cost accounting is essential for this process. In fact, the earliest costing exercises in this century were more generally addressed to this issue (Todman 1922). Later in the 1930s and 40s, cost accounting was important for defence purchases as they bought from monopoly producers and prices had to be negotiated.

**Costing in defence**
Mohammed Shoaib of the Indian Defence Accounts Service is the father of Indian costing. He used it for the costing of defence purchases.

One of the founders of Indian costing was Muhammed Shoaib, a brilliant officer of the Indian Defence Accounts Service (IDAS), who later became the finance minister of Pakistan. Pakistan issued a stamp in June 2000 to honour his role in the costing movement. Cost accounting analysis was used in the fixation of the scale of reimbursements in medical insurance. Public pricing policies rely on cost analysis. We shall use several examples in later chapters showing these applications of cost accounting. Table 1.1 points out the differences between financial, management, and cost accounting.

**Table 1.1** Difference between financial accounting, management accounting, and cost accounting

| Financial accounting | Management accounting | Cost accounting |
|---|---|---|
| Reports to those outside the organization—owners, lenders, tax authorities, and regulators. | Reports to those inside the organization for planning, directing and motivating, controlling, and performance evaluation. | Reports to those inside the organization and regulatory authorities. |
| Emphasis is on summaries of financial consequences of past activities. | Emphasis is on decisions affecting the future. | Emphasis is on product costing and activity-based costing. |
| Objectivity and verifiability of data are emphasized. | Relevance of items relating to decision-making is emphasized. | Assists in formulation and execution of budgets and standards. |
| Precision of information is required. | Timeliness of information is required. | To be defined according to purpose. |
| Only summarized data for the entire organization is prepared. | Detailed segment reports about departments, products, customers, and employees are prepared. | Emphasis on profit or loss of each product, job, service, or division. |
| Must follow Generally Accepted Accounting Principles (GAAP). | Need not follow Generally Accepted Accounting Principles (GAAP). | Follows rules set by the Cost Accounting Standards Board (CASB). |
| Mandatory for external reports. | Not mandatory. | Not mandatory. |

## COST AUDIT REGULATIONS IN INDIA

**Statutory cost audit in India**
Unique in India are the powers of Central Government to prescribe cost accounting procedures and audit by cost accountants. Forty seven industries are currently in the list.

Innumerable examples of the use of cost accounting data for external applications can be provided. The most important of these is a very unique piece of legislation in the Indian Companies Act (Section 233 B and Section 209), which empowers the Central Government to prescribe the cost accounting record rules for industries which are of public importance. Cost accountants could be appointed to examine them and give them a report. Forty-seven industries are now included in this list. They have been listed in Annexure 1.2.

The industries in this list could be typically of the following types:

1. Products which are of wide consumption and their prices hit hard on the standard of living of vulnerable sections of the population.
2. Products in which there are dominant producers who may tend to have exploitative prices.
3. Products which have a criticality in ensuring the development of certain sections of the population, say, rural populations.
4. Products whose production is regulated by the government and it may be important that those who have been permitted to produce do not misuse the favours given to them.

The list has been conditioned by the prevalent public policy postures. Since the postures have been shifting, we still have the residuals of the obsolete policies left in the listing. India is now veering more towards freer markets and less of government interference in industry and this necessitates the de-listing of certain industries. Threatened by the possibility of public cost audit, some of these industries have often attempted to get their products de-listed. This game of power politics shows the strategic importance of this legislation and the deference required from the related managers to the social purposes of cost accounting in India.

### Public Regulations to Control Cost Accountants

The scope of cost accounting in problem-solving, scorekeeping, and attention drawing in organizations is wide and all pervasive. Notwithstanding the wide-ranging applications described earlier in the discussion of the external uses of cost accounting, the greater power of cost accounting is in this internal role. Just as the ICAI certifies chartered accountants, the ICWAI is the professional council having the powers for certifying the professional competence of cost accountants. Most other countries of the world have similar professional bodies to regulate the work of cost accountants such as the Institute of Management Accountants (IMA) of the US.

# MANAGEMENT ACCOUNTING

**Management accounting**
It integrates financial and non-financial data to help in all-round improvement of performance and achievement of strategic goals.

On tracing the history of financial accounting and cost accounting, we would notice that the scope of these subjects would seamlessly and imperceptibly move towards their greater use in managerial non-financial decisions. All such decisions would surely have financial repercussions in the long run. However, these will not be obvious in the short term.

Thus, using correlated training costs and effectiveness, customer servicing time and customer satisfaction, customer sales and customer profitability is a typical application of management accounting. As the Institute of Management Accounting of the US defines it, management accounting is *a value adding continuous process of planning, designing, measuring, and operating both non-financial information systems and financial information systems that guides management action, motivates behaviour, and supports and creates the cultural values necessary to achieve an organization's strategic, tactical, and operating objectives.*

Let us now consider two examples of extensions, one from financial accounting and the other from cost accounting, which show their transitions to management accounting (Examples 1.1 and 1.2).

**Tools to aid management accountants**
Budgeting, balanced scorecards, standard costing variance analysis, cash flow analysis, and so on are the tools to help management accountants.

The examples discussed indicate how much accountants use budgeting and capital investment appraisals in conjunction with report cards for helping the management to achieve strategic objectives. These report cards are known as *balanced scorecards*. The jurisdiction of accountants extend across the value chain of the organization, as shown in Fig. 1.1.

In every one of these segments of the value chain, management accountants help in identifying the key controllable factors and success factors, cost and efficiency, quality, time management, innovation, and benchmarking. They use standard costing and variance analysis to help the management to correct themselves for achieving operational and strategic targets. These functions are briefly described as under:

*Research and Development*: Keeping a tag on the project cost and achievement of milestones, warning of the likelihood of future excess over project cost based on PERT cost analysis, choice of projects based on likely internal rate of return.

## Example 1.1 Rashmi Detergents

The published financial results of three detergent companies were studied by Raghu, the financial accountant of Rashmi Detergents, and he found that as against debtor to sales showing 1 to 1.2 months of sales in all other companies, Rashmi Detergents had four months. Raghu drew the attention of the management to this gap between Rashmi Detergents' data and the industry norm. Rashmi Detergents decided that it would bring it down to the industry average. This was built into the month's budget. This can be labelled as planning. Raghu ensured that the invoices were promptly raised on the customers. He also checked the daily balance of customer outstanding and sent reminders to the customers who were exceeding the permitted credit period, now of one month. This activity can be labelled as scorekeeping. When Raghu spoke to a few employees of Rashmi Detergents, he came to know that in many cases, the packaging got broken in transit and the sale was returned. This was a problem that resulted in large outstanding debts. He solved the problem by suggesting inspection before secondary packing. This activity can be labelled as problem solving. The entire exercise can be presented as in Table 1.2.

**Table 1.2** Management control from financial accounts at Rashmi Detergents

| Observation/Setting up system | Action |
|---|---|
| Attention drawn to high debtor balance (industry average of 1–1.2 months sales) | Budgeting and planning for bringing down to one month balance (planning) |
| Set up documents to watch debtor balance – scorekeeping system against budget | Prompt invoicing and reminders for debtors exceeding credit limit (scorekeeping) |
| Ascertaining that the delay in payment is due to packaging damages | Inspecting primary packing before secondary packing is done (problem solving) |

*Design:* The goals in this department being of shorter lead time and uncertainties being less, short-period reports would be useful on lines similar to research and development. More importantly, the design department is the critical part of target costing and cost reduction. Management accountants would, therefore, develop data to enable one to judge the use of the new design for achieving the goals. Significantly, the data would not be available off the shelf from the historical cost accounting data of an organization, and would have to be built up.

*Production:* This typically includes evaluating asset acquisition proposals. Other operational processes are evaluated against physical and financial parameters and in relation to the responsibilities specified by the organization.

## Example 1.2    Elixir Engineering—Electric Grinder Divisions

Jyoti, the cost accountant who was preparing the product-wise profitability of Elixir Engineering, found that the price of the competitor's product was 20 per cent higher than theirs, but Elixir's market share was much lower. She found that the sales returns were high at 15 per cent, and expenses against warranty/guarantee were high at 5 per cent of the cost of sales. She found that the product was running at a loss. She analysed why this was happening and found the reasons to be low volumes (therefore, high fixed costs per unit) and low prices. Elixir decided to improve the quality of its product; increase its prices; and sell it aggressively. Budgets were set accordingly. Amounts of warranty expenses were budgeted as 2 per cent of sales, sales returns as 5 per cent of sales, and ceilings for customer complaints as 5 per cent of the number of sales. This also meant an increase in the cost of inspection by 5 per cent and design costs by 5 per cent. Jyoti advised that if all this were done, the electric grinders would give handsome profits. Therefore, all these steps were budgeted and watched. After these were carried out, the salespersons realized that the grinder could improve in sales if one attachment for grinding hard substances such as pepper were added to it. This attachment was thus provided so as to widen the market segment. However, it involved some extra capital investment. Jyoti worked out the profitability implications and found that the cash flows would increase considerably and the internal rate of return could be very high. The scheme is presented in Table 1.3.

**Table 1.3**    Management control flowing from cost accounting for electric grinders

| Observation/Setting up system | Action |
|---|---|
| Product profitability low. Prices are lower than competition. Sales returns high. Warranty expenses high. Volumes low and high fixed cost/unit. | Increasing prices, reducing returns, reducing warranty expenses, pushing product, increasing inspection costs and design costs, setting budgets accordingly (planning) |
| Set up documentation to watch performance against budget. | Watching performance (scorekeeping) |
| Sales force suggested the widening of market segments by providing special attachment. This seemed to give high return on further investment. | Changing strategy based on cost analysis (problem solving) |

*Marketing:* Assessing advertisement expenses and other marketing efforts in trade shows, TV, and other media.

*Distribution:* Assessing channel costs and channel effectiveness, correlating with customer satisfaction.

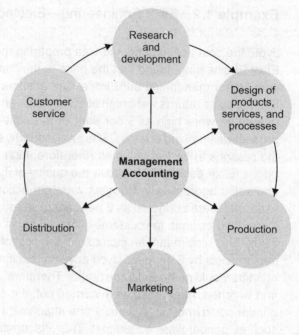

**Fig. 1.1**  Helping managers in the different segments of the value chain

*Customer service:* Computing customer costs and assessing customer profitability, special volume customer discounts, special extra prices for small orders, and so on.

From a review of the literature on management accounting, one may conclude the following:

1. Management accounting practices can be divided between those which involve decision making, and those which focus on evaluation and control by identification, measurement accumulation, analysis, interpretation, and communication.

2. The second stream of functions has sometimes been used as umbrella expressions to cover several detailed activities such as tax administration, protection of assets, or reports to the government. These have always been part of the traditional functions of accountants, which have been variously described as internal audit, tax management, etc. There is a general tendency to treat management accounting as an omnibus word which covers all the good things that could be done to an organization because it feels grand to call it all management accounting. These topics have not been dealt with in this book as it focuses on strategic costs. These topics are usually covered in detailed texts of management control systems.

# THE ACCOUNTANT IN THE ORGANIZATIONAL STRUCTURE

**Organizational structure**
Reporting relationships of accountants are sometimes to the divisional management and sometimes to the central controller.

Like all other functional disciplines, accountants could be spread over several levels of hierarchy, but the more significant aspect of accountants and the organizational structure is the reporting relationship between the divisional accountants and the divisional manager. Two alternative patterns are followed, which are shown in Fig. 1.2.

*Pattern 1:* The divisional accountant reports primarily to the controller, while he has a dotted working relationship with the divisional manager. This could cause immense tension with the divisional manager and emphasize the role of an accountant as a keeper of scorecards.

*Pattern 2:* The divisional accountant reports primarily to the divisional manager, while she has a dotted working relationship with the controller. This pattern of reporting relationships emphasizes the problem-solving and attention-drawing roles of the accountant.

## A Day in the Life of a Management Accountant

Some interesting data are available on how management accountants spend their time now and how they are likely to spend their time in the coming decades (Horngren 2003). The major work activities on which they spend their time are indicated in Exhibit 1.1.

In terms of importance, management accountants indicate the following work aspects:

- oral and written communication
- ability to work as a team
- solid understanding of accounting

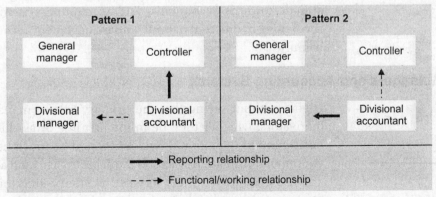

**Fig. 1.2** Patterns of reporting relationships of accountants

**Exhibit 1.1** Major work activities on which management accountants spend their time

- Accounting systems and financial reporting 62%
- Managing accounting and finance function 42%
- Internal consulting 42%
- Short-term budgeting 37%
- Long-term strategic planning 25%
- Financial and economic analysis 24%

- Computer systems operation 21%
- Process improvement 20%
- Performance evaluation 17%
- Tax compliance 14%
- Accounting Policy 13%
- Consolidations 11%

- understanding how business functions
- computer skills

Management accountants also predict future trends, as shown in Table 1.4.

**Table 1.4** Decreasing and increasing trends of preoccupation among management accountants

| Decreasing trends | Increasing trends |
|---|---|
| Accounting systems and financial reporting | Internal consulting |
| Consolidations | Long-term strategic planning |
| Managing accounting and finance function | Computer systems operation |
| Accounting policy | Process improvement |
| Short-term budgeting | Performing financial and economic analysis |
| Project accounting | |

## ATTITUDES TOWARDS ACCOUNTING SYSTEMS

In this section, we shall discuss the need for managers to have a positive attitude towards accountants and accounting systems, attitudes towards accounting in different nations, and management accounting in developing countries.

### Managers and Accounting Systems

It goes without saying that the primary role of managers is to be active innovators, whether they be in the first line or as chief executives. Their decisions and operational methods would be much better informed if the enormous information system is available to them and accounting personnel are also available at their service for interpreting this information. This two-way relationship between the manager and the accountant calls for mutual trust and not subservience of one to the other.

However, there has been extensive ambivalence in this relationship. Thus, an intuitive understanding has resulted in massive investment of resources in accounting systems, but contrarily, its utilization has often been inadequate (Krumviede 2005). There could be three reasons for this situation. First, the manager's fear of the complexity of accounting data and information, which needs to be dispelled by education and continued counselling at the individual level as well as the organizational level. The second reason may be the secretiveness of accountants in sharing their knowledge; they have to learn to be transparent and lucid. The third unfortunate reason could be the lack of ethics on the part of managers—there can be no quick remedies for this, but a major effort of organizational transformation supported by punitive measures, as typically contained in the Sarbanes–Oxley Act of the US, which savagely punishes wrong statements in the published accounts, could be helpful.

## Comparative Survey of National Attitudes towards Accounting

We have shown that Indian accounting practices have generally followed from Anglo-Saxon practices, in particular those of institutions in the UK. The US practices tend to be compliance-oriented, which means that they lay down rule, which are to be followed. If they are not, there would be punishment. The impact on judgements is less and actors are, therefore, free to choose their action and decisions with implicit faith in the system to be supportive of free market capitalism. This discipline enforced by an external legal force often makes managers in the US view accounting systems as impositions. The UK has a tradition of a commonly shared social concern and expects managers to share in this concern.

The German and Japanese economies are strongly driven by financial institutions working in collaboration with major industrial groups (Rajan and Zingales 2000). They are very strongly inclined to taking management accounting seriously. Thus, the cost accounting systems followed in Germany are elaborate and complicated, and the German term for it is a tongue twister—*grenzplankostenrechnung*—known simply as GPK in other parts of the world (Clinton and Webber 2004). Significantly, German managers have taken the complexities of these systems in their stride and have not got tired out. The systems are entirely computerized in enterprise resource planning (ERP) systems such as PROGRESS, SAP, etc. This has taken the drudgery out of the system and enables them to handle complexity with ease.

The Japanese system, with no trace of individualism as in Germany, has a paternalistic and educative attitude towards its managers and has management accounting methods which are strongly conditioned by their impact on behaviour rather than their absolute logic (Hiromoto 1988).

## Management Accounting in Developing Countries

Hopper, Wickramasinghe, Tsamenyi, and Uddin have done extensive fieldwork in the state of management accounting in developing countries such as India, Bangladesh, Srilanka, and Ghana (Hopper et al. 2003). They work on the implicit understanding that the implementation of the Anglo-Saxon accounting practices and standards would undoubtedly be beneficial to developing countries—a hypothesis which has not been demonstrated to be true (Larson and Kenny 1995).

Be that as it may, Hopper et al. show that standard management accounting practices developed in advanced countries are used in developing countries, but their extensive use is inhibited due to a few factors:

- A large part of the industry is in family-owned business where compulsions are in different directions.
- The cost benefits available in manipulating markets and state regulators are more rewarding than genuine cost control, cost reduction, and better resource allocation decisions.
- Many small activities have operated quite successfully with indigenously developed accounting and control systems, typically the self-help groups of Bangladesh.
- A large part of the activities in developing countries are rural and agricultural in nature, whereas much of western management accounting is based on manufacturing.

In their appreciation of the situation in developing countries, Hopper et al. have missed out the recent boom in IT and pharmaceutical industries in India. Due to these newer developments, we would undoubtedly witness major convergence in management accounting practices in the world in future.

## STATUTORY CONTROLS ON ACCOUNTING

We have alluded to the existence of statutory regulations governing both financial accounting and cost accounting, the most fundamental being the certification of professional competence. We shall now discuss some more legal controls on accounting.

In financial accounting, the Indian Companies Act in its Schedule VI prescribes the details which must be shown, for instance, the profit and loss account must show the opening stock, purchases and closing stocks, raw material consumed, spare parts consumed, sales of each class of goods, brokerage and discount in sales, bad debts, repairs, miscellaneous income, depreciation on categories of assets as specified, categories of working capital as specified, share capital, and so on. Similar are the provisions all over the world.

As mentioned earlier, the statutory support for cost accountants in India is unique in so far as it provides for the cost audit of firms. Both financial accountants and cost accountants are also regulated by the directions issued by their respective professional councils. These directions are issued after detailed consultation with industry and the professional members. Networking with other professional councils all over the world brings in some standardization. It must be noted that unlike the standardization imposed by the Indian state from time immemorial, the current modern effort is to bring it all about by mutual consultation and participatory processes.

## Moral and Ethical Imperative of Accountants

**Ethics of accountants**
Accountants have special need to be ethical as their roles are fiduciary.

The professional councils of financial accountants and cost and management accountants all over the world have, in addition to a set of instructions on the content of their professional work, laid down guidelines for moral and ethical behaviour. The need for ethical behaviour is very high in this profession as the nature of work is highly intricate and not easily understandable by the users of their outputs. Society, therefore, has very high expectations of honesty, trustworthiness, and professional competence from the accountants. Accountants therefore have to be above suspicion.

A summary of the codes of conduct followed by accountants is provided in Annexure 1.1. Exhibit 1.2 shows a typical process by which

**Exhibit 1.2**  Typical process of ethical negotiation of a management accountant

| | |
|---|---|
| If the policies of an organization do not resolve ethical conflict, practitioners should consider the following:<br>• The problem should be discussed with the immediate superior except when it appears that the superior is involved, in which case the problem should be presented to the next higher managerial level. If the next superior level is the chief executive, it may be submitted for acceptable review to the audit committee or its equivalent. | • Relevant ethical issues should be clarified by confidential discussion with objective advisor.<br>• One's attorney should be consulted regarding legal obligations.<br>• If the ethical conflict still exists after exhausting all levels, then one can resign and submit an informative memorandum to an appropriate representative of the organization. After resignation, it may also be appropriate to notify other parties. |

*Source: Management Accounting, vol. LXXXIX, no. 1.*

an ethical management accountant could get his/her ethical bearings in the organization.

## COST OF ACCOUNTING

**Cost of accounting**
It should be consciously kept low.

As in any other managerial activity, the cost of accounting should be an important consideration. However, we often lose sight of this. There is, therefore, always a continuous dialogue between the prescribing authorities in accounting, whether it be the government or professional councils, and the industry, which has to implement the prescription. Even in internal prescriptions, this aspect may be overlooked, in spite of the fact that computers have made the task easier. One may roughly say that the cost of accounting should not generally exceed one per cent of the total costs of the product or service.

---

## SUMMARY

Accountants are expected to be trusted problem solvers, scorekeepers, and attention drawers. They keep accounts for the accounter, who is accountable to the accountees. This makes them prone to tension-ridden power struggles. The law and professional councils lay down codes of conduct which can help to steer them through difficult dilemmas. Accountants have the benefit of an ancient lineage of skills. Double-entry bookkeeping is one such system and can be considered one of the greatest innovations of the human mind. It is the foundation of the current computerized systems of accounting which are engaged in aggregating the results of transactions.

The main concern in financial accounting is true and fair balance sheets, whereas cost accountants specialize in tracing resources to products and processes. Both have to use the data in their possession for the achievement of the strategic and operational goals and objectives of an organization. This is termed as management accounting.

Budgeting, balanced scorecards, and standard costing are some of the tools used by accountants. The law has laid down several directions for financial accountants and cost accountants regarding the structure and details of their accounts. India has a unique legal provision for the cost audit of firms. Professional councils of accountants also have codes of conduct as they are only too aware that the profession is esoteric, and trustworthiness is the most important quality expected of accountants. One must consciously attempt to restrict the cost of accounting to reasonable levels.

---

## KEY POINTS

- Management accounting is a value adding continuous process of planning, designing, measuring, and operating both financial and non-financial information systems, which guides management action, motivates behaviour, and supports and creates the cultural values necessary to achieve an organization's strategic, tactical, and operating objectives.
- Scorekeeping is the task of indicating performance levels against benchmarks available in targeted plans.
- Attention drawing is a task done by an accountant to tell the accounter that mid-course correction may be called for.
- Problem solving is a task done by an accountant in identifying problems and suggesting solutions.
- Codes of conduct of accountants are norms of behaviour prescribed by professional councils of accountants.
- Double-entry bookkeeping is based on the principle that every transaction in an organization will increase or decrease what it owns and owes with a corresponding decrease or increase in what it owns and what it owes in a different item of account. This basic concept is used both in manual and computerized accounting systems.
- The business entity concept distinguishes the owner from the business entity and presumes that the profit of a business entity is its liability, which is owed to the owner, and, conversely, loss is to be made good by the owner to the business entity, thus balancing the balance sheet.
- True and fair is a concept used in the presentation of financial statements, conforming to professional standards of clarity, transparency, and unbiasedness, even if it is a subjective assessment.
- Schedule VI of the Indian Companies Act contains mandatory and recommendatory provisions for disclosure in published accounts of Indian companies.
- Cost audit is a verification and report on the reliability of cost records maintained by an organization, usually used in the context of the provisions of the Indian Companies Act empowering the central government to prescribe and direct cost audits.

## CONCEPT REVIEW QUESTIONS

1. What, according to Horngren, are the three types of roles an accountant is expected to play in an organization?

2. What, according to Ijiri, are the expectations from an accountant?
3. Has the concept of double-entry bookkeeping become obsolete with the computerization of accounting?
4. Why is what an organization owes always equal to what it owns?
5. What is the role of cost accounting in the construction of a balance sheet?
6. Is a balance sheet only an aggregate summary of the transactions in an organization, or does it involve some judgmental estimation? Explain.
7. Mention the most important provision for external reporting by cost accountants which is unique in India.
8. Indicate three important techniques which enable management accountants to help in achieving strategic goals.
9. What could be the role of a cost accountant in research and development activity?
10. List three types of activities which are likely to take an increasing share of the time of management accountants of the future.
11. Why are ethics very critical for the profession of accountancy?
12. Rate the three ethical values of truthfulness, loyalty, and competence, on a scale of 1–10. Explain the reasons for the ratings chosen by you.

## PROJECTS

1. Form a group of three or four students and interview a financial accountant and a cost accountant and summarize and critically analyse their perceptions of their roles in the organization.
2. Form a group of three or four students and interview a chief executive, a middle-level financial executive, and a junior-level non-financial executive regarding the role of a Cost Accountant in a manufacturing organization. Critique it.
3. Form a group of three or four students and study the role played by accountants and auditors in the happenings of Enron and WorldCom. Draw lessons.
4. Form a group of three or four students and study the role of accountants in the Tata Finance scam.
5. Form a group of three or four students and study the cost accounting rules prescribed by the Institute of Cost and Works Accountants of India (ICWAI) for any two industries.

| CASE STUDY 1 | Cost Benefit of Kaup Power Plant |
| --- | --- |

Energy International (EI), a multinational organization, proposed the setting up of the Kaup power plant on the western coast of India in the state of Karnataka. The plant would be based on imported oil. EI had, it seems, a cast-iron case. Even if they priced power at the existing tariffs prevailing in Karnataka, the project was shown to have an internal rate of return of 30 per cent. It would also provide a much-needed fillip to industrialization in the west coast of Karnataka. The project was supported by the political leadership of the state, which also had a strong representation at the national government. MJ, the American Chief Executive of Kaup Power Company (KPC)—the wholly owned subsidiary of EI—had close personal relations with political leadership in India, and had convinced EI that he could carry the project through the cost–benefit scrutiny of the Central Power Authority of India which had to clear the project.

EI had employed one of the well-known applied economists in the US, who showed that the benefits of poverty alleviation far outweighed the drainage on foreign exchange, which the project would entail in the early years. He also showed that even the foreign exchange would be recouped by increasing exports of horticultural products which the power availability would induce. MJ arranged for a blazing publicity campaign in the Indian media highlighting the benefits of the project. He soon found that he had indeed been over-optimistic.

The political opponents of his friends had whipped up an agitation against the destruction of the heritage temples at the site of the project. MJ assured them that he could compensate the affected population by helping in re-establishing the heritage constructions in a new site. He asked his cost accountant, GR, to prepare a note for the Planning Commission, which would take into consideration all these points. GR had a close friend, DK, who was an environmentalist. He was unassuming and was not given to categorical assertions without sufficient proof. He privately told GR that he had an apprehension that the air circulation in the area was such that the smoke which the power plant would spew could ruin vast areas with their ash deposits from the skies. Further, he felt that the powdery ash which the plant would produce might pose a disposal problem as it would occupy enormous space which could be made available to the plant only by diversion of land currently being used for agriculture. These were probably remediable with some costs. The smoke problem could be corrected with strong electrical precipitators fitted into the chimney. The powdery ash could be used up in making firebricks or cement, but in the net it would cost some money.

No one in the environmental analysis group of the planning commission was even remotely aware of all these possibilities. DK did not wish to pass on this concern to the opponents of the project either, as he felt that his ideas were at the best only tentative at present. However, GR felt that the issue as posed by the American social cost–benefit study was nothing but a smoke screen, and many more problems lay behind the project than could be discerned by a superficial examination done by them. GR introduced DK to MJ and explained his apprehensions. MJ pointed out to GR that DK's ideas were tentative and it would be unwise to bring this up in his report at this stage. GR sought a few days to think about it. In those few days, GR's suspicions of the intentions of MJ became strong due to some developments. MJ said that he could arrange for GR's son's admission to a reputed institution in Pennsylvania as a company sponsor. He also said that he could arrange to send GR and his wife on an educational tour of the powerhouses in the US so that he could familiarize himself with power plant accounting. GR knew that social cost–benefit analysis is a hazy subject and the ultimate decisions often depend on the reputation of the analyst. He had a good reputation in the field as he had worked as a consultant to the planning commission. If he gave a favourable report, it was likely that the project would be passed. Even if he brought in DK's views, he could bend the data to show that on the whole the project was positive in social cost benefits.

## Discussion Questions

1. What are the options GR has?
2. Should he avail MJ's offer even if he is sure that it would not affect his report?
3. Would it be fair to the company if he revealed the concerns of DK to the public even if they are not scientifically proven?
4. Would he be fair to society if DK's views were not made public so that they could be debated?
5. Why should he, an accountant, concern himself with non-financial matters like pollution? Can you cite any support from the codes of conduct of accountants to support your arguments?

| CASE STUDY 2 | Excellent Engineering: Submersible Pump Division |
|---|---|

Excellent Engineering was one of the prime engineering companies of India. AG, the Finance Director, had introduced many new ideas on the use of management accounting for achieving the strategic objectives of the company. The submersible pump division was one of its star units. The strategic goal of the division was to capture a major chunk of the domestic and South-East Asian and African markets. AG had therefore worked out a scheme in consultation with the Divisional Manager, JS, wherein bonus would not be based on the profits of the division but more on the long-term objectives.

Bonus would be paid if the cost of quality was less than 10 per cent of the revenue, customer complaints was less than 4 per cent of the number of sales transactions, and delivery was on time on more than 92 per cent of occasions. They defined 'cost of quality' as a total of inspection costs, cost of warranty liability, cost of product testing, cost of scrap, and cost of design engineering. AG had recently recruited GN, an MBA from the Badami Institute of Management, whom he asked to work out these parameters for the division for the first month of the scheme. GN used the figures available in the accounting and production planning records of the division. He did not, however, depend solely on the number of complaints on record in their factory. He interviewed all the customers and used his findings in his report.

His numbers for the month in consideration were as follows:

### I. Based on data collected from JS's department:

Sales: ₹50,00,000
Inspection: ₹45,000
Warranty liability: ₹1,30,000
Production testing: ₹1,05,000
Scrap: ₹1,15,000
Design engineering: ₹1,00,000

### II. Data collected by GN

Percentage customer complaints: 5 per cent
On time delivery: 93 per cent

As directed by AG, GN gave a copy of the report to both AG and JS. JS was utterly disappointed with the report and thought that GN had gone out of the way to ferret out complaints from the customers. 'If the customers had a genuine complaint, they would come out on their own. Why should we instigate them to do so?', he said. AG thought that there was a point in what JS said. GN, however, felt that the complaints were genuine and the customers were very angry with some of the supplies. He said that the warranty liability is an indication of the customer dissatisfaction. Confiding in AG, GN said that he felt that the other quality cost data had also been doctored. He wanted permission to re-check them from the basic account records. AG did not want to do anything like that. 'We will introduce mistrust into the system, which is the last thing I want to do,' said AG.

### Discussion Questions

1. What is the total cost of quality as percentage of sales?
2. What should GN do now—modify the report or persist in his findings?

### Annexure 1.1   Code of Conduct of Accountants

## Code of ethics for American management accountants

The standards of ethics for American management accountants has four basic stipulations: competence, confidentiality, integrity, and objectivity. It is significant that competence is part of the code. Other than the obvious directive not to accept gifts, etc., management accountants are expected to adhere to the truth even it be unfavourable to the company. Objectivity must always be maintained.

*Ethics for Indian Accountants*

The first schedule to the Chartered Accountants Act is an attempt to legislate ethical norms. It is in three parts, the first is for accountants in practice, the second for accountants in employment, and the third is a general one.

*Part 1: For practising chartered accountants*

Misconduct of a chartered accountant is defined as the following:

*Clause 1:* If he allows any person to practise as a chartered accountant if he is not one.

*Clause 2:* If he pays any brokerage or fee out of his remuneration to a non-chartered accountant.

*Clause 3:* If he shares the profit with a lawyer or broker.

*Clause 4:* If he enters into a partnership with a person other than a chartered accountant in practice and shares the fees with him.

*Clauses 5,6, and 7:* If he advertises or solicits work.

*Clause 8:* If he accepts a position held by another chartered accountant without communicating with him.

*Clause 9:* If he accepts an auditor's position in a company and he is legally prohibited from doing so.

*Clause 10:* If his charges are based on a percentage of profit.

*Clause 11:* If he engages in a profession other than chartered accountancy without the permission of the council.

The second schedule lists misconduct in the auditing profession.

*Clause 1:* He discloses confidential information about his client.

*Clause 2:* He certifies a statement without adequate scrutiny.

*Clause 3:* He lends his name to any financial projection for the future of the company.

*Clause 4:* He does not disclose his interest in any financial report.

*Clause 5:* He omits to mention any important fact of which he is aware in a financial statement.

*Clause 6:* He fails to report any major misstatement in the accounts of his client.

*Clause 7:* He is grossly negligent in work.

*Clause 8:* He fails to get adequate information from his client for certifying the accounts.

*Part II: For employees*

- If he discloses the confidential information of his employer.
- If he accepts gratification from a lawyer, broker, or customer dealing with his organization.

*Part III: General, applicable to all*

A person would be regarded as indulging in misconduct if he gives wrong information to the council.

## Codes of conduct of the Institute of Cost and Works Accountants of India

The Institute of Cost and Works Accountants of India (ICWAI) also has norms similar to that of chartered accountants. The July 1980 declaration of its professional council also requires them to be straightforward, respect confidentiality, and be technically competent (Saxena and Vashist 2000). The emphasis is not on listing misdemeanor as in the codes of chartered accountant.

## Code of conduct of the US Institute of Management Accountants

Practitioners of management accounting and financial management have an obligation to the public, their profession, the organization they serve, and to themselves to maintain the highest standards of ethical conduct. Practitioners will commit accepts contrary to the standards prescribed in this regard by the Institute nor Condone the Commission of such acts by others within their organization. The codes are grouped under the four objectives of the profession: competence, confidentiality, integrity, and objectivity.

**Annexure 1.2** List of Industries and the Products Covered under Section 209(1)(D) of the Companies Act, 1956

| No. | Industry | Products | GSR NO. and Date | Effective from | Remarks |
|---|---|---|---|---|---|
| 1. | Cement | Cement, Clinker | 536 (E) dt. 11.9.1997* | 11.9.1997* | The Rules,1997 notified in suppression of GSR 1402 dt. 12.9.66 |
| 2. | Cycles | Cycles, component of cycles | 311 dt. 2.3.1967 | 1.04.67 | |
| 3. | Tyres & Tubes | Rubber tyres and tubes for all types of vehicles | 1260 dt 10.8.1967 | 1.10.67 | |
| 4. | Air-Conditioners | Air conditioning system or device by which air is controlled for the fulfillment of required condition of the confined space through controlling temperature, humidity, air purity and air motion for human comforts | 1447 dt. 16.9.1967 | 1.10.67 | Application clause and tile from 'Room-Airconditioners' to Air -conditioners' changed vide GSR 668(E) dt. 28.9.1999 |
| 5. | Refrigerators | Refrigerators | 1448 dt. 18.9.1967 | 1.10.67 | |
| 6. | Batteries other than Dry Cell Batteries | Batteries of all types other than Dry Cell Batteries | 1467 dt. 20.9.1967 | 1.01.68 | Application clause and tile from 'Automobile Batteries' changed vide GSR 667(E) dt 28.7.1999. |
| 7. | Electric Lamps | Electric lamps of all types 27.9.1967 | 1503 dt. | 1.01.68 | Application clause changed vide GSR670(E) dt 28.9.1999 |
| 8. | Electric Fan | Any type of electric fan | 2298 dt. 15.9.1969 | 1.01.70 | |
| 9. | Electric Motors | All types of electric motors | 2574 dt. 24.10.1969 | 1.01.70 | |

| No. | Product | | Notification | Date | Remarks |
|---|---|---|---|---|---|
| 10. | Motor Vehicles | (a) All types of passenger cars, jeeps and station wagons<br>(b) All types of commercial vehicles, delivery and pick up vans<br>(c) Motor cycles, scooters, scooterettes and mopeds<br>(d) Three-Wheeler Vehicles<br>(e) All types of tractors<br>(f) Heavy Earth Moving Equipments | 537 (E) dt. 11.9.1997* | 11.9.1997* | The Rules, 1997 notified in suppression of GSR 1465 dt. 17.5.1969<br><br>No (e) added vide GSR 328(E) dt.3.6.1998.<br><br>CAR (Tractors) Rules, 1971 applicable before 1.4.1999 vide GSR 329(E) dt. 3.6.98<br>No.(f) added vide GSR 280(E) dt. 24.4.2001 |
| 11. | Aluminum | 1. Alumina<br>2. Aluminium<br>3. Aluminium ingots in any form or alloy<br>4. Aluminium rolled products including foil<br>5. Aluminium extruded products<br>6. Properzirod or Aluminium wire rod<br>7. Any other aluminium product or its alloy | 334 dt. 25.2.1972 | 1.04.72 | Application clause amended vide GSR NO 703(E) dt. 28.9.2001 |
| 12. | Vanaspati | Refined vegetable oils and vegetable oil products as also Industrial Hard Oil. | 1529 dt. 27.11.1972 | 1.01.73 | Application clause amended vide GSR 287 dt. 29.5.1992 |
| 13. | Bulk Drugs | Bulk Drugs under any system of medicine including Ayurvedic, Homeopathic, Siddha and Unani systems of medicine and Intermediates thereof | 130(E) dt. 14.3.1974 | 1.04.74 | Application clause amended vide GSR NO 707(E) dt. 28.9.2001 |

*(Contd)*

Annexure 1.2 (*Contd*)

| No. | Industry | Products | GSR NO. and Date | Effective from | Remarks |
|---|---|---|---|---|---|
| 14. | Sugar | Sugar by vacuum pan process and excludes jaggery and khandsari | 388(E) dt. 15.7.1997* | 15.7.1997* | The Rules, 1997 notified in suppre-ssion of GSR 982(E) 4.9.1974 |
| 15. | Industrial Alcohol | 1. Absolute Alcohol<br>2. Rectified spirit<br>3. Denatured and special denatured spirit<br>4. Power alcohol | 532 (E) dt. 17.9.1997* | 17.9.1997* | The Rules, 1997 notified in suppre--ssion of GSR 594(E) dated 30.12.1975 |
| 16. | Jute Goods | Jute goods - Yarn, Twine, Fabrics or any other product made wholly from, or containing not less than 50 % by weight of, jute including bimlipattam jute or mesta fibres | 590(E) dt. 29.12.1975 | 1.01.76 | |
| 17. | Paper | Paper - used for printing, writing and wraping, newsprint, paperboard, and exercise note books | 601(E) dt. 31.12.1975 | 1.01.76 | |
| 18. | Rayon | 1. Viscose staple fibre in all forms<br>2. Viscose filament yarn<br>3. Viscose tyre yarn/cord/Fabric<br>4. 100% Viscose Yarn Fabric<br>5. Acetate yarn/fibre<br>6. Rayon film ( Cellophane Film) | 606 dt. 20.4.1976 | 1.05.76 | Application clause amended vide GSR 694 dt. 31.8.2000 |
| 19. | Dyes | Acid dyes, basic dyes, direct dyes, sulphur dyes, vat dyes, azoic dyes, ingrained dyes, metal complex dyes, disperse dyes, reactive dyes, oil dyes, and water soluble dyes | 605 dt, 22.4.1976 | 1.05.76 | |
| 20. | Polyester | 1. Polyester fibre<br>2. Polyester filament yarn | 126(E) dt. 24.3.1977 | 1.04.77 | No (3) to (7) inserted vide GSR 692(E) dt. 31.8.2000 |

3. Polyester Chips
4. Polyester Fibre Fill ( PFF)
5. Partially Oriented Yarn ( POY)
6. Processed Polyester yarn (texturised, twisted, dyed, crimped, etc.)
7. 100% Polyester fabric

| Sr. | Industry | Products | Notification | Date | Remarks |
|---|---|---|---|---|---|
| 21. | Nylon | 1. Nylon chip 2. Nylon fibre 3. Nylon filament yarn 4. Nylon partially oriented yarn 5. Nylon tyre yarn or cord 6. Nylon tyre cord fabric 7. 100% Nylon fabrics | 157(E) dt. 1.4.1977 | 1.04.77 | Application clause amended vide GSR 695)E) dt. 31.8.2000 |
| 22. | Textiles | Any art silk cloth, cloth, cotton yarn or cotton cloth, processed yarn and processed cloth, man-made fibre yarn or man made fibre cloth, silk yarn or silk cloth, wool, woollen yarn or woollen cloth, yarn or other textiles products. | 417(E) dt. 28.6.1977 | 1.07.77 | Application clause amended vide GSR 29(E) dated 19.1.1994 |
| 23. | Dry Cell Batteries | All types of dry cell batteries and components thereof | 45(E) dt. 31.1.1979 | 1.02.79 | |
| 24. | Steel Tubes and Pipes | Steel Tubes and Pipes (including stainless steel) both black and galvanized | 506(E) dt. 10.5.1984 | 26.05.84 | |
| 25. | Engineering | 1. Power driven pumps 2. Internal combustion engines 3. Diesel Engines 4. All type of automotive parts and accessories 5. Power Transformers | 688 dt. 25.6.1984 | 7.07.84 | No. 4 to 7 added GSR 279(E) dt. 24.4.2001 |

*(Contd)*

Annexure 1.2 (*Contd*)

| No. | Industry | Products | GSR NO. and Date | Effective from | Remarks |
|---|---|---|---|---|---|
| | | 6. Electric generator | | | |
| | | 7. Machine tools | | | |
| 26. | Electric Cables and Conductors | (a) Power cables (All types—PILC, PVC, XLPE etc.) | 767 dt. 7.7.1984 | 21.07.84 | |
| | | (b) VIR/Rubber covered cables and flexible wires of all types | | | |
| | | (c) PVC Insulated cables, flexible wires of all types including switchboard wires and cables | | | |
| | | (d) Enamelled covered wires and strips | | | |
| | | (e) Wire and strips covered with paper, glass, silk and any other types of insulating materials | | | |
| | | (f) AAC/ACSR Conductors | | | |
| | | (g) Telecommunication cables | | | |
| 27. | Bearings | Bearings of various types e.g. ball and roller bearings, needle bearing of various sizes | 664 dt. 1.7.1985 | 13.07.85 | |
| 28. | Milk Food | Infant Milk Food or Milk Food as malted milk food, energy food or food drink under any brand name | 704(E) dt.28.9.2001* | 29.9.2001* | CAR (Infant Milk Food) Rules 1974 and CAR (Milk Food) Rules,1986 merged and application clause amended vide GSR 704(E) dt. 28.9.2001 |
| | | (a) "Infant Milk Food" includes all types of milk food intended for the routine, complementary or supplementary food of infants and children up to the age of five years and other types of modified milk foods for infants | | | |

which are intended for the feeding of infants and children during the treatment of gastro-intestinal disorders;

(b) "Milk Food" means any food produced by mixing whole milk, partly skimmed milk or milk powder with ground barley malt or any other malted cereal grain, wheat flour or any other cereal flour or malt extract, with or without addition of flavouring agents and spices, edible common salt, sodium or potassium bicarbonate minerals and vitamins, cocoa powder, sugar or sweetening agents or other edible materials

29. Chemical    596 dt. 8.8.1987    8.08.87    Application clause amended vide GSR 562(E) dated 2nd September, 2004

01. Acetic Acid
02. Acetic Anhydride
03. Acetone
04. Aluminium Fluoride
05. Aniline
06. Benzene
07. Boric Acid
08. Butadiene
09. Butanol
10. Calcium Carbide
11. Carbon Black
12. Caustic Soda
13. Chloro Methanes
14. Diacetone Alcohol
15. Diethylene Glycol

(Contd)

Annexure 1.2 (*Contd*)

| No. | Industry | Products | GSR NO. and Date | Effective from | Remarks |
|-----|----------|----------|------------------|----------------|---------|
| | | 16. 2-Ethyl Hexanol | | | |
| | | 17. Ethylene | | | |
| | | 18. Ethylene Dichloride | | | |
| | | 19. Ethylene Glycol | | | |
| | | 20. Ethylene Oxide | | | |
| | | 21. Formaldehyde | | | |
| | | 22. Isopropanol | | | |
| | | 23. Linear Alkyl Benzene | | | |
| | | 24. Maleic Anhydride | | | |
| | | 25. Methanol | | | |
| | | 26. Methyl Ethyl Ketone | | | |
| | | 27. Methyl Isobutyl Ketone (MIBK) | | | |
| | | 28. Nitrobenzene | | | |
| | | 29. Ortho Nitro Cholro Benzene | | | |
| | | 30. Para Nitro Chloro Benzene | | | |
| | | 31. Penta Erithritol | | | |
| | | 32. Phenol | | | |
| | | 33. Polyethylenes viz. LDPE, HDPE, LLDPE | | | |
| | | 34. Polypropylene | | | |
| | | 35. Polythylene Glycol | | | |
| | | 36. Propylene | | | |
| | | 37. Soda Ash | | | |
| | | 38. Sodium Tripoly Phosphate | | | |
| | | 39. Sulphuric Acid | | | |
| | | 40. Resins (excluding natural resins), Paints, Varnishes and Plastics | | | |
| | | 41. Synthetic Rubber | | | |
| | | 42. Titanium Dioxide | | | |
| | | 43. Toluene | | | |
| | | 44. Xylenes | | | |

| No. | Name | Description | Notification | Date | Remarks |
|---|---|---|---|---|---|
| 30. | Formulations | All formulations under any system of medicine including Ayurvedic, Homeopathic, Siddha and Unani | 452 dt. 22.4.1988 | 4.06.88 | Applicability clause revised vide GSR 706(E) dt. 28.9.2001 |
| 31. | Steel Plant | Steel and steel products, Steel products includes Ingot Steel, Blooms, Billets, Slabs (code as well as semi-finished); steel products produced by backward integration like Coal based Sponge Iron, Gas based hot briquetted Iron, steel products produced by forward integration like Beams, Angles, Tees, Sees, Channels, Pilings, Rails, Crane Rails, Joint Bars, Bare (Round Squares, Hexagonal, Octagonal, Flat, Triangular, Half Round); Wire, Wire Ropes, Nails, Wire Fabrics, Plates, Pipes and Tubes, HR Coils/Sheets, CR Coils/Sheets | 574 dt. 31.7.1990 | 8.09.90 | 'Steel Products' defined vide circular no. 52/378/CAB-86-(CLB) dt. 29.6.1992<br><br>The words 'Steel Plant' substituted for 'Mini Steel Plants' vide GSR 281(E) dt.24.4.2001 |
| 32. | Insecticides | 1. Insecticides<br>2. Fungicides<br>3. Redenticides<br>4. Nematicide<br>5. Weedicide<br>6. Plant growth Regulant<br>7. Herbicides<br>8. Fumigants<br>9. Bio-pesticides | 258 (E) dt. 3.3.1993 | 4.03.93 | |
| 33. | Fertilizers | 1. Straight Nitrogenous Fertilizers<br>2. Straight Phosphatic Fertilizers | 261(E) dt. 5.3.1993 | 5.03.93 | |

*(Contd)*

Annexure 1.2 (*Contd*)

| No. | Industry | Products | GSR NO. and Date | Effective from | Remarks |
|-----|----------|----------|------------------|----------------|---------|
| | | 3. Straight Potassic Fertilizers<br>4. N. P. Fertilizers<br>5. N. P. K. Fertilizers<br>6. Micro Nutrients<br>7. Fortified Fertilzers | | | |
| 34. | Soaps and Detergents | Cleansing material used for cleaning, laundry/washing, bathing/toilet purposes and includes soaps and detergents (Whether in the form of cake, powder or liquid) | 677(E) dt. 29.10.1993 | 29.10.93 | |
| 35. | Cosmetics and Toiletries | Powders, Creams, Toothpastes, Toothpowders, Shaving Creams, After shave lotions, Shaving soaps, Shaving foams, Perfumes, Hair oils, Hair creams, Oxidation hair dyes, Mouthwash, Cologne, Shampoos - soap based, Shampoos - synthetics, detergent based, Room fresheners, Deodorants, Surfactants | 678(E) dt. 29.10.1993 | 29.10.93 | |
| 36. | Footwear | Shoes, boots, sandals, chappals, slippers, play shoes and moccasins | 186(E) dt. 12.4.1996 | 12.04.96 | |
| 37. | Shaving Systems | 1. Shaving blades<br>2. Razors<br>3. Any part or component thereof | 202(E) dt. 6.5.1996 | 6.05.96 | |

(*Contd*)

| | | | |
|---|---|---|---|
| | 4. Any other shaving instrument | | |
| 38. | Industrial Gases | Oxygen Gas, Nitrogen Gas, Acetylene Gas, Hydrogen Gas, Nitrous oxide Gas, Argon Gas, Helium Gas, Carbon dioxide Gas | 271(E) dt. 9.7.1996   9.07.96 |
| 39. | Mining and Metallurgy | List of products (metals and non-metals, their minerals, ores and alloys) 1. Uranium 2. Thorium 3. Zirconium 4. Titanium 5. Lead 6. Copper 7. Zinc 8. Nickel 9. Cobalt 10. Chromium 11. Gallium 12. Germanium 13. Platinum 14. Molybdenum | 276(E) dt. 24.4.2001   24.04.2001 |
| 40. | Electronic Products | 1. All Consumer electronics such as television both black and white and colour, video cassette recorder, video cassette player, audio compact disc player, video compact disc player, digital video compact disc player, radio receiver, tape recorder and combination, | 277(E) dt. 24.4.2001   24.04.2001 |

Annexure 1.2 (*Contd*)

| No. | Industry | Products | GSR NO. and Date | Effective from | Remarks |
|-----|----------|----------|------------------|----------------|---------|
| | | electronic watch and electronic clock, etc. | | | |
| | | 2. Industrial electronics including all control instrumentation and automation equipment. | | | |
| | | 3. Computer including personal computer, laptop, note book, server, workstations, super-computers, data processing equipment and peripherals like monitors, keyboards, disk drivers, printers, digitizers, SMPs, modems, networking products and add-on cards. | | | |
| | | 4. Communication and broadcasting equipment including cable television equipment. | | | |
| | | 5. Strategic electronics and systems such as navigation and surveillance systems, radars, sonars, infra-red detection and ranging system, disaster management system, internal security system, etc. | | | |
| | | 6. Other electronic component and equipment such as picture tube, printed circuit board, etc. | | | |
| 41. | Electricity | Generation of electricity from: 1. (a) thermal power (b) gas turbine (c) hydro-electric | G.S.R. No 913(E) dt. 21.12.2001 | 21.12.2001 | Ammended vide G.S.R.709(E) Dated 7th December 2005 and G.S.R.387(E) Dated 27th |

(Contd)

June 2006

|  |  |  |  |
|---|---|---|---|
| | power (d) atomic power (e) solar power (f) wind power (g) and other source of energy; | | |
| | 2. transmission and bulk supply of electricity | | |
| | 3. Distribution and bulk supply of electricity | | |
| 42. Plantation Product | 1. Tea and tea products | G.S.R. 685(E) dt. 8th Oct., 2002 | 8.10.2002 |
| | 2. Coffee and coffee products | | |
| | 3. Other commercial plantation products including seeds thereof | | |
| 43. Petroleum Industry | Manufacturing crude oil, gases (including compressed Natural Gas or Liquified Natural Gas and re-gasification thereof) or any other petroleum products | G.S.R. 686(E) dt. 8th Oct., 2002 | 8.10.2002 |
| 44. Telecommuni-cation | Processing of any one or more of the telecommunication activities namely: | G.S.R. 689(E) dt. 8th Oct., 2002 | 8.10.2002 |
| | 1. Basic telephony: | | |
| | (a) Telephone access | | |
| | (b) Local call | | |
| | (c) Subscriber Trunk dialing (STD) | | |
| | (d) International subscriber dialing (ISD) | | |
| | 2. Cellular mobile | | |
| | 3. Telex | | |
| | 4. Telegraphy | | |
| | 5. Voice mail/Audiotex service | | |
| | 6. Internet operations including gateway service/E-mail | | |

Annexure 1.2 (*Contd*)

| No. | Industry | Products | GSR NO. and Date | Effective from | Remarks |
|---|---|---|---|---|---|
| | | 7. Packet switched public data network(PSPDN) service | | | |
| | | 8. Wireless in local loop (WILL) service | | | |
| | | 9. Public mobile radio trunk service | | | |
| | | 10. Very small Aperture Terminal service | | | |
| | | 11. Global mobile personnel communication service | | | |
| | | 12. Leased circuits | | | |
| | | 13. Internet ports | | | |
| | | 14. National Long Distance Operator | | | |
| | | 15. Internet Telephony | | | |
| | | 16. Radio Paging | | | |
| | | 17. Any other telecommunication service for commercial use. | | | |

*Amendment Rules

*Note*: *Cost Accounting Records Rules are not applicable to a company*:

a. the aggregate value of the machinery and plant installed wherein, as on the last date of the preceding financial year, does not exceed the limits as specified for a small scale industrial undertaking under the provisions of the Industries (Development and Regulation) Act, 1951 (65 of 1951); and

b. the aggregate value of the turnover made by the company from sale or supply of all its products during the preceding financial year does not exceed ten crore rupees.

*Source*: http://www.mca.gov.in/Ministry/RecordRules44.html

## CHAPTER 2

# Financial Accounting and Financial Statement Analysis

## Learning Objectives

After reading this chapter, you will be able to understand

- the basic concepts in financial accounting
- the systematic documentation of transactions
- the practical application of the concepts discussed in the chapter
- cash flow and fund flow analysis
- financial ratio analysis through standard ratios
- accounting standards and analysis of the origins of some of the biggest accounting frauds in accounting practices

## INTRODUCTION

This chapter provides an in-depth understanding of financial accounting and financial statement analysis. It discusses the mechanics and documentation of financial transactions and also deals with a more sophisticated analysis of financial statements which qualify to be described as *management accounting* as defined in Chapter 1. The chapter also deals with the basic concepts and conventions in financial accounting which have acquired importance in ensuring transparency and in contributing to their prevention of frauds such as those perpetrated by Enron and WorldCom in the US, the Parmalat in Italy, Shell and Baring in the UK, and Tata Finance in India. These also aid rational economic decisions of investors from the share markets. The conventions also include an up-to-date version of the Indian Accounting Standards. The chapter has largely built on the pedagogy suggested by the well-known publication of the International Labour Organization, *How to Read a Balance Sheet* (ILO 1991), which builds up the concepts analytically from the fundamentals rather than mysterious formulae and rules of thumb often used by accounting professionals such as the secretive craft guilds of the past.

## BASIC CONCEPTS IN FINANCIAL ACCOUNTING

We have discussed the need for financial accounting in detail in Chapter 1. The most important output of the system of financial accounting is the balance sheet and profit and loss account to be made available to the stakeholders, the main ones being the owners and shareholders.

In a somewhat simplified understanding, financial accounting deals with all the processes which enable the organization to present to the external stakeholders of an organization, the *balance sheet* on specified dates. This shows what are owed and owned by an organization, which are described in technical language as liabilities and assets. It has an attached exploratory statement of changes in the amount owed to the owners of an organization in the balance sheet from the previous date to the next. In a later part of this chapter, we shall explain why any amount should be owed to the owners at all and what its meaning in financial analysis is. The latter is basically the *profit and loss account*, which shows the profit or loss generated in the intermediate period, as explained earlier. This also provides a neat summary to all concerned of the financial performance of the managers in charge of the organization in this period. Their salaries and careers depend on the numbers thrown up in the profit and loss account. Some non-profit-oriented organizations could have an *income and expenditure account* instead of a profit and loss account.

Financial accounts are audited by accountants whose qualifications are prescribed by law. Usually, they are chartered accountants who are qualified under the certifying procedure of the Institute of Chartered Accountants of India (ICAI)—a body constituted under an act of the parliament. Every country has similar arrangements.

This entire scheme of making a balance sheet and profit and loss account to provide a true and fair picture of an organization is often considered, rightly or wrongly, as the crucial engine of the capitalist system of free markets, and a primary prerequisite for development (May and Sundem 1995).

What does a balance sheet and profit and loss account look like? In Chapter 1 we mentioned that the Indian Companies Act, Schedule VI, statutorily prescribes the form and contents of both balance sheets and profit and loss accounts. A brief mention was also made of the prescribed contents. The form is elaborate and may be of interest only to specialists. It would suffice to indicate that there are options available to show the liabilities and assets in a horizontal form, with liabilities on the left hand side and assets on the right hand side. This, however, is a matter of convention and there are countries where liabilities are shown on the right hand side and assets on the left hand side. The law also allows for vertical presentation wherein the liabilities are shown first and then the assets. Liabilities can also be described as sources of funds and assets as application of funds. Most modern companies show it in this manner. A brief preview of the way profit and loss accounts and balance sheets look is shown in Tables 2.4 and 2.5 respectively.

## Entity Concept

**The entity concept**
Financial accounting always presumes that the organization is an entity distinct from the owner.

The foremost concept in financial accounting is the *entity of the organization* for which the financial accounts are generated. This was briefly alluded to in Chapter 1, and is being elaborated here.

Organizations function under varying legal structures–individual ownership, partnership, state ownership, public limited companies, private limited companies, cooperatives, societies under the Societies Registration Act, and so on. Whatever be the form of ownership, financial accounting is understandable and meaningful only if the transactions of the entity are kept separate from that of the owner. This separation of the entity from the ownership is less explicit in individual ownership and partnership but is more explicit in the other legal forms. The dramatic impact of this was articulated in the famous case *Salomon* v. *Salomon Co Ltd*, when Salomon, the company, went into liquidation and creditors wished to enforce the recovery of their dues from Salomon, the owner. However, the court ruled that Salomon, the company, was an entity distinct from Salomon, the owner.

**Salomon versus Salomon**
A famous court judgement which reaffirmed the concept of corporate entity as distinct from the owners in the company form of organization.

An entity would have to periodically produce, for its own information and for the information of all stakeholders, a balance sheet. A balance sheet is a statement, on a particular date, of what the entity owes to others and what it owns. This is a plain language description of what is known by the accountants as the assets and liabilities of the entity.

What is the implication of the relationship between the entity and the owner we have described thus far?

### Entity–owner relationship

Let us consider a typical situation when the owner puts in, say, ₹10,000 in the business. At the end of the transaction, the entity would owe the owner ₹10,000. Thus, the entity will show the owner as liability. This enunciation often intrigues managers who are fresh to accounting. Even more puzzling would be the case of a society that receives a donation of ₹10,000 from a donor. The donor would similarly appear as a liability in the financial accounts. These statements do not mean that the entity will be obliged to return ₹10,000 to the owners or the donors. It only means that it would be returnable only if the condition under which the monies were paid explicitly requires it to be done. Even more intriguing for a fresh manager would be the situation where, at the end of the time period of operations, the money paid by the owner is used to generate an extra sum of ₹10,000. This would obviously be a profit. By the logic of entity, this extra money would also be owing to the according. Contrarily, if the transactions resulted in a loss of ₹10,000, this is money which the owner will owe to the entity and conversely, the entity will own this money. This will be treated as an asset.

Thus, by this logic of the entity, *the amounts owed by the entity will always be equal to what it owns, and the balance sheet will always balance, irrespective of what happens in the affairs of the entity.*

## Duality Concept

**The duality concept**
Every change in the figure of what an entity owes and owns always has a corresponding change in the opposite direction under some other head of account.

The second important concept in financial accounts is that of *duality*. Financial accounts, as we have seen, produce figures of what the entity owes and what it owns. The concept of duality means that every transaction which changes either what we owe or what we own always has a corresponding change in what we own or what we owe. We have described these as *liabilities* and *assets*. Liabilities are of varied descriptions, typically shares, loans, bank credit, trade credits, and so on. Assets similarly could be fixed assets of different types, investments, current assets such as cash, bank and trade dues, etc.

A little reflection will show that the concept of duality is a logical consequence of the entity concept, and not as sometimes held that it is vice versa. Pacioli, the famous friend of the even more famous Leonardo Da Vinci, captured this in his writings. We have already illustrated typical transactions in Chapter 1. We shall discuss many more situations in Example 2.1. We are not yet using the concepts of debit and credit.

### Example 2.1   Situation Showing the Concept of Duality

1. ₹10,000 worth of raw material is purchased on credit: Stock (purchase) owned will go up by ₹10,000 and what we owe to the vendor will increase by ₹10,000.
2. ₹10,000 is paid to the vendor: What we owe to the vendor will decrease by ₹10,000 and cash (what we own) will come down by ₹10,000.

3. Material worth ₹10,000 is issued to works: Stock (what we own) will come down by ₹10,000 and work-in-progress (what we own) will increase by ₹10,000.
4. Labour is paid ₹5000 for the work: Work-in-progress (what we own) will increase by ₹5000 and cash (what we own) will decrease by ₹5000.
5. Completed production costing ₹15,000 is transferred to finished good stock: Work-in-progress (what we own) will decrease by ₹15,000 and finished goods (what we own) will increase by ₹15,000.
6. The goods are sold for ₹20,000 in credit: Finished goods (what we own) will decrease by ₹15,000 and expenses account (profit and loss account) will increase by ₹15,000. At the same time, income account (profit and loss account) will increase by ₹20,000 and debtors account (what we own) will increase by ₹20,000. Net monies owing to owners will increase by profits being ₹5000 (₹20,000 minus ₹15,000).

## Accounting Equation

We are now in a position to understand what is known as the accounting equation. The logical outcome of the entity concept and the duality concept is the accounting equation concept. This concept can be expressed as a formula:

$$\text{Asset } (A) = \text{Liability } (L) + \text{Beginning of Owners' Funds } (E_0)$$
$$+ \text{ Income } (Y) - \text{Expense } (X).$$

### Example 2.2   A Clean Mess

Leela and Prasad, two freshers in the MBA programme of a premium business school, were heroes for their classmates when they said that they would, between themselves, serve the students three meals a day at ₹1000 per month, which was much cheaper than the rates seniors were paying to the contractor at ₹1500 per month for three meals a day. Leela, a graduate in home science, was quite sure of her ability to cook and her friends, who had sampled her cooking, would vouch for it. Prasad was a man about town who struck his class fellows as an expert in practical management. Of the hundred students of the year, only Janki had doubts about Prasad's financial prudence; she had also heard from his previous class-fellows that he threw extravagant parties. Janki, a gold medallist chartered accountant, offered to keep accounts for the venture, but Prasad would have none of it as he felt that she would restrict his freedom and style of working. 'I cannot function with her constant nagging,' he said.

Leela and Prasad started the mess with the initial funds provided by their class fellows. Prasad had computed the initial start-up costs of ₹20,000 for vessels and a gas stove and a deposit of ₹5000 required by the gas supplier.

The initial supply of grocery for a month was also to be provided, but he thought that he could manage part of it on credit. He calculated that he would need ₹1,00,000 as a start-up fund, which would imply that each student would have to deposit ₹1000. Prasad bought gas cylinders in cash at ₹300 per cylinder. The mess was started on 1st July .The venture went very well for the first month and the seniors were obviously envious of the juniors.

The second month, August, saw some disillusionment as the teachers complained that Leela and Prasad were neglecting their studies. By the end of August, Leela and Prasad were fed up and closed the mess. They had no alternative but to seek Janki's help to settle the accounts with all the students. Janki checked Prasad's cash box and found ₹3000. The bank passbook showed ₹2000. She found a bill of ₹24,000 from the shop which had supplied the vessels. Prasad did not remember if he had paid the bill, but Janki checked with the shopkeeper and he confirmed that he had received cash from him. Janki asked the supplier if he would be willing to buy back the vessels. He said he could buy it back for ₹10,000. She took the balance grocery which was left in the mess to the grocer, who was willing to take back the material for ₹5000, but he said that he had ₹1,40,000 due from Prasad and, after adjusting this, Prasad still owed him ₹1,35,000. She found three half-empty gas cylinders. The gas deposit receipt was available. The gas dealer was willing to pay back the deposit only if the cylinders were returned, but he was not willing to give any credit for the gas still left in the cylinders. Janki found a scribbled note in Prasad's diary that three of the students had not paid their dues for July or even the initial deposit of ₹1000. The note, however, had not mentioned the names of these students. After detailed enquiry, Janki identified these three students, who admitted that they had not paid anything to the mess so far. All hundred students were to pay the dues for August, that is, ₹1000, by 1st September.

By the end of August, most of the students who were taught accounts had understood its importance. They wanted Janki to provide the balance sheet as on 1st July and a second one on 31st August, but wondered if she could make one without a cash book, day books, and ledgers, which had been taught in their course. Janki confirmed that Prasad did not maintain any such records. Let us see if we can first construct the balance sheet on 1st July. Here it is in Table 2.1.

**Table 2.1** Balance sheet of the student mess as on 1st July

| What we owe (liabilities) | | What we own (assets) | |
|---|---|---|---|
| Item | Amount (₹) | Item | Amount (₹) |
| Student deposit | 97,000 | Cash | 97,000 |
| Total | 97,000 | Total | 97,000 |

Thus, Janki could have constructed the balance sheet for both 1st July (Table 2.1) and 31st August (Table 2.2) without any double entry or single entry in the books. These figures would show that the students would have to pay for the loss, which, on an average, amount to ₹545 per month for each student. Thus, the total monthly bill for each student was ₹1545 (₹1000 old rate + share of loss ₹545) against ₹1500 of the seniors. It seems that running the mess was no great idea, considering the fact that it was done at the cost of studies. Was the problem one of inefficiency or cheating? Although it was possible to make the balance sheet, it would not be possible for Janki to make the profit and loss account with all details which will stand scrutiny of the stakeholders. That purpose would be served only if every transaction was entered in the books, summarized in subsidiary records, and made available to the stakeholders. We will see in the remaining part of the chapter how this is usually done.

**Table 2.2**  Balance sheet of the student mess as on 31st August

| What we owe (liabilities) | | What we own (assets) | |
|---|---|---|---|
| Item | Amount (₹) | Item | Amount (₹) |
| Student deposit | 97,000 | Cash in hand | 3000 |
| Due to grocer | 1,40,000 | Cash in bank | 2000 |
| | | Assets | 10,000 |
| | | Debtors July | 3000 |
| | | Debtors August | 1,00,000 |
| | | Gas deposit | 5000 |
| | | Gas in cylinder | 0 |
| | | Grocery in stock | 5000 |
| | | Net loss | 1,09,000 |
| **Total** | **2,37,000** | **Total** | **2,37,000** |

Thus, starting with the proof that independent of double entry bookkeeping, using the duality concept, a balance sheet will balance, we have shown in the accounting equation concept that it would continue to do so after we pass the adjustments required for several transactions, in the accounts using double entry booking. It is well to remember that the balance sheet will balance whether we use double entry booking, single entry booking, or no entry booking.

Why do we then continue to extensively use Pacioli's double entry bookkeeping even in the most advanced modern computerized format? The following example of two fresh management students, Leela and Prasad, starting a mess for their class (Example 2.2), will help us understand this.

### Relationship between balance sheet and profit and loss account

Let us now understand the relationship between the balance sheet and profit and loss account from Tables 2.1 and 2.2, in which balance sheets are prepared without accounting records, and Tables 2.4 and 2.5, which we propose to prepare using account records that we will develop now.

Tables 2.1 and 2.2 do not have the profit and loss account, whereas Table 2.4 shows the profit and loss account for the period 1st July to 31st August, which explains the difference between the balance as on 1st July and 31st August, showing, among other things, the break up of the loss of ₹1,09,000. One may see the relationship between the other figures in the profit and loss account and the balance sheet in Tables 2.4 and 2.5. Depreciation has been shown in the balance sheet as a deduction from gross assets, whereas it figures as an expense in the profit and loss account. Similarly, material consumed in the profit and loss account is ₹2,97,600 purchases less closing stock of ₹5000. This closing stock appears in the balance sheet too. If one had a suspicion that a part of debtors may turn bad and we are not sure how much of it would, the profit and loss account would show that provision as an expense and debtors would be reduced in the balance sheet to that extent. This would, of course, correspondingly reduce the profit figure both in the profit and loss account and the balance sheet. The technicalities of performing these transactions/operations are detailed in several remaining parts of the chapter.

## THE MEANING OF DEBIT AND CREDIT

**Debit or credit**
*Debit* means increase in assets, decrease in liabilities, or decrease in owner's fund. *Credit* means just the opposite.

Having understood some of the basic concepts in accounting, we can now learn to use the typical jargon used by accountants—the terms *debit* and *credit*. Debit means increase in what we own or decrease in what we owe. Conversely, credit means increase in what we owe or decrease in what we own. Extending this understanding, income (sale) would increase what we owe to the owner and, therefore, would be credit. Expenses would decrease what we owe to the owner and would, therefore, be debit. The abbreviations 'Dr' and 'Cr' are usually used for debit and credit, respectively.

If an account balance is 'debit', it means it would go to the assets side of the balance sheet or the expense side of the profit and loss account. If an account is 'credit', it would go to the liability side of the balance sheet or the income side of the profit and loss account. The reader must be clear about the way the words 'debit' and 'credit' are used in common parlance.

If an organization has a cash balance, it would be a debit balance and an asset. If an organization has some money in the bank, it will similarly show a debit balance in the books of accounts. The banks would say that the organization has a credit balance as, in its books, the bank will be owing that money to the organization. The concepts often confuse managers and one should be clear about them.

It is usual for accountants to use a formula to know when to debit and when to credit the accounts and commit this rule to memory. If we use logical thinking, this learning by rote would no longer be required.

## Money Measurement Concept

Financial accounting will obviously deal only with transactions which are expressed in monetary terms, but it is good that this is recognized as a basic concept. It may be tremendously important for an organization to enter into a memorandum of understanding (MoU) that they will collaborate in the future with some other organization. If there are no monetary implications spelt out in the MoU, there is no way this 'transaction' can figure in the financial accounts. Conversely, if there has been a robbery and valuable property being lost but no cash stolen, it would still figure in the financial accounts as the related asset which has a money tag would have to be removed from the balance sheet.

## Cost Concept

In Example 2.2 (Table 2.2), we should normally have indicated the value of the assets at its costs, namely, ₹24,000 or the cost minus depreciation. The situation of the mess was unusual as it was closing down and Janki, the chartered accountant, brought it down to a realizable value of ₹10,000. Accountants are more comfortable with recording values at cost as it is more objective and verifiable with past records. We will see how significant this concept is in giving a true and fair view of accounts.

## Going Concern Concept

While dealing with the cost concept, we observed that Table 2.2 did not follow the cost concept but the current realizable value of assets. That is because the mess was not a going concern; it was not going to last any more. But if it were a going concern, it would be confusing to all users of financial statements to adjust the assets at the current realizable value. We shall later consider situations in which the cost concept would be used or those where the alternative of the going concern would be considered more appropriate.

## Periodicity Concept

Financial accounting usually provides for periodic reporting through a balance sheet and statement of income and expense or profit and loss account, which explain the change in owners' funds as brought out in the accounting equation. The frequency of such reports is usually legally prescribed by the company's act or other regulations, which will be described later in the chapter.

## Accrual Concept

In Table 2.2, a true and fair balance sheet required that monies due to others be shown as liability and amounts others owe to the mess be shown as assets so that the profit and loss could be correctly worked out. This can be done only if we accept the idea that accounting cannot be limited to cash transactions. When one buys material and uses it in production, even if it is not paid for, the *accrual concept* requires that it should be shown in the accounts. The easy and prompt way of recording this would be to use the duality concept and record this transaction by debiting purchases and crediting vendors.

Similarly, if one sells one's products or services on credit, even before the cash is received, one needs in an 'accrual concept' to credit sales and debit parties using the duality concept. If this 'accrual concept' is not followed, one can be totally misinformed of the performance, as would be clear from Exhibit 2.1.

The inadequacy of doing only cash accounting is reflected in a specific provision of the Income Tax Act in India that accrual accounting must be followed. Even government accounting in India is considering the introduction of accrual accounting, as have several other countries.

**Exhibit 2.1**   The myth of cash accounting

Darbara Singh felt that he could try nothing more sophisticated than keeping a cash book faithfully. He bought goods worth ₹2,00,000 on credit but sold the entire goods on a cash basis for ₹1,80,000. At the end of this period he had in hand ₹1,80,000 and was quite happy with his performance. If he had followed accrual accounting, he would have known that he had actually lost ₹20,000 as sales would show ₹1,80,000 and purchases ₹2,00,000.

## Matching Concept

We have repeatedly indicated why organizations would not only like to produce a balance sheet but would like to explain to the stakeholders the details of how the status in the balance sheet have changed in the intervening periods. This is necessary for managerial evaluation and control as well. The profit and loss of the intervening period is the difference between the income of the period and the expenses 'matching' with this income. Conversely, income received in one year may produce a stream of expenses and profit and loss statements would need to 'match' the income with the corresponding expenses to arrive at a true and fair profit and loss account.

There are innumerable situations that require 'matching', which calls for innovations on the part of the accountants. We will describe three of such simpler situations on how this matching is done:

1. Fixed assets purchased in a given year lasts, say, for five years and produces a stream of income. A typical way of matching these lump sum costs is not to show the cost of fixed assets as an expense in the year it is bought but to show part of it in the form of depreciation as an expense. One can see that this calls for a subjective judgement on how much of it could be shown in that manner. The Income Tax Act and rules, the Companies Act, and several other rules and laws provide guidelines on how this can be done.

2. The second is the accounting of material purchased in one year, used in the following years and goods produced in one year, sold in the following years. Such a situation will usually arise in manufacturing organizations, but could also exist in service industry in respect of raw material. In such a situation, accountants use the method of inventory accounting. Material not used and finished goods not sold would be kept under the head inventory as an asset and converted to expenses to come only in the period they are used/sold. As in depreciation accounting, a lot of judgement is involved in this process.

3. In the third set, a typical set of examples would be from (a) holiday homes and (b) warranty provisions in standard supply contracts. Holiday homes receive a lump sum from those who purchase time-sharing rights, say, for ten years of use. Income is received in the first year but expenses are spread over ten years. Many holiday homes came to grief in India as they took the entire income in the first year. Proper matching would require that only, say, one-tenth of the income is taken in the first year (or use some other method which would attempt to match income with expense). The other situation of warranty requires that from the income in the year of transaction some amounts should be set apart for meeting warranty expenses during the pendency of the warranty.

## Prudence or Conservatism Concept

One might have noticed several situations in which judgement is involved in financial accounting. The normal precept followed by accountants is 'anticipate no profits but provide for all possible losses'. Thus, in valuing inventories, they use the principle of cost or market, whichever is less. Continuing the inventory values do not include marketing costs but only production costs. Assets which have appreciated in the market are not usually revalued with increased values, but assets which have lost in market value may be reduced in value to that extent. Accountants always tend to be prudent and conservative in their judgement.

## Realization Concept

When do we show a sale as an income? The *realization concept* would require that three conditions are met:

1. when the goods are accepted by the buyer
2. when the buyer accepts the correct consideration
3. when the risk on the loss of the goods finally passes on to the buyer

It may be seen that this is a direct consequence of applying the concept of prudence.

## Materiality Concept

Often it is seen that being accurate in one's facts and judgements may involve a lot of time and energy. Among other things, the judgement would take into consideration the materiality, both in terms of the gain or loss, of the transaction and its importance and relevance to the stakeholder for whom the statement is intended. The concept of materiality is described in accounting standards as follows:

The concept of materiality recognizes that some matters, either individually or in the aggregate, are important for fair presentation of financial statements in conformity with generally accepted accounting principles, while other matters are not important.

## SYSTEMATIC DOCUMENTATION OF TRANSACTIONS

We noted in Example 2.2, in the case of the students mess, that accountability could not be established as the transactions were not documented. This would be unacceptable to stakeholders, most of all, the tax authorities.

What are the standard operating procedures accountants that have evolved to keep track of the transactions?

They develop standard heads of accounts to pigeonhole and aggregate the transactions, so that the stakeholders may understand where the monies came from and where they go. Very often, laws prescribe the minimum standards of transparency and disclosure.

Accountants use vouchers to record the transactions:

- An *expense voucher* would show a debit for an expense or an asset and credit from cash/bank or a creditor.
- A *receipt voucher* would show a credit to a receipt head and debit to a debtor or cash/bank.
- A *journal voucher* is a general purpose adjustment of accounts.
- A *contra voucher* would indicate a transfer to and from cash in hand and bank.

## Columnar Sales Day Books, Purchase Day Books, Cash Books, and Bank Books

The transaction entries mentioned earlier can be repetitive and add to the drudgery of work without adding anything useful to information. This repetition is avoided in manual systems if the voucher transactions are entered in day books with columnar facilities. They would roughly look as follows:

Sales day book

| SI no./date | Document detail | Amount | Sale item 1 | Sale item 2 | Sale item *n* |
|---|---|---|---|---|---|
|  |  |  |  |  |  |
| Total for period |  |  |  |  |  |

Purchase day book

| SI no./date | Document detail | Amount | Purchase item 1 | Purchase item 2 | Purchase item *n* |
|---|---|---|---|---|---|
|  |  |  |  |  |  |
| Total for period |  |  |  |  |  |

Cash book/Bank book (Receipt Side)

Dr

| Sl no./ date | Documen- tation | Cash | Bank | Account 1 ledger folio | Account 2 ledger folio | Account 3 ledger folio | Account n ledger folio |
|---|---|---|---|---|---|---|---|
| | | Opening balance | Opening balance | | | | |
| | | | Closing balance | | | | |
| Total/ closing balance | | | | | | | |

Cash book/Bank book payments

Cr

| Sl no./ date | Documen- tation | Cash | Bank | Account 1 ledger folio | Account 2 ledger folio | Account 3 ledger folio | Account n ledger folio |
|---|---|---|---|---|---|---|---|
| | | | | | | | |
| Total | | | | | | | |

When voucher entries have to be made into the books periodically, the totals can be posted through journal vouchers. In a computerized system, this intermediary step would be redundant.

## T Accounts, General Ledgers, Subsidiary Ledgers, and Group Ledgers

Vouchers for the transactions described earlier in the chapter are then 'posted' in what is known as *T accounts*, which are counters intended to aggregate the transactions for a period. They would typically look as follows:

Ledger Folio No.

| | Debit | | | | Credit | | |
|------|-------------|-------------------|--------|------|-------------|-------------------|--------|
| Date | Particulars | Journal folio | Amount | Date | Particulars | Journal folio | Amount |
| | | | | | | | |
| | | | | | | | |
| Total | | | | | | | |

These basic T accounts can be constituted as detailed ledgers or as general group ledgers. Thus, the group ledger can have a consolidated account of sundry debtors, and the subsidiary ledgers can consist of individual debtors. The group ledger can be sundry creditors and the subsidiary ledgers can be individual creditors, and so on. In a computerized system, the general ledger and subsidiary ledger would be updated simultaneously. In a manual system, they could be posted from independent sources and reconciled.

One should note that the cash book is a combined day book and T account. Intriguingly, unlike the other T accounts, the debit entries of the cash book is usually on the right hand side of ledgers, whereas, in other accounts, they are on the left hand side. Credit entries are just the opposite. This is only a matter of convention.

## Trial Balance

Due to the duality principle, the figures extracted from the T accounts would automatically balance if the postings and castings are right. The purpose of the trial balance in a manual system is to do this. In a computerized system, the trail balance could show opening balance transactions and closing balance and helps the accountant to review if there are any obviously erroneous entries.

Even after these processes, there could be errors in the accounts due to deliberate or accidental mistakes. An independent confirmation of the debtor's balances from the debtors and bank balances from the banks is usually done in one's own effort and those of the auditors.

## Periodic Adjustments in Accounts

At the end of the specified period, a review is done and adjustments are made. Typical entries are as follows:

1. After review of debtors, one may assess that some could turn out bad. This adjustment is done by debiting the profit and loss account with a provision and crediting provision for bad debts. The latter will come in the balance sheet.
2. At the end of the period, the value of the assets is reduced by deducting depreciation. This is done by crediting depreciation provision and debiting depreciation as an expense. The former will appear in the balance sheet.
3. Closing inventories will be credited to the profit and loss account and debited to inventory to be shown in the balance sheet.

### Balance sheets from trial balance

Once these transactions are put through, from the adjusted trial items going to profit and loss and balance sheet would go to their respective places to show the stakeholders a transparent account, which will be a true and fair description of the financial state of the entity.

## Practical Application of Concepts

We shall demonstrate the practical application of the concepts discussed by picking up the data from Example 2.2, that is, the students' mess. The first step is to decide the accounts heads to be able to satisfy the stakeholders. We could decide as follows:

1. *Expenses:* material consumed, gas used, depreciation
2. *Receipt:* income
3. *Liability:* student deposit (with subsidiary ledgers), creditors
4. *Assets:* cooking vessels, debtors (with subsidiary ledgers), gas deposits, grocery stock (purchase), cash in hand, and cash in bank

Let us have the likely transactions that would have been available to Janki if the accounts records had been kept properly. We would list twelve transactions, clubbing several of them together to make the presentation simpler. The thirteenth transaction could be to adjust the value of assets from the purchase price to the current realizable value.

1. Students deposit ₹27,000.
2. ₹5000 is deposited with gas dealer.

3. Eight cylinders of gas purchased in cash at the rate of ₹300 per cylinder.
4. Grocery worth ₹2,97,600 purchased at various times on credit in July–August.
5. Vessels purchased on credit for ₹24,000.
6. Received ₹97,000 from 97 students for July mess bill.
7. Paid grocer in several instalments ₹1,57,600.
8. Paid for vessels ₹24,000.
9. Adjustment for July overdue from students for ₹3000.
10. Adjustment for August dues from students ₹1,00,000.
11. Adjustment for material used in mess from stocks from time to time ₹2,92,600.
12. Cash transferred from cash to bank by contra ₹2000.

We can use a spreadsheet from excel programs to put these transactions through T accounts. The results are summarized in Table 2.3.

The bottom row would be the net balances of the T account without the thirteenth transaction of bringing the asset value at costs from ₹24,000 to ₹10,000.The difference may be treated as depreciation.

We would now be in a position to provide the stakeholders a full account of the profit and loss account and balance sheet using the figures from the bottom column of Table 2.3. This is shown in Tables 2.4 and 2.5.

It would be interesting to note that while debit items come on the right hand side of the profit and loss account, they appear in the right hand of the balance sheet. This is just a convention. There could be several variations of the presentation; some could be even vertical.

## FINANCIAL STATEMENT ANALYSIS

Following the description of the concepts and mechanics of accounting systems, this part of the chapter deals with the interpretation of their outcomes. This truly qualifies to be described as *management accounting*.

Throughout this section, one must remember that a lot of judgement is incorporated in financial statements and, therefore, one must keep in mind the limitations of these analyses. The three major types of financial statements are as follows:

**Income statement (profit and loss accounts)**   A summary of the revenue and expenses for a specific period of time.

**Statement of retained earnings**   A summary of the changes in the retained earnings that have occurred during a specific period of time.

**Table 2.3** Students' mess transaction summary

| Transaction | Cash | Bank | Asset | Debtors Jul-Aug | Gas deposit | Stock (grocery purchase) | Material used | Gas used | Student deposit | Creditors | Income | Total |
|---|---|---|---|---|---|---|---|---|---|---|---|---|
| 1. Deposit | 97,000 | | | | | | | | -97,000 | | | 0 |
| 2. Cylinder | -5000 | | | | 5000 | | | | | | | 0 |
| 3. Gas | -2400 | | | | | | | 2400 | | | | 0 |
| 4. Grocery | | | | | | 2,97,600 | | | | -2,97,600 | | 0 |
| 5. Assets | | | 24,000 | | | | | | | -24,000 | | 0 |
| 6. July mess bill | 97,000 | | | | | | | | | | -97,000 | 0 |
| 7. Pay grocer | -1,57,600 | | | | | | | | | 1,57,600 | | 0 |
| 8. Payment vessels | -24,000 | | | | | | | | | 24,000 | | 0 |
| 9. July overdues | | | | 3000 | | | | | | | -3000 | 0 |
| 10. Aug dues | | | | 1,00,000 | | | | | | | -1,0,0,000 | 0 |
| 11. Material used | | | | | | -2,92,600 | 2,92,600 | | | | | 0 |
| 12. Cash-bank | -2000 | 2000 | | | | | | | | | | 0 |
| Total at end of Aug | 3000 | 2000 | 24,000 | 1,03,000 | 5000 | 5000 | 2,92,6000 | 2400 | -97,000 | -1,40,000 | -2,00,000 | 0 |

**Table 2.4**  Profit and loss of the mess (July–August)

| Expenses (₹) | | Income (₹) | |
|---|---|---|---|
| Material consumed | 2,92,600 | Income: | 2,00,000 |
| Gas consumed | 2400 | Loss July–August | 1,09,000 |
| Depreciation (purchase value-current value) | 14,000 | | |
| **Total** | **3,09,000** | | **3,09,000** |

**Table 2.5**  Balance sheet of the mess as on 31st August

| Liability (₹) | | Assets (₹) | |
|---|---|---|---|
| Student deposit | 97,000 | Cash in hand | 3000 |
| Due to grocer | 1,40,000 | Cash in bank | 2000 |
| | | Debtors July–August | 1,03,000 |
| | | Gas deposit | 3000 |
| | | Assets: | |
| | | Gross | 24000 |
| | | Less depreciation | 10,000 |
| | | Grocery in stock | 5000 |
| | | Cumulative loss | |
| | | July–August | 1,09,000 |
| **Total** | **2,37,000** | | **2,37,000** |

**Balance sheet**  A list of the assets, liabilities, and owner's equity as of a specific date. The purpose of the balance sheet is to report the financial position of an accounting entity at a particular point in time.

Various account heads in a balance sheet are given in Table 2.6.

**Table 2.6**  Various account heads in a balance sheet

| Liabilities | Assets |
|---|---|
| NET WORTH/EQUITY/OWNED FUNDS<br>• Share capital/partner's capital/paid up capital/owners funds<br>• Reserves (general, capital, revaluation and other reserves)<br>• Credit balance in P and L A/c | FIXED ASSETS (LAND AND BUILDING, PLANT AND MACHINERIES)<br>• Original value less depreciation<br>• Net value or book value or written down value |
| LONG-TERM LIABILITIES/BORROWED FUNDS<br>• Term loans (banks and institutions)<br>• Debentures/bonds, unsecured loans<br>• Deposits, other long-term liabilities | NON-CURRENT ASSETS<br>• Investments in quoted shares and securities<br>• Old stocks or old/disputed book debts<br>• Long-term security deposits<br>• Other misc. assets which are not current or fixed by nature |

*(Contd)*

**Table 2.6** (*Contd*)

| Liabilities | Assets |
|---|---|
| • Bank working capital limits such as CC/OD/bills/export credit<br>• Sundry/trade creditors/creditors/bills payable, short duration loans or deposits<br>• Expenses payable and provisions against various items | • Cash and bank balance<br>• Marketable/quoted govt. or other securities<br>• Book debts/sundry debtors, bills receivables<br>• Stocks and inventory (RM,SIP,FG) stores and spares, advance payment of taxes, prepaid expenses, loans and advances recoverable within 12 months |
| | INTANGIBLE ASSETS<br>• Patent, goodwill, bebit balance in P and L A/c<br>• Preliminary or preoperative expenses |

## Cash Flow and Fund Flow Statements—Accounting Standard 3 of the Institute of Chartered Accountants of India

One of the confounding features of financial accounting is that it is built up on accrual basis and on judgements, both of which prevent stakeholders from understanding the happenings inside organizations. Accounting standards in all parts of the world, therefore, mandate organizations to append a cash flow statement to their published accounts. So is it in India as per Accounting Standard (AS) 3, whose status is indicated in Annexure 2.1.

AS 3 allows organizations to present the cash flow analysis in two ways:

- the direct method
- the indirect method

The *direct method* requires major classes of gross cash receipts and gross cash payments and reconciles the closing balance of cash. It is another form of receipt and payment account. It is possible to compile this by directly coding the cash vouchers into broad categories. A second method used could be the classification of debtors and creditors according to specified groups and arriving at this figure by using the following calculations in published accounts:

1. Cash inflow from sales = Opening balance debtors + Sales – Closing balance debtors
2. Cash outflow for purchase = Opening balance creditors + Purchases – Closing balance creditors
3. Cash outflow on assets = Closing balance – Opening balance + Depreciation provided

4. Cash inflow on equity and loan = Closing balance – Opening balance + Repayment

Those who prepare cash flow forecasts for internal control are used to this method as it is used in many organizations.

The *indirect method* starts from profits, adding back heads which give cash generated without adjusting for working capital changes and adding miscellaneous items to arrive at the net cash. Similarly, cash from investing activities are computed and in financing activities are added back. The summary of the cash flow statements of Hindustan Lever Limited (HLL) is reproduced in Table 2.7.

**Table 2.7** Cash flow statement of HLL (in lakh ₹)

| | 2004 | 2004 | 2003 | 2003 |
|---|---|---|---|---|
| Profit before tax | | 1,46,181 | | 2,15,883 |
| Adjustments: | | | | |
| Depreciation | 19,568 | | 19,999 | |
| Loss investment | –2488 | | –6010 | |
| Loss on assets | 2444 | | –1131 | |
| Others | –2880 | | –10,725 | |
| Total before WC | | | | |
| adjustments | | 1,62,825 | | 2,18,016 |
| Receivables | 3253 | | 1356 | |
| Inventories | –8152 | | –14,997 | |
| Payables | –5557 | | 3950 | |
| Total operations | 1,52,369 | | 2,08,325 | |
| Income tax | –25,102 | | –42,307 | |
| VRS | –4386 | | –2489 | |
| Others | 1,22,652 | | | |
| Net operations | | 1,22,652 | | 1,57,416 |
| Asset purchase | –33,849 | | –24,038 | |
| Investments | –8,54,273 | | –1,11,064 | |
| Sale business | 0 | | 8517 | |
| Other invest | 9,14,853 | | 1,16,634 | |
| Net investing activities | | 26,731 | | –9951 |
| Dividends | –1,20,968 | | –2,84,099 | |
| Tax on profits | –16,323 | | –36,729 | |
| Borrowings | 78,109 | | 56,410 | |
| Borrowing repayment | –89,896 | | –28,072 | |
| Others | –11,393 | | 1,34,246 | |
| Net financing activities | | –1,60,471 | | –1,58,244 |
| Change in cash | | –11,088 | | –10,780 |
| End balance | | 89,241 | | 97,723 |

*Source:* Hindustan Lever Limited Report on Accounts 2004, p. F 42.

The indirect method is nearly the same as a fund flow statement, and therefore, we are not explaining fund flow statements. We could, however, ask ourselves what the managerial uses of cash flow or fund flow statements are.

Vasudevan (2005) holds that the purpose of making cash flows could be to understand the following:

1. Are cash flows truly reflective of the working results?
2. Do cash flow statements make it credible that it is possible to service debts and sustain returns to the investors?
3. Do they give us a glimpse of the future operations or financial soundness?

If we were to think about it carefully and reflect on the cash flow statement of HLL, one would come to the conclusion that it hardly provides a more profound insight than many other analyses that would be explained later in this chapter. Nevertheless, it is a useful addition to our armoury.

## FINANCIAL RATIO ANALYSIS THROUGH STANDARD RATIOS

One of the most fascinating ways of understanding financial statements is through a variety of financial ratios. One can come to important conclusions by studying the ratios across organizations, across industries, and also the changes in the values for the same organization across time. The perspectives with which they are examined would be different and what would be considered excellent in one perspective may turn out to be inadequate from another. It is also usually important to combine several ratios to get a composite understanding. The meaning of this would be clear as we describe the different ratios used and some practical illustrations of how the ratios can be combined into a common understanding.

Before we describe the ratios, we shall briefly summarize the understanding of the descriptive categories used in balance sheets and profit and loss account.

*Current assets* include items which have transient existence in the cycle of operations in an organization. They usually change their composition within a year of their creation. They typically include cash in hand, cash in bank, trade debtors, inventories of raw material and finished goods, works-in-progress, etc. They are, therefore, more easily convertible to disposable forms.

*Fixed assets* are assets which are not current.

*Current liabilities* are those liabilities which are expected to be cleared within a short period of time, usually one year. These include sundry creditors, dues to workers and employees, dividend declared and payable, etc.

*Equity* includes shareholders' investments, and *debt* includes long-term borrowings.

## Liquidity Analysis Ratios

The status of liquidity is of critical interest to those who sell services and goods to an organization or lend monies to them. It is obviously important for the organization itself to make sure that it is always in funds to be able to pay its dues to others. It is measured as:

1.  Current ratio = Current assets/Current liabilities
    Whenever the organization is down and out and needs money to pay to service current liabilities, it can convert some current assets into liquid cash to do the needful.
2.  Quick ratio = Quick assets/Current liabilities
    Quick assets = Current assets – Inventories
    Quick assets are more liquid than the total current assets as inventories can sometimes be sticky.
3.  Net working capital ratio = Net working capital/ Total assets
    Net working capital = Current assets – Current liabilities

It shows the policy of the organization in optimally using their resources.

The norms for these ratios would be different for different organizations, different industries, and on different occasions. Thus, trading concerns would be well advised to have a high working capital ratio as a strategy. The construction industry would be required to have a high current ratio and quick ratio as its work would otherwise suffer. As we would show later in the chapter, Hindustan Lever can afford to have a current ratio of less than one as their cash management is so sophisticated and sensitive that they can always compel their creditors pay their dues on time.

## Profitability Analysis Ratios

Profitability ratios are intended to capture how well the organization is using its resources to generate value for its owners, shareholders, and other stakeholders. The Du Pont Company of the US used these ratios extensively in its organization to bring home to its executives the segment in which the resource utilization needed improvement. They used a cascading set of ratios from the top to the bottom of the organization. Stakeholders outside the organization can also judge for themselves if an organization has used its resources well, and therefore, is likely to continue to do so in the future too.

It is important to note that profitability measures are just in contrast to liquidity ratios. Organizations with very high profitability ratios may not always have high liquidity ratios. Contrarily, there would be pressures to reduce these ratios. Thus, a highly profitable organization may land itself in bankruptcy due to its inability to meet its liabilities in time. The ratios are as follows:

1. Return on assets (ROA) = Net income/Average total assets
   Average total assets = (Beginning total assets + Ending total assets)/2

   This ratio is an important measure for internal management and those who would like to know if resources are used effectively.
2. Return on equity (ROE)= Net income/Stockholder equity
   This is important for the stockholder.
3. Return on common equity (ROCE) = Net income/Average common stockholder's equity
4. Profit margin = Profit/Sales

## Activity Analysis Ratios

Ratios capture the performance of the organization in generating activity with its resources. They are as follows:

1. Assets turnover ratio = Sales/Average total assets. It may be seen that

   Profit/Assets = Profit/Sales × Sales/Assets.

   Thus, the insight into the impact of increasing activity on profitability can be roughly guessed. (In Chapter 3 we will see that this relationship is a little more complex and depends on the breakdown of costs into fixed and variable costs.)
2. Accounts receivable turnover ratio = Sales/Average accounts receivable when average receivable = (Opening receivables + Closing receivables)/2.

   An excellent ratio does not indicate the optimum situation. Tightening this may result in the restricting of sales.
3. Inventory turnover ratio = Cost of goods sold/Average inventories
   Average inventories = (Opening inventories + Closing inventories)/2

(The definition of cost of goods sold would be available in Chapter 3). As in the previous case, an excellent inventory turnover ratio may result in its stock outs. Some industries need to have low ratio, e.g., in the books industry. Amazon.com has high stocks of books to give adequate choice to the purchasers.

## Capital Structure Analysis

This primarily concerns the risk perception of the investors in the organization. The ratios are as follows:

1. Debt equity ratio = Total liabilities/Total equity
   Higher the ratio, the more highly geared are the finances. A small drop in earnings would have a sharp reduction in dividend on equity. The risk is, therefore, increased. Organizations going for long-gestation and highly capital intensive projects may prefer to have a low ratio to begin with to reduce risk.
2. Interest coverage ratio = Income before interest and income tax/ Interest expenses
   Those who lend monies to the organization may carefully watch this ratio so that their interest is secure with a high ratio.

## Capital Market Ratios

1. Tobin quotient = Market value of debt and equity/Historical cost of debt and equity
   This ratio, conceived by Tobin, a Nobel Laureate in Economics, is the perception of the market of the quality of corporate governance of the organization. There can be variations of the same concept, such as Market to book ratio = Market price of common stock per share/Book value of equity per share.
2. PE ratio = Market price of common stock per share/Earnings per share
   Higher the ratio, the higher is the perception of the future earnings expected by the market. It is analogous to the Tobin quotient.
3. Dividend yield = Annual dividends per common share/Market price of common share
4. Dividend payout ratio = Cash dividends/Income

## Discernment Analysis

An important method of identifying the extent of risks is typically using *discernment analysis*. It is a statistical method by which the data is statistically analysed to determine the combination of ratios which could partition the outcomes into different categories with a desired reliability. Thus, the analysis could show if a debtor would turn bad. If, say, 80 per cent of those who turned into bad debts had a particular combination of indicators and 80 per cent of those who did not turn bad had a different combination of indicators, one could use those indicators for fairly deciding the risk of the debt turning bad. However, it is still an intelligent guesswork as in 20 per cent of the cases the indicators could turn out to be wrong in prediction. One can use any of the several computer software programmes to do this exercise; the most well known of these is the statistical package for social sciences (SPSS) programme. Let us see an example done manually without the aid of computers.

### Discriminant analysis combining different ratios

An organization may not know how safe it is to lend money to different parties. If it typically has data on the past cases of defaulters and the corresponding figures of its profit, investments and current assets, current liabilities, it can plot these on the graph and the results may look as shown in Fig. 2.1.

As can be seen from Fig. 2.1, parties above the line generally did not default. The line can be defined by an equation. The equation can be described by a Z value $= AP + BW$, where A and B are the coefficients of P and W. This was roughly the method used by Altman (1993) with remarkable success to help his clients to forecast failures.

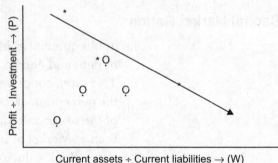

Current assets ÷ Current liabilities → (W)

∗ Parties not defaulting. ○ Parties that default.

**Fig. 2.1**  Graphical analysis of defaulting parties

HLL publishes its ratios in its reports. These are reproduced in Table 2.8.

One can see that the precipitous fall in the earnings per share not only falls in the ratio earnings/sales but also falls in the asset turnover ratio. This is in spite of rapid improvement in working capital turnover. This may be due to severe competition in the market and inadequate product innovations, which will improve sales with respect to assets and price with

**Table 2.8**  Some ratios of HLL

|  | 1995 | 1996 | 1997 | 1998 | 1999 | 2000 | 2001 | 2002 | 2003 | 2004 |
|---|---|---|---|---|---|---|---|---|---|---|
| Sales (crore ₹) | 3775 | 7120 | 8343 | 10215 | 10918 | 11392 | 11781 | 10952 | 11096 | 10888 |
| Earning per cent sales before interest and tax ₹ | 9.4 | 8 | 8.8 | 9.5 | 10.7 | 12.3 | 14 | 17.6 | 18.4 | 13.4 |
| Fixed asset turnover | 9.5 | 9.9 | 10.5 | 9,7 | 10 | 9.5 | 8.9 | 8.3 | 8.1 | 7.2 |
| Working capital turnover | 8.3 | 18.8 | 68.2 | 45.2 | 58.3 | WC minus | WC minus | WC minus | WC minus | WC minus |
| Earnings per share | 1.64 | 2.08 | 2.81 | 3.67 | 4.86 | 5.95 | 7.46 | 8.04 | 8.05 | 5.44 |
| Profit % after tax/sales | 6.3 | 5.8 | 7 | 8.2 | 9.8 | 11.5 | 13.1 | 15.8 | 16.3 | 11 |
| ROCE per cent | 49 | 53 | 61 | 59 | 62 | 65 | 62 | 59 | 60 | 46 |

*Source:* Hindustan Lever Limited Report 2004, p. 12.

reference to costs. The price–earning ratio was, however, high even in 2005, at approximately 30, which was much higher than other companies, which showed that the markets continued to have faith in the company in spite of poor recent performance.

Tables 2.9–2.14 show how to use the particulars given in the balanced sheet and calculate the various ratios.

## Example 2.3  Calculation of Financial Ratios

**Table 2.9**  Balance sheet as on 31 March 2011

| Particulars | Beginning of year (₹) |
|---|---|
| Inventory | 25,000 |
| Total assets (a) | 2,40,000 |
| Owners' equity | 58,000 |
| Number of common shares | 50,000 |

| Particulars | Annual (₹) |
|---|---|
| Current assets | 86,000 |
| Fixed assets | 1,60,000 |
| Total assets (b) | 2,46,000 |
| Average total assets (a+b)/2 | 2,43,000 |
| Cash and cash equivalents | 28,700 |

*(Contd)*

**Table 2.9** (*Contd*)

| Particulars | Beginning of year (₹) |
|---|---|
| Inventory | 28,700 |
| Average inventory | 26,850 |
| Current liabilities | 51,200 |
| Total liabilities | 2,50,000 |
| Owners' equity | 56,000 |
| Number of common shares | 50,000 |
| Average number of common shares | 50,000 |
| Average owners' equity | 57,000 |
| Market price per share | 100 |
| Cash flow | 13,70,000 |
| Cash flow per share | 27 |
| Dividends paid | 40,000 |
| Total sales | 11,23,200 |
| Operating expenses | 5,44,000 |
| Operating income | 5,79,200 |
| Advertising expense | 1,44,000 |
| Marketing expense | 88,000 |
| Earnings before interest and taxes | 3,47,200 |
| Interest expense | 1,20,000 |
| Net income | 2,27,200 |

**Question** Calculate liquidity, asset, profitability, debt and market ratios using the balance sheet provided above.

**Table 2.10** Liquidity ratio

| Liquidity ratio definition | | Annual |
|---|---|---|
| Current Ratio | $= \dfrac{\text{Current Assets}}{\text{Current Liabilities}}$ | $1.7 = \dfrac{86,000}{51,200}$ |
| Industry Average | | 2.0 |
| Variance | | −0.3 |
| Quick Ratio | $= \dfrac{\text{Current Assets} - \text{Inventory}}{\text{Current Liabilities}}$ | $1.1 = \dfrac{86,000 - 28,700}{51,200}$ |
| Industry Average | | 2.0 |
| Variance | | −0.9 |
| Net Working Capital Ratio | $= \dfrac{\text{Current Assets} - \text{Current Liabilities}}{\text{Total Assets}}$ | $0.1 = \dfrac{86,000 - 51,200}{2,46,000}$ |
| Industry Average | | 2.0 |
| Variance | | −1.9 |

(*Contd*)

| Currrent Liabilities to Inventory Ratio | = $\dfrac{\text{Current Liabilities}}{\text{Inventory}}$ | 1.8 = $\dfrac{51,200}{28,700}$ |
|---|---|---|
| Industry Average | | 2.0 |
| Variance | | –0.2 |
| Cash Ratio | = $\dfrac{\text{Cash and Cash Equivalents}}{\text{Current Liabilities}}$ | 0.6 = $\dfrac{28,700}{51,200}$ |
| Industry Average | | 2.0 |
| Variance | | –1.4 |
| Operating Ratio | = $\dfrac{\text{Operating Expenses}}{\text{Operating Income}}$ | 0.9 = $\dfrac{5,44,000}{5,79,200}$ |
| Industry Average | | 2.0 |
| Variance | | –1.1 |

**Table 2.11**  Asset ratio

| Asset ratio definition | | Annual |
|---|---|---|
| Inventory Turnover Ratio | = $\dfrac{\text{Total Sales}}{\text{Average Inventory}}$ | 41.83 = $\dfrac{11,23,200}{26,850}$ |
| Industry Average | | 2.00 |
| Variance | | 39.83 |
| Fixed Assets Turnover Ratio | = $\dfrac{\text{Total Sales}}{\text{Fixed Assets}}$ | 7.02 = $\dfrac{11,23,200}{1,60,000}$ |
| Industry Average | | 2.00 |
| Variance | | 5.02 |
| Total Assets Ratio | = $\dfrac{\text{Total Sales}}{\text{Total Assets}}$ | 4.57 = $\dfrac{11,23,200}{2,46,000}$ |
| Industry Average | | 2.00 |
| Variance | | 2.57 |
| Asset of Equity | = $\dfrac{\text{Total Assets}}{\text{Owners' Equity}}$ | 4.39 = $\dfrac{2,46,000}{56,000}$ |
| Industry Average | | 2.00 |
| Variance | | 2.39 |

**Table 2.12** Profitability ratio

| Asset ratio definition | | Annual |
|---|---|---|
| Return on Assets Ratio | $=\dfrac{\text{Net Income}}{\text{Average Total Assets}}$ | $0.93 = \dfrac{2,27,200}{2,43,000}$ |
| Industry Average | | 2.00 |
| Variance | | (1.07) |
| Return of Equity Ratio | $=\dfrac{\text{Net Income}}{\text{Average Owners' Equity}}$ | $3.99 = \dfrac{2,27,200}{57,000}$ |
| Industry Average | | 2.00 |
| Variance | | 1.99 |
| Profit Margin Ratio | $=\dfrac{\text{Net Income}}{\text{Total Sales}}$ | $0.20 = \dfrac{2,27,200}{11,23,200}$ |
| Industry Average | | 2.00 |
| Variance | | (1.80) |
| Basic Earnings | $=\dfrac{\text{Earnings Before Interest and Taxse}}{\text{Total Assets}}$ | $1.41 = \dfrac{3,47,200}{2,46,000}$ |
| Industry Average | | 2.00 |
| Variance | | (0.59) |
| Earnings per Share Ratio | $=\dfrac{\text{Net Income}}{\text{Average Number of Common Shares}}$ | $4.54 = \dfrac{2,27,200}{50,000}$ |
| Industry Average | | 2.00 |
| Variance | | 2.54 |

**Table 2.13** Debt ratio

| Debt ratio definition | | Annual |
|---|---|---|
| Total Debt Ratio | $=\dfrac{\text{Total Liabilities}}{\text{Total Assets}}$ | $1.02 = \dfrac{2,50,000}{2,46,000}$ |
| Industry Average | | 2.00 |
| Variance | | (0.98) |
| Interest Coverage Ratio | $=\dfrac{\text{Earnings Before Interest and Taxes}}{\text{Interest Expense}}$ | $2.89 = \dfrac{3,47,200}{1,20,000}$ |
| Industry Average | | 2.00 |
| Variance | | 0.89 |
| Debt/Equity Ratio | $=\dfrac{\text{Total Liabilities}}{\text{Owners' Equity}}$ | $4.46 = \dfrac{2,50,000}{56,000}$ |
| Industry Average | | 2.00 |
| Variance | | 2.46 |

**Table 2.14** Market ratio

| Market ratio definition | | Annual | |
|---|---|---|---|
| Earnings per Share (EPS) Ratio | $=$ $\dfrac{\text{Net Income}}{\text{Average Number of Common Shares}}$ | 4.54 | $= \dfrac{2,27,200}{50,000}$ |
| Industry Average | | 2.00 | |
| Variance | | 2.54 | |
| Price to Earnings Ratio | $=$ $\dfrac{\text{Market Price per Share}}{\text{Earnings per Share}}$ | 22.01 | $= \dfrac{100}{4.54}$ |
| Industry Average | | 2.00 | |
| Variance | | 20.01 | |
| Price to Cash Flow Ratio | $=$ $\dfrac{\text{Market Price per Share}}{\text{Cash Flow per Share}}$ | 3.65 | $= \dfrac{100}{27}$ |
| Industry Average | | 2.00 | |
| Variance | | 1.65 | |
| Payout Ratio | $=$ $\dfrac{\text{Dividends Paid}}{\text{Net Income}}$ | 0.18 | $= \dfrac{40,000}{2,27,200}$ |
| Industry Average | | 2.00 | |
| Variance | | (1.82) | |

## ACCOUNTING STANDARDS

Here we shall briefly deal with the legal and professional norms for accounting policies and disclosures. As mentioned in chapter 1, they are laid down by the company laws of the related country and its accounting standards are laid down by its professional councils. A large part of it is left to the self-control of the professional councils. The range of areas covered by these norms are contained in the norms laid down by the Institute of Chartered Accountants of India in the statement in Annexure 2.1 provided at the end of the chapter. It is not proposed to get into the details of each of these norms. Readers who are interested in it could go through detailed texts in financial accounting.

However, in keeping with the trends of globalization in all other aspects of business, Accounting Standards in India have also started conforming to the international standards followed by the International Accounting

Standards Board (IASB). IASB has been instrumental in developing accounting standards or further improvising the existing ones and has ushered in the International Financial Reporting Standards (IFRS) since 2001 thereby replacing the erstwhile International Accounting Standards (IAS). In India, the government has mandated that IFRS be adopted by organizations in three phases starting from 1 April 2011 and latest by 1 April 2014.

## Accounting Origins of the Enron, WorldCom, Parmalat, and Tata Finance Frauds

International attention has been drawn to the measures necessary in accounting practices to pre-empt accounting frauds perpetrated by some of the world's biggest companies. These are briefly described here.

In Enron, the directors invested in several joint ventures in which they had a partnership and the entire scheme was that if they made profits they would siphon it off for themselves. They though could palm off the risk of failure onto Enron, while the fruits of success would be theirs. The Enron balance sheets never showed the true picture of the recoverability of these investments. Many of them turned out to be disastrous investments. When the full investigation was done, the truth came out and Enron collapsed and totally destroyed a vast number of shareholders.

In WorldCom, revenue expenses were systematically shown as capital and the profits were bloated and the benefits went to the Chief Executive, who had a substantial share in the company. When the fraud came to public notice, the Chief Executive pleaded that he had signed the accounts without understanding them. In Tata Finance, the modus operandi had similarities to Enron. The company invested in A, which invested in B, which invested in C, and so on, in which the Chief Executive was interested. It turned out a bad investment. This was not explicitly disclosed in the balance sheet. When the fraud was discovered, the chief executive was jailed. He pleaded that it had the approval of his board and his chairman. It turned out that the minutes of the board was false and fabricated. Tata Sons, the parent company, made good all the losses from its own sources.

Parmalat, one of the industrial giants of Italy and one of the world's largest dairy companies, had a massive fraud perpetrated by the Tanzi family, which owned the major part of the shares of Parmalat (Sverige 2004). Clear cases of forgery, siphoning off monies to the family companies, and a range of other frauds were perpetrated. The published financial accounts, as expected, covered up everything. The facts came out when a bank, reportedly having received 4.98 billion dollars in the published accounts of Paramalat, said it had received nothing of it. Tanzi was jailed and his account chief committed suicide.

In similar cases, Shell had falsely claimed that it owned a reserve of oil far more massive than it actually had. The Chief Executive worked out profits on the basis of this and got his portion of the dividends. The top executive of the Barings Bank had an unholy deal with a junior officer that he would use the bank's money in speculating with derivatives. They suppressed the information on consequent losses in the accounts till it became obvious as there was not enough cash to support further activities. The bank went into liquidation.

Shocked by such worldwide scandals, and afraid that this would shake the foundations of modern capitalism, President George Bush rushed to enact the Sarbeanes–Oxley Act, which, among other things, had savage punishments for chief executives who sign fraudulent balance sheets. If not anything else, it should compel managers to be aware of the consequences of breaching, directly or indirectly, the canons of the accounting standards of the type available in Annexure 2.1 at the end of this chapter.

## SUMMARY

There are four features of financial accounting. First are the basic concepts, the second is the mechanics used in implementing these concepts, the third are the techniques of analysing the results reported in financial statements, and the fourth are the conventions and norms prescribed by law and professional councils of accountants for transparent disclosure. These are intended to ensure the smooth functioning of capitalism using market mechanisms for ensuring free choice for investors.

The basic outcome of financial accounting is the published balance sheet and profit and loss account (or its equivalent), which inform the stakeholders of an organization. The importance of this document may be adjudged by the fact that false or wrong facts in published accounts would entail severest punishment, which may extend upto 25 years of jail, for the chief executive who signs such a report. The US has taken a lead in this regard through its Sarbeanes–Oxley Act.

## KEY POINTS

- Entity has an identity distinct from that of the owner and has to periodically prepare its balance sheet on specific dates which exhibit what the entity owes and what it owns, which are known as liabilities and assets.
- The accounting equation requires that the difference between what it owes or what it owns with respect to outside parties is in the net what it owes or owns in respect of the owners. Therefore, balance sheets on the whole will always balance what is owed and what is owned.
- Mandatory disclosures dictate the nature of the documentation required to record the financial transactions. Accrual accounting is important to understand the financial situation, accounting standards require appending cash flow statements. There are two options provided, one, the direct method, such as the receipt of a payment account, and a second, which is derived from published profits and making adjustments for non-cash aspects of the accounts.

## CONCEPT REVIEW QUESTIONS

1. Why does the balance sheet balance?
2. What is the difference between double entry bookkeeping and single entry bookkeeping?
3. Can one prepare a balance sheet without any accounting entries of financial transactions that precede such a preparation?
4. A credit purchase is made of an asset. How will it figure in the balance sheet?
5. List three situations which require the application of the concept of mutual matching of expense with revenue?
6. State the basic stipulations under which a sale transaction would be recorded as a sale in the books of accounts.
7. What are the two methods recommended for making cash flow statements in Accounting Standard 3 of the ICA of India?
8. An organization has reduced its current ratio from 1.5 to 0.80. What are the questions that a management accountant should ask?
9. What is the significance of the difference between the current ratio and the liquidity ratio?
10. In an organization, profit/sales is 30 per cent and sales/assets was 3. In the next year, profit/sales continued to be 30 per cent, but sales/asset became 2. What are the questions that a management accountant should ask?
11. Sales/accounts receivable reduces from 4 to 3. What are the questions that a management accountant should ask?

12. Is the increase of ratio of debt/equity a signal of increased or reduced risk?
13. The price earning (P/E) ratio has come down in an organization. What are the questions that a management accountant should ask?
14. The Tobin quotient has increased in an organization. Is it a good or bad signal?
15. Can you cite a method invented by Altman by which a liquidity ratio and a profitability ratio can be studied together to forecast the risk of default of a party in paying its dues?

## NUMERICAL PROBLEMS

1. An organization has an opening balance of ₹1,00,000 on 1 August in its debtor's account and a closing balance of ₹80,000 on 31 August for its debtors. The sales of the month on cash was ₹30,000 and sales on credit was ₹3,00,000. What was the total cash flow on account sales in August?
2. The opening owner's account for the year starting on 1 April 2004 was ₹20,00,000. The year's expenses were ₹10,00,000 and income was ₹12,00,000. There was no fresh infusion of owner's funds. Prepare an accounting equation to incorporate this information.

## PROJECTS

1. Form groups of four students and choose a company of your choice and critically comment on their segment profitability ratios.
2. Form groups of four students and compare the ratios of three companies in the same industry and prepare a report. Also, prepare an analysis of five years of their comparative performance as revealed by their critical ratios.

 **CASE STUDY 1**   **Kamath's Student Mess**

Kamath, an enterprising restaurant owner, was approached by the students of Badami Institute for taking over the mess. They showed him the balance sheet prepared by Janki, the chartered accountant. He was impressed by the facilities available and the ready customers. He agreed to take over the mess on an as-is-where-is condition provided they agreed to his monthly

Table 2.15   Balance sheet of the mess as on 31st Aug

| Liability (₹) | | Assets (₹) | |
|---|---|---|---|
| Student deposit | 97,000 | Cash In hand | 3000 |
| Due to grocer | 1,40,000 | Cash in bank | 2000 |
| | | Debtors July–Aug. | 1,03,000 |
| | | Gas deposit | 3000 |
| | | Assets: | |
| | | Gross | 24,000 |
| | | Less depreciation | 10,000 |
| | | Grocery in stock | 5000 |
| | | Cumulative loss | |
| | | July–Aug. | 1,09,000 |
| Total | 2,37,000 | | 2,37,000 |

charge of ₹1500 per head for a month for three meals. He said that he would take over the liabilities and assets. He decided to show the equivalent of the past losses of the mess as goodwill in his books, as shown in Table 2.15.

The gas dealer agreed to transfer the deposit in his name.

His transactions in September were as follows:

He paid back the student deposit of ₹97,000. He further borrowed ₹1,00,000 from a bank. He collected all the outstanding student dues of ₹1,03,000 and paid back the vendor dues of ₹1,40,000.

He bought grocery worth ₹1,00,000 and paid ₹80,000.

He bought further capital assets worth ₹30,000.

He paid for three gas cylinders for ₹900.

He employed three cooks and paid them cash ₹10,000. Nothing else was due to them.

At the end of the month, grocery worth ₹3000 was available.

He assessed that he should depreciate his assets at 20 per cent per annum.

The student dues at the rate of ₹1500 per student were not yet collected from September.

## Discussion Questions

1. If you were Kamath, how would you prepare the balance sheet as on 1st September?
2. Prepare the profit and loss account for September and balance sheet as on 30th September.
3. How would you prepare the cash flow statement for September based on the first and second method prescribed under Accounting Standard 3 of the ICAI (you may refer to Annexure 2.1)?

| CASE STUDY 2 | Jyoti Prakash Highway Restaurant |

Prakash and his wife Jyoti decided to start a restaurant on the highway between Mangalore and Bangalore.

Jyoti advised Prakash that they needed a smart person who could handle the customers and that she knew a person, Kumar, who would fit the bill. Jyoti and Prakash promised to put in ₹1,00,000 and she persuaded Kumar to put in ₹20,000 of his money. They decided that they would share the profit and loss in the ratio of 10:2, representing the investment ratios. The partnership was, however, only between Prakash and Kumar. Jyoti's name was not included, even though she had desired to be included as a partner. The business started on 1st January and Prakash handed over his ₹1,00,000 to Jyoti, who acted as the cashier. He saw Kumar similarly hand over his ₹20,000. Prakash arranged an overdraft arrangement with the Karnataka Bank for ₹1,00,000. Cooks were appointed for ₹8000 per month in addition to free food. Prakash looked after the cooking and Jyoti generally agreed to keep the cash and cash book and accounts. Prakash would not trust cheque signing to her and he kept the cheque drawing powers all to himself. However, Jyoti collected all the receipts, which were all in cash. Cash payments were intended for gas cylinders, the cooks' wages, and small miscellaneous items. The grocer was paid by cheque by Prakash after Jyoti checked it with her records of purchases. Prakash wrote the details of the cheques issued in the stubs. At the end of every month, he checked the cash balances and deposited the surplus as estimated by him in the nearby branch of the Karnataka Bank. He kept the paying slips in his personal custody. The business was roaring success and all seemed to be going on wonderfully. However, after six months, that is, from 1st July, he started noticing some changes in Jyoti's attitude. She seemed cold and aloof. Even though his customers did not appear to be reducing in number, he was getting less and less surpluses from the cash box for depositing in the bank. Prakash did not understand why this was happening. Jyoti said that the income was coming down and the cash expenses going up. Somewhat tragically, one day he found his bedroom door wide ajar, and the cash box was empty. The cash book which Jyoti used to maintain was also gone, as also the vouchers that supported the cash book entries. He looked first for Jyoti and then for Kumar. Both were gone. He later learnt that Jyoti and Kumar had started a restaurant near Goa.

Prakash complained to the police. The police said that they could file a case against Kumar for adultery, but Jyoti, when approached, complained in turn of cruel treatment by Prakash. The police said that Prakash could file a civil suit. Prakash's lawyers said that he would have to estimate the likely amount of cash which must have been taken by Jyoti and Kumar. If Prakash could roughly work out the cash surpluses and profits in the first six months, it would be helpful for preparing the estimate. Prakash provided the following data:

*January:*

**1 Jan:**     Paid into JPH account in bank ₹1,00,000
                  Cheque issued to gas dealer for deposit ₹5000
**30 Jan:**   Issued cheque to grocer ₹60,000 for supplies till date

*February:*

**10 Feb:**   Issued cheque to kitchen equipment supplier ₹30,000
**28 Feb:**   Issued cheque to grocer ₹68,000 for supplies till date
                  Deposited in JPH bank ₹1,13,000

*March:*

**1 Mar:**    Paid for A/c of deluxe room ₹25,000
**31 Mar:**   Paid for grocer ₹80,000 up to date payment
                  Deposit in bank ₹1,33,000

*April:*

**1 Apr:**    Paid for special furniture and room decorations ₹40,000
**30 Apr:**   Paid grocer for up to date receipts ₹90,000
                  Paid to bank ₹1,50,000

*May:*

**31 May:**   Paid to grocer up to date payment ₹1,00,000
                  Deposited in bank ₹1,70,000

*June:*

**30 June:**  Paid grocer up top date ₹1,10,000
                  Deposited in bank ₹1,76,000

*July:*

                  Paid to grocer bill up to date ₹1,20,000
                  No money deposited in bank as there did not appear to be any surplus

Prakash had checked on 31ˢᵗ July that the grocery in the kitchen was worth ₹30,000. Jyoti had taken away the records of the grocery purchased. Prakash found gas cylinders worth ₹600 still in stock and the gas dealer confirmed that his deposits were intact. The cooks were not paid for the month of July. Prakash decided that he could provide depreciation for the equipment at 20 per cent per annum.

## Discussion Questions

1. Prepare a balance sheet at the end of July.
2. How would you prepare the profit and loss account for January–July (including the loss due to the theft of the monies by Jyoti and Kumar)?
3. Draft your estimates for profit for the period January–June (giving clear assumptions) and for Kumar's share.
4. Prepare an estimate of the money stolen by Jyoti and Kumar (make your assumptions clear).
5. Was the overdraft ever used by Prakash?

# ANNEXURE

## Annexure 2.1

### Accounting Standards Issued By ICAI

| AS No. | Title of the Statement | Effective date |
|---|---|---|
| 1 | Disclosure of Accounting Policies | 01/04/1993 |
| 2 | Valuation of Inventories (Revised) | 01/04/1999 |
| 3 | Cash Flow Statement (Revised) | 01/04/2001 |
| 4 | Contingencies and Events Occurring after the Balance Sheet Date | 01/04/1998 |
| 5 | Net Profit or Loss for the Period, Prior Period Items and Changes in Accounting Policies (Revised) | 01/04/1996 |
| 6 | Depreciation Accounting (Revised) | 01/04/1995 |
| 7 | Construction Contracts (Revised) | 01/04/2002 |
| 8 | Research & Development | Withdrawn |
| 9 | Revenue Recognition | 01/04/1993 |
| 10 | Accounting for Fixed Assets | 01/04/1993 |
| 11 | The Effects of Changes in Foreign Exchange Rates (Revised) | 01/04/2004 |
| 12 | Accounting for Government Grants | 01/04/1994 |
| 13 | Accounting for Investments | 01/04/1995 |
| 14 | Accounting for Amalgamations | 01/04/1995 |
| 15 | Employee Benefits | 01/04/2006 |
| 16 | Borrowing Costs | 01/04/2000 |
| 17 | Segment Reporting | 01/04/2001 |
| 18 | Related Party Disclosures | 01/04/2001 |
| 19 | Leases | 01/04/2001 |
| 20 | Earning Per Shares | 01/04/2001 |
| 21 | Consolidated Financial Statement | 01/04/2001 |
| 22 | Accounting for Taxes on Income | 01/04/2001 |
| 23 | Accounting for Investment in Associates in Consolidated Financial Statement | 01/04 2002 |
| 24 | Discontinuing Operations | 01/04/2004 |

| 25 | Interim Financial Statement | 01/04/2002 |
| 26 | Intangible Assets | 01/04/2003 |
| 27 | Financial Reporting of Interests in Joint Ventures | 01/04/2002 |
| 28 | Impairment of Assets | 01/04/2004 |
| 29 | Provisions, Contingent Liabilities and Contingent Assets | 01/04/2004 |
| 30 | Financial Instruments: Recognition and Measurement | |
| 31 | Financial Instruments: Presentation | |
| 32 | Financial Instruments: Disclosures | |

*Source:* http://en.wikipedia.org/wiki/Accounting_Standards_Issued_by_ICAI

## CHAPTER 3

# Terminology of Costing

## Learning Objectives

After reading this chapter, you will be able to understand

- the terminology of costing used in this book and the practical uses of the concepts they imply
- the difference between the natural classifications used in financial accounts and the functional classification used in cost accounting
- the meaning of cost objects and distinguish it from the objective of costing
- the meaning of responsibility centres, cost centres (expense centres), revenue centres, and investment centres
- the behaviour of costs classified as fixed costs, variable costs, and semi-variable costs
- the use and misuse of the concept of unit cost for managerial purposes

- the managerial meaning of controllable costs and uncontrollable costs
- the meaning of direct costs, indirect costs, overheads, prime costs, conversion costs, and out-of-pocket costs
- the interface between cost accounting and financial accounting in the computation of cost of goods sold in manufacturing and non-manufacturing organizations, cost of goods manufactured in manufacturing organizations, inventoriable costs, non-inventoriable costs, period costs, and product costs
- the need for defining costs differently for different purposes

## INTRODUCTION

**Standardization**
Accounting terminologies are not fully standardized and caution is necessary in using them.

Cost accountants can fulfil their role of scorekeepers, problem solvers, and attention drawers, probing into the internal workings of an organization, only if they had at their disposal a variety of concepts and techniques, which could cope with the complexity of organizations and also simultaneously be clear enough for extensive and easy understanding of non-finance managers. These concepts and techniques are captured by the terminology used by accountants. There are varying meanings for the words used by cost accountants across the world though several efforts have been made to standardize them.

This text uses words in the manner they are used by Horngren (2002) in his well-known books. The reader is advised to adhere to the definitions used in this book for understanding the text and desist from seeking out alternative definitions. The words and concepts common across all the chapters of the book are described in this chapter. The list contained in this chapter is, therefore, not a comprehensive glossary. In introducing the basic terminology, a glimpse has been provided to the range of practical uses of cost accounting as a domain of knowledge. Individual chapters have definitions of words more specific to the respective chapters.

## NATURAL DESCRIPTIVE CLASSIFICATION AND FUNCTIONAL CLASSIFICATION

**Natural descriptive classification**
Financial accounting uses natural classification to suit legal requirements.

In aggregating the results of the transactions of an organization, financial accounting and cost accounting use different categories of ledgers (counters). Financial accounting involved in preparing and presenting balance sheets and profit and loss accounts to the outside world, uses what is known as natural classification. Typically, they are sales, sale returns, salaries and wages, expenses, depreciation, purchases by class of stores say packing material, and so on. This follows the usual requirements of law; in India they are prescribed by the Indian Companies Act and other legislations applicable to different forms of organizations. The description of this manner of classification as natural could be intriguing. It attracted the sardonic comment of Shillinglaw (1971), the well-known professor at Columbia University.

He preferred to rename the principle as a descriptive classification. Cost accounting, on the other hand, interested in tracing use of resources to products and services, classifies the transactions according to their functions in application. Thus, could be purchase department, cutting department, machining department, polishing department—all of which are called overheads, and say grinders, juice makers, sale of grinders, sale of juice makers, and so on, which are all product categories.

A few statutes covering financial accounting may require some functional break down of revenue and expenses. For example, the GAAP of the US would require a segment profitability to be published along with the audited balance sheet; so would the latest amendments to Indian accounting standards that have been explained in Chapter 1.

**Functional classification**
Cost accounting uses functional classification in conjunction with natural classification.

These require functional classification to a limited extent. Very importantly, it should be possible, if need be, to relate the functional breakdown of expenses and revenues back to their aggregated numbers across functions and unscramble and restore the pristine purity of the natural descriptive classifications. This posed one of the major problems in introducing cost accounting and programme budgeting concepts in budgeting for public administration in the US. They had to devise what is known as crosswalk or cross over network between the two types of classifications (Anshen 1965).

We will show later that this is simple in computerized accounting. The relationship between natural classification of financial accounts and functional classification of cost accounting in an organization in household appliances business, would be clear in Table 3.1. The organization buys parts, assembles them, packs them, and markets them in their brand name.

The natural classification could, therefore, be opening and closing stocks, purchase and consumption of purchased parts, purchases and consumption of packing material, manufacture and sale of finished goods, salaries and wages, power expenses, and depreciation. Functional classification could be say two products, grinders, juice makers, and a third head which is an overhead. Since overheads would ultimately have to be used in products, there could be one more head of account, which could be called overhead allocated.

For overhead allocated, the accountant would show a negative figure in the functional classification and a positive figure against each product cost centre. The net overhead will be zero in cost classification (spent minus allocated to products) and neither the plus nor the minus would appear at all in financial accounts. As mentioned in Chapter 1, the figures for inventory would be provided by cost accountants as they have the wherewithal and the data to compute cost per unit of each product and they could use this to value closing stocks as well as opening stocks prudently at cost or market, whichever is lower. If one were to analyse why grinders are losing, we could trace the records to show why costs are high and for this purpose, the breakdown under natural classification within the cost centre would be necessary.

Thus, financial accounts and cost accounts are integrated. Such an integration was a great travail when accounts were kept manually. With computerization, the simple matrix shown in Table 3.1 could be made for a large number of products and services, enormous number of overheads, innumerable allocations, and a long list of natural heads of accounts developed for financial accounting.

**Table 3.1** Matrix of natural and functional classification in Sowbhagya Household Appliances (in ₹)

| | Financial accounts | Cost/Revenue object grinders | Cost/Revenue object juice makers | Cost object overhead |
|---|---|---|---|---|
| 1a. Parts opening stock | 0 | | | 0 |
| 1b. Purchases | 3,00,000* | | | |
| 1c. Closing stock | 0 | | | |
| 1d. Consumption a+b-c | 3,00,000* | 1,20,000 | 1,80,000 | |
| 2a. Packing material Opening stock | 0* | | | 0 |
| 2b. Purchases | 40,000* | | | |
| 2c. Closing stock Consumption a+b-c | 0* 40,000* | 20,000 | 20,000 | |
| 3. Salaries/wages | 4,00,000 | 80,000 | 40,000 | 2,80,000 |
| 4. Power | 40,000 | 20,000 | 15,000 | 5000 |
| 5. Depreciation | 1,00,000 | | | 1,00,000 |
| 6. Overhead allocated | | 2,15,000 | 1,70,000 | (3,85,000) |
| 7. Cost of manufacture Σ(1–6) | 8,80,000* (300+40+ 400+40+ 100 all in thousands) | 4,55,000 | 4,25,000 | 0 |
| 8a. Finished goods Opening stock | 0* | 0 | 0 | 0 |
| 8b. Manufacture | 8,80,000* | 4,55,000* | 4,25,000* | |
| 8c. Closing stock | 30,000* | 20,000* | 10,000* | |
| 8d. Cost of good sold | 8,50,000* | 4,35,000* | 4,15,000* | |
| | Financial accounts | Cost object grinder | Cost object juice maker | Cost object overheads |
| 9. Sales | 9,35,000 | 4,00,000 | 5,35,000 | 0 |
| 10. Profit 9–8d | 85,000 | (35,000) | 1,20,000 | 0 |

*Data from cost analysis
Brackets are negative figures.

# COST OBJECTS

**Cost object**
Cost object is a thing or a person on whom cost is accumulated. These are sometimes described as cost centres in UK.

For the purposes of directing the activities of the organization towards achievement of its goals, we had seen in Table 3.1 the various types of heads and how useful information was aggregated (cost accumulated) under cost objects, grinders, juice makers, and overheads. Cost objects are things or persons on which the aggregation (accumulation) is done. Traditionally in UK (Lucey 2002), cost objects are also described as cost centres but not by Horngren. Such aggregation is done for several managerial purposes.

It could be to ascertain the cost of a product, a process, or the cost incurred by a set of managers who are accountable for such expenses. The cost of products could be important for pricing, product mix decisions, or production planning. The cost of process may be useful in choosing between different processes. Cost incurred by a set of managers may be necessary for them to set budgets, targets, and for the evaluation of their performance. To summarize, cost objects are designed to fulfil operational and strategic objectives. The cost objects are, therefore, a valuable help to achieve the objectives of the cost management. Table 3.2 illustrates the variety of cost objects.

**Table 3.2** Variety of cost objects

| Cost object | Illustrations |
| --- | --- |
| Product | Coking coal Gr 1, Disco Diwane—a music album, *Costing a Strategic Emphasis*—a book, Dabur Red toothpaste (small tube), Whole wheat bread (half kg), electric grinder, electric juice maker, Laser printer 222, Lifebuoy (green), Lifebuoy (red) |
| Service | MBA general programme, Mobile telephone transmission towers, Rajdhani Express, ICU unit of Dayanand Hospital |
| Project | Karkardooma flyover, Kalimati Open Cast Project, launching of Fair and Lovely |
| Customer | Senior citizen accounts, students accounts, women customers |
| Brand category | Amul brand, Tomco brand, Bata brand |
| Activity | Heat treatment, lathe operations, dough mixing, baking, packing, customer after sales service, assembly, AC unit, boiler house, invoicing, computer data entry |
| Distribution | Super markets, wholesalers, retail, franchisees |
| Department | Accounts department, administration department, advertisement department |
| Responsibility centres | Salesman A, works manager, purchase manager, general manager, personnel manager, maintenance manager, power house manager |

It can be seen that there could be vastly different reasons for the manner in which information of transactions have to be aggregated (accumulated) and shown against a cost object. With computers, one can have the same transactions classified and deconstructed in more than one way. Thus, expenses can be classified under product cost objectives for understanding product costs say grinders, juice mixer, etc. and simultaneously under responsibility centres namely Salesmen A, B, and C to find out their performance, and against distribution channels as wholesales, retailers, etc. (Nadani 2000).

## RESPONSIBILITY CENTRES

**Responsibility centres**
Organizational devices to ensure accountability to achieve organizational goals and strategies. Four categories: cost centre, revenue centre, profit centre, investment centre.

The role of cost accountants as scorekeepers, attention drawers, and problem solvers can be seen from two distinctly different perspectives, one for decision-making and a second for budgeting, performance evaluation, and management control. Cost objects are designed to provide information for both perspectives. Responsibility centres address themselves to the second perspective. Responsibility centres emerge out of organizational structures which are intended to bring in accountability to the functioning of managers. Responsibility is aligned with accountability and is described both in terms of work to be done by the responsibility centre and also has a corresponding financial provision. These are discussed in detail in Chapters 6, 7, 8, and 9.

It is sufficient to indicate in this chapter that responsibility centres are of the following four types:

*Cost Centres:* Managers who are responsible for costs incurred with reference to the activity.

*Revenue Centres:* Managers who are responsible for revenue earned with reference to the activity.

*Profit Centres:* Managers who are responsible for both costs and revenue and, therefore, for profits with reference to the activity.

*Investment Centres:* Managers who are responsible not only for absolute profits but also for investments that the activity used to make that profit. The relationship between the different types of responsibility centres for performance evaluation and responsibility centres for decision-making would be clear from Table 3.3, which may be seen as an extension of column of grinders (third column) in Table 3.1.

One can note that information for accountability and for decisions are intertwined and can be served quite well by a well designed and integrated accounting system as also shown in Table 3.3.

**Table 3.3** The hierarchy of responsibility centres

| Profit centre | Grinder division divisional manager (Overall)–DM | | | | | | | | | | |
|---|---|---|---|---|---|---|---|---|---|---|---|
| Responsibility decisions RD | Divisional manager (Direct)-RD1 | General manager reporting to DM-RD2 | | | | | | | Divisional manager (Direct) RD3 | Marketing manager reporting to DM-RD4 | |
| Responsibility implementation R 1–6 | R & D manager R1 | Production manager R2 | | Maintenance manager R3 | | Purchase manager R4 | | | Personnel manager R5 | Marketing and sales manager R6 | |
| Cost centre C 1–10 and Revenue centres 1 (Grinder) | General activity C1 | Project A C2 | Manufacture C3 | Packing C4 | Mechanical C5 | Electrical C6 | Ordering C7 | Inspection C8 | Personnel C9 | Selling and Distribution C10 | Revenue Rev 1 |

Costs are equal to

$C1+C2+C3+C4+C5+C6+C7+C8+C9+C10 = \Sigma C_n$ and

$Profit = Rev\ 1 - \Sigma C.$

But the responsibility of R1, R2, R3, R4, R5, and R6 are separately ascertainable in financial and non-financial terms, which include working harmoniously with the other responsibility centres.

Responsibility centres could sometimes get further broken down into responsibilities of individual activities as shown in Table 3.3.

Let us take the next important step that has been immensely helped by the availability of computers. Let us presume that the responsibility centres in Table 3.3 represent the following:

R1 Research and development: C1–General activity and C2–Specific project

R2 Production: C3–Manufacture C4–Packing

R3 Maintenance: C5–Mechanical engineering C6–Electrical engineering

R4 Purchase: C7–Ordering C8–Inspection and receipt

R5 Personnel: C9–Personnel

R6 Marketing and selling: C10–Selling and distribution expenses, Rev 1–Revenue

One may come to understand that both for better control and better decisions, it may be important to gather a more discriminating detail as the following, which is called activity-based costing (ABC), dealt with in detail in Chapter 6:

1. Under C3: Activities A1 to N, A1–Casting, A2–Machining, A3–Heat Treatment, A4–Polishing. This would enable cost of these activities to be differentiated between Product X and Y using the same methodology as we used for allocating costs of cost centres.
2. Under C7: A5–Orders against rate contracts, A6–Normal ordering including bulk ordering.
3. Under C8: A7–Inspection and receiving for Product X, A8–Inspecting and receiving for Product Y.
4. Under C10: Selling A9–Selling of Product X through Channel D, A10–Selling of Product X through Channel E, A11–Selling Product Y through Channel D, A12–Selling of Product Y through Channel E.

A1–10 may also be perceived as low responsibility centres subordinate to the high-level responsibility centres. This reorganization of data would also give a more accurate picture of product costs of X and Y. Activity based costs are basically to classify overheads. The two purposes of accountability and product costing, therefore, now stand better integrated.

The issues of accountability and decision-making in ABC system is much simplified if we assume that activity costs are all fixed in the short run and all variable in the long run. This means that if we find that the cost of a product results in our inability to sell it, the manager at responsibility centre RD in Table 3.3 can take steps to have the other related responsibility centres to reduce costs or can as a last alternative discontinue the product.

## CLASSIFICATION OF COSTS ACCORDING TO BEHAVIOUR TOWARDS DRIVERS AND OVER A RANGE

**How cost drivers drive costs**
Cost drivers drive variable costs in short range changes, semi-variable costs in the medium range changes, and fixed costs in the long range changes. They share a cause and effect relationship and can be explained by a plausible theory and empirical observation.

One of the most important aids to decision-making is discovering the optimum level of activity for an organization. This arises from the fact that activities act as cost drivers, and alter costs in the short run and long run, over short ranges of changes in activities and over long range of changes.

Costs that change within short range of changes are defined as variable costs, those which change over medium ranges are known as semi-variable costs, and those which change only over a very large change in activity are known as fixed costs. All these categories of costs have their cost drivers. This pattern is shown in Fig. 3.1.

The changes in costs can be linear, quadratic, or can take odd shapes. These are described in Chapter 12. Some costs may also have multiple cost drivers, a problem we will handle in Chapter 4. An understanding of these changes in cost and revenue can aid both in decision-making and in performance evaluation. Cost drivers have a direct cause and effect

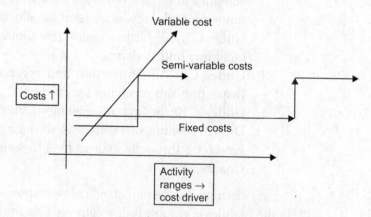

**Fig. 3.1** Behavioural patterns of costs

relationship to costs as could be seen in Fig. 3.1. But beyond a range, patterns of relationship would change as can be seen from Example 3.1.

**Fixed overhead** This represents overhead expenses which tend to remain unaffected by the fluctuations in the volume of production or sale within a relevant range and during a defined period of time. Examples are rent, rates, insurance, executive salaries, audit fees, etc. Fixed cost is also termed as period cost or policy cost, since most of the expenses are incurred over a period of time and arise out of the policy of the management. Fixed overheads remain unchanged within a relevant range of activity, because if the activity exceeds or recedes the range, expenses on certain items of fixed overheads may increase or decrease. Again, fixed overheads change with the change in price levels. For example, prices of indirect materials, executive and supervisory salaries, insurance premia, power tariff, etc. may change over a period of time, resulting in the change of fixed overheads. However, such changes do not occur in a short period, say, one year. Hence, fixed overheads are said to remain fixed within a short period of time. Total fixed overheads remain unchanged with the increase or decrease of output in a short period, but the fixed overhead cost per unit changes with the change in the activity level, as shown in Table 3.4.

**Variable overhead** Variable overhead expenses tend to follow (in the short run) the level of activity. The variation may not always be in the same proportion as the production or sales volume changes, but, by and large, there is a linear relationship between the variable overheads and output, represented in Fig. 3.2. Examples of variable overheads are indirect

**Table 3.4** Illustrations of use of cost behaviour for managerial purposes

| | Cost Diffrentiation | | |
|---|---|---|---|
| **Units produced** | **Variable** | **Fixed** | **Total** |
| – | – | 2,000 | 2,000 |
| 100,000 | 400 | 2,000 | 2,400 |
| 200,000 | 800 | 2,000 | 2,800 |
| 300,000 | 1,200 | 2,000 | 3,200 |
| 400,000 | 1,600 | 2,000 | 3,600 |
| 500,000 | 2,000 | 2,000 | 4,000 |
| 600,000 | 2,400 | 2,000 | 4,400 |
| 700,000 | 2,800 | 2,000 | 4,800 |
| 800,000 | 3,200 | 2,000 | 5,200 |
| 900,000 | 3,600 | 2,000 | 5,600 |
| 1,000,000 | 4,000 | 2,000 | 6,000 |

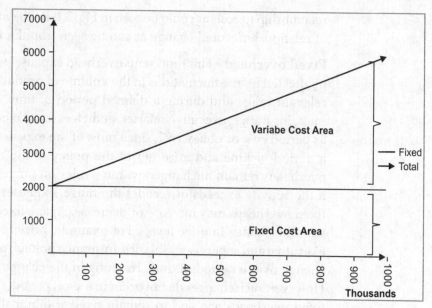

**Fig. 3.2** Cost differentiation

material, indirect labour, power and fuel, lighting and heating expenses, salesmen's commission, etc. Although the amount of variable overhead changes, the cost per unit of output tends to remain constant at different levels of output. This is, again, true only within a limited range of output.

## Example 3.1 Cost Behaviour in a Business School

The cost driver that could be logically considered is the number of students: the cost of photostatting reading material would increase linearly with it. More the number of students more the photostatted material as one copy is given to each. Beyond a point when the capacity is stretched, overtime maybe demanded and the costs would change direction as in Fig. 3.1.

The cost of faculty would be constant initially but if the number of students increases, faculty would also increase, and again remain constant at an enhanced level. The cost of facilities will remain constant for large changes in the number of students, but ultimately it cannot contain vast increase in the number of students without increasing. In summary, the cost driver logically continues to be the number of students but the cost behaviour changes as items of costs may be different over short term, medium term, and long term.

Atkinson et al. (2004) have noted that the costs which change over a long range have an in-built feature that they will have idle capacity in lower levels of activity. Management accountants should highlight this in their reports. Another feature of cost drivers is that the proximate causes of costs may be different from the ultimate causes of costs. This is illustrated in Example 3.2.

### Example 3.2 Proximate and Ultimate Cost Drivers

In the example of a business school depicted in Example 3.1, the proximate cost driver for costs is the number of class room sessions. That is, a visiting faculty may be paid according to the number of sessions taught. But once the teaching module is decided, the number of sessions would remain constant for it. So the number of students could be used for practical purposes as a cost driver which is the cause of the costs. But if the number of students increase beyond a point, we would need one more section which would increase the number of sessions and, therefore, costs would go up accordingly. Since revenues go up with the number of students, it would be convenient for decisions to treat number of students both as cost and revenue drivers.

A third kind of problem is that the most logical and scientific cost driver may not be easily measurable and a proxy may be used for practical reasons. Example 3.3 would illustrate this.

### Example 3.3 Choice of More Easily Measurable Cost Drivers

Canteen expenses would logically be driven by the number of heavy eaters, vegetarians, non-vegetarians, and a combination of these two factors, which would require a four-way classification of activity. But this would put a lot of difficulty in measuring. Therefore, worker strength which is more easily measured can be used as a proxy cost driver, which would serve our purposes normally.

A fourth kind of problem is that some costs have multiple cost drivers. Example 3.4 would illustrate this.

### Example 3.4 Power Cost Drivers

Power costs are directly driven by horse-power of motors per hours run. But this is difficult to measure. If we wish to develop a proxy for this, we could get three sources, product mix, ambient temperature that drives the AC unit. The only proxy cost driver that we could get, is a formula based on product mix and weights for summer and winter.

A fifth kind of issue is that costs which are variable with reference to one cost driver may be fixed with reference to another driver. This can be seen in Example 3.5.

### Example 3.5 Variable with Reference to One Cost Driver and Fixed with Reference to Another

Lawn maintenance costs are fixed for an institute, as it does not change with its universal cost driver, namely the number of students. But for an entrepreneur who is in lawn maintenance business it is variable with reference to the area of lawn maintained, which is the cost driver. One must, therefore, be cautious in describing any cost as fixed or variable without specifying the cost driver.

Fixed costs are not constant non-varying costs. They are fixed because they have no short-term cost–effect relationship with reference to a chosen cost driver. We will see this in Example 3.6.

### Example 3.6 Fixed Costs not Same as Constant and Non-Varying Costs

In an engineering firm, salaries and wages were ₹2 lakhs in April, ₹2.5 lakh in May, ₹2.4 lakh in June; production in April was 1000 units, 800 units in May, and 750 units in June. No engineer could explain the cause and effect between salaries and wages and changes in production in the short run. On the other hand, the entire workforce comprised permanent employees. It transpired that in May, there were machine breakdowns and overtime had to be used to set the plant right. In April, a large number of workers were absent and they had taken leave without pay. In June, the manpower got its yearly increment and salaries and wages went up. These changes did not make the head for expenses variable. They could be described only as fixed but not invariant. Lastly, separation of costs into fixed and variable costs must be based on sound theoretical understanding of the engineering cause and effect relationship between the cost driver and the item of cost as also confirmed by actual empirical verification of this theory. The way this could be done is explained in Chapter 12. Lastly, we will note that just as drivers of cost there could be drivers of revenue. When the same driver drives cost and revenue, it is convenient to plot them together in a chart to take several decisions. Thus if sale of chocolates drives both costs and revenue, we may choose the optimum sale volume of chocolates.

We now have an example from the aviation industry (Example 3.7).

**Example 3.7**    Dichotomy between Revenue and Cost Drivers
in the Aviation Industry

Aviation industry has its costs driven by hours of flight, both the variable and
fixed costs as depreciation in the industry are computed by flight hours. But
revenue is driven basically by number of passengers and to some extent by
flight hours; longer the flight higher the revenue, but not quite in proportion.
How do we make managerial decision on this parameter? Aviation accountants
use a parameter that finds a solution to this problem. They use a parameter
described as occupancy ratio, and in conjunction with flight hours, it could help
aviation executives take several decisions.

To summarize, for describing any element of cost as variable, semi-
variable, or fixed costs, one would have to specify the cost driver with
reference to which this assertion is made and should be able to establish a
cause and effect relationship with a plausible theory. Further, the range of
values for the cost driver has to be specified. If the same driver also drives
revenues, it is possible to put the two bits of information together to take
several decisions. Having got the basic ways in which cost and revenue
behaviour could be predicted, let us now have a set of illustrations for the
several uses of this fixed–variable analysis. This can be seen in Table 3.5.

Horngren et al. (2002) ranks the managerial uses of such study of cost
behaviour. This is shown here:

1. Pricing
2. Budgeting
3. Profitability analysis—existing products
4. Profitability analysis—new products
5. Cost-volume-profit analysis
6. Variance Analysis

One may see that according to Horngren, the two most important uses
are one in decision-making, that is in pricing, and a second in performance
evaluation and controls, namely budgeting.

The internal perception of the Japanese shows the emphasis on target
pricing, cost reduction, and profit planning, that is, the Japanese would use
the analysis to reduce the variable cost per unit, fixed costs per period, and
then concern themselves last of all in adjusting sales volume to achieve
target prices. On the other hand, Anglo Saxons use fixed–variable cost
analysis for deciding volume with given prices and elasticity of demand,
and a given target of profits. A flow chart and a table depicting the value
functions and cost drivers of the publishing industry are given in Table 3.6
and Fig. 3.3.

**Table 3.5** Illustrations of the use of cost behaviour for managerial purposes

| Used in | Illustration |
|---|---|
| Pricing | Mobile phones were seen to fetch higher profits with low price and high volume. This conclusion could come only by understanding cost behaviour with change in volume. |
| Budgeting | Large multi-product companies can do product planning using linear programming exercises using cost information of fixed and variable costs. This is used in budgeting. Flexible budgets with provision for flexing for volume can be prepared only with fixed–variable analysis. |
| Profit analysis—new products | Profit analysis would require to be done at different levels of sales and this is possible only with separate treatment of fixed and variable costs. Only after such analysis, new telecom products are introduced by all the companies. |
| Profit analysis—existing products | Before budgets are decided, product mix decisions require fixed–variable analysis. |
| Cost-volume-profit analysis | CVP analysis cannot be done and break-evens cannot be decided without fixed–variable analysis. |
| Cost reduction | The Japanese success in telecom products came after they understood how much of fixed costs for a period and variable cost/unit should be reduced and the rest of target price could be made up by volumes; all these use fixed and variable cost analysis. |
| Variance analysis | Any variance analysis would have to identify variance in profits as due to volume variance and efficiency and price variance. Volume variance requires fixed–variable analysis. |

**Table 3.6** Value chain activities and its corresponding cost drivers

| Value chain activity | Activity | Cost driver |
|---|---|---|
| Product development | Identify the customer's need | Number of schools the marketing representative visits to market the book |
| | Find an author | Number of potential authors interviewed |
| | Author writes book | Amount paid to the author for number of pages of text |
| | Editor edits book | Number of changes editor makes number of pages of text |
| | Author rewrites book | Number of times author must do rewrites |
| Printing and binding of the book | Print and bind the books | Machine hours for running the printing and binding equipment |
| Marketing | Market the book to faculty | Number of schools the marketing representative visits to market the book |

*(Contd)*

| | Process orders from bookstores | Hours spent with prospective customers to sell the book<br>Number of deliveries made to bookstores<br>Number of schools that adopt the new book<br>Number of books ordered by bookstores |
|---|---|---|
| Distribution | Receive unsold copies of book from bookstore<br>Deliver the book to bookstore | Number of deliveries made to bookstores<br><br>Number of unsold books sent back from bookstores |
| Customer service | Provide assistance to faculty and students (study guides, test) | Number of faculty that adopt the new book<br>Number of books ordered by bookstores |

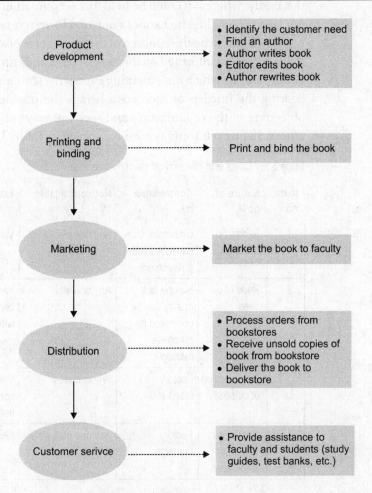

**Product development** ┄┄┄►
- Identify the customer need
- Find an author
- Author writes book
- Editor edits book
- Author rewrites book

**Printing and binding** ┄┄┄►
Print and bind the book

**Marketing** ┄┄┄►
Market the book to faculty

**Distribution** ┄┄┄►
- Process orders from bookstores
- Receive unsold copies of book from bookstore
- Deliver the book to bookstore

**Customer serivce** ┄┄┄►
- Provide assistance to faculty and students (study guides, test banks, etc.)

**Fig. 3.3** Publishing industry value functions and cost drivers

## CONTROLLABLE COSTS AND UNCONTROLLABLE COSTS

**Controllable costs**
Costs that can be controlled by a specified responsibility centre are controllable costs.

Identifying controllable costs are a part of daily controls in management at all levels of the hierarchy. Discussions on this are ubiquitous in any organization.

This is intimately interlinked with the ideas we have described earlier in responsibility centres. Some items of costs are controllable by some responsibility centres and not controllable by other responsibility centres and the debates and conflicts on deciding the area of responsibility can make for a lot of organizational turbulence. It must be clearly understood that controllability or otherwise has nothing to do with the costs being fixed and variable, though often variable costs are understood wrongly to be controllable and fixed costs as uncontrollable.

Lastly, whereas it could be held that accountability of any manager should not be for costs he/she cannot control, Horngren holds that uncontrollable costs should also be the concern of the manager for two reasons. The manager may be the best informed on the item of costs and can apprise the organization of the patterns which are emerging even if he/she cannot control it. Secondly, bearing the burden of such costs brings the manager closer to the overall objectives of the organization and seek out ways of jointly achieving it with others. Let us see some typical examples in Table 3.7.

**Table 3.7**  Costs and hierarchical responsibility

| Item no. | Nature of cost | Controllable by | Not controllable by | Fixed/variable | Cost driver short term |
|---|---|---|---|---|---|
| 1 | Excise on dispatch | Chairman who can lobby with government | Any one else | Variable | Dispatch value |
| 2 | Price of oil seed | No one but quality can be controlled by purchase manager | Any one else | Variable in conjunction with item 3 | Oil production in conjunction with item 3 |
| 3 | Consumption of oil seed | Factory manager | Any one else | Variable in conjunction with item 2 | Oil production in conjunction with item 2 |
| 4 | Overtime to permanent employees | Factory manager | Any one else | Fixed | nil |

*(Contd)*

| 5 | Process losses in dairy industry | Factory manager | Any one else | Variable | Volume of milk input |
| 6 | Tape consumption in music cassette industry | Factory manager | Any one else | Variable | Cassette production |

# DIRECT AND INDIRECT COSTS

**Direct and indirect costs**
Direct costs can be traced to cost object with minimum effort. Indirect costs, also called overheads, can be allocated to cost objects using a base.

Direct and indirect costs are one of the most important issues in cost management. We saw an illustration of this in Table 3.1. Certain costs can be directly traced to a product with least cost and effort, whereas it is very difficult to trace some other types of costs.

Such costs that cannot be directly traced to a product in an economically feasible manner are known as indirect costs, variously called overheads and burden. Such costs are pooled in a cost pool and assigned to the products using the measure of activity of the cost driver we have described earlier in the chapter. These measures of activity are usually described as the cost allocation bases for cost allocation. The two costs, one that is traced and the second that is allocated, can be together described as the process of cost assignment.

Direct costs can be fixed or variable, controllable or uncontrollable. Thus, keeping in view the earlier categories we have discussed, we could have 2(direct, indirect) × 3(fixed, variable, semi-variable) × 2(controllable and non-controllable) = 12 combinations. Table 3.8 shows a typical matrix

**Table 3.8**    Direct, indirect, fixed, and variable costs in a garment factory

| Cost behaviour pattern with changes in production | | Direct cost | Indirect cost |
| --- | --- | --- | --- |
| | Variable cost | Cloth, power for machines dedicated to each product | Power costs on common machine for pressing and packing and allocated to product on cost allocation base machine hours |
| | Fixed cost | Depreciation of machine and time-rated labour dedicated to each product | Depreciation of common machine for pressing packing and common time-rated labour and allocated top product on cost allocation base machine hours |

of direct, indirect, fixed, and variable costs, which can exist in an organization.

We will have several practical examples of measurement of direct and indirect costs and methods of cost allocation in Chapters 5, 6, 14, 15, and 16. Suffice to indicate at this stage that marking costs as direct or indirect can be done in the wage sheets, material issue notes, and expense and journal vouchers.

One of the features of modern industry is that the proportion of indirect costs in the total costs of a product has steeply increased. Such costs are mostly committed capacity costs.

In Table 3.9, a set of items of costs are shown along with the cost driver and cost allocation base used for them. Some of the items could have the option of being treated as direct costs, but for reasons of materiality and difficulties in measurement in a tracing exercise, they are treated as indirect costs. Activity-based costs described earlier in the chapter are indirect costs with reference to the product. Because of breaking down the broader classification of overheads to smaller segments of activities, cost assignment to the products becomes more accurate.

We have so far emphasized the ease of measurements to put an item of cost into the basket of direct costs or indirect costs. Apart from this trivial issue of measurement, there could also be some other reason of logic in one typical case of overtime payment to workers. Overtime is paid to workers usually working beyond normal specified working hours. It is usually paid at the double the normal rate.

**Table 3.9**  Cost allocation practices for indirect costs

| Item | Direct cost object that could be considered | Indirect cost object usually chosen | Cost allocation base associated with it |
|---|---|---|---|
| Cotton waste | Machine cost object | Factory overhead | Machine hours |
| Power | Metered power for each machine | Factory overhead | Machine horse power × machine hours |
| Canteen expenses in a labour intensive process | Value of food consumed by each worker working in a product cost object | Factory overhead | Labour hours spent on cost object |
| Labour expenses including perquisites in a labour intensive telecom manufacture | Tracing each labour to product cost object | Factory labour cost pool as cost object | Labour hours spent on product cost object |

Thus if a worker's hourly rate is ₹10, he would be paid an overtime at a rate of ₹20. If a product is made during the overtime hours, the worker would be paid ₹10 normal rate plus a premium rate of ₹10. Should this extra ₹10 be considered a direct cost or an indirect cost? There is no such doubt for the normal portion of the payment. If there is a general labour shortage in the organization, some product would be made in the extra hours, one cannot load this extra premium to the product. The cost of this extra overtime will have to be borne by all the products and, therefore, it should be an indirect cost. On the other hand, if the overtime was done only because this product had to be completed in overtime hours because it could not be postponed, then the costs would be a direct cost. This issue is a common occurrence in organizations that have rush orders. Rush orders cost the organization more, and are based on cause and effect logic and thus overtime premium would have be treated as direct cost of the product.

A second conceptually intriguing item of cost is that arising from idleness in an organization. Labour can be idle and machines can be idle and in both cases some committed costs cannot be cut down for this period. Which cost object should these costs be charged to? If there are short stints of inevitable idleness in between production runs, it should certainly be charged directly to the product.

On the other hand, if idleness is caused due to abnormal breakdown of machines it can be charged to the cost object described as maintenance. If the idleness is due to inadequate load or a mistake in capital investment scheduling, the cost object would have to figure it out in a manner that product price decisions do not get vitiated by abnormal costs. This would also affect inventory valuation of closing stock of products.

## PRIME COSTS, OUT OF POCKET, AND CONVERSION COSTS

**Prime costs**
Prime costs equal direct material + direct labour + direct expenses.

There are two expressions in common usage, one is prime costs and the second is conversion costs. The words are quick summaries of the easily ascertainable and apparently sure cost structure of a product.

Prime cost is equal to the cost of direct material plus direct labour, and directly measurable expenses and excludes all overheads. Thus any ambiguity and sophistry in the cost structure is avoided. If one had a repair job to be done, prime costs would be the basic minimum charges to be charged and it would seem that the overhead could be the subject for negotiation.

If labour were paid on piece rate and were not in permanent employment, as is true in the unorganized sector in India, prime costs would approximately be equal to variable costs. This could also be approximately equal to the cash outflow and could in that sense often be described by a word of mouth, and not necessarily accurately, as out-of-pocket costs. This expression is now used rarely in practice except in medical insurance. The expenses to be shared by insured party from her own pocket are described as out-of-pocket expenses.

Another quick and unambiguous understanding of costs is to focus on the most palpable element of costs, namely material, and treat all other elements including manufacturing overhead as conversion costs.

## UNIT COST AND AVERAGE COST

One of the most common queries raised when discussing pricing of products and services is to ask for its unit cost. Again in issues raised in public policy when monopolistic pricing is suspected, one needs to ask for its unit cost. Unit cost is equal to total cost divided by production and is, therefore, an average figure. This figure is mostly used in managerial decisions, typically in the decisions required in Example 3.8.

**Example 3.8** Pricing Entry Tickets for a Theatre Show

A theatre show is expected to cost ₹1,00,000 with the following breakdown:

| | |
|---|---|
| Hall charges | ₹10,000 |
| Costumes | ₹20,000 |
| Sound systems | ₹20,000 |
| Artist payments | ₹45,000 |
| Printing tickets | ₹5000 |
| **Total** | **₹1,00,000** |

It could be seen that none of the costs vary with the size of the audience. If the organizershave to fix the ticket price, one way would be to fix it low. This will ensure maximum amount of collection, assuming more people will buy it if tickets are priced lower. If this is not the real situation as there is an inelastic demand for tickets and that the organizers are expected not to make profit, the tickets would be priced at the unit cost which is equal to the total costs divided by the expected audience.

Unit costs could also vary seasonally, as shown in Example 3.9.

**Example 3.9** Seasonal Unit Cost in Industries

It is well known that milk production of cattle varies seasonally. In lean season prices are higher and the production is less. With most cost in the dairy industry being fixed in nature, the unit cost would be high in lean seasons and low in flush seasons. Similarly, unit cost in hotel industry will be high in periods of low occupancy and low in periods of high occupancy. In engineering industry, similarly, there could be seasonal fluctuation of both costs and production.

**Fallacy of unit cost**
Unit cost is equal to total cost divided by production. It is useful information but cannot be used for many decisions involving cost analysis. Total cost and total revenue is more useful.

In all these cases, how should we use the concept of unit costs?

We would see in Chapters 4, 11, and 13 that the use of unit or average costs is deceptive and analysis is clearer if we use total cost and total revenue broken down into fixed costs and variable costs. It is an apocryphal story that Robert McNamara would sack any one who committed the McNamara fallacy by using unit costs in their analysis instead of using total cost and total revenue. But unit costs necessarily have to be used for valuation of closing inventories. That is why we ought to be careful in inclusion or exclusion of the cost of idleness in the computation of unit costs.

## COST OF GOODS SOLD

**Inventory valuation**
Inventory valuation is done by the cost accountants, which is used in financial accounting in the preparation of balance sheets.

In Table 3.1 we presented the cost of goods sold which could enable the financial accountant to transparently show the profit and loss account of Sowbhagya Household Appliances Ltd. Sowbhagya was a manufacturing concern, and an oversimplified account was presented. The essential purpose of the presentation was to demonstrate the accounts in natural classification and its relation to cost accounting.

We will now show a more fully explicit version of the cost of goods sold. Before we do that we will show in Figs 3.4 and 3.5 the flow of transactions in two types of organizations, the first doing only merchandizing and the second doing manufacturing as well as merchandizing.

One may see that both in Fig. 3.4 in respect of merchandizing firms and Fig. 3.5 in respect of manufacturing firms, the extreme left side shows items exhibited in the income statement, the central portion shows the balance sheet items, and the right side again contains items from the income statement. One may see that the important flow of information of raw material consumed and cost of finished goods sold from central portion to the right side. Both these sets of information are generated by the costing

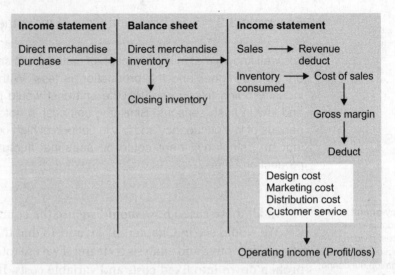

**Fig. 3.4** Flow of transactions in a merchandising firm

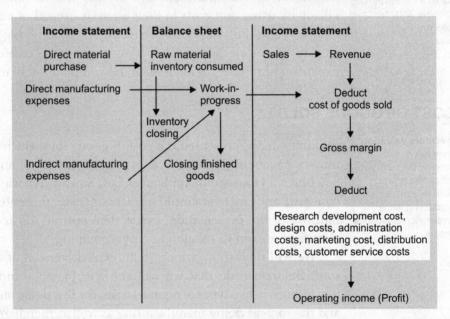

**Fig. 3.5** Flow of transactions in a manufacturing firm

system. Therefore, work-in-process in the central portion is also organized on functional classifications of costing to enable transfer of costs to the right side, product wise.

Further both the income side items (extreme left and the right) could be desegregated into natural classifications in financial accounting reports to external parties, and would be available in functional classification in cost accounting. It all seems very complicated and in the manual systems it is usually done twice over, once in financial accounting and a second time in costing records. In a computerized system, it can all be done in one stroke with a common and well structured data entry system and a properly crafted chart of accounts.

## COST OF GOODS MANUFACTURED

One may note that the expenses were transferred to work-in-process in the central portion of Fig. 3.5. The total expenses are what would constitute cost of goods manufactured. But there is a bit of adjustment required for opening work-in-process and closing work-in-process. The cost of goods manufactured divided by the units produced will be equal to cost per unit. This data can be used to value closing inventory and cost of goods sold.

The entire exercise would be clear from Table 3.10, which gives the full income statement of Hind Consumer Products Ltd for the year ending 31 December 2005.

It had sold 12,00,000 units at ₹2 per unit. It had produced 11,50,000 units and put 50,000 units in stock.

Cost of goods sold is shown as

Opening stock + Cost of goods manufactured − Closing stock
(100 + 1730 − 75 = 1755)

Cost of goods manufactured = Opening work-in-process + Production costs − Closing work-in-process (0 + 1730 − 0 = 1730).

Therefore, cost/unit is ₹1.50 (1730 ÷ 1150 units)

Direct material consumed = Opening stock + Purchases − Closing Stock (100 + 700 − 200 = 600)

### Work-in-process

Table 3.10 does not show the product-wise breakdown of work-in-process, finished goods, and cost of goods sold. But this detail has to be available with Hind Consumer Products Ltd.

It may also be seen that the entire indirect manufacturing expenses have been considered for transferring to work-in-process. We will see a little later that many organizations may choose to do this differently by transferring only the variable costs.

It may also be seen that the transfer to finished goods will be only for goods completed in production, whether the production was commenced in the year or if the commencement was earlier and is completed this year. But the average costs or unit costs for computing the value for the transfer would be a heterogeneous pool of product costs that includes the costs incurred in several periods, during which periods, prices, and costs may have varied. In this process, we could follow the first in first out method, the last in first out method, or any other method of our choice. In Hind Consumer Products Ltd, they seem to follow the first in first out methods as the inventory is valued at the current year's cost of production.

In summary, the statement is a fair estimate with several assumptions that have to be made explicit in any published document.

Let us see if the data in Table 3.10 can be used to make the budget for 2006. Let us plan for zero raw material closing inventory, same prices of raw material and finished goods as in 2005, zero closing work-in-process, zero closing finished goods, and a sale of 15,00,000 units as against 12,00,000 units in 2005. One can see that the production will only be 14,50,000 units as 50,000 are already in stock. Variable production costs will go down but fixed costs would not go up. This illustration shows how unit cost of goods manufactured may show some unexpected results due to averaging effect. The projected results for the year 2006 would thus be as shown in Table 3.11.

## PERIOD COSTS AND PRODUCT COSTS

**Inventoriable costs**
These elements of costs are considered for valuation of inventories and also described as product costs.

In Figs 3.4 and 3.5 and in Tables 3.10 and 3.11, we have taken some costs into account in computing the cost of goods sold, cost of goods manufactured, finished goods inventory, while we have taken some costs after working out gross profits. The latter included marketing, distribution, research and development costs, and customer service. Is this governed by logic or by accounting conventions? The answer is more by the latter than the former, though logic could also support it. Costs incurred after the product leaves the factory cannot be considered for valuing the inventory at the factory as these stocks have not benefited from these later costs.

**Period costs**
Costs not inventoried are known as period costs.

Costs considered for inventory are labelled, somewhat inappropriately, as product costs. They should preferably be described by the accounting treatment they receive in inventory valuation, that is, they should be called inventoriable costs. These figure in the balance sheet are devices to match expenses with revenue. Expenses in one accounting period are carried forward to the next accounting period through the process of inventorying

**Table 3.10** Income statement of Hind Consumer Products Ltd for year ending 31 December 2005

| in ₹ thousand | | |
|---|---|---|
| Revenues | | 2400 |
| Cost of goods sold | | |
| Opening finished goods | 100 | |
| Cost of goods manufactured | 1730 | |
| Cost of goods available for sale | 1830 | |
| Closing finished goods | 75 | |
| Cost of goods sold | | 1755 |
| Gross margin (profit) | | 645 |
| Operating costs | | |
| Marketing distribution | | |
| Customer service (variable with reference to sales) | | 300 |
| Operating income | | 345 |
| **Cost of goods manufactured breakdown** | | |
| Direct material | | |
| Opening stock | 100 | |
| Purchases | 700 | |
| Material available for use | 800 | |
| Closing stock | 200 | |
| Direct material consumed (Variable) | | 600 |
| Direct manufacturing labour (Variable) | | 600 |
| Indirect manufacturing costs | | |
| Indirect manufacturing labour (Fixed) | 100 | |
| Supplies (Fixed) | 50 | |
| Power and energy (Variable) | 150 | |
| Depreciation plant (Fixed) | 100 | |
| Depreciation plant building (Fixed) | 80 | |
| Miscellaneous (Fixed) | 50 | |
| Total indirect manufacturing costs | | 530 |
| Total Manufacturing costs | | 1730 |
| Add work-in-process opening | | 0 |
| Deduct work-in-process closing | | 0 |
| Cost of goods manufactured | | 1730 |

**Table 3.11** Budgeted income statement of Hind Consumer Products Ltd for year ending 31 December 2006

| | (in ₹ thousand) |
|---|---|
| Revenues | 3000 |
| Cost of goods sold | |
| Opening finished goods | 75 |
| Cost of goods manufactured | 2082.174 |
| Cost of goods available for sale | 2157.174 |
| Closing cost of finished goods | 0 |
| Cost of goods sold | 2157.174 |
| Gross margin | 842.826 |
| Customer service (variable) | 375 Proportionately more |
| Operating income | 467.8261 |
| Cost of goods manufactured | |
| Director material | |
| Opening stock | 200 |
| Purchases | 556.517 |
| Material available for use | 756.521 |
| Closing stock | 0 |
| Material consumed (Variable) | 756.5217 (adjusted for production) |
| Direct labour (Variable) | 756.5217 (ditto) |
| Indirect labour (Fixed) | 100 |
| Supplies (Fixed) | 50 |
| Power energy (Variable) | 189.13 (adjusted for production) |
| Dep plant (Fixed) | 100 |
| Dep plant bldg | 80 |
| Miscellaneous (fixed) | 50 |
| Cost of goods manufactured | 2082.174 |

them. Costs that are not inventoriable are called period costs as they are shown in the income statement wholly in the period they are incurred.

Manufacturing companies typically have one or more of the following three types of inventory:

1. *Direct materials inventory* Direct materials in stock and awaiting use in the manufacturing process.
2. *Work-in-process inventory* Goods partially worked on but not yet completed, also called *work-in-progress.*
3. *Finished goods inventory* Goods completed but not yet sold.

*Direct material costs* are the acquisition costs of all materials that eventually become part of the cost object (work-in-process and then finished

**Table 3.12** Schedule of cost of goods manufactured and income statement for the year ended 31 December 2010 (in ₹ lakhs)—Singh Corporation

| Cost of goods manufactured | | |
|---|---|---|
| Direct material cost | | |
| Beginning inventory 1 January 2010 (Add) | 600 | |
| Purchase of direct material | 13,000 | |
| Cost of direct material available for use | 13,600 | |
| Ending inventory 31 December 2010 (Deduct) | 800 | |
| Direct material used (a) | | 12,800 |
| Direct manufacturing labour cost (b) | | 5000 |
| Indirect manufacturing cost | | |
| Indirect manufacturing labour cost | 300 | |
| Plant supplies used | 400 | |
| Plant utilities | 1200 | |
| Depreciation—plant equipment | 400 | |
| Plant supervisory salaries | 500 | |
| Miscellaneous plant overhead (c) | 1200 | 4000 |
| Manufacturing cost incurred during 2010 (a+b+c) | | 21,800 |
| Beginning work-in-progress inventories 1 January 2010 (Add) | | 500 |
| Total manufacturing cost | | 22,300 |
| Ending work-in-progress 31 December 2010 (Deduct) | | 200 |
| Cost of goods manufactured | | 22,100 |

goods), and can be traced to the cost object in an economically feasible way.

*Direct manufacturing labour costs* include the compensation of all manufacturing labour that can be traced to the cost object (work-in-process and then finished goods) in an economically feasible way.

**Interpretation of statements**

1. The income statement schedule in Table 3.13 can become a schedule of cost of goods manufactured and sold shown in Table 3.12 simply by including the beginning and ending finished goods inventory figures in the supporting schedule, rather than directly including them in the body of the income statement. Note that the term *cost of goods manufactured* refers to the cost of goods brought to completion (finished) during the accounting period, whether they were started before or during the current accounting period. Some of the manufacturing costs incurred are held back as costs of the ending work-in-process; similarly, the costs of the beginning work-in-process inventory become a part of the cost of goods manufactured for 2010.

**Table 3.13** Income statement for the year ended 31 December 2010 (in ₹ lakhs)—Singh Corporation

| Income statement | | |
|---|---:|---:|
| Revenues/sales (i) | | 50,000 |
| Cost of goods sold | | |
| Beginning finished goods inventory 1 January 2010 | 3500 | |
| Cost of goods manufactured | 22,100 | |
| Cost of goods available for sales | 25,600 | |
| Ending finished goods inventory 31 December 2010 | 2,000 | 23,600 (ii) |
| Gross margin iii = (i − ii) | | 26,400 |
| Marketing, distribution, customer service cost (iv) | 15,000 | |
| Operating Income (iii − iv) | | 11,400 |

2. The sales manager's salary would be charged as a marketing cost as incurred by both manufacturing and merchandising companies. It is basically an operating cost that appears below the gross margin line on an income statement. In contrast, an assembler's wages would be assigned to the products worked on. Thus, the wages cost would be charged to work-in-process and would not be expensed until the product is transferred through finished goods inventory to cost of goods sold as the product is sold.

3. The direct indirect distinction can be resolved only with respect to a particular cost object. For example, in defense contracting, the cost object may be defined as a contract. Then, a plant supervisor working only on that contract will have his or her salary charged directly and wholly to that single contract.

4. Direct materials used = $1,28,00,00,000 \div 1,00,000$ units = ₹12,800 per unit
   Depreciation on plant equipment = $4,00,00,000 \div 1,00,000$ units = ₹400 per unit

5. Unit costs are averages, and they must be interpreted with caution. The ₹12,800 per unit direct materials unit cost is valid for predicting total costs because direct materials is a variable cost; total direct materials costs indeed change as output levels change. However, fixed costs like depreciation must be interpreted quite differently from variable costs. A common error in cost analysis is to regard all unit costs as one—as if all the total costs to which they are related are variable costs. Changes in output levels will affect *total variable costs*, but not *total fixed costs*.

## Different Costs for Different Purposes

The discussion in the previous paragraph covers one type of situation in which different costs are used for different purposes. Let us explore a variety of options for definition of product costs. These are shown in Table 3.14. Table 3.10 shows that some organizations that want to be prudent do not desire to inventory any part of fixed costs, even if they are manufacturing in nature. Majority of US firms prefer to do this. Income tax authorities and the US Generally Accepted Accounting Principles (GAAP) also permit this if one is consistent.

**Different costs for different purposes** Definitions of costs have to be adapted for the issues to be handled. Costs relevant only to that context are to be included. Costs to be included in definition of product costs, therefore, vary.

Even if we do not inventory certain costs, it is obvious that a large part of marketing, distribution, and customer service costs can be traced to the product cost object. Rational decision-making has to use that information. Variable costs that have their cost effect relationship to a product, even if they are not manufacturing costs, have to be used for short-term decisions in which fixed costs are not relevant. Lastly, if a negotiated reimbursement formula is to be worked out, usually with government, they allow a mark up which takes into account all costs of an organization.

Inventory valuation will be studied in detail in Chapter 10.

**Table 3.14**  Varying definitions of product cost

| Definition of product costs | Used for purpose |
| --- | --- |
| Includes all manufacturing costs | Preferred when production in one accounting period would be sold in the next accounting period |
| Includes only variable manufacturing expenses | Used for short run pricing decisions and prudent finished goods valuation |
| Includes all manufacturing and marketing and distribution expenses | Long-term product mix and product pricing |
| Includes variable manufacturing and variable marketing | Short run product mix and pricing decisions |
| All manufacturing, marketing, and administrative and corporate office | When negotiating cost to reimbursed say in insurance, government health schemes, etc. |

## FRAMEWORK FOR COST MANAGEMENT WITH EMPHASIS ON STRATEGY

In this chapter we have seen cost managers as problem solvers, score-keepers, and attention drawers. This, however, has been discussed in a generic sense. Several chapters in the book would deal with this idea in greater depth.

Changes in volume of production raise many fundamental issues on the products and services in which volume should be increased or decreased. But even as we adjust and readjust the volumes and product mix at each stage we may keep targets for costs. The ideas on cost behaviour dealt with in this chapter would form the basis for further development. This theme would figure repeatedly in several chapters of the book. Many decisions dealt with in some of the chapters of the book would discard the assumption that future costs can be predicted on basis of past cost patterns. These discontinuities would be dealt with in more complex cost and revenue models in several chapters of the book.

The interweaving of cost and revenue information described in this chapter with physical data on performance is one of the important features of modern cost management. This will be dealt with in Chapter 16. No cost analysis would be worthwhile if the cost of costing information is too high. Careful crafting of chart of accounts and process of data entry has enabled computers to reduce cost of costing and it is possible now to make some bold demands on the system without our adding up to much costs.

## Summary

Costing terminology could vary. Financial accounts follow a natural descriptive classification to facilitate preparation of account statements for external users. Cost accounts use functional classifications that also capture natural classifications. Cost accounting provides data inventory valuation. Cost objects are things and persons on which (on whom) costs are accumulated. They are devised to help the cost accountant in being the scorekeeper, problem solver, and attention drawer. Responsibility centres are devices to ensure accountability to achieve operational and strategic objectives. They are of four types: cost, revenue, profit, and investment. Behaviour of costs towards changes in the activity of a cost driver determines whether they are variable costs, semi-variable costs, or fixed costs. Costs are variable if they change in short range, semi-variable if they change in medium range, and fixed if they change in long ranges. Cost that can be traced more easily to a cost object is direct for that cost object. Costs that cannot be traced easily to a product but have a theoretical cause and effect relationship to that cost object are indirect costs and are also called overheads. Controllable costs are those costs that can be controlled by a specified responsibility centre and have a greater weight in measuring performance. Prime costs are a sum of direct material, direct labour, and direct expense and make for a useful number for taking snap decisions.

Cost of goods manufactured is equal to cost of production plus or minus changes in work-in-process. Cost of goods sold is cost of goods manufactured plus or minus changes in finished goods. Cost of material consumed is purchases plus or minus changes in the stocks. Definitions in costs have to be adapted to the context and may have different meanings for decision processes and control processes. In the former (decision processes), costs may be discontinuous from the past. Cost of costing should be kept within reasonable limits and in this, computers have helped.

## KEY POINTS

- Natural or descriptive classification of accounts is used in financial accounting, which is usually guided by legal requirements of disclosure to external users of accounting statements.
- Functional classification of accounts is used in cost accounting, which follows cost objects created for the purpose.
- Cost objects are things or persons on which costs are accumulated. They are known as cost centres in UK tradition.
- Cross walk from natural to functional classifications and back are needed by organizations and are called crosswalks or network crossovers, terms used in the literature of programme budgeting in the US.
- Responsibility centres are of four types, cost, revenue, profit, and investment, all of which are devices to assist in budgeting, performance evaluation, and achievement of operational and strategic goals.
- Cost drivers are those that drive costs in a plausible cause and effect relationship with cost object.
- Revenue drivers are those that drive revenues.
- Costs that vary in short range changes in cost driver activity are variable costs, those which change over medium range changes are semi-variable costs, and those which change only with long range changes are fixed costs.
- Costs that can be more easily traced to a cost object are direct costs. Those which cannot be traced easily but have a logical relationship are the related indirect costs or overheads.
- Sharper discrimination of cost of product is available when overhead cost objectives are broken down to activities in activity-based costing (ABC).
- Indirect costs can be allocated to cost object using a cost allocation base which has cause–effect relationship with the cost object.
- Activity-based costs refer to smaller segments of overheads wherein the cause–effect relationships with the cost driver are more accurate resulting in more accurate cost assignment to the product.

- Costs of finished goods usually include total manufacturing costs but some organizations include only variable manufacturing costs. This is acceptable to tax authorities provided it is followed consistently.
- Costs included in inventory are known as inventoriable or product costs.
- Costs not included in inventory are period costs and are charged to income statement in the account period in which it is incurred.
- Cost definitions are adapted to the context and the issues that come up for a decision.
- Cost definition of product costs could include marketing, distribution, and customer service costs for product planning and pricing purposes, even if these are not considered product costs for inventory valuation.
- A controllable cost refers to its controllability by a specific responsibility centre.
- Identifying fixed and variable elements of costs has several uses, the most significant of which is pricing and profit planning and budgeting.
- Unit cost, which is obtained by dividing total costs by total activity, is sometimes managerially useful short hand information, but it may be fallacious support in most situations where total cost and total revenue are more amenable for meaningful analysis.
- Cost of goods manufactured = Cost of production ± Change in work-in-process.
- Cost of goods sold = Cost of goods manufactured ± Change in finished goods.
- Gross profit = Revenue – Cost of goods sold.
- Operating income = Gross profit – Operating expenses.

## CONCEPT REVIEW QUESTIONS

1. Give three examples of natural classification in accounts.
2. Why do financial accounts prefer natural classification in their accounts?
3. Give three examples of a cost object.
4. What are the four categories of responsibility centres?
5. What is the conceptual difference between responsibility centres as cost objects and products as cost objects?
6. Relate the concept of cost drivers with that of cause and effect relationship.
7. Conceptually, does a fixed cost have a cost driver? Explain.
8. All costs are direct to some or the other cost object. Is this a true or a false statement?

9. Give an example where it is possible to trace an item of cost directly to a particular cost object but we may not choose to do so and may prefer to use the process of cost allocation.

10. Which process gives a more accurate cost ascertainment, direct measurement or the process of allocation?

11. Activity-based costs refer to indirect costs. True or False.

12. Are fixed manufacturing costs inventoriable?

13. Should idle time costs be treated as period costs or product costs?

14. Is overtime a direct cost or an indirect cost?

15. Define prime cost.

16. Is marketing cost a period cost or a product cost?

17. Can a cost be fixed with reference to one cost driver and variable with reference to another cost driver?

18. Should the same transaction need to be posted once in financial accounts and a second time in cost accounts?

19. Will financial accounts show the cost of overheads distinctly and separately?

20. Can the inventory of finished goods include advertisement expenses?

21. Give examples of a revenue driver and cost driver being the same.

22. Give examples of driver of revenue being different from a driver of costs.

23. Define controllable costs.

24. What are the two most important managerial purposes of identifying fixed and variable elements of total costs?

25. Why can unit costs be sometimes fallacious support for decision making?

26. Explain the concept of crosswalk in the structure of accounting classifications.

## COMPUTER-BASED NUMERICAL PROBLEMS

### 1. Cat Biscuit A

Fill in the space marked **?** for the Cat Biscuit company. Indicate computations: V means variable costs, F means fixed costs. Variable manufacturing costs vary with production and variable marketing costs vary with sales. Two alternatives are provided—Alt 1 and Alt 2. Alt 1 uses total manufacturing costs for valuing inventory. Alt 2 uses only variable manufacturing costs to value inventory. Sales price is the same in both alternatives, that is, ₹400 per unit. But sales quantity differs. Work-in-process opening and closing are zero. All gross amounts are in rupees thousand. Unit cost is in ₹/unit and quantities are in numbers. Please be careful in noting this.

| | Alt 1 Full cost inventory | Alt 2 Variable cost inventory |
|---|---|---|
| **Physical units numbers** | | |
| Production | 1000 | 1000 |
| Sales | 800 | 900 |
| Opening finished goods | 0 | 0 |
| Closing finished goods | ? | ? |
| **All in ₹000** | | |
| Direct material consumed (V) | 100 | 100 |
| Indirect manufacture (V) | 50 | 50 |
| Direct manufacture (F) | 10 | 10 |
| Indirect manufacture (F) | 30 | 30 |
| Cost of goods manufactured | ? | ? total costs |
| Cost of finished goods ₹0000 | ? | ? at variable costs |
| Cost of goods sold ₹000 | ? | ? |
| Revenue ₹000 | ? | ? |
| Gross profit ₹000 | ? | ? |
| Marketing (V) ₹000 | 20 | ? |
| Marketing (F) ₹000 | 10 | ? |
| Net income ₹000 | ? | ? |
| Cost of finished goods/unit (₹) | ? at total costs | ? at variable costs |

## 2. Cat Biscuit B

Fill in the space marked **?** for the Cat Biscuit company. Indicate computations: V means variable costs, F means fixed costs. Variable manufacturing costs vary with production and variable marketing costs vary with sales. Two alternatives are provided–Alt 1 and Alt 2. Alt 1 uses total manufacturing costs for valuing inventory. Alt 2 uses only variable manufacturing costs to value inventory. Sales price is the same in both alternatives, that is, ₹400 per unit. But sales quantity differs. All gross amounts are in rupees thousand. Work-in-process opening and closing are zero. Unit cost is in ₹/unit and quantities are in numbers. Please be careful in noting this. Data are different from Problem 1.

| | Alt 1 Full cost inventory | Alt 2 Variable cost inventory |
|---|---|---|
| **Physical units numbers** | | |
| Production | 1000 | 1000 |
| Sales | 900 | 800 |
| Opening finished goods | 0 | 0 |
| Closing finished goods | ? | ? |
| **All in ₹000** | | |
| Direct material consumed (V) | 100 | 100 |
| Indirect manufacture (V) | 50 | 50 |
| Direct manufacture (F) | 10 | 10 |
| Indirect manufacture (F) | 30 | 30 |
| Cost of goods manufactured | ? | ? total costs |
| Cost of finished goods ₹0000 | ? | ? at variable costs |
| Cost of goods sold ₹000 | ? | ? |
| Revenue ₹000 | ? | ? |
| Gross profit ₹000 | ? | ? |
| Marketing (V) ₹000 | 20 | ? |
| Marketing (F) ₹000 | 10 | ? |
| Net income ₹000 | ? | ? |
| Finished goods/unit (₹) | ? at total costs | ? at variable costs |

## 3. Cost of goods manufactured

The following are the balances (all in ₹ thousand) abstracted from Raghuram Auto Parts which supplies ancillaries to major automobile companies in India and abroad:

| Item | Beginning of 2005 | End of 2005 |
|---|---|---|
| Direct material inventory | 44,000 | 52,000 |
| Work-in-process | 42,000 | 40,000 |
| Finished goods inventory | 36,000 | 46,000 |
| Purchase direct material | | 75,000 |
| Direct manufacturing labour | | 50,000 |
| Indirect manufacturing labour | | 30,000 |
| Plant insurance | | 18,000 |
| Depreciation plant building and equipment | | 22,000 |

*(Contd)*

*(Contd)*

| Repair and maintenance plant | | 8000 |
|---|---|---|
| Marketing, distribution, customer service | | 1,86,000 |
| General administrative costs | | 58,000 |

3.1 Prepare a schedule of cost of goods manufactured.
3.2 Prepare an income statement.

## NUMERICAL PROBLEMS

### 1. Unit Costs in Erode Garment Exports

Erode Garment Exports makes standardized bed sheets, room furnishings, car furnishings in three dedicated weaving lines. It plans its production in terms of number of units produced in each category. It keeps track of direct labour and direct material expenses and one overhead account that it distributes to the products on the basis of direct manufacturing labour costs. The overheads include pre-weaving yarn preparation and post-weaving process of calendaring and pressing and packing. The overheads for the month of June 2005 were ₹15 lakh of which ₹5 lakh was fixed. Their report is also based on unit costs as they use it for the next month's quotation for the export. The cost and production reported in June 2005 was as follows:

| Item | Bed sheets | Furnishing | Car furnishing |
|---|---|---|---|
| Direct material cost/unit (₹) | 100 | 130 | 150 |
| Direct labour cost/unit (₹) | 50 | 70 | 100 |
| Indirect manufacturing cost/unit (₹) | 220 | 315 | 440 |
| Units produced | 3000 | 2000 | 500 |

They plan to produce 2000 units of bed sheets, 2500 units of furnishing, and 1000 units of car furnishing in July 2005.

1.1 Can they safely use the data of June as shown in the analysis for quotation for July 2005?
1.2 Is their identification of direct and indirect costs conceptually sound? If not what is your suggestion?
1.3 If the cost driver for indirect costs, both fixed and variable are correctly direct labour costs, what would be the July costs/unit? Why would be this be a better approximation than the present method of going by the unit costs of June even if it is not the ideal or a permanent remedy?

1.4 If the cost driver for indirect costs, both fixed and variable, are correctly direct material costs, what would be the cost/unit in July 2005? Why would this be a better approximation than the present method of going by the unit costs of June even if it is not the ideal or a permanent remedy?

1.5 If we apply the permanent remedy, would it be necessary to present the unit costs in the manner presented in the table?

## 2. Classifying Costs

There are a set of ten cost items indicated here. Making reasonable assumptions, which you must explicitly state, classify them as direct or indirect, fixed or variable. Give full reason and your understanding of the related cost drivers:

(i) Expenses paid for collecting information in an interview for understanding the attributes preferred or attributes not desired in a new product to be launched shortly.

(ii) Subscription for marketing magazine used by everyone in the marketing department.

(iii) Telephone expenses of the marketing department for contacting various persons for fixing interviews for various products.

(iv) Retainer fees paid to an agency who does field interviews for understanding customer perceptions.

(v) Air travel bill of the managing director who attended a negotiation for technical collaboration with a foreign firm to produce a new product.

(vi) Petrol expenses of the wife of the managing director who took the car to a hill station to attend a social gathering, which was televised as part of the promotion campaign for a product.

(vii) Cost of books and periodicals bought by a firm for a consultant who was engaged to suggest a strategic plan for the organization.

(viii) Expenses of buying gift for the best worker of the year.

(ix) Performance bonus to a worker who is dedicated to the production of a particular product.

(x) Study leave for an executive to acquaint himself with the latest developments in information technology.

## 3. Kerala Rare Earths

Kerala Rare Earths (KRE) owns a beach on an island close to the west coast of India. The beach sand is a source of thorium, a valuable atomic mineral that could be used for making fissile material for nuclear power stations. It has costs in four areas:

(i) Payment to sub-contractor who charges ₹160 per ton of beach sand, which is returned to the beach after it is processed in the mainland beneficiating plant.

(ii) Royalty payable to the Kerala Government at ₹100 per ton of beach sand.

(iii) Payment made to a barge operator at the rate of ₹30,00,000 per month if beach sand transported ranges from 0–100 tonnes per day, round trips, from the beach and back to beach. Even if no sand is transported, this ₹15,00,000 will be paid for the month. The payment will be ₹30,00,000 per month if 101–200 tonnes are transported. Even if in a single day the transport is more than 100 tonnes, this amount of ₹30,00,000 would be payable up to 200 tonnes per day. The amount will become ₹45,00,000 per month if the transport ranges between 201–300 tonnes. Even if on a single day the transport is more than 200 tonnes and up to 300 tonnes, this will be the amount. The barges will be available on 25 days a month.

(iv) A fixed amount of ₹50,00,000 per month on the beneficiating plant which separates the titanium oxide from other rare earth compounds. The expenditure does not vary with the quantity of beach sand handled unless it goes beyond 15,000 tonnes per month.

3.1 Identify the cost driver that drives the costs.

3.2 Identify items of variable costs, semi-variable costs, and fixed costs.

3.3 Plot the costs with cost driver in the X-axis and individual items of costs on the Y-axis in the form used in Fig. 3.1.

3.4 Calculate total cost/tonne of beach sand for (a) 100 tonnes per day (b) 200 tonnes per day (c) 150 tonnes per day (d) 300 tonnes per day (e) 301 tonnes per day. Comment on the results.

3.5 What would be an important measure to be taken for controlling costs arising from production and transportation scheduling?

## 4. Cost Drivers in Hindustan Foods

Chandra, the professor of costing, was engaged for a training programme for Hindustan Foods, a firm dealing with a variety of food items and having a large export business. He had prepared a list of cost drivers matched with business functions. But due to some confusion it all got jumbled up. The jumbled up data are in the table below:

4.1 Identify the cost driver and explain the logic.

4.2 Suggest a second cost driver for the chosen department.

| Business function | Representative cost driver |
|---|---|
| A. Production | 1. Minutes in TV advertising |
| B. Research and development | 2. No. of calls to toll-free customer phone line |
| C. Marketing | 3. No. of packages shipped |
| D. Distribution | 4. Hours spent in designing tamper-proof consumer pouches of milk |
| E. Design of products and services | 5. No. of hours the oil packaging line is in operation |
| F. Customer service | 6. No. of patents filed in Indian and foreign patent offices |

## 5. Reconstruction Accounts of Balujas and Ramkinkers

The accounts of Balujas and Ramkinkers were destroyed and the following balances were available with significant gaps A, B, C, D, E, F, G, and H. Figures are in ₹ thousand.

5.1 Supply the required numbers indicating calculations.

| | Balujas | Ramkinkers |
|---|---|---|
| Accounts receivable closing balance | 6000 | 2100 |
| Cost of goods sold | A | 23,000 |
| Accounts payable opening balance | 3000 | 1700 |
| Accounts payable closing balance | 1800 | 1500 |
| Finished goods closing balance | B | 5300 |
| Gross margin | 11,300 | E |
| WIP opening balance | 0 | 800 |
| WIP closing balance | 0 | 3000 |
| Finished goods opening balance | 4000 | 4000 |
| Direct material used | 5000 | 12,000 |
| Direct manufacturing labour | 5000 | 5000 |
| Indirect manufacturing cost | 10,000 | F |
| Purchase direct material | 9000 | 7000 |
| Revenues | 32,000 | 33,000 |
| Accounts receivable opening balance | 2000 | 1400 |
| Costs of production | C | G |
| Cost of goods manufactured | D | H |

## 6. Fire in Kottayam Rayons

Kottayam Rayons (KR) had been having trouble in its industrial relations for long, which culminated in one of the employees setting fire to the factory on 1 June 2005. KR had to put in a claim on the insurance company. They were able to get historical information on assets from its permanent records stored in a separate office. But the details of finished goods, raw material inventory, and work-in-process proved a little difficult to get. They had salvaged data for the month of May, which is shown below. All values are in ₹.

| | |
|---|---|
| Direct materials purchased | 25,00,000 |
| WIP opening balance | 30,00,000 |
| Direct material opening inventory | 20,00,000 |
| Finished goods opening inventory | 3,50,000 |
| Indirect manufacturing expenses | 40 per cent of conversion cost |
| Revenues | 60,00,000 |
| Direct manufacturing labour | 20,00,000 |
| Prime cost | 50,00,000 |
| Gross margin | 20 per cent of revenue |
| Cost of goods available for sale | 55,00,000 |

6.1   Estimate the cost of closing stock of finished goods, work-in-process, and direct material inventory.

6.2   If the insurance covers replacement cost, how would you revalue the closing stock of finished goods in stock?

6.3   If you are told that all the indirect manufacturing costs were fixed in nature and you had planned to meet the market demand that was expected to be 10 per cent more in June over May, and the insurance also covered estimated loss of gross margin, calculate the claim of Kottayam Rayon on this account.

## 7. The Rush Printing at Kalimata Printing Press

Kalimata Printing Press (KPP) of Kolkata was famous for its quality and adherence to promised delivery. It was, therefore, much sought after. In the first week of July 2005, it was negotiating its rates with New Age Publishers, for their two publications—Durga Mahima and Modern Physics. The manuscript for Modern Physics was ready and that of Durga Mahima was expected in September. Both were to be released in October 2005 and were more or less of the same size and the number of print copies was the same. Modern Physics had many mathematical formulations, which were more time consuming to compose. They were intrigued by the fact the quotations were different.

| Item | Durga Mahima | Modern Physics |
|---|---|---|
| Paper (entirely variable) | ₹7,00,000 | ₹7,00,000 |
| Composing overhead based on labour hours (20% fixed and 80% variable) | ₹20,000 | ₹40,000 |
| Printing overheads based on machine hours (80% fixed and 20% variable) | ₹4,00,000 | ₹4,00,000 |
| Binding overheads based on labour hours (10% fixed and 90% variable) | ₹1,00,000 | ₹1,00,000 |
| Direct overtime premium on labour costs: Composing Printing Binding | ₹15,000 ₹1,00,000 ₹85,000 | 0 0 0 |
| Total cost | ₹14,20,000 | ₹12,40,000 |
| No of copies | 10,000 | 10,000 |
| Cost per copy | ₹142 | ₹124 |

New Age got the breakdown of the quotation as under:

New Age asked if Modern Physics would be printed only in normal hours and stood the risk of delay in delivery. KPP said that there was no surety that Modern Physics would be printed only in normal hours and New Age need not worry about the delivery, as if need be, they will use overtime hours to print it. They also said that the overhead rates for composing, printing, and binding included their projected overtime hours for all the books using the services of the composing, printing, and binding departments, irrespective of whether they were actually worked in normal hours or overtime hours. The labour was paid the normal hourly wages plus an extra premium of 100 per cent if they worked for overtime hours.

Turning to the Durga Mahima, they asked why the same treatment could not be had for this book. KPP said that the manuscript was arriving just when the Puja holidays commence and when the press does not normally work. So the extra premium was an extra cost they would be incurring only for Durga Mahima. New Age having understood the issue was still worried as the cost per copy would make it difficult to price the book for general consumption. It would neither be possible for them to prepone the delivery of the manuscript, nor be desirable to postpone the release of the book, as it will sell best during the fortnight between Durga Puja and Saraswati Puja.

7.1 Do you think principle followed by KPP in cost estimation in respect of overtime payments fair to everyone?

7.2 Why should KPP charge extra premium overtime to all products even if they were not incurred during the execution of that particular work?

7.3 Is there anything else that New Age could do to reduce the cost/book of Durga Mahima. Suggest a list with detailed arguments.

7.4 In their cost analysis, would New Age work only with unit cost of all items of costs or would they use some other manner of cost analysis?

## 8. Cost of Goods Manufactured

Data in ₹ thousand for year ending 2004

| Cost of goods manufactured | | Cost of goods manufactured | |
|---|---|---|---|
| WIP opening balance | 5 | Plant expenses | 4 |
| Direct material closing inventory | 10 | Indirect manufacturing labour | 20 |
| Finished goods closing | 15 | Depreciation plant equipment, building | 10 |
| Accounts payable closing | 20 | Revenues | 300 |
| Accounts receivable opening | 30 | Miscellaneous manufacturing overhead | 5 |
| WIP closing balance | 4 | Marketing distribution customer service | 80 |
| Accounts receivable closing | 30 | Direct material purchase | 90 |
| Account payable opening | 30 | Plant supplies used | 45 |
| Direct material inventory opening | 30 | Property tax on plant | 1 |
| Finished goods opening | 35 | | |

8.1 Calculate the material consumed, the cost of production, the cost of goods manufactured, the cost of goods sold, and the profit for the year 2004.

## PROJECTS

### 1. Exploring firm practices

(a) Form a group of four to five students. Visit a successful and large size hotel. Find out how they fix the prices of their products and services and how they monitor their cost and performance.

(b) Form a group of four or five students. Visit a successful manufacturing organization and find out how they fix the prices of their products and how they monitor cost and performance.

2. **Learning to explore costing systems from published accounts (1)**

   (a) Form a group of four or five students and choose a large organization in the service sector. Study their Chairman's report to the General Body and their audited and published accounts. Prepare a list of their likely financial heads of accounts and cost objects.

   List out and explain the kind of problems the organization is likely to have in decision-making. Have an imaginative method of problem solving, scorekeeping, and attention drawing functions that these accounts classifications and cost objective is likely to support.

   (b) Form a group of four or five students and choose a large organization in the manufacturing sector. Study their Chairman's report to the General Body and their audited and published accounts and prepare a list of their likely financial heads of accounts and cost objects.

   List out and explain the kind of decision-making problems the organization is likely to have. Have an imaginative method of problem solving, scorekeeping, and attention drawing functions that these accounts classifications and cost objective are likely to support.

| CASE STUDY 1 | Bansiram Bhujias |
| --- | --- |

Bansiram Bhujias was now a world famous brand of ready-to-eat vegetarian snacks. They had rapidly grown in the last few years and Lala Bansiram was the Chairman of this public limited company that had branches and franchisees all over the world. All important towns and cities in India had several branches.

Their main products had been packets of crisp bhujias in six different flavours—plain, lime, pudina, asli masala, chatpata, and khatta–mitha. During the last few years they also developed another line of business, that of ready-to-cook noodles. The production line-up for both these product lines was similar. They had a central plant in Bikaner in Rajasthan. Both bhujias and noodles were prepared from the dough from wheat and maida flour. The flour was centrally procured from some specified flour mills in Punjab and Haryana. They were fermented very slightly before being partially cooked and were then transported in refrigerated containers to ten different locations in India for preparing the bhujias and instant noodles near the location of their sale. They used their own transport. One of the plants was dedicated for exports. The special mixes which were added to the prepared dough were also prepared centrally at Bikaner. These special mixes had market of their own and some of these packets were sold by the Bansiram outlets. The plants had product lines with extrusion devices each for one product line. They were fed with the dough, which were prepared after the addition of the special mixes. The bhujias were extruded on to special frying pans, which had hot oil. The oil was also procured centrally from Bikaner but the suppliers delivered to the plants where it was tested for quality. The fried bhujia was packed in nitrogen filled aluminium foil pouches, sealed after the food inspectors sample check the quality, and inspectors of the standard weights and measures act check for weight and proper details on the packages. The packages were transported in vans to Bansiram's own outlets and the outlets they had franchised. Sixty per cent of the outlets were franchised, whereas 40 per cent were owned by Bansiram. The transportation was through either the transport fleet owned by them or transported by contractors.

The noodles line-up was that the extrusion was into hot water and on to steam cookers and dehydration chambers. The packing was done in plastic cups with aluminium foil. The outlet managers had on their own initiative tried out catering for special parties. This was an instant success as the managers could improvise many new dishes with their mechanized cooking arrangements. The central office tacitly accepted this activity and the local branches advertised through cable TV and local newspaper for the bhujias, noodles, and the catering arrangements. The central office controlled the central advertisement budget and ran promotional campaigns in India and abroad. The central office had a small but very active research group that was trying to invent new products, and also monitoring quality controls of existing products. Market research was usually done by consultants. The corporate office has the usual work of managing shares and dividends.

## Discussion Questions

1. Suggest a list of natural classification accounts for the financial accounts.
2. Suggest cost objects keeping in view cost of costing.
3. Indicate the kinds of problems the organization will face in which the cost accountants' help will be useful.
4. What kind of scorekeeping and attention drawing could be supported by accounting information which the classifications will throw up.

| CASE STUDY 2 | Matsyaraja Moulded Boats |
|---|---|

Matsyaraja Moulded Boats (MMB) was a ten year old organization, which was founded by Dr Arumughan, a scientist from the Chennai Institute of Science for People (CISP). CISP had been doing marine research and spearheaded the movement against big trawlers fishing in the seas surrounding India. These trawlers were taking away the fish that used to provide livelihood to a large number of fishermen.

There was objection to bringing legislation against big trawlers as, in the view of several people, fishermen with country boats called kattamarans made of logs of wood, are dangerous on the high seas and have very low productivity. This would also affect the price of fish, which is an important part of the nutritional requirement of the Indian population. Dr Arumughan conceived of boats made from moulded plastic, which would be light and tough. They could be carried single handedly by a fishermen. They could also resist fungus and other climatic causes of deterioration of the boats. He made boats of two sizes, big and small. He designed a mould for both and had mould makers to make these. Plastic raw material was melted and poured into the moulds and once they set, they could be opened up and the boats brought out. They were then trimmed and polished. The boats were fitted with motors and a few accessories, which were again designed by Dr Arumughan and bought out. These were fitted into the boats. The motor and accessories were different for the two boats. The moulds had a lifespan, in terms of the number of boats that could be made from one mould; there was wear and tear. Other machines used by them would generally last for five years. The buildings were of thirty years life. The production process used a common facility in moulding. As the workers worked simultaneously in more than one boat, it was difficult to find out how much of the labour cost is ascribable to which product. The labour for trimming and polishing could be identified to each product.

Dr Arumughan priced the products at cost plus a mark up to give 15 per cent return on investment. But the government persuaded him to sell the boats to poor fishermen at what they described as variable costs. They said they would give them a subsidy for this. After the Tsunami disaster, they bought the boats at total costs, which included all costs, excluding marketing costs plus a 15 per cent mark-up on the costs.

Even though Dr Arumughan had developed the product for the Indian fishermen, he soon found that several sportsmen and fun lovers found it exciting. The interest spread to foreign countries and Dr Arumughan found ways of being able to pack the boats nicely and fitted into sea going containers. He however, had to spend considerable amounts in advertisement, demonstrations, and educational films on his product.

## Discussion Questions

1. Suggest a list of natural classification accounts for the financial accounts.
2. Suggest cost objects keeping in view cost of costing.
3. Indicate the kinds of problems the organization will face in which the cost accountants' help will be useful.
4. What kind of scorekeeping and attention drawing could be supported by accounting information which the classifications will throw up.
5. Is the cost of using the mould a fixed cost or variable cost?
6. What information would Dr Arumughan need for pricing his products.

# PART II

## Tools for Management Accounting

# Cost-Volume-Profit Analysis

## INTRODUCTION

This chapter builds on some of the concepts introduced in Chapters 1 and 3. In Chapter 1, it was indicated that in many situations, organizations have to contend with capacities built up in anticipation of demand. In Chapter 3, the concepts of fixed, variable, and semi-variable costs were introduced. This chapter indicates the consequences of increasing utilization of existing capacities, which can be assessed by the possible patterns of increased revenues and variations in the behaviour of variable costs, semi-variable costs, and fixed costs. This results in variation of profits due to variations in volume of activity. There is another aspect of cost, volume, and profit variations that depend on the variations in cost per unit activity due, which is known as *economies of scale*. It is a common experience that plants that have larger capacities result in lower fixed cost per unit of activity. Thus music cassette bodies cost nearly ₹4 per unit in India, where licensing regulations restricted plant capacities to small numbers. With larger plants, Singapore could produce the same cassette bodies at 50 paise per cassette. This chapter will not be handling situations of this type. We shall discuss such situations in greater detail in Chapter 11.

# CHANGES IN COSTS AND PROFITS WITH CHANGES IN VOLUME

In the following section, we shall discuss why cost per unit and revenue per unit change with volume. We shall also look at the need to forecast the total profits in addition to the total expenses when volume changes.

## Why do Cost Per Unit and Revenue Per Unit Change with Volume?

In Chapter 1, we mentioned that cost per unit is useful information in some situations, typically, in the pricing of products. But we also mentioned that the figure of cost per unit could sometimes be deceptive.

A look at Figs 4.1 (a) and 4.1 (b) shows that unit fixed cost is an indeterminate figure affected by the level of activity. Consequently, it is also very confusing if used to predict the total cost for a given level of activity. On the other hand, as would be seen in Example 4.1, it would be easy to predict costs rapidly at different levels if we approached the problem differently from that of the total unit cost.

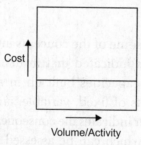

**Fig. 4.1**    (a) Unit fixed cost

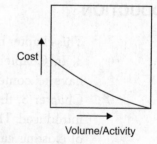

**Fig. 4.1**    (b) Unit variable cost

## Example 4.1    Hiring a Fruit Stall

If we have to decide on hiring a fruit stall selling oranges in, say, a college campus, which costs ₹1,000 a month and we have to consider the cash outlays, then we would have to plan for different levels of activity of 200 kg, 300 kg, or

1000 kg a month. If each costs ₹10, one can compute the monthly cash outlay as follows:

$$\text{For 200 kg, } ₹1000 + 200 \times 10 = ₹3000$$
$$\text{For 300 kg, } ₹1000 + 300 \times 10 = ₹4000$$
$$\text{For 1000 kg, } ₹1000 + 1000 \times 10 = ₹11,000$$

To summarize,

$$\text{Total cost (TC)} = \text{Fixed cost for month (F)} +$$
$$\text{Variable costs/unit (V)} \times \text{quantity (Q)}$$

Does this equation hold true in every situation? The answer is no. It is true only if we can mange with a stall which costs ₹1000 per month on operational size of 1000 kg. Again, we have to presume that we will not get a discount in the price for buying 1000 kg. That is, we presume a linear relationship between cash outlays and the quantity purchased.

Let us now turn to the question of revenue per unit. This does not have the problem of a fixed portion and a variable portion that is associated with costs. However, there is another problem associated with revenue per unit—increased volume can usually be established only if we reduce the unit price. That is, the linearity of revenues with volume cannot always be presumed. We will see later in the chapter that in many situations one can have simplified assumption of linearity in both variable costs and revenues.

## Changes in Total Profits with Change in Volume

Very often in managerial situations, one has to forecast not only the total expenses but also total profit when volume changes. This task is totally impossible only with the unit cost approach.

In Example 4.2, we will show how this can be done very quickly in an alternative approach, which makes one more assumption apart from the linearity of variable costs and fixity of fixed costs. It will presume that what we produced is equal to what we sold and that inventories were neither increased nor decreased. We could alternately also presume that work-in-progress and finished goods inventory are valued only using variable costs, as we described in Chapter 3. If we did so, fixed costs would be charged to the profits when the expenditure was made, whether the goods produced were sold or not.

## Example 4.2   Profitability in the Fruit Stall

We will further develop the earlier example (4.1). Let us assume the price at which the oranges can be sold is ₹20 per kg. Let us also make a practical assumption that the fixed costs per month are fixed, the variable cost and revenues are linear.

The profits in the different situations will be as follows:

For 200 kg, 200 × {20 (price) – 15 (variable cost/unit)} – 1000 = 0
For 300 kg, 300 × {20 (price) – 15 (variable cost/unit)} – 1000 = 500
For 1000 kg, 1000 × {20 price – 15 (variable cost/unit)} – 1000 = 4000

The figure within the brackets is known as Contribution/unit (C) and Contribution/unit × Quantity (Q) is called Total contribution (T.C.) Thus fitted in a formula:

$$\text{Profit} = (\text{Contribution/unit} \times \text{Quantity}) - \text{Fixed costs}$$

$$\text{Pr} = (C \times Q) - F \qquad (A)$$

Where, $(C \times Q) = \text{T.C.}$

We should not forget the assumptions we have made to arrive at this formula.

## BREAK-EVEN ANALYSIS

Often in business, one needs to understand what minimum quantity should be sold to make sure that one does not incur a loss. This minimum quantity is called the *break-even point* (BEP). Let us now discuss the methods of determining the break-even point.

### Methods of Break-even Analysis

There are three methods used to determine the break-even point, namely, the algebraic equation method, the contribution margin method, and the graphical method (Horngren et al. 2003).

### *The algebraic method*

**Break-even analysis**
A simple management tool limited in scope because of the need for critical assumptions

We can arrive at the desired quantity $(Q_{bep})$ by substituting $\text{Pr} = 0$ in the Equation A. Rearranging the terms,

$$C \times Q_{bep} = F \text{ (for a month)}$$

Therefore, $Q_{bep}$ for a month $= F \div C$ (Contribution per unit quantity sales)

### The contribution margin method

If we wish to get the break-even point in value of sales, we can use another concept of contribution margin ratio (CMR), which is computed by dividing contribution per unit by price per unit $(C \div P)$.

$$CM = C \div P \qquad (B)$$

This contribution margin means the contribution for every rupee sales. So,

$$\text{Sales}_{bep} \text{ for a month} = \text{Fixed cost (month)} \div \text{Contribution margin}$$

Hence,

$$\text{Sales}_{bep} = F \div CM \qquad (C)$$

Example 4.3 shows the BEP of the fruit stall.

### Example 4.3 BEP of the Fruit Stall

Let us calculate the break-even point both in quantity $(Q_{bep})$ and sale value $(\text{Sales}_{bep})$ for the data given in Example 4.1 and 4.2.

$Q_{bep}$ for a month = 1000 ÷ 5 = 200
$\text{Sales}_{bep}$ for a month = 1000 ÷ (5 ÷ 20) = ₹4000
     Fixed  Contribution
     cost  margin

We can check that $\text{Sales}_{bep} = Q_{bep} \times \text{Price (20)}$

### Example 4.4 Break-even Analysis

Let us assume that a company manufactures gel pens each of selling price ₹30 and variable cost ₹22. Now the fixed cost per annum is ₹1,20,000. To break even, the firm's contribution from the sale of the pens should be equal to ₹1,20,000.

**Note:** Each pen sold will cover its own variable cost and leave a remainder called contribution to cover the fixed cost.

Sale of one pen will yield a contribution of ₹8 (30 – 22). Number of pens that should be sold to realize total contribution of ₹1,20,000 to cover fixed cost: 1,20,000/8 = 15,000, i.e., in order to achieve break even, the company must sell 15,000 pens.

| | |
|---|---|
| Sales revenue (15,000 pens @ ₹30) | 4,50,000 |
| Less variable cost (15,000 pens @ ₹22) | 3,30,000 |
| Contribution | 1,20,000 |
| Less fixed costs | 1,20,000 |
| Profit/loss | 0 (No profit, no loss) |

Case 1. Now consider that number of pens sold are 18,000. Calculating the profit/loss:

| | |
|---|---|
| Sales revenue (18,000 pens @ ₹30) | 5,40,000 |
| Less variable cost (18,000 pens @ ₹22) | 3,96,000 |
| Contribution | 1,44,000 |
| Less fixed costs | 1,20,000 |
| Profit/loss | 24,000 (Profit) |

Case 2. Now consider that number of pens sold are 12,000. Calculating the profit/loss:

| | |
|---|---|
| Sales revenue (12,000 pens @ ₹30) | 3,60,000 |
| Less variable cost (12,000 pens @ ₹22) | 2,64,000 |
| Contribution | 96,000 |
| Less fixed costs | 1, 20,000 |
| Profit/loss | 24,000 (Loss) |

It can be observed that it is necessary for a positive break even to occur so that the selling price is greater than the variable cost per unit.

### The graphical method

In a CVP graph, sometimes called a break-even chart, unit volume is commonly represented on the horizontal (X) axis and amount on the vertical (Y) axis. Let us understand this method with the help of an example.

### Example 4.5   The Graphical Method

Following is the net profit calculation of a company.

| | ₹ | ₹ |
|---|---|---|
| Estimated sales (600 UNITS SOLD @ ₹250) | | 1,50,000 |
| **Variable cost** | | |
| Direct material | 20,000 | |
| Direct labour | 40,000 | |
| Factory overheads | 10,000 | |
| Administration and selling overheads | 20,000 | 90,000 |
| Contribution | | 60,000 |
| **Fixed cost** | | |
| Factory overhead | 18,000 | |
| Administrative | 17,000 | 35,000 |
| Net profit | | 25,000 |

Preparing a CVP graph involves three steps.

1. Draw a line parallel to the volume axis to present total fixed expenses. For example, we assume total fixed expenses ₹35,000.
2. Choose volume of sales and plot the point representing total expenses (fixed and variable) at the activity level for example 600 units. Total expenses at that activity level is as follows:

| | |
|---|---|
| Fixed expenses | ₹35,000 |
| Variable expenses | ₹90,000 |
| Total cost (expenses) | ₹1,25,000 |

After the point has been plotted, draw a line through it back to the point where the fixed expenses line intersects the rupee axis.

3. For a volume of 600 units sales at this activity level are ₹1,50,000 (600 units × ₹250). Draw a line through this point back to the origin. The break-even point is where the total revenue and total expense lines cross. See the graph (Fig. 4.2) and note that break-even point is at 350 units. It means when the company sells 350 units the profit is zero. When the sales are below the break-even, the company suffers a loss. When sales are above the break-even point, the company earns a profit and the size of the profit increases as sales increase.

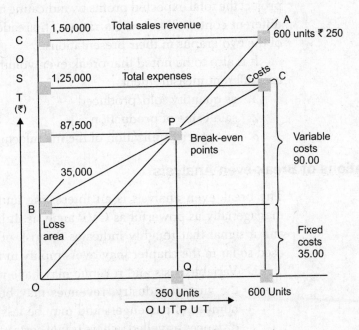

**Fig. 4.2** Cost-volume-profit graph

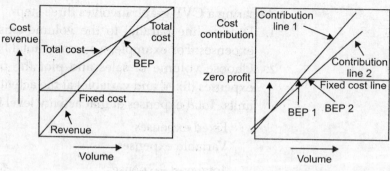

**Fig. 4.3** (a) Break-even point      **Fig. 4.3** (b) PV graph

The CVP dynamics can be graphically demonstrated in several ways, two of which are shown in Fig. 4.3 (a) and (b). In both cases, volume is on the X-axis. In Fig. 4.3 (a), Y-axis has fixed costs, total costs, and total revenue. The origin of Y-axis is zero costs. Figure 4.3(b) has only one plot on Y-axis namely contribution. Its origin is minus fixed costs. It has also two alternative products shown in one graph, to offer a comparison.

As one might see, Fig. 4.3 (a) has more details on cost than Fig. 4.3(b). But if one has to predict profits, one has to measure the distance between the total cost line and the revenue line. Figure 4.3(b) is clearer in indicating the profits by directly reading it from the graph. One can use the graph to project the total expected profits by indicating alternative decisions having different contribution margin ratios. The readers may like to choose any of the two graphs in their presentations.

It is also to be noted that break-even volume shown in the X-axis can use different measurements

1. as quantity sold/produced
2. sale value of production
3. as capacity utilization of the manufacturing plant

## Limitations of Break-even Analysis

The break-even analysis is an interesting and useful tool. But it is not managerially as powerful as CVP analysis. It is at best a useful indicator and a signal that roughly indicates the risk of a venture. The approach used so far in the chapter may oversimplify in many respects:

1. Variable costs and revenue may have multiple drivers. Typical to the aircraft industry, revenues may be driven obviously by the number of passengers and may be less strongly correlated to the distances travelled, whereas fuel costs would be directly correlated

to the distance travelled. Catering costs would be directly proportional to the number of passengers.

2. The analysis ignores what is known as the time value of money. That is, if the revenues are spread over a longer period than costs, one has to account for this time lag. This is usually done more expertly in texts of financial management.

**Cost-volume-profit (CVP) analysis**
BE analysis is often crude like the use of a butcher's knife, but CVP analysis is more sophisticated like the use of a lancet by an expert surgeon.

3. Organizations having multiple products have to make several adjustments in their calculations. These adjustments would be demonstrated in some of the remaining portions of this chapter.

4. If a decision increases the BEP, it is no reason to feel that it is an undesirable decision. Every new investment would increase the BEP as it will increase fixed costs, but the total profits may increase, which is what is desirable. This can be predicted in CVP analysis. We will see later in the chapter how one should decide on the appropriateness of the decision.

## BREAK-EVEN ANALYSIS AND CVP ANALYSIS FOR MULTIPLE PRODUCTS

The framework for both CVP and break-even analysis in the chapter has been till now based on a single product. We will now extend it to multiple products. We will first show the formula which can be used:

$$\text{Profit (P)} = (C_1 \times Q_1 + C_2 \times Q_2 \dots \Sigma\, C_n \times Q_n \text{ Contribution of product}$$
$$n \times \text{Quantity of product } n) - \text{Fixed cost (F)} \qquad \text{(D)}$$

Similarly, the average contribution per unit quantity can be calculated as under:

$$(\Sigma C_n \times Q_n) \div \Sigma Q_n = C_{avg} \qquad \text{(E)}$$

$$\text{BEP} = F \div C_{avg} \qquad \text{(F)}$$

In the break-even analysis, in addition to the earlier assumptions, one needs to have one more assumption that the product mix would be constant. No such assumption would be required in the CVP analysis as the profits get automatically adjusted for varying quantities of individual products. An example of the CVP analysis in an FMCG company is shown in Example 4.6.

One may see from the example that the more complex CVP analysis would enable one to decide that all the three products should be produced. One can make the problem even more interesting by testing if the profit would go up or come down if we increase or decrease the prices and consequently change the volume.

## Example 4.6 Profit Forecast in a Multi-product FMCG Company

The data of a well-known FMCG company, in regard to a select group of products, is provided in Table 4.1 for understanding profit forecasting and break-even analysis in multi-product situations.

**Table 4.1** Data for three products at India Cosmetics

| Product | Unit variable (in ₹) | Unit sale price (in ₹) | Unit contribution (in ₹) | Fixed cost (in ₹) | BEP product (in ₹) |
|---|---|---|---|---|---|
| Gori Sundari | 10 | 20 | 10 | 1,00,000 | 10,000 |
| Tandrusti Soap | 6 | 8 | 2 | 3,00,000 | 1,50,000 |
| Safi | 15 | 18 | 3 | 4,00,000 | 1,33,333 |
| Common | 0 | 0 | 0 | 10,00,000 | |
| Total | | | 15 | 18,00,000 | 1,20,000 |

Gori Sundari has the highest contribution margin ratio 0.50, Tandrusti soap has the next highest 0.25, and Safi, which has severe competition, has the lowest contribution margin ratio at 0.17. Each of them has their direct fixed costs, but they also have common fixed costs. If the product is produced, the respective fixed costs cannot be avoided. Common fixed costs cannot be avoided if any one of the products is produced. It is simple enough to get the BEP of every product. But the BEP for all the products together would require us to compute the contribution margin of all the three together. This can be done only if we presume a particular product mix. The table has presumed equal quantities of each product, that is, one of each. If we vary the product mix, the BEP will change.

In such situations, CVP analysis yields richer dividends. Thus, if it is known that the market demand for Gori Sundari is 1,00,000 pieces and for Tandrusti soap and Safi is 2,00,000 pieces each, we may need to know what the profit would be if we produce all the products up to the market demand. Alternatively, what is the profit if Safi, having the lowest contribution ratio, is not produced, or both Safi and Tandrusti, which have lower profitability than Gori Sundari, are not produced? The analysis is available in Table 4.2.

**Table 4.2** CVP analysis of three products at India Cosmetics

| | Production | Contribution (in ₹) | Fixed costs (in ₹) | Profit (in ₹) |
|---|---|---|---|---|
| **Product** (when all products are produced) | | | | |
| Gori Sundari | 1,00,000 | 10,00,000 | | |
| Tandrusti Soap | 2,00,000 | 4,00,000 | | |
| Safi | 2,00,000 | 6,00,000 | | |
| Total | 5,00,000 | 20,00,000 | 18,00,000 | 2,00,000 |

*(Contd)*

| Product (when Safi is not produced) | | | | |
|---|---|---|---|---|
| Gori Sundari | 1,00,000 | 10,00,000 | | |
| Tandrusti Soap | 2,00,000 | 4,00,000 | | |
| Safi | 0 | 0 | | |
| Total | 3,00,000 | 14,00,000 | 14,00,000 | 0 |
| **Product** (when Tandrusti Soap and Safi is not produced) | | | | |
| Gori Sundari | 1,00,000 | 10,00,000 | | |
| Tandrusti Soap | 0 | 0 | | |
| Safi | 0 | 0 | | |
| **Total** | 1,00,000 | 10,00,000 | 11,00,000 | −1,00,000 |

Thus, CVP analysis is more powerful and richer than break-even analysis.

## Planning for Target Income

Example 4.6 shows how the CVP approach can be used in budgeting for a target income.

If there is only one product whose production is to be planned or if we convert a multi-product situation to the analogy of a single product by presuming a uniform product mix to be converted to one product, we can use the formula as follows:

Production to be planned = (Fixed costs + Target income) ÷ Contribution margin ratio

Thus, if the target income is ₹1,00,000, fixed cost is ₹2,00,000 and the contribution margin ration is 0.40.

Production to be planned = ₹3,00,000 ÷ 0.40 = ₹7,50,000

This means, in essence, target income could be treated as fixed cost in a manner similar to the treatment to ascertain the break-even formula earlier. But as mentioned earlier, the BEP is one of the less important features in CVP analysis. The number of products to plan for an organization of even modest size would be in the range of 100–200. To plan for this number one can use the base data as shown in Example 4.6 and load it on to a spreadsheet. One can then try various alternatives and arrive at a product mix that may yield the desired target income. This could include varying the costs and the sale price with target income in mind. Thus, if fixed costs increase, the target volume for the desired profit will increase. Same would be the case if variable cost per unit increases or sale price per unit decreases. Opposite would be the case if fixed cost decreases, variable cost per unit decreases, or sale price increases. One can also build into this analysis other multiple causes for changes in costs, for example, fluctuations in labour strength due to absenteeism, ambient weather conditions, etc. These manipulations are most easily done on the computer.

## Adjusting Plan for Taxation

Since organizations are usually interested in predicting dividend payment to the shareholders, they should have an easy way to fit in projections of post-tax income. This is projected by the formula:

$$\text{Net post-tax income} = \text{Pre-tax income} \times (1 - \text{Tax rate } t)$$

Thus,

$$\text{Desired quantity to be produced} = [\text{Fixed Cost} + \text{Pre-tax income} \times (1 - \text{Tax rate } t)] \div \text{Contribution margin ratio}$$

Again using the CVP model and spreadsheet on the computer, one can play around with varying combinations of product mix and cost data to plan the production plan.

## 'WHAT IF' AND SENSITIVITY ANALYSIS USING COMPUTERS

The previous section will lead us on to the concept of *sensitivity analysis* or what is known as answering 'what if' questions.

Exhibit 4.1 is the output of sensitivity exercise done on a computer using spreadsheets. It has constructed a matrix of information leading up to the net income based on the variations of product mix of five products. The variations incorporated are the changes in the product mix, variations affecting the contribution ratio, and variations in fixed costs. Managers armed with such information can be well warned. The variations in the data could be deliberately planned or could be caused by statistical probabilities not within the managers' control. But the managers can hypothesize the probability of such occurrences and see the consequences. They can also work out an estimate of the likely profits. Since this involves some statistical refinement in the data, it has not been presented here. It has been explained in Annexure 4.1.

**Exhibit 4.1** 'What if' exercise

| Product | Prod Alt1 | Prod Alt 2 | Prod Alt3 | Prod Alt 4 | Prod Alt 5 |
|---|---|---|---|---|---|
| Gori Sundari | 1,00,000 | 1,20,000 | 80,000 | 70,000 | 50,000 |
| Tandrusti soap | 2,00,000 | 1,80,000 | 2,00,000 | 2,20,000 | 2,30,000 |
| Safi | 2,00,000 | 2,50,000 | 2,80,000 | 3,00,000 | 3,20,000 |
| Sparkling Teeth | 3,00,000 | 2,50,000 | 1,75,000 | 2,00,000 | 2,50,000 |
| Shampoochi | 5,00,000 | 6,00,000 | 7,00,000 | 8,00,000 | 90,000 |
|  | **Cont Alt 1** | **Cont Alt 2** | **Cont Alt 3** | **Cont Alt 4** | **Cont Alt 5** |
| Existing contribution rate | 49,00,000 | 52,00,000 | 48,80,000 | 52,000,00 | 46,60,000 |
| Change in contribution rate (multiplication factor) | 1.1 | 1.2 | 0.9 | 0.95 | 0.8 |
| Revised contribution | 53,90,000 | 62,40,000 | 43,92,000 | 49,40,000 | 37,28,000 |
|  | **Fix cost 1** | **Fix cost 2** | **Fix cost 3** | **Fix cost 4** | **Fix cost 5** |
| Fixed costs | 20,000,00 | 22,000,00 | 25,000,00 | 28,000,00 | 22,000,00 |
| Net at present contrib. | 29,000,00 | 30,000,00 | 23,80,000 | 24,000,00 | 24,60,000 |
| Net revised contrib. | 33,90,000 | 40,40,000 | 18,92,000 | 21,40,000 | 15,28,000 |

# MEASURES OF RISK

In the following section we shall discuss concepts such as margin of safety, operating leverage, risk sharing, and changing of time horizon for analysis.

## Margin of Safety

We had mentioned earlier in the chapter that break-even analysis does give insights into the status of risk in chosen decisions. The *margin of safety* is one of the concepts used in break-even analysis, which articulated this feature.

The margin of safety is the safety gap between the present level above the BEP and the level of break-even. This could be seen in Fig. 4.4.

It is obvious from Fig. 4.4 that we can increase the margin of safety by reducing the fixed costs, and hence, shifting the BEP eastward. Alternatively, if we make the contribution line steeper, the BEP will also be shifted eastward, thereby increasing the margin of safety.

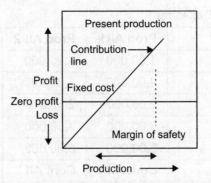

**Fig. 4.4**  The margin of safety from the PV graph

---

## Example 4.7  Margin of Safety

The margin of safety can also be expressed in percentage form. This percentage is obtained by dividing the margin of safety by total sales. The following equation is used for this purpose:

$$\text{Margin of safety ratio} = \frac{\text{Budgeted sales} - \text{Break-even sales}}{\text{Budgeted sales}}$$

|  | ₹ |
|---|---|
| Sales (500 units @ ₹200) | 1,00,000 |
| Break-even sales | 87,500 |
| Margin of safety | 12,500 |
| Margin of safety as a percentage of sales | 12,500/1,00,000 |
|  | = 12.5% |

It means that at the current level of sales and with the company's current prices and cost structure, a reduction in sales of ₹12,500, or 12.5%, would result in just breaking even.

The margin of safety indicates the extent to which sales may fall before the firm suffers a loss. Larger the margin of safety, safer the firm. A high margin of safety is particularly significant in the times of depression when the demands for the firm's product are falling. When the margin of safety is low management must think of possibilities of increasing the selling price, provided it does not adversely affect the sales volume, or reducing the variable costs by bringing improvements in the manufacturing process.

## Operating Leverage

The risk profile of a particular option is also seen often in terms of its *operational leverage*. Operational leverage is measured (Horngren et al. 2003) as:

Contribution at a given level of production ÷ (Contribution at that level of production − Fixed costs)

In other words, it is a measure of the cover that the contribution provides to profits. Thus, the operational leverage would vary with the chosen reference level of production. Higher the cover lower is the operational leverage and higher is the risk of the impact of tumbling down from the peak of profits by the slightest downward trend in production. But lower the cover of profits accounted by contribution, lower is the leverage, which means profits increase and decrease only gradually in sympathy with production. It also means that the slope of the contribution line is less steep. Obviously, the lowest possible operational leverage will be one wherein contribution will be equal to profits. The concept is useful in comparing the risks and rewards of alternative options. Managers decide how to structure the cost function for their organizations. Often, potential trade-offs are made between fixed and variable costs. For example, a company could purchase a vehicle (a fixed cost) or it could lease a vehicle under a contract that charges a rate per mile driven (a variable cost). One of the major disadvantages of fixed costs is that they may be difficult to reduce quickly if activity levels fail to meet expectations, thereby increasing the organization's risk of incurring losses.

The degree of operating leverage is the extent to which the cost function is made up of fixed costs. Organizations with high operating leverage incur more risk of loss when sales decline. Conversely, when operating leverage is high an increase in sales (once fixed costs are covered) contributes quickly to profit. The formula for operating leverage can be written in terms of either contribution margin or fixed costs, as shown here

$$\text{Degree of operating leverage in terms of contribution margin} = \frac{\text{Contribution margin}}{\text{Profit}} = \frac{(P-V) \times Q}{\text{Profit}}$$

$$\text{Degree of operating leverage in terms of fixed costs} = \frac{\text{Fixed cost}}{\text{Profit} + 1}$$

Managers use the degree of operating leverage to gauge the risk associated with their cost function and to explicitly calculate the sensitivity of profits to changes in sales (units or revenues).

$$\% \text{ Change in profit} = \% \text{ Change in sales} \times \text{Degree of operating leverage}$$

Let us illustrate it with Example 4.8.

## Example 4.8 Degree of Operating Leverage

Find out the degree of operating leverage of Venus Beauty Clinic.

| | | ₹ |
|---|---|---|
| Variable cost per visit | | 25 |
| Fixed cost | | 50,000 |
| Estimated visits | | 3000 |
| Revenue per visit | | 55 |
| Total revenue (55 × 3000) | | 1,65,000 |
| Total variable cost (25 × 3000) | | 75,000 |
| Contribution margin | | 90,000 |
| Estimated profit (contribution margin – fixed cost) | | **40,000** |
| Degree of operating leverage | Contribution Margin/Profit | 2.25 |

We arrive at the same answer of 2.25 if we use the fixed cost formula:

Degree of operating leverage in terms of fixed costs = Fixed cost/Profit + 1

$$= 50,000/40,000+1= 2.25$$

The degree of operating leverage and margin of safety percentage are reciprocals.

Margin of safety percentage = 1/Degree of operating leverage

If the margin of safety percentage is small, then the degree of operating leverage is large. In addition, the margin of safety percentage is smaller as the fixed cost portion of total cost gets larger. As the level of operating activity increases above the break-even point, the margin of safety increases and the degree of operating leverage decreases. For Venus Beauty Clinic, the reciprocal of the margin of safety percentage is 2.25 (1/0.444). The reciprocal of the degree of operating leverage is 0.444 (1/2.25).

## Example 4.9 Meals on Wheels

Madhuri Mehra, an MBA, decided that she would not like to be away from her baby daughter for too long in the day and came up with an idea that could give her enough earnings staying at home. She started a meals on wheels business. She picked an enterprising widow who was a great cook and could make north Indian, south Indian, and Chinese meals at a standard cost of ₹120 per meal. Madhuri found that delivering these meals piping hot at homes could fetch ₹200 per meal. She had three offers for the delivery. Gopal quoted a standard ₹2000 per day irrespective of the number of deliveries. Renuka quoted a retention charge of ₹800 per day but charged ₹30 per delivery. Bhaskar quoted a straight charge of ₹50 per delivery but no other fixed charge. Madhuri was wondering which option she should choose. She did a CVP and sensitivity analysis and posted it in a table as under (Table 4.3).

**Table 4.3** Meals on wheels

| Option | Fixed cost/day (C1) | Variable cost/meal (C2) | Variable transport/ meal (C3) | Price per meal (C4) | Contribu- tion meal (C5 = C4 – C2 + C3) | Profit @ 0 sale (0*C5 – C1) | Profit @ 40 sale (40* (C5 – C1) | Profit @ 16 sale (16* C5 – C1 | Profit @ 25 sale (25* C5 – C1) | Profit @ 60 sale (60* C5–C1) |
|---|---|---|---|---|---|---|---|---|---|---|
| Gopal | 2000 | 120 | 0 | 200 | 80 | –2000 | 1200 | –720 | 0 | 2800 |
| Renuka | 800 | 120 | 30 | 200 | 50 | –800 | 1200 | 0 | 450 | 2200 |
| Bhaskar | 0 | 120 | 50 | 200 | 30 | 0 | 1200 | 480 | 750 | 1800 |

A perusal of the table will show that at high levels of sales, Gopal's scheme will give high profits but at low levels it will be disastrous. Bhaskar's scheme will never go into a loss and give higher profits at lower levels of sales. Renuka's proposal was in between. At a daily sale of 40 meals, all the three gave an identical profit. Which scheme should Madhuri choose? If she is sure that the sale will be round about 40, she would choose Bhaskar as it will also be the most secure. If she is sure that the sale will be definitely 60 or more, she will choose Gopal. But if she is unsure, her choice depends upon her propensity to take risks. These types of situations will be more elaborately and precisely detailed in Annexure 4.1. It is sufficient at this stage to show it in a graphical form and work out the operational leverage for all the three options (Fig. 4.5).

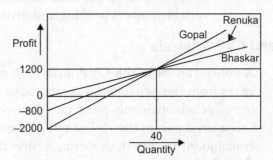

**Fig. 4.5** PV graph of decision options

We have to choose a reference level of sales to compute operational leverage. It is most illustrative to choose the level of sales as 40 meals as the profit at this level is the same for all the three options (Table 4.4).

**Table 4.4** Operational leverage for decision options

| | Gopal | Renuka | Bhaskar |
|---|---|---|---|
| Contribution | 3200 | 2000 | 1200 |
| Fixed cost | 2000 | 800 | 0 |
| Profit | 1200 | 1200 | 1200 |
| Operational leverage | 2.667 | 1.667 | 1 |

It may be seen from Table 4.4 that Gopal has the highest operational leverage and is most risky. The reader may practise calculating the operational leverage with reference to other levels of sales. The figures would change (except for Bhaskar, which will be constant at 1) but the relative rankings of the three options will remain the same.

There are several managerial situations that are similar to the one in Example 4.10.

Here is a typical illustrative list:

1. Should we pay our wages by piece rate, that is, by output, by fixed salary, or by partly fixed salary and partly production bonus?
2. Should we open retail outlets with high fixed costs and low variable costs, or should we sell through distributors with some fixed costs and middling variable costs, or completely through franchisees with no fixed costs but very high variable costs?
3. Should we hire a large number of faculty on monthly salaries, or fewer faculty with provision for paying extra for extra classes, or should there be only hired faculty paid only by the hours taught?
4. Should we buy assets or lease them and if we lease should the payment be by usage or time-based rental?
5. Should we allow for retail sales in small lots involving increased variable costs in packing and invoicing or in larger lots?

## Risk Sharing and CVP Analysis

Another variant of the CVP analysis flows out of the alternatives. This arises from the behavioural assumptions of risk sharing. If for example, one pays salesmen only piece rate, if there is no sale, there is no payment and a large part of the risk of reduced sales is passed on to them. But consequent to this the salesmen directly get a stake in ensuring the risk of drop in sales is avoided. They work for even higher sale than would have happened if the payment had been time-rated. Similarly, competence in distribution arrangement with distributors may take them to much higher level of sales than would be possible if the entire retail sales were directly conducted.

### Strategy of varying share of fixed and variable costs

Earlier discussions would show that managers have wide options in varying the shares of fixed and variable costs and their choice depends upon CVP and probability analysis. Break-even analysis by itself would be inadequate to reach a conclusion. Let us see Example 4.10 concerning decisions for a management development programme on ethics called Om Shanti.

## Example 4.10 Om Shanti

Om Shanti is a short three-day Indian ethics training programme, which was popular in Europe. A tentative cost analysis of the programme is available in Table 4.5, which is self-explanatory. There are three alternative plans A, B, and C under consideration. Plan A is to hire Prof. Grundig as a faculty. Posted in Germany and most willing to gain experience, he is a 'cheap alternative'. However, he is little known and it is apprehended that he would attract only limited participation. Alternative B is to hire Prof. Chandra from India who has a very good reputation. In this alternative, Prof. Chandra would get a fixed fee plus reimbursement of travel expenses. Alternative C is a further variation of alternative B, wherein he would be given only travel expenses as a fixed sum but would get a 30 per cent share in the surplus before consultant fees. Prof. Chandra would then be motivated to contact institutions and individuals he knew to get them to sponsor participants. As can be understood at the end of it all, the number of participants was an uncertain figure. Plan C passes considerable part of the risk to Prof. Chandra.

The net surpluses shown in Table 4.5 are at best estimates. With the rough information available, it seems that the Om shanti programme would choose Plan C. Would the choice of Prof. Chandra be the same? The answer is yes if he has self-belief and also has an understanding of CVP and probability analysis in addition to ethics, which was his chosen subject of specialization.

**Table 4.5** Cost analysis of Om Shanti

| Participant no. | Building hire (in ₹) | Reading material (in ₹) | Food (in ₹) | Total cost (in ₹) | Fees (in ₹) | Surplus before consultant charges (in ₹) | Faculty fixed cost (in ₹) | Faculty variable cost (in ₹) | Total (in ₹) | Net surplus (in ₹) |
|---|---|---|---|---|---|---|---|---|---|---|
| 50 | 50,000 | 50,000 | 1,00,000 | 2,00,000 | 3,50,000 | 1,50,000 | 1,00,000 | 0 | 1,00,000 | 50,000 |
| 100 | 50,000 | 1,00,000 | 2,00,000 | 3,50,000 | 7,00,000 | 3,50,000 | 2,00,000 | 0 | 2,00,000 | 1,50,000 |
| 200 | 50,000 | 2,00,000 | 4,00,000 | 6,50,000 | 14,00,000 | 7,50,000 | 1,00,000 | 2,25,000 | 3,25,000 | 4,25,000 |

## Changing Time Horizon for Analysis

In Chapter 3, we showed that some costs that do not vary in the short run may vary in the medium term or the long term. These variations are not spontaneous consequences of 'time' but due to conscious and elaborate decisions that are taken at longer time gaps. Thus one may very aptly describe them as related to longer time horizons. Following are two typical examples:

1. In aviation industry, fuel costs behave like fixed costs in the short run as the distance travelled is more or less constant. But in the

medium term, the routes are changed. A flight from Delhi to Chennai may be extended to Trichy and Colombo, which would make flight travel distance a variable cost driver for fuel costs, etc.

2. An ore handling plant would generally be set for a specified number of shifts in a day in a short-term horizon. But in a longer time horizon, it may run a second or a third shift. The pattern of fixed and variable costs would change.

## DECISION OPTIONS

CVP analysis is used in various decision processes, even in non-profit organizations. Let us now look at some of these decision options.

### Cost-volume Analysis for Non-profit Organizations

Cost–volume relationship in non-profit organizations has a slightly different focus. Typical issues are as under:

1. In a school, the cost of education consists of fixed costs and variable costs. The distribution of this can be varied with typically hiring whole time teachers on time-rated basis, teachers paid by the number of classes taken, or paid by number of students taught. The total cost incurred and cost per student could be planned by appropriate mix of fixed and variable costs.

2. In a charitable dispensary, one can have whole time doctors or part time doctors, have pathological tests done by the dispensary or by sending the cases to an outside agency paid by the number of tests, etc. These govern the cost per patient.

3. In an organization involved in counselling drug addicts, one can similarly have permanent counsellors paid by time or counsellors paid by the number of addicts handled. This will show up as cost per drug addict.

### Using Multiple Cost Drivers

We have described organizations whose cost and profits are driven by product mix. But there could be other cost drivers.

1. In dairy industry, which uses boiler to produce hot water and oil fired dryers, the energy cost may be driven not only by the product but also by the seasonal external ambient temperatures. The energy cost may have a fixed element that is common for all seasons and

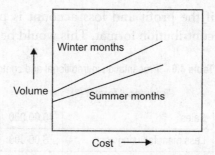

**Fig. 4.6**   Energy cost in dairy for one product (milk)

a variable element that depends on product mix. The cost line may look as in Fig. 4.6.

2. The cost may be driven not only by the quantity sold but also by the lot size of each sale. More the lot size, more may be packing costs, invoicing costs, etc.

3. In some cases multiple cost drivers may be converted to single cost drivers by the use of compound cost drivers. Patients and number of days in a hospital can be combined to patient-days. In hotels, we could have room-days; in transport industry, tonne-kilometres, etc.

## Decisions on Advertising Plans

Advertisement plans are made with an expectation of an estimated increment in sales. These estimates are at best inspired guesses, but one can roughly apply CVP analysis to the decision by relating the advertisement expenses and alternative fixed costs in alternative advertisement plans and see the corresponding benefits in profits.

## Decisions in Raising or Reducing Sale Prices

Change in sale prices will result in change in sales quantity due to price elasticity of demand. Change in sales prices also result in change in unit contribution. But as the purpose of managerial decision is to maximize total profit and, therefore, total contribution rather than contribution per unit sale, the formula should be:

If $Q_1 \times C_1 > Q_2 \times C_2$ even if $C_1 < C_2$, one should choose the option of $C_1$ and therefore a lower sale price associated with it.

## Presentation of Profit in the Contribution Format

Finally, as a modified understanding of the way profit and loss is exhibited in Chapters 2 and 3, cost-volume-profit relationships are brought out sharper if the profit and loss account is presented in what one could call the contribution format. This would be clear from Table 4.6.

**Table 4.6** Presentation in traditional and contribution format

| Traditional format (₹) | | Contribution format (₹) | |
|---|---|---|---|
| Sales | 10,00,000 | Sales | 10,00,000 |
| Less manufacturing costs | 8,00,000 | Less variable costs | 4,50,000 |
| Gross profit | 2,00,000 | Contribution | 5,50,000 |
| Marketing administrative costs | 1,00,000 | Less fixed costs | 4,50,000 |
| Net profit | 1,00,000 | Net profit | 1,00,000 |

What is the advantage of the contribution format? Suppose, we like to estimate the profit if the sales increases by say 20 per cent, it can be easily found by multiplying contribution by a factor of 1.20, which will result in a contribution of 6,60,000. Net profit would be computed by deducting 4,50,000, yielding a profit of ₹2,10,000. Such computation would not be possible with the traditional presentation.

## SUMMARY

Prediction of future costs and profits is critically based on understanding the nature of costs—whether they are fixed, variable, or semi-variable–and on the ranges of activity. Prediction of future costs and profits offer themselves as targets and budgets. Break-even analysis predicts the level of activity at which profit is zero or costs equal revenue. The absolute figure of contribution is the difference between sales and variable costs.

Contribution minus fixed costs equals profits. Contribution per unit activity multiplied by quantity sold/produced is equal to absolute contribution. Break-even activity can be expressed as activity for a given time period, sales per given time period, or capacity utilization of the plant. Break-even analysis presumes linear function of revenue and variable costs with reference to activity. It also assumes that what is produced is sold and inventory increase or decrease is not involved. Break-even analysis enables one to understand the margin of safety that is the measure of risk. Another measure of risk is the operational leverage, which equals contribution divided by profit at a given level.

CVP analysis is more comprehensive and complex than break-even analysis and is used in varied decision processes and even in non-profit organizations. Sensitivity analysis indicates the consequences or outcomes of variations in the independent variables and is done easily on the computer. It may enable a decision-maker to take a good decision consistent with risk propensities. However, this may result in good decisions sometimes giving bad outcomes.

## KEY POINTS

- Break-even point (BEP) equals fixed costs contribution per unit (expressed as in units of production in a given time period) or fixed costs ÷ contribution margin ratio (expressed in sales value in a given time period).
- Contribution margin ratio equals contribution ÷ sales.
- Production required for achieving target income equals (fixed costs + target income) ÷ contribution per unit production.
- The PV graph plots contribution against activity with point of origin on Y-axis as zero profits and fixed costs as a negative figure.
- Margin of safety is the distance between the present level of production and the break-even level.
- Operational leverage equals contribution divided by profit (contribution minus fixed costs) at a given level of activity. Operational leverage changes with the level of activity.
- Sensitivity analysis indicates the consequences of variations in independent variables and forewarns managers to take calculated risks.

## CONCEPT REVIEW QUESTIONS

1. What are the basic assumptions in break-even analysis?
2. Does a higher operational leverage mean a higher risk? Give reasons.
3. Can we have a break-even analysis for a multi-product organization? Explain.
4. Explain why CVP analysis is more complex and provides richer insights than break-even analysis.
5. Explain the limitations of CVP analysis.
6. What is sensitivity analysis? How does it help managers?
7. What are the advantages of exhibiting profits in the contribution format?
8. How can a good decision sometimes result in bad outcomes?

## NUMERICAL PROBLEMS

1. Fill in the answer in the space marked **?** with appropriate figures.

| Case | Revenue | Variable cost | Fixed cost | Total cost | Operating income | Contribution margin |
|------|---------|---------------|------------|------------|------------------|---------------------|
| A | 1000 | 500 | 300 | ? | 200 | ? |
| B | ? | 800 | 400 | 1200 | ? | 0.6 |
| C | 4000 | 3000 | ? | 3100 | 900 | ? |
| D | 5000 | 1000 | 3500 | 4500 | ? | ? |

2. **Seeta Travels**

Seeta Travels is into air ticket business. The airlines give it a 10 per cent commission on the sale price of air tickets. The average value of the air ticket is ₹10,000, that is, its average commission is ₹1000 per ticket.

Its monthly fixed costs are ₹25,000. In addition, its variable cost is ₹50 per ticket.

2.1 What is its BEP in terms of number of monthly tickets?

2.2 What would be the BEP if the average value of tickets will increase by 10 per cent?

2.3 What would be the BEP if the present conditions prevail but variable costs are reduced by 10 per cent?

2.4 What would be the BEP if in addition to decrease in variable costs by 10 per cent the fixed costs are also reduced by 10 per cent?

2.5 What would be the BEP if the monthly advertisement expenses are incurred of ₹10,000 over and above the present levels?

2.6 How may more tickets should they have to sell over the present level to justify spending ₹10,000 per month in advertisement over and above the present level?

3. **Sishu Sadan**

Sishu Sadan, a charitable school, gets an annual grant of ₹10,00,000 from the government. It provides scholarship to poor children. Every scholarship involves a monthly expense of ₹500 and a lump sum payment of ₹1000 every year. Sishu Sadan also spends a yearly sum of ₹2,00,000 for maintaining infrastructure and the teachers.

How many scholarships can be afforded by Sishu Sadan?

4.  **Bahujan Hardware**

Bahujan Hardware's break-even monthly sales is ₹1,00,000. Its fixed costs are ₹40,000.

4.1  What is its contribution margin ratio?

4.2  What is its sale price per unit if its variable cost per unit is ₹1.20?

4.3  If 80,000 units are the present sales, what is its margin of safety?

5.  **Bengal Handloom and Handicrafts**

Bengal Handloom and Handicrafts (BHH) had organized a grand sale for three days at the Pragati Maidan, Delhi for Murshidabad economy carpets that it sells at ₹1000 a piece. It buys these at ₹700 a piece with provision for unlimited return of unsold carpets. The Pragati Maidan scheme, sponsored by government to encourage Indian handicrafts, had two options:

(i)  A fixed payment of ₹10,000 as a lump sum for the three days rental.

(ii)  A 10 per cent of sale value for the period.

5.1  Compute the BEP for options (i) and (ii).

5.2  Calculate the level of sales where both options will give same net income.

5.3  List the conditions under which BHH should prefer option (i) and option (ii)

5.4  What is the operational leverage of the two options at a sale of (a) 100 carpets, (b) 200 carpets? Interpret the results obtained.

6.  **Vapi Pharma**

Vapi Pharma was selling its products through wholesale distributors at 18 per cent commission. This was the situation throughout 2004 and the financial results are presented in the following table (Table P 6).

**Table P6**  Vapi Pharma's income statement for year 2004 (in ₹)

| Revenue | | 26,00,000 |
|---|---|---|
| **Cost of goods sold:** | | |
| Variable | 11,70,000 | |
| Fixed costs | 2,87,000 | 14,57,000 |
| Gross profit | | 11,43,000 |
| **Marketing costs:** | | |
| Commission | 4,68,000 | |
| Fixed costs | 3,42000 | 8,10,000 |
| Operating income | | 3,33,000 |

Vapi was contemplating switching from wholesale distributors to direct selling. This would increase annual fixed costs further by ₹2,00,000. But commission would decrease from 18 per cent to 10 per cent of sales.

6.1 Calculate BEP for 2004 with present cost and distribution structure.
6.2 Calculate BEP for 2004 if the new structure had been in place and comment on the result.
6.3 What is the operating leverage in the two systems at the year 2004 level of sales, say ₹26,00,000? Comment on the result.
6.4 If the sales force demanded the same commission as is being given to the distributors, suppose 18 per cent, would it be wise to agree to it with some additional stipulations?

7. **Bengal Tent Manufacturers**
Bengal Tent sells its tents at ₹4000 a piece. Its variable costs are ₹2000. Its annual fixed costs are ₹10,00,000. It has budgeted to sell 1700 tents in 2005 and budgeted a net income of ₹24,00,000 but a mid-year review showed that for the first five months only 350 tents were sold. Its income tax rate was 20 per cent. A review showed the following:

(i) If they reduce the price to ₹400, they could sell 2700 units in the remaining seven months without changing the variable cost/unit or fixed costs.
(ii) If they lower the variable costs by ₹100 and use lower quality goods, the selling price can be reduced by ₹300 and sales would be 2200 units in the remaining part of the year.
(iii) If they reduce fixed costs by ₹10,000, lower price by 5 per cent, and keep variable cost/unit the same, they can sell 2000 units in the remaining part of the year.

7.1 If we do not change and price structure, what is the BEP sale?
7.2 Which alternative should they choose?

## Computer-based Numerical Problems

8. **PV Graph**
Two products A and B have the cost structure as in the following table. All values are in ₹.

| Product | Fixed cost/annum | Variable cost/unit | Price/unit |
| --- | --- | --- | --- |
| A | 1,00,000 | 3 | 20 |
| B | 20,000 | 8 | 10 |

1.1 Using a spreadsheet, calculate contribution and profit at a sale of 5883, 10,000, 15,000, and 3,000 units.

1.2 Draw a PV graph for both products A and B and comment on the results.

9. **Switching from Gross Profits to Contribution Format**

Zeeta was a multi-product company whose 2004 record showed a sale of ₹20,00,000, variable manufacturing cost of ₹10,00,000, a fixed manufacturing cost of ₹5,00,000, variable marketing costs of ₹2,00,000, and fixed administrative costs of ₹2,00,000.

2.1 Present the data to show gross profit and net profit.

2.2 Present the same data in the contribution format.

2.3 Use the answer in 9.2 to project the figures for the year 2005 at three levels of sales:

(i) ₹30,00,000 (ii) ₹15,00,000 (iii) ₹25,00,000. State your assumptions clearly.

## PROJECTS

1. Form several groups of four or five and visit a local restaurant, pan shop, cinema house, vehicle repair shop, etc., and identify their fixed cots, variable costs, semi-variable costs, the corresponding ranges, and related cost drivers. From this basic data, forecast their contribution margins for different products, profits at different levels of sales and product mixes, break-even sales, margin of safety, and operational leverage.

**CASE STUDY 1**     **Gummidipundi Sintered Products**

Gummidipundi Sintered Products (GSP), situated in the Gummidipundi industrial estate close to Chennai in Tamil Nadu, was well known for its standard product used in automobiles made in powder metallurgy. Natarajan, its Managing Director, was a brilliant engineer from IIT Chennai but was a little impatient with complex ideas of management and cost accounting. 'Keep it simple stupid' (KISS) was his favourite slogan. He preferred to delegate authorities to his subordinates with simple guidelines and liked to enjoy with his filmstars and cricketer friends in Chennai. He persuaded his nephew Raman, a chartered accountant, to join his firm. Raman was quite good in financial accounting but was not always comfortable with cost analysis. Egged on by his uncle seeking out a formula, he first produced the data as shown in Table CS 1(a). Natarajan wanted him to produce a weekly profit and loss account as his production plans were also based on forecast three weeks ahead. He did not keep inventories. His single shift production weekly capacity was 600, but beyond 500 units he had to stretch the direct labour with inducements such as overtime. This could also work up to 700 units. But beyond 700, he would have to start a second shift.

**Table CS 1(a)** Weekly cost sheet

| | Units of output | Direct material | Direct labour | Indirect labour | Indirect material | Electricity | Factory depreciation, etc. | Other overheads |
|---|---|---|---|---|---|---|---|---|
| Week 1 | 400 | 3000 | 5000 | 1800 | 3000 | 1150 | 1250 | 3100 |
| Week 2 | 500 | 3750 | 6250 | 2000 | 3000 | 1250 | 1250 | 3600 |
| Week 3 | 600 | 4500 | 7500 | 2200 | 3000 | 1350 | 1250 | 4100 |

In addition, he found that office and administrative expenses were steady at weekly ₹7810. He also found that the prices were usually ₹70 per piece. Raman thought he could analyse these further to identify fixed costs, variable costs, and semi-variable costs and do a CVP and a break-even analysis.

He produced a table as shown in Table CS 1(b).

**Table CS 1(b)** Weekly profit statement

| | Week 1 | Week 2 | Week 3 |
|---|---|---|---|
| Sales @ std price ₹70 | 28,000 | 35,000 | 42,000 |
| Cost of goods sold (actual) (₹) | 18,300 | 21,100 | 23,900 |
| Gross profit (₹) | 9,700 | 13,900 | 18,100 |
| Less other expenses (₹) | 10,610 | 11,310 | 12,010 |
| Net profit (loss) (₹) | (910) | 2590 | 6090 |

Raman realized the obvious that profit increased with sales. But he was puzzled that the cost of production/unit fell with increased production as under:

When sales were 400 units: ₹45.75/unit
When sales were 500 units: ₹42.2/unit
When sales were 600 units: ₹39.80/unit

He was puzzled and asked Gopika who was a masters in statistics and was working in the office. Gopika said that there was no need to be puzzled by the drop in cost of production with increased sales and could be understood by segregating the fixed costs and variable costs. Raman, too proud to get Gopika's help, did the segregation himself. He produced what he called a standard cost sheet as under:

| | |
|---|---|
| Average variable cost per unit | ₹28 |
| Average fixed cost per unit | ₹14.20 |
| Total | ₹42.20 |
| Average fixed administrative costs | ₹15.60 |
| Average commission per unit sold | ₹7 (10 per cent of ₹70) |
| Added rounding errors | ₹1.20 |
| Total cost | ₹66 |

He summarized a decision rule for Natarajan:

(i)   At a price of ₹70 make only ₹4 per piece.

(ii)   Decision rule #1: Never sell at less than ₹66 as that is the break-even level.

(iii)   Decision rule #2: For sales directly from the office that do not bear commission, never sell at less than ₹59, which is the break-even level.

Natarajan appreciated Raman's work and accordingly issued a circular. Raman showed it proudly to Gopika who rubbished the analysis. Natarajan, after issuing the circular and brimming with confidence, went for a spree with his actor friends.

A week after he came back he was shown the following transactions:

(i)   The salesmen had sold 450 units at ₹70.

(ii)   The salesmen turned out a request from an irregular customer for 50 units at ₹65 per unit.

(iii)   One telephone order directly to the office (not bearing commission) was accepted at ₹65 for 80 units but another at ₹57.50 for 50 units was rejected.

(iv)   Gopika received a call from Reddy who was making the same part but was closing down. He told her his cost was ₹55 and he would like to have 100 pieces at the same price. This was the last time he would be ordering from GSP as he was closing down his business. Gopika, more self-confident than others to break the 'rule', accepted the offer and thought it would please Natarajan.

Raman also prepared a profit analysis for the week as shown in Table CS 1(c):

**Table CS 1(c)**   Profit analysis for the week

| Source | No. of units | Price/unit (in ₹) | Cost per unit (in ₹) | Profit per unit (in ₹) |
|---|---|---|---|---|
| **Orders accepted** | | | | |
| Salesmen | 450 | 70 | 66 | 4 |
| Office | 80 | 65 | 59 | 6 |
| Gopika | 100 | 55 | 59 | (4) |
| **Orders rejected** | | | | |
| Salesmen | 50 | 65 | 66 | (1) |
| Office | 50 | 57.50 | 59 | (1.50) |

Natarajan studied the profit analysis and decided as follows:

(i) He advised the salesmen that he would increase their commission to 15 per cent if they sold at ₹80. He argued as follows

| | New (in ₹) | Old (in ₹) |
|---|---|---|
| Revenue | 80 | 70 |
| Cost | 59 | 59 |
| Contribution | 21 | 11 |
| Commission | 12 | 7 |
| Profit | 9 | 4 |

(ii) He fired Gopika.

## Discussion Questions

1. What do you think about Natarajan's decision?
2. What should be the decision rule for pricing the product? What is the extra information you need to make it practical?

| CASE STUDY 2 | Franchising Money Order Business |
|---|---|

Jyoti Rao was running a utility store in the new campus of the Badami Institute that was far away from city limits. The Indian postal authorities were receiving complaints from the construction and road workers working near the Badami Institute that they had to go long distances to be able to send money orders to their homes. The workers' families lived in the villages of Belgaum and Golkunda districts and were very much dependent on the money order remittances of these workers. The postal authorities were impressed with Jyoti's efficient operations and offered her a franchise for handling money order transactions.

While Jyoti was contemplating, she got to understand that Ramya of the Badami Institute was looking out for a costing study assignment that she could do without travelling very long distances. She asked Ramya to advise her. Ramya was glad to accept the job.

On scrutiny of the available invoices of the store, she found that the average purchase was for ₹50 though it peaked in some periods to ₹100. The contribution margin on these sales was 20 per cent. On a random sample she found that the time the shop assistant took to handle the sale was within a narrow range around 30 seconds. But there were sometimes periods of idleness for the assistants in between the sales. She got to understand that the postal authorities would charge ₹250 per month for renting a machine that could process the money orders. It would also take about a minute to process a money order. The postal authorities would also charge fifty paise per money order. Ramya also found that most banks and other informal institutions charged their customers ₹1 per transaction; the facilities were as little far away. Jyoti said she proposed to charge 70 paise per transaction to meet competition.

Jyoti was paying her staff ₹72 for an eight-hour shift, that is, ₹9 per hour. Jyoti additionally told Ramya that if her assistants did not promptly attend to her regular customers, they may transfer their loyalties to the other store in the campus, whereas if she made the money order clients wait a little, they may stray into the main store and buy some items from the store. However, they would get irritated if they were made to wait too long.

## Discussion Questions

1. What is the BE number of money orders that has to be sustained?
2. Is this a simple exercise or does it depend upon other factors? What are those factors?
3. What other information does Ramya need to collect to improve the reliability of the decision?

| CASE STUDY 3 | Choice of Umbrella Designs |
| --- | --- |

The ladies of Goa were fashion conscious and chose the colour of their umbrellas to match their wardrobe. But it was always difficult to predict the way the fashion would go. Goa Fashions had to order umbrellas for the coming monsoon season from the manufacturers in bulk to get discount on prices and an assurance that they would not supply to any other party. For this purpose, they had to pay a fixed commitment charge. This commitment plus other fixed costs amounted to an annual figure of ₹40,000. They had zeroed in on two designs—'plain green' and 'striking red'. If striking red caught on, it would probably sell in large quantities. But plain green is steadier. Once chosen, the manufacturer could supply at short notice. The distribution of the probabilities of sale is as shown in Table CS 3.

**Table CS 3**  Distribution of the probability of sales

| Probability of Demand | Plain Green (in %) | Striking Red (in %) |
| --- | --- | --- |
| 500 | 0 | 10 |
| 1000 | 10 | 10 |
| 2000 | 20 | 10 |
| 3000 | 40 | 20 |
| 4000 | 20 | 40 |
| 5000 | 10 | 10 |
| Total | 100 | 100 |

The variable cost for each product is ₹80 and selling price is ₹100.

### Discussion Questions

1. What is the BEP of the sale of green and red umbrellas?
2. Which product should be chosen if they have to maximize their income?
3. If management is definite that 3000 red umbrellas will sell but cannot improve on the probability information on plain green as contained in the table, would the decision be any different?

CASE STUDY 4

**Deciding Where to Produce**

Maharashtra Power Supplies has two power plants, one near the coal mines in Wardha and a second near the coast at Mumbai. The Wardha plant with capacity of 400 units per day is coal based and has lower variable cost than the Mumbai one, which is oil based and has a daily capacity of 320 units per day. The cost data of the two plants is given in Table CS 4:

**Table CS 4**  Cost data of the two plants

| | Wardha Plant | | Mumbai plant | |
|---|---|---|---|---|
| Selling price/unit | | ₹2.50 | | ₹2.50 |
| Variable manufacturing cost/unit | 0.72 | | 0.88 | |
| Fixed manufacturing cost/unit | 0.30 | | 0.15 | |
| Variable distribution cost/unit | 0.14 | | 0.14 | |
| Fixed distribution cost/unit | 0.19 | | 0.145 | |
| Total cost/unit | | 1.35 | | 1.315 |
| Operating income/unit | | 1.15 | | 1.85 |
| Production/day | 400 units | | 320 units | |

All fixed costs/unit are calculated on 240 days per annum. If it exceeds 240 days, variable cost of manufacture increases by ₹0.30/unit in Wardha and ₹0.80 in Mumbai plant.

Presently, to supply 1,92,000 units to the grid they have planned to operate Mumbai plant for 300 days and Wardha for 240 days. The logic of this is that Mumbai gives a profit of ₹1.85/unit as against ₹1.50/unit at Wardha.

**Discussion Questions**

1. Calculate the BEP of the Wardha and Mumbai plant.
2. What will be the operating income if 96,000 units are produced in each of the plants as proposed?
3. Can you improve the profitability by changing the allocation? Show calculations.

| CASE STUDY 5 | Dada Pawar Wrestling Match |
|---|---|

The famous wrestler, Bhim Singh, is a star wrestler and Dada Pawar, the cable company owner, desires to arrange a wrestling match of an upcoming wrestler, Laxman Singh, with Bhim Singh. Bhim Singh will charge ₹50,000 plus a share of 20 per cent from the cable viewers. Dada's own fixed costs in addition to the payment to Bhim Singh would be ₹50,000. Every cable viewer will pay ₹50 for watching the show out of which Pawar will pay Bhim Singh ₹10. Dada Pawar will, however, have to spend ₹5 per home of the viewers. Dada was uncertain of the likely number of viewers and he wishes to be careful before he commits to Bhim Singh. His estimate of the probability of the number of viewers are as shown in Table CS 5:

**Table CS 5**   Estimate of the probability of the number of viewers

| Demand | Probability |
|---|---|
| 1000 | 0.05 |
| 2000 | 0.1 |
| 3000 | 0.3 |
| 4000 | 0.35 |
| 5000 | 0.15 |
| 10000 | 0.05 |
| Total | 1 |

## Discussion Questions

1. What is the break-even number of viewers that Dada will have to ensure?
2. What is the amount Bhim Singh could expect from the fight?

# ANNEXURE

## Annexure 4.1

### Analysing uncertainty and sensitivity using some mathematical tools

We will demonstrate the use of the mathematical tools with the example of Jyoti Rao who was planning to start a utility store. Jyoti Rao had an offer from the new campus of the Badami Institute of Management to run a utility store. She could choose one of three modes of payment to the institute:

(a) A monthly rental of ₹20,000

(b) A monthly rental of ₹10,000 plus a royalty of 5 per cent of sales

(c) A royalty of 10 per cent of sales

Jyoti did some preliminary survey and found that she could sell her wares at a mark-up of 20 per cent. That is, if she bought a product at ₹100 she could sell it at ₹120. But she was not certain about the quantum of sales. She may get customers from the Badami campus but some from outside the campus may also buy from the store. She roughly worked out that 60 per cent chances were that the sale would be ₹1,00,000 per month. But there were 40 per cent chances that the sale may touch ₹4,00,000. How could she decide amongst the options?

### Step 1

Identify the choice criterion. It could be cost minimization or profit maximization. Jyoti could choose profit maximization.

### Step 2

Decide the specifics of the alternatives to be considered. The three modes of payments are stated in the preamble to the problem.

### Step 3

Identify the set of events that would affect profit outcome. It is identified as sale of ₹1,00,000 and ₹4,00,000 as stated in the preamble. They are mutually exclusive.

### Step 4

Assign probabilities for the events from independent market research. Make sure these probabilities add up to one, which shows they are mutually exclusive.

### Step 5

Compute the outcome.

The information fed into a spreadsheet would give the matrix information as in Table A4.1

## Interpretation of Table A4.1

Table A4.1 shows that for an event which is more probable, that is monthly sale of ₹1,00,000, the income would be much better if Jyoti chooses option C. But since the profitability of option A is immensely high if the sale is ₹4,00,000, the weighted income is tilted in favour of choosing option A. Thus if Jyoti is comfortable with taking risks, it would be perfectly logical for her to choose option A. However, she would have to remember that the probability of the decision turning out bad is high.

*Good decisions resulting in bad outcomes*

The interpretation of the data would show that a perfectly sound decision consistent with risk propensities of the decision-maker can turn out to have bad outcomes.

**Table A4.1** Jyoti Rao Income estimates (in ₹)

| Option | Fixed cost | Sale | Sale margin | Variable cost | Operating income | Probability | Weighted income |
|---|---|---|---|---|---|---|---|
| A | 20,000 | 1,00,000 | 20,000 | 0 | 0 | 0.6 | 0 |
| B | 10,000 | 1,00,000 | 20,000 | 5,000 | 5,000 | 0.6 | 3,000 |
| C | 0 | 1,00,000 | 20,000 | 10,000 | 10,000 | 0.6 | 6,000 |
| Option | Fixed cost | Sale | Sale margin | Variable cost | Operating income | Probability | Weighted income |
| A | 20,000 | 4,00,000 | 80,000 | 0 | 60,000 | 0.4 | 24,000 |
| B | 10,000 | 4,00,000 | 80,000 | 20,000 | 50,000 | 0.4 | 20,000 |
| C | 0 | 4,00,000 | 80,000 | 40,000 | 40,000 | 0.4 | 16,000 |

## CHAPTER 5

# Job and Process Costing

## Learning Objectives

After reading this chapter, you will be able to understand

- the manner of choosing cost objects based on production and operational processes in an industry
- when a job would be an appropriate cost object and when a process or department would be more appropriate
- the manner in which resource outlays in production computed in the chosen accounting periods could be tied up with resource outlays in jobs that typically follow a time schedule out of step with those accounting periods
- both manufacturing and service industries where job costing is a useful device
- the need for job costs to be computed

- immediately after a job is finished, and the short cuts used in cost accounting in estimating indirect costs to be charged to the job in normal costing system
- the problems arising in incorrect forecasting in normal costing systems and its remedies
- the use of job costing in pricing of products with negotiated cost-plus arrangements
- the role of process costing and unit cost calculation
- the various methods of costing of inter-process transfers
- appreciate the role of unit cost calculation by using equivalent unit method

## INTRODUCTION

This chapter deals primarily with the concepts of job and process costing. However, it also unfolds the detailed processes in cost accounting and thus discusses the features considered in choosing the costing systems. In the previous chapters, we highlighted the difference in the structure of financial accounting and cost accounting. Financial accounts are based on summarizing transactions according to natural classification, whereas cost accounting uses functional classification indicating the use of resources in products and services. The latter governs the choice of cost objects. But the story was incomplete.

Job costing and process costing are the two basic methods of costing. Job costing is adopted when each activity is *unique in nature* and is based on orders received from the customers, whereas in process costing there is a uniform product or products which go through a homogeneous production process. It involves more than one department. Raw materials are added usually in each process, though in some cases the whole or nearly the entire raw materials are introduced at the first department itself.

## Job Costing vs Process Costing

In this section, we will discuss the similarities and dissimilarities between job costing and process costing.

### *Similarities*

It may be noted that the above two types of costing can be applied in the same industry for specific functions. A soft drink company may use process costing for all its repetitive activities, but may adopt job costing for customer specific products. Similarly, a heavy industry factory may use job costing for specific orders involving unique features but may adopt process costing for components of a repetitive nature which are mass produced and have a general demand.

The two methods of costing use similar costing terminology and source documents for materials, labour, and overhead are identical. Both systems calculate the unit cost for the items produced and arrive at the cost of production by using appropriate cost sheets. They use similar concepts and exclude certain items of cost which are usually included in the financial accounts. Obviously the costing systems under both the above categories are meant for the internal use of the organization and not for the external stakeholders.

### *Dissimilarities*

However, the two systems of costing differ from each other in a number of ways as shown in Table 5.1.

There is one more issue that comes up in jobs whose commencement and completion does not coincide with the time periods for which costing is done in financial accounting. On the other hand, in continuous process industries there is no such mismatch. Departments have also no such go and no-go problem. The situation is graphically shown in Fig. 5.1.

Figure 5.1 is a typical situation in organizations. At the end of 30 days, the organization must be in a position to calculate the resource locked up in work-in-process and in finished goods transferred to stocks, both for products that are in the job mode of production and for those in the process

**Table 5.1**  Differences between job costing and process costing

| SI no. | Job costing | Process costing |
|---|---|---|
| 1. | End products are not identical. | End products are identical. |
| 2. | The jobs undergo different processes depending upon the nature of the job. | The processes are uniform and all products pass through the same set of processes. |
| 3. | Each job requires specific set of tools, equipments, and expertise. | All products use the same set of tools, equipments, and expertise. |
| 4. | Production is against the specific orders of the customers. | Production is against the expected levels of market demand |
| 5. | Costs are ascertained for each job. | Costs are ascertained for each department. |
| 6. | Costs are determined when the job is completed. | Costs are determined on a periodic basis. |
| 7. | In the cost sheet there is no unfinished work. | The periodic cost sheet usually contains work-in-process. |
| 8. | Unit cost determination is relatively easier as cost can be directly traced to jobs with the overheads constituting a lesser proportion of the total cost. | Unit cost determination is complicated and requires careful allocation and apportionment of overheads. |
| 9. | Materials inventory consists of items relevant to the job and hence cannot be planned in advance. | Materials inventory is predictable and hence can be planned in advance. |
| 10. | The question of costing unfinished products does not arise. | The cost of work-in-process is done periodically by adopting equivalent unit method. |

## Example 5.1   Central Avantica Fruit Juices Ltd

Central Avantika Fruit Juices (CAFJ) Ltd produces a number of fruit juices which are sold in tetra pack containers all over India. These juices contain natural fruit extracts from orange, pineapple, and apple. They are sold in two standard sizes. Besides, the company gets orders from specific airlines and hotels to supply the fruit juices in smaller sizes with the names of the airline or hotel mentioned separately. CAFJ adopts a combination of process costing and job costing to arrive at the unit cost of the major products under the two standard packing sizes and also for the smaller orders from the hotels and airlines in varying sizes. The company charges slightly higher rates for the smaller orders from the airlines and hotels for the non-standard packing size and for printing the name of the client.

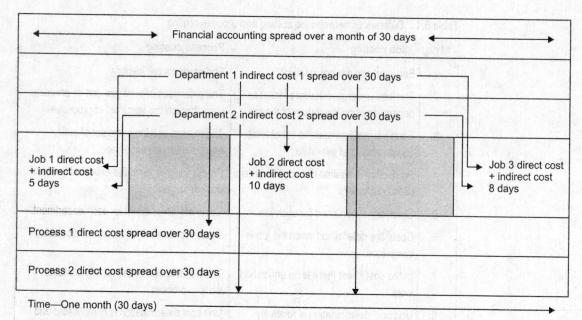

**Fig. 5.1** Job and process direct costs and overheads

mode of production. This information should be available in the costing system and used in the financial accounts for valuing closing stocks. This chapter will describe how the resource calculation is done in job order and process industries.

Several industries would fall into one of these three categories–job order industries, process industries, and joint product industries. Some could be hybrid combinations. These hybrids take various forms. For example, products, which are inherently in process mode of production, could be produced in batches and each batch would need treatment as in job costing. We will also study several methods to charge indirect costs in these variations. In some industries, this charging is critical for product costs and needs great accuracy. In some others, the direct costs are more dominant and rough and ready methods to charge overheads would suffice.

Whatever technique we follow in costing and whatever ingenuity we exercise in analysing the data, the ultimate considerations will be the following:

1. The cost of costing should be justified by the benefits the system provides.
2. Every system should be tailor made to fit into the operational structure.

Costing systems must help in control revolving around responsibilities, and decisions revolving around products and processes.

Information from the costing system should correlate with more easily ascertainable non-financial data.

Concepts summarized in Fig. 5.1 distinguishing job costing from process costing could be understood better if we have an illustrative list of industries grouped under these categories, as shown in Table 5.2.

**Table 5.2**    Illustrative list of industries grouped under job and process costing

|  | Service sector | Merchandizing sector | Manufacturing sector |
|---|---|---|---|
| Job costing | • An audit assignment<br>• A movie/TV serial<br>• A consultancy<br>• A landscaping contract<br>• A lawyer's case<br>• A repair job in auto-repair shop | • A promotion project for a new product | • Biscuits with varying specifications using same facility and produced in batches<br>• An aircraft<br>• A ship<br>• A river dam<br>• Batch of special purpose lubricant in refinery<br>• Batches in pharmaceutical industry |
| Process costing | • A letter sorting line in a post office | • A continuous process in grain handling<br>• Timber handling | • A continuous production of single product in refinery<br>• Production line dedicated to one tier product |

One may note that process costing is applicable to a continuous production of a single product in a production line and job costing is used when same facilities are used by several products whose production is on a go and no-go mode. Further, job costing is an appropriate concept both when the products move from one facility to another in the process of being made or when the facilities move one by one to the product as in aircraft making, ship building, or dam building. Documentation will obviously be more cumbersome for job costing. But some basic methodologies are common to all product and process costing, which we will describe later in the chapter.

## COST FLOWS IN A MANUFACTURING JOB COSTING SYSTEM

Costs flow through an accounting system because they accumulate as the product progresses through the various stages of production. Before a product is started, no costs have been incurred. Workers stand ready to make the product, inventory waits patiently in the warehouse, and the manufacturing plant contains all the resources necessary to perform the manufacturing operation. First of all, material is added into production from the inventory. At the same time the accounting department transfers the cost of inventory items to the work-in-process account, and the product or job now has a value. Next the workers start to convert the raw inventory into a product. As labour is added, the accounting department transfers payroll costs to the work-in-process account, increasing the value of the product or job. Overhead costs are allocated to the product or job, based on the costing method used. As work progresses on the product or job, it accumulates labour, materials, and overhead costs. Finally, the total finished product or job cost is transferred to finished goods, and when it is sold the cost is transferred to cost of goods sold. This practice allows inventory to be reported at cost on the balance sheet, and cost of goods sold to be matched against revenues on the income statement. Thus, job costing in a manufacturing organization assigns costs first to inventory and then to cost of goods sold when jobs are completed and sold, as shown in Fig. 5.2.

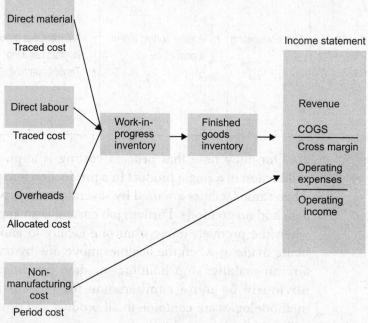

**Fig. 5.2** Cost flows in a manufacturing job costing system

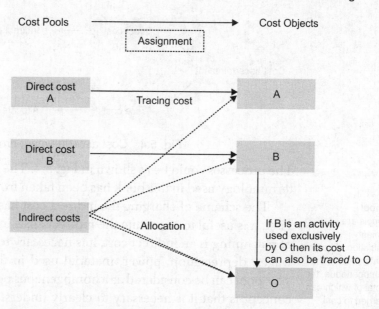

**Fig. 5.3** Cost pools and cost objects

The following five terms constitute the building blocks that will be used in this chapter (see Fig. 5.3):

1. A *cost object* is anything for which a separate measurement of costs is desired.
2. *Direct costs of a cost object* are costs that are related to the particular cost object and can be traced to it in an economically feasible way.
3. *Indirect costs of a cost object* are costs that are related to the particular cost object but cannot be traced to it in an economically feasible way.
4. *Cost pool* is a grouping of individual cost items.
5. *Cost allocation base* is a factor that is the common denominator for systematically linking an indirect cost or group of indirect costs to a cost object.

## COSTING OF PRODUCTS AND PROCESSES

We had a preview of the steps to be taken in costing of products and services in Chapter 3. Readers may re-look at Table 3.1 dealing with a household appliances organization, Table 3.8, a garment factory, and Fig. 5.1 of this chapter. All these show the interplay between direct costs and indirect costs and the need for *tracing* direct costs to the product and *allocating* indirect costs. Both these processes can be described as *cost ascertainment* processes.

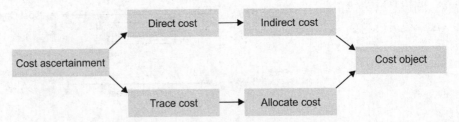

**Fig. 5.4** Cost ascertainment processes

The processes could be as shown in Fig. 5.4. The readers may note that the terminology used in this book has been taken from Horngren et al. (2003).

**Cost pool**
Cost pools are convenient accumulation of several elements of costs that are homogeneous, the sum total of which can be charged to cost object to avoid repetitive effort of charging individual elements of the pool.

The scheme of charging the indirect cost has two important concepts. First, it is useful to constitute the indirect costs into a *cost pool*. Thus, if cost of machining is an indirect cost, it is necessary to put in this pool typically wages, depreciation, power, material used in the process of machining. This pool can be considered as a homogeneous pool. The second important concept is that it is necessary to clearly understand what is the nature of the cost driver which drives these costs. Thus machine hours would drive the machine costs through a logic of cause and effect. Therefore, it is legitimate to assume that the total machining costs (included in the cost pool) divided by the machine hours would yield a rate, which would be logically charged to the product on the basis of overhead rate multiplied by the hours used. Machine hours is described in costing literature as the *cost allocation base*. There could be several sophistications that could be considered in modification of this logic. This basic understanding would suffice at this stage.

## Steps in Cost Ascertainment

The process summarized somewhat simplistically in Fig. 5.4 and conceptually explained in the previous paragraph involves seven detailed steps, which are described here:

**Cost allocation base and cost pools**
Costs accumulated in cost pools are charged to cost objects using cost allocation bases usually chosen on an understanding of cause–effect relationship between base and pool.

### Step 1: Identifying the product cost object

The first step is to identify the product cost object. Thus, in Table 3.1 in Chapter 3, the cost objects are the different household appliances—the grinder and the juice maker. Again in Table 3.8 the cost objects are the different garments.

### Step 2: Identifying the direct cost of the job

Identifying the direct costs of a job has two considerations. First, the physical inputs for the making of the product are to be identified as the cost object.

Second, the economically feasible way these inputs can be measured are to be identified. We will describe later in the chapter how these measurements can be made in an economically feasible way.

### Step 3: Selecting the cost allocation base to use for allocating costs to the job

The cost allocation bases may be simple measures that can be tracked with simple documentation. Machine hours or labour hours could be counted as such simple measures. But even such measures can sometimes prove difficult to record. But some cost pools may require complex compound measures. For example, power expenses may have compound bases, such as horsepower hours, if there are no meters to measure power consumption. Similarly, transport costs can have a base of kilometres × weight or volume × kilometres.

### Step 4: Judging the optimum number of indirect cost pools

More the number of homogeneous cost pools, more accurate will be the cost allocation. But this will increase the cost of costing. One may, therefore, decide to have less number but more heterogeneous cost pools.

### Step 5: Computing rate per unit of each allocation base

This is simple arithmetic. The rate will look as follows:

$$\text{Actual indirect cost rate} = \text{Actual cost in indirect cost pool}/\text{Actual quantity of cost base}$$

For example, if actual cost in indirect cost pool is ₹25,00,000 and the actual quantity of cost base is 25,000 machine hours, then actual indirect cost rate would be ₹25,00,000/25,000 = ₹100.

### Step 6: Computing the charge

Ascertain the machine hours used by the cost object and compute as shown here:

$$\text{Charge} = ₹100 \text{ (actual indirect cost rate)} \times 2000 \text{ hrs (actual number of machine hours used by cost object)} = ₹2,00,000$$

### Step 7: Calculating the total cost of job

$$\text{Total costs} = \text{Direct material} + \text{Direct labour} + \text{Direct expenses} + \text{Indirect costs}$$

$$\text{Cost per unit} = \text{Total costs} \div \text{Total units produced}$$

## Source Documents

The following comes under source documents.

### Material

We had a purview of the accounting of material used in production in Chapter 3. We had shown the direct material consumed as the following:

Direct material consumed = Opening stock of raw material +
Purchases – Closing stock

This system is described in accounting terminology as periodic inventory accounting. However, this system is of no use in cost accounting, which we have described in the previous paragraph. First, this would not provide the material consumed when the job is finished or in progress. Second, the material consumed figure is fine for the purpose of financial accounts, which considers the total for a period, but not for individual processes and jobs. For this purpose, we need to use a perpetual inventory accounting system wherein with every issue from the inventory, the purpose for the issue is recorded. Thus in this case the formula should be as the following:

Closing stock = Opening stock + Purchases – Consumption

For documenting this transaction, every issue is supported by a Goods Issue Note or Material Requisition Note or an executed Bill of Material for a production run. These documents would show the cost object in which it is used. These can be manually posted in the job-cost record or process-cost record or entered through computers. In more advanced organizations, the material and cost object codes are bar coded and are read by machines in real time arrangements.

**Perpetual and periodic inventory accounting system** Financial accounting can be managed with periodic inventory accounting system but cost accounting would need a perpetual inventory accounting system.

### Labour

Labour hours spent on the cost object would be available in primary attendance records or subsidiary records containing work done. This multiplied by the labour rate would give the labour cost to be posted in the cost sheets.

### Expenses

Expenses can be recorded through journal vouchers described in Chapter 2.

### Overhead

Records of the activity are kept in log books and these are totalled and journal entries passed to record in the cost records.

| Material consumed | | | | | |
|---|---|---|---|---|---|
| Date | Requisition No. | Mat Code | Qty | Rate | Amount |
| | | | | | |
| Total | | | | | ₹7,00,000 |

| Labour applied | | | |
|---|---|---|---|
| Week ending | Skilled Hrs Normal OT | Rate | Amount |
| | Unskilled Hrs Normal OT | Rate | Amount |
| Total Week ending | | | |
| | | | ₹2,00,000 |

| Expense | |
|---|---|
| Week ending Power | |
| ----- | |
| Week ending Total 0 | |

| Indirect cost | | | |
|---|---|---|---|
| Week ending | Composing labour hrs amount | Printing machine hrs amount | Binding labour hrs amount |
| Week ending Total | ₹20,000 | ₹4,00,000 | ₹1,00,000 |

| Work-in-process ₹ | | | | | | | | |
|---|---|---|---|---|---|---|---|---|
| Week ending | Balance from previous week | Material 7,00,000 | Labour 2,00,000 | Expense 0 | Overhead 5,20,000 | Total ₹14,20,000 | Transferred Finished goods qty ₹10,000 | Amount ₹14,20,000 | Balance 0 |

**Fig. 5.5** Job cost sheet for cost object book *Durga Mahima* with some data provided illustratively (see Problem 7 of Chapter 3 and Annexure 5.1)

After all these entries have been made, the job cost sheet will look as shown in Fig. 5.5.

## NORMAL COSTING

The fifth of the seven steps of cost ascertainment procedure requires the calculation of the overhead rate. The overhead rate is calculated by dividing the overhead expenses by the overhead activity. Should it be on actual or budgeted numbers, calculated every week, every month, or once a year to coincide with yearly closing of accounts? Before we decide on this, we need to know a few features of overhead activity:

1. Overhead costs would include costs that are fixed in nature or variable with respect to the base, which is the cost driver.

2. Overhead activity may have seasonal pattern and, therefore, overhead rate would vary if averaged over the whole year or averaged within periods, which coincide with the seasonal patterns.
3. Expenses themselves maybe seasonal, for example, winter and summer holiday periods.
4. The flow of expenses cannot be linked with the flow of activity and averaging over very short periods would give completely wrong measurement of the cause and effect of expenses and activity.
5. The overhead expenses would, therefore, never match in the time horizon, with the go and no-go pattern of activity in job order industries.

Keeping all these in consideration, it is usual to use normal costing in computing the overhead rate.

Normal costing implies that a time period is chosen judiciously (month, quarter, year, three or five years) and a budgeted expense and budgeted activity is forecast and a budgeted overhead rate is calculated. It is more usual to choose a year as it usually covers a full circle of high level and low level activity and is the natural time span of planning. The charge to the cost object is computed by multiplying actual activity used by the cost object and multiplying it by budgeted overhead rate.

The advantages of this normal costing are as follows:

1. The moment the job is finished, the cost of the job can be made 'online' by adding direct costs, which are usually on real time with indirect cost charges as activity is available on real time and the rates are budgeted.
2. At the end of the accounting period, if there is a discrepancy between the overhead incurred and charged, managerially useful information is available for further investigation of why there is such a discrepancy. The fixed expense may be deviant from the budget. The variable cost per unit activity of cost base may not be in line. Activity may have fallen short of or exceeded the budgets. Each one of this has a managerial implication.
3. It helps in keeping a uniform pricing structure for the products and provides an incentive for uniform demand and stabilized capacity utilization.

The disadvantages of normal costing are as follows:

1. The overhead charged is different from the overhead incurred during actual production of product.
2. It puts a premium on accuracy of forecasting, which may be sometimes unrealistic.

3. In negotiated prices based on cost-plus contracts, revision of rates due to discrepancy gives rise to doubts on the dependability of the costing system.

Let us see the consequences of *underabsorbed* or *overabsorbed* overheads. These are shown in Table 5.3.

How do we remedy the situation when we find overabsorption or underabsorption resulting in incorrect estimation of work-in-process and finished goods in financial accounts as a result of the errors in cost accounting?

1. If the variation is marginal, one can ignore it.
2. The difference can be carried forward to the next accounting period and the rates for the next accounting period adjusted accordingly.
3. The rates can be worked retrospectively and all figures corrected. That is an enormously difficult exercise but there is no way it can be avoided if the prices are negotiated on cost-plus basis, as happens in government contracts or public utility pricing where mandatory pricing has to conform to costs. This could happen in water and electricity rates, and expensive machinery made-to-order.
4. The difference can be proportionately distributed between work-in-process and finished goods and cost of goods sold based on the relative value. In this process when the work-in-process and finished goods are corrected, the balance will automatically get adjusted in the cost of goods sold in financial accounts. If, for a company, we assume underabsorbed overhead as 2,00,000, cost of goods sold as 50,00,000, work-in-process as 5,00,000 and finished goods as 2,00,000, then it would work out as follows:

Underabsorbed overhead/(Cost of goods sold + Works-in-process + Finished Goods)
2,00,000 /(50,00,000) + (5,00,000) + (2,00,000)

**Table 5.3** Impact of incorrect overhead rate in normal costing

| | Work-in-process | Finished goods | Cost of goods sold (financial accounts) | Pricing of product in markets and in negotiation | Profit |
|---|---|---|---|---|---|
| Underabsorbed underallocated | Understated | Understated | Overstated as financial account overheads will be more than allocated | Likely to be underpriced | Understated in financial accounts. Profit in cost accounts will be higher |
| Overabsorbed overallocated | Overstated | Overstated | Understated in financial accounts as actual overhead will be less than allocated | Likely to be overpriced | Overstated in financial accounts. Profit in cost accounts will be lower |

Add to work-in-progress = 5,00,000 × 0.035 = ₹17,544

Add to finished goods = 2,00,000 × 0.035 = ₹7000

Since the overheads in the financial accounts would be ₹2,00,000 and all of it would have been charged in the profit and loss account, it would be more than the overheads in the cost accounts, and hence, profits would be less to that extent. That reduction would be made good by ₹24,544 (17,754 + 7000) as increased work-in-process and finished goods would increase profits or reduce losses.

## Accounting Mechanics of Normal Costing

The technical features of accounting mechanics of normal costing are shown in Annexure 5.1 as a continuation of the earlier description of the mechanics associated with Fig. 5.5 relating to Kalimata Printing Press's product *Durga Mahima.*

## NON-MANUFACTURING COSTS AND JOB COSTING

We have indicated in Table 5.1 that the concepts of joint costing are used not only in the manufacturing sector but also in merchandizing and service sectors. In all such cases the seven-step exercise of costing is no different from the examples provided so far in the chapter. But there are differences. The strong cause and effect relationship between the indirect cost pool and the chosen base (cost driver) observed in manufacturing sector is less obvious in service sectors. In audit and consultancy projects, overheads such as telephone and computer expenses can be traced as direct expenses. But often these are charged to the product based on the hours spent by the major actors in the project–the senior personnel.

The more important deviation is in respect of direct labour costs (also direct consultant costs). It is seen that while direct consultant hours are more easily available, costs are somewhat unpredictable. Therefore, even direct costs are estimated in the same manner as normal costing in respect of overheads.

## Multiple Overhead Cost Pools

The illustration of the job cost sheet in the Kalimata Printing Press in Fig. 5.5 shows three indirect cost pools–composing, printing, and binding. The organization would have to assess if there is a need of increasing their documentation work by having three cost pools instead of only one. If they do so, their costs for the two books *Durga Mahima* and *Modern Physics* would be different. *Modern Physics*, which uses complicated composing, would be charged less but there would be no difference in printing and binding as both follow the same printing and binding process, and the physical characteristics of these two books are identical. But this may not be the case if the books are printed and bound in different ways and the length of production runs is different. The management would have to consider if the information in a multi-cost pool arrangement gives added information, thus making its costs justifiable. In Chapter 6, we would explore the need for a prolific multiplication of indirect cost pools in 'activity based costing'.

## NEGOTIATED OR ADMINISTERED PRICES AND COST-PLUS CONTRACTS

Prices are often not based on market forces but are administered by law or regulations, or are negotiated usually on a cost-plus basis.

As mentioned in Chapter 1, the history of the development of costing systems was pioneered in India by Mohammed Shoaib for providing a 'fair pricing system' in cost-plus contracts for the defence forces. But at this stage one may note that these pricing arrangements need certain caution. Most of the products would usually need a job costing, though process costing, batch costing, and joint costing are not uncommon.

**Cost-plus contracts in India**
Mohammed Shoaib pioneered cost accounting in India mainly to provide a basis for price fixation in cost plus contracts for supply to the defense forces.

In regard to direct costs, they usually have to settle a physical norm for consumption of raw material and labour and expenses. They have also to state the price level of the raw material, labour, and expense (say cost per kilowatt hour).

In indirect costs, they have to agree to a set of prohibited items, say entertainment and extravagant perquisites. They have to agree to a cost base and the method of measuring these activities. They have to be mutually convinced of the cause and effect relationship between the indirect cost pool and the cost base. They would then have to agree on the documentation so that the bookings in the accounts are a fair depiction of the transactions. Often, ethical issues of honest accounting crop up between the negotiating parties. If there were a dispute, there would be the need for an agreed arbitrator.

## BATCH COSTING

Table 5.1 described how products that could be manufactured by continuous processes could be manufactured in batches so that the same facilities could

**Several aspects of batch costing**
Bunching production in batches uses normal job costing techniques. In addition, ABC techniques for set-up costs (discussed in Chapter 6) and mathematical techniques for optimal batch size are required.

be used for making several products. The processes of tracing direct costs and allocating indirect costs for these batches are no different than for job costs. But there are two other features of batch costs. First, batches have to be set up and this process is often costly. This aspect of cost ascertainment will be dealt with in Chapter 6 on activity-based costing (ABC).

The second feature involves the decision of the quantities to be produced in each batch. Higher the quantity higher will be the average inventory of the finished product. This aspect of optimal batch size will be dealt with in Chapter 10 while discussing inventories.

## CONTRACT AND PROJECT COSTING

In Table 5.1, we covered in the gamut of job costing, landscaping projects, dams, aircraft, ships, etc. The activities are characterized by the fact that they usually last more than the stretch of an accounting period, and that facilities visit them rather than jobs visiting facilities. Projects may be handled directly by an organization for itself or may be contracted out. Parties who get the contract and the principal project authorities keep an account of their costs in a manner that may be useful to understand as an extension of the concepts we have used in this chapter.

Contract costing uses systems of recording their costs, which is slightly different from that shown in Fig. 5.5. It is shown in Table 5.3 (Owler and Brown 1978).

There could be variation of Table 5.4. Large projects may have different item lines, each having its own estimate. The different sections of the project may jointly have a material at site account as a subsidiary account to the main project/contract account. Return of material would be of very minor importance. All these amounts would be under work-in-progress.

The work is usually measured and checked by an architect or a valuer. Their payments can then be billed to the client if it were a contractor's account we are dealing with.

Since projects/contracts are spread over a long period, a contractor may have to decide how he/she would prepare his/her profit account for

**Table 5.4** Contract ledger account

| Week ending | Ref | Debit | Debit | Debit | Debit | Debit | Credit | Credit | Credit | Total Direct | Over head | Total to date |
|---|---|---|---|---|---|---|---|---|---|---|---|---|
| | | Material store | Material direct | Plant used | Wages | Direct expense | Total | Store returned | Other income | Total | | | |

tax purposes as well as for division with partners and for dividends to the shareholders.

Until the final work is competed, certified and paid for, one could never say if the certified values are a safe guide for estimating profits. Further, as the contract is proceeding along, there may be unexpected losses. Contractors have, therefore, to be cautious in declaring profits for incomplete works. The general practice is to use the formula:

$$2/3 \times \text{Notional profit} \times \text{Cash received/Work certified}$$

As the projects are nearing completion, the formula could be:

$$\text{Notional profit} \times \text{Work certified/Contract price}$$

# PROCESS COSTING

Process costing is ideally suited for industries producing products, such as paper, brick, dairy products, soft drinks, etc. It is extensively used in agricultural processes, such as flour, *atta*, food processing units, breweries, petroleum industry, metal processing industry, automobile plants, etc.

## Cost Flow

Assume that there are two departments A and B in a company that adopts process costing. The cost flow between the departments will be as follows.

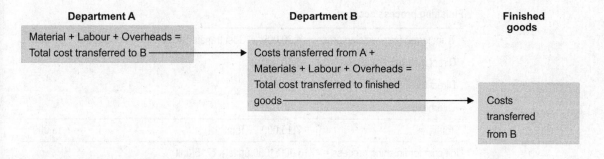

## Solved Problem 5.1

A company has two departments called welding and finishing. It makes an end product at the completion of the finishing process. Costs are compiled on a weekly basis. The following costs were incurred for the week 25.

**Welding**
Direct material = ₹2,00,000
Direct labour = ₹1,50,000

### Finishing

Direct material = ₹1,50,000

Direct labour = ₹75,000

The company had incurred common overheads amounting to ₹1,40,000 which are to be apportioned on the basis of direct material. During the week 25, 1000 units were introduced at the welding process and there was no process loss.

You are required to calculate the cost of each process and also the unit cost.

The above problem is easy to answer as there is no work-in-progress at the beginning or end of each process and there is also no loss in production.

### Solution

**Welding process account**

| | ₹ | | ₹ |
|---|---|---|---|
| Direct material | 2,00,000 | Cost transferred to finishing process | 4,30,000 |
| Direct labour | 1,50,000 | | |
| Overheads | 80,000 | | |
| Total | 4,30,000 | Total | 4,30,000 |

Unit cost for welding process = ₹430,000/1000 units = ₹430/unit

**Finishing process account**

| | ₹ | | ₹ |
|---|---|---|---|
| Transferred from welding process | 4,30,000 | Cost transferred to finished goods a/c | 7,15,000 |
| Direct material | 1,50,000 | | |
| Direct labour | 75,000 | | |
| Overheads | 60,000 | | |
| Total | 7,15,000 | Total | 7,15,000 |

Unit cost for finishing process = ₹715,000/1000 units = ₹715/unit

Note: The overheads are apportioned on the basis of direct materials, i.e., 2,00,000 : 1,50,000 = 4 : 3

The total cost of finishing process is transferred to finished goods account. Thus, in process costing the total cost of the first process (welding) is transferred to the second process (finishing). The unit cost of each process is obtained by dividing the total cost of the process by the number of units transferred.

## Equivalent Units of Production

In the above example it was assumed that there was no incomplete unit at the beginning or end of the process. But it often happens that there are some unfinished units at the time of accounting. The cost sheet must assign a value to such units in proportion to the level of completion. For this purpose a method is adopted to convert these units into an equivalent number of fully completed units based on the percentage of completion of these units which is calculated through technical estimates and cost records.

The advantage of this method is to arrive at cost of production for each process on a more accurate basis. If the incomplete units are ignored, the cost will be deflated. On the other hand, if they are taken as fully completed units, the closing stock will be disproportionately valued. Hence, the equivalent unit of production is a scientific method to arrive at the cost of each process in a more realistic manner.

Based on the above concept it is usual to show the equivalent units at the beginning and end of each process. Therefore, the composition of units in a process for a given period will consist of the

  (a)   work completed on the opening work-in-process. This is calculated by the percentage of unfinished work of the opening equivalent units, which is completed during this period;

  (b)   work completed on the new units introduced and fully completed; and

  (c)   work done on the partially finished closing work-in-process.

### *Cost Constituents of Equivalent Units*

The costs of production are taken under three heads namely material, labour, and overheads. The cost of material is calculated based on the issue of material to the process. The labour and overheads are calculated based on cost records and technical estimates. Since labour and overheads generally go in direct proportion, they are termed as *conversion costs* and are taken as a single composite unit of cost. However, some organizations may treat them separately under process costing.

## Cost Sheet

The cost sheet under process costing consists of computation different from job costing. The basic elements in process cost sheet are the

(a) opening work-in-process where additional work has been done to complete them;

(b) additional costs incurred on units introduced during this process;

(c) units completed and transferred out of the process to next process or to finished goods account; and

(d) work-in-process at the end of the process.

### Flow Chart

Assume that the milling department started December operations with 200 units (30% complete). 3000 units were introduced into production and 2500 completed units were transferred to the next department. The ending work-in-process was 50 per cent complete.

**Milling Department**

| Opening W.I.P. | + | Introduced | = | Completed | + | Closing W.I.P. |
|---|---|---|---|---|---|---|
| 200 units | | 3000 units | | 2500 units | | 700 units |
| **Work completion** | | | | | | |
| 30% completed earlier | | | | - | | - |
| 70% work done now | | | | 100% work done | | 50% work done |

### Quantity Schedule

The above illustration can be taken forward to compile a quantity schedule. It can be done using the weighted average method or the first-in-first-out (FIFO) method.

(a) Weighted average method:

**Milling Department**

| | Quantity Schedule | Month: December |
|---|---|---|
| No. of units to be accounted for | EU | |
| Opening W.I.P. | 200 units | |
| Introduced into process | 3000 units | |
| Units to be accounted for | 3200 | |
| Completed and transferred | 2500 | 2500 |
| Closing W.I.P. (50% completed) | 700 | 350 |
| Units to be accounted for | 3200 | 2850 |

(b) FIFO method:

**Milling Department**

| | Quantity Schedule | Month: December |
|---|---|---|
| | | EU |
| No. of units to be accounted for | | |
| Opening W.I.P. | 200 units | |
| Introduced into process | 3000 units | |
| Units to be accounted for | 3200 | |
| Completed and transferred | | |
| - from opening W.I.P. | 200 units | 140 |
| - introduced in December | 2300 units | 2300 |
| Closing W.I.P. (50% completed) | 700 units | 350 |
| Units to be accounted for | 3200 | 2790 |

The cost flow also will be shown under the weighted average method or the FIFO method. A comparison of the two methods is given below.

### Weighted Average Method

This method is relatively simple as the total costs incurred are divided by the equivalent units to calculate the cost of equivalent units. No separate treatment is given for the cost of completing the opening work-in-process.

### FIFO Method

Here the opening incomplete units are supposed to be completed first and are accordingly assigned the cost. The closing inventory will be typically assigned costs actually incurred in the process.

The main difference between the two methods is that while the weighted average method distributes the costs evenly to all the units produced as well as in process, the FIFO method assigns costs on the basis of the time of completion. Hence, the opening inventory is costed first and the units introduced during the process are costed subsequently. While the FIFO method involves more calculations, it is considered as more reflective of current cost for inventory valuation.

Based on the method selected, quantity schedule and cost sheets can be prepared.

### Solved Problem 5.2

A company adopting process costing system has the following cost data gathered for the month of May.

For department A, the opening work-in-process was 25,000 units completed up to 60 per cent for materials and 40 per cent for conversion cost. It introduced 1,60,000 units into production during May. By the end of the month, it has transferred 1,70,000 units to Department B. The closing work-in-process was 15,000 units which were 60 per cent complete for materials, and 50 per cent of the conversion cost.

Calculate equivalent units of production for May under the
(a) weighted average method
(b) FIFO method

## Solution

Weighted average method – Equivalent units (EU)

|  | Materials (in ₹) | Conversion (in ₹) |
|---|---|---|
| Units completed and transferred to process B | | |
| 1,70,000 × 100% | 1,70,000 | 1,70,000 |
| Ending work-in-process | | |
| 15,000 × 60% | 9000 | - |
| 15,000 × 50% | - | 7500 |
| Total equivalent units | 1,79,000 | 1,77,500 |

FIFO method - Equivalent units

|  | Materials (in ₹) | Conversion (in ₹) |
|---|---|---|
| Beginning work-in-process | | |
| 25,000 × 40% | 10,000 | - |
| 25,000 × 60% | - | 15,000 |
| Units started and completed during May | | |
| 1,45,000 × 100% | 1,45,000 | 1,45,000 |
| Ending work-in-process | | |
| 15,000 × 60% | 9000 | |
| 15,000 × 50% | | 7500 |
| Total equivalent units | 1,64,000 | 1,67,500 |

Based on the calculation of equivalent units, the cost of the processes can be assigned to the total output of the process. The following problem clarifies the unit cost calculation.

## Solved Problem 5.3

A company using process costing has the following data for its Department A for the month of October.

| | Material (₹) | Conversion (₹) |
|---|---|---|
| Opening work-in-process | 38,000 | 33,000 |
| Expenses incurred during October | 2,50,000 | 2,00,000 |

The equivalent units of production were 40,000 for materials and 35,000 for conversion.

Calculate the cost per equivalent unit for material and conversion and the total cost per equivalent unit, using the weighted average method.

### Solution

Weighted average method – Equivalent units

| | Materials (₹) | Conversion (₹) |
|---|---|---|
| Opening work-in-process | 38,000 | 33,000 |
| Expenses incurred during October | 2,50,000 | 2,00,000 |
| Total cost | 2,88,000 | 2,33,000 |
| Equivalent units of production | 40,000 | 35,000 |
| Cost per equivalent units (₹) | 7.20 | 6.65 |

Total cost per equivalent unit (EU)

| | ₹ |
|---|---|
| Material cost per EU | 7.20 |
| Conversion cost per EU | 6.65 |
| Total cost per EU | 13.85 |

## Process Loss

In most of the process industries some reduction in value/spoilage/wastage occurs, which leads to process losses. It can arise due to a variety of reasons such as the following:

- shrinkage
- losses due to cutting and issuing
- evaporation

- material quality
- drying
- loading/unloading
- inefficient tools/workmanship, etc.

Most of the above causes lead to some inevitable process loss which cannot be avoided. This type of loss is called *normal loss*. There is generally no normal gain, but abnormal gain is calculated for costing purposes. Any other loss which arises due to abnormal circumstances is called *abnormal loss*. This could happen due to serious power/equipment breakdowns, floods, civic commotion, fire, etc. and also due to human errors. While normal loss is uncontrollable and unavoidable, abnormal loss is controllable. Due to the above nature of process losses it is possible to determine normal loss in advance and absorb it by the good production. It is usually expressed as a percentage. Any loss above the normal loss is treated as abnormal loss and is transferred out of the process costs, to be written off from the costing profit and losses. As a corollary, any loss below the normal loss is termed as *abnormal gain,* which is shown in the costing profit and loss account. Both abnormal gain and loss require managerial action, if significant.

## Solved Problem 5.4

The US based Fun Products Company makes health foods based on cereals. The following particulars of Department A are available for the month of December:

Direct material          $10,000
Direct labour            $6000

Overheads charged at 50% of direct labour

The normal loss for Department A is estimated at 5 per cent of the material input. In December the input was 500 pounds. Prepare Department A account assuming that the output was as per estimate.

**Department A account**

|  | Units/Pds | Amount ($) |  | Units/Pds | Amount ($) |
|---|---|---|---|---|---|
| Direct materials | 500 | 10,000 | Normal loss | 25 |  |
| Direct labour |  | 6000 | transferred to | 475 | 19,000 |
| Overheads |  | 3000 | Department B |  |  |
|  | 500 | 19,000 |  | 500 | 19,000 |

Cost per unit for Department A = $19,000/475 units= $40

In this case the normal loss is not shown as fetching any salvage value. Assuming that the normal loss has a salvage value of $5 per Pds, the process account will look as under.

## Solved Problem 5.5

Innovators Ltd is a company having three processes X, Y, and Z. At the first two stages the end products do not have a market-determined price, whereas the end product of process Z has a market value. Hence, the company has the following principle for inter-process pricing.

(a) Process X to Y: 20 per cent margin on transfer price to be charged
(b) Process Y to Z: 25 per cent margin on the total costs actually incurred by the process to be charged
(c) Process Z to finished stock: Transferred at the market price of ₹20/unit

Prepare process accounts based on the above data from the following information.

Units produced at the end of process Z were 10,000. There was no process loss at any stage.

| Process | Material + Conversion costs |
|---------|-----------------------------|
| X | 70,000 |
| Y | 40,000 |
| Z | 80,000 |

Assume no opening/closing stocks.

### Solution

**Process X account**

| | | | |
|---|---|---|---|
| Materials + Conversion cost | 70,000 | Process Y - transfer | 87,500 |
| Profits | 17,500 | | |
| | 87,500 | | 87,500 |

Note:
Profits = 20% on transfer price = 25% on cost
70,000 x 25/100 = 17,500

**Process Y account**

| | | | |
|---|---|---|---|
| Transfer from Process X | 87,500 | Process Z - transfer | 1,37,500 |
| Materials + Conversion cost | 40,000 | | |
| Profits | 10,000 | | |
| | 1,37,500 | | 1,37,500 |

Note:
Profits = 25% of 40,000 = 10,000

**Process Z account**

| Transfer from Process Y | 1,37,500 | Finished goods - transfer | 2,00,000 |
|---|---|---|---|
| Materials + Conversion cost | 80,000 | Loss | 17,500 |
| | 2,17,500 | | 2,17,500 |

Note: In Process Z, the market price is used to calculate the transfer cost. The profit or loss is the net figure.

## Abnormal Loss

Assume that for the above example the output was 460 units.

The abnormal loss will be = 500 – 25 – 460 = 15 units

The cost of abnormal loss = 15 x 39.74 = $596

Process account will look as under

**Department A account**

| | Units/Pds | Amount($) | | Units/Pds | Amount($) |
|---|---|---|---|---|---|
| Direct materials | 500 | 10,000 | Normal loss | 25 | 125 |
| Direct labour | | 6000 | Abnormal loss | 15 | 596 |
| Overheads | | 3000 | Transferred to Department B | 460 | 18,279 |
| | 500 | 19,000 | | 500 | 19,000 |

If there is any abnormal gain, the process account is debited with the amount of such gain. In this process, the cost per unit is not affected by abnormal gain or loss.

## Inter Process Profit

In the above cases, the cost of completed units is transferred to the next process at cost. But certain organizations add an element of profit to the cost of a process which becomes the input cost of the next process. This is usually adopted when the organization treats each process as a *profit centre*. In this manner the transferring process is able to show a profit or loss which can be the basis for performance measurement such as department bonuses, etc.

Organizations may adopt different bases for adding the profit. If the end product of a process has an identifiable market price, then the transfers can be made at such market prices. In this way the transferring process can be rewarded for controlling costs and adopting efficient production techniques. For the transferee department the products are charged at market price and hence its own cost can be monitored effectively. In this way no department is responsible for the inefficiencies of other departments; nor can it benefit at the cost of other efficient departments.

However, it is not often easy to obtain market prices for all intermediary products. In such cases a company may adopt standard costing method and add profits on that basis. Another method is to add a percentage to the cost per unit of the transferring department. Figure 5.6 gives an overview of job costing method.

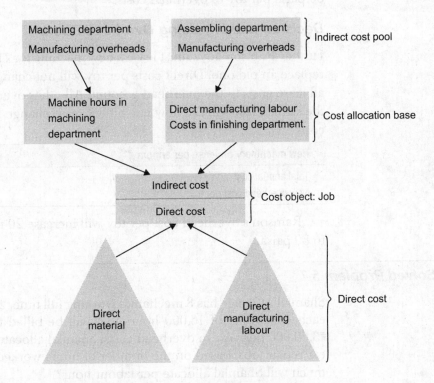

**Fig. 5.6** An overview of job costing method

## Simple Overhead Allocation

The simplest form of overhead allocation is to treat all annual overhead as a single cost pool, and allocate it to one annual cost driver.

## Solved Problem 5.6

Ramson Toyz produces 50,00,000 toys per year, and incurs ₹3,00,000 in annual overhead cost. How much overhead cost must Ramson allocate to each toy?

## Solution

$$\frac{\text{Total annual overhead}}{\text{Units of cost driver}} = ₹1 \text{ unit of cost driver}$$

| | |
|---|---:|
| Toys per year | 5,00,000 |
| Annual overhead cost | ₹3,00,000 |
| Overhead cost per toy | 60 paisa |

In addition to direct costs (labour and materials), Ramson will allocate 60 paisa per toy to overhead costs.

### Decision-making Using Overhead Costs

Further Ramson Toyz must lease a new machine for ₹1,00,000 per year, to replace an old one. Direct costs per toy will not change. Ramson charges all lease costs to the overhead account. All other overhead costs will stay the same. How will the new machinery lease change Ramson's overhead costs?

| New machinery on lease per annum | ₹1,00,000 |
|---|---:|
| Total annual cost | ₹4,00,000 |
| New overhead cost per toy | 80 paisa |

Ramson's overhead cost per toy will increase 20 paisa, from 60 paisa to 80 paisa.

## Solved Problem 5.7

Shamlal's Garage has 8 mechanics working full time, 2,000 hours per year each, for a total of 16,000 hours that will be billed to jobs. They incur ₹3,60,000 per year in overhead costs. Shamlal allocates overhead costs to car repair jobs, based on the number of hours worked on each job. How much will Shamlal allocate per labour hour?

### Solution

$$\frac{\text{Total annual overheads}}{\text{Total annual labour hours}} = \frac{₹3,60,000}{16,000 \text{ hours}}$$

$$= ₹22.50 \text{ overhead per labour hour}$$

Shamlal's Garage will allocate ₹22.50 per labour hour for overhead.

## Solved Problem 5.8

Shamlal's Garage is working on the delivery truck belonging to Ramson's Toyz Store. The job will take 2 hours. How much overhead cost will Shamlal allocate to this job?

## Solution

Overhead per labour hour × labour hours = Overhead allocated to job
$$= ₹22.50 × 2 = ₹45$$
Shamlal Garage will allocate ₹45 in overhead costs to the delivery job.

### Solved Problem 5.9

Sharma & Sons uses an estimated overhead rate for allocating production overhead to job orders. The rate is on a machine hour basis for the machining department and on a direct labour cost basis for the finishing department. The company estimated the budget for 2010 in Table 5.5:

**Table 5.5**    Cost heads of Sharma & Sons for 2010

| Cost pools | Machining | Assembly |
|---|---|---|
| Production overhead | ₹45,00,00,000 | ₹20,00,00,000 |
| Direct labour cost | ₹3,60,00,000 | ₹16,00,00,000 |
| Direct labour hours | 50,000 | 1,80,000 |
| Machine hours | 2,00,000 | 33,000 |

During the month of January 2010, the cost record for Job Order 807 shows the following (Table 5.6):

**Table 5.6**    Cost heads of Sharma & Sons for January 2010

| Job Order 807 | | |
|---|---|---|
| Cost pools | Machining | Assembly |
| Production overhead | ₹6,00,000 | ₹1,50,000 |
| Direct labour cost | ₹30,000 | ₹50,000 |
| Direct labour hours | 40 | 60 |
| Machine hours | 130 | 10 |

The actual cost and machine hours for the year 2010 were as follows (Table 5.7):

**Table 5.7**    Total cost and machine hours for 2010

| Cost pools | Machining | Assembly |
|---|---|---|
| Actual production overhead | ₹40,00,00,000 | ₹36,00,00,000 |
| Actual direct labour cost | ₹3,60,00,000 | ₹12,00,00,000 |
| Actual machine hours | 2,50,000 | 40,000 |

Based on the data given above, answer the following questions.
1. What is the budgeted overhead rate that should be applied to the machining department and the assembly department?
2. Determine the total overhead cost of job order no. 807.
3. Suppose that job order 807 manufactures 300 units of product, then what is its unit cost?

4. Based on the actual data, find the overapplied or underapplied overhead for each department.

## Solution

1. Overhead allocation rate: Budgeted manufacturing overhead divided by allocation base
   (a) Machining department:

   $$\frac{₹45,00,00,000}{₹2,00,000} = ₹2250 \text{ per machine hour}$$

   (b) Assembly department: Direct labour cost is calculated as under:

   $$\frac{₹20,00,00,000}{₹16,00,00,000} = 125\% \text{ of Direct manufacturing labour cost}$$

2. Total overhead allocated to Job 807
   Machining department overhead = ₹2250 × 130 hours = ₹2,92,500
   Assembly department overhead = 125% of ₹50,000
   Direct manufacturing labour cost = ₹62,500
   Total manufacturing overhead = ₹2,92,500 + ₹62,500 = ₹3,55,000

3. Suppose Job 807 manufactures 300 units of product, the total cost per unit can be calculated as follows:
   Direct material Machining department = ₹6,00,000
   Assembly department = ₹1,50,000

| Cost pools | Machining | Assembly |
|---|---|---|
| Production overhead | ₹6,00,000 | ₹1,50,000 |
| Direct labour cost | ₹30,000 | ₹50,000 |
| Overhead allocated | ( ₹2250 X 130 hours) | (125% of ₹50,000) |
| | ₹2,92,500 | ₹62,500 |
| Total | ₹9,22,500 | ₹2,62,500 |
| 300 units produced in Job Order 807 | | |
| Total cost | (₹9, 22,500 + ₹2,62,500) | ₹11,85,000 |
| Per unit cost of Job 807 | (₹11,85,000/300 units) | ₹3950 |

4. Total amount of over/under applied overheads in each department is as follows:

| Cost pools | Machining | Assembly |
|---|---|---|
| Production overhead | ₹40,00,00,000 | ₹36,00,00,000 |
| Direct labour cost | ₹3,60,00,000 | ₹12,00,00,000 |
| Machine hours | 2,50,000 | 40,000 |

| Matching department Overhead allocation | (2,50,000 hours × ₹2250) | ₹56,25,00,000 |
|---|---|---|
| Actual overhead in machining | | ₹40,00,00,000 |
| Over applied overhead | (₹56,25,00,000 – ₹40,00,00,000) | ₹16,25,00,000 |

| Matching department Overhead allocation | (125% of ₹120,000,000 ) | ₹15,00,00,000 |
|---|---|---|
| Actual overhead in Finishing | ₹36,00,00,000 | ₹36,00,00,000 |
| Under applied Overheads | (₹15,00,00,000 – ₹36,00,00,000) | (₹21,00,00,000) |

## SUMMARY

The chapter deals with the seven-step processes of cost ascertainment and basic documentation. The seven steps include identifying the cost object, tracing its direct costs in an economically feasible way, identifying an indirect cost pool, identifying a cost base to allocate these costs, calculating the overhead rate by dividing costs accumulated in the cost pool by activity measure of cost base, measuring the activity applied to the cost and the allocated amount to the cost object, and computing the total costs, direct and indirect put together. Inventory accounting for costing purposes has to be a perpetual one, which means that the data entries on transactions have to be as close as possible to real time.

Job costing is done when the cost object has a staccato production schedule, whereas process costing is done when the production is a steady stream. Overhead can be applied on the basis of overhead calculated on normal rate of budgeted cost divided by budgeted activity. This method may result in under- or overallocation of overhead. There are several methods to adjust this mismatch in allocation. This normal costing has several advantages, such as quick availability of costs, evening-out seasonal variations in activity and expenses, etc.

Negotiated and administrative pricing mechanisms require clear and mutually acceptable norms for costs and a clear documentation.

## KEY POINTS

- Job costing is used for staccato production and process costing for continuous steady production.
- Cost ascertainment involves tracing of direct costs and allocation of indirect costs from the cost pool.
- Cost base for allocation of indirect cost is the related cost driver in a cause and effect relationship.
- Job cost sheet records and accumulates all the costs assigned to a specific job. Cost of each cost object is accumulated in records subsidiary to financial accounts.
- Indirect cost can be charged based on normal costing principles, which means a budgeted overhead rate = budgeted cost divided by budgeted activity.
- These cost exercises result in the working out a fair estimate of work-in-process and finished goods stock used in financial accounting.
- This may result in underallocation (underabsorbed costs) or overallocation (overabsorbed costs) of overheads which can be adjusted in several ways as suits the management.
- Equivalent units represent the number of incomplete units at the beginning and the end of a process multiplied by the percentage of completion of these units.
- Work-in-process is the unfinished quantum of work at the end of the period for which costs are compiled.
- Inter-process profits represent the profits that are added to the total cost of the process by a pre-determined method.
- Process loss is the avoidable/unavoidable loss that arise in the course of a process and includes normal and abnormal loss.

## CONCEPT REVIEW QUESTIONS

1. Distinguish between cost tracing and cost allocation.
2. Explain the relationship between cost pool and cost allocation base.
3. Describe the seven steps in cost ascertainment.
4. Explain the basic source documents in job costing.
5. Explain why overhead rates in normal costing are usually averaged round the year.
6. Describe broadly how online computerized systems can be used in job costing.

7. In each of the situations below, choose the most appropriate costing design—job costing, process costing, or batch costing.

 (i) An audit firm  (ii) An oil refinery
 (iii) A tyre manufacturer  (iv) A publisher of books
 (v) A garment export company (vi) A rice mill which de-husks rice
 (vii) A hospital  (viii) A hotel
 (ix) A landscaping company  (x) A TV serial producer
 (xi) An aircraft manufacturer  (xii) A catering service
 (xiii) An auto repair garage  (xiv) A ship repair firm
 (xv) A building contractor

8. What is process costing?
9. What are the similarities between job and process costing?
10. Explain the differences between job and process costing.
11. Explain the term equivalent units of production.
12. What are the cost constituents of equivalent units?
13. What is the main difference between weighted average method and FIFO method of assigning cost under process costing?
14. What are the methods of charging inter-process costing?
15. Explain the terms process loss, normal loss, abnormal loss, and abnormal gain.

## NUMERICAL PROBLEMS

1. **Howrah Engineering Works**

 Howrah Engineering Works (HEW) is an engineering firm that produces a variety of custom-made products, some part of which are manufactured in-house and some parts bought out and assembled along with their own manufactured components. Since its products have varying proportions of own manufacture and bought-out items, they decided to have two cost pools—one for machining department and one for the assembly department. The machining department employs more skilled employees than the assembly department. The machining department charges are based on machine hours and that of the assembly department are based on labour costs. Their budgeted cost for 2005 is shown in the following table.

**Budget for 2005**

| | Machining department | Assembly department |
|---|---|---|
| Manufacturing overhead (₹) | 1,80,00,000 | 3,60,00,000 |
| Direct manufacturing labour cost (₹) | 14,00,000 | 20,00,000 |
| Direct manufacturing labour hours | 10,000 | 20,000 |
| Machine hours | 50,000 | 2,00,000 |

During June 2005, their job cost record was as shown in the following table.

| | Machining department | Assembly department |
|---|---|---|
| Direct material used (₹) | 4,50,000 | 7,00,000 |
| Direct man labour costs (₹) | 1,40,000 | 1,50,000 |
| Direct man labour hours | 1000 | 1500 |
| Machine hours | 2000 | 1000 |

1.1. Compute cost of this project.

1.2. At the end of 2004, overhead cost of machining department and assembly department was ₹2,10,00,000 and ₹3,70,00,000 respectively. 55,000 actual machine hours were used and labour cost in the assembly department was ₹22,00,000. Compute the under- and overallocation of costs.

1.3. Since machining department has a very high wage complement of labour with high wages rates, should not machining cost be allocated according to labour hours and not machine hours?

Would it be more rational to allocate assembly costs on labour hours rather than labour costs? Does it matter in this case? Why or why not?

## 2. Dedicated Shoe Makers

Dedicated Shoe Makers (DSM) manufactures two brands (Jaipuria and Punjabi) of shoes for a national shoe company. Jaipuria had no closing work-in-process at the end of May 2005 as all of the 15,000 shoes produced were shipped to the purchasers. Punjabi was all bottled up as work-in-process awaiting some finishing material. The data for May was as shown in the following table.

| | Jaipuria | Punjabi |
|---|---|---|
| Direct material (₹) | 7,50,000 | 5,00,000 |
| Direct labour (₹) | 30,00,000 | 20,00,000 |
| Direct labour hours | 37,500 | 25,000 |

Manufacturing overhead was ₹30 per labour hour.

2.1. Compute the total cost of Jaipuria.

2.2. Compute the unit cost of Jaipuria.

2.3. Prepare a journal entry transferring cost of Jaipuria to finished goods and cost of goods sold.

2.4. Calculate the closing work-in-process.

### 3. Arora Fabricators—End Period Adjustment in Normal Costing

Arora Fabricators has a very simple fabricating outfit in the Okhla Industrial Estate in Delhi. Their budget for their single indirect cost pool for 2004 was as follows:

Direct manufacturing labour (base for allocation) = ₹42,00,000

Manufacturing overhead (indirect cost pool) = ₹25,00,000

At the end of 2004, two jobs were incomplete: Job 301 (total manufacturing labour costs ₹1,00,000) and Job 302 (direct manufacturing cost ₹4,00,000). Machine time for the Job 301 was 300 hours and for Job 302 was 650 hours. Actual manufacturing overhead cost incurred for the year turned out to be only ₹18,00,000 against a budget of ₹25,00,000. The total labour cost for all the jobs for the year was ₹40,00,000 and the labour hours for all jobs was 20,000. There were no beginning inventories. In addition to work-in-process, ending finished goods was ₹16,00,000 (including direct manufacturing costs of ₹4,00,000). Revenue totalled ₹30,00,000, cost of goods sold ₹16,00,000 according to cost books (without adjusting for under/overabsorbed overheads). Marketing cost was ₹8,50,000. All their contracts were in principle of cost including marketing costs plus a mark-up of 40 per cent over costs.

3.1.  What is the under/overallocated overhead?

3.2.  Distribute the under/overallocated overhead based on ending balances work-in-process, finished goods, and cost of goods sold, before proration.

3.3.  Distribute the under/overallocation based on total overhead allocated to work-in-process, finished goods, and cost of goods sold.

3.4.  What is the possible explanation of the fact that revenue is not equal to cost of goods sold plus marketing costs plus 40 per cent mark-up?

### 4. Wadia Industries—A Defence Deal

Wadia industries was one of the first to offer to supply defence forces with specialized electronic equipment in response to the policy shift of the defence authorities in India to privatize. They had also supplied similar equipment to the British authorities during war-time. Wadias, however, have complaints against them that they occasionally indulged in corrupt practices. Piyush Desai, Secretary Defence Production, was therefore not surprised to get the following anonymous letter:

*Dear Sir,*

I wish to bring to your attention gross cheating by Wadias in their supplies to you of mine detectors. Taxpayers' money is going down the drain.

- *Direct Material has been billed ₹2.50 lakh. The parts have not been purchased on market rates, which are 10 per cent lower as they have been purchased from vendor firm in which Mrs Wadia has an 80 per cent partnership.*
- *Direct manufacturing labour has been billed for ₹6,00,000. This includes 16 hours of set-up time at ₹200 per hour which is already included in manufacturing overhead and has been double counted. This ₹6,00,000 also includes 120 hours of design cost calculated at ₹400 per hour. Design cost were to be excluded as the designs were the property of Wadia and could be used for other supplies.*
- *Manufacture overhead was charged as 150 per cent of direct labour already includes set-up costs as stated earlier.*

CC Arun Rajpal, Editor of Machalka

Juggi Wadia Chief Executive of Wadia Industries

4.1. What is the total cost billed on this product to the defence establishment?

4.2. Should Piyush Desai act on this letter?

4.3. What precautions should the defence establishment take while entering into such contracts in future?

5. **Sharing Profits in an Audit Firm**

Geeta, Arvind, and Jyotirmoy were three partners of a firm of chartered accounts. The arrangement was that 60 per cent of the profits of each of their audit assignments would be paid to them and the balance would be put in the bonus pool for the staff and other infrastructural investments. The partners were also paid a fixed monthly sum of ₹15,000 plus ₹500 per consultant hour for Geeta, ₹700 per hour for Arvind, and ₹800 per hour for Jyotirmoy. The budget and the actual figures for 2004 are given in the following two tables. Based on budget the overhead to cover telephone, computer costs, miscellaneous travel not directly billed to the partners' accounts was ₹20 per consultant hour. The charging was done on normal costing basis, that is, budgeted rate per actual consultant hours.

5.1. Compute net earnings after charging all direct and indirect expenses for each of the three partners and the partnership.

5.2. Compute net earnings on normal cost basis for each of the partners and on actual basis for partnership.

5.3. Compute net earnings on actual cost basis for partners.

**Budget for 2004 of Geeta, Arvind, and Jyotirmoy**

| | Geeta | Arvind | Jyotirmoy | Total |
|---|---|---|---|---|
| Consultant hours | 1250 | 1400 | 1500 | 4150 |
| Direct expenses other than salary (fixed and variable) ₹ | 1,20,000 | 1,50,000 | 2,00,000 | 4,70,000 |
| Overhead charged | 3,01,205 | 3,37,349 | 3,61,446 | 5,00,000 |
| Audit fee | 12,00,000 | 16,00,000 | 20,00,00 | 48,00,000 |

**Actual figures for 2004 of Geeta, Arvind, and Jyotirmoy**

| | Geeta | Arvind | Jyotirmoy | Total |
|---|---|---|---|---|
| Consultant hour | 1500 | 1400 | 1200 | 3100 |
| Direct expenses other than salary (fixed and variable) ₹ | 1,30,000 | 1,45,000 | 2,00,000 | 4,75,000 |
| Overhead charged at budgeted rate Actual consultant hours ₹ | ? charged on normal cost basis | ? charged on normal cost basis | ? charged on normal cost basis | Actual expenses ₹4,00,000 |
| Audit Fee ₹ | 14,00,000 | 15,00,000 | 15,00,000 | 34,00,000 |

6. **Badami Institute Swimming Pool**

Kinni and company had contracted with the Badami Insitute of Management for constructing a swimming pool building and other hot water facilities. The contract was for ₹27,50,000. It commenced work in July 2004 and was supposed to complete it in 18 months, that is, by December 2005. By December 2004, most of the excavation work was completed. The architect measured the work and certified it in December 2004. The certified value on that date was ₹8,00,000. Kinni estimated that the amount of work done from 15–31 December 2005 was ₹70,000. Badami was contracted to pay stage payment of 85 per cent of the certified value, that is, ₹6,80,000. Badami paid this amount promptly by 31 December 2005.

Kinni's contractor's ledger shows the following figures:

Value of plant at site = ₹12,50,000
Stores sent from depot = ₹3200
Material purchased, cement = ₹46,000
Reinforcement rods = ₹92,000
Sand ballast = ₹27,200
Wages = ₹1,36,000.

Wages accrued but not paid = ₹5200

Insurance = ₹4000

Miscellaneous expenses and overheads = ₹3,02,000.

The value of the plant used at site that cost ₹12,50,00 is now ₹10,60,000.

Material available at site that can be used in 2006 was ₹17,500.

6.1.   Compute the profit on the contract for the year ending December 2005.

## 7.   Sarup & Co.

Sarup & Co. is a confectionery company. During March they had an opening W.I.P. of 40,000 kgs. They introduced 2,00,000 kg into production during the month and had 60,000 kg of W.I.P. on 31 March.

The Chief Engineer estimates that the following percentage of work was completed for the opening and closing W.I.P.

| Materials | Conversion | |
|---|---|---|
| W.I.P 1st March | 80% | 60% |
| W.I.P 31st March | 70% | 40% |

7.1   Calculate the quantity schedule for March and the quantity completed for transfer to next process under the following:

(a)  Weighted average method

(b)  FIFO method

## 8.   Perfecto

Perfecto, a company manufacturing cosmetic soaps, has an opening work-in-process of 15,000 units (40% complete). On 1st May Department A introduced 2,50,000 units into production and had 28,000 units (50% complete) of work-in-process on 31st May.

8.1   Prepare a quantity schedule and a computation of equivalent units for May using the following:

(a)  Weighted Average Method

(b)  FIFO Method

## 9.   Shyamal & Co.

Shyamal & Co. has two departments in its manufacturing process. Data for Department A for the week 42 was:

| | Units | % of Completion | | |
|---|---|---|---|---|
| | | Materials | Labour | Overheads |
| W.I.P. at the beginning | 10,000 | 80% | 70% | 70% |
| W.I.P. at the ending | 15,000 | 60% | 50% | 50% |

The department introduced into production 50,000 units and transferred 45,000 units to the next department. The cost data (in ₹) for Department A shows the following:

|  | Materials | Labour | Overheads |
|---|---|---|---|
| W.I.P. at the beginning | 6000 | 5000 | 4000 |
| Costs added during the process | 70,000 | 40,000 | 30,000 |

The company adopts weighted average method.
9.1 Prepare quantity schedule.
9.2 Compute equivalent units.
9.3 Calculate the cost per equivalent unit.

# PROJECT

(A) Make groups of 4 to 5 students and choose any one of the following organizations:
A medium-sized motor repair shop, an engineering firm ancillary to a big industry, an engineering firm producing for the market, a large restaurant, a plastic products unit, an audit firm, a firm doing consultancy work, a garment manufacturing unit, a textile spinning mill, a textile weaving mill, a software company, a printing press. Make a flow chart of the processes. Suggest the seven steps for cost ascertainment.

**CASE STUDY 1**      **Poornima Biotech**

Poornima Rawat was a brilliant biotechnologist and had recently developed three products, A, B, and C. They all use the same unit process plants but in varying intensities. She proposed to price A, B, and C at ₹72.60/unit, ₹52.80/unit, and ₹46.20/unit, respectively. She had fixed the price on the basis of her cost estimates as follows (Table CS 1).

She assessed the overheads as ₹10,00,000 per annum. Not knowing how best she should distribute the overheads, she decided to distribute in the ratio of 10:6:4, that is, 50 per cent to go to A, 30 per cent to go to B, and 20 per cent to C.

The sales were going on briskly, and she thought she should increase the capacity. Meanwhile some more biotechnologists started making the same products and priced them very differently. Each of them decided to

**Table CS 1**  Cost estimates for Products A, B, and C

|  | Product A | Product B | Product C |
|---|---|---|---|
| Material cost/unit (₹) | 6 | 12 | 18 |
| Labour cost/unit (₹) | 10 | 6 | 4 |
| Overheads/unit (₹) | 50 | 30 | 20 |
| Total/unit (₹) | 66 | 48 | 42 |
| Profit at 10 per cent/ unit (₹) | 6.60 | 4.8 | 4.2 |
| No. of units produced | 10,000 | 10,000 | 10,000 |
| Sale price/unit (₹) | 72.60 | 52.80 | 46.20 |

make only one of the products. Ramchander made only A, Elizabeth only B, and Rahman only C. They were, however, pricing their products A, B, and C very differently from her. A was being priced at ₹39.60, B at ₹52.80 (same as Poornima), and C at ₹79.20. Poornima asked the summer training students of Badami Institute to do some industrial espionage and find out more about her competitors. They were all producing only 10,000 annual units as did Poornima. Their costs were identical to Poornima's on material and labour but their overhead was ₹20, ₹30, and ₹50 for A, B, and C, respectively. They also kept the profit margin at 10 per cent of the cost. Poornima, rather proud of her business sense said, 'Surely Ramchander will crash due to his losses and no one will buy Rahman's expensive product. They are totally inefficient. We are much more cost effective. We can beat them hollow.' Poornima decided to double the production of C with the same price and delay the production of A and B. She hoped Ramchander would crash with his present prices and she would rule the roost ultimately. She could also wipe out Rahman in competition.

## Discussion Questions

1. Why do you think that there is difference between Poornima and the competitors in only one cost item?
2. If she persists in the proposed action, what will be the scenario say after six months?
3. If you were Poornima's consultant, what would you advise her?

**CASE STUDY 2**  Bonda Earthmover Repairs

Bonda area had just been explored and opened up for iron ore exports. Bonda Iron Exports had put up a beneficiation plant for iron ore at Bonda, which could use the low-grade ore of the area and produce high-class ore. Many iron ore mines mushroomed in the area. They all used earth moving equipment but the repair facilities for such equipment were far away at Goa. Bonda Earthmover Repairs (BER) was opened to meet this demand.

BER had the following shops in its unit:

  (i)    Machining, which had lathes and shaping machines, etc.
 (ii)    Casting and forging
(iii)    Electroplating
 (iv)    Hydraulic equipment unit
  (v)    Heat treatment
 (vi)    Electric welding machines
(vii)    Fabrication shop
(viii)   Spray painting unit
 (ix)    Auto electric shop
  (x)    Assembly line

Each one of these shops had a foreman in charge. But they ranged widely in seniority and salaries. Some of the very highly specialized employees were dedicated to the shops. But there were many employees who were floating around and were allotted by the scheduling and estimation department as requisitioned by the foremen.

BER's services could be broadly divided into the following categories:

(a)  Planned maintenance for the yearly contract with clients. The machines came for overhauling. The contracts included replacement of parts at the cost of the clients. Once the job was done, it was covered by a year's guarantee for performance. Such contracts had post-maintenance hiccups that had to be corrected at BER's costs. Tyre re-treading was not covered by these contracts.
(b)  Breakdown maintenance for clients who were not in yearly contracts.
(c)  Special jobs like total rebuilding of some machines and making them look new.
(d)  Re-treading jobs coming from outside Bonda area.

BER's costing process was as follows:

The scheduling and estimation department allots job number for each job. The machine goes to the shop along with the job card. Material is requisitioned by the shops, cleared by estimation department, and is issued by the store department. One copy with values goes to the shop. The accounts department books these materials as consumption. The job numbers are not noted on this as they argue that often the material being surplus is returned or is used by the shops for other jobs. The wage sheets are prepared on a monthly basis. Every employee has a card to record the hours worked in a job countersigned by the foreman.

The foreman notes the material and wages in the job card. At the end of the month, all the cards are sent to the accounts department, who prepare a job cost sheet, which indicates both completed jobs and unfinished jobs. The accounts department charges the overhead (there was only one omnibus rate for the unit), tabulates the result, and shows it to the management. This is the basis of the monthly cost meetings. The unit had a rate card for all types of jobs on the basis of which labour and overheads are charged. Material is charged to clients in categories 2, 3, and 4 in the list of jobs performed (these are indicated earlier in the case). Fernandes, the MD of BER, had some problems in costing and pricing his services to the earth mover industry.

The problems which usually occurred were as follows:

(i) The total material consumed in the job cards did not reconcile with the material consumed in financial accounts.

(ii) The total wages charged did not reconcile with the wages showed in the wage sheet.

(iii) Many clients complained that the total charges were much higher than what the Goa repair shops were charging.

(iv) Some of the foremen who were working in Goa before they joined Bonda complained on the other hand that the Bonda clients were being undercharged.

## Discussion Questions

1. How can we ensure that the discrepancy in wage and material booking could be easily solved?
2. Is it a good idea to have only one indirect cost pool?
3. Suggest a set of cost effective steps to help management improve.

**Prakash Computer Hardware**

Prakash Computer Hardware was a new venture, which assembled in India the following lines of products:

(i) Desktop computers
(ii) Laptop computers
(iii) Network servers
(iv) Printers

They did not do any manufacturing but bought 85 per cent of the value of components in India and 15 per cent from several countries all over the world. Their basic activity was, therefore, assembling, testing, and marketing. Of its total manufacturing costs, components were 60 per cent and wages 40 per cent. Due to wages being low in India, they were able to compete in the international markets for their products.

The company provided an ambience for high productivity in its assembly lines and excellent canteen facilities for its employees. It employed a large number of high-class staff in testing components, semi-finished products, and final production. The company spent a lot of money in research and design and in keeping in touch with foreign makers of parts. There was a great variation in the efforts put in for each of the products. It had also to spend considerable amounts in promotion, marketing and selling activity, especially in its export.

### Discussion Questions

1.  What are the period and product costs of the company?
2.  What will be the nature of the cost objects of the organization?
3.  Suggest the seven-step process of cost ascertainment for the company.

| CASE STUDY 4 | Siva Enterprises |
|---|---|

Siva Enterprises has two processing departments cutting and finishing. Each department calculated the costs by adopting a simple process costing system developed by the CEO, Mr Sivam. He called it the *cost computer* and Sivam was quite proud of it for its simplicity. 'I am not a qualified accountant', he used to say, 'but look at this, anytime I want, the computer can trace my process costs.' The costs incurred directly in the process (consisting of direct material and direct labour) were included in the *cost computer* through the system network. These costs were distributed over the units completed and transferred to the Finishing Department (from Cutting Department) and to the finished goods (from Finishing Department). The semi-finished units were ignored as Sivam felt it was just an accounting jugglery and added no real value. Besides, it could not be captured through the available software.

Due to increasing work load, Sivam had recently recruited Ram, a young and inexperienced accountant who did his masters in commerce. Ram was not too comfortable with the existing system and prepared the following revised cost sheets for the month of May.

## Cutting Department

| Direct materials (₹) | 15,00,000 | Normal loss (₹) | 25,000 * |
|---|---|---|---|
| Direct labour (₹) | 8,00,000 | Transferred to finishing department (₹) | 26,75,000 |
| Overheads (₹) | 4,00,000** | | |
| | 27,00,000 | | 27,00,000 |

## Finishing Department

| Transfer from cutting department (₹) | 26,75,000 | Normal loss (₹) | 25,000* |
|---|---|---|---|
| Direct materials (₹) | 6,00,000 | Transferred to finishing goods (₹) | 47,25,000 |
| Direct labour (₹) | 10,00,000 | | |
| Overheads (₹) | 5,00,000** | | |
| | 47,75,000 | | 47,75,000 |

* Ram discovered that the scrap sales was ₹50,000 which was equally distributed between the two processes.
** 50% of direct labour.

He proudly showed his revised cost sheets in the place of the existing *cost computer* to Sivam.

Sivam: Why you are changing the cost computer. This is confusing.

Ram: Sir, the earlier system ignored some process costs. I have included them now in the cost sheet.

Sivam: Our system was perfect and was completely software driven with no messing around by human beings. Why did you include overheads? And what is this normal loss?

Ram: The process should bear the proportionate share of overheads. The normal loss head is the sale amount of scrap.

Sivam: See Ram. Overheads are common costs. I calculate the gross costs after finishing and then deduct the overheads less the recovery from the scrap to calculate the net costs. You are now apportioning the overheads manually and what is the benefit? Distorting the figures... That is what you achieve. Now why a credit amount against the entry 'Normal loss'? Losses should appear in the debit side you know.

Ram was confused. He thought probably his boss was right. After all Sivam was a successful businessman. 'Theory is probably useless in practice', he sighed.

**Discussion Questions**

1. What is Sivam's reason for supporting the *cost computer*?
2. Is Sivam right in his treatment of overheads?
3. Explain the treatment of normal loss by Ram (he is not too sure of the difference between normal loss and abnormal loss)
4. Both Ram and Sivam have ignored equivalent units. What is its likely impact on costs?

| CASE STUDY 5 | The Ethical Dilemma |
|---|---|

Sampath, the Departmental Manager of the VT – II process, was rapidly going through the cost figures for the month of July. It showed the following:

There was negligible work-in-process in the beginning and hence was excluded from the costs. During the period 1,00,000 units were received from VT – I process and 90,000 units were completed and sold. The ending work-in-process was nearly half-finished. The cost data was as follows:

| Costs transferred from VT – I | ₹3,00,000 |
|---|---|
| Costs incurred in VT – II | |
| Materials | ₹75,000 |
| Labour | ₹50,000 |
| Overheads | ₹37,700 |

He was almost near his target profit figure, but not sure whether he could ultimately reach it, as only a week was left for the end of the financial year. He called his Accountant, Sanyal and explained the situation.

Sampath: Look Sanyal, we have to show some profits and I can't get more sales. Now the only method is to adjust the cost. I do not understand the word equivalent unit. Can you explain?

Sanyal (explains)

Sampath: Oh! I see, I see. Now you see, the profits can be boosted up in this simple way. All you have to do is show to a different percentage of completion in the final process so that the profit figures are fine.

Sanyal (hesitantly): I really do not know how I can do it?

Sampath: It is all very simple. You have given 40 per cent as the stage of completion of finished process. Change it suitably. That's all.

Sanyal: Well, it was done by Chief Engineer, Gupta and I think I cannot do much about it. It is based on technical estimates.

Sampath: Just send a note to me saying that it was wrongly calculated and I will endorse it, nobody in the corporate office knows anything about it. Ok.

Sanyal: Really I do not know whether I should do it...........

### Discussion Questions

1. What is the impact of percentage of completion on profit?
2. Should the percentage be increased or decreased for meeting the target?
3. Is Sanyal right in following Sampath's advice?

# ANNEXURE

## Annexure 5.1

### Accounting Mechanics

The annexure shows the ledger entries that are usually made in respect of the job cost entries shown in Fig. 5.3. The entries are not exhaustive but only indicative of the manner of ledger keeping.

| Dr | Paper Stock Purchase Account (??) | | Cr |
|---|---|---|---|
| To Creditors | ₹7,20,000 | By profit and loss account | ₹7,20,000 |

| Dr | Paper Stock Issue Account (cost ledger) | | Cr |
|---|---|---|---|
| | | By work-in-process *Durga Mahima* | ₹7,20,000 |

| Dr | Works-in-process *Durga Mahima* (cost ledger) | | Cr |
|---|---|---|---|
| To paper stock account issue (cost ledger) | ₹7,20,000 | By finished goods account *Durga Mahima* | ₹14,20,000 |
| To wages applied account (cost ledger) | ₹2,00,000 | | |
| To composing overhead applied account (cost ledger) | ₹20,000 | | |
| To printing overhead applied account (cost ledger) | ₹4,00,000 | | |
| To binding overhead applied account (cost ledger) | ₹1,00,000 | | |

| Dr | Finished Stock Account *Durga Mahima* (Cost ledger) | | Cr |
|---|---|---|---|
| To work-in-porcess *Durga Mahima* | ₹14,20,000 | By cost of goods sold *Durga Mahima* | ₹14,20,000 |

| Dr | Cost of goods sold Durga Mahima (Cost ledger) | | Cr |
|---|---|---|---|
| To finished stock account *Durga Mahima* | ₹14,20,000 | | |

| Dr | Sales *Durga Mahima* | | Cr |
|---|---|---|---|
| To profit and loss account | ₹14,20,000 | By debtors account | ₹14,20,000 |

| Dr | Composing department account | | Cr |
|---|---|---|---|
| To creditors | ₹1,00,000 | By profit and loss account | ₹1,00,000 |

| Dr | Printing department account | | Cr |
|---|---|---|---|
| To creditors | ₹10,00,000 | By profit and loss account | ₹10,00,000 |

| Dr | Binding department Account | | Cr |
|---|---|---|---|
| To creditors | ₹5,00,000 | By profit and loss account | ₹5,00,000 |

| Dr | Wages account | | Cr |
|---|---|---|---|
| To creditors | ₹40,00,000 | By profit and loss account | ₹40,00,000 |

One may see that the concept of 'applied accounts' has been used, which is different from the expenditure account ledgers. The entire exercise would leave the expenses accounts intact for being transferred to the profit and loss account in financial accounting. The applied accounts only help in computing the work-in-process of each cost object and thereafter the value of finished goods. Similarly stock issue accounts in cost ledgers enable one to arrive at closing stocks of raw material using the formula described in Chapter 3:

$$\text{Opening Stock} + \text{Purchases} - \text{Issues} = \text{Closing stock}$$

Purchase accounts and creditors accounts will be available as usual in the financial accounts. Chapter 10 will show how this complex accounting can be simplified in what is known as *back flush costing*.

*Accounting Mechanics of Normal Costing*

Let us deal with the same data of *Durga Mahima* as given in job cost sheet with an additional information that in all three overhead departments there has been an under/overallocation of overheads in a system of normal costing. Only the relevant ledgers are shown:

| Dr | | Composing department account | | Cr |
|---|---|---|---|---|
| To creditors | ₹1,00,000 | By profit and loss account | | ₹1,00,000 |

| Dr | Composing overhead account application account | | Cr |
|---|---|---|---|
| | | By WIP *Durga Mahima* | ₹20,000 |
| | | By WIP *Modern Physics* | ₹40,000 |
| | | By *Modern History* | ₹15,000 |
| | | By *Fairy Tales* | ₹10,000 |

| Dr | | Printing department account | | Cr |
|---|---|---|---|---|
| To creditors | ₹10,00,000 | By profit and loss account | | ₹10,00,000 |

| Dr | Printing overhead account application account | | Cr |
|---|---|---|---|
| | | By WIP *Durga Mahima* | ₹4,00,000 |
| | | By WIP *Modern Physics* | ₹4,00,000 |
| | | By *Modern History* | ₹2,00,000 |
| | | By *Fairy Tales* | ₹1,00,000 |

| Dr | | Binding department account | | Cr |
|---|---|---|---|---|
| To creditors | ₹5,00,000 | By profit and loss account | | ₹5,00,000 |

| Dr | Binding overhead account application account | | Cr |
|---|---|---|---|
| | | By WIP *Durga Mahima* | ₹1,00,000 |
| | | By WIP *Modern Physics* | ₹1,00,000 |
| | | By *Modern History* | ₹1,00,000 |
| | | By *Fairy Tales* | ₹1,50,000 |

One may see that there is underallocation of ₹15,000 in the composing department, ₹50,000 in the binding department, and overallocation of ₹1,00,000 in printing. There is a net overallocation of ₹35,000. Considering the insignificance of the amount, one can ignore it, absorbing it in the cost of goods sold in financial accounts. But if the parties, who were quoted on an actual cost-plus contract, come to know, they may demand a rework of their costs.

## CHAPTER 6

# Activity-based Costing

## Learning Objectives

After reading this chapter, you will be able to understand

- activity bases in operations in manufacturing, merchandising, and service organizations
- activity-based costing (ABC) as a more recent extension of indirect cost allocation methods used for a long time in industries
- the need to be judicious and cost effective in adopting the number of activity centres for cost allocation

- alternate methods to measure and quantify activities including time-driven methods devised by Kaplan and his associates, work sampling, and the German computerized real time systems
- the limitations of ABC analysis and circumstances in which it is useful or not useful

## INTRODUCTION

The history of the activity-based costing (ABC) movement has been one of great initial euphoria (Kaplan 1983), strong disillusionment, and apologetic revival in a recently modified form by the same authors of the first movement (Kaplan and Anderson 2004). These somewhat irrational movements in its fortunes are undoubtedly due to the unnecessary mystique surrounding its first exposition as a magic wand. If it had been understood right from the beginning as an extension of the simple concept of the need for more than one overhead cost pool (multiple indirect cost pools), which we described in Chapter 5, the disillusionment and its aftermath may have been less pronounced.

Thus, if we have two products—one that is manufactured using ones own machines and another that only assembles our parts albeit using some machinery—both of them use machine hours and labour hours, if we use one common indirect cost pool, it would most certainly distort costs. As operational processes become more complicated, there are greater compulsions to increase the number of cost pools. Typically,

**Mystique of ABC**
ABC should be viewed with pragmatic scepticism and not as a magic wand.

1. in manufacturing, costs of casting, machining, heat treatment, and polishing activities have to be differentiated between products X and Y using the same methodology as we used for allocating costs of cost centres. In purchasing/ordering, orders against rate contracts, normal ordering, bulk ordering, etc. are different activities.
2. in merchandising, ordering, deliveries, shelf stocking, and customer support in supermarkets may be activities which are differentially required by customers or different classes of customers.
3. in service organizations, making demand drafts, letters of credit, deposits, savings account transactions, current account transactions, and inspection of customers in banks may be activities whose overheads need to be allocated.

**Computer software**
The most effective use of ABC is reported with online computer software.

The potential opening for this concept has not caught on as rapidly as one would have expected to. Dhavale (1989) quoting Schwarz and Howell reports that nearly one-third to half organizations have only one plant-wide overhead or at the most departmental overheads (say a two-third of them). That leaves only about a third who may be using ABC. Later in this chapter, we will see the variation in the practices across the world. Kaplan and Anderson (2004) said, 'In the classroom, activity-based costing looks a great way to manage a company's limited resources. But many managers who have tried to implement ABC in their organizations on any significant scale have abandoned the attempt.' All is not lost, as we will see in this chapter, provided we are armed with two supports, a healthy pragmatic scepticism and a sophisticated computer software.

## ABC—AN EXTENSION OF INDIRECT COSTS

One of the features of modern industry is that manufacturing cost as a share of total cost of the product is rapidly reducing as the share of manufacturing in GDP is rapidly reducing and the share of service sector costs are rapidly increasing, being 72 per cent in developed countries and about 50 per cent in developing countries. Thus in software industry research and development costs are 75 per cent and manufacturing costs 0 per cent (Atkinson et al. 2004). Further in many other manufacturing industries, easy and economically traceable direct costs are getting less than in the traditional industries (Dhavale 1989).

At least that is the situation in the US, where there is a pronounced tendency to abandon strenuous efforts to trace direct costs as contrasted to Japan (Shields et al. 1991). In view of this, the compulsions for a more accurate allocation of indirect costs are now much greater. Global competition has also made it very important to use resources more carefully whether the cost of these resources behave like variable costs or like fixed costs as described in Chapter 3. There was a realization that cost and managerial analysis was veering dangerously to assume that fixed costs can be taken for granted and need not be adequately analysed. The German and Japanese industries gave the Anglo-American industries a rude jolt that woke them up to the importance of accurate costing, which inter alia meant the use of ABC.

## ABC and the Seven Steps in Cost Ascertainment

Since conceptually ABC is no different from the universally followed concepts of allocation, the seven steps followed for indirect cost allocation described in Chapter 5 apply to ABC as well. These seven steps are briefly summarized here.

*Step 1: Identifying the product cost object*

The first step is to identify the product cost object.

*Step 2: Identifying the direct cost of the job*

Identifying the direct costs of a job has two considerations. First, the physical inputs for the making of the product should be identified as a cost object. Second, the economically feasible way of measuring these inputs is to be identified.

*Step 3: Selecting the cost allocation base to use for allocating costs to the job*

The bases may be simple measures, which can be tracked with simple documentation. Machine hours or labour hours could be counted as such simple measures. But even such measures can sometimes prove difficult to record. But some cost pools may require complex compound measures. For example, power expenses may have compound bases such as horsepower hours if there are no meters to measure power consumption. Similarly transport costs can have a base of kilometres 'weight or volume' kilometres.

*Step 4: Judging the optimum number of indirect cost pools*

More the number of homogenous cost pools, more accurate will be the cost allocation. But this will increase the cost of costing. One may, therefore, decide to have less number of but more heterogeneous cost pools.

*Step 5: Computing the rate per unit of each allocation base*

This is a simple arithmetic.

*Step 6: Computing the charge*

It will include ascertaining the activity used by the cost object and computing it.

*Step 7: Calculating the total cost of the job*

## Normal Costing and ABC

In Chapter 5, the use of normal costing for overhead allocation was explained. This provides that for indirect cost, a pre-determined overhead rate is calculated at Step 5 of the process by dividing expected overhead expense by expected overhead activity. This may result in underabsorbed or overabsorbed overheads after the actual is known. This method is even more forcefully useful in ABC. This arises partly from the difficulties of concurrently recording activities of the myriad activity centres in manual systems. We will explain this in the next paragraph. The advantages of normal costing are, therefore, reaped even more in ABC. We will see in Chapter 9, dealing with standard costing, how an extension of the concept of normal costing in conjunction with standard costing would give rich insights in ABC.

## PROBLEMS OF MEASUREMENT OF ACTIVITIES IN ABC

Kaplan and Anderson (2004) addressed themselves in one of the great problems in ABC. Since Kaplan was one of the originators of the ABC concept, their worries are very significant. The myriad activity centres do not hold any serious problem in gathering the costs planned or actually incurred in the activity centres. The documentation is not difficult for this and cumulating them can be aided by computers. But the greater problem is keeping track of the activities that have a logical cause and effective relationship with these activity-based cost pools. According to Kaplan and Anderson (2004),

> 'As the activity dictionary expands, the demands on the computer programs used to store and process the data escalate... if the company has 150 activities and applies the costs to 600,000 cost objects (products and services) and runs the model monthly for two years... it will involve storage of 2 billion bytes.'

But more than the processing problems is the cost of gathering data. As they say,

**Table 6.1** Older method of ascertaining costs and activities in ABC

| Activity | Per cent time spent | Quantity | Total cost assigned in dollars in proportion of time spent | Cost/unit dollar = total cost ÷ quantity |
|---|---|---|---|---|
| Process customer orders | 70 | 49,000 | 3,92,000 | 8 |
| Handle customer inquiries | 10 | 1400 | 56,000 | 40 |
| Perform credit checks | 520 | 2500 | 1,12,000 | 44.80 |
| Total | 100 | | 5,60,000 | |

'In one large bank's brokerage operation, the ABC data-gathering process required 70,000 employees at more than 100 facilities to submit monthly reports of time allocation. The company employed 14 people full time just to manage data collection.'

As can be seen the present process required employees to record the percentage of their time in each of the activities. This posed unexpected behavioural problems as employees would never frankly reveal the fact that they have idle time.

Kaplan and Anderson resolved this problem by requesting the top management to assess the standard time for merging complex set of processes. Precision was not as important as identifying the variety of complex operations. They contrast the results of the previous method of cost assignment and the revised method in Tables 6.1 and 6.2.

**Table 6.2** The revised time-driven way of cost ascertainment in ABC

| Activity (Col. 1) | Quantity (Col. 2) | Standard unit time as per management (Col. 3) | Total time used in minutes (Col. 4 = Col. 3 × Col. 2) | Cost driver rate dollars (Col. 5 = Col. 6 ÷ Col. 2) | Total cost assigned (Col. 6 = in proportion of Col. 4) |
|---|---|---|---|---|---|
| Processing customer orders | 51,000 | 8 | 4,08,000 (8 × 51,000) | 6.40 | 3,26,400 |
| | 1150 | 44 | 50,600 (44 × 1150) | 35.20 | 40,480 |
| | 2700 | 50 | 1,35,000 (2700 × 50) | 40 | 1,08,000 |
| Total used | | | 5,93,600 | | 4,74,880 |
| Total supplied | | | 7,00,000 | | 5,60,000 |
| Unused capacity | | | 1,06,400 | | 85,120 |

One can see that the cost assigned to product in Table 6.2 as proposed by Kaplan and Anderson is short of total cost incurred as the total time used is less than total time available. This idle time would be the equivalent of underabsorbed overhead on the analogy of normal costing. We must also note that the example given by Kaplan is in the service sector. As the activities are in service industry they do not inventorize product costs. The mechanics described in Annexure 5.1 of Chapter 5 would, therefore, not apply in this case.

## USE OF WORK SAMPLING IN ABC

Work sampling could be described as 'a large number of random observations on output and activity levels are made on the job. These observations are used to determine the number and type of steps for the job in normal operating mode' (Failing et al. 1988).

Let us see an example of how work sampling can be used for ABC, in a manner that avoids taking a subjective judgement of the management suggested by Kaplan and Anderson in Example 6.1.

If similar work sampling is done in several branches, the standards can be surmised. It could sometimes embarrass the worker as the observation shows 60 minutes wasted out of 390 minutes, that is, 15 per cent of the time. But this may be necessary to keep the productivity up. One can also note the waiting time in the queue. Often the branch managers may themselves come out and see what is happening. One can note that this method can be used only if (a) the transactions happen in a closed room which can be sampled easily through a random process, (b) if the workers are not hostile to these observations being taken.

## GPK—THE GERMAN COSTING AND FLEXIBLE MANUFACTURING SYSTEMS

Whereas Kaplan takes a defensive posture in regard to ABC in the service sector in the US, coping with the enormous difficulty of keeping track of a great number of cost objects and activity bases, the manufacturing sector in Germany has implemented computerized costing systems that capture the most complex processes and diversified products often with incredibly short production runs, small batch sizes, sometimes even with a single unit of production. (See Dhavale 1989; Krumwiede 2005; Smith 2005; Compton 1996; Clinton and Webber 2004.)

## Example 6.1 Work Sampling in a Bank

A small branch of a bank wished to assess the cost of its activities. It had only one assistant working in several functions. The functions were (1) cashing cheques, (2) preparing drafts, (3) preparing bankers' cheques, (4) attending to balance enquiries, (5) entering inward cheques on the computer, and (6) opening new accounts. The duration of 390 minutes in a working day (leaving out lunch break of 30 minutes) also had periods of tea drinking, gossiping, and some period of idleness. We may label them 7, 8, and 9 following the six already described earlier. The assistant's daily wages are ₹500 including perks. Cost per minute is, therefore, ₹1.28. The work sampling was done by noting the work done by the clerk when the observation was made. Observations were made by random number choice of throw of dice. Seventy-nine observations were made. The number of occasions he was observed doing the work item is in Table 6.3.

**Table 6.3** Data collected for work sampling

| Activity* | 1 | 2 | 3 | 4 | 5 | 6 | 7 | 8 | 9 |
|---|---|---|---|---|---|---|---|---|---|
| Number of observations | 8 | 7 | 6 | 16 | 11 | 19 | 4 | 4 | 4 |
| Per cent total | 10 | 8 | 8 | 21 | 14 | 24 | 5 | 5 | 5 |
| Time in minutes | 39 | 32 | 32 | 80 | 55 | 92 | 20 | 20 | 20 |
| Units done | 6 | 3 | 3 | 10 | 20 | 5 | - | - | - |
| Time per unit | 6 | 10 | 10 | 8 | 2.75 | 18.4 | | | |
| Cost per unit Rs | 7.68 | 12.8 | 12.8 | 10.24 | 3.52 | 21 | | | |

*Note*: See the description of the activities given earlier along with the numbers 1, 2, 3, 4, 5, 6, 7, 8, and 9.

How does one understand this difference in approach? The processes in manufacturing are structured and in one place, unlike in the service and merchandising sectors. They can all be hooked on to real-time systems for recording measures of activities to be used for cost allocation. Complexity of transactions is no bar for such real time recording of events. Second, 'their evolution has been conditioned by the strength of American capitalist markets systems giving more emphasis to financial accounting and external reporting. Because of this, US management accounting systems aren't as sophisticated as those in some other developed countries of the world' (Clinton and Webber 2004).

Let us see some details.

The steps in introducing real time computerization are as follows:

*Step 1:* The entire operational model is reproduced in the software. This would include identification of the batch process too. Every component is linked with the model with operational and financial details (Blankley 2000).

*Step 2:* These models provide an option to decide the number of cost pools. German firms have up to 20,000 of such resource centres (another name for indirect cost pools). These may include batch identities. However, the number of resource centres is a managerial choice. US firms usually have much less number of cost pools (Krumwiede 2005). Even in German–US collaboration this divide causes problems between the groups. When DaimlerChrysler opened a factory in Germany, the Daimler side implemented a large number of resource centres but the US side was reluctant to follow suit.

*Step 3:* The software is a collaborative effort of consultants and academics (Krumwiede 2005).

*Step 4:* Cost centre application rates are periodically set, usually annually.

*Step 5:* Routing and setting of machines can be adjusted periodically.

*Step 6:* The computer automatically allocates maintenance overhead, tool room expenses, office overheads to machine centres. These, in turn, are charged to the cost objects usually based on machine hours. Batch costs are accumulated and rate applicable to the cost object depends on lot size. The ultimate output of the system would look somewhat like Table 6.4 (Dhavale 1989).

**Table 6.4**　Transformation cost for Product C 100

| Programming cost | |
|---|---|
| 1. Process analyst programming | $ 10,600 |
| 2. Trial run | $1560 |
| 3. Dyes special tools | $4310 |
| Capitalised programme costs | $16470 |
| Expected no. of units to be made over a period of time | 8000 units |
| Amortization expenses per unit | $2.06 |
| **Production set up costs/unit** | |
| Tool setter | $40 |
| Set-up operator | $40 |
| Loader/unloader | $15 |
| **Total** | $ 95 |
| Average lot size | 25 |
| Production set-up expenses for unit | $3.80 |
| Total programme production expenses | $5.86 |

*Step* 7: Material expenses are most easily available on the computer automatically as the material issue are read straight by the computer using bar codes, optical characteristics or magnetic stripes (Dhavale 1989). Thus product costs are now available. Do we incorporate this in financial accounts? We will answer this later in the next paragraph.

## ACCOUNTING MECHANICS AND ABC

**ABC and financial accounts**
It is now more usual to use ABC as a supplement to normal financial accounts and not as its substitute. Inventory accounting is usually done more on traditional costing than the data of the ABC system.

The enormous versatility of computerized systems detailed in the previous paragraph has had one profound consequence on the relationship between ABC costing and financial accounting. 'Cost accounting is no longer constrained to use data prepared for financial accounts' (Dhavale 1989). 'Most companies do not use the data from the ABC costing system for inventory valuation to fulfil the requirements of accounting standards', says Ted Compton (1996).

Thus the accounting mechanics detailed in Annexure 5.1 of Chapter 5 would usually not be relevant for ABC system. Nevertheless, its integration and links with the rest of financial accounting exists.

Thus, the total expenses incurred figure of $560,000 in Table 6.1 and 6.2 will be available with the financial accounts and the departmental or cost centre. The further breakdown into activity centres would not be linked in the financial books. Similarly, Table 6.3 may have links with financial accounts at the basic source, for example, total batch costs, or cost on maintenance, etc. But its further distribution up to the product would be quite remote from financial accounts. Moreover, Table 6.3 may not be used to value inventories.

## ABC AND COST-VOLUME-PROFIT ANALYSIS

**ABC for long-term analysis**
ABC costing categories presume all fixed costs can change in the long run and therefore differentiating fixed and variable costs for CVP analysis is usually not attempted.

One may note in all our ABC analysis, we have not separated fixed and variable costs in each activity centre. There is nothing theoretically absurd in trying to do so. But one message comes out of this. The preoccupation of the perpetrators of the ABC culture was different from those using BEP and cost-volume-profit (CVP) analysis. Accountants using CVP analysis and simulation techniques (described in Chapter 4) try to modify volumes to get higher profitability or to reach an optimum product mix with maximum contribution. The focus is on maximization of profit and not on reduction of fixed costs. On the other hand, ABC analysis concentrates on the long run. It considers that all costs—whether fixed or variable—are really variable in the long run (Horngren et al. 2003; Atkinson et al. 2004).

So it would ignore the focus on CVP analysis. Since short-term analysis also have a place in management, the alternative of using the CVP framework is not abandoned in this book after 'indoctrination in the ABC culture'. It finds prominence in several later chapters. Chapter 11 expounds the theory of constraints, which is conceded as a desirable complementary approach to ABC by the very authors of ABC. As they say, 'In theory, there is no reason why Theory of Constraints and ABC cannot be used together' (Atkinson et al. 2004).

## ABC HIERARCHY OF COSTS

One of the most significant outcomes of the ABC approach is that in the search of the activities in an organization, which are the true origins of the cost variations between products, it was realized that the activities could vary in nature across what is described as the hierarchies in an organization.

They are summarized as follows:

**Cost implications of batch size**
One of the most profound implications of ABC system is the insights into the impact of set-up costs and batch size on product costs.

1. *Output unit level costs:* They directly move in sympathy of production, that is, if output increases, these costs would increase. These include direct material, direct energy, etc.
2. *Batch level costs:* They move in sympathy with number of batches, that is, one needs to accumulate and allocate costs of activities to the products based on the number of units produced in each batch. The batch concept is applicable not only in the production process but also in the purchasing process, dispatching process, and even billing process.
3. *Product-sustaining costs:* These are costs incurred independent of the number of units/batch produced. Designing and research and development costs are typical of this category. These costs are allocated based on the total output it is expected to serve.

**Charging facility-sustaining costs to product**
It becomes important when management is guided by costs for pricing.

4. *Facility-sustaining costs:* These are costs of those activities that sustain the entire organization. They have the least cause and effect relationship with production.

Allocating these costs becomes important for organizations that are compulsive believers in fixing selling prices based on costs.

We will illustrate the implication of cost hierarchies in Example 6.2.

Both products were selling well at this price. But how could they afford to lose so heavily on Peaberry. If they increased the price, sales may have rapidly fallen and batch related costs would have further increased on per unit computation.

## Example 6.2   United Coffee Works

United Coffee Works was a well-known coffee manufacturer, which prided itself in giving its customers the best choice in products. They offered about 50 blends, many of which were exported. They priced their products on cost plus a mark-up of 30 per cent. It seemed to be working out fine till a new cost accountant said one of their products Robusta was overpriced and another product Peaberry was heavily underpriced. He showed his computations in Table 6.5. The existing price was based on existing cost estimate of ₹150/kilo for Robusta and ₹179/kilo for Peaberry.

**Table 6.5**   United Coffee Works

|  | Per kg (₹) | | Total amount (₹) | | | |
|---|---|---|---|---|---|---|
|  | Robusta | Peaberry | Robusta | Peaberry | | |
| Direct material | 96 | 125 | 9,60,000 | 25,000 | | |
| Direct labour | 9 | 9 | 90,000 | 1800 | | |
| Total direct cost | 105 | 134 | 10,50,000 | 26,800 | | |
| Overhead | 45 | 45 | 4,50,000 | 9000 | | |
| Production | 10,000 | 200 | | | | |
| Total cost | 150 | 179 | 15,00,000 | 35,800 | | |
| **ABC cost** | | | | | Activity | Cost/unit activity |
| Purchase orders | 0.6 | 30 | 6000 | 6000 | Order | ₹1500 |
| Material handling | 3.6 | 72 | 36,000 | 14,400 | No set up | ₹1200 |
| Quality control | 0.72 | 14.4 | 7200 | 2880 | No batches | ₹720 |
| Roasting | 3 | 3 | 30,000 | 600 | Hrs | ₹30 |
| Blending | 1.5 | 1.5 | 15,000 | 300 | Hrs | ₹30 |
| Packing | 0.3 | 0.3 | 3000 | 60 | Hrs | ₹30 |
| Total ABC overhead | 9.72 | 121.2 | 97,200 | 24,240 | | |
| Total ABC cost/unit | 114.72 | 255.2 | 11,47,200 | 51,040 | | |
| Existing sale price | 195 | 232.7 | | | | |

The ABC analysis shows that whereas a differential of ₹29 per kg (125 – 96) in direct material cost for the two products could not be avoided and customers were getting a value of higher quality of Peaberry coffee seeds with finer flavour, the purchase order costs, material handling costs, and quality control costs are entirely due to low batch sizes of production for Peaberry. If we increase the batch size, the average inventory will go up and loss of flavour obsolescence due to storage of coffee powder would escalate costs. Similarly, if we reduce the number of purchase orders, inventory of raw material would increase and so would obsolescence. Management could seek remedies for this. For example, if they improve packaging, flavour could be maintained. If they enter into a rate contract, ordering costs could come down; a telephonic advice should suffice. Efforts could be made to reduce the cost per unit activity for purchase, set-up and quality control. We will address ourselves to this issue later in the chapter. The exposition in Example 6.2 showed the role batch costs play on the product cost, ABC, and target pricing. It presented the interplay of target pricing and ABC analysis. In Chapter 13 we will further explore this concept with examples from Japanese industries that use ABC costing for fixing target cost and prices.

Example 6.2 also showed the availability of leads for cost reduction provided by ABC costing, which wisely avoid fiddling around with only variations in volume of production to reduce per unit costs of the product. It attempts to have a close look for making fundamental changes in the structure of costs.

## ABC IN SERVICE AND MERCHANDISING SECTORS

ABC is extensively used in service and merchandising sectors. The instruments and techniques used in these sectors are very different from those in the manufacturing sectors as would be clear from the several examples indicated in this chapter. Customer-wise profitability is one typical use of ABC analysis. Let us see Example 6.3.

One can see that due to the nature of the products and less quantities for each transaction, *Papa di Dukaan* is becoming unsustainable. Some marketing solution could surely be innovated for this small and intimate shop. The pricing patterns could be adjusted and home delivery can be given only for orders above a particular value, etc.

## Example 6.3  Bansal Supermarkets

Bansal supermarkets have two branches served by the same management. The first branch called *Sitara* was slightly away from the cluster of residences, and had good car parking arrangements. The management was in the hands of the younger members of the Bansal family—the two sons and their wives. The other shop known as *Papa di Dukaan* was located right within the crowded campus and was in the charge of the senior Bansal and his elderly wife. The finances, purchase and ordering, and central services were controlled by the senior couple. Both branches had home-delivery system. They both had a common list of stocking items but had also large variations. Bansal had presented a month ago the financial performance (Table 6.6) of both the branches for one month, which seemed to show that *Papa di Dukaan* was doing better than *Sitara*. One of the daughter-in-laws was a cost accountant and respectfully suggested that this may not be the case and an ABC analysis would be necessary. She did the preliminary work and her ABC rates are shown in Table 6.7. She applied the results to rework the profitability of the two branches (see Tables 6.8 and 6.9).

**Table 6.6**  Financial performance of Bansal Supermarkets

|  | *Papa di Dukaan* | *Sitara* |
|---|---|---|
| Sales | 2,00,000 | 20,00,000 |
| Cost of goods sold (₹) | 1,85,000 | 19,50,000 |
| Gross margin (₹) | 15,000 | 50,000 |
| Profit/sale (₹) | 0.075 | 0.025 |

**Table 6.7**  Preliminary ABC analysis

| Activity | Cost (₹) | Activity base | Activity quantity | Cost/activity (₹) |
|---|---|---|---|---|
| Purchase | 8000 | Number | 200 | 40 |
| Line item | 6000 | Number | 2000 | 3 |
| Delivery | 10,000 | Number | 200 | 50 |
| Handling | 10,000 | Number | 1000 | 10 |
| Shelf stock | 8000 | Hrs | 80 | 100 |
| **Total overhead** | **42,000** | | | |

**Table 6.8**   Detailed ABC analysis for Bansal Supermarkets

| | Papa di Dukaan quantity | Papa di Dukaan cost (₹) | Sitara quantity | Sitara cost (₹) | Total cost (₹) |
|---|---|---|---|---|---|
| Purchase | 20 | 800 | 180 | 7200 | 8000 |
| Line item | 240 | 720 | 1760 | 5280 | 6000 |
| Delivery | 180 | 9000 | 20 | 1000 | 10,000 |
| Handling | 300 | 3000 | 700 | 7000 | 10,000 |
| Shelf stocking | 10 | 1000 | 70 | 7000 | 8000 |
| **Total overhead** | | **14,520** | | **27,480** | **42,000** |

**Table 6.9**   Net profit for Bansal Supermarkets (in ₹)

| | Papa di Dukaan | Sitara | Total |
|---|---|---|---|
| Gross profit | 15,000 | 50,000 | 65,000 |
| Overhead | 14,520 | 27,480 | 42,000 |
| Net profit (loss) | 480 | 22,520 | 23,000 |

Activity based costing (ABC) assigns manufacturing overhead costs to products in a more logical manner than the traditional approach of simply allocating costs on the basis of machine hours. Activity based costing first assigns costs to the activities that are the real cause of the overhead. It then assigns the cost of those activities only to the products that are actually demanding the activities.

## ACTIVITY-BASED COSTING WITH TWO ACTIVITIES

Company X has an annual manufacturing overhead costs of ₹8,00,00,000 of which ₹80,00,000 is directly involved in setting-up the production machines. During the year the company expects to perform 400 machine set-ups. Also suppose that the batch sizes vary considerably, but the set-up efforts for each machine are similar.

The cost per set-up is calculated to be ₹20,000 (₹80,00,000 of cost per year divided by 400 set-ups per year). Under activity based costing, ₹80,00,000 of the overhead will be viewed as a batch-level cost. This means that ₹80,00,000 will first be allocated to batches of products to be manufactured and then be assigned to the units of the product in each batch.

Batch A consists of 5000 units of product, the set-up cost per unit is ₹4 (₹20,000 divided by 5000 units). If Batch B is 50,000 units, the cost per unit for set-up will be ₹0.40 (₹20,000 divided by 50,000 units). The remaining ₹7,20,00,000 of manufacturing overhead is caused by the production activities that correlate with the company's 1,00,000 machine hours, as shown in Tables 6.10 and 6.11.

**Table 6.10** Various cost heads of Company X

| Annual Manufacturing Overhead Costs | ₹8,00,00,000 |
|---|---|
| Production overhead | ₹80,00,000 |
| Expected machine set-up during year | 400 |
| Cost per set-up | ₹20,000 |

**Table 6.11** Cost overheads of Company X

| Particulars | With ABC | Without ABC |
|---|---|---|
| Mfg overhead costs assigned to set-ups | ₹80,00,000 | 0 |
| Number of machine set-ups | 400 | 0 |
| Mfg overhead per set-up | ₹ 20,000 | 0 |
| Total manufacturing cost | ₹8,00,00,000 | ₹8,00,00,000 |
| Less cost traced to machine set-ups | ₹80,00,000 | 0 |
| Mfg overhead costs allocated to machine hours | ₹7,20,00,000 | ₹8,00,00,000 |
| Machine hours (mh) | 1,00,000 | 1,00,000 |
| Mfg overhead cost per machine hour (mh) | ₹720 | ₹800 |
| Mfg cost overhead | ₹20,000 per set up + ₹720 per mh | ₹800 per set |

## Impact of Different Allocation Techniques and Overhead Rates on the Per Unit Cost

A company manufactures a batch of 5,000 units and it produces 50 units per machine hour. Here is a comparison between the cost assigned to the units with activity based costing and without activity based costing (Table 6.12):

**Table 6.12** Comparison of cost overheads between ABC and without ABC

| Particulars | With ABC | Without ABC |
|---|---|---|
| Mfg overhead per set-up | ₹20,000 | 0 |
| Number of units | 5000 | N.A. |
| Mfg overhead per set-up (i) | ₹4.00 | N.A. |
| Mfg overhead cost per MH (a) | ₹720 | ₹800 |
| No. of units produced per machine (b) | 50 | 50 |
| Mfg overhead costs allocated to machine hours (ii) = (a/b) | ₹14.40 | ₹16.00 |
| Total overhead cost per unit (i) + (ii) | ₹18.40 | ₹16.00 |

If a company manufactures a batch of 50,000 units and produces 50 units per machine hour, here is a comparison between the cost assigned to the units with ABC and without ABC (Table 6.13):

**Table 6.13**   Comparison of cost overheads between ABC and without ABC for a batch size of 50,000 units

| Particulars | With ABC | Without ABC |
|---|---|---|
| Mfg overhead per set-up | ₹20,000 | 0 |
| Number of units | 50,000 | N.A. |
| Mfg overhead per set-up (i) | ₹0.400 | N.A. |
| Mfg overhead cost per MH (a) | ₹720 | ₹800 |
| No. of units produced per machine (b) | 50 | 50 |
| Mfg overhead costs allocated to machine hours (ii) = (a/b) | ₹14.40 | ₹16.00 |
| Total overhead cost per unit (i) + (ii) | ₹14.80 | ₹16.00 |

With activity-based costing the cost per unit decreases from ₹16.00 to ₹14.80 because the cost of the set-up activity is spread over 50,000 units instead of 5,000 units. Without ABC, the cost per unit is ₹16.00 regardless of the number of units in each batch. If companies base their selling prices on costs, a company not using an ABC approach might lose the large batch work to a competitor who bids a lower price based on the lower, more accurate overhead cost of ₹14.80. It is also possible that a company not using ABC may find itself being the low bidder for manufacturing small batches of product, since its ₹16.00 is lower than the ABC model of ₹18.40 for a batch size of 5,000 units. With its bid price based on manufacturing overhead of ₹16.00 but a true cost of ₹18.40 the company may end up doing lots of production for little or no profit.

## OTHER USES OF ABC

Let us now focus our attention on some other uses of ABC.

### ABC and Controls

The ultimate aspect in controls is the use of standard costing, which will be discussed in Chapter 9. Can ABC be used in conjunction with standard costing? William Stammerjohan (2001) is sure this can be done. We will see in the later chapter on standard costing that one dimension of the analysis depends on the segregation of the fixed and variable elements in the budget. This goes against one of the basic foci of ABC. But we will see in the chapter on standard costing, if we can bypass the problem somehow.

### ABC and Product Mix Decisions

ABC can surely be of use to take product mix decisions. But it would be wiser to use it for long-term decisions. Such decisions may involve major shifts in the structure of facilities and manpower and may merge with capital investment decisions.

## WHEN TO AND WHEN NOT TO USE ABC

In conclusion, the use of ABC would be strongly recommended when the following conditions are met:

1. The first condition is that the incidence of indirect costs should be very high with reference to direct costs. Thus even in a techno-logically advanced and modern organization such as Hindustan Lever Limited, the products are dominated by direct costs (mostly material) and even with availability of the most up-to-date computer software, they do not have to have the multiplicity of cost pools as envisaged in ABC. Accuracy in costing need not always mean increasing the indirect cost pools using ABC. It can also be achieved by a more thorough examination of the process of tracing direct costs so that a larger portion of indirect costs are identified as direct costs.

2. The introduction of ABC should substantially alter the overhead distribution between the products. This would be the case when the products are extremely heterogeneous in the use of activity centres. One can make a rough sensitivity analysis to see if increasing the activity centres changes the cost pattern.

3. Measurement problems should not be tortuous and expensive as to make the whole exercise cost ineffective.

4. Lastly, ABC analysis needs much greater effort than the traditional systems and further it focuses sharply on inefficiencies in the crevices of the organization all over. This results in hostility to introduction of the system. It has to be consciously overcome by education and persuasion.

## SUMMARY

If there are great difficulties in tracing direct costs to products in an economically feasible way and if indirect costs are a very high proportion of total costs of the product, there may be a prima facie case for having a multiplicity of indirect cost pools to allocate costs. The use of a large number of indirect cost pools maybe described as activity-based costing (ABC). The cost benefits of this multiplicity of cost pools needs to be verified before introducing the ABC system. ABC in manufacturing sector effectively uses real time computer packages. Automated real-time systems hooked on to machines and production plans and routing and scheduling programmes are often used in this sector. These are more popular in Europe (called GPK) and Japan than in Anglo-Saxon countries. ABC is used extensively in merchandising and service sector for tracing sources of cost-ineffective activities and cost-ineffective products and services. In merchandising sector, time recording for activity is not always done for the individual actual activity but the budgeted total time can be compared with total available time, enabling both control and an estimate of the process costs. Often inventory valuation is not done with ABC figures but by the more traditional cost systems. The impact of batch set-up costs and batch size on product cost is one of the most important contributions of ABC analysis. ABC's focus is on long-term decisions of pricing, cost reduction, and product mix and does not emphasize on the segregation of fixed costs and variable costs, which is crucial for short-term decisions. Accuracy of costing need not always use ABC; it may well lie in the process of tracing direct costs to the product. ABC systems need much greater managerial effort than traditional systems and are more effective in spotting inefficiencies in grass root level operations and, therefore, invite some hostility in implementation.

## KEY POINTS

- Activity-based costing (ABC) identifies activities of an organization that represent the resources used by its products and services.
- Work sampling involves making a large number of random observations on output and activity levels of the job. These observations are used to determine the number and type of steps for the job in normal operating mode.
- Cost hierarchy is a classification of costs into different cost pools depending on the difficulty in determining cause–effect relationships.

## CONCEPT REVIEW QUESTIONS

1. Does the ABC concept essentially deal with indirect costs or direct costs?
2. What is the reason for the tardy and hesitant adoption of ABC in non-manufacturing sectors?
3. Please explain GPK.
4. Is the primary focus of ABC on short-term or long-term decisions? What is the consequence of this focus?
5. What are the implications of ABC for set-up costs and batch size?
6. Explain the concept of work sampling and its use for ABC.
7. Why does Hindustan Lever not use ABC costing for its soaps, detergents, and cosmetic products?
8. What is the test one would apply for increasing or decreasing the number of indirect cost pools?
9. What is the approximate percentage of organizations who use ABC systems? Why do you think they are not rapidly increasing?
10. Are there some differences between US, Japan, and Germany in their preference to trace costs to product direct instead of allocating it via an indirect cost pool?

## NUMERICAL PROBLEMS

### 1. Bhaichara Bank

Bhaichara Bank has recently had a spurt of increased business as it gives many services free of cost to those who choose to be covered under their Bhaichara scheme that means brotherhood scheme. The members of the scheme were expected to keep a minimum balance of ₹1000. The management of Bhaichara Bank believed that the scheme was successful as it yielded a spread of 3 per cent being the difference between the interest they pay to the members and the interest they receive on the loans they make on the scheme. If a member had a balance of ₹2000, it gave the bank a gross profit of ₹60 per annum. But this does not take into account the other administrative costs. They had a group of young MBAs who did their summer project with them for ascertaining these costs through work sampling. They also checked three representative account holders—Mrs Malati, Mr Punja, and Mr Prahlad. The results of their findings are shown as follows:

| | ABC cost per transaction (₹) | Malati usage | Punja usage | Prahlad usage |
|---|---|---|---|---|
| Deposit/withdrawal teller | 2.50 | 40 | 50 | 5 |
| Deposit/withdrawal ATM | 0.80 | 10 | 20 | 16 |
| Prearranged withdrawal | 0.50 | 0 | 12 | 60 |
| Bankers cheques issued | 8 | 9 | 3 | 2 |
| Foreign currency draft | 12 | 4 | 1 | 6 |
| Inquiries about balance | 1.50 | 10 | 18 | 9 |
| **Average balance in 2003 (₹)** | | **1100\*** | **800\*** | **25,000\*** |

\* Assume the balance of Malati and Prahlad were always above ₹1000 and Punja always below ₹1000.

## Questions

1.1 Compute the profitability of Malati, Punja, and Prahlad.

1.2 Would you recommend some changes in the scheme? Why or why not?

2. **Friendly Credit Cards**

Friendly Credit Cards, introduced in India by the Richmond Bank of the US, was adopted across the country. It enables cardholders to buy goods and services on credit. The bank pays the sellers and recovers the money from the cardholders. The bank allows a month's credit to its cardholders. As part of their promotion policy, the bank has inducted some members in the lifetime promotion programme. They will not pay any annual service charges as long as they use the cards at least twice a year. Let us call one such lifetime customer 'B'. The bank has a special scheme of zero annual fees for students in prestigious universities. Let us call one such student 'D'. The bank charges interest to the outstanding overdue at 19 per cent per annum, wherein overdue means due for more than a month. Since the bank has to borrow the money to finance the purchases, it has to pay an interest of 10 per cent per annum. The spread between the two is 9 per cent per annum. That is, if the outstanding is ₹2000 it will gain ₹180 per annum. The bank also receives commission of 2 per cent from the retail merchants. Unfortunately due to some debts turning out bad, they have to make a provision of 0.5 per cent. This makes a net gain of 1.5 per cent on purchases made by their card. If we deduct the amount of interest the bank pays of one month credit it provides at the rate 10 per cent per annum (0.83 per cent per month), the net benefit on purchases is 1.50 minus 0.83 per cent = 0.67 per cent.

Timely receipt of payments yields the bank this gain of 0.67 per cent, whereas defaulters get them a 9 per cent gain per annum on the defaulted overdue amounts and the period for which they are overdue. Recently, a gambling outfit was offering to advance ₹500 to its cardholders. It is estimated that this would be highly profitable as it will give them high volume of business with practically no transaction costs even if there was a little apprehension of the possibility of bad debts. A summer trainee from a business school estimated the following transaction costs:

Each customer transaction costs ₹0.50. Each customer enquiry for balance costs ₹5. Replacing a lost card costs ₹120. Annual cost of maintaining an account is ₹108. As against these costs the only charge, if at all it is levied, is the annual fee; B and D are exempted from this and only A and C pay. The summer trainees were asked to collect data on A, B, C, and D and present it. This is given in the following table.

| | A | B | C | D |
|---|---|---|---|---|
| Annual retail purchase (₹) | 80,000 | 26,000 | 34,000 | 8000 |
| No. of purchases transactions | 800 | 520 | 272 | 200 |
| Annual fee (₹) | 50 | 0 | 50 | 0 |
| Average overdue balance (₹) | 6000 | 0 | 50 | 0 |
| No. of inquiries at bank | 6 | 12 | 8 | 2 |
| Credit card replacement | 0 | 2 | 1 | 0 |

## Questions

2.1 Compute the consumer profitability.

2.2 Describe the profile of a profitable cardholder and an unprofitable cardholder.

2.3 Should Richmond Bank charge for bank inquiries and card replacement?

2.4 Richmond was wondering if they should withdraw the cards from unprofitable customers. What if they did not?

2.5 Should they accept the proposal of the gambling outfit? What are the issues connected with this proposal?

## 3. Student Cooperative Bank of Badami

The alumni of the Badami Institute of Management ran a cooperative bank. They needed to fix its service charge and wished to install an

ATM facility, if they could save money. They used work sampling methods to study the situation. They took random observations of the work being done over three days. Of the 100 observations they made in the three days work, 20 were of the manual system of cheques cashing, 10 of cash deposit, 20 of fixed deposits, 10 of new account opening, 10 of attending to balance enquiry, 10 of preparing accounts statements, and in the balance 20, the staff were idle. The hours of work were seven hours per day, which means 1260 minutes for three days. The cost per minute of an assistant was ₹1.28. In these three days, 60 cheques were cashed, 30 cash deposits made, 30 fixed deposits made, 10 new accounts were opened, 10 balance enquiries were entertained, 30 balance statements were made. An ATM installation would cost ₹100 per day and this could do away with the manual work of cashing cheques.

## Questions

3.1 Calculate the cost of each one of these services.

3.2 Is it worth introducing an ATM? Should there be any non-financial consideration for installing an ATM?

### 4. Pondicherry Delight

Pondicherry Delight was a new concept in India of large-scale manufacture of cakes. It was established by a French couple settled down in the Auroville campus of Pondicherry. They started in 2002 with only one product—Pondicherry plain. They used normal costing for their cost estimation. In 2005 they introduced a new product—Auroville Special. They budgeted for making 1600 kg of plain cake and 400 kg of Auroville, totalling to 2000 kg. They budgeted the material cost at ₹90/kg for plain and ₹140/kg for Auroville and labour cost at ₹14/kg for plain and ₹20/kg for Auroville. They budgeted the overhead at ₹1,60,000. As the year was progressing, the sale of plain did not catch up with the budget. On the other hand, demand for the newly introduced product Auroville spurted up. At the end of the year, it was seen that plain sold 1200 kg but Auroville sold 800 kg. Thus the total remained 2000 kg. The overhead went up to ₹1,77,670. The material and labour cost/kg remained as in the budget. Francoise, the daughter of the family and a management graduate, felt that probably the plain cake is overpriced and Auroville underpriced and that could explain the pattern of demand. The basic data she collected is as follows.

| Activity | Measure of activity | Cost/rate (₹) | Quantity of activity | Plain quantity | Auroville quantity |
|---|---|---|---|---|---|
| Mixing | Labour hours | 8 | 1240 | 700 | 540 |
| Cooking | Oven hours | 25 | 500 | 250 | 250 |
| Cooling | Cool room hours | 20 | 1400 | 800 | 600 |
| Creaming | Machine hours | 25 | 2450 | 0 | 2450 |
| Packaging | Packaging | 12 | 5500 | 2600 | 2900 |

## Questions

4.1 What is the cost/kg of plain cake and Auroville cake, assuming that the normal costing method is followed?

4.2 What is the cost/kg if Pondicherry Delight followed the ABC system using actual overheads that were used for deriving the cost unit activity in the table?

4.3 List the reasons why the overheads might have gone up over the budget. Would this surprise have been there if the budgeting had also been done on ABC?

4.4 Would you recommend Pondicherry Delight to follow the traditional system or the ABC system?

5. **Bhattacharya and Bhattacharya**

Bhattacharya and Bhattacharya (B & B) is a firm of legal consultants at Kolkata, which had two clients, Purulia Quarries and Burdwan Plastics. They charge the clients on actual cost plus a margin. Purulia Quarries were unhappy with the charges even if B&B thought they were charging the actual with reasonable mark-up. B&B had been charging direct costs at ₹70/professional labour hour and indirect costs at ₹105/labour hour. That is, it totalled to ₹175/hour. The last month's labour hours were 104 hrs for Purulia Quarries and 96 hours for Burdwan Plastics. B & B asked a trainee manager to attempt analyse the current month's indirect costs of ₹21,000 and to see if any part of it could be identified as direct costs.

| Direct costs | Purulia Quarries (₹) | Burdwan Plastics (₹) |
|---|---|---|
| Contract labour | 1200 | 3400 |
| Computer charges | 500 | 1500 |
| Travel expenses | 500 | 5000 |
| Telephone/telex | 200 | 1000 |
| Photocopy | 250 | 800 |
| Total (₹) | 2650 | 11,700 |

They came out with the analysis as in the following table and reported that out of ₹21,000 shown as indirect costs, ₹14,350 were actually direct costs.

## Questions

5.1 What would be the charge to the two clients following the old system of costing?

5.2 If you use the newly found data and identify ₹14,350 as direct costs, remove it from the indirect cost pool, and allocate to the two parties using professional labour hours as the base, what would be the charge to the two parties?

5.3 Would ABC system using more indirect cost pools improve the accuracy of the costing and satisfy both their clients?

## 6. Joshi Calculators

Joshi Calculators of Pune in Maharashtra manufactured two types of calculators, a mathematical model and a financial model. Both the models had identical direct costs and same input–output relationship of indirect activity except that the batch size was smaller for the mathematical model and hence the inspection hours was double pro-rata (being proportional to the number of batches). The data is shown in the following table.

| | Mathematical | Financial |
|---|---|---|
| Production nos | 5000 | 10,000 |
| Direct material costs (₹) | 5,00,000 | 10,00,000 |
| Direct labour (₹) | 1,00,000 | 2,00,000 |
| Direct man labour hour units | 10,000 | 20,000 |
| Machine hours | 2500 | 5000 |
| No. of production runs | 50 | 50 |
| Inspection hours | 100 | 50 |

The combined overheads of Joshi Calculators were as follows:
Machining costs: ₹4,00,000
Set-up costs: ₹2,00,000
Inspection costs: ₹1,00,000

## Questions

6.1 What is the cost of the two calculators?

6.2 Why are the two calculators costing differently though they have the same raw material costs and the manufacturing processes are identical?

## 7. Shree Corporation

The new CEO of Shree Corporation wants to introduce an activity-based costing. He constituted a team which identified three cost pools, namely receiving, production, and distribution. The finance division provided the following figures of expenditure

|  | ₹ |
|---|---|
| Payroll | 24,00,000 |
| Administrative | 32,00,000 |
| Others | 10,00,000 |

The ABC team made a detailed analysis and made the following distribution of costs.

| Cost pools | Receiving | Production | Distribution | Total |
|---|---|---|---|---|
| Payroll costs | 10% | 60% | 30% | 100% |
| Administrative expenses | 20% | 40% | 40% | 100% |
| Other overheads | 20% | 50% | 30% | 100% |

The activity levels were identified as:

| Receiving | 100,000 man-hours |
|---|---|
| Production | 6,000 units |
| Distribution | 500 customers |

## Question

7.1 Calculate the activity rates for each cost pool.

## 8. Kedar & Co.

Kedar & Co. is a printing company based at Bangalore. It has an Activity Based Costing system. The main activities are Collecting Orders, Printing, and Binding & Distribution. The associated costs are ₹50,000, ₹120,000 and 72,000 respectively. The corresponding activity levels are 250 orders, 1200 machine hours and 6000 direct labour hours.

Job 24 involves direct materials cost of ₹1000 and 15 hours of direct labour at ₹20/hour. It involves 25 machine hours.

## Question

8.1 Calculate the cost of Job 24.

## 9. A manufacturing company

A manufacturing company wants to shift to activity-based costing system. Its CEO Ramesh and Chief Engineer Takur have recently attended a training session on ABC and were quite impressed. Ramesh called his CFO Raj and Chief Engineer Takur for a discussion. They discussed about specific items of expenditure to be brought under ABC.

(a) **Indirect labour costs: 440,000**   Raj wants to use direct labour-hours for allocating this overhead. Ramesh feels this should not be used as a measure of activity in an activity-based costing system. 'This is okay under the traditional systems, not under modern ABC concept,' he argued.

(b) **Fixed expenses: ₹678,000**   Takur feels that ABC has no role to play as far as fixed expenses are concerned. Ramesh is not sure but said, 'I think ABC is used for variable costs only.'

(c) **Overhead costs of SBU 'TINA' ₹1,37,200 (Turnover of TINA is ₹4 crores)**   Ramesh feels that ABC may not be used for TINA as its overhead costs are a low percentage of its total activity.

(d) **Idle capacity in finishing dept: ₹12,000**   Nobody is clear about this. Raj feels that costs of idle capacity should not be assigned. He could not explain it though.

(e) **Total overheads allocated under ABC: ₹22,45,000, but under earlier method it came to ₹27,54,000**   Ramesh advised Raj to see which items are omitted under ABC. 'You cannot have two figures under two systems,' he said.

## Question

9.1  Review each item of expenditure and give your views on the right treatment for each under ABC.

## PROJECT

Make a group of 4 or 5 students. Choose a multi-product organization, which, in your understanding, may benefit from ABC analysis. Briefly record in your notes why you think ABC may be useful in the organization. After visiting the unit, note the products manufactured by it and prepare a flow chart of the processes involved in the production. Use a computer package that you know to record it. Then again review if ABC would be useful in the unit. Now discuss with the management. Then prepare the cost/unit of one product both in traditional single or at the most two indirect cost pools. Re-prepare the same costs using ABC. Compare the results and present your recommendations.

| CASE STUDY 1 | New Age Bank |
| --- | --- |

Jugal Kishore, the Additional Managing Director of the New Age Bank, was contemplating his unfinished analysis of the Mangalore Baikampady branch and the Delhi Parliament Street branches. Karanth, his MD, had asked him to give him a report on these branches as one of the inputs for deciding the promotion of Ramamurthy of the Baikampady branch and Sahadev of the Parliament Street branches. Both of them had served as the managers of these two branches for three years now and it was considered fair to evaluate them. His unfinished analysis is presented in Tables CS 1(a)–(e).

**Table CS 1(a)**  Summary of Financial Results for 2003 in ₹Lakhs

| Income | Delhi | Mangalore |
| --- | --- | --- |
| Interest on deposits* | 45 | 20 |
| Interest on current/savings accounts* | 2 | 5 |
| Loans/cash credit* | 80 | 30 |
| Letters of credit | 7.2 | 9.6 |
| Demand draft | 1.92 | 2.16 |
| Gross Income | 136.12 | 66.76 |
| Expenses | | |
| Provision for non-performing assets | 1.6 | 0.9 |
| Brokerage | 18 | 0 |
| Salaries supervisory staff | 10 | 8 |
| Salaries others | 27.224 | 33.38 |
| Overheads | 27.224 | 20.028 |
| Total expenses | 84.048 | 62.308 |
| **Net Income** | **52.072** | **4.452** |

*Net of interest payable and interest receivable for corresponding funds both calculated at standard rates

**Table CS 1(b)**  Pattern of Deposits in ₹Lakh

| | Delhi | Mangalore |
| --- | --- | --- |
| Less than ₹1000 | 0 | 20 |
| ₹1000 < ₹10 lakh | 0 | 200 |
| >=₹10 lakh < 20 lakh | 0 | 50 |
| >=₹20 lakh < ₹50 lakh | 100 | 0 |
| >=₹50 lakh | 800 | 0 |
| **Total (₹lakh)** | **900** | **270** |

**Table CS 1(c)**    Pattern of Loans/Cash Credit in ₹Lakh

|  | Delhi | Mangalore |
|---|---|---|
| Up to ₹1 lakh | 0 | 10 |
| >₹1 lakh <= ₹10 lakh | 0 | 10 |
| >₹10 lakhs <= ₹20 lakh | 0 | 55 |
| >₹20 lakh <= ₹100 lakh | 0 | 300 |
| >₹100 lakh <= ₹300 lakh | 333.33 | 0 |
| **Total amount (₹lakh)** | 333.33 | 375 |

**Table CS 1(d)**    Work Sampling Data for Delhi

|  | Demand draft | Letter of credit | Deposit making | Savings/current account opening/closing | Savings/current account transactions | Inspection cash credit loan | Idle | Total |
|---|---|---|---|---|---|---|---|---|
| No. of observations | 18 | 28 | 0 | 50 | 40 | 20 | 100 | 256 |
| Total allocated hours including idle hours | ? | ? | ? | ? | ? | ? | 0 | 320 |
| Labour cost | ? | ? | ? | ? | ? | ? | 0 | ₹ 52,354* |
| Overhead | ? | ? | ? | ? | ? | ? | 0 | ₹ 52,354* |
| Total cost | ? | ? | ? | ? | ? | ? | 0 | ₹ 1,04,708 |
| Activity units | 36 | 28 | 0 | 10 | 200 | 4 |  |  |
| Cost/unit (₹) | ? | ? | ? | ? | ? | ? |  |  |

*52,354 × 52 (weeks) = ₹27.224 lakh {in Table CS 1(a)}

He had large gaps (shown by question marks) that need filling up. It showed the observations he had obtained in a week's work-sampling exercise. The work sampling could capture only the work done at the counters. He had also noted some observations on the two branches. They are as follows:

1. On the basis of the sample study, he found that at the Delhi branch, the time elapsed from the date of application for loan and its sanction

**Table CS 1(e)**   Work Sampling Data for Mangalore

| | Demand draft | Letter of credit | Deposit making | Savings/ current account opening/ closing | Savings/ current account transac- tions | Inspec- tion cash credit loan | Idle | Total |
|---|---|---|---|---|---|---|---|---|
| No. of obser- vations | 16 | 22 | 16 | 29 | 38 | 100 | 14 | 235 |
| Total allocated hours including idle hours | ? | ? | ? | ? | ? | ? | 0 | 520 |
| Labour cost | ? | ? | ? | ? | ? | ? | 0 | ₹ 64,192* |
| Overhead | ? | ? | ? | ? | ? | ? | 0 | ₹ 38,515* |
| Total cost | ? | ? | ? | ? | ? | ? | 0 | ₹ 1,02,707 |
| Activity units | 56 | 38 | 80 | 30 | 700 | 100 | | |
| Cost/unit (₹) | ? | ? | ? | ? | ? | ? | | |

*64,192 × 52 (weeks) = ₹33.38 lakh #38,515 × 52= 20.028 lakh (both in Table 6.10)

was one month, whereas it seemed to take four months in Baikampady. He roughly assessed that the time elapsed is not only important for customer satisfaction but it affected the costs. Every month's time lapsed after the initial one month invited much more attention of the supervisory staff and cost approximately ₹5000 per month extra for this. This was in addition to the initial cost of negotiating the loan, which was approximately ₹10,000. This work was done basically by the supervisory staff and was not captured in the work-sampling data in tables. In calculating the profitability of loans this additional cost has to be considered. The total costs have, however, been incorporated in the income statement in Table 6.10; only the allocation of this cost to the specific product line namely loans and cash credit has to take this into account. These costs are included in the supervisory salary of ₹10 lakh shown against the Delhi branch and ₹8 lakh against the Baikampady branch. Besides this activity, this ₹10 lakh and ₹8 lakh has also included other supervisory work.

2. Table 6.10 is self-explanatory. But he noted that the overheads were higher for the Delhi branch due to greater use of computers. He proposed to charge overhead cost on the basis of labour cost. He believed that the week's work sampled was fairly representative of the year's transactions, in both branches except the zero transaction at the Delhi branch for deposits, which had very few but heavy deposits. The deposit making and cashing was a rare event at the Delhi branch that operated through brokers. For the other activities if we apply the week's sample of activity and the corresponding time spent and multiply it by 52 being the number of weeks in the year, it would approximate to the year's results shown in the summary financial report.

3. He found that at the Baikampady branch the customers had to wait in a long queue before the tellers, whereas at the Delhi branch they had no reason to use the tellers as ATMs were available. Since he knew that an ATM requires only a cost ₹20,000 per month he had asked Ramamurthy why he had not initiated action for an ATM in his locality. Ramamurthy said that he thought opening ATMs was at the discretion of the head office and anyway the ATM had been franchized out to a third party. It would take away his business and could cause disaffection among his staff.

   Ramamurthy's observation that ATMs were franchized out and the decision is taken at the headquarters were correct, but he was a little disappointed that Ramamurthy did not respond to the problems of his customers who stood in long queues at the tellers.

   He, however, found that indifference to the working of the ATMs was quite widespread in his bank; ATMs not working or working wrongly did not immediately evoke reactions among the other managers of the bank as well.

4. Sahadev confidentially told him that he had excellent networking with government and the public sectors. He preferred to operate through the brokers as they managed to pay the government and public sector bosses under the table for giving preferential treatment to deposit with the New Age Bank.

5. Ramamurthy took seriously the mission statement of the bank that they would encourage small entrepreneurs. Sahadev did not seem to care particularly for this. Moreover, Baikampady was anyway close to small business geographically.

## Discussion Questions

1. Complete the blanks in the data (indicated by question marks).
2. Indicate the profitability of the different activities of each of the two branches.

| CASE STUDY 2 | Mudaliar Auto Parts |
| --- | --- |

Mudaliar Auto Parts was a Bangalore-based auto parts manufacturing unit. It had been started by Radhakrishna Mudaliar and was doing quite well till liberalization opened up the industry to widespread competition. Sales and profits started falling. Some products of Mudaliar had some unique features of quality where they could dictate the prices. But most of them had competition. Mudaliar thought their costing system needed to be reviewed and he felt a good management graduate may give him fresh ideas. Mudaliar employed Jayaram, an MBA. Jayaram went about collecting information about his cost and activity centres. He identified action centres as stamping, assembly, die casting, machining, and grinding. He believed these centres should charge the product on labour hours used in the operation. He computed cost per hour including overhead. He got all the other overheads of the factory loaded on to the action centres. He prepared his analysis of a few randomly chosen parts (A, B, C, and D) as shown in Table CS 2. All of them had a large volume of sales. The existing costing system had one overall overhead rate for the plant and charged it on the basis of direct labour hours used by the product. Jayaram was satisfied with the manner of collecting direct material and labour costs of the products.

Mudaliar was convinced that the present costing system needs to be changed. He did not wish to change anything unless his officers were convinced. He asked Jayaram to make a presentation. Mudaliar started with asking Iyer, the chief accountant. Iyer said, 'I have heard about all these ABC systems being talked about in management schools. It is all developed for big companies with computer facilities. It would be a waste of time to introduce it in our company. Where do we stop multiplying cost centres? Why complicate matters and increase our costs of costing? Jayaram found the tracing of material and labour costs to the products satisfactory. That should be enough. Jayaram is pleading for homogeneous cost pools. Homogeneity, my foot. No two processes, no two products are alike. If we have to have total homogeneity, we will have to have hundreds of indirect cost pools. Where do we draw the line?' Kapoor, the sales manager pointed out, 'If we have to use Jayaram's figures, we will have to increase the prices of B and D by a huge margin. I cannot sell these products at that price.' Mudaliar countered, 'If you think prices have to be fixed by ascertaining costs first, don't you think Jayaram's figures have to be considered?' Kapoor said, 'Prices are not set by seeing cost data. It is competition that determines the prices.' Mudaliar argued, 'But in some products we have no competition as our quality is far superior.'

**Table CS 2**  Mudaliar Auto Parts

### (a) Existing method

|   | Labour hours | Cost hour (₹) | Total cost (₹) |   |   |
|---|---|---|---|---|---|
| A | 0.45 | 8 | 3.6 |   |   |
| B | 0.47 | 8 | 3.76 |   |   |
| C | 1.5 | 8 | 12 |   |   |
| D | 1 | 8 | 8 |   |   |

### (b) Proposed method

| A |   |   |   |   |   |
|---|---|---|---|---|---|
| Stamping | 0.15 | 8 | 1.2 |   |   |
| Assembly | 0.3 | 5 | 1.5 |   |   |
| Total | 0.45 |   | 2.7 |   |   |
| **B** |   |   |   |   |   |
| Die casting | 0.25 | 14 | 3.5 |   |   |
| Machining | 0.22 | 10 | 2.2 |   |   |
| Total | 0.47 |   | 5.7 |   |   |
| **C** |   |   |   |   |   |
| Grinding | 0.7 | 8 | 5.6 |   |   |
| Machining | 0.3 | 10 | 3 |   |   |
| Assembly | 0.5 | 5 | 2.5 |   |   |
| Total | 1.5 |   | 11.1 |   |   |
| **D** |   |   |   |   |   |
| Die casting | 0.25 | 14 | 3.5 |   |   |
| Stamping | 0.25 | 8 | 2 |   |   |
| Machining | 0.35 | 10 | 3.5 |   |   |
| Assembly | 0.15 | 5 | 0.75 |   |   |
| Total | 1 |   | 9.75 |   |   |

### (c) Comparison of cost

|   |   | A | B | C | D |
|---|---|---|---|---|---|
| Present |   | 3.6 | 3.76 | 12 | 8 |
| Proposed |   | 2.7 | 5.7 | 11.1 | 9.75 |
| Variation |   | −0.9 | 1.94 | −0.9 | 1.75 |

Balusubramanian said, 'I think we are doing fine with the present system. Moreover, I do not control costs by seeing cost reports. I control them by personal visits to the factory and making sure that productivity is maintained.' Mudaliar said, 'If you all feel this way about Jayaram's system, I will not change the old system.' In spite of this hostility of his senior executives, Mudaliar decided that he should have a firm of consultants to examine Jayaram's proposal. Assume that you are appointed as the consultant and answer the following questions.

### Discussion Questions

1. Do you feel that the difference between the old and new systems is significant?
2. Which system of costing is correct?
3. How would you think Mudaliar should proceed further?
4. Why do you think the executives were hostile to Jayaram's ideas?

| CASE STUDY 3 | Diamond Computers |
| --- | --- |

Diamond computers were computer hardware manufacturers in Chennai. They made custom-made products. They employed cost accountants to ascertain the cost of their products. But many of the traditional wisdom in product costing seemed to need modification in the product lines of the company. Typically they found that every single component sometimes took enormous time to be spotted in the market, a lot of time in developing the know-how and fixing the specifications. The cost of procurement of a component had no relation to its price. Thus, the normal practice in industry of charging a flat purchase overhead as percentage of the value of the purchase would have distorted the costs. The overhead would seem to require a charge per component. Even if we used an average charge for this purpose, it would have led to less distortion. These peculiarities resulted in Diamond computers deciding activity centres and the basis of their charges to be decided by team consensus—the team having persons from different functional areas. The ascertainment of direct costs was not very difficult. But the overheads did pose a problem. They could not use the standard packages used by other manufacturing industries. The teams decided that several activity centres could be considered. They could not follow the GPK practices of huge number of such centres. They decided they would have only 10 key activities and concentrate on this.

**Discussion Questions**

1. Was it a good idea to have decisions on activity centres taken by a multi-functional team?
2. Was it a good strategy to limit activity centres to only 10 in number?
3. Do you think conventional job costing system could have served Diamond computers better?

## CHAPTER 7

# Responsibility Accounting and Budgeting

## Learning Objectives

After reading this chapter, you will be able to understand

- the concept of responsibility accounting and the matrix of ties of accountability that bind in an organization
- the distinction and the relatedness between product and process costing and responsibility accounting
- the variations in the responsibility ranging from cost (expense) to revenue, profits, and investments
- the four levers of control and budgets as some

- of the key instruments for effective responsibility accounting
- the budgeting process and the key factors, the administrative machinery, and the structure and content of budgets
- the difference between discretionary costs and engineered costs in budget formulation and in evaluation
- the limitations of and behavioural distortions triggered by some standard budgetary practices

## INTRODUCTION

**Responsibility accounting**
It concentrates on the 'who' aspect of the organizational functioning.

Chapter 1 explained that the basic objective of management accounting is to optimally apply resources to products and services. Chapter 3 explained not only how management accounting would show the ways to identify and assign the costs of the resources but also who controls the processes that use these resources. The intertwining of these two complementary instruments used by management accountants has been depicted in Table 3.3 in Chapter 3.

We can describe the former as the 'what' and 'how' of costing and the latter as the 'who' of it. Chapters 4, 5, 6 and several later chapters in the book concentrate on the 'what' and 'how' aspects of management accounting. But this chapter and Chapters 8 and 9 give prominence to the 'who' aspects of management accounting.

But throughout the book both aspects are discussed conjointly as in all management accounting literature. This chapter introduces the basic aspects of responsibility accounting. But ramifications of these are complex in large organizations and in multinationals. They are dealt with in later chapters.

## RESPONSIBILITY ACCOUNTING

Whereas the concept of responsibility accounting and reporting and its meaning and objective would be dealt with in some depth later in the chapter and will be expanded further in later chapters, a simple preview of the ideas is given at this stage. Since any organization with a typical pyramidal chart shows the lines of responsibility and these responsibilities would need appropriate accounting information, the structure of such accounting information is responsibility accounting. This accounting information would be incomplete without a description of inputs provided to those responsible and outputs they produced. The nature of accounting information and the inputs and outputs would have to suit the nature of such a responsibility centre (Hansen and Mowen 2007). These will be described later in the chapter. Responsibility may be collective as in 'department' or may be individualized, which is often the case in modern organizations.

The arrangement among other things presumes the assessment of the contribution of that responsibility towards the strategic goals and objectives of the organization. This tenuous relationship may be quite hard to establish at every stage of evaluation. The first step of this is described in this chapter but would be clearer in later chapters, particularly Chapter 16 on balanced scorecards.

## ACCOUNTABILITY IN ORGANIZATIONS

**Accountability in organizations**
It may be seen as a social contract governed either by hierarchy or market-driven forces.

The other word for responsibility is accountability. The modern concept of accountability has a strong element of empowerment and democracy. These are succinctly summarized by the term social contract. These are captured by inter-relationships shown in Fig. 7.1. Box 1 of Fig. 7.1 shows that everyone could have expectations from others in the organization. Box 2 shows how they get settled whether it be driven by market-oriented systems or hierarchy-oriented systems (these two expressions are explained a little later in the paragraph), but it gets converted to a social contract in Box 2. Because the social contract is settled, there could be the question of accountability as shown in Box 3. The terms markets and hierarchy were coined by the economist Oliver Williamson (1975) and need explanation. It is more commonly understood that the members of an organization are

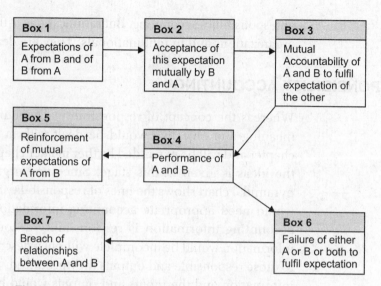

**Fig. 7.1** Accountability as governed by expectations
*Source*: Sekhar 2005

enabled to work together for a common purpose of optimizing the use of its resources by a fiat from the top. Such an arrangement could be roughly described as a social contract driven by hierarchical system. On the other hand, they can hope to work for a common purpose if they are individuals or members of a departmental group, working as if they are in an open market for their own profits. This is labelled by Williamson as *market systems of control.* We will mostly deal with the former situation in this chapter and briefly allude to the latter.

# RESPONSIBILITY CENTRES

We will reiterate what we said in Chapter 3 about responsibility centres (see Fig. 7.2):

Responsibility centres emerge out of organizational structures that are intended to bring in accountability to the functioning of managers. Responsibility is aligned with accountability and is described in terms of both work to be done by the responsibility centre and its corresponding financial provision.

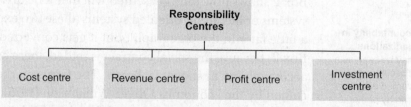

**Fig. 7.2** Types of responsibility centres

| Cost centre | Revenue centre |
|---|---|
| Raw material variance<br>Labour variance<br>overhead variance | Sales price variance<br>Sales quantity variance<br>Sales mix variance |

| Profit centre | Investment centre |
|---|---|
| Gross profit<br>Contribution margin | Return on investment<br>Residual income<br>Economic value added |

**Fig. 7.3**  Responsibility centre evaluation model

Figure 7.3 shows the responsibility centre evaluation model.

One has to be aware all the time that the information for taking decisions on products and services, crucial as it is, has to be distinguished from the information required for enforcing accountability. The former would be labelled as product or process costing, indicating the resources used by a product or process. As stated earlier in the chapter, one may describe it as the 'what' or 'how' of costing. The latter, on the other hand, would show the resources used by the person responsible for the product and process and is accountable for its results. One or more persons may be responsible for a product or a process. That person may or may not be responsible for the ultimate product or process decisions and may only be implementing decisions made by others and serve as one link in the chain of activities. In short, this concerns the 'who' of costing and could be labelled as *accountability*.

Let us illustrate this differentiation with an example. Assume that an organization has two departments A and B headed by a supervisor. The organization changes this overheads of the central unit on the basis of the investments made in each department. Example 7.1 shows the cost departmentwise.

According to Horngren et al. (2003),

**Responsibility centres**
They can be cost (expense) centres, revenue centres, profit centres, or investment centres.

'Each manager, regardless of the level is a responsibility center. A responsibility center is a part, segment, or sub-unit of an organization whose manager is accountable for a specified set of activities. The higher the manager's level, broader the responsibility center and, generally, larger the number of his subordinates.'

Thus, a responsibility centre is not just an accounting concept but a generalized management concept. Nevertheless, since every activity that has a target or physical goal has to be performed within a financial constraint, every responsibility centre has a related dimension of responsibility accounting.

## Example 7.1 Product Cost and Responsibility Cost

| Departments | Department A | Department B | Total |
|---|---|---|---|
| Direct costs ₹/unit | 10 | 15 | 25 |
| Overheads in departmental control (₹) | 5 | 3 | 8 |
| Overhead not in departmental control (₹) | 10 | 12 | 22 |
| Total (₹) | 25 | 30 | 55 |

Costs for accountability would be ₹15 for Department A and ₹18 for Department B and ₹22 for the central unit. But the product costing information would cover all of the ₹55. One must remember the targets for these numbers could be handed over from the central authority or be determined by common consent. It should be obvious that product and process costing is not divorced from accountability and is in fact intertwined with it. Well-designed costing systems generate information for both the needs with ease and at minimum cost as would be evident from the typical illustration in Example 7.1. Organizational structures are skeletal arrangements of the lines of responsibility and are clothed with detailed understanding of expectations from the different managers.

## Types of Responsibility Centres

There are four types of responsibility centres:

**Cost centres or expense centres** A manager is expected to perform a specified task within a specified cost or expense. This can be spelt out either as a lump sum for a specified period or as the cost or expense for a unit of corresponding specified physical activity. A manager is expected to perform a specified task within a specified cost or expense. This can be spelt out either as a lump sum for a specified period or as the cost or expense for a unit of corresponding specified physical activity.

A cost centre is a responsibility centre in which inputs, but not outputs, are measured in monetary terms. Responsibility accounting is based on financial information relating to inputs (costs) and outputs (revenues).

In a cost centre of responsibility, the accounting system records only the cost incurred by the centre but the revenues earned (outputs) are excluded. An expense centre measures financial performance in terms of cost incurred by it. A manager's performance can be evaluated on the basis of raw material variance, labour variance, and overhead variance from budgeted costs. Many companies offer good incentives to the mangers on cutting down the cost of their respective divisions. This not only motivates managers but also helps in utilizing the material efficiently and henceforth reduces waste.

**Revenue centres**   A manager is expected to garner specified gross revenue within a period or revenue for unit sales. Revenue centres are departments or divisions that have direct interaction with consumers to sell goods and services. For example, rooms depart-ment and food-and-beverages department of a hotel are its revenue centres. Companies prepare projected budgets and forecast financial goals for revenue centres; these goals typically are reviewed periodically to determine favourable or unfavourable vari-ances and to make corrections to revenue centre operations. A manager's performance can be evaluated on the basis of sale price variance; sale quantity variance, and sales mix variance from budgeted costs.

**Profit centres**   The manager is accountable for both revenues and costs as well as expenses. A centre in which both the inputs and outputs are measured in monetary terms is called a profit centre. In other words both costs and revenues of the centre are accounted for. Since the difference between revenues and costs is termed as profit, this centre is called the profit centre. In a centre, there are financial measures of the outputs as well as of the inputs. It is possible to measure the effectiveness and efficiency of performance in financial terms. Profit analysis can be used as a basis for evaluating the performance of a divisional manager, a profit centre as well as additional data regarding revenues. Therefore, the management can determine whether the division was effective in attaining its objectives. This objective is presumably to earn a 'satisfactory profit'. The concept of divisional profit is referred to as 'profit contribution' since it is the amount of profit contribution coming directly from the division.

The performance of the managers is measured by profit. In other words managers can be expected to behave as if they were running their own business. For this reason, the profit centre is a good training for general management responsibility.

**Investment centres**   A manager is accountable for investment, revenues, and costs. One can consider them as a special case of profit centres.

It is commonly known as the DuPont return on investment (ROI) model (Fig. 7.4). This model consists of a margin subcomponent (Operating Profit/Sales) and a turnover subcomponent (Sales/Invested Capital). These two

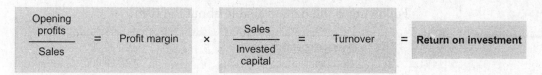

**Fig. 7.4**   DuPont return on investment model

subcomponents can be multiplied to arrive at the ROI. Thus, ROI = (Operating Profit/Sales) × (Sales/Invested Capital). ROI can be reduced to a much simpler formula: Operating Profit/Invested Capital.

## Return on Investment vs Residual Income

### Return on investment

The performance of each investment centre is measured by using a variety of tools some of which are briefly discussed as under:

Total returns are divided by total invested capital. For example, in 2010, the returns (Operating Profit) were ₹1,20,00,000 while investments were ₹4,00,00,000 and the ROI being 30% (1,20,00,000/4,00,00,000). Suppose the company has benchmarked a minimum required rate of return as 25%. ROI comes out to be greater than minimum rate of return required by the company.

### Residual income (RI)

It is the net operating income which an investment centre earns over and above the minimum required return on its operating assets. Like ROI, RI is another approach to measuring an investment centre's performance.

$$\text{Residual Income} = \text{NOPAT} - \text{Required profit}$$
$$= \text{NOPAT} - \text{Cost of capital} \times \text{Investment}$$
$$= \text{NOPAT} - \text{Cost of capital} \times (\text{Total assets} - \text{Non-interest bearing current liabilities})$$

where NOPAT is Net Operating Profit After Taxes.

Residual income (RI) overcomes the underinvestment problem of ROI since any investment earning more than the cost of capital will increase the residual income.

Though ROI and RI have the same roots and results, RI proves to be better in certain circumstances as follows:

The company XYZ Ltd had been using ROI measure to evaluate the Investment Centre Manager. The director of the company wants to compare both ROI and residual income measure of investment centre.

Following is the data available about the firm:

| | |
|---|---|
| Average operating assets | ₹20,00,000 |
| Net operating income | ₹5,00,000 |
| Minimum required rate of return | 15% |

Since the company has invested ₹20,00,000 in the division in the form of operating assets, the company should be able to earn at least ₹3,00,000 (15% × ₹20,00,000) on this investment. Since the division's net operating income is ₹5,00,000, the residual income above and beyond the minimum required return is ₹20,00,000. If residual income is adopted as the performance measure to replace ROI, the manager of the division would be evaluated based on the growth in residual income from year to year.

**Return on investment vs residual income**

| Performance measure | | ROI | Residual income |
|---|---|---|---|
| Average operating assets (a) | | ₹20,00,000 | ₹20,00,000 |
| Net operating income (b) | | ₹5,00,000 | ₹5,00,000 |
| ROI (b/a) | | 25% | |
| Minimum required rate of return (c) | 15% | | ₹3,00,000 |
| Residual income (b–c) | | | ₹2,00,000 |

## Performance evaluation using residual income return on investment

Suppose the manager wants to purchase a new equipment. The equipment would cost ₹3,00,000 and is expected to generate additional operating income of ₹65,000 a year. From the stand point of the company, this would be a good investment since it promises a rate of return of 21.7% [(₹65,000/₹3,00,000) × 100], which is in excess of the company's minimum required rate of return of 15%.

**Performance evaluation using return on investment**

| | Present | New project | Overall |
|---|---|---|---|
| Average operating assets (a) | ₹20,00,000 | ₹3,00,000 | ₹23,00,000 |
| Net operating income (b) | ₹5,00,000 | ₹65,000 | ₹5,65,000 |
| ROI (b/a) | 25% | 21.7% | 24.6% |

The new project reduces the ROI from 25% to 24.6%. This happens because the 21.7% rate of return on the new machine, while above the company's 15% minimum rate of return, is below the division's present ROI of 25%. Therefore, the new equipment would tow the division's ROI down even though it would be a good investment from the perspective of the company as a whole. If the manager of the division is evaluated based on ROI, he would be hesitant to even propose such an investment.

## Performance evaluation using residual income

Since the project would increase the residual income of the division, the manager would want to invest in the new machine.

The key reason for preferring residual income measure over return on income is that managers view new investment under the two performance measurement schemes. The residual income approach encourages managers to make investments that are profitable for the entire company but that would be rejected by managers who evaluate using ROI formula. Basically, a manager whose evaluations are based on ROI will reject any project whose rate of return is below the division's current ROI even if the rate of return on the project is above the minimum rate of return for the entire company. In contrast, any project whose rate of return is above the minimum required rate of return of the company will result in an increase in residual income. Since it is in the best interest of the company as a whole to accept any project whose rate of return is above the minimum rate of return, managers who are evaluated on residual income will tend to make better decisions concerning investment projects than managers who evaluate using ROI.

**Performance Evaluation using Residual Income**

|  | Present | New project | Overall |
|---|---|---|---|
| Average operating assets | ₹20,00,000 | ₹3,00,000 | ₹23,00,000 |
| Net operating income | ₹5,00,000 | ₹65,000 | ₹56,5000 |
| Minimum required rate of return | ₹3,00,000 | ₹45,000 | ₹3,45,000 |
| Residual income | ₹2,00,000 | ₹20,000 | ₹2,20,000 |

**Economic value added (EVA)**   Economic value added concentrates only on one of the factors of production, that is, capital. It measures surplus value created by total investments which include funds provided by banks, bondholders, and shareholders. It is more useful than the rate of return (ROI) in evaluating operations of an enterprise.

EVA = NOPAT − (WACC × Invested capital)
EVA = NOPAT − Capital charge
  = [NOPAT/Invested capital − WACC] × Invested capital

NOPAT = Net operating profit after taxes, which is the profit after depreciation and taxes, but before interest, WACC = Cost of capital to a firm is the opportunity cost to investors for investing in the firm.

Value of a firm = Invested capital + Present value of projected EVA

EVA is the residual income after charging the company for the cost of capital provided by lenders and shareholders. It represents the value added to the shareholders by generating operating profits in excess of the cost of capital employed in the business.

Let us now look at Example 7.2 to see how a typical task of a responsibility centre looks like.

## Example 7.2  Different Types of Responsibility Centres

1. In March 2009, the factory manager is expected to produce 3000 units of good quality X all for ready dispatch to the customer by 31 March 2009 at a maximum cost of ₹15,00,000 with no overtime payment to workers. With one month's notice they should produce 6000 units on similar stipulations at a maximum cost of ₹24,00,000. The production manager's cost will include the charge of ₹5,00,000—the expenses of the maintenance department, ₹2,00,000—the expenses of the personnel department, and the purchasing cost 2 per cent of the cost of material used by them and will receive good quality of raw material at the time specified in the schedule supplied by them at the cost of ₹12 per kg.
2. The maintenance manager is expected to keep the machines in working condition for 80 per cent of a single shift operation at a cost of ₹5,00,000 in March 2009 which is the exact amount also figuring in the production manager's costs.
3. The personnel manager was expected to ensure that labour costs per shift was pegged in March 2009 to a figure of ₹100 per man shift. They will ensure there will be no strike or go-slow in this period. For this purpose their budget will be ₹2,00,000.
4. The purchase manager will be expected to procure good quality raw material at a maximum price of ₹12 per kg and have the raw material delivered in time as per consumption schedule provided to them. For this purpose they will not spend more than 2 per cent of the cost of raw material as their departmental expenses.
5. The sales manager would be expected to sell 3000 units in March 2009 earning a minimum revenue of ₹22,00,000 and expected to collect the cash from its related debtors by 30 April 2009. For this they will spend a maximum amount of ₹1,00,000 as the department's selling expenses.
6. The CEO of the organization would be expected to make a profit of ₹5,00,000 after charging selling expenses and research and development expenses in March 2009 for which the CEO will get a 5 per cent of profit as commission.
7. The research and development manager will be expected to reduce the cost of production by fifty paise per unit for which they will get a monthly budget of ₹1,00,000. A review of their progress will be made every three months.

The actual descriptions of the tasks would be very much more complicated than in this simplistic example. But the meaning of responsibility centres/expense centres/revenue centres/profit centres would be clear from this.

## Hierarchy of Responsibility Centres

**ABC analysis**
It strengthens both
product costing and
responsibility costing.

Every responsibility centre could have a whole lot of cost centres and revenue centres under it as information or more details may be necessary for several other purposes, as will be clear from the paragraphs that follow. But an overall view will be available in Table 7.1 which is a reproduction of Table 3.3 of Chapter 3.

One can note that information for accountability and for decisions are intertwined and can be served quite well by a well designed and integrated accounting system as also shown in Table 7.1. Costs are equal to $C1+C2+C3+C4+C5+C6+C7+C8+C9+C10 = \sum C_n$ and Profit = Rev 1 – $\sum C$. But the responsibility of R1, R2, R3, R4, R5, R6 are separately ascertainable in financial and non-financial terms which include working harmoniously with the other responsibility centres. The reader may now refresh what was learnt in Chapter 3 and 6 on the need for the further break up of information along the lines of activities, which not only enables more accurate costing of the product or process but also enables more detailed delineation of responsibilities and accountability.

## Responsibility Centre Report

The information contained in a responsibility centre report is essential to monitor, control, and direct each business unit. The details and form of a performance report varies according to a particular organization and the nature of the responsibility centre. The reports shall provide a comparison between budgeted and actual data, with the difference being reported as a variance from budget. These performance reports should be consistent with the organizational structure of the firm.

Suppose Fast Food Pvt. Ltd, New Delhi, has 4 stores located at Rajouri Garden, Shadipur, Janakpuri, and Dwarka. Rajouri Gardens' performance report is very detailed, and it provides a basis for analysis of numerous features of the fast food business (Table 7.2). The report is 'specialized' to show the product mix proportions. The report provides sufficient detail to show if the objectives are being met.

The results for Rajouri Garden shows that the budgeted goal for Fast Food Pvt. Ltd sales was not met. But, the profit objectives were nevertheless exceeded because the product mix of garlic bread and pasta produced higher margins.

The Senior Manager of Store Operations is supposed to keep a check on whether each store is making profits. Underperforming stores are

**Table 7.1** The hierarchy of responsibility centres

| Profit centre | Grinder division divisional manager (Overall)–DM | | | | | | | | | | |
|---|---|---|---|---|---|---|---|---|---|---|---|
| Responsibility Decisions RD | Divisional Manager (Direct)–RD1 | | General Manager reporting to DM-RD2 | | | | | | Divisional Manager | Marketing Manager reporting to DM-RD4 (Direct) RD3 | |
| Responsibility Implementation R 1-6 | R & D Manager R1 | | Production Manager R2 | | Maintenance Manager R3 | | Purchase Manager R4 | | Personnel Manager R5 | Marketing and Sales Manager R6 | |
| Cost Centre C1–10 and Revenue Centres 1 (Grinder) | General Activity C1 | Project A C2 | Manufacture C3 | Packing C4 | Mechanical C5 | Electrical C6 | Ordering C7 | Inspection C8 | Personnel C9 | Selling and Distribution C10 | Revenue Rev 1 |

**Table 7.2**  Responsibility centre report

| Performance Report of Fast Food Pvt. Ltd, Rajouri Garden, New Delhi for the year ending 31 March 2011 | | | | | |
|---|---|---|---|---|---|
| | Actual results | | Budgeted results | | Variance |
| Particulars | % age of total sales | Total (₹) | % age of total sales | Total (₹) | Total (₹) |
| Sales: | | | | | |
| Pizza | 40 | 10,00,000 | 43 | 1,100,000 | (100,000)U |
| Garlic bread | 24 | 6,00,000 | 22 | 5,50,000 | 50,000 F |
| Pasta | 36 | 9,00,000 | 35 | 8,75,000 | 25,000 F |
| Total sales | 100 | 25,00,000 | 100 | 25,25,000 | (25,000)U |
| Variable expenses: | | | | | |
| Food cost | 19 | 4,75,000 | 20 | 5,05,000 | (30,000)U |
| Other variable cost | 7 | 1,75,000 | 8 | 2,02,000 | (27,000)U |
| Total variable cost | 26 | 6,50,000 | 28 | 7,07,000 | (57,000)U |
| Contribution margin | | 18,50,000 | | 18,18,000 | 32,000F |
| Less traceable fixed cost* | | 11,00,000 | | 11,00,000 | – |
| **Location margin** | | **7,50,000** | | **7,18,000** | **32,000F** |

* **Traceable fixed cost:** A traceable fixed cost is a fixed cost that is incurred because of the existence of a segment. If the segment had never existed, the fixed cost would not have been incurred; and if the segment were eliminated, the fixed cost would disappear.

identified, problems are studied, and corrective measures are taken. Very little attention is given to the profitable stores. It can be noticed in the performance report (Table 7.3) that there is ₹9,00,000 of fixed costs associated with store operations that are not traceable to any specific location; nevertheless, the Senior Manager of Store Operations must control this cost and it is subtracted while calculating the overall margin. Thus, the total fixed cost for all store operations is ₹57,00,000 (₹48,00,000 + ₹9,00,000). The Senior Manager should immediately pay attention to the Dwarka Store as it is currently incurring losses and the traceable cost associated with the Dwarka Store is needed to be examined and controlled.

**Table 7.3**  Store-based responsibility centre report

| Sales | Combined (₹) | Rajouri Garden | | Shadipur | | Janakpuri | | Dwarka | |
|---|---|---|---|---|---|---|---|---|---|
| | | % age of Total Sales | Total (₹) | % age of Total Sales | Total (₹) | % age of Total Sales | Total (₹) | % age of Total Sales | Total (₹) |
| Pizza | 38,84,000 | 40 | 10,00,000 | 45 | 9,45,000 | 42 | 1,13,400 | 35 | 8,05,000 |
| Garlic bread | 24,28,000 | 24 | 6,00,000 | 23 | 4,83,000 | 20 | 5,40,000 | 35 | 8,05,000 |
| Pasta | 32,88,000 | 36 | 9,00,000 | 32 | 6,72,000 | 38 | 10,26,000 | 30 | 6,90,000 |
| Total sales variable expenses | 96,00,000 | 100 | 25,00,000 | 100 | 21,00,000 | 100 | 27,00,000 | 100 | 23,00,000 |
| Food cost | 16,82,000 | 19 | 4,75,000 | 15 | 3,15,000 | 16 | 4,32,000 | 20 | 4,60,000 |
| Total variable cost | 25,65,000 | 26 | 6,50,000 | 22 | 4,62,000 | 24 | 6,48,000 | 35 | 8,05,000 |
| Contribution margin | 70,35,000 | | 18,50,000 | | 16,38,000 | | 20,52,000 | | 14,95,000 |
| Traceable fixed cost | 48,00,000 | | 11,00,000 | | 10,00,000 | | 12,00,000 | | 15,00,000 |
| Location margin | 22,35,000 | | 7,50,000 | | 6,38,000 | | 8,52,000 | | (5,000) |
| Common fixed cost | 9,00,000 | | | | | | | | |
| Store margin | 13,35,000 | | | | | | | | |

**Common fixed cost:** A common fixed cost is a fixed cost that supports the operations of more than one segment, but is not traceable in whole or in part to any one segment. Even if a segment were entirely eliminated, there would be no change in true common fixed cost.

## EFFECTIVE RESPONSIBILITY ACCOUNTING

In the paragraphs that follow we would be pursuing the multiple requirements for effective responsibility accounting which would be armed with proper delineation of responsibilities. Among other things, total managerial support would be required to enable the whole apparatus to function smoothly. The support would not be just an unstructured emotional one but also well considered and orchestrated in the several manners we will describe. It calls not only for desirable attitudes but also for desirable processes.

## The Four Levers of Control

**Accountability**
It is ensured by using one or more of the four levers of control: diagnostic systems, interactive systems, belief systems, or boundary systems.

The instruments for guiding accountability would be quite inadequate if they were only based on accounting numbers though much of accounting literature appeared to give that impression. The effective instruments, on the one hand, are far more complex and on the other hand, draw upon very simple traditional skills of social living used by any parent in keeping a family together or any ancient society to keep the community together. These are described as following 'ecological rationality' by the Nobel Laureate Vernon Smith (2003) and are categorized by Robert Simons (2000) in a simpler manner as the four levers of control—diagnostic systems, interactive systems, belief systems, and boundary systems.

*Diagnostic systems* usually require a set of achievements to be set for the organization and is followed through with a system which monitors the achievement. *Interactive systems* require constant interaction between the members of an organization, more particularly down the hierarchical levels. This helps in constant corrections to strategy and targets. *Belief systems* require the organization to build up some belief among the members of an organization so that they can be self-regulating. *Boundary systems* specify some prohibited behaviour which would call for severe penalty. One may realise that these instruments are precisely what all societies from time immemorial have been using for social cohesion and effective coordinated action.

## Participative Budgets

One of the most important instruments for helping to accountability and controls is the budget. 'A budget is (a) the quantitative expression of a proposed plan of action by management for a specified period and (b) an aid to coordinate of what needs to be done to implement the plan' (Horngren et al. 2003).

It is usually guided by a budget committee. It serves four purposes. It

1. compels strategic planning and a process for its implementation;
2. provides a set of expectations for performance for every manager;
3. motivates managers and employees; and
4. promotes communication and coordination among sub-units within the company.

These are the normative virtues of the instrument of budgeting. But, as actually practised, it has had severe critics, which we will deal with later in this chapter. Nevertheless, budgeting is widely used all over the world and its benefits seem to outweigh its problems.

# STRATEGY AND ITS RELATION TO BUDGETS

**Strategy**
Strategy as a well
thoughout plan of
action is the jumping
board for budgets.

The concept of strategy is too profound to be trivialized. But, it is obvious if we have to have budget to help an organization in a purposeful, coordinated fashion it would be important to tie it to a sign post which we may call a strategy. Simons (2000) notices enormous variations in the meaning of the word *strategy* and he suggests they could be of six categories:

1. Corporate strategy deals with the area of business of the organization.
2. Business strategy is concerned with the way to compete in defined product markets.
3. Strategy can just be a perspective or vision statement of sorts.
4. Strategy can be a position in the marketplace—how we create value for the customer or how we differentiate our products and services from our competitors.
5. Strategy as a plan will have performance goals.
6. Strategy can be a pattern of action.

Mintzberg et al. (1998) gives greater importance to the processes of arriving at a pattern of action as has been seen in category 6 of Simons' list rather than a formal document titled 'plan of action'. But we do not propose to deal with it in the book. This is dealt with extensively in the growing literature on the subject and summary of it could be seen in Chapters 10 and 11 of *Management Control Systems: Text and Cases* (Sekhar 2005). Suffice to indicate that Simons (2000) would consider this pattern of action as available to the managers who are in the process of making budgets. Leaving semantics alone, a strategy acquires its status as a strategy when reversing it would be expensive both in money and time. Nevertheless, we could still do the reversal if we find it is worthwhile. The pattern of action being embedded in the organization would guide them in the process of making budgets at every stage. This pattern of action is sometimes called a business plan. We would explain in the later part of the chapter that one of the great concerns of many organizations is that it should not be a straight jacket which stifles original thinking and innovation.

# THE BUDGETING PROCESS

The process by which one could arrive at the operating budget could be developed as shown in Fig. 7.5 for business organizations. The budgets of

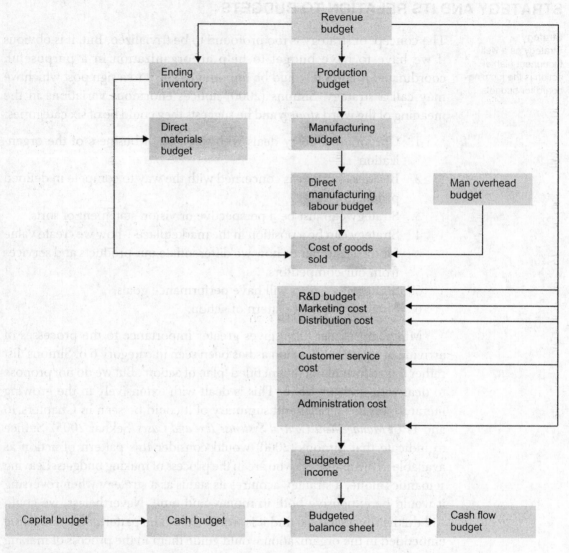

**Fig. 7.5** The budgeting process

non-profit organizations have a less self-evident logic tied to a sharply focused concept of profits and would, therefore, be a little different. All budgetary processes are reiterative and have to be participative with all managers. They can, therefore, be described ideally and normatively as interactive systems and could take anything up to five months to complete. Even then it often requires several corrections and updates. All financial arrangements with financial institutions such as banks are critically dependent on the ultimate outcomes of this exercise.

## The Budgeting Cycle

A budget is usually framed for a period of 12 months as explained here:

1. The annual accounts have a 12 month periodicity as required under company legislation.

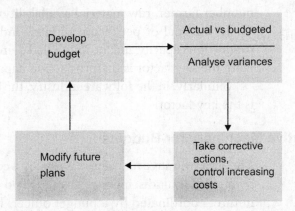

**Fig. 7.6** Budgetary cycle

**Budget cycle**
A budget cycle usually takes an entire year, consisting of six month's preparation, implementation, investigation of variances, and then back to the preparation for the next year.

2. A 12 month cycle is usually a climatic cycle.
3. The taxation legislations are made once in 12 months, which trigger changes in the demand patterns for products.

A shorter period of budget, such as quarterly, is also used in conjunction with the 12 month budgets. Budget reviews are, however, most usual at half-yearly intervals.

Some companies use rolling budget which is applicable for the next 12 months and is constantly rolled over.

A budgeting cycle would cover the cycle of preparation, fixing expectations, investigating variances, and planning again in the light of feedback (Fig. 7.6). It would be seen that the cycle would usually cover a period of one year.

## Key Factors in Budget Making

The expression 'key factor in budgets' or 'principle budget factor' was very popular sometime ago (Owler and Brown 1978). But recent books make much less use of the concept. Nevertheless, it is important to build up a perspective on where to begin the reiterative process.

Most organizations will use sales as the key factor. They start with an understanding of how much a product can be sold considering their sales

**Sales**
In most organizations the key factor in the budget is sales, in some such as petroleum and coal it is the production capacity, in software industry it is the availability of skilled manpower, etc.

force, distribution network, and the intrinsic worth of a product. Even if it is the starting point, after a round of reiteration one may also have to change one's estimate of sales.

Thus, the key factor is not always an unchanging one. In a cooperative dairy industry where the vision is to market whatever is produced by a member farmer, raw material availability is usually the key factor.

In the coal or petroleum refinery industry, usually demand exceeds production capacity and the unfulfilled demand is imported by the customer. Here the key factor is the production capacity.

Similarly, in the software industry, the availability of skilled manpower is the key factor.

## Administrative Machinery for Budgets

The administrative machinery is usually a compact one which is coordinated by a small multidisciplinary group called a 'budget committee', which is, in turn, coordinated by a budget officer. It is very important to keep this committee transparent in its workings and open to suggestions. They will do all the preparatory work for the budget.

The preparatory work is to

1. work on the perspectives, the vision, and the action plan;
2. provide findings of research on demand and market trends;
3. indicate the errors in the past forecasts; and
4. analyse the strengths and weaknesses of the past period performance.

Later, we will describe the more elaborate administrative machinery which organizations use in the analogous process of building up balanced scorecards, which are far more advanced processes of budgeting.

## Structure and Content of Budgets

The structure and content of business budgets would be self-evident from the process of making budget shown in Fig. 7.5. We will now describe with examples each of the boxes in the figure and the summing up what is usually described as 'master budget'. We will show some reiteration in the building of the budget in one of the most volatile and uncertain industries—the music industry. It is a typical industry if a straight jacket of a budget may inhibit efforts to seek out opportunities in the industry. But if indeed one can make budgets work in a music industry, there is much hope for its application in other less uncertain industries.

### *Revenue budget*

**Master Budget**
It is the summary of all the individual sections of the budget highlighting the most critical aspects that touch on strategy.

As mentioned earlier, in most cases the key factor of the budget is revenue. These budgets are first drafted by the salesmen of a music company, by say Muthu at the grass root level. They would look somewhat as shown in Table 7.4. He would do so after getting to know from the artist and repertoire (A&R) manager the kind of products he is planning and how exciting it will be for the market.

Muthu may be expecting a big hit from an exciting film for which he should prepare himself. They are classified as 'top hits'. In a year he may expect four or five of such numbers. But an unexpected bonanza may also come their way. The A & R manager may indicate that he is expecting an Amitabh Bachchan—Shah Rukh Khan—Rani Mukherjee starrer with Javed Akhtar givng the lyrics and A.R. Rahman directing the music. He will also tell Muthu on the plans of the competitors. Muthu may also give the A&R manager information about his customers and what they expect from their company and from their competitors. Steady sellers as the name implies may be depended upon to give a large share. Some advertisements

**Table 7.4**   Quarterly sales budget for the year 2006

|  | Sale price (₹/Piece) | Sale Q1 no. | Sale Q2 no. | Sale Q3 no. | Sale Q4 no. | Year Sale no. | Year sale value (₹) |
|---|---|---|---|---|---|---|---|
| Cassettes – top hits (six new releases) | 40 | 0 | 5000 | 5000 | 0 | 10,000 | 4,00,000 |
| Cassettes – steady sellers (film) (1000 old and new releases) | 30 | 2000 | 4000 (Salary bonus season for customers) | 2000 | 2000 | 10,000 | 3,00,000 |
| Cassettes – first releases (60 new releases) | 35 | 100 | 200 | 100 | 100 | 500 | 17,500 |
| Cassettes – classical and semi-classical (500 old and new releases) | 60 | 1000 | 2000 (Salary bonus season for customers) | 1000 | 1000 | 5000 | 3,00,000 |
| Total | 39.90 |  |  |  |  | 25,500 | 10,17,500 |

may also be promised. Muthu can be told of the expected first releases, many of which may have only a small initial sale but some may also blossom into top hits of the year. Classical and semi-classical repertoire has a segmented market, which needs to be nurtured through dealers who are networked with such segments. Muthu may suggest modifications and ultimately produce Table 7.4.

The next stage is to consolidate all the sales forces projection to form first the regional numbers and then the national numbers.

At that stage one must check if the repertoire can produce products which have been included in the budget.

This is not the final end of the revenue budget. It may take several reiterative attempts to finally fix the revenue budget of the company, the region and of Muthu, the salesman. During the implementation, some surprises have to be provided for and the budgets adjusted in an interactive system, which has already been described in the chapter.

### Production budget

Production budgets are made by the production department. They follow the logic that is mentioned here:

Production quantities = Closing inventory – Opening inventory + Sales

The management may have plans to tighten working capital control and keep a very low closing inventory subject to minimized stock-outs. This is usually very effectively planned on computers. These decisions can be taken by the production department only in consultation with other departments as among other things, level of inventory has a corresponding consequence in supply efficiency and stock-outs.

The production budget will be in quantitative terms, multiplied by rates to get values. But this step will need interaction with the personnel manager and purchase manager.

### Direct material budget

This will be the task for the production manager. Each product has a bill of material which can be projected by a computer. This will give total material to be consumed.

**Table 7.5**  Material purchase budget

| Item | Unit | Price (₹/unit) | Opening quantity | Q1 purchase | Q2 purchase | Q3 purchase | Q4 purchase | Total | Closing inventory |
|---|---|---|---|---|---|---|---|---|---|
| Jombo type rolls | No. | 10,000 | 100 | 1000 | 1200 | 1500 | 1800 | 5500 | 70 |
| Plastic chips | Kgs | 50 | 10,000 | 1,00,000 | 1,20,000 | 1,50,000 | 1,80,0000 | 5,50,000 | 700 |

## Purchase budget

This has to be prepared by the purchase manager.

In the case of finished goods, the purchase has to be hemmed in by the inventory policy for raw material.

$$\text{Purchases} = \text{Opening inventory} + \text{Consumption}$$
$$\text{(manufacturing budget)} - \text{Closing inventory}$$

As in the case of finished goods inventory, the level of inventory has a corresponding consequence on the promptness of supply and of stock-out which the organization will have to accept.

These quantities to be purchased will be extended by expected rates. This step is important to define the accountability of the purchase manager. The material budget would then be as shown in Table 7.5.

## Manufacturing budget

Each product will have a bill of material. The computers will provide the direct material in quantity. Similarly, it can also provide direct labour in quantity. These will be extended.

## Manufacturing overhead budget

The production manager will marshal all his activities and may prepare a budget for each activity or each department depending on the nature and extent of activity.

There may be several overheads not in the control of the production manager. For example, in the music industry, the A & R manager may budget the number of ordinary recordings and the number of special recordings requiring costly instruments and accompanists.

## Cost of goods sold

As we have seen in Table 3.14 of Chapter 3, we can compute the manufacturing costs, cost of goods manufactured, and the cost of goods sold.

### Research and development cost

This is a typical discretionary expenditure and the expenditure has to be debated extensively and settled usually at the top level. We will discuss the nature of discretionary costs later in the paragraph. Wise decisions in this budget is critical for long-term growth and survival. Often this budget is most prone to be viewed by accountants with great suspicion and even cynicism. In a music industry, R&D may include developing new equipment, which focuses primarily on combating piracy. However, this may or may not succeed.

### Distribution cost

Currently, this budget is gaining great importance. In music industry typically, one may have to take a bold step of distributing by expensive modes to avoid expensive stock-outs.

### Consumer service costs

Consumable durables usually have to be backed by warranty expenses.

### Administrative costs

The item is self-explanatory. It is desirable that the administrative costs are also under the critical scrutiny of all the managers who feel obligated to zealously advise.

### Capital budget

The contents of the capital budget are relevant to build up the budgeted balance sheet.

### Cash budget and cash flow budget

We have seen cash flows in the end chapter exercises of Chapter 2. They are also mandated by AS 3 of the Institute of Chartered Accountants of India (ICAI). They were intended among other things to provide transparency to the accounting system and to assist the stake holders in taking their own decisions.

In this chapter, however, cash flow statements are shown as extremely critical and necessary instruments to carry on operations of an organization. They are prospective (for the future) in nature and not postmortem. But as shown in our discussion on the mandatory direction in published accounts there could be both direct method of constructing cash flow statements by forecasting inflows of cash on account of sales and outflows on account of purchases and other expenses. There could also be an indirect method by deriving it from the accounts prepared on an accrual basis. Considering its importance, we will show in detail how cash budgets can be derived directly from the projected budgeted balance sheets and capital budgets. Cash flow budgets are also prepared for short time horizons to assist operational planning. The preparation of cash flow budgets having considerable accounting mechanics are detailed in Annexure 7.1.

## Example 7.3  Production Budget

Prestige Pvt. Ltd expects sales of 2,00,000 units of bathtubs in the current year. Beginning Inventory for the current year is 10,000 bathtubs; target inventory is 15,000 bathtubs. Compute the number of bathtubs budgeted for production in the current year.

| Production Budget | Amount (₹) |
|---|---|
| Budgeted sales in units | 2,00,000 |
| Target inventory (Add) | 15,000 |
| Total requirement | 2,15,000 |
| Beginning finished goods inventory (Deduct) | 10,000 |
| Bathtubs to be produced | 2,05,000 |

## Example 7.4  Revenue and Production Budget

Mr Ritesh Verma, Marketing Manager, Groomlet Pvt. Ltd, projects the monthly sales of two products, namely wooden comb and hairbrush as 50,000 and 1,00,000 respectively.

1. For 2011, the average estimated selling prices are ₹50 per wooden comb and ₹30 per hairbrush. Prepare the revenue budget for the company for the year ending December 31, 2011.
2. The company begins 2011 with 70,000 wooden combs in inventory. The Senior Operations Manager wants ending inventory to be no less than 60,000 wooden combs on December 31, 2010. Based on the sales projections as budgeted above, what is the minimum number of wooden combs Groomlet must produce during 2011?
3. The company begins 2011 with 1,20,000 hairbrush in inventory. The Senior Operations Manager wants ending inventory to be no less than 1,50,000 hairbrushes on December 31, 2010. Based on the sales projections as budgeted above, what is the minimum number of hairbrushes Groomlet must produce during 2011?

**Revenue Budget**

| | Monthly sales | Price ₹ | Units sold per year | Total revenue |
|---|---|---|---|---|
| Wooden Combs | 50,000 | 50 | 600,000 | 30,000,000 |
| Hair Brushes | 100,000 | 30 | 1,200,000 | 36,000,000 |
| Total Revenue | | | | 66,000,000 |

**Production Budget**

| Wooden comb | | Hairbrush | |
|---|---|---|---|
| Beginning Inventory | 70,000 | Beginning Inventory | 120,000 |
| Ending inventory | 60,000 | Ending inventory | 150,000 |

| Wooden Comb | | Hairbrush | |
|---|---|---|---|
| Units sold per year | 6,00,000 | Units sold per year | 12,00,000 |
| Adding ending inventory | 60,000 | Adding ending inventory | 1,50,000 |
| Total requirement | 6,60,000 | Total requirement | 13,50,000 |
| Deduct beginning inventory | 70,000 | Deduct beginning inventory | 1,20,000 |
| **Minimum production** | **5,90,000** | **Minimum production** | **12,30,000** |

# BUDGETING FOR DISCRETIONARY COSTS AND ENGINEERED COSTS

We have already seen from the descriptions of the seven responsibility centres that there exists a clear relationship between the expected outcomes and the cost outlays in case items 1 (production), 4 (purchase), and 5 (revenue). The relationship is most uncertain in item 7 (research and development). In items 2 (maintenance), 3 (personnel) and 6 (overall profits), it is nebulous. Items 1, 4, and 5 are described as engineered costs and item 7 as discretionary costs, while the remaining being hybrids. It can be seen that accountability has willy-nilly to be perceived differently in engineered and discretionary costs. We can see the difference between these two in Exhibit 7.1.

It is said of discretionary cost that half of it is a waste, but the problem is that we do not know which half it is.

A very significant aspect of discretionary costs is in costs which create infrastructure and capacity typically for design offices, sales offices, or public counters, such as ticketing in railway stations or airlines. Actual activity

**Exhibit 7.1**  Difference between engineered costs ands discretionary costs (Atkinson et al. 2003)

| Characteristic | Engineered costs | Discretionary costs |
|---|---|---|
| Process | a. Detailed and physically observable<br>b. Repetitive | a. Black box (Knowledge of process is sketchy or unavailable.)<br>b. Non-repetitive |
| Level of uncertainty | Moderate or small (E.g., shipping or manufacturing setting) | Large for example R & D or advertisement setting |

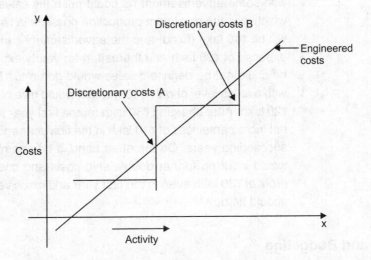

**Fig. 7.7**  Discretionary costs to cushion fluctuating activity

often may not catch up with capacity. But peak activity may require the capacity. The organization would then have to decide if it would keep idle capacity just to meet the peak demand or down-size to reduce costs. Similarly, if one starts a new product or process, there could be a period of learning before costs come down. Advertisement and promotion costs are also typically discretionary. We can see the relationship between such discretionary costs and the exact engineering needs in Fig. 7.7.

In Fig. 7.7, the line of engineered costs is straight, whereas that of discretionary costs are in the form of a stepladder. If one has to fulfil peak activity, one may have to provide for discretionary costs and hope activity will hover around B, the bottom of the step-up of the ladder than point A which is in the top of the step-up. This dilemma for accountability could be more comprehensively and strategically handled through balanced scorecards. An illustrative example would show the dilemmas discretionary costs would pose.

Budgeting for discretionary costs is therefore always problematic. But without these the organization will never be able to move forward.

## Example 7.5 Discretionary Cost Dilemma

Jadeja was currently running his plant for one shift. He had achieved the maximum possible production of 5000 units per month. He was advised that with some advertisement he could push his sales to 10,000 units per month which was the maximum production possible in two shifts. The extra shift cost will be ₹40 lakh (fixed) and the advertisement campaign would be a one time expense of ₹30 lakh and thereafter, an yearly expense of ₹15 lakh. However, he could not be definite if sales would go up to 10,000 and he could land up with a sales level of only 8000, which would give him a net incremental profit of ₹20 lakh. After charging ₹30 lakh for the first year advertisement he will have a net incremental loss of ₹10 lakh in the first year and small positive profits in the succeeding years. On the other hand, if he can manage a sale of 10,000 he would incur no further double shift costs and could make a net incremental profit of ₹30 lakh even in the first year and massive profits in later years. What should he do?

## ABC and Budgeting

As explained in Chapter 6, the ABC system is essentially for overheads in which there is a definite correlation between the input and the output. Thus, in heat treatment plant, costs have a correlation with the hours of treatment. Therefore, wherever ABC is used, budgeting becomes extremely useful to determine the norms for application of the cost of the activity. ABC also considerably improves the predictability of the budgets.

## Responsibility and Controllability

**Zero-based budgets** These budgets, starting from the scratch, are a must for all discretionary costs and also useful for engineered costs.

Horngren clearly distinguishes between responsibility and controllability (Horngren et al. 2003). For example, a purchase manager in a vegetable oil industry may not be able to control oil seed prices. But he is responsible to the organization to warn the management of an impending increase in prices and provide information on alternate oil seed. He can prepare a forecasting model to understand the causes for the fluctuation and plan the production accordingly.

## Incremental, Kaizen, and Zero-based Budgets

One can reduce the efforts in making the budgets if we follow incrementalism, that is, starting with the present and making adjustments for changes. This approach preempts fresh thinking but it is mostly followed in industries.

Zero-based budgets, on the other hand, start from the scratch and examine every budget line afresh. They were made famous by the US President, Jimmy Carter. Discretionary costs would greatly benefit from this approach (Anthony and Govindarajan 2003).

But even engineered costs could use it in periods where reengineering and cost reduction drives are on. Budgets would be the appropriate instruments which can incorporate these improvements.

## Loose Budget and Slack Budget

A budget prepared with participation enhances accountability as would be evident from the structure proposed in Fig 7.1. But there is one lurking fear in this approach. Some proposals for the budget may not 'stretch the capabilities' and there could be an inevitable slack. Moreover, if budgets are treated as instruments for 'negotiation', the first proposal may be kept loose in order to provide adjustments during bargaining (Sekhar 2005).

Budgets can also be 'tight' or 'achievable' according to the style of management control of an organization. A budget which has a 50 per cent probability of achievement is usually considered an achievable budget. Those who work on a tight budget may compensate with less severe reprimand for failure to meet the budget. Those who use achievable budgets may find it more useful because of the following reasons (Horngren et al. 2003). Tight budgets

1. can be shared with external agencies, such as banks, stock brokers, etc. with greater confidence;
2. drive managers to sacrifice long-term for short-term plans;
3. drive managers to manipulate;
4. are only 50 per cent probable and an overoptimistic budget may commit to too much resources being tied up; and
5. creates a winning atmosphere.

## BEHAVIOURAL PROBLEMS IN BUDGETS

The picture as built up so far in this chapter is that budgets are ideal means to smoothly coordinate and communicate in organizations to help them to achieve strategic objectives. But there have been rumblings against this 'orderly' manner of coordinating organizations. On the basis of field work, Hopwood (1972) had felt that budgeting resulted in distorted behaviour as the managers often bend and corrupt the data to show achievement of the budgeted numbers. Otley (1978) also analysed field data and found that such distortions take place only if the managers do not agree with the goals of the budget. This means that the congruence of belief systems and the goals is important before one uses budgets.

Sigmund Ginsburg (Atkinson et al. 2003), in a brilliant satirical piece on manipulations managers do in pushing their budgets, describes them as belonging to nine types:

1. The gardener who waters the garden to grow all that is available. At the budget time she makes a slick presentation of what she needs and smuggles in all the jungle and tires out the sanctioning authority so that no questions are asked.
2. The duck hunter who presents ducks and decoys. He veers the discussion on the decoys which are presented in complex terms. The ducks which are the items he wants get through.
3. The entrepreneur who promises the moon and if she fails says that she had to take risks.
4. The gambler who says, 'Cut my budget and I will resign.'
5. The surgeon who claims she has cut the budget to the bare bone and she cannot take any more cuts.
6. The good soldier who flatters by showing he has followed all company policies faithfully.
7. The drowning man who projects panic and hopes to get his projects through that way.
8. The saviour who claims she will save the firm.
9. One who pretends to be an honest person, who shows he has put all the cards on the table.

All these gimmicks are more than plausible in real life if the organization is bureaucratic and power is centralized.

It is precisely such practices which made Jack Welch (2005), the legendary GM of General Electric, to burst out on budgets as follows:

Mr Welch believes that budgets are 'the worst invention ever'.[*] They result from the two opposing sides of the budget, headquarters and

_____

[*] Adapted from a report of a speech by Jack Welch in Chicago Business Line, 10 November 2005.

departments, trying to con each other. The decisions are made by people sitting in a room with no window.

Be that as it may, the experience of several has not been as dismal as that of Jack Welch and Ginsburg. However, the moment one feels that budgets cramp the style of the managers, it is time to look into the internal processes and take corrective steps.

## SUMMARY

Accounting information can focus attention on accountability of the managers to the physical and financial results expected of them. This information is intertwined with that which would enable an organization to take decisions on products and services. Responsibilities and accountability of managers can be of four types—cost (expense), revenue, profits, and return on investments. Budget is a quantitative expression, both physical and financial, of proposed plan of action for a specified period and acts as an aid to what needs to be done to implement the plan. It involves a participatory and reiterative process. Budgets have typically components of sales, production, manufacturing, material purchase, labour, expenses, overheads, operating income, capital, and cash flow projections. Budgets raise several behavioural problems which need to be tackled before they seriously harm the organization. As a wrap up, one may say that responsibility accounting irrespective of what its detractors can achieve the following:

1. It can help in controlling controllable costs through positive efforts of the executives.
2. It can help in taking alternative decisions if forewarned about even non-controllable costs
3. It sharply focuses in reporting systems.
4. It would help in sharpening corporate objectives.
5. It will make planning and budgeting more purposeful.
6. It will improve the quality of information.
7. It will make for much better monitoring and control and come up with better ideas for cost reduction.

## KEY POINTS

- Hierarchical systems are those which rely on superior, peer, and subordinate monitoring and counseling to perform.

- Market systems of control are those which signal performance as do market systems namely through profit.
- Accountability in an organization arises through a matrix of mutual expectations.
- Budgets are devices to formally spell out physical and financial expectations, which enable an organization to coordinate activities and communicate the strategy chosen by the organization and the shape of the activities proximate to the manager.
- Budgets, if misused, or made too rigid, can inhibit initiative when it is most required to identify opportunities.
- Budgets loaded on a spread sheet enables one to do a sensitivity analysis to see the effect of changing one or more parameters on the ultimate outcomes in profits, or cash flows.

## CONCEPT REVIEW QUESTIONS

1. Is it better to compare actual performance with past performance or budgeted performance?
2. What are the four levers of control that could aid in establishing and monitoring accountability?
3. What are the four types of responsibility centres that managements usually use?
4. What are discretionary costs and engineered costs?
5. Are cash flow budgets useful in interacting with external authorities?
6. Describe the key factors in a budget.
7. What are the components of a budget cycle?
8. Are zero-based budgets useful for engineered costs?
9. What is a Kaizen budget?
10. What is the meaning of sensitivity analysis with reference to budgeting? How is it useful?
11. What is the relationship between strategy and budgeting?

## NUMERICAL PROBLEMS

1. **Rashmi Detergents**
   Rashmi Detergents expects sales of 10,000 kg of its product in 2005. Its opening inventory is 2000 kg. It desires that it should have a maximum of 1000 kg as inventory at the end of the year. What should its production be?

## 2. Charu Containers

Charu Containers makes standard containers for its market. It plans to sell 40,000 containers in 2006. It has 2000 containers in the opening inventory and desires to have a closing inventory of 3000 containers. Every container has a standard quantity of aluminium sheets weighing 1 kg. The purchase price of 1 kg of aluminium is ₹50. Each can needs a standard electrode costing ₹10. What should be the material purchase budget for Charu for the year 2006?

## 3. Bansal Stores

Bansal Stores follows ABC system for its two outlets—Papa di Dukaan and Sitara. Their actuals for 2004 are as follows:

| | Papa di Dukaan (₹) | Sitara (₹) | | | |
|---|---|---|---|---|---|
| Sales | 2,00,000 | 20,00,000 | | | |
| Cost of goods sold | 1,85,000 | 19,50,000 | | | |
| Gross margin | 15,000 | 50,000 | | | |
| Profit/sale | 0.075 | 0.025 | | | |

| Activity | Cost (₹) | Activity base | Activity quantity | Cost/ activity | |
|---|---|---|---|---|---|
| Purchase | 8000 | Number | 200 | 40 | |
| Line item | 6000 | Number | 2000 | 3 | |
| Delivery | 10,000 | Number | 200 | 50 | |
| Handle car | 10,000 | Number | 1000 | 10 | |
| Shelf stock | 8000 | Hours | 80 | 100 | |
| Total overhead | 42,000 | | | | |

| | Papa di Dukaan quantity | Papa di Dukaan cost (₹) | Sitara quantity | Sitara cost (₹) | Total cost (₹) |
|---|---|---|---|---|---|
| Purchase | 20 | 800 | 180 | 7200 | 8000 |
| Line item | 240 | 720 | 1760 | 5280 | 6000 |
| Delivery | 180 | 1000 | 20 | 1000 | 10,000 |
| Handling | 300 | 3000 | 700 | 7000 | 10,000 |
| Shelf stocking | 10 | 1000 | 70 | 7000 | 8000 |
| Total overhead | | 14,520 | | 27,480 | 42,000 |

| | Papa di Dukaan (₹) | Sitara (₹) | Total (₹) | | |
|---|---|---|---|---|---|
| Gross profit | 15,000 | 50000 | 65000 | | |
| Overhead | 14,520 | 27,480 | 42,000 | | |
| Net profit (loss) | 480 | 22,520 | 23,000 | | |

Bansals propose to reduce the cost per activity by 24 per cent over the actual figures for 2004. Its activities will be as indicated in the following table. The sales for Papa di Dukaan will remain the same as 2004, but that of Sitara will increase by 30 per cent and will increase the activity correspondingly. Papa di Dukaan activity will remain the same as in 2004. The gross margin percentages will be the same as in the first table, namely 7.5 per cent in Papa di Dukaan and 2.5 per cent in Sitara.

## Questions

3.1 Fill up the cells marked with a question mark.

| | Papa di Dukaan quantity | Papa di Dukaan cost | Sitara quantity | Sitara cost | Total cost |
|---|---|---|---|---|---|
| Purchase | ? | ? | ? | ? | ? |
| Line item | ? | ? | ? | ? | ? |
| Delivery | ? | | ? | ? | ? |
| Handling | ? | ? | ? | ? | ? |
| Shelf stocking | ? | ? | ? | ? | ? |
| Total overhead | | ? | | ? | ? |
| | Papa di Dukaan | Sitara | Total | | |
| Gross profit | 15,000 | 50,000 | 65,000 | | |
| Overhead | ? | ? | ? | | |
| Net profit (loss) | ? | ? | ? | | |

3.2 Instead of planning a straight reduction in cost per activity of 24 per cent and 30 per cent increase in sales of Sitara, the plan now is to follow the Kaizen approach and plan a 2 per cent reduction in cost in the first month and 2 per cent over the first month level in the second month, and so on. Similarly, in sales of Sitara, a 3 per cent increase is planned in the first month and 3 per cent of that level for the second month, and so on. What would be the budget in the sixth month?

## 4. Diamond Computers

Diamond Computers supplies computers to schools at competitive rates. It supplies them at ₹25,000 per piece. The peak demand is in June/July/August when the new school sessions start and the schools are ready with the infrastructure and buildings for the computers. The average supply for each school will be ten computers. Its pattern of demand and the material cost structure is shown in the following table.

Diamond has a monthly salary bill of ₹30,000. Transportation cost for each computer will be ₹150. The schools are invoiced immediately after installation, which takes half a day. 20 per cent of the invoices are usually paid in the month of invoice, 30 per cent in the next month, and balance in the third month. Purchases have to be paid within 30 days of the invoice. If they are paid in cash, all items would be supplied 5 per cent cheaper.

## Question

4.1 Prepare a cash flow budget for every month from June–October with and without availing cash discount of 5 per cent. Comment on the results.

## 5. Srivatsa Corporation

Srivatsa Corporation has started a marketing company recently. It is planning to buy 2,000 units of a product in January, which will be sold in the same month. It has calculated the following costs:

1. Purchase price ₹100 per unit*
2. Administrative expenses (all fixed) ₹40,000 per month
3. Variable selling expense (mainly commission on sales) ₹25.00 per unit**
4. Depreciation ₹10,000 p.m on straight line method
5. Fixed marketing expenses ₹15,000 per month
6. Selling price ₹160 per unit***

## Question

5.1. Prepare the cash budget for January for Srivatsa Corporation

## 6. Paschim Oshadalaya Ltd

Paschim Oshadalaya Ltd (P.O. Ltd) makes rare Ayurvedic preparations. One of their products Omsakthi is a popular household medicine. It is based on a herb which is available in the Himalayan regions only during March and September. It costs ₹2000 per kg. One kg of the herb can make 5 bottles of Omsakthi.

The production plan of P.O. Ltd. for Omsakthi (in bottles) for the four quarters is as follows:

---

* 20% of purchases will be paid next month
** ₹5 per unit payable in the current month; balance payable in the next month
*** 75% will be realized in the current month.

| Period | Unit |
|---|---|
| I Quarter (Apr.–June) | 30,000 |
| II Quarter (Jul.–Sep.) | 40,000 |
| III Quarter (Oct.–Dec.) | 50,000 |
| IV Quarter (Jan.–Mar.) | 45,000 |

Since the herb is a rare commodity, P.O. Ltd. wants to buy during each season (i.e. March and September) enough quantity to cover 150% of the requirements of the next two quarters.

## Question

6.1 Prepare a material budget for the herb showing the quantities and amount during March and September.

## 7. Ram Shakti Ltd

A company, Ram Shakti Ltd, sells all its products on cash. The company has the following sales projections based on the current *cash-sales-only* policy:

| Month | ₹ |
|---|---|
| January | 15,00,000 |
| February | 20,00,000 |
| March | 22,00,000 |
| April | 25,00,000 |

Market surveys have shown that the products can fetch higher prices if it adopted a suitable credit sales policy. If it sells on credit, the following collection pattern is expected:

| | |
|---|---|
| On the month of sales | 70% |
| The month succeeding sales | 15% |
| The second month succeeding sales | 10% |
| Bad debts | 5% |

The company is concerned about the high bad debt percentage.

## Questions

7.1 Calculate the collection situation for April at current price levels under the two options. (Ignore interest computations)

7.2 Will your answer differ if the price increases by 10% and the 'bad debts' no longer exist? They will be collected in the second month succeeding sales (i.e., it becomes 15% instead of the present 10% in the second month succeeding sales). The increase in price is not possible if credit is not offered to the buyers.

## 8. Shivpur Concerns

The cost accounts of Shivpur Concerns for the latest completed year, based on actual figures read as under:

| | | (figures in lacs of ₹) |
|---|---|---|
| Sales | (10,000 units) | 10.00 |
| Direct materials | | 5.50 |
| Direct labour | | 1.00 |
| Variable manufacturing costs | | 0.75 |
| Variable selling costs | | 0.50 |
| Fixed Costs | | 1.75 |
| Profits | | 0.50 |

The management is confident that it can increase production and sales by 20% during the current year. The other information is as follows:

- Sale prices will remain the same
- Advertising costs of ₹75,000, included in fixed costs, will no longer be needed.
- The variable manufacturing and selling costs will increase by 10%
- New substitutes for materials will reduce costs by 15%
- Labour costs will register a 10% jump.

New regulations of quality controls require an external agency to do the testing. The company has accepted their quotation of standing charges of ₹25,000 plus ₹2.50 per unit.

## Question

8.1 Prepare a budget for the current year assuming the same cost behavior as in the last year.

## PROJECT

Form a group of 3 or 4 students, choose an organization, and offer to help them to prepare a year's cash flow budget. Explain the advantages of making one.

| CASE STUDY 1 | Responsibility and Controllability |
|---|---|

Consider each of the following situations in an organization which has responsibility centres as production manager, purchase manager, maintenance manager, personnel manager, and the chief executive and determine where responsibility and controllability lay.

1. The Production Manager rang up the office of the Purchase Manager and advised him the purchase scheduled for the next month. He did not follow it up with a formal indent as required by the rules of business of the company. The Purchase Manager who got the message from his secretary confirmed to the Production Manager that he would do the purchase. But he forgot. He was reminded a day before the due delivery time. He moved heaven and earth and made a rush purchase and stuck to the new schedule but he had to pay a higher price.

2. The Purchase Manager operates through an agent. The arrangement was in a firm price contract. The supplier increased the price which the agents wish to pass on to them.

3. The Production Manager used more than expected amount of raw material which was traced to sub-standard quality of raw material and consequently a rush order had to be purchased at a higher price.

4. The situation was the same as the three mentioned before but the excess quantity was due to defective machine.

5. The situation was the same as before but the excess was due to the machines not being available for maintenance on time as the factory was running short of machines and could not be spared for maintenance.

6. The organization was reporting high costs as the retiring Personnel Manager gave away a gift of packages for the labour which enhanced their costs. He felt this step would increase the loyalty and productivity of the existing workers.

7. The Production Department A produced only to 80 per cent of capacity even though the manager's budget required him to produce 100 per cent of capacity. He argued that it was wasteful to do so as the succeeding Department B was a bottleneck department and increasing production would only add to his inventory which would add to the interest costs which the central office charged to him.

8. The Production Department B was glad to produce to its capacity and the manager did not initiate action to de-bottleneck his department. The Chief Executive felt that he should continue to produce to capacity in Department A as he felt that once de-bottling is done, the inventory would be used in no time.

| CASE STUDY 2 | Gurukul University |

Gurukul University was well-known for its contribution to the national teams in several sports (Sekhar 2005). The case focuses on the problems of Harichand, the Head of Sports Department, to find funds for his department. Harichand had been in the Indian hockey team in three Olympics. Gurukul had four sources of funds:

1. Tuition fees
2. Sponsorship of industries
3. Government grants
4. Special training programmes

Its expenses were as follows:

1. Capital Expenses
2. Running expenses in faculty salaries
3. Other administrative expenses
4. Scholarships provided for students under several schemes

Every department's accounts were maintained to show the surplus or deficit. Considerable autonomy was given to the individual departments including seeking funds. If there was deficit, the Vice Chancellor made an application to the government to fill the deficit. The Vice Chancellors were a little wary of asking for a government grant as it brought along with it interference in their work. Gurukul was not shy of making money for its use wherever an opportunity was available. Its trustees were well known industrialists who believed in the utility of markets and its commands. Harichand had built a formidable reputation due to his sportsmen and he had been able to get a deficit in the region of ₹30 lakh per annum from government grants. But this year he had to contend with a new Vice Chancellor, Premavati, who was not happy with his department for several reasons:

1. She said that the department had not been encouraging women sports persons.

2. She felt that Cricket had been given undue importance and proper attention was not given to other sports.
3. Many of the cricket heroes were atrocious in academic achievement and were objects of public ridicule.
4. The cricket coach, Mohinder Singh, was a white elephant. A test player of reputation, he had produced top class cricketers in the university. But Premawati was not sure if that was a good enough reason for him to get a salary higher than several distinguished professors in the university who were world authorities in their respective subjects.
5. Athletics was not getting its due share and the students were not given enough options.

Premawati told Harichand that he would have to balance his budget. She gave him a fortnight to recast his budget. Every time he tried to open the subject she shut him up by saying, 'Nothing doing'. Harichand had a look at the budget that he had prepared (Table CS 2). It showed a deficit of ₹90 lakh. He did not wish to spread his resources thin by covering too many sports. He was also clear that Mohinder Singh brought in several donations. He knew that his department's reputation was not only based on producing star sports persons, but also in attracting academically bright young persons who liked to cultivate their talents. They paid the high tuition fees to the main courses they had registered for; they partook in the activities of the sports department and paid nominal extra fees for this purpose which meagre amount was added to the tuition fees shown in his accounts. Premawati's peevish arguments were self-contradictory but he had to live with her irritability as she had the support of the violently feminist Minister for Education.

**Table CS 2**  Budget of the sports department of Gurukul University (₹ lakh)

| Game→ <br> Revenue cost↓ | Cricket | Hockey | Football | Athletics | Common | Total |
|---|---|---|---|---|---|---|
| Tuition (men) | 86 | 15 | 10 | 15 | - | 126 |
| Costs (men) | 74 | 30 | 3 | 3 | - | 110 |
| Scholarship (men) | 30 | 20 | 5 | 4 | - | 59 |
| **Net (men)** | (18) | (35) | 2 | 8 | - | (43) |
| Tuition (women) | 5 | 1 | 1 | 1 | - | 8 |
| Cost (women) | 24 | 2 | 2 | 2 | - | 30 |
| Scholarship (women) | 12 | 4 | 4 | 4 | - | 24 |
| **Net (women)** | (31) | (4) | (5) | (5) | - | (46) |
| Donation (common) | - | - | - | - | 34 | 34 |
| Costs (common) | - | - | - | - | 35 | 35 |
| **Net (common)** | - | - | - | - | - | (1) |

Total deficit equals 43 + 46 +1 = 90

## Discussion Questions

1. Can Harichand argue his case logically on the basis of goal congruence between the multiple constituents?
2. Does the university have a single or multiple objectives? In either case, what would you suggest the process of making budgets should be.
3. How can we evaluate the performance of the Sports Department?
4. If you were Harichand, how would you tackle the situation?

# ANNEXURE

## Annexure 7.1

### Accounting Mechanics of Cash Budgets

## Cash budget of Sangeeta Ltd
## (All figures in ₹ lakh)

We can see the budgeted income statement in Table A7.1 and the budgeted balance sheet in Table A7. 2. The cash flow statement using direct method of assessment from the primary data available in the organization is in Table A7.3. The pattern can be derived by the indirect method (Table A7.4) which uses the accounting data on accrual system to come to the same conclusion. Thus, the cash on account of sale can be derived as follows:

Cash inflow on account of sales = Sales + Opening balance debtors – Closing debtors

Similarly, cash outflow on account of purchase is

Purchases + Opening sundry creditors – Closing creditors

Cash outflow due to other items = Expenses + Opening creditors – Closing creditors

**Table A7.1** Budgeted income statement

| Budgeted income statement | Qr 1 | Qr 2 | Qr 3 | Qr 4 | Full Year |
|---|---|---|---|---|---|
| Sales | 1000 | 1200 | 1400 | 1500 | 5100 |
| Closing finished goods | 80 | 70 | 60 | 50 | 50 |
| Closing raw material | 30 | 20 | 15 | 15 | 15 |
| Total | 1110 | 1290 | 1475 | 1565 | 5165 |
| Opening finished goods | 90 | 80 | 70 | 60 | 90 |
| Opening raw material | 35 | 30 | 20 | 15 | 35 |
| Purchase raw material | 200 | 220 | 300 | 350 | 1070 |
| Labour | 100 | 110 | 105 | 110 | 425 |
| Overhead expenses | 200 | 210 | 215 | 220 | 845 |
| Depreciation | 100 | 100 | 100 | 100 | 400 |
| Marketing/Administrative expenses | 200 | 210 | 210 | 210 | 830 |
| Net profit before tax | 185 | 330 | 455 | 500 | 1470 |
| Total | 1110 | 1290 | 1475 | 1565 | 5165 |
| Tax | 46.25 | 82.5 | 113.75 | 125 | 367.5 |
| Profit after tax | 138.75 | 247.5 | 341.25 | 375 | 1102.5 |
| Dividend | 0 | 0 | 60 | 0 | 60 |

**Table A7.2**    Budgeted balance sheet

|  | Qr 1 | Qr 2 | QR 3 | Qr 4 | Open Bal |
|---|---|---|---|---|---|
| Capital | 2000 | 2000 | 2000 | 2000 | 2000 |
| Sundry creditors purchases | 20 | 22 | 25 | 25 | 25 |
| Sundry creditors expense | 22 | 24 | 23 | 24 | 24 |
| Profit less dividend | 638.75 | 886.25 | 1167.5 | 1542.5 | 500 |
| **Total liabilities** | 2680.75 | 2932.25 | 3215.5 | 3591.5 | 2549 |
| Assets | 4200 | 5000 | 5200 | 6000 | 3800 |
| Depreciation | −1600 | −1700 | −1800 | −1900 | −1500 |
| Debtors | 120 | 100 | 110 | 120 | 120 |
| Cash | −149.25 | −557.75 | −369.5 | −693.5 | 4 |
| Inventory finished goods | 80 | 70 | 60 | 50 | 90 |
| Inventory raw material | 30 | 20 | 15 | 15 | 35 |
| **Total** | 2680.75 | 2932.25 | 3215.5 | 3591.5 | 2549 |

**Table A7.3**    Cash flow direct method

|  | Qr 1 | Qr 2 | Qr 3 | Qr 4 |
|---|---|---|---|---|
| Opening balance | 4 | −149.25 | −557.75 | −369.5 |
| Inflow |  |  |  |  |
| Debtors Opening balance | 120 | 120 | 100 | 110 |
| Cash sale | 300 | 400 | 500 | 500 |
| I month old | 500 | 600 | 600 | 700 |
| 2 months old | 80 | 100 | 190 | 180 |
| Total cash available | 1004 | 1070.75 | 832.25 | 1120.5 |
| **Cash outflow** |  |  |  |  |
| Sundry credit (purchase from opening balance) | 25 | 20 | 22 | 25 |
| Sundry credit (other expenses from opening balance) | 24 | 22 | 24 | 24 |
| Purchase cash | 50 | 50 | 50 | 50 |
| 1 month old | 100 | 100 | 100 | 100 |
| 2 months old | 30 | 28 | 125 | 175 |
| Labour | 100 | 110 | 105 | 110 |
| Other expenses | 378 | 416 | 402 | 405 |

*(Contd.)*

**(Table A7.3** *contd.*)

| Assets | 400 | 800 | 200 | 800 |
|---|---|---|---|---|
| Dividend | 0 | 0 | 60 | 0 |
| Income tax | 46.25 | 82.5 | 113.75 | 125 |
| Total ouflow | 1153.25 | 1628.5 | 1201.75 | 1814 |
| Closing cash | −149.25 | −557.75 | −369.5 | −693.5 |

**Table A7.4**   Cash flow indirect method

| Opening balance | 4 | −149.25 | −557.75 | −369.5 |
|---|---|---|---|---|
| Inflow | | | | |
| Sales | 1000 | 1220 | 1390 | 1490 |
| Total cash available | 1004 | 1070.75 | 832.25 | 1120.5 |
| **Outflow** | | | | |
| Purchases | 205 | 198 | 297 | 350 |
| Other expenses | 502 | 548 | 531 | 539 |
| Dividend | 0 | 0 | 60 | 0 |
| Tax | 46.25 | 82.5 | 113.75 | 125 |
| Assets | 400 | 800 | 200 | 800 |
| **Outflow** | 1153.25 | 1628.5 | 1201.75 | 1814 |
| Closing balance | −149.25 | −557.75 | −369.5 | −693.5 |

The cash flow budget shows a mounting negative cash balance rapidly increasing from ₹1.49 crore at the end of the first quarter to ₹6.93 crore. On the other hand, a minimum of at least one week's turnover is necessary to ensure payment in time for the creditors. This minimum balance would be ₹80 lakh. Why does this grim picture emerge in spite of the years after tax profit of ₹11.02 crore? The answer lies in the capital expansion programme of ₹22 crore for the year.

What is the remedy?

(i) Increasing share capital

(ii) Increasing loan

(iii) Increasing cash credit with bank

(iv) All of them put together

Some of the decisions would already have been tentatively taken when the capital proposal were floated.

Once these financing decisions are firmed up, the cash budgets can be recast.

Finally, since Table A7.1-A7.4 would be on spread sheet, they can be tested for sensitivity by changing one or more assumptions. Typically,

(i)   what would happen if the sale price is increased and sales volume is kept intact?

(ii)  as in one above but if sales quantity falls.

(iii) if credit terms are made more liberal.

(iv)  if capital expenses are postponed, etc.

## CHAPTER 8

# Flexible Budgets and Variance Analysis

## Learning Objectives

After reading this chapter, you will be able to understand

- the factors which could enhance or diminish the achievement of financial performance targets
- these factors as material prices and efficiency of material usage, labour rates, and labour efficiency, energy tariffs and energy efficiency, machine availability and efficiency of machine usage, machine capacity utilization, and variable and fixed overhead expenses
- the financial impact of such deviant factors, and express them as variances using the contrivance of flexible budgets and standard costing systems
- the impact of the variances to overall profits, individual product costs, activity costs, and individual responsibility centres of the organization
- that evaluation, only in terms of efficiency is not the same as evaluating them for the efficacy in achieving organizational goals and strategies
- the limitations and negative behavioural repercussions of standard costing and variance analysis, and the remedial steps required to enhance cooperation among executives, and maintain the cohesiveness and sustainability of organizations
- the shifting focus in some organizations following lean production systems, away from standard costing and variance analysis, and towards timely delivery, lower inventories, higher customer satisfaction, etc.

## INTRODUCTION

This chapter will deal with issues of measuring the impact of different factors on the profitability of an organization. These are labelled as variances. These measurements are made against a point of reference, which is the budget we dealt with in Chapter 7.

**Variances**
Variances measure the financial impact of deviations in the different factors which went into the building up of the budgets.

This chapter will deal extensively with the mechanics of it all and will have some number crunching. Chapter 9, on the other hand, will deal with some standard methods and processes to set up such reference points for comparison with actual performance, in addition to the necessary but not sufficient condition spelt out in Chapter 7, namely, one of participation.

These descriptions will revolve around the rubric of what is known as standard costing and budgetary controls, but Chapter 9 will also deal with some of the typical managerial uses of standard costing other than variance analysis. The precise and rigorous preparation required for this distinguishes it from the general domain of budgeting. In this chapter, we will build up the concepts around the numerical example of an open cast Indian coal mine, the Agnikundala Mines.

## RELATIONSHIP BETWEEN ACTUAL COST AND STANDARD COST

The following illustration (Fig. 8.1) is intended to demonstrate the very basic relationship between actual cost and standard cost. AQ means the 'actual quantity' of input used to produce the output. AP means the 'Actual price' of the input used to produce the output. SQ and SP refer to the 'standard' quantity and price, respectively, that was anticipated. As you will soon see, variance analysis can be conducted for each factor of productive input: material, labour, and overhead. Variances are simply the differences between the actual cost incurred and the standard cost that was appropriate for the achieved production.

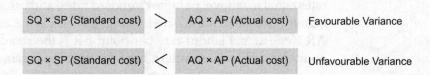

| SQ × SP (Standard cost) | > | AQ × AP (Actual cost) | Favourable Variance |
| SQ × SP (Standard cost) | < | AQ × AP (Actual cost) | Unfavourable Variance |

**Fig. 8.1**  Favourable and unfavourable variances

## Variances Related to Direct Material

**Materials price variance**  A variance that exposes the difference between the standard price for materials purchased and the amount actually paid for those materials {(Standard price – Actual price) × Actual quantity}.

**Materials quantity variance**  A variance that compares the standard quantity of materials that should have been used to the actual quantity of materials used. The quantity variation is measured at the standard price per unit {(Standard quantity – Actual quantity) × Standard price} (see Fig. 8.2).

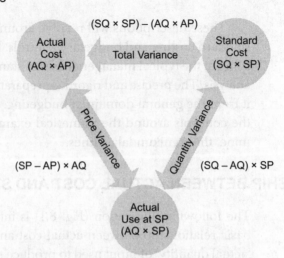

**Fig. 8.2** Variance related to direct material

## VARIANCES RELATING TO DIRECT LABOUR

The intrinsic logic for direct labour variances is very similar to that of direct material. The total variance for direct labour is found by comparing actual direct labour cost to standard direct labour cost. The overall labour variance could result from any combination of having paid labourers at rates equal to, above, or below standard rates, and using more or less direct labour hours than anticipated. In Fig. 8.3, AH is the actual hours worked, AR is the actual labour rate per hour, SR is the standard labour rate per hour, and SH is the standard hour for the output achieved.

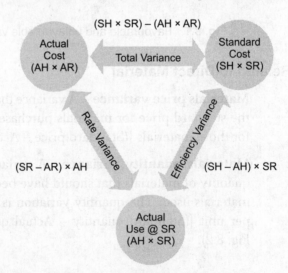

**Fig. 8.3** Variance related to direct labour

The total direct labour variance can be separated into two types:

**Labour rate variance**   A variance that reveals the difference between the standard rate and actual rate for the actual labour hours worked {(Standard rate – Actual rate) × Actual hours}.

**Labour efficiency variance**   A variance that compares the standard hours of direct labour that should have been used to the actual hours worked. The efficiency variance is measured at the standard rate per hour {(Standard hours – Actual hours) × Standard rate}.

## DEFINITION OF STANDARD COSTING

**Simple production system**
Even an apparently simple production system has several inter-related activities

This chapter will weave together budgeting and standard costing. Budgeting has already been defined in Chapter 7. A simple (almost simplistic) definition of standard costing provided by the Chartered Institute of Management Accountants (CIMA 2000) states the following: *The planned unit cost of products, components, or services produced in a period. The standard cost may be determined in a number of bases. The main use of standard costs is in performance measurement, control, stock evaluation, and in establishing selling prices.*

There are several ancillary activities which go towards making the flow of work in the Agnikundala Mines possible. These include seeking the right spot for the mines by geological drilling and planning the sites. The mining operations involve the removal of the overburden of earth and exposing the coal. This involves the use of drilling and explosives. Once the coal is exposed, holes are drilled on it and filled with explosives to dislodge the coal and fragment it. A dozer pushes the coal into heaps. The shovel loads it into dumpers that transport it to the coal handling plant, where it is loaded on to wagons and weighed. The roads for the dump truck have to be made and maintained in good condition. The costly machinery has to be kept in good order all the time. The shovels run on electricity, whereas the dumpers and dozers run on diesel. Therefore, power stations, and diesel and lubricant stores have to be maintained. There are, of course, the administration purchase and accounts offices that support all these activities. Figure 8.4 shows the types of variances.

### Comparative Analysis of Variations of Actual Profits from Budgets

Table 8.1 shows the variance between the budgeted and actual profits of Agnikundala for the month of June 2005. The difference between the budgeted profit of ₹12,00,000 and the actual profits of ₹3,96,000 is ₹8,04,000. We could describe this as the *zero level analysis*. If we consider that it is the function of the general manager of the mine to be fully responsible for this fall in performance, and we do not propose to help him any further, we

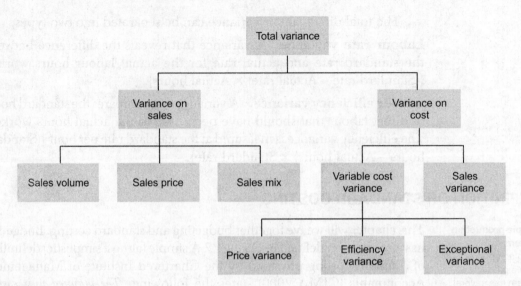

**Fig. 8.4**  Types of variances

**Table 8.1**  Zero level analysis of variances in June 2005 for Agnikundala Mines

|  | Budget | Actual | Variance |
|---|---|---|---|
| Production/sales tonne | 1,50,000 | 1,00,000 | −50,000 |
| Revenue (₹) | 75,00,000 | 55,00,000 | −20,00,000 |
| Costs (₹) | 6,30,000 | 5,10,400 | +11,96,000 |
| Profit (₹) | 12,00,000 | 3,96,000 | −8,04,000 |

would not be doing the organization any service. Unfortunately, this is precisely what is done by organizations that take the concept of responsibility accounting to its brutal extreme of fixing the responsibility only on the unit head.

In Table 8.1, we have followed a convention where variances that have decreased profits are shown in the negative and those that have increased profits have been shown as positive. It is more common to label the minus figures as unfavourable (U) and the positive ones as favourable (F). In all future tables, we will either show it algebraically to facilitate direct manipulation in an excel spreadsheet, or as U and F, if no such spreadsheet is envisaged.

More progressive organizations would provide helpful comparisons as shown in Table 8.2. They have shown the numbers under the financial account heads, even if they do not show them under cost heads.

Royalty costs have been ignored as they cannot be controlled by the local management of the mines. We have the option to add it on as an item of variable costs.

**Table 8.2** Comparative analysis of expenses and revenue of Agnikundala Mines against the budget for June 2005

|  | Budget | Actual | Variance |
|---|---|---|---|
| Production/sales tonne | 1,50,000 | 1,00,000 | −50,000 |
| Revenue (₹) | 7,50,000 | 5,50,000 | −2,00,000 |
| Salaries | 5,00,000 | 5,50,000 | −50,000 |
| Diesel (₹) | 1,50,000 | 1.10,000 | +40,000 |
| Lubricant (₹) | 3,50,000 | 2,20,000 | +1,30,000 |
| Explosives (₹) | 9,00,000 | 4,00,000 | +5,00,000 |
| Other mining material (₹) | 1,50,000 | 72,000 | +78,000 |
| Spare parts (₹) | 4,50,000 | 4,00,000 | +50,000 |
| Road maintenance material (₹) | 50,000 | 52,000 | −2000 |
| Power (₹) | 5,00,000 | 4,00,000 | +1,00,000 |
| Depreciation (₹) | 10,00,000 | 10,50,000 | −50,000 |
| Marketing (₹) | 50,000 | 48,000 | +2000 |
| Admin/Accts/Purchase (₹) | 4,00,000 | 3,80,000 | +2000 |
| Total costs (₹) | 63,00,000 | 51,04,000 | +11,96,000 |
| Profit (Loss) (₹) | 12,00,000 | 3,96,000 | −8,04,000 |

In the analysis, Table 8.2 shows that the total unfavourable variance of ₹8,04,000, is accounted for by the following conditions:

1. The production, sales, and revenue have fallen precipitously giving an unfavourable variance of ₹20,00,000.
2. Under many accounting heads such as diesel, lubricants, explosives, and other variable items, the expenses are considerably less than the budget, and have compensated for the unfavourable variance.
3. Under many heads the expenses are at par.
4. There have been minor excesses under some of the heads.

Does this mean that barring production and sales all others have been working satisfactorily or even superbly? As we will discover with further analysis, aligning it with responsibility centres, this is true.

## Example 8.1  Variance Analysis

Do the variance analysis using the data given below.
Standard cost on material and labour for the making of one lot of a Fair Skin soap is estimated as follows:

**Standard Price**

| Material | 800Kg | @ ₹40 per kg |
|---|---|---|
| Labour | 100hrs | @ ₹20 per hr |

**Actual Price**

| | | |
|---|---|---|
| Material | 750Kg | @ ₹45 per kg |
| Labour | 80hrs | @ ₹30 per hr |

**Material Cost Variance** (Standard cost of material – Actual cost of material)

(800 kg × ₹40 – 750 kg × ₹45) = – 1750  **Unfavourable**

**Material Price Variance** (i) Actual usage (Standard price – Actual price)

750 kg (₹40 – ₹45) = – 3750  **Unfavourable**

**Material Usage Variance** (ii) Standard price (Standard usage – Actual usage)

₹40 (800 kg – 750 kg) = 2000  **Favourable**

**Labour Cost Variance** Standard cost of labour – Actual cost of labour

(100 hrs × ₹20 – 80 hrs × ₹30) = – 400  **Unfavourable**

**Labour Rate Variance** (i) Actual time (Standard rate – Actual rate)

80 hrs (₹20 – ₹30) = – 800  **Unfavourable**

**Labour Efficiency Variance** (ii) Standard rate (Standard time – Actual time)

₹20 (100 hrs – 80 hrs) = 400  **Favourable**

## Factors that Deviate from Budgets and Isolate the Variances for Responsibility Centres

Before we venture into a more detailed analysis, let us describe the expectations from each of the responsibility centres. This is presented in Table 8.3.

**Table 8.3** Expectations from responsibility centres at Agnikundala Mines

| Budget line item | Responsibility |
|---|---|
| 1. Revenue | Sales price depends on quality, i.e., the geologist and mines manager, quantity maintenance manager for availability of machines, the civil engineer for road conditions, personnel manager for motivation and industrial peace, the mines manager for production, and the marketing manager for marketing, which will include the wagons being available from the railways and positioned under the coal handling plant |
| 2. Salaries | General manager who regulates recruitment |
| 3. Diesel | Diesel litres/hour—maintenance manager, price/litre—purchase manager, output/hour—mines manager and civil engineer |
| 4. Lubricants | Same as diesel |
| 5. Explosives | Quantity mines manager, price purchase manager |
| 6. Other variables | As for explosives |
| 7. Spare parts | Quantity maintenance engineer, price purchase manager |
| 8. Road material | Quantity civil engineer, price purchase manager |
| 9. Depreciation | Regulated by the general manager, as assets are controlled by him/her |
| 10. Marketing | Marketing manager |
| 11. Administration, etc. | General manager |

It may be seen that much as we may have clear cut organizational structures and definitions of responsibility, many of the tasks require great cooperation among the responsibility centres, even in a production system as simple as that of the Agnikundala Mines.

## Cause for Deviation from Budget–Sales and Second Level Analysis of Variances

**Production and sales**
These are preferred cost drivers in flexing budgets.

One of the most overwhelming causes for the deviation from the budget is the result of changes in the production and sales volumes. That is why, production and sales are usually chosen as cost drivers, both for costs and revenue. Consequently, it is customary for many companies to prepare budgets for different levels of production.

These budgets are described as *flexible budgets*. One can flex the budget in several ways, but flexing it on the lines of the volume of production is the most popular option. Flexing can be done at the same time as preparation; it can also flex the budget *ex post facto* to match the actual production achieved, and compare it with the original budget, which is described as *static budgets*. This can be seen in Table 8.4. While doing this, we will register the profound impact of the revenues rapidly (and usually linearly) changing with production and sales.

The analysis shown in Table 8.4 is another powerful stage in tracing variances to responsibility centres and the expectation described in Table 8.3.

Static budgets are built on certain assumptions and expectations on the variability of revenues and costs with production/sales volume. Thus, if we show salaries as being fixed, it is an assertion of the fact that we will not as a principle wish to change our personnel for short-term changes in production. Similarly, spare parts may be required for preventive maintenance which is fixed in nature, and some segments that need change in order to change production. Depreciation is treated as fixed as by and large life does not change with use, or more possibly, we may not like the manager to think so and regulate his production accordingly. Having invested heavily, management may want to indicate to the manager that he must produce and sell as much as he can and match the demand. There may be a base charge for the connected load and a variable charge for usage of power. Roads must be maintained and always kept in good condition irrespective of the level of production, and so on.

**Table 8.4** Flexible budgets and sales volume and flexible budget variances in Agnikundala Mines for June 2005

| Item | Static budget (1) | Actual (2) | Flexible budget (3) | Total variance 1–2 (4) | Sales volume variance 1–3 (5) | Flexible budget variance 3–2 (6) | Per tonne Budgeted fixed costs (7) | Per tonne budgeted variable costs (8) |
|---|---|---|---|---|---|---|---|---|
| 1. Production tonnes | 1,50,000 | 1,00,000 | 1,00,000 | –50,000 | –50,000 | 0 | | |
| 2. Revenue | 75,00,000 | 55,00,000 | 50,00,000 | –20,00,000 | –25,00,000 | 5,00,000 | | 50 |
| 3. Salaries (F) | 5,00,000 | 5,50,000 | 5,00,000 | –50,000 | 0 | –50,000 | 3.333333 | 0 |
| 4. Diesel (V) | 15,00,000 | 11,00,000 | 10,00,000 | 4,00,000 | 5,00,000 | –1,00,000 | 0 | 10 |
| 5. Lubricants (V) | 3,50,000 | 2,20,000 | 2,33,333.3 | 1,30,000 | 1,16,666.7 | 13,333.33 | 0 | 2.33 |
| 6. Explosives(V) | 9,00,000 | 4,00,000 | 6,00,000 | 5,00,000 | 3,00,000 | 2,00,000 | 0 | 6 |
| 7. Other variables | 1,50,000 | 72,000 | 1,00,000 | 78,000 | 50,000 | 28,000 | 0 | 1 |
| 8. Spare parts (50% V) | 4,50,000 | 4,00,000 | 3,75,000 | 50,000 | 75,000 | –25,000 | 1.5 | 1.5 |
| 9. Road main material (F) | 50,000 | 52,000 | 50,000 | –2000 | 0 | –2000 | 0.333333 | 0 |
| 10. Power (75% V) | 5,00,000 | 4,00,000 | 3,75,000 | 1,00,000 | 1,25,000 | –25,000 | 0.833333 | 2.5 |
| 11. Depreciation | 10,00,000 | 10,50,000 | 10,00,000 | –50,000 | 0 | –50,000 | 6.666667 | 0 |
| 12. Marketing (F) | 5,00,000 | 4,80,000 | 5,00,000 | 20,000 | 0 | 20,000 | 3.333333 | 0 |
| 13. Admin. accts purchase (F) | 4,00,000 | 3,80,000 | 4,00,000 | 20,000 | 0 | 20,000 | 2.666667 | 0 |
| 14. Total cost (3 to 13) | 63,00,000 | 51,04,000 | 51,33,333 | 11,96,000 | 11,66,667 | 29,333.33 | 18.666 | 23.333 |
| 15. Contribution (50–23.333)* 1,50,000 | 40,00,000 | | | | –13,33,333 | | | |
| 16. Contribution/tonne (Item 15 ÷ item 1) | 26.667 | | | | | | | |
| 17. Fixed costs (item 14 minus 23.33* 1,50,000) | 28,00,000 | | | | | | | |
| 18. Profit item 2 minus item 14 or item15 minus item 17 | 12,00,000 | 3,96,000 | –1,33,333 | –8,04,000 | –13,33,333 | 5,29,333.3 | | |

Column 1 and 2 are self-explanatory. Column 3 is the flexed version of the static budget in Column 1, i.e., the figures are computed as follows:

Revenue is actual sale value at budgeted prices, i.e., 1,00,000 × 50.

Expenses are budgeted fixed cost in the static budget (Column 1) + budgeted variable cost shown in Column 8 × Actual production/sale, i.e., 1,00,000.

Therefore, by simple logic of CVP analysis the variance between Column 1 and Column 3 is the effect only of change in sales volume, all other things being the same. This figure is shown in Column 5. The total profit variance in Column 5 can be seen to be ₹13,33,333. This is equal to contribution/unit × Δ production, i.e., change in production, plus or minus, as the case may be. Thus, it is also equal to 26.667 × 50,000, or 13,33,333.

Now comes the task of aligning this amount along the responsibility centres. One can do this with some reservations, as many of the causes are overlapping and are usually of joint responsibility. But the flavour of it would be available in Table 8.5 (the basic data and calculations are not shown here).

An analytical statement as in Table 8.5 may be useful for seeing why the deviation took place and to determine how it can be avoided in the future. But if it focuses too sharply on determining the responsibility centre that should be penalized for it, it would lead to endless disputes of figures and mutual blame throwing.

Thus, we have dealt with a factor of sales volume that could explain ₹13,33,333, which is 1.65 times of the total variance of ₹8,04,000. Obviously some compensating factors must have helped in restoring a portion of these variances.

**Table 8.5** Responsibility for sales volume variance

| Responsibility centre | Impact on production/ sales variance | Qty. of variance in tonnes | Impact on profit (₹) = Impact on production × contribution per unit = ₹26.6667 |
|---|---|---|---|
| Maintenance | Against 80% machine availability, only 70% was achieved | 10,000 | –₹26,668 |
| Civil (road) | For three days the roads were slushy and dumpers could not move fast | 3000 | –₹8000 |
| Mines manager | Low productivity | 17,000 | –₹45,334 |
| Purchase manager | Delays in supplying spares resulting down time of machines and delay, and supply of diesel and explosives | 10,000 | –₹26,667 |
| Personnel manager | One day go slow strike by workers | 5000 | –₹13,335 |
| Marketing manager | Two days wagon not placed in time leading to choking of coal handling plant | 5000 | –₹13,335 |
| Total Agnikundala | | 50,000 | –₹13,33,333 as shown in column 5 of Table 8.4 |

Table 8.4 shows that the compensating factors are available in the numbers in Column 6. One can see that the dominant share is due to sales price variance which is favourable (+ ₹50,000). In deciding the responsibility centre that should take credit for it, one can impetuously conclude that it should be the marketing department. But the credit may also be due to the quality, which may be the result of good geological planning and better selective mining, and more careful fragmentation to suit customer needs. It may also be due to a different product mix. Thus, in coal, different fractions may have different prices. In many other industries the impact of product mix can be profound and a third level analysis may be necessary for this.

After doing all this, we would still not have seen all the facets of the alignment of variances with responsibility centres and would need a third level analysis.

## Third Level Analysis of Variances

The third level variance is due to the flexible budget variance being composed of factors which are controlled by more than one responsibility centre. Let us take one unfavourable variance, i.e., diesel. Its analysis may appear simple but may turn out to be quite difficult. Against a permissible amount of ₹10,00,000, they have spent ₹11,00,000, i.e., they have an unfavourable variance of ₹1,00,000. This could be composed of three major factors, namely, litres per machine hour, output per machine hour, and price per litre. These have been analysed in Table 8.6.

The analysis of lubricants will follow the same method as for diesel, as it also has the involvement of three responsibility centres.

The analysis of power would be even more complicated as the consumption of power involves several departments. Its use in production machinery such as shovels, and the relationship of the responsibility centres of maintenance, the mines manager, and power purchasers are analogous.

Item 6 (explosives) would have a less complex analysis as only two departments are involved. This could be worked as the following:

$$\text{Price variance} = \Delta \text{ Price} \times \text{Actual quantity purchased}$$
$$\text{Efficiency variance} = \text{Standard quantity required for actual production} - \text{Actual quantity used}$$

**Table 8.6**　Diesel cost—level three analysis

| | Flexible budget | Actual | Responsibility | Formula for variance | Amount (₹) |
|---|---|---|---|---|---|
| 1. Diesel qty/machine hour | 43 | 44 | Maintenance | | −24,000 |
| 2. Diesel for machine hour actually used | *44,806 | 45,848 | Maintenance | Δ usage × standard prices | rounded |
| 3. Output/machine hour | 99 | 96 | Mines manager | | −31,000 |
| 4. Machine hours for actual output | **1010 | #1042 | Mines manager | Δ machine hrs × standard diesel per machine hour × standard price | rounded |
| 5. Price/litre (₹) | 23 | 24 | Purchase manager | | |
| 6. Diesel actually used (litres) | ***45,833 | 45,833 | Flexed | | |
| Total cost of actual diesel used (₹) | 10,54,166 | 11,00,000 | Purchase manager | Δ price × actual diesel used | − 45,000 rounded |
| 7. Cost/tonne ₹(item 1 × item 5 ÷ item 3) | 10 | 11 | | | |
| Variance total rounded off | | | | | −1,00,000 |

\* 1042 * 43
\*\* 1,00,000 ÷ 99
\# 1,00,000 ÷ 96
\*\*\* 11,00,000 ÷ 24 = 45,833

Item 7 (other variable), item 8 (spare parts), and item 9 (road material) are composed of several individual items, which are of small value by themselves but may add up to significant numbers. It is usually easier to compare actual consumption with static budgets for the more significant items which can be described as 'A' items. Flexing individual items to match production may not be theoretically sound although in the aggregate it may have statistical significance, as random errors in the behaviour of one item may be compensated by the behaviour of another item in order to keep the expenses as typically semi-variable in the aggregate. The concept of 'A' items in inventory management is dealt with in Chapter 10. The price variances of these items can usually be compiled every day on the computer, as shown in Table 8.7.

Such an analysis can easily be generated by the computer and can be discussed in periodic cost meetings. The remedy could be to change the vendor or change the design and specifications of the part concerned.

**Labour-oriented industry**
In labour-oriented industries unlike in Agnikundala, wages would be usually piece-rated and variance analysis would be analogous to material cost variances.

Since Agnikundala is a heavily mechanized mine and labour costs are only peripheral, and the wages are paid in time rate, there can be no particular benefit in working out the variances in labour costs. If, on the other hand, it were a more labour oriented industry and workers were paid by piece rate, it would give rise to variances exactly on the analogy of material, i.e., broken into labour efficiency and labour rate variance.

**Table 8.7**  Price variance analysis on 22 June 2005

| Item | Standard price (₹) | Actual price (₹) | Unit price variance (₹) | Quantity bought | Total price variance on date (₹) | Cumulative price variance for month (₹) | Cumulative price variance for year (₹) |
|---|---|---|---|---|---|---|---|
| Air cleaner ___ | 2000 | 2300 | 100 | 20 | 20,000 | 30,000 | 40,000 |

The fixed costs can be scrutinized according to each responsibility centre.

It is a common failing that the attention of organizations is often drawn exclusively to variable costs.

## Sales Mix

A sales mix variance can arise in organizations selling more than one product. In practice it is caused by the use of average prices for families of products or customers. At the individual product line level the only variances which can arise are price and volume. An example will illustrate the cause of the variance.

A company budgets to sell 1000 products – being 500 units of Deo Freshy at ₹100 per product and 500 units of Talcum Fragzz at ₹110. The company actually sold 1200 products – being 800 units of Deo Freshy at ₹90 and 400 units of Talcum Fragzz at ₹120.

Conventional variance analysis is shown in Table 8.8.

**Table 8.8**  Variance analysis of Deo Freshy and Talcum Fragzz

| Budgeted Sales | Deo Freshy | Talcum Fragzz | | |
|---|---|---|---|---|
| Total no. of products to be sold | 500 | 500 | 1000 products | |
| Price per product | ₹100 | ₹110 | | |
| Actual sales | Deo Freshy | Talcum Fragzz | | |
| No. of products sold | 800 | 400 | 1200 products | |
| Price per product | ₹90 | ₹120 | | |
| | Actual | Budgeted | Variance | |
| No. of products | 1200 | 1000 | 200 | *Favourable* |
| Average price | ₹100 | ₹105 | ₹(5) | *Unfavourable* |
| | Actual | Budgeted | Variance | |
| Sales Deo Freshy | ₹72,000 | ₹50,000 | ₹22,000 | *Favourable* |
| Sales Talcum Fragzz | ₹48,000 | ₹55,000 | ₹(7000) | *Unfavourable* |
| Total | ₹1,20,000 | ₹1,05,000 | ₹15,000 | *Favourable* |

*(Contd)*

**Table 8.8**  *(Contd)*

| Budgeted Sales | Deo Freshy | Talcum Fragzz | |
|---|---|---|---|
| The 15,000 favourable variance could be analysed as | | | |
| Sales volume | 21,000 | (1200 – 1000) × 105 | *Favourable* |
| Sales price | ₹(6000) | (100 – 105) × 1200 | *Unfavourable* |
| Sales Volume | | | |
| Deo Freshy | 31,500 | (800 – 500) × 105 | *Favourable* |
| Talcum Fragzz | (10,500) | (400 – 500) × 105 | *Unfavourable* |
| Sales Price | | | |
| Deo Freshy | ₹(8000) | (90 – 100) × 800 | *Unfavourable* |
| Talcum Fragzz | ₹4000 | (120 – 110) × 400 | *Favourable* |
| Sales Mix | | | |
| Deo Freshy | ₹(1500) | (800 – 500) × (100 – 105) | *Unfavourable* |
| Talcum Fragzz | ₹(500) | (400 – 500) × (110 – 105) | *Unfavourable* |

From the example above the variable costs and margins would need to be calculated to identify if the results of the sales tactics of lower price of Deo Freshy to gain more volume was 'better' than those of the manager of Talcum Fragzz.

## The General Problem of Sharing of Common Variance

The analysis in Table 8.6 shows a controversial feature in respect of variances for which there is joint responsibility, e.g., diesel, where responsibility is shared between three departments. The material price variance has been calculated on the actual quantity used, which means that the impact of other responsibility centres in excess usage is also partly passed on to the purchase manager. Conversely, if the usage is less than standard, and it is because material of higher quality has been purchased at higher prices, he/she will stand to gain.

The quantity of diesel used is seen to be a function of output per machine hour and the fuel used per hour, which are in two different responsibility centres as per the organizational structure. The presentation in Table 8.6 shows the impact of bad engine quality computed on an inefficient use of the machines, thus placing the responsibility for the joint variance entirely on the maintenance department. An alterative analysis would be if the variance had been costed against the mines manager as the following:

Δ Machine hours × Actual diesel per machine hour × Standard price
= ₹32,384, (item 4 of Table 8.6).

If this had been done, the variance against the maintenance department would be as follows:

$1 \times 1010 \times 23 = 23,230$, (item 1 of Table 8.6). The total variances would be the same (subject to rounding off). The problem of forcibly allocating joint causes to one responsibility centre can be appreciated with Fig. 8.5.

**Division of responsibility**
The division of responsibility of material variances between price and usage needs to be done with caution and imagination to make sure purchase managers and production managers do not indulge in throwing blame on each other.

Figure 8.5 shows the original flexible budget as the inner rectangle IEGH (in white) built up by multiplying the standard prices by standard usage. The rectangle BIEC (shaded) extending on top of the earlier rectangle is Δ price × standard quantity as a variance belonging to purchase and is clear enough. The rectangle to the left, DIHF is Δ quantity × standard price (shaded grey) belonging to production, and is also clear enough. But the black portion on left hand top corner, ABID, i.e., Δ quantity × Δ price, is controversial and can cause friction.

Good organizations, therefore, use these analyses as trends and do not attempt to ruthlessly fix responsibilities.

**Responsibility of purchase manager**
Purchase manager's responsibility extends to forecasting price trends and getting information on alternate substitute material.

Lastly, if prices are not under the control of the purchase manager, what is his/her role in the management of materials? Apart from making sure of quality and timely delivery, he/she has to make sure that production is helped to adhere to targets, and in this, his/her responsibility is collective. Moreover, as in the case of diesel cost variance elaborated in Table 8.7, the purchase manager is responsible for forecasting the future trends of prices and alternative fuels. This information would stimulate the users of diesel to develop and maintain machines that are efficient in fuel use. This has been discussed in Chapter 7, in the paragraph on 'Responsibility and Controllability'.

The allocation of the blackened portion on the right hand top of the rectangle, as in Fig. 8.5, between the mines manager and the maintenance department shown in numbers in Table 8.6, would pose a similar ticklish problem. Incorrect operation of machines by the mines manager can

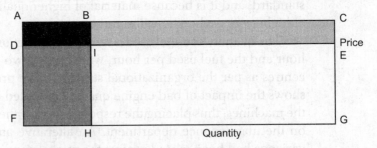

**Fig. 8.5** Joint responsibility of material variances

increase the fuel use per hour, as machines may get spoilt by harsh handling, over speeding, etc. So, who should bear the brunt of Δ fuel per machine hour × Δ machine hours used, for a given production? Variance analyses are full of such issues and one must beware of coming to rash conclusions by using simplistic formulae.

## VARIED MEANING OF OVERHEADS

**Overheads**
The concept of overheads can also be used for the measurement of performance of separate responsibility centres and the allocation of standard costs to products, segregating the variances of responsibilities to the generators and users of the services.

The expression overheads has been used in Chapters 3, 5, and 6, as those expenses which cannot be traced with ease and low costs to product or service are described as indirect costs or overheads. Thus far it is a good definition. But the concept of overhead can also be used as a construct arising from organizational responsibilities. Thus, in Agnikundala Mines we have described the responsibility of the maintenance department to make machines available and ensure that the engines are in good condition so that fuel and lubricant use/machine hour or power used/machine hour is optimal. This can be built into the cost accounting system by the maintenance department supplying the machine to the mining department at standard hourly rates, which could include the variable cost of diesel and lubricants. Machine hours then become the cost driver for this department, and its budgets have to be flexed to machine hours and not to production. The flexible budget variance, i.e., the spending variance, would then be judged with reference to the diesel consumed for actual machine hours and not the standard machine hours for production.

Its flexible budget would be as follows:

Machine hours actually used × Standard fuel used per machine hour

and the actual can be compared with this. The difference could be costed at standard fuel prices. The figure is worked out as –₹24,000, against item 2 of Table 8.6.

It may be noted that flexing is not done for production but its proximate cost driver, namely, machine hours. The costs are related to the ultimate cost driver, namely, production, when the services rendered by the overheads are converted by the direct production department.

The responsibility of the mines manager could be to get the best possible output per machine hour. Its efficient use of machine hours would then be computed by the variations in machine hours which should have been taken for the actual production, and the actual machine hours costed at standard fuel per hour and at standard prices. The figures are worked out as –₹31,000, against item 4 in Table 8.6.

## Efficiency Variance due to Change in Batch Size in Actual and Budget

If for some reason the actual batch size is different from the budgeted batch size, the variance can be computed as the following:

(Actual number of batches for actual production – Budgeted batch size allowed for actual production) × Standard cost/batch

This standard cost may only be labour cost, material cost, labour plus material costs, or a sum of standard costs of several activities. This is illustrated with an example (Example 8.2).

## Production Volume Variance, Fixed Spending Variance, and Capacity Utilization

We have hitherto computed variances so that they could tie up with profit variance. We, therefore, used the concept of contribution per unit production as an easy way of explaining the variations in profit due to variation in production and sale, using the following formula:

$$\Delta \text{ Profit} = \Delta \text{ Production/Sale} \times \text{Contribution/Unit}$$

### Example 8.2   Batch Size Variance

The budget proposed that 3000 units of part X would be manufactured in 5 batches. The standard cost of each batch was ₹10,000. Thus, the total overhead to be charged to the product cost was ₹50,000. But unfortunately, it took six batches to manufacture these. Consequently, the negative variance was (6 – 5) × 10,000 = ₹10,000 (unfavourable).

But there could be occasions when we do not sell the product and services but would like to understand the variations in costs per unit due to change in volume. Typical examples are

1. the cost per student when this is reimbursed by some arrangement with a donor,
2. the cost per unit when a price regulating authority is externally regulating the prices, and
3. the cost per unit when there is a managerial need to fix transfer prices from one department to another.

To understand the mechanics, let us scrutinize the analysis in Table 8.4. The budgeted and actual cost per unit and the corresponding production are restated in Table 8.9.

Table 8.9    An analysis of cost per tonne in Agnikundala Mines for June 2005

| Item | Budget | | Actual | |
| --- | --- | --- | --- | --- |
| Production tonnes | Amount (₹) | ₹per tonne | Amount (₹) | ₹per tonne |
| Fixed cost | 2,80,000 | 18.667 | | |
| Variable cost | 3,50,000 | 23.333 | | |
| Total cost | 6,30,000 | 42 | 51,04,000 | 51.04 |

**Loss or gain valuing**
Loss or gain in value due to change in production volume can be computed either on contribution per unit or budget fixed cost per unit. The latter is very subjective, whereas the former is based on market values and is sharper in its insights.

Total variance = $1,00,000 \times (42 - 51.04) = ₹9,04,000$, (U).

Explained by flexible budget variance from Table 8.4 = ₹29,333, (F).

Balance to be explained = $9,04,000 + 29,333 = ₹9,33,333$

Or, Fixed cost per unit × Δ Production volume = ₹9,33,350, (rounded off)

This figure is labelled as production volume variance.

This is an alternate way of valuing the loss or gain due to capacity utilization.

It may be seen that this figure is different from the variance computed using contribution per unit which was ₹13,33,333 as per Table 8.4.

This production volume variance can be ascribed to the different responsibility centres as has been done in Table 8.5. Thus, the efficient use of the resources provided can be measured in terms of fixed cost per machine hour gained or lost.

It may be seen that the contribution based figure relates the value loss to the market value and the figure based budgeted fixed cost per unit production, and the estimates of capacity appropriate to the budget fixed costs, and is therefore very subjective. It would be seen that both measures have appropriate applications. Spending variance of fixed expenses is the difference between the actual expenses and the flexible budget, which for fixed expenses is the same as the difference between the actual and the static budget.

## Formulae for Calculating Variance Analysis—A Memory Aid

The entire discussion on variance analysis has sandwiched formulae in between descriptions and arguments. It would be useful at this stage to provide, in a tabular form and at one place, all the formulae that have been used so far. This is given in Table 8.10.

**Table 8.10** A summary of variances used in cost analysis

| | Item | Formula | Position in chapter | Value |
|---|---|---|---|---|
| 1. | Sales volume | Contribution per unit × Δ volume | Item 18, Col. 5 of Table 8.4 | –₹13,33,333 |
| 2. | Production volume | Budgeted fixed cost unit × Δ volume | Text following Table 8.8 | –₹9,33,333 |
| 3. | Flexible budget | Flexible budget – Actual expenses | Item 18, Col. 6 of Table 8.4 | +₹5,29,333.3 |
| 4. | Sale price | (Actual sale price – Budgeted sales price) × Actual quantity sold | Item 2, Col. 6 of Table 8.4 | +₹5,00,000 |
| 5. | Purchase price | (Budgeted price – Actual price) × Actual quantity purchased/used | Item 7 of Table 8.6 | –₹45,000 |
| 6. | Material usage efficiency | (Budgeted quantity for actual production – Actual quantity for actual production) × Budgeted price | Item 1 and 3 of Table 8.6 | –(₹24,000 + ₹ 31,000 = ₹55,000 |
| 7. | Labour rate | (Budgeted labour rate – Actual labour rate) × Actual labour hours | See discussion on pages 263–264 | Not computed |
| 8. | Labour efficiency | (Budgeted labour hours for actual production – Actual hours for actual production) × Budgeted labour rate | See discussion on pages 263–264 | Not computed |
| 9. | Variable overhead spending | (Budgeted variable cost for actual service rendered – Actual variable cost for actual service rendered calculated at budgeted prices | Item 2 of Table 8.6 | –₹24,000 after excluding price variance shown against Item 5 of this Figure |
| 10. | Variable overhead efficiency | (Budgeted measure of service required for actual production – Actual measure of services used for actual production) × Budgeted cost per unit measure of the service | Item 4 of Table 8.6 | –₹31,000 |
| 11. | Fixed cost spending | Actual expenses – Flexible budget also = Actual expense – Static budgeted expenses | Col. 6 of Table 8.4, read items shown as fixed costs | –₹50,000 salaries; ₹2000 road material; –₹50,000 dep.; + ₹20,000 marketing; + ₹20,000 admin. |
| 12. | Batch size variance (efficiency) | (No. of standard batches for actual production – Actual number of batches) × Standard cost of batch | Explained in Example 8.1 | Not computed anywhere |

## Investigating a Variance

As mentioned earlier in the chapter, variance analysis should never be used to *fix responsibility* but to investigate matters further (Horngren et al. 2003). The first criterion should be that investigations should be made for both positive and negative variances because an abnormally positive variance in one department may be the cause of a corresponding bad variance elsewhere. Thus, if purchase price variance is highly positive, it may be because quality is compromised and results in excess quantity which is reflected in some other responsibility centre, for example, in this case the maintenance department.

**Variance analysis**
It should help to initiate investigation and could be triggered by a variance more than an accepted threshold of both positive and negative variances in absolute amount, and as a percentage of the budget. It can also be watched like quality performance in a chart.

The threshold is chosen both for the absolute amount and the percentage variation from budget. This would make sure there is an even spread of concern and attention across all departments and responsibility centres, big or small. Thus, one can use the rule that variances of more than ₹10,000 in any month or more than ± 5 per cent variation are taken for investigation. One can also use variance control charts as one uses in quality control as shown in Fig. 8.6.

Thus, if we get 52 weeks of variance for a particular responsibility centre, one can see if its mean is around 120 as can be seen in Fig. 8.6. If not, there is a need to investigate this. The standard deviation of the plots from the mean can be calculated. This is also easily obtained from a spreadsheet which has a formula that automatically works this out. One can see

1. the weekly plots outside the line marking ± 2.33 standard deviation, which would indicate the figure has not arisen by the operation of the principle of random statistical distribution; and
2. the weekly plots are not unduly aligned either north or south of the central line of the standard.

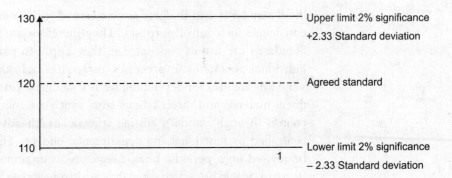

**Fig. 8.6**  Graph of control limits (Lucey 2002)

**Table 8.11** Comparison between standard costing and normal costing

| Item | Normal costing | Standard costing |
|---|---|---|
| Direct material/direct labour | Actuals charged to product | Standard based on rigorous exercise and charged to product |
| Overheads | Budgeted rate charged to product based on expected activity sometimes including cost of idleness | Standard rate charged to product based on budget for normal activity, i.e., normally excluding idle capacity costs |
| Manner of fixing overhead rate | Based on less rigorous exercise | Rate fixed with rigorous exercise |
| Treatment of variances in accounts (and inventory of finished goods) | 1. Carried forward to next year, or 2. Absorbed in product, or 3. Charged to profit and loss of the year, as considered expedient | Usually absorbed in the profit and loss account as higher or lower value of finished goods inventory or work-in-process |

## Comparison of Normal Costing and Standard Costing

In Chapter 5 on job costing, we dealt with the concept of normal costing which used budgeted overhead rates to be applied to the product. Since we have also used the concept of budgeted overheads in this chapter as part of the standard cost approach to costing, we need to know the difference between normal costing and standard costing. This is shown in Table 8.11.

## Difference between Budgetary Control and Control through Standard Costing

In this chapter we have happily and easily moved to and from budgetary controls to controls through standard costing and back. The two terms are closely related and yet they do not mean the same, as the emphasis is different. According to Lucey (2002),

'Both standards and budgets are concerned with setting performance and cost levels for control purposes. They therefore are similar in principle. Standards are a unit concept, i.e., they apply to particular products, to individual operations or processes, or services.... In this way detailed unit standards are uses for developing realistic budgets. This is particularly so for direct material and direct labour costs which are more amenable to close control through standard costing whereas overheads would normally be controlled by functional and departmental budgets. Further budgets would be revised on a periodic basis, frequently as an annual exercise, whereas standards would be revised when they are inappropriate for current operation.'

# VARIANCE ANALYSIS AND INVENTORY VALUATION

As has been indicated in Table 8.11, inventory valuation of finished goods and work-in-process is always in standard costing but can accommodate variations in overheads allocated to products from expectations in normal costing. Raw material is also valued at standard costing. Thus, price variances are recognized immediately on purchase. Purchases in financial accounts will always be at actual prices, and the variances will be absorbed in the profit and loss account of the year.

## The Tediousness and Paperwork Involved in Variance Analysis

The elaborate working out variances shown in the chapter may give an impression to the reader that standard costing and variance analysis is a tedious process involving a lot of paperwork and time. So would it be, if we insist that for every product cost figure there should be availability of both standard cost and actual costs. As we shall see, if standard costing has been introduced with enough preparation and the products are by and large not too variegated and are repetitive, there are remedies for the situation.

## Keeping All Accounts at Standards and Reducing Work of Accounting

If all products and processes are at standard and if the accounting is completely computerized, the accounting can be online and can typically follow the flow of accounting entries as detailed here:

*Step 1:*  *When raw material is purchased:*
Debit stock at standard prices
Credit vendors at actual prices for actual quantities
Credit or debit the difference between D prices for actual quantities
Thus, stocks are at standard and entries are made from invoices.

*Step 2:*  *When raw material is consumed:*
Debit cost of the product standard quantity at standard prices (omitting the stage of work-in-process)
Credit stock of actual quantity at standard price
Debit/credit efficiency variance for the difference
Therefore, product cost is kept at standard costs in the inventory. The whole entry will be automatic the moment the quantity issued to works is fed into the computer.

*Step 3:* *When sale is made:*
Debit party at actual prices
Credit sale at standard prices
Credit or debit sale price variance for the difference
The entry will be made the moment the sales invoice is made.
Also,
Debit cost of products sold at standard costs
Credit stocks at standard costs
This will clear the stock of finished goods.

*Step 4:* Profit as per cost books = Sales at standard prices – Cost of goods sold at standard costs ± Raw material price variance ± Raw material efficiency variance ± Sale price variance.
This will be equal to profit as per financial account books.

## ABC ANALYSIS, STANDARD COSTING, AND VARIANCE ANALYSIS

In Chapter 6, the problems of keeping track of gathering data on individual activity centres, and keeping a tab on cost drivers of each activity centre have been discussed. Further, difficulties in keeping the fixed and variable portions of ABC were detailed. In the examples provided in the chapter, it was assumed that ABC would increase linearly with the increase in activity, which would be valid if the increase is over a long range. These problems militate against using the activity based overheads in variance analysis. According to Cheatham and Cheatham (1996),

> 'ABC is a cost accumulation rather than a cost control system... ABC can have cost management features but there is no day-to-day monitoring system to assure that cost are within certain parameters... ABC can be used for analysis outside the main record-keeping system...and standard costing system can be used for direct costs within the main record-keeping system.'

This assertion is a strong one to make, but on the balance it is a reasonable summary of the present status of ABC system vis-à-vis standard costing system.

### Limitations of Standard Costing and Its Negative Impact on Behaviour

In Chapter 7 we expressed a concern that budgeting may cramp the style of management in so far as its focus is not on radical improvement and seeking new opportunities but on enthusiasm deadening methods to make every manager a conformist. This objection is even more drastically applicable to standard costing, as its rigidities are infinitely more pervasive.

The behavioural impact on standard costing is now shown to be even more aggressively devastating. Karen Kroll (2004) says it may result in

1. the overlooking for timely delivery,
2. ignoring customer satisfaction for the sake of quality,
3. designing products without considering the specific needs of the customer, and
4. a tendency to boost production to get the benefit of lower costs/unit, resulting in a massive build up of inventory.

Using lean accounting in preference to systems driven by standard costs resulted in dramatic results in Landscape Structures Ltd (Kroll 2004),

1. Manufacture lead times dropped down by 90 per cent
2. Inventory turnover jumped by 50 per cent
3. Production capacity was freed by 25 per cent in each year.

Further, standard costing needs too much preparation and is useful only if production is standardized for a substantial part (Lucey 2002). Quite often standards would have to be modified too often if they have to be current and effective.

Many executives may feel de-motivated and threatened by an aggressive enforcement of standard costing systems.

## Example 8.3  Flexible Budgeting (I)

Unlived Pvt. Ltd manufactures toothbrushes for which market demand exists for each additional quantity. Presently sales of ₹50,000 per month make the most of only 50 per cent of the plant. Mr Malhotra, Marketing Manager of Unlived Pvt. Ltd, is of the view that with the reduction of 16.67 per cent in price, he can push the sales by 25 per cent to 30 per cent.

The following data has been given:

|  |  |  |
|---|---|---|
| (I) | Selling price | ₹12 per toothbrush |
| (II) | Variable cost | ₹3 per toothbrush |
| (III) | Semi variable cost | ₹6,000 fixed + 0.5 paisa per toothbrush |
| (IV) | Fixed cost | ₹20,000 |

Prepare the operating profit at 50 per cent, 60 per cent and 70 per cent levels at ₹12 per toothbrush and operating profit at proposed selling price at the above levels.

| Statement of cost and profit at ₹12 per toothbrush | | | | |
|---|---|---|---|---|
| Units | 50% capacity 5000 | 60% capacity 6000 | 70% capacity 7000 | ₹12 per toothbrush |
| Fixed Cost | 20,000 | 20,000 | 20,000 | |
| Semi Variable cost: Fixed cost | 6,000 | 6,000 | 6,000 | |
| Variable @ 50 paisa per toothbrush | 2,500 | 3,000 | 3,500 | |
| Variable @ ₹3 per toothbrush | 15,000 | 18,000 | 21,000 | |
| Total cost | 43,500 | 47,000 | 50,500 | |
| Sales | 60,000 | 72,000 | 84,000 | |
| Profits (Sales –Total cost) | 16,500 | 25,000 | 33,500 | |
| Statement of cost and profit at ₹10 per toothbrush | | | | |
| Total cost | 43,500 | 47,000 | 50,500 | |
| Sales @ ₹10 per toothbrush | 50,000 | 60,000 | 70,000 | |
| Profits (Sales – Total cost) | 6,500 | 13,000 | 19,500 | |

With 16.67 per cent reduction in price per toothbrush, sales and profits also decreased considerably rather than rising up.

## Example 8.4   Flexible Budgeting (II)

Prepare a flexible budget with the following data for production of 50,000 units and 85,000 units, showing fixed cost, variable cost, and total cost distinctly. Also indicate element wise cost per unit. Budgeted output is 1,00,000 units and budgeted cost per unit is as follows:

| | |
|---|---|
| Direct material | 85 |
| Direct labour | 55 |
| Production overheads fixed | 5 |
| Production overheads variable | 30 |
| Administrative overheads | 5 |
| Selling overheads (10% fixed) | 10 |
| Distribution overheads (20% fixed) | 15 |

| Variable cost | 1,00,000 units | | | 50,000 units | | 85,000 units | |
|---|---|---|---|---|---|---|---|
| | Per unit | Per unit | Total Amount (₹) | Per unit | Total Amount (₹) | Per unit | Total Amount (₹) |
| Direct material | 85 | 85 | 85,00,000 | 85 | 42,50,000 | 85 | 72,25,000 |
| Direct labour | 55 | 55 | 55,00,000 | 55 | 27,50,000 | 55 | 46,75,000 |
| Production overheads variable | 30 | 30 | 30,00,000 | 30 | 15,00,000 | 30 | 25,50,000 |
| Selling overheads (10% fixed) | Variable 90 % | 9 | 9,00,000 | 9 | 4,50,000 | 9 | 7,65,000 |
| Distribution overheads (20% fixed) | Variable 80% | 12 | 12,00,000 | 12 | 6,00,000 | 12 | 10,20,000 |
| Total variable cost | | 191 | 1,91,00,000 | 191 | 9,550,000 | 191 | 1,62,35,000 |
| **Fixed cost** | **Per unit** | **Per unit** | **Total** | **Per unit** | **Total** | **Per unit** | **Total** |
| Production overheads fixed | 5 | 5 | 5,00,000 | 10 | 5,00,000 | 5.9 | 5,00,000 |
| Administrative overheads | 5 | 5 | 5,00,000 | 10 | 5,00,000 | 5.9 | 5,00,000 |
| Selling overheads ( 10% fixed) | 10% Fixed | 1 | 1,00,000 | 2 | 1,00,000 | 1.2 | 1,00,000 |
| Distribution overheads (20% fixed) | 20% Fixed | 3 | 3,00,000 | 6 | 3,00,000 | 3.5 | 3,00,000 |
| Total fixed cost | | 14 | 14,00,000 | 28 | 14,00,000 | 16.5 | 14,00,000 |
| Total cost | | 205 | 2,05,00,000 | 219 | 1,09,50,000 | 207.5 | 1,76,35,000 |

## SUMMARY

The chapter has detailed various instruments to measure performance aligning with responsibility centres, and to value deviation from predetermined plans, budgets, and standards. These are expressed as material price and efficiency variance, labour rate and labour efficiency, sale price variance, sales volume variance, production volume variance, variable overhead spending variance and variance of efficiency in using overhead services, and spending variance. The efficiency in the use of the services would typically include the use in batch preparation, which is reflected in proliferation of the number of batches for a given production. It advises the use of these variances in a constructive manner and not in an accusing and threatening style. The purpose of variance analysis should also be to induce cooperation among working executives. The distinction between budgetary control and control through standard costing as part of the overall rubric of responsibility accounting is detailed. The difficulties in using ABC data for overheads in the usual manner of variance analysis used for less detailed overhead measurements are explained.

---

## KEY POINTS

- Sales volume variance is the profit foregone or gained by changes in volume of sales, and is measured as contribution per unit × D sales quantity deviant from budget.
- Production volume variance is the loss or gain on changes in capacity utilization measured as budgeted fixed cost/unit × Δ production quantity deviant from budget.
- Flexible budget variance is the difference between allowed expenditure for actual activity and the actual expenses, and may also be described as spending variance.
- Purchase price variance is equal to Δ price between budget and actual × Actual quantity purchased.
- Material usage efficiency variance is Δ standard usage for actual production × Budgeted price.
- Variable overhead spending variance is equal to the difference between actual expenses and the allowed expenses for actual activity of the overhead (measured as machine hours or any other chosen cost driver).
- Variable overhead efficiency variance is equal to the difference of activity of the cost driver (say, machine hours) allowed for actual production and the actual activity used × Budgeted cost per unit activity of the chosen cost driver.
- Labour rate variance is equal to actual labour hours used × Δ Labour rates.
- Labour efficiency variance is equal to Δ standard usage for actual production × Standard labour rates.
- Part of the labour efficiency and material efficiency variance can be further attributed to the difference between the standard batch size for actual production and the actual batch size for actual production.
- Raw material, work-in-process, and finished goods are kept at standard costs in the standard costing system, and the variance absorbed in the financial accounts.
- Standard costing systems may inhibit innovation.
- Standard costing may induce high levels of production and high inventories, and ignore timely deliveries and quality of products.

## CONCEPT REVIEW QUESTIONS

1. Distinguish between static budgets and flexible budgets.
2. Does standard costing help to improve cooperation among executives?
3. Explain how some variances may have joint responsibilities of more than one responsibility centre?
4. Explain the use of statistical control charts for watching variances?
5. Distinguish between controls through standard costing and controls through budgeting?
6. Explain the concept of variable overhead spending variance?
7. What are the two ways of measuring the economic impact of change in sales/production volume from budgets?
8. Can ABC system incorporate the concept of standard costing?
9. Why is batch size one of the measures of efficiency variance?

## NUMERICAL PROBLEMS

### 1. BRF Tyres

BRF Tyres of Gurgaon budgeted for manufacturing 3000 tyres in December 2005 at a variable cost of 300 per tyre, and total fixed costs of ₹10,00,000. It proposed to sell each tyre at ₹850. Actual results in December 2005 were 2800 tyres at a selling price of ₹800 per tyre. The total variable cost was ₹9,00,000, and a fixed cost of ₹9,85,000.

### Questions

1.1 Prepare a report as shown in Table 8.4.
1.2 Comment on the results.

### 2. Road Raja Bus Services

Road Raja Bus Services operating from Bengaluru in Karnataka has a fleet of fifty buses. The buses operating in Karnataka, Kerala, and Tamil Nadu have maintenance facilities in Bengaluru, Thiruvananthapuram, Cochi, and Mangalore. The maintenance department was expected to keep forty-five buses on the road in fit condition. The central planning department was expected to provide 1000 km per day for 25 days for each bus, and the marketing department was expected to have occupancy of 55 passengers on every route. The operations department was in charge of drivers and was expected to fulfil mileage targets and keep to the time schedule.

Table P2 shows its static budget for December 2005 as well as the actual for the same month. All amounts are in ₹.

**Table P2**   Budget—actual for December 2005

| | Static budget | Actual | Flexible budget | Total variance | Sales volume variance | Flexible budget t variance |
|---|---|---|---|---|---|---|
| Bus km | 11,25,000 | 8,00,000 | ? | ? | ? | ? |
| OP staff 80% variable | 40,50,000 | 35,00,000 | ? | ? | ? | ? |
| Fuel variable | 32,00,000 | 30,00,000 | ? | ? | ? | ? |
| Repair & maintenance 25% variable | 20,00,000 | 30,00,000 | ? | ? | ? | ? |
| Rates taxes fixed | 10,000 | 10,000 | ? | ? | ? | ? |
| Depreciation fixed | 10,00,00,000 | 10,00,00,000 | ? | ? | ? | ? |
| Administration, marketing, accounts fixed | 2,00,000 | 2,30,000 | ? | ? | ? | ? |
| **Total** | 11,12,66,000 | 11,14,10,000 | ? | ? | ? | ? |
| Revenue | 49,50,000 | 32,00,000 | ? | ? | ? | ? |
| Profit | 124,90,000 | 314,10,000 | ? | ? | ? | ? |

## Questions

2.1   Fill in the question marks.

2.2   What other information will you seek to explain the variances more fully?

## 3.   Viswakarma Furnitures I

Viswakarma Furnitures made furniture for several parties who had showrooms at Panchkuin Road, which was the biggest furniture centre in Delhi. They sold their furniture as basic structures. The painting and upholstery work was done by the Delhi buyers. This made their cost analysis simple, as only the wood and labour costs had to be accounted for. The labour rates included the minor materials which are used in the furniture, apart from wood. The present problem concerns school desks which they supply in large numbers to Delhi schools.

The standard cost sheet for these school desks was as per Table P3(a).

**Table P3(a)**   Standard cost sheet of school desk

| | Price (₹) | Quantity kg/hr | Total cost |
|---|---|---|---|
| Wood | 7 | 30 | 210 |
| Labour | 25 | 8 | 200 |
| Total | | | 410 |

Viswakarma had a planned budget for making 200 such desks in April 2005 and selling them at ₹500 per desk.

They actually succeeded in making 250 desks in the month and sold them for ₹550 each. Their costs were as shown in Table P3(b).

**Table P3(b)**  Actual for December 2005

|  | Price (₹) | Quantity (kg/hr) purchased and used | Total cost |
|---|---|---|---|
| Wood | 8 | 8000 | 64,000 |
| Labour | 30 | 2250 | 67,500 |
|  |  | Total | 1,31,500 |

## Questions

3.1  What are the price variance, material usage, labour rate, and labour efficiency variances for Viswakarma Furnitures for the month of December 2005?

3.2  Reconcile these numbers with the total expected contribution and the actual total contribution.

### 4.  Viswakarma Furnitures II

Viswakarma bought 9000 kgs and used only 8000 kgs of wood as shown in the previous problem. They value inventories of raw material and finished goods at standard prices/cost.

## Questions

4.1  What are the price variance, material usage, labour rate, and labour efficiency variances for Viswakarma for the month of December 2005?

4.2  Reconcile these numbers with the total expected contribution and the actual total contribution.

4.3  Why are the answers different from those in Question 8.11?

### 5.  CD India

CD India was the pioneer in India in the manufacture of rewritable CDs. Their budget for December 2005 was as follows:

* Average selling price per CD = ₹40
* Total direct material cost per CD = ₹8.50
* Direct manufacturing labour:

  Labour cost per hour = ₹15

  Productivity of CDs per hour = 300

* Direct marketing cost per CD = ₹3
* Fixed overhead = ₹9,00,000
* Projected sales = ₹1,50,000

The actual results for December 2005 were as follows:

- Unit sales of the plan = 70 per cent
- Actual selling price on the average = ₹38
- Actual labour cost per hour = ₹15
- Actual labour productivity per hour = 250 CDs
- Actual material cost per CD = ₹8
- Actual direct marketing cost per unit = ₹3.50
- Fixed costs contained = ₹8,00,000

## Questions

Calculate the following:

(i)   Income in static budget and actual income

(ii)  Total profit variance between static budget and flexible budget

(iii) Total flexible budget variance

(iv)  Total sales volume variance (total impact of reduction of sales volume on profits)

(v)   Price and efficiency variance for labour

(vi)  Spending variance of fixed costs

(vii) Production volume variance (Total impact of cost per CD × Actual volume of production, due to reduction in volume).

6. **Vigrahams India**

Vigrahams India manufactures realistic reproductions of the images of several gods and goddesses of India in special quality plastic material. It produces them in batch quantities. After each batch, the parts of the moulding machine have to be cleaned completely to get rid of the dyes and colours of the product made earlier. One of the most popular products was that of Ganesha, made in black with a granite-like appearance. The date for the budget for 2005 and the actual are given in Table P6.

**Table P6** Budget—actual comparison

|  | Static budget | Actual |
|---|---|---|
| Number of images | 10,000 | 9000 |
| Batch size | 250 | 200 |
| Batch cleaning labour hours per batch | 3 | 3.5 |
| Cleaning labour cost per hour | ₹12.50 | ₹12 |

## Questions

6.1  What is the variance due to reduction in batch size?

6.2  What is the labour rate and labour efficiency of cleaning operations of the 45 batches so cleaned?

### 7.  Bankura Horses

Bankura Horses manufactured terracotta sculptured horses which were famous in the art market. The horses were all of the same size.

*The following information was the static budget for 2004:*

The expected sale was 5000 units at ₹300 per horse. The sales manager was responsible for this.

The production manager was expected to produce the quantity that the sales manager could sell.

The standard quantity of the special mud required for this was 10 kg per horse.

The purchase manager was expected to buy the material at ₹10 per kg.

The production manager was expected to use 4 hours labour per horse.

The personnel manager was to hire labour at ₹40 per hour.

Other fixed costs were ₹1,00,000, controlled by the general manager.

*The actual results for the year were as follows:*

Produced and sold 6000 horses at ₹590 each

Direct material 54,000 kg at ₹11 per kg

Direct labour 25,000 hours at ₹38 per hour

Actual fixed costs ₹1,05,000.

It was decided that a bonus of 5 per cent on favourable variances and penalty of 1 per cent on unfavourable variances will be distributed to the responsibility holders.

### Question

Suggest the amount of variances to be distributed to each responsibility centre. Be explicit and comprehensive on the logic of the distribution, dwelling on the inter-departmental cooperation.

### 8.  Laksmi Mysore Pak

Laksmi Mysore Pak was very famous for its fine texture and flavour, and attractive appearance and was even exported. It was expertly packed in one kilo cartons, which retained its flavour and softness for a long time after it was made. Laksmi made 2000 kilograms a month. Its prices commanded a premium in the market; whereas competitors market their mysore pak at ₹88, Laksmi marketed theirs at ₹120 per kilogram. Its standard cost sheet is shown in Table P8(a).

**Table P8(a)**    Standard cost sheet of Laxmi Mysore Pak

| Cost item | Quantity | Price | Standard cost |
|---|---|---|---|
| Besan gms | 300 | 0.03 | 9 |
| Ghee gms | 200 | 0.12 | 24 |
| Sugar gms | 600 | 0.02 | 12 |
| Boxes no. | 1 | 1 | 1 |
| Labour min. | 30 | 1 | 30 |
| Overhead mins | 30 | 0.4 | 12 |
| Total | | | 88 |

It charged overhead on the base of labour hours.
In January 2006, it sold 1800 kilograms. Its other data are shown in Table P8(b).

**Table P8(b)**    Budget—actual report, January 2008

| | Price (₹) | Quantity | Amount | Financial summary January 2004 | Budget | Actual |
|---|---|---|---|---|---|---|
| Besan | 0.04 | 5,76,000 | 23,040 | Production | 2000 | 1800 |
| Ghee | 0.13 | 3,60,000 | 46,800 | Direct material | 90,000 | 93,340 |
| Sugar | 0.02 | 10,80,000 | 21,600 | Direct labour | 60,000 | 72,000 |
| Boxes | 1 | 1900 | 1900 | Revenue | 2,40,000 | 2,16,000 |
| Labour hrs | 1.2 | 60,000 | 72,000 | Overhead | 24,000 | 24,000 |

## Questions

8.1  Static budget for January 2006 and flexible budget for 2006
8.2  Material price and efficiency variance
8.3  Labour price and efficiency variance
8.4  Overhead efficiency variance

### 9.  Allah Bux Tailors

Allah Bux Tailors was one of the well-known tailors from old times and has now transformed into a supplier of designer suitings of the latest designs. Since the suits were customer specific designs, its direct material costs varied and could not be contained in the standard cost framework. But Allah Bux tried to keep a control over labour costs and their overheads. The overheads arose from a cutting and a stitching machine. The overheads had both variable elements and fixed elements. They charged the standard labour costs and overheads for every individual suit. Variable overhead was charged on the basis of labour hours. Thus, more the labour hours a product took, more was the overhead costs. Fixed overheads consisting of depreciation, rent for floor space, etc. have been charged to the product at budgeted cost per piece.

At the end of the month they tried to see if all had been well with the overheads.

The relevant data had to be analysed . These are as indicated in Table P9.

**Table P9** Overhead analysis for December 2004

|  | Budget | Actual |
|---|---|---|
| Production numbers | 1500 | 1250 |
| Labour hours | 6000 | 5625 |
| Variable overhead per labour hour (₹) | 20 | 22 |
| Variable overhead costs (₹) | 1,20,000 | 1,23,750 |
| Fixed costs (₹) | 1,20,000 | 1,10,000 |
| Total overhead cost per piece (₹) | 160 | 187 |

On examining the data he commented, 'I have lost ₹33,750 in December 2005, being the difference in cost per piece, namely, ₹27 multiplied by the actual production of 1250 pieces.'

## Questions

9.1 Indicate the variances in a table as follows:

| Nature of variance | Amount (₹) |
|---|---|
| Variable cost spending variance (flexible budget variance) | |
| Variable cost user efficiency variance | |
| Fixed cost spending variance | |
| Fixed cost production volume variance | |
| Total variance | |

9.2 Can you suggest a better economic measure than production volume variance to measure the economic loss due to lower production? What further information would you need in order to compute this?

# PROJECT

1. Form batches of four students and visit chosen organizations such as a fairly large hotel, restaurant, catering establishment, engineering goods industry, or a garment manufacturing unit, and describe the process by which they monitor their costs and productivity.

## CASE STUDY 1                                    Delhi Mail

Arun Nagpal had started a new daily paper at Delhi, which was intended to provide balanced news to its readers. There were to be twenty pages per issue. Arun was examining the accountant's report on the financial performance of the newspaper for December 2005 and was disappointed that profits were far below his budget. He asked you to report on this. The investigations showed that the press had printed 7,00,000 pages. The marketing department said that it had a daily circulation of 10,000 issues. You have computed that this would need 6,20,000 pages (31 × 10,000 × 20), and therefore, 80,000 pages more than required had been printed. Production department said that the paper supplied was bad and tore during printing, and 10,000 pages were lost in the process. They also said that all their variable costs were driven by the number of print pages. The circulation manager said that he sent more than the targeted circulation to the market, as he did not want the circulation to be affected due to insufficient stock in some pockets of the city. This accounted for 70,000 print pages, i.e., a little more than 1000 copies daily. The financial data is provided in Table CS 1. You are informed that the prices and labour rates did not change during this period. Arun Nagpal said that he would need to talk to the advertisement and personnel managers. The price of the newspaper did not change during the period.

Table CS 1    Financial data for Delhi Mail

|  | Budget (₹) | Actual (₹) |
|---|---|---|
| Direct material (variable) | 6,80,000 | 7,00,000 |
| Direct labour (fixed) | 3,00,000 | 3,50,000 |
| Variable indirect costs | 6,80,000 | 7,20,000 |
| Fixed indirect costs | 5,00,000 | 5,60,000 |
| Circulation revenue | 9,30,000 | 9,50,000 |
| Advertisement revenue | 15,00,000 | 14,00,000 |
| Profit | +2,70,000 | +20,000 |

## Discussion Question

1. Prepare a cogent analysis to help Nagpal to control his financial results.

| CASE STUDY 2 | Maharaja Garments |
|---|---|

Maharaja Garments is an export oriented garment manufacturing concern. Its young, new managing director, Govind Sakhlani, a textile fashion designer from the Institute of Fashion Technology, Ahmedabad, had one look at its cost reports and came to the conclusion that the low volumes and absence of cost controls were the main reasons why it was operating at low profit levels. He thought that standard costing systems could streamline the organization. He found that the garments had a great variety and prices varied from ₹500 to ₹2000. He decided to have only three or four standardized products. He could mass produce them and use computerized designers to change the designs once every two months, and create four more products for the next period. The standardized products had standard material costs, standard labour costs, and standardized overhead costs of mechanized cutting and stitching of garments. Operations for stitching buttons and some fancy collars could be given to piece rated workers who worked from their homes. As the production and sales boomed, Govind saw the organization booming with profits, as costs drastically reduced. But the profits were reckoned after valuing the stocks at standard costs, including fixed overheads. He followed the principle of cost or market, whichever was lower. In the second year, he found that the demand was not picking up sufficiently enough to enable him to clear his opening stocks. Even heavy discounts did not work and he had to offload them as export quality garments at a very heavy discount. Often the prices were below direct material and labour costs. The export markets also complained that Maharaja Garments was perpetually behind time (may be only by two months or so) and their customers who were interested in Indian garments were put off by too many other people wearing identical clothes. A young MBA who worked with Maharaja Garments said, 'Computers can be used as a great opportunity for designing a tremendous variety at very short notice. But the targets of standard costs have been devastating.'

## Discussion Questions

1. How should Govind proceed from this point?
2. Should standard costing targets be applied to direct material as well as overheads?
3. Should variable overheads be treated differently from fixed costs included in the overhead?

# Developing Standard Costs and Their Use in Pricing and Estimations for Contract Bids

## Learning Objectives

After reading this chapter, you will be able to understand

- the use of standard costs in fixing the sales prices of products and services
- the role played by standard costs in bidding for public works and public services
- the processes of standard setting
- internal and external benchmarking
- the use of secondary data in benchmarking
- the use of agencies that specialize in inter-firm comparison and benchmarking
- creative benchmarking as enabling innovation

- rather than negatively restricting and cramping the style
- the scope of competitive benchmarking and effective use of standards, which revolve around externalities and avoidance of destructive and socially undesirable competition typically in environmental and safety issues
- the ethics of benchmarking
- learning curves and the upwardly shifting standards in the horizon of time and experience

## INTRODUCTION

Chapter 8 dealt with the enabling instrument of budgeting to operate bearing in mind the strategy of an organization. We used standard costing to make the instrument sharper and more precise. This enabled us to prepare a variance analysis of deviation from the budget and align it with the structure of responsibility centres. This chapter explores the other uses of standard costing and the way standards can be developed, and how they can be used to liberate the organization from mediocrity and propel them towards excellence.

# STANDARD COSTING FOR PRICING

In Chapter 8, standard costing has been defined as a formal process of setting standards of performance in organizations. But standard costing de facto has existed informally everywhere, in business and trade. Informal standards are used extensively. The terminology of costing has a built-in concept that by definition, standard costing data are those used for pricing of products and services (Chartered Institute of Management, 2000).

Similarly, there are formal and informal standards that are used for millions of products in the market. This is true of the products of multinationals, as well as those of small local producers. If one asked a small restaurant how it arrived at the price of, say, Mysorepak, the famous south Indian sweet, it will provide a statement as in Table 9.1.

Table 9.1   Pricing statement for Mysorepak (Mysorepak cost per kg)

| Cost item | Quantity | Price (₹) | Cost (₹) |
|---|---|---|---|
| Gram flour (*besan*) (grams) | 300 | 0.03 | 9 |
| Ghee (grams) | 200 | 0.12 | 24 |
| Sugar (grams) | 600 | 0.02 | 12 |
| Boxes (no.) | 1 | 1 | 1 |
| Labour (mins) | 30 | 1 | 30 |
| Overhead (mins) | 30 | 0.4 | 12 |
| | | Total | 88 |

Less sophisticated statements may not use the concept of overheads but the direct costs would invariably be considered in the working sheets for determining prices. Engineering repair shops, e.g., automobile or earthmover repair shops, or even other delicate machinery which may have a random unpredictable flow of repair orders and seemingly not amenable for standard fixation, may find that the orders have a certain pattern and would benefit from having a standard booklet indicating the charges for labour and material, for a variety of jobs. They would then be in a position to quote for the jobs quickly and acquire more business than competitors who may not be having standard estimates.

## Standard Cost in Public Services and Bidding

Indian government agencies that are involved in estimating and constructing vast networks of infrastructure perform one of the most sophisticated exercises in standard costing. These relate to roads, dams, powerhouses, and hospitals all over the country. The construction is done by departmental agencies or is contracted out and has to be done in a most transparent manner, as the authorities are answerable to the public for prudent expenditure.

The different state agencies usually set up 'expert committees' who build up the standard costs by first gathering basic rates, for example, the costs of a road roller, cement, steel, labour, power, aluminium, glass, wood, bitumen, pipes, explosives, etc.

They then analyse the rates for a vast range of works, which they can build up based on past records. These indicate the efficiencies possible in each of the operations involved.

Using the basic rates and analysis, they usually publish a schedule of rates on their websites as shown in Table 9.2.

In India, there are at least 300 published schedules of rates, which form the core of building standard costs and engineering specifications in the country. These have helped to stabilize construction costs and control

**Table 9.2** Schedule of rates

| Item | Unit | Rate (₹) |
| --- | --- | --- |
| Earthwork in excavation and dressing of surface with lead of 15 m and lift 1.5 m | | |
| (a) Ordinary soil | Cum | 72.40 |
| (b) Hard rock pick work | Cum | 94.50 |
| (c) Soft rock blasting work | Cum | 237.00 |
| (d) Hard rock blasting work | Cum | 329.70 |
| Cement concrete for reinforced concrete in superstructure | | |
| (a) M 25 grade | Cum | 5696.90 |
| (b) M 30 grade | Cum | 6023.70 |
| Construction of trapezoidal drain with RCC 1:2:$ 15 cm thick with nominal reinforcement HYSD steel @ 50 kg/m3 of concrete with internal dimension of 30 cm base, 60 cm depth excluding earthwork and carriage of material | Rm | 1129.50 |
| Brick masonry in cement mortar 1:3 in foundation complete excluding pointing and plastering as per drawing and specifications | Cum | 3779.00 |
| Stone masonry in cement mortar 1:3 for foundation | | |
| (a) Cursed rubble masonry (first sort) | Cum | 3284.30 |
| (b) Random rubble masonry | Cum | 3371.10 |
| Providing storage tank riveted angles from frame with 40m nominal bore GI scour pipe with fitting, with fittings for mosquito-proof coupling 1800 litres net capacity with 3.15 mm thick MS steel riveted with 30×30×30 mm angle with iron frame | Each | 13,856.90 |

*Source:* A random sample from the website of the Mizoram government.

haphazard bidding by contractors who bid for these jobs. The process of converting the basic rates to a schedule of rates can be understood from a worked example in Table 9.3.

**Table 9.3**  A worked out schedule of rates (Chakraborti 1987)

| Particulars | Quantity | Rate (₹) | Amount (₹) |
|---|---|---|---|
| Stone | 11.7 cum | 1000 per cum | 11,700 |
| Cement | 0.57 cum = 17 bags | 200 per bag | 3400 |
| Sand medium | 3.40 cum | 1100 per cum | 3740 |
| Mason days | 16 | 250 per day | 4000 |
| Unskilled worker days | 24 | 100 per day | 2400 |
| Total for 10 cum | | | 25,240 |
| Total for 1 cum | | | 2524 |

*Schedule of rates for stone masonry in cement mortar (1:6) in a superstructure calculated for 10 cum.*

## Processes of Standard Setting

**Degrees of standards**
Three degrees of standards:
1. Basic
2. Ideal
3. Attainable

In organizations, standard setting is a long drawn process if it has to be a benchmark for performance and has to be sustained for a long time as an internal benchmark.

One also has to be clear whether one opts for a basic, ideal, or attainable standard, keeping in mind the prevailing conditions (Lucey 2002).

Basic standards are long-term standards and are not useful for analysing present performance. They can at best be used as a starting point for working out current standards.

Ideal standards do not make any concession to present conditions and have, for example, zero wastage, zero idle time, etc. Such standards may result in frustration and performance level may decline, as workmen may perceive these standards to be elusive and unachievable.

Attainable standards take into account present conditions and are realistic. For this reason, they may need to be revised from time to time.

There are several methods to arrive at a standard, some of which are quicker and more acceptable to workers and executives. These can briefly be summarized into five types:

1. Based on the internal past records of the organization, both accounting and non-accounting
2. Based on internal brainstorming in organizations, and conditioned to see beyond past performance and norms followed by the organization.
3. By using the studies of those industrial engineers.

4. By starting from the target price set by the organization and working on designs and processes outlined by the industrial engineers, to enable the cost to be contained within the target price. This is a method emanating from Japan.
5. By gathering data and information from sources external to the organization, including public sources and competition.

Each of these methods has its advantages and disadvantages, and often a combination of these methods have to be used.

## Using Past Internal Data and Internal Benchmarking

Internal accounting and productivity records can often provide a wealth of information on standards. These can initiate the lines of investigation and could also serve as internal benchmarking.

The records would provide data on material prices and labour rates which have prevailed, as well as on the trends. In conjunction with records of efficiency that have prevailed at different times and with different operators, it is possible to prepare a chart of a range of possible efficiency and choose the most attainable, and also spot the conditions under which this efficiency could be attained. Thus, if in addition to the Agnikundala Mines, there were other mines in the Coal Federation of India, the data could be studied to arrive at an analysis as indicated in Table 9.4.

**Table 9.4** Productivity data of three mines of Coal Federation of India

| Item | Agnikundala | | Kailash | | Swargaseema | |
|---|---|---|---|---|---|---|
| | Average | Best month | Average | Best month | Average | Best month |
| % Availability dumpers | 60 | 70 | 80 | 100 | 50 | 60 |
| Trip/hour | 2 | 3 | 1 | 2 | 3 | 4 |
| Haul distance/km | 2 | 1.8 | 2 | 1.5 | 1 | 0.5 |
| Diesel/machine hour litre | 43 | 40 | 40 | 38 | 48 | 42 |

Several improvements in standards could be achieved from the analysis in Table 9.4. Swargaseema and Agnikundala could examine if the low availability is due to (a) poor spare parts inventory management, (b) bad choice of machines, (c) age of the machines, (d) poor workshop training, and (e) bad speeding practices of the dumper operators, etc.

1. Agnikundala may check if the mine layout needs to be altered in order to shorten the distance of haulage.

2. Kailash may assess whether diesel is being pilfered or Swargaseema engines are better maintained.
3. Kailash may want to confirm whether the haul road maintenance is bad.

Another sophisticated method of analysing the existing data is through statistical technique of multiple regressions (Sekhar 1979).

Thus, the data of 500 underground coal mines were fitted into a regression equation:

$$Y = a P + AX + BZ + CR + DS + ET + \ldots\ldots,$$

where, Y is manshifts for a month

$\alpha$, A, B, C, D, and E are coefficients

P is the month's production

X is haul distance from fine face to surface

Z is 0 or 1 depending upon whether the seam is less than 3 metre high

R is 0 or 1 depending on whether the seam is more than 5 metre high

S is 0 or 1 depending on whether the coal face is mechanized or not

T is 0 or 1 depending on whether methane emission is high or low and so on.

The plausible hypothesis is that with the increase of output each month, manpower may, within some ranges, tend to be proportional. Similarly, the difficulties in mining increase with a very thin seam of coal mines, as also with very thick mines above a particular size. Gaseous mines with methane emissions need a lot of precaution and manpower. Manpower increases with haulage distance and behaves like fixed cost vis-a-vis output. Face mechanization reduces manpower requirement.

The computer will work out a regression line of best fit and the actual as plotted as *, and the expected as the line, and would appear as shown in Fig. 9.1.

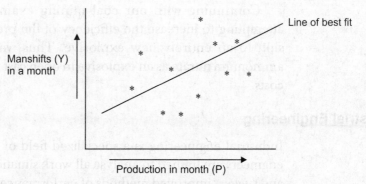

**Fig. 9.1** Regression analysis of manshifts per month

**Inter-unit comparisons in HUL**
HUL India provides a powerful motivation for their production units to achieve and excel in efficiency norms by providing online mutual information.

The line of best fit is the expected manshifts on the basis of the regression equation. If the $R^2$ (a statistical measure of the goodness of fit) is high, we can be sure that the manshifts are not random numbers, but establish a pattern; a deviation from the line could be a managerially significant measure of efficiency or lack of it. The technicalities of this statistical tool will be more fully explained in Chapter 12.

By studying the mines in the north of the line we may be able to assess if the sources of their inefficiency can be pinpointed, so that they can be brought down to at least the line of best fit if not improved to the manpower in the mines south of the line. A simpler method of influencing the bad ones to emulate the good ones can be seen in the Indian FMCG company, Hindustan Unilever, which has a transparent system where production units throughout the country have real time access through Internet facilities to the goings on in all other production units on material usage efficiency. This provides a powerful impetus not only to implement standards but also shift them from those currently available to ideal ones.

## Focus Groups and Participative Processes

Learn from people.
Plan with the people
When the task is accomplished, the people will remark,
'We have done it.'
    –Lao Tse

There is much to be said for the use of participative processes in standard setting and internal benchmarking as described. As Lao Tse observes, participative processes give a sense of ownership to the standards set by organizations. Moreover, new ideas emerge much faster in the process of breaking from the past.

One of the most effective processes of participative discussions is what is known as 'brain-storming', which is an uninhibited exchange of views, often without an agenda. Typically, in such a discussion, the emphasis would shift from doing the same thing in a cheaper way to doing something in a totally different way. Thus, the emphasis would shift from efficiency to efficacy.

Continuing with our coal mining example then, instead of just attempting to increase the efficiency of the present explosive, one could shift to an entirely new explosive. Thus was born the idea of using ammonium nitrate as an explosive in open cast mines to drastically reduce costs.

## Industrial Engineering

Industrial engineering is a specialized field of knowledge, and industrial engineers are trained to analyse all work situations to their basic elements, and suggest improved methods of performance and the standard time that the operations should take. Its great modern founder was the American, Fredrick Taylor. Although many accused him of treating human beings as mere machines, the Soviet leader Lenin, saw him as a saviour of humanity from unnecessary drudgery (Lenin 1960).

The technique of work sampling described in Chapter 6 was one of the typical methods used by industrial engineers to ascertain the distribution of the time taken for various tasks.

One of the difficulties in using industrial engineers to set standards is the hostility of the affected workers and executives, and the consequent alienation of the lone wolf industrial engineer.

## Working Back to Target Costs from Target Prices and Using Value Engineering

*Target costing can be attempted only if one has a standard costing and budgetary system in place in the organization.*
*– M. Sakurai*

The work of the industrial engineer in fixing standards receives added gusto if he does not function in isolation in just a theoretical exercise, but in product development, working towards customer satisfaction and with a target price for the product. This approach has been a Japanese gift to the world (Sakurai 1989).

The steps in the process are the following:

1. Develop a product that satisfies the customer need.
2. Choose a target price.
3. Derive a target cost per unit by subtracting target operating income per unit from target price. If this cost is well below one's present cost there is a 'gap which has to be bridged'.
4. Perform value engineering to cut costs by identifying those processes and components that do not add value for the customer, but increase cost. This may also result in an increase in costs in some places, but may add much in terms of value to the customer, for example, after-sales services.

One would immediately conclude that much of the costs in products and services get 'locked in' at the design stage. Therefore, target costing should usually start with designs. The phenomenon of 'locked in costs' is depicted in Fig. 9.2.

As evident from this, even though costs are incurred gradually, most of it is already committed and locked in the design.

Therefore, standard setting is required right from the start and usually revolves around the

*Target costing*
*Target costing should not result in retrenchment and redundancy. Surplus labour should be redeployed in new activity or expansion.*

1. number of parts to be tested before assembling,
2. number of parts to be assembled,

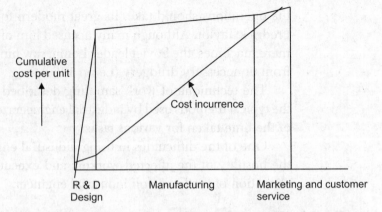

**Fig. 9.2** Locked in costs (adapted from Horngren et al. 2003)

3. number of vendors to be approached for part development,
4. number of occasions on which purchases have to be negotiated,
5. time taken for testing the final product, and
6. complexity or simplicity of components to be used.

## External Benchmarking

Comparisons with outsiders can highlight the best practices in any industry.
– Tucker et al. (1987)

Whereas internal benchmarking discussed earlier can yield rich dividends, it may tend to become myopic and may not induce radically new learning. Ever since the Xerox Company made extraordinary efforts in 1979 to learn from others through benchmarking, there has been a revolution in the approach of business and industry towards the use of external benchmarking (Tucker et al. 1987).

Xerox started with an analysis of unit production. Their main motivation was to match the extremely low cost prevailing in their Japanese counterparts. The company used the Japanese costs as target costs, and discarded their existing standard cost and budgetary standards. They started with product costs but soon extended their benchmarking to costs and efficacy of services. They also started benchmarking with some notable organizations outside their industry.

The benchmarking was possible in a less furtive atmosphere where one is not probing a competitor and can be done for mutual benefit. The most famous of these was L. L. Bean, a sports company, from whom they could borrow some excellent ideas to control inventory and warehousing management.

The comparative features of internal and external benchmarking (including external to industry) are made by Harrington and Harrington (1995) and are shown in Table 9.5.

**Table 9.5**  A comparison of different benchmarking practices

| Benchmarking type | Cycle time for full solution | Benchmarking partners | Results |
|---|---|---|---|
| Internal | 3–4 months | Within organization | Major improvements |
| External competitive | 6–12 months | None | Better than competition |
| External industry | 10–14 months | Same industry | Creative breakthrough |
| External generic | 12–24 months | All industries worldwide | Changes the rules |
| Combined internal and external | 12–24 months | All industries worldwide | Best in class |

Benchmarking, as it is developing now, is vastly variegated. This is not limited to the narrow confines of standard costing. It envelops attitudes and styles of management and is used for structuring and speeding up new product innovation and development (Cooper et al. 2000).

The choice of organizations for benchmarking is important and bias should be avoided. A typical bias is to choose only apparently successful companies. However, companies that have failed could also offer useful education and enable one to see if they did share some points with successful companies. The cause of the success may also not be so obvious and easily identifiable (Jerker 2005) and may need careful study.

## Using Secondary Data for Benchmarking

Xerox, who were the pioneers in benchmarking, relied much on trade journals, annual reports and other company publications in which 'statement of pride' appear, and the presentations made by the companies at professional and other forums.

In India, organizations such as the Bureau of Standards and National Productivity Council have a range of publications where standards are widely publicized. The domain of the Indian Bureau of Standards does not cover standard costs, but standards of the output. However, since they are decided after discussion with producing and using industries, they accommodate the implication of being able to produce the goods at affordable prices. The National Productivity Council has a large number of productivity studies which establish inter-firm comparisons (Nandi et al. 1992).

The rules of public disclosure in the Indian Company's Act enable several agencies to publish useful inter-firm data. Tables 9.6 and 9.7 are extracts from publicly available data.

The data is amenable for triggering standard costs by carefully seeing what is common or different between organizations.

**Table 9.6** Productivity in a sample of Indian banks

| Name of bank | Business per employee (₹ in lakh) |
|---|---|
| **Private sector banks (2002)** | |
| Bharat Overseas Bank | 259 |
| Lord Krishna Bank | 246 |
| Bank of Rajasthan | 136 |
| Karnataka Bank | 247 |
| HDFC | 778 |
| Global Trust Bank | 709 |
| ICICI | 487 |
| **Public sector banks (2001)** | |
| State Bank of India | 170 |
| Allahabad Bank | 140 |
| Andhra Bank | 200 |
| Bank of Baroda | 169 |
| Bank of India | 190 |
| Canara Bank | 191 |
| Central Bank | 126 |
| Corporation Bank | 246 |
| Punjab National Bank | 142 |
| Syndicate Bank | 134 |
| UCO Bank | 97 |

*Source:* www.indiastat.com

**Table 9.7** Energy consumption in a sample of Indian textile companies

| Company | Product | Energy source | Energy consumption |
|---|---|---|---|
| Arvee Denim | Yarn | Electricity | 1050 Kwh/tonne |
| Arvee Denim | Cloth | Electricity | 1.05 Kwh/metre |
| Aditya Birla | Fabric | Electricity | 1.02 Kwh/metre |
| Banswara Textile | Cloth | Electricity | 0.28 Kwh/metre |

*Source:* Prowess (V 2.0) Centre for Monitoring Indian Economy, Mumbai.

The textile industry, which is one of the largest industries in India and is dominated by the private sector, has extensive inter-firm comparisons available to it. ATIRA of Ahmedabad in weaving, BITRA of Mumbai in post-weaving processing, and SITRA of Coimbatore for yarn, have extensive data on inter-firm comparisons and these are used by the textile industry.

The US Bureau of Mines used to have detailed statistical information for all the mines in the US. Similar data is provided for Indian open cast

**Table 9.8**  International cost and productivity comparisons of open cast mines in 1980

|  | US | Australia | South Africa | Canada |
|---|---|---|---|---|
| Labour productivity output worker hour | 14–21 | 3–25 | 4–5 | 11–20 |
| Mining costs | $5.52–6.30 | $9.05–37.71 | $3.56–5.25 | $4.78–12.25 |
| Labour costs | $1.35–1.72 | $1.41–4.69 | $1.07–1.47 | $1.23–2.2 |
| Health welfare safety included in labour costs | $0.7–1.14 | $0.28–0.36 | $0.24–0.44 | $0.56–1.59 |

mines, in Table 9.8 (Bureau of Mines, 1993) and shows the possible beneficial impact of continuous inter-firm comparisons provided by the US Bureau of Mines. There could have been other geological factors too. The low costs of US mines were traced by the author to the low idle time of the US machinery as a result of excellent maintenance.

One more area where benchmarking studies have been universally used is in public road transport. Road transport, widely nationalized now, have had bitter critics. Public road transport is always under public scrutiny A typical letter to the South Indian daily, *The Hindu,* reads as follows:

'The proper maintenance of the fleet has taken a beating and we find only rickety buses. The only plus point of the nationalization is service to far-flung villages. The only solution is to privatize the whole city bus service while the government retains control over its operation' (*The Hindu,* 11 August 2003).

On several occasions, practising transport managers have exchanged data and views which help them to benchmark. Academicians have also worked extensively in this field (Indian Journal of Transport Management). A sample of the related comparative data is shown in Table 9.9.

**Table 9.9**  Productivity ratios in Indian transport undertaking

| Name of organization | Passenger kms per employee (× 10³) | Passenger kms per litre diesel | Passenger kms per bus held | Employees per bus held | Road staff per road bus | Road staff per employee |
|---|---|---|---|---|---|---|
| Maharashtra | 476 | 176 | 3591 | 7.58 | 5.29 | 0.63 |
| Andhra Pradesh | 513 | 198 | 4255 | 8.35 | 5.85 | 0.67 |
| Karnataka | 596 | 175 | 3865 | 6.49 | 4.75 | 0.65 |
| Gujarat | 590 | 197 | 3899 | 6.61 | 5.31 | 0.69 |
| Uttar Pradesh | 382 | 161 | 2659 | 6.95 | 5.38 | 0.66 |
| Kerala | 439 | 169 | 3897 | 9.01 | 7.03 | 0.61 |
| Rajasthan | 545 | 183 | 3620 | 6.76 | 4.98 | 0.65 |
| Madhya Pradesh | 351 | 155 | 2805 | 8.01 | 4.67 | 0.48 |
| Punjab | 636 | 156 | 3320 | 5.22 | 3.52 | 0.63 |

To what extent can such benchmarking be useful? The study of the World Bank by Mishra and Nandagopal (1991) is a sobering report which shows that more than all such benchmarking, it is the existence of competition in Tamil Nadu that had made them more efficient.

Sanjay Kumar Singh has also shown that increase in the route length per bus results in decrease in overhead costs. This is because while route length itself may increase overhead costs, an increase in the number of buses which would increase revenue proportionately, would result in reduction of overhead costs per bus. He also notes that fleet utilization has no correlation with expenses incurred. This means that fleet utilization is a factor of managerial efficiency and of using agencies for benchmarking.

There are several international organizations that have specialized in benchmarking. Their assistance can be availed of. Some of these organizations are the following (Cook 1995):

1.  European Foundation for Quality Management, Brussels, Belgium
2.  Benchmarking Clearance House of IFS International, Bedford, UK
3.  Benchmarking Centre, Hertfordshire, UK
4.  American Productivity and Quality Centre, International Benchmarking Clearance House, Houston, US
5.  National Productivity Council, New Delhi.

Benchmarking can also be done by an organization in consultation with the suppliers of their equipment. As equipment manufacturers have experience from several organizations, they are a good clearing house of best practices. Joy Company, which supplied long haul equipment to the Norwegian mining company SNSG, achieved an unbelievable monthly production of 4,02,200 tons in September 2001, with just 40 underground workers (Coal International Mining and Quary World, May–June 2001).

## Competitive Benchmarking and Externalities

The issue of standards and of benchmarking has now proceeded in a direction that is very different from those in earlier times. They now have greater concern for standards which affect the world outside the organization, and involve the safety and welfare of society. These inevitably affect the standard cost of production, but it is socially desirable that they should be used in parallel.

1.  Standardization of products is a proof against a monopolist stranglehold on the consumer, who is left with no free choice in buying equipment which does not fit in with the system for equipment made by other manufacturers. Fixing such standards is

**Safety standards**
In 2004, 6000 miners died in China in accidents, i.e., 3.28 persons for a million tonne production. In UK there were no deaths with 23 million tonnes of production.

usually fraught with power struggles within the industry to ensure that the standards conform to their own specifications. This is presently the case with the telecommunications industry (Schwaber and Wright 2004).

2. Pollution standards have to be common for everyone and should allow a level playing field for all product manufacturers and service providers.

3. Safety standards should be the same for all producers of goods and services. Thus, there are complaints (Sowman 2005) that China, with poor safety standards, was able to sell coal to the West who could not compete on prices as their safety standards were high. In China, for every million tonnes of coal produced in the year 2004, 3.28 persons were killed. In contrast, in the UK 23 million tonnes were produced without the loss of a single life.

## Learning Curve

Anyone who tries to learn a new skill knows that in the initial stages performing the task can be a struggle, but it becomes easier with experience.

This feature would be significant for fixing standards in modern industry, where new products emerge fast. This was discovered during the great world war when it was found that the learning followed a pattern.

One of the bothersome features of standard setting in modern times is that there may be rapid changes in product designs, and standards are uncertain. These have to accommodate what is known as 'the learning curve'. This was discovered during the Second World War when contracts based on standard costs were used in defence contracts. It was found that it was possible to bring order to the understanding by projecting a learning curve. This recorded the improvement of productivity with the learning associated with increased production. There are several ways of measuring this. One of the methods is to have a formula to indicate the average hours of the cumulative number produced. Another is to indicate the time taken for the latest production. We will illustrate the learning curve using the latter formula.

A learning curve is a function that measures how labour hours per unit decline as units of production increase because workers are learning and becoming better at their jobs. Two models used to capture different forms of learning are as follows:

**Cumulative average time learning model**  The cumulative average time per unit declines by a constant percentage each time the cumulative quantity of units produced doubles.

**Incremental unit time learning model** The incremental time needed to produce the last unit declines by a constant percentage each time the cumulative quantity of units produced doubles.

The illustration below shows this model by using 70% learning curve.

70% Learning Curve

| Learning curve: Cumulative average time learning model | | | |
|---|---|---|---|
| Cumulative number of units (x) (1) | Individual unit time for the unit (y) labour hours (2) | Cumulative total time: Labour hours (3) | Cumulative average time per unit: Labour hours (4) = (3)/(1) |
| 1 | 100 | 100 | 100.00 |
| 2 | 70.00 | 170.00 | 83.00 |
| 3 | 56.82 | 226.82 | 75.61 |
| 4 | 49.00 | 275.82 | 68.95 |
| 5 | 43.68 | 319.50 | 63.90 |
| 6 | 39.77 | 359.28 | 59.88 |
| 7 | 36.74 | 396.01 | 56.57 |
| 8 | 34.30 | 430.31 | 53.79 |
| 9 | 32.28 | 462.60 | 51.40 |
| 10 | 30.58 | 493.18 | 49.32 |
| 11 | 29.12 | 522.29 | 47.48 |
| 12 | 27.84 | 550.13 | 45.84 |
| 13 | 26.72 | 576.82 | 44.37 |
| 14 | 25.72 | 602.57 | 43.04 |
| 15 | 24.82 | 627.39 | 41.83 |
| 16 | 24.01 | 651.40 | 40.71 |

| Learning curve: Cumulative average time learning model | | | |
|---|---|---|---|
| Cumulative number of units (x) (1) | Individual unit time for the unit (y) labour hours (2) | Cumulative total time: Labour hours (3) | Cumulative average time per unit: Labour hours (4) = (3)/(1) |
| 1 | 100 | 100 | 100.00 |
| 2 | 70.00 | 170.00 | 85.00 |
| 4 | 49.00 | 275.82 | 68.95 |
| 8 | 34.30 | 430.31 | 53.79 |
| 16 | 24.01 | 651.40 | 40.71 |

A learning curve can be defined by the following equation:

$$Y = aX^b$$

where $Y$ is the cumulative average time, $X$ is the cumulated number of products produced, $a$ is the time (labour hours) taken to produce the first unit, and $b$ is the learning factor. Cumulative average time $Y$ can be calculated as under:

$a = 100$, $X = 1, 2$, or 3 etc. and $b = -0.514573$, which gives

When $X=2$, $Y=100 \times 2^{-0.15457} = 70$, which can also be calculated as: $100 \times 70\%$

When $X=3$, $Y=100 \times 3^{-0.15457} = 56.89$

When $X=4$, $Y=100 \times 4^{-0.15457} = 49$, which can also be calculated as: $70 \times 70\%$

When $X=8$, $Y=100 \times 8^{-0.15457} = 34.30$, which can also be calculated as: $49 \times 70\%$

When $X=16$, $Y=100 \times 16^{-0.15457} = 24.01$, which can also be calculated as: $34.40 \times 70\%$

Value of learning factor $b$ can be determined as follows:

$$b = \frac{\ln(\text{learning curve \% in decimal form})}{\ln 2}$$

$$\begin{array}{ll} -0.356674944 & \dfrac{\ln(0.70)}{\ln(2)} \\ 0.693147181 & \\ -0.514573173 & b \end{array}$$

Note that only units which are double the previous units produced can be calculated by simply multiplying unit time labour hours with learning curve percentage.

**Learning curve incremental unit time learning model**   The incremental time needed to produce the last unit decline by a constant percentage

| Learning curve: Cumulative average time learning model | | | |
|---|---|---|---|
| Cumulative number of units (x) (1) | Cumulative average time per unit (y) labour hours (2) | Cumulative total time: Labour hours (3) = (2) × (1) | Individual unit time for Xth unit: Labour hours (4) |
| 1 | 100.00 | 100.0 | 100.00 |
| 2 | 70.00 | 140.0 | 40.00 |
| 3 | 56.82 | 170.5 | 30.45 |
| 4 | 49.00 | 196.0 | 25.55 |
| 5 | 43.68 | 218.4 | 22.42 |
| 6 | 39.77 | 238.6 | 20.21 |
| 7 | 36.74 | 257.2 | 18.54 |
| 8 | 34.30 | 274.4 | 17.22 |
| 9 | 32.28 | 290.5 | 16.15 |
| 10 | 30.58 | 305.8 | 15.25 |
| 11 | 29.12 | 320.3 | 14.48 |
| 12 | 27.84 | 334.1 | 13.24 |
| 13 | 26.72 | 347.3 | 13.24 |
| 14 | 25.72 | 360.0 | 12.72 |
| 15 | 24.82 | 372.3 | 12.26 |
| 16 | 24.01 | 384.2 | 11.85 |

| Learning curve: Incremental unit time learning model | | | |
|---|---|---|---|
| Cumulative number of units (x) (1) | Cumulative average time per unit (y) | Cumulative total time: Labour hours (3) = (2) × (1) | Individual unit time for Xth unit: Labour hours (4) |
| 1 | 100.00 | 100.0 | 100.00 |
| 2 | 70.00 | 140.0 | 40.00 |
| 4 | 49.00 | 196.0 | 25.55 |
| 8 | 34.30 | 274.4 | 17.22 |
| 16 | 24.01 | 384.2 | 11.85 |

each time the quantity of units produced doubles. The illustration below shows this model by using 70% learning curve:

By comparing the cumulative average time learning model with the incremental unit time learning model, it can be noticed that to produce 4 cumulative units, the 70% incremental unit–time learning model predicts 196 labour hours versus 275.82 labour hours by cumulative average time learning model. This is because the average labour hours needed to produce all 4 units is 68.5 hours while under the incremental unit time learning it is 25.55 hours, which is much less than 68.5 hours.

In Fig. 9.3(a) and (b), Plot A graphically illustrates cumulative total labour hours as a function of cumulative units produced for each model.

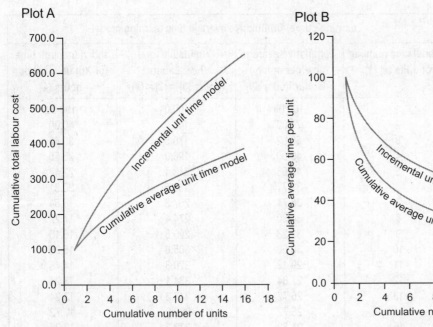

**Fig. 9.3a** Cumulative total labour cost

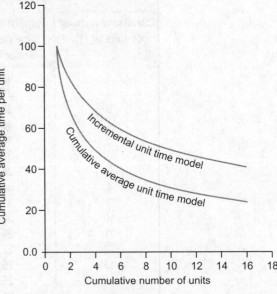

**Fig. 9.3b** Cumulative average time per unit (labour hours)

**Table 9.10** Learning curve model

| Cumulative number of units (x) (1) | Cumulative average time per unit (y) labour hour (2) | Cumulative total time: Labour hours (3) =(2) × (1) | Cumulative cost @ ₹200 per labour hour | Additions to cumulative costs Amount(₹) |
|---|---|---|---|---|
| 1 | 100 | 100 | 20,000 | 54,000 |
| 2 | 70 | 140 | 28,000 | 8000 |
| 4 | 49 | 196 | 39,200 | 11,200 |
| 8 | 34.3 | 274.4 | 54,880 | 15,680 |
| 16 | 24.01 | 384.16 | 76,832 | 21,952 |

Plot B graphically illustrates cumulative average time model per unit as a function of cumulative units produced for each model.

The incremental unit time model predicts a higher cumulative total time to produce two or more units than the cumulative average–time model assuming 70% learning rate for both the models.

We can use the learning curve model to predict variable costs as shown in Table 9.10.

While choosing the models managers make choices on case-to-case basis.

We can define the learning curve as the proportion of the time taken by production of the double of the previous unit of production. Thus, 80 per cent learning curve means that if the first unit took 200 hours, the second unit will take $200 \times 0.80 = 160$ hours, the fourth unit will take $160 \times 0.80 = 128$ labour hours, and so on. This 80 per cent learning curve is described in Table 9.11.

**Table 9.11** Data of a learning curve

| Production number | Labour time/ minute | Cumulative time | Cumulative average time |
|---|---|---|---|
| 1 | 200 | 200 | 200 |
| 2 | 160 | 360 | 180 |
| 3 | 144 | 504 | 168 |
| 4 | 128 | 632 | 158 |
| 5 | 121.6 | 753.6 | 150.72 |
| 6 | 115.2 | 868.8 | 144.8 |
| 7 | 108.8 | 977.6 | 139.6571 |
| 8 | 102.4 | 1080 | 135 |
| 9 | 100.04 | 1180.04 | 131.1156 |
| 10 | 97.28 | 1277.32 | 127.732 |
| 11 | 94.72 | 1372.04 | 124.7309 |
| 12 | 92.16 | 1464.2 | 122.0167 |
| 13 | 89.58 | 1553.78 | 119.5215 |
| 14 | 87.01 | 1640.79 | 117.1993 |
| 15 | 84.47 | 1725.26 | 115.0173 |
| 16 | 81.92 | 1807.18 | 112.9488 |

An 80 per cent learning curve is a product that is easier to learn than a product with a 90 per cent learning curve, and more difficult to learn than a product with a 70 per cent learning curve. If one roughly assesses the complexity of a product, one can approximately guess its learning curve, and estimate the standard production time and its related standard costs. One can use algebra (Horgren et al. 2003) to forecast as can be seen here:

$$Y = aX^b$$

where $Y$ = Time taken to make last single unit, $X$ is the cumulative number produced, $a$ is the time taken to produce the first unit and $b$ is the factor.

$b$ = Log learning curve in percentage expressed in decimal form divided by log 2.

This is depicted graphically in Fig. 9.3.

We can define the learning curve by an alternative equation as shown here:

$$Y = aX^b$$

where $Y$ is the cumulative average time, $X$ is the cumulated number of products produced, $a$ is the time (labour hours) taken to produce the first unit, and $b$ is the learning factor. The same 80 per cent learning curve will depict a different data as shown in Table 9.12.

One can note that if the same 80 per cent represented in Fig. 9.4 defined as the time for the last unit is now changed to cumulative average time, the 16th unit will take 43.67 minutes instead of 81.92 minutes. This means that the learning curve will show a much steeper climb down, and will appear as shown in Fig. 9.5.

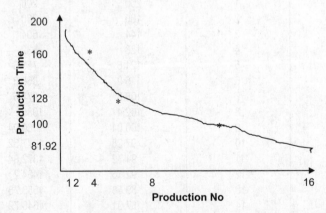

**Fig. 9.4**  A plotted 80% learning curve defined as time for last unit

**Table 9.12** Cumulative average time learning model

| (1)<br>Production | (2)<br>Cumulative average<br>labour time<br>per unit | (3)<br>Cumulative<br>labour time<br>1 × 2 | (4)<br>Individual time<br>for last unit (4)<br>derived from Col. 3 |
|---|---|---|---|
| 1 | 200 | 200 | 200 |
| 2 | 160 | 320 | 120 |
| 3 | 144 | 432 | 112 |
| 4 | 128 | 512 | 80 |
| 5 | 121.6 | 608 | 96 |
| 6 | 115.2 | 691.2 | 83.2 |
| 7 | 108.8 | 761.6 | 70.4 |
| 8 | 102.4 | 819.2 | 57.6 |
| 9 | 100.04 | 900.36 | 81.16 |
| 10 | 97.28 | 972.8 | 72.44 |
| 11 | 94.72 | 1041.92 | 69.12 |
| 12 | 92.16 | 1105.92 | 64 |
| 13 | 89.58 | 1164.54 | 58.62 |
| 14 | 87.01 | 1218.14 | 53.6 |
| 15 | 84.47 | 1267.05 | 48.91 |
| 16 | 81.92 | 1310.72 | 43.67 |

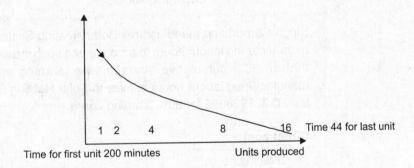

**Fig. 9.5** A plotted 80% learning curve as related to cumulative time

Which of these models is preferable? Horngren (2003) says that this should be decided on a case by case basis. Engineers associated with the production process would be able to advise as to which model is closer to reality.

The data in Tables 9.10 and 9.11, and Figs 9.4 and 9.5 assume that learning curves extend only to labour time. It can also extend to other variables such as direct material usage, quality of product, etc. This is used by Yokogawa Hewlett Packard.

Learning curves are useful when bidding for orders. They can be influenced by several factors such as training, job rotation, and working as teams, when learning becomes faster.

## Element of Strategic Innovations

The discussions so far in this chapter have not harked back to the concerns expressed in Chapter 8 that standard costing may inhibit rapid innovations. We have tried to show that in the process of setting standards and with internal and external benchmarking, brain storming and target pricing, organizations can venture into unexplored areas. But many more favourable conditions may be necessary in order to be more explosively innovative. Among others who have held the view that standard costing can truly and fully destroy innovation is Vijay Govindarajan, one of the leading votaries of standard costing and budgeting. No amount of apologies would convince him to the contrary (Govindarajan and Trimble 2005).

### Example 9.1   Learning Curve Cumulative Average Time Learning Model

Singh Corporation manufactures Solar Heating Systems. It takes 4000 direct manufacturing labour hours to produce one such system. Corporation believes that an 80% cumulative average time learning model applies for direct manufacturing labour hours applies to Solar Heating Systems.
$b = -0.321928095$ for 80% learning curve.

**Direct cost:**

| Direct cost | 1 Unit |
| --- | --- |
| Direct material | ₹8,00,000 |
| Direct manufacturing labour | ₹12,00,000 |
| (₹300 per unit) x 4000 labour hours | |
| Variable manufacturing overheads | ₹8,00,000 |
| (₹200 per unit) x 4000 labour hours | |
| Total variable cost | ₹28,00,000 |

Calculate the total variable cost producing 2, 4, 8, 16 units.

80% learning curve model is shown below:

| Learning curve: Cumulative average time learning model | | |
|---|---|---|
| Cumulative number of units (x) (1) | Individual unit time for the unit (y) labour hours (2) | Cumulative total time |
| 1 | 4000 | 4000 |
| 2 | 3200 | 6400 |
| 4 | 2360 | 10,240 |
| 8 | 2048 | 16,384 |
| 16 | 1638 | 26,214 |

Value of $b$ is determined as below:

| $b$ = ln (learning curve % in decimal form)/ln 2 | |
|---|---|
| −0.223143551 | ln (0.80) |
| 0.693147181 | ln (2) |
| −0.321928095 | B = ln (0.8)/ln 2 |

We know that learning curve equation is given as follows:

$$Y = aX^b$$

where $Y$ is the cumulative average time, $X$ is the cumulated number of products produced, $a$ is the time (labour hours) taken to produce the first unit, and $b$ is the learning factor.

$a = 4000$, $X = 2, 4, 8, 16$ and $b = -0.321928095$ for 80% learning curve, which gives

When $X = 2$, $Y = 4000 \times 2^{-0.321928095} = 3200$, can also be calculated as: $4000 \times 80\%$

When $X = 4$, $Y = 4000 \times 4^{-0.321928095} = 2560$, can also be calculated as: $3200 \times 80\%$

When $X = 8$, $Y = 4000 \times 8^{-0.321928095} = 2048$, can also be calculated as: $2560 \times 80\%$

When $X = 16$, $Y = 4000 \times 16^{-0.321928095} = 1638$, can also be calculated as: $2048 \times 80\%$

| Direct cost | 1 unit | 2 units | 4 units | 8 units | 16 units |
|---|---|---|---|---|---|
| Direct material | 8,00,000 | 16,00,000 | 32,00,000 | 64,00,000 | 1,28,00,000 |
| Direct manufacturing: (₹300 per unit) × (4000:6400:10240:16348:26214) labour hours | 12,00,000 | 19,20,000 | 80,72,000 | 49,15,200 | 78,64,320 |
| Variable manufacturing overheads: (₹200 per unit) × (4000:6400:10240:16348:26214) labour hours | 8,00,000 | 12,30,000 | 20,48,000 | 82,76,800 | 52,42,880 |
| Total variable cost | 28,00,000 | 48,00,000 | 83,20,000 | 1,45,92,000 | 2,59,07,200 |

**Example 9.2** Learning Curve Incremental Unit Time Learning Model

Based on the same data provided by Singh Corporation, determine the variable cost for producing 2, 4, 8, and 16 units using incremental unit time learning Model.

| Learning curve: Incremental unit time learning model | | |
|---|---|---|
| Cumulative number of units (x) (1) | Individual unit time for the unit (y) labour hours (2) | Cumulative total time |
| 1 | 4000 | 4000.0 |
| 2 | 3200.00 | 7200.0 |
| 3 | 2808.41 | 1008.4 |
| 4 | 2560.00 | 12,568.4 |
| 8 | 2048.00 | 21,383.7 |
| 16 | 1638.40 | 35,680.5 |

$a = 4000$, $X = 2, 4, 8, 16$ and $b = -0.321928095$ for 80% learning curve, which gives

When $X = 2$, $Y = 4000 \times 2^{-0.321928095} = 3200$, can also be calculated as: $4000 \times 80\%$

When $X = 4$, $Y = 4000 \times 4^{-0.321928095} = 2560$, can also be calculated as: $3200 \times 80\%$

When $X = 8$, $Y = 4000 \times 8^{-0.321928095} = 2048$, can also be calculated as: $2560 \times 80\%$

When $X = 16$, $Y = 4000 \times 16^{-0.321928095} = 1638$, can also be calculated as: $2048 \times 80\%$

| Direct cost | 1 unit | 2 units | 4 units | 8 units | 16 units |
|---|---|---|---|---|---|
| Direct material | 8,00,000 | 16,00,000 | 32,00,000 | 64,00,000 | 1,28,00,000 |
| Direct manufacturing: (₹300 per unit) × (4000:6400:10240:16348:26214) | 12,00,000 | 19,20,000 | 80,72,000 | 49,15,200 | 78,64,320 |
| Variable manufacturing: (₹200 per unit) × (4000:6400:10240:16348:26214) | 8,00,000 | 14,40,000 | 25,13,683 | 42,76,731 | 71,36,109 |
| Total variable cost | 28,00,000 | 52,00,000 | 94,84,207 | 1,70,91,827 | 3,06,40,274 |

**Cumulative Average Time Learning Curve versus Incremental Unit Time Learning Curve**

| | Variable cost of production (₹) | | | | |
|---|---|---|---|---|---|
| Cumulative average time variable cost | 28,00,000 | 48,00,000 | 83,20,000 | 1,45,92,000 | 2,59,07,200 |
| Incremental unit time Variable cost | 28,00,000 | 52,00,000 | 94,84,207 | 1,70,91,827 | 3,06,40,274 |
| difference | – | 4,00,000 | 11,64,207 | 24,99,827 | 47,33,074 |

Total variable costs for manufacturing 2, 4, 8, and 16 units are lower under the cumulative average time learning curve relative to the incremental unit time learning curve. Direct manufacturing labour hours required to make additional units decline more slowly in the incremental unit time learning curve relative to the cumulative average time learning curve when the same 80% factor is used for both curves. The reason is that, in the incremental unit time learning curve, as the number of units double only the last unit produced has a cost of 80% of the initial cost. In the cumulative average time learning model, doubling the number of units causes the average cost of *all* the additional units produced (not just the last unit) to be 80% of the initial cost.

# SUMMARY

Standard costing, rigorously or roughly developed, is extensively used for pricing. The standardized schedule of rates for public works is based on standard prices and standard efficiencies applicable to different regions in India. Fixation of standards uses five basic methods. First, they internally benchmark using data in the internal records of the company; second, they use internal brain storming; third, they use industrial engineering studies; fourth, they use target prices as a reference point; and fifth, they use external benchmarking within and outside the industry. Creative benchmarking is usually triggered by relating to organizations outside the industry. External benchmarking pioneered by Xerox is extensively used not only for product and service costs but also for product and service quality. Standard setting and benchmarking is also used for environmental impact and safety standards to ensure a level playing ground and social benefits. Learning curves discovered during the world war follow an algebraic logic and are useful for setting standards for new products that have a period before standards of performance could stabilize.

# KEY TERMS

- Standard costs are used for pricing.
- Schedule of rates in public works is based on region-based standards.
- Standards are of three levels, of which the basic is perennial and minimal; attainable, which is currently useable and needs continuous modification; and ideal, whose enunciation is necessary to drive an organization to excellence.
- External benchmarking can be done within and beyond the boundaries of an industry.
- Publicly available published data can be a good starting point for benchmarking.
- Benchmarking is extended from standards to be followed from inputs to production, to standard qualities and attributes, to outputs of an organization.
- Benchmarking would also cover environment, pollution, and safety.

# CONCEPT REVIEW QUESTIONS

1. What are the advantages and disadvantages of internal and external benchmarking?
2. What is the use of brain storming in setting standards?
3. What is the difference between basic, attainable, and ideal standards?
4. What is the algebraic rule for the learning curve?
5. What are the biases to be avoided during benchmarking?
6. What is the relevance of environmental standards for standard costing?
7. Standard costing is the enemy number one of strategic innovation. Comment.
8. Why could an industrial engineer be alienated from the other workers and executives in an organization?
9. Give two instances of public and published sources of data which could initiate benchmarking.

# NUMERICAL PROBLEMS

## 1. Standard Costs for Stone Masonry

Shailaja, a student of architecture, had an assignment to estimate the costs of a stone masonry construction.

On investigation she found that the work involved buying the stone, dressing it, during which some of the stone is lost, making cement mortar with cement and sand, and laying the stone and applying mortar; and the labour included skilled masons and unskilled helpers.

She saw the past records of the data left behind by the previous batch of students and observed the following:

- For 10 cum of stone work, most often 11 cum stone was used, but even with bad stones resulting in losses, it was never more than 12.5 cum. In exceptional situations it was as low as 10.5 cum per 10 cum stone work, i.e., the losses were only 0.5 cum. Stone prices were high (at ₹1300 per cum) when the export markets boomed or where environmental regulators stopped nearby stone quarries. It became very low (₹750 per cum) when exports became dull and when domestic building was also low. Normally, prices hovered around ₹1000 per cum.
- For 10 cum stonework it is usually a steady use of 17 bags of cement and 3.40 cum of sand. Cement has a steady price, currently of ₹200 per bag, but sand prices fluctuated from ₹800 per cum to ₹1300 per cum, with an average of ₹1100 per cum.
- Skilled labour use for 10 cum ranged from 12 to 20, with an average of 16. Unskilled labour used was steady at 24 days per 10 cum. Labour rates were steady as it is governed by negotiation with unions. This was ₹200 per day for skilled and ₹100 per day for unskilled labour.

## Question

Calculate the basic, attainable, and ideal standard costs for stone masonry per cum. State your presumptions clearly.

### 2. Krishanlal Garments

Krishanlal was a well known shirt manufacturer. He had been employed by the army in the Kanpur garment factory. After the war he was retrenched and he started his own manufacturing unit using the machines which the army had disposed of. Trained as he was in the army, he introduced standard costing in his factory. The data for December 2005 was as indicated in Table P2.

**Table P2**  Data of Krishanlal Garments for December 2005

| Item | Budgeted amounts | Actual amount |
|---|---|---|
| Shirts manufactured | 8000 | 8976 |
| Direct material cost (₹) | 4,00,000 | 4,03,920 |
| Rolls of clothes used | 800 | 816 |
| Direct manufacturing labour costs (₹) | 3,60,000 | 3,69,240 |
| Direct manufacturing labour hours | 2000 | 2040 |

Krishanlal never kept inventories. He had based the standard provided by an industrial engineering consultant, approximately six months ago. Krishanlal wondered how his workers seemed to be close to the standard productivity targets, when he had personally caught many of them gossiping in the pan shop in front of his factory; sometimes they were also seen gambling.

Krishanlal had recently attended a workshop on benchmarking and wondered if he should subscribe to benchmarking clearing house monthly bulletins, and if it could enable him to clear his mind about the paradox in his factory.

## Questions

2.1 Work out the price and efficiency variance for December 2005.

2.2 What could have possibly gone wrong with the industrial engineers' efforts and how could the workers have led him astray?

2.3 Will benchmarking set the problem right?

2.4 Discuss the pros and cons of benchmarking exercises in this context.

3. Siva and Patil came out of the monthly financial performance review meeting in opposite frames of mind. Siva was distraught that the company MD was very critical of the performance of his division. The new MD had taken over the charge recently and this was the first time they had met officially. Both Siva and Patil were old timers, and had grown within the organisation together. In the last two years though, Siva had been promoted as Senior Manager due to his higher productivity and quality adherence. Hence this meeting had come as a shock to him. Patil on the other hand was praised for adhering to the newly introduced standard costing system. Siva went back to his cabin at the shop floor and called for Ms Gupta, his trusted accountant.

*Siva:* I can't understand. I have the highest production amongst all the three divisions, and my rejections are zero percent. Still Patil, whose entire production on Monday's first shift was rejected, has met the H.O. standards. What is the reason?

Ms. Gupta collected the report of the Head Office and went to her cabin. She came back after an hour.

*Ms. Gupta:* I went through the papers. Well, I think the standards are set too hastily. Look at this. Material price variance in our case is high as we use JIT purchases. Other divisions do not do it. Quality rejections are ignored by H.O. and material and labour spent on reworks are ignored. We do preventive maintenance during office hours, and others work on holidays using extra rates. It is ignored. Since we produce more we get a higher share of H.O. overheads which comes to nearly 30% of our costs.

*Siva:* Send a report to H.O. on these lines.

### Question

3.1 What are the problems with the standard costing in this case? Do you agree with Ms Gupta that they are set hastily?

4. Office Items Fabricators is a company which specializes in special furniture and office equipment for commercial organizations. During the year the firm manufactures 50,000 boxes using 60,000 kg of material. The standard specifications for the product are 1.3 kg of material per box at a cost of ₹20 per kg.

   The purchases account shows that the company has purchased 70,000 kg of the material at a price of ₹22 per kg during the year. There was no opening stock.

### Questions

4.1 Calculate the material price and quantity variances for the above boxes.

4.2 Can the company continue with the same standards next year? It is expected that the prices will go up during next year by 15 per cent and new technology may reduce the material usage by 10 per cent.

5. Chelon is a popular chemical which needs three units of material dye for producing one unit of Chelon. Actual quantity of dye used was 48,000 units for achieving a production of 15,000 units of Chelon. The material quantity variance was ₹9,000 unfavourable.

   The accounts department informs that the material dye was purchased at ₹3.50 per unit.

### Question

5.1 Calculate the material price variance. Do you need any extra information?

6. A product goes through two processes namely welding and assembly. The associated costs per unit of the product are

   **Welding**

   | | |
   |---|---|
   | Standard time | 5 hrs |
   | Standard rate | ₹10 per hour |

   For the month of January the actual time taken was 24,000 hours at the rate of ₹11 per hour

### Assembly

| Standard time | 8 hrs |
|---|---|
| Standard rate | ₹15 per hour |

For the month of January the actual time taken was 42,000 hours at the rate of ₹14 per hour

During January 5,000 units were processed in each of the two processes.

### Questions

6.1 Calculate the labour rate and efficiency variances.

6.2 Which process (welding or assembly) is more efficient?

7. A company had the following variances at the end of April for its fabrication department.

| Material price variance | ₹25,000 (U) |
|---|---|
| Material quantity variance | ₹40,000 (F) |
| Labour rate variance | ₹ 3000 (F) |
| Labour efficiency variance | ₹ 35,000 (U) |

### Question

7.1 Based on the above, comment on the performance of the fabrication department.

# PROJECT

Form groups of 4 or 5 students, browse through the websites giving public information and data, tabulate and analyse it. Suggest what further questions you could pose to the organization and assist them in setting up standard costs.

 **CASE STUDY 1**    **Janapriya Watch**

Janapriya Watch came into the market when there was severe competition in the Indian market. Nilima Khaitan, a brilliant MBA graduate from the Badami Institute of Management, was its managing director. Janapriya was manufactured using Japanese technology and enabled Nilima to make it 'cheap'. She sold 50,000 watches per annum at a price of ₹406.

But she soon realized that her competitors were selling good watches for ₹348. She was distraught and desperate to reduce her costs. Her costs at that time were as follows:

Direct material (variable) ₹8,50,000
Direct manufacturing labour costs (variable) ₹3,00,000
Direct machining cost fixed 5000 hrs × ₹30 per hour, i.e., ₹1,50,000.

In addition, overheads on account of set up costs, testing and engineering had to be charged.

Nilima decided to use ABC system for this purpose and she got the following data as shown in Table CS 1.

**Table CS 1**   Data for Janapriya Watch

| Activity | Cost driver | Cost per unit of cost driver |
|---|---|---|
| Set up | Set up hours | ₹250 per set up hour |
| Testing | Testing hours | ₹20 per testing hour |
| Engineering | Complexity of process | Cost assigned by special study |

Over a long time horizon Nilima thought she could consider these ABCs as variable, with reference to activity.
She also gathered the following data:

Production batch size = 500 units
Set up time per batch = 12 hours
Testing and inspection time per units produced = 2.5 hours
Engineering cost allocated = ₹17,00,000

Nilima wanted to introduce a new product Janamohini, and price it at the competitors' price of ₹348. That was the target price and she asked her consultants to cut costs in order to sell it at that price. She assessed that if she did this, she could maintain her present volume of sales. She did not consider increasing sales beyond that.

The new design for Janamohini was expected to achieve the following:

i.    Direct material cost was expected to reduce by ₹30 per unit.
ii.   Direct manufacturing labour costs would reduce by ₹7.50 per unit.
iii.  Janamohini would take up only 6 set up hours.
iv.   Time taken for testing would be 2 hours instead of 2.5 hours, as in the previous model.
v.    Engineering cost would remain the same.
vi.   Machining costs being fixed would not change.
vii.  Batch size would remain the same, i.e., 500.
viii. The cost per unit cost driver would remain the same.

## Discussion Questions

1. What would be the cost per watch of Janapriya and Janamohini?
2. How much profit margin (mark up) can Nilima manage now with Janamohini?
3. Should she go in for the new watch?
4. Do you perceive of any issue that may disturb the executives of the company if Janamohini is introduced and the sales are pegged at 50,000 per annum, as Nilima desired?

| CASE STUDY 2 | Marathe Research Labs |
| --- | --- |

Rear Admiral Marathe was a brilliant engineer who had risen to the top position in the Indian Navy but retired prematurely because of a difference with the defence minister. He started his own research lab and designed a new sea-going boat that could be used in conjunction with the warship. The defence authorities were impressed with the design and asked the admiral to submit a quote. He said that the prototype had cost him ₹7,25,000 but if more numbers are ordered it could be cheaper. The authorities placed an order for seven units. His costing data for the first prototype was as follows:

Direct material = ₹1,00,000

Direct manufacturing labour = 10,000 labour hours at ₹30 per hour, ₹3,00,000

Tooling costs (will not be required for subsequent production as the initial tooling can be used for all the seven units = ₹50,000

Variable manufacturing overhead in proportion to direct labour hours = ₹2,00,000

Other fixed manufacturing overheads (it was usual to charge a flat 25 per cent on direct manufacturing labour costs) = ₹75,000

Total = ₹7,25,000

The admiral assesses that the task has an 80 per cent learning curve.

## Discussion Questions

1. What should Marathe quote for the seven boats?
2. How much would he lose if the boats are more difficult to make and actually have a 90 per cent learning curve?

## CHAPTER 10

# Cost Information for Inventory Valuation and Inventory Management

**Learning Objectives**

After reading this chapter, you will be able to understand

- the various ways in which inventories are valued in industry and business
- the implications of direct (variable) costing, total (absorption) costing, and throughput costing on profits, and its behavioural impact on works managers and marketing managers who fix prices
- the impact of capacity utilization on inventory valuation and pricing
- ways of optimizing average inventory levels and safety stocks by balancing ordering costs, carrying costs, and stock out costs in an ambience of uncertainty, using an economic order quantity (EOQ) module as well as economic batch quantity (EBQ) model
- the cost of prediction errors in the EOQ and EBQ model
- the imputed cost of capital in inventory

- management and methods of converting this into real costs in accounts, to force managers to take full cognizance of it
- the cost implications of using just in time (JIT) systems
- the cost implications of supply chain management
- the use of material resource planning (MRP) and economic resource planning (ERP) systems and their inventory and cost implications
- the back flush costing system and its implication on the size of the inventory, and its valuation
- the managerial uses of cost information in Pareto analysis of consumption (ABC analysis) and inventories (XYZ analysis), and the speed of movement of inventories (fat slow non-moving or FSN analysis)

## INTRODUCTION

This chapter has three themes, all in respect of inventory management. Firstly, it describes the various ways in which inventories are valued responding to the legal requirements of accounting standards, the stipulation of tax regulations, which are different in different countries, and the compulsions of regulating the behaviour of operational managers with delegated authority. The second theme regarding inventory, covers the issue of maintaining optimum inventory by regulating purchases and intelligent production planning, and by using the size of the batches judiciously. The third theme dwells upon the managerial possibilities of maintaining near zero inventories by using fast and instantaneous communications. These require radically different accounting processes.

## VALUATION OF INVENTORIES

Inventories of raw materials, work-in-process, and finished goods can be valued in several ways. In Chapter 1 we suggested inventory valuation as a means to ensure the 'matching concept', in order to show the expenses in the accounting period in which the corresponding revenue is realized. Expenses made in, say, 2009 will be 'inventoried' and parked at the end of the accounting period 2009, and will be charged to the period when the corresponding sales take place in 2010. Even if this is an unexceptionable concept, the actual meaning of it in computing the 'inventoriable expenses' could be quite debatable. The debate on this issue of product costs which are inventoried and period costs which are not has been initiated in Chapter 3. Chapter 4 describes the process and periodicity of arriving at the inventory value in the two alternate systems of perpetual and periodic inventory.

The accountancy standards used by Indian accountants following the guidelines laid down by the Institute of Chartered Accountants of India (1994) (AS 2) are extremely liberal and pragmatic in all the features described so far. In a few issues they differ from the International Accounting Standards recommended by the World Bank (International Accounting Standards, A Practical Guide, 2001, IAS 2) and the generally accepted accounting principles (ARB 43) applicable in the US (Williams 1997). The options available in these standards are detailed below. Wherever a system of standards does not permit a practice, this has been indicated against that practice.

### Actual Cost Options

1. The first in first out (FIFO) method faithfully follows the physical flow of goods. In periods of rapidly rising costs, the closing inventory will be valued high and the cost of goods sold will be correspondingly lower. Therefore, it may give shareholders a wrong signal. However, all accounting standards give unfettered discretion

in their use. For those who lend money to the organization, the balance sheet would indicate a better security since it is valued high, as is usual in an inflationary economy.

2. In the last in first out (LIFO) method, the implication is just the opposite of FIFO and is favoured by those who wish to be current in their understanding of profitability.

3. In the weighted average method, the total value of the inventory purchased/manufactured is divided by the quantity purchased/manufactured to arrive at the unit rate.

4. The moving average method works out the rate at the end of every transaction with a receipt or issue of stock.

5. The retail inventory method values stock at a resale value less the standard mark-up on purchase price when fixing the sale price.

6. The base stock method is one in which a minimum quantity of stock, valued at the cost of initial acquisition, is required to be kept in stock. None of the accounting standards favour this method.

The various methods can be illustrated by two examples as shown in Tables 10.1 and 10.2.

Beginning inventory = 10,000 units at ₹5
Closing inventory = 14,000 units
Consumption = 1,16,000 i.e., 1,20,000 plus opening balance 10,000 minus 14,000 which has been consumed in the period.
Under FIFO the closing inventory would come from
5000 units of December @ ₹5.50 = ₹27,500
5000 units of October @ ₹530 = ₹26,500
4000 units from October @ ₹5.40 = ₹21,600
Total = ₹75,600

**Table 10.1**  FIFO, LIFO, and weighted average methods

| Date | Units purchased | Cost per unit | Total costs |
|---|---|---|---|
| 15th January | 10,000 | ₹5.10 | ₹51,000 |
| 20th March | 29,000 | ₹5.20 | ₹52,000 |
| 10th May | 50,000 | ₹5.00 | ₹2,50,000 |
| 8th June | 30,000 | ₹5.40 | ₹1,62,000 |
| 12th October | 5000 | ₹5.30 | ₹26,500 |
| 21th December | 5000 | ₹5.50 | ₹27,500 |
| Total | 1,20,000 | | ₹6,21,000 |

**Table 10.2** Moving average method

|  | Units in inventory | Inventory value | Unit cost |
|---|---|---|---|
| Beginning | 1000 | ₹5000 | ₹5 |
| Issue 200 | 800 (1000 minus 200) | ₹4000 (800*5) | ₹5 |
| Purchase 1200 @ ₹6 | 2000 (800 + 1200) | ₹4000 + 7200 = ₹11,200 | ₹5.60 |
| Issue 1000 | 1000 (2000 minus 1000) | ₹5600 | ₹5.60 |
| Purchase 1000 @ ₹5 | 2000 | ₹10,600 (5600 + 1000* 5) | ₹5.30 |

The consumption will be equal to ₹6,71,000 (opening balance plus purchases) minus ₹75,600 (closing balance) = ₹595,400

If you use LIFO the inventory will be as follows:

10,000 units @ ₹5 = ₹50,000

4000 units @ ₹5.10 = ₹20,400

Total = ₹70,400

Consumption will be ₹6,71,000 – ₹70,400 = ₹6,00,600

This will result in lower profits.

In the weighted average method, cost per unit will be ₹5.165 and inventory will be ₹72,261. Consumption will be 6,71,000 – ₹72,261 = ₹5,98,739

The moving average will also require issues from the inventory and the values would be as shown in Table 10.2.

## Example 10.1   Inventory Cost Flow Methods

Use the following data to calculate the cost of goods sold and ending inventory under LIFO, FIFO, and weighted average cost methods:

**Inventory Data**

| | |
|---|---|
| January 2 (beginning inventory) | 2 units @ ₹20 per unit = ₹40 |
| January 8 purchase | 3 units @ ₹30 per unit = ₹90 |
| January 19 purchase | 5 units @ ₹50 per unit = ₹250 |
| COGS available | 10 units          = ₹380 |
| Units sold during January | 7 units |

### Solution

Value the 7 units sold at the unit cost of the first units purchased. Start with the earliest units purchased.

## FIFO cost of goods sold

| | |
|---|---|
| From beginning inventory | 2 units @ ₹20 per unit = ₹40 |
| From first purchase | 3 units @ ₹30 per unit = ₹90 |
| From second purchase | 2 units @ ₹50 per unit = ₹100 |
| FIFO COGS available | 7 units                     = ₹230 |
| Ending inventory | 3 units @ ₹50 per unit = ₹150 |

## LIFO cost of goods sold

| | |
|---|---|
| From second purchase | 5 units @ ₹50 per unit = ₹250 |
| From first purchase | 2 units @ ₹30 per unit = ₹60 |
| FIFO COGS available | 7 units                     = ₹310 |
| Ending inventory | 2 units @ ₹20 PER UNIT + ₹70 |
| | 1 unit @ ₹30 PER UNIT |

**Table 10.3**   Summary of FIFO, LIFO, and weighted average

| Weighted average cost of goods sold | | |
|---|---|---|
| Average cost per unit | ₹380/10 units = | ₹38 per unit |
| Weighted average cost for 7 units | units @ ₹38 per unit | ₹266 |
| Ending inventory | 3 units @ ₹38 per unit | ₹114 |
| **Summary** | | |
| *Inventory* | *COGS* | *Ending Inventory* |
| FIFO | ₹230 | ₹150 |
| LIFO | ₹310 | ₹70 |
| Weighted average | ₹266 | ₹114 |

It can be noticed that prices and inventory levels were rising over the period and purchases during the periods were same for all cost flow methods.

During inflationary periods and stable or increasing quantities LIFO COGS is higher than FIFO cost (see Table 10.3). This is because the last unit purchased has a higher cost than the first unit produced. Under LIFO, the more costly last units purchased are the first units sold. Higher COGS will diminish the net profit and will result in lower net income.

Using similar logic LIFO ending inventory is lower than FIFO ending inventory (see Table 10.4). Under LIFO, ending inventory is valued using older lower costs.

During deflationary periods and unstable or decreasing quantities cost flow will be reversed, that is, FIFO COGS is higher than LIFO cost; this is because the first unit purchased will have a higher cost than the last unit produced. Under LIFO, ending inventory will be higher (see Table 10.5). This makes sense because the most recent lower cost purchases are sold first under LIFO, and the units in the ending inventory are assumed to be the earlier purchases with higher costs.

**Table 10.4** Inventory valuation and COGS under different economic environments

| Economic environments | Account | LIFO | FIFO |
|---|---|---|---|
| Inflationary | Ending inventory | Higher | Lower |
| | COGS | Lower | Higher |
| Deflationary | Ending inventory | Lower | Higher |
| | COGS | Higher | Lower |

**Table 10.5** Outcomes of LIFO and FIFO methods

| LIFO results in ... | FIFO results in ... |
|---|---|
| High COGS | Higher COGS |
| Lower taxes | Higher taxes |
| Lower net income | Higher net income |
| Lower inventory levels | Higher inventory levels |
| Lower working capital | Higher working capital |
| Higher cash flow | Lower cash flow |
| Lower net gross margins | Higher net gross margins |
| Lower current ratio | Higher current ratio |
| Higher inventory turnover | Lower inventory turnover |
| Higher debt/equity ratio | Lower debt/equity ratio |

A firm's choice of inventory valuation method can have a significant impact on profitability, solvency, liquidity, and activity ratios.

**Profitability ratio**   LIFO results in higher COGS, which in turn will give lower earnings in the income statement. Any profitability measure that includes COGS will be lower under LIFO. For example, higher COGS will result in lower gross margin, operating margin, and lower net profit margin.

**Liquidity ratio**   As compared to FIFO, LIFO results in lower inventory value on balance sheet. Since inventory value is a current asset in balance sheet, it will result in lower liquidity ratios that include inventory. For example, current ratio is a leading indicator of the liquidity of a firm. Working capital under LIFO is lower because of lower current assets.

It is to be noticed that quick ratio shall remain unaffected as it excludes inventories.

**Activity ratio**   Inventory turnover (COGS/average inventory) is higher for the firm that uses LIFO inventory valuation. Higher inventory turnover will result in lower days of inventory on hand (365/inventory turnover).

**Solvency ratio**   LIFO results in lower total assets in comparison to FIFO which will further result in lower stockholder's equity (Assets – Liabilities). Since total assets and stockholder's equity are lower under LIFO, debt ratio and debt equity ratio will be higher under LIFO.

## Standard Cost

**Transition from actual to standard costing**
This transition via normal costing results in reduction in paper work with improved controls, but published accounts would accept only a minimal sacrifice of accuracy.

In Chapter 8 we had examined the advantages of keeping inventories at their standard costs. This can result in reducing paper work and considerably quicken the computations of costing. All the standards permit the use of this provided there is a review from time to time to ensure that the variances of actual costs from standards are not too high, and corrections are made whenever necessary.

## Normal Costing

Normal costing as described in Chapter 5 uses overhead rates as developed in the budgets. In a way, it is a variation of standard costing and would be acceptable with the same stipulations.

The comparative features of normal and standard costings were illustrated in Chapter 8, Table 8.11.

## Items to be Included in Inventory Costs

**Absorption costing**
Absorption costing in which all fixed costs are traceable to a product directly or through a process of allocation is closest to the orthodox concept of matching expenses with the corresponding revenue and is most favoured even if it leads to undesirable behavioural consequences on managers.

The following list of items is to be included in the inventory costs.

1. Absorption costing includes all direct costs (variable) as well as variable and fixed overhead. There should be an acceptable allocation base for fixed costs. This follows the matching costing (see Chapter 1) very strictly and the more orthodox prefer it. All standards have a precaution that the capacity utilization used for charging fixed costs should be reasonable. Thus, if the fixed cost is ₹10,00,000 and the reasonable capacity utilization can produce 1,00,000 units, the costs charged to the product should be charged at ₹10 per unit. If the actual production turns out to be only 10,000, the charge has to be restricted to ₹10 and not increased to ₹100 (1,00,000 ÷ 10,000).

2. Direct costs (variable costs) plus only indirect variable costs.

3. Overheads are not allowed in IAS 2 but are allowed in Indian and US standards. This method is called the direct costing method of inventory valuation, as against absorption costing, which includes fixed costs (direct as well as indirect).

4. Only direct cost (variable costs) excludes all overheads and is not permissible in any of the standards.

5. In throughput, only direct material costs are included in the finished goods inventory. This is absolutely prohibited even it be highly favoured by many for managerial purposes.

## Periodicity of Inventory Valuation

**Perpetual inventory**
Perpetual systems of inventory which keep on line the quantity and value of inventory provides much better control though it is costlier than periodic inventory systems. But with computers, cost can come down.

All the standards permit both the perpetual and periodic inventory maintenance system but require that adequate stock verification is done. As mentioned in Chapter 5, a perpetual system of inventory would greatly enhance the credibility of the costing data thrown up by the system. All standards require inventories to be valued at cost or market, whichever is lower.

# INCOME TAX PROVISIONS

Income tax provisions generally follow the accounting standards of the respective countries. Thus, according to Taxman's Master Guide to Income Tax, 1996, Section 145 is an omnibus provision of the Indian Income Tax Act which says the following:

'The valuation of … inventory … shall be: in accordance with the method of accounting regularly employed by the assessee.

In the case CIT versus Carborondum Universal Ltd (1984 149 ITR 759 Madras) specifically, the direct cost method of valuing inventory excluding fixed overheads was accepted as one of the options organizations could use.'

But US internal revenue codes allow only full costing, i.e., absorption costing for inventory valuation (US Internal Revenue Code 1-471-11).

## Implications of Categories of Costs Included in Inventory Valuation

Let us first see the implications on the reports provided to the external stakeholders in the published audited accounts. The impact on profits would be as shown in Table 10.6.

**Table 10.6**   Impact of absorption and direct costing on profits

| If | Then |
| --- | --- |
| Production greater than sales | Absorption costing profit > direct costing |
| Sales greater than production | Absorption costing profit < direct costing |
| Sales = production | Absorption costing profit = direct costing |
| If yearly difference between sales and production are fluctuating | Absorption costing will give steadier profit figures than direct costing |

Direct costing is highly geared and profits go up and down violently with build up of inventories and its liquidation. Managements and shareholders may not like to see this happen.

On the other hand, for internal control, managers may try to pile up unsaleable goods if rewards are on profit and absorption costing is used in inventories. For the same reason, managements may want to have 'lean inventories' by not including any item other than raw materials for inventory valuation.

An illustration of this phenomenon will be seen in Table 10.7.

One can see that for the same set of base data for production, sales, sale price, and costs, the inclusion or exclusions of items to be inventorized results in varying profits. A manager who gets a bonus on profits and with full freedom to produce goods would add up to inventories if absorption costing is used and be extremely careful not to add to inventories if throughput costing is adopted. The economics of adding to inventory would be of no concern to him/her. Thus, managerial precaution would require that throughput costing is used.

**Table 10.7**    Impact of inventory valuation on profit

| Item | Absorption costing | Direct costing | Throughput costing |
|---|---|---|---|
| Production quantity | 10,000 | 10,000 | 10,000 |
| Sales quantity | 6000 | 6000 | 6000 |
| Sale price/unit | 10 | 10 | 10 |
| Raw material cost (₹) | 10,000 | 10,000 | 10,000 |
| Other variable cost (₹) | 3000 | 3000 | 3000 |
| Fixed cost (₹) | 5000 | 5000 | 5000 |
| **Cost of goods manufactured (₹)** | **18,000** | **18,000** | **18,000** |
| Closing finished goods (₹) | 7200 | 5200 | 4000 |
| Cost of goods sold (₹) | 10,800 | 12,800 | 14,000 |
| Revenue (₹) | 60,000 | 60,000 | 60,000 |
| **Profit (₹)** | **49,200** | **47,200** | **46,000** |
| Cost/unit (₹) | 1.8 | 1.3 | 1 |
| Quantity inventory FG | 4000 | 4000 | 4000 |

If this is not approved by accounting standards and tax laws, they may opt for different methods of inventory valuation for taxation, tax returns, and internal reporting (Horngren 2003). Horngren has interesting statistics of international practices. This is shown in Table 10.8.

In summary, a great variety of systems are available for inventorizing costs as well as sequencing their charge to the cost of goods sold. It

**Table 10.8** Comparative global practices in absorption/variable costing of inventory

|  | Australia (%) | Japan (%) | UK (%) |
|---|---|---|---|
| Add fixed overhead at year end | 41 | 39 | 25 |
| Variable costing internal report and adjusted year end | 11 | 8 | 4 |
| Use both as dual system | 23 | 33 | 31 |
| Do not inventory fixed overhead | 25 | 3 | 35 |
| Other systems | 0 | 17 | 5 |

**Inventorizing costs**
A great variety of options are available for inventorizing costs and sequencing their charge to cost of goods sold. Knowing the consequences of every system, management has to consciously decide what suits them.

would be unwise to declare any system as superior to the others. But a clear understanding of the consequences of the choice in published accounts, the direction of the tax authorities, and the internal impact on managerial behaviour has to be considered before deciding on an accounting policy.

## IMPACT OF INVENTORY ACCOUNTING ON PRICING

We have touched upon some impacts of inventory accounting systems on the behaviour of managers. We need to amplify the impact on their pricing policies. A large number of organizations use product costing data for pricing rather than opt for market data as a determining factor.

We must realize that product costing is the other side of the coin of inventory valuation. What does not go into the value of inventory goes into the cost of goods sold and determines product costs. As seen earlier, one may use differing accounting practices for computing product costs for internal purposes rather than for external reporting.

Table 10.9 outlines a few extreme cases of the behavioural impact on product pricing.

A downward spiralling of sales will follow if pricing is done with absorption costing using fixed overheads with low capacity utilization of resources.

**Table 10.9** Behavioural impact of accounting practice on pricing

| Accounting practice (If) | Consequence (Then) |
|---|---|
| First in first out (FIFO) | Managers will price their products too low if there is an inflationary situation. |
| Absorption costing if calculated on either actual or budgeted, but low capacity utilization | Cost as well as the price will be too high. Sales and the capacity utilization will come down further, resulting in a further increase in price, and a further lowering of sales and the spiralling down effect. |
| Variable costing and throughput costing | Managers may lose sight of the fact that fixed costs need recovery and strenuous sales effort. This can be looked after by a minimum mark up which is mandatory for pricing. |

# HOW MUCH STOCKS SHOULD ONE HAVE AND WHEN?

Quite different from the theme of valuation of stocks is the more substantive issue of inventory management and the decision on how much stock of raw material, work-in-process, and finished goods the inventory should hold, and how their acquisition should be timed. The routine issues of inventory management are best learnt through standard books on inventory management. But the basic conceptual issues that are based on the logical use of cost information will be dealt with in this chapter. The third issue that will be dealt with is the manner in which the inventories are budgeted, as described in Chapter 7, and how they are appraised in the financial ratios described in Chapter 2. This issue has a large divergence (Hector 1964) from the economic logic developed in this chapter, but we will describe how an organization can cope with these divergences.

# FUNCTIONAL CLASSIFICATION OF INVENTORIES

- Cycle inventories
- Safety stocks
- Anticipation stocks
- Pipeline (or work-in-process) inventories

## Cycle Inventories

These are inventories that vary with lot size. They help in reducing the lot size and streamlining the order placement.

Reduction in the lot size will minimize the material, ordering, and holding costs. The longer the cycle, the bigger the lot size ($Q$). Ideally,

cycle inventory varies from $O$ to $Q$ or average of $\dfrac{O+Q}{2} = \dfrac{Q}{2}$

In Fig. 10.1, Quantity ($Q$) varies directly with the elapsed time (cycle) between orders. A one-month cycle means an average lot size of one month's supply.

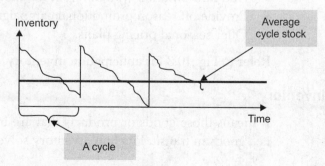

**Fig.10.1**   Average cycle stock

## Safety Stock

Safety stock means storing extra stock. Safety stock or inventories are used to meet uncertainities in demand and supply. Safety stock inventory is shown in Fig. 10.2. The primary purpose of maintaining safety stock is as follows:

- Place order closer to the time it may be received. This may lead to unacceptable customer service level.
- Improve demand forecast.
- Cut lead time of produced or purchased items.
- Reduce supply uncertainties.
- Rely more on equipment and labour buffers.

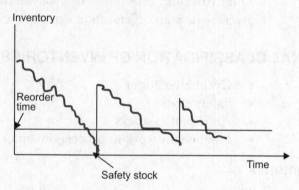

**Fig. 10.2** Safety stock

## Anticipation Inventory

It means the inventory that businesses maintain in anticipation of events that are most likely to occur. The reasons for keeping anticipation inventory are as follows:

- Match demand rate with production rate.
- Level customer demand.
- Add new products with different demand cycles.
- Provide off season promotional campaigns.
- Offer seasonal pricing plans.

Refer to Fig. 10.3 for anticipation inventory.

## Pipeline Inventory

It means those goods or products that are in the process of distribution, i.e., goods in transit. Pipeline inventory solves the following purposes:

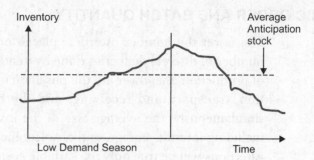

**Fig. 10.3** Anticipation inventory

- Reduce lead time (because pipeline inventory is a function of demand during lead time).
- Improve the shipping time between two stocking locations.
- Decrease lot size—at least in those cases where lead time depends on lot size.
- (or work-in-process) Goods-in-transit, between levels of a supply chain, between workstations.
- Sometimes it is 0 (nothing on order) and sometimes $Q$ (one open order). But on the average, it is given by

$$\text{Average pipeline inventory} = \overline{D}_L = dL$$

## Example 10.2 Cycle and Pipeline Inventory

A plant makes monthly shipments of iron rods to a wholesaler in average lot size of 240 rods. The wholesaler's average demand is 60 rods a week, and the lead time from the plant is 3 weeks. The wholesalers must pay for the inventory from the moment the plant makes a shipment. If the wholesaler is willing to increase its purchase quantity to 300 units, the plant will guarantee a lead time of two weeks. What is the effect on cycle and pipeline inventories?

| | |
|---|---|
| Cycle inventory | $= Q/2$ |
| | $= 240/2$ |
| | $= 120$ rods |
| Pipeline inventory | $= DL = dL$ |
| | $= (60 \text{ rods/week}) (3 \text{ weeks})$ |
| | $= 180$ rods |

## ECONOMIC ORDER AND BATCH QUANTITY

The fewer the number of orders placed on a vendor, the fewer are the number of discrete deliveries done by vendors, and the fewer the batches of production, the lower are the purchase order (including cost of inspection, transport, and receiving) and the batch preparation costs. But simultaneously, the average size of the inventory and its carrying costs including interest, storage, and obsolescence will also be high. Both these assertions will be true only for variable costs and not for the fixed costs of purchasing, or batch preparation, or variable costs of carrying. For the present, we will leave the task of identification of the fixed elements and the variable elements of the costs. Conceptually, we can visualize these two costs of purchasing and storage; the former decreasing and the latter increasing with order size. This is shown in Fig. 10.4.

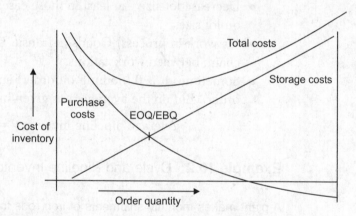

**Fig. 10.4**  Order/batch quantity and cost of inventories

Figure 10.4 shows that the cost is lowest when the order quantity is at the point of intersection of the purchase order costs and storage costs. This point is the economic order quantity (EOQ). If we substitute purchase order costs by batch costs, we will get economic batch quantity (EBQ). We can calculate the EOQ using differential calculus as follows:

Let the total cost of inventory management for the year be TC. Then,

$$TC = F_p + B/Q \times P + Q/2 \times S + F_{s+} B \times V$$

Where, $F_p$ is fixed cost of purchases including material receipt costs; $B$ is the annual quantity to be purchased; $Q$ is the quantity of one batch; $P$ is the variable cost of purchase per purchase order; and $F_s$ is the fixed cost of storage; $S$ is the variable cost of storage which is equal to $I + C + O$; where $I$ is the cost of capital multiplied by the variable cost of one unit of material, namely, $V$; $C$ is the variable storage cost including floor space cost, etc.; and $O$ is the obsolescence cost.

$V$ is the purchase price and incidental costs not dependent on quantity purchased rather than number of orders or number of times the deliveries are made, or on quantity stored.

Let us assume that $TC$ varies with batch size $Q$.

Therefore, to get optimum value of $TC$, we can differentiate $TC$ with reference to $Q$ using the formula that if $Y = X^n$, then $dY/dx = nX^{n-1}$

$$dTC/dQ = -BP/Q^2 + Q/2 \times S = 0; \quad Q^2 = 2BP/S$$
$$\text{So, } EOQ = \sqrt{2BP/S}$$

We can confirm that this is the minimum and not the maximum by differentiating this again as shown here:

$$d^2(TC)/dQ^2 = +2\,RS/Q^3$$

Since it is positive, it is the minimum cost point. Let us apply the formula in an example (Example 10.3).

## Example 10.3   The Coffee Powder Shop

An audio cassette shop has an annual purchase of 20,000 packets of coffee powder at ₹35 per packet. Each time a purchase is made, ₹300 is spent and every consignment, irrespective of its size, is charged ₹200.

The interest rate of capital is 15 per cent per annum, storage cost per annum per packet is ₹10, and obsolescence is 20 per cent as coffee becomes unsaleable very fast due to loss of flavour. Calculate the EOQ.

$$EOQ = \sqrt{2 \times 20000 \times 500/(0.15 \times 35 + 10 + 0.20 \times 35)}$$
$$= \sqrt{40000 \times 500/22.25} = ?\ 3809524$$
$$= 948$$

This means 21 orders.

## Example 10.4   Time between Orders

A customer has been ordering 1040 units at the rate of 20 units per week. Production cost is ₹60 per unit. Inventory carrying cost is 25% of the production cost. Processing cost of one order is ₹45. Calculate the EOQ

Annual demand   $D$ = (20 /week)(52 weeks) = 1040 units

$H$ (Holding cost) = 0.25 × (₹60/unit) = ₹15

$S$ (Ordering cost) = ₹45

**Case 1:**

$$Q = 400 \text{ units}$$

$$\text{Total cost} = \frac{Q}{2}(H) + \frac{D}{Q}(S) \ (400/2)(15) + (1040/\ 400)(45) = ₹3117$$

**Case 2:**

$$Q = 450 \text{ units}$$

$$\text{Total cost} = \frac{Q}{2}(H) + \frac{D}{Q}(S) \ (450/2)(15) + (1040/450)(45) = ₹3488$$

**Case 3:**

$$Q = EOQ = 79 \text{ units}$$

$$Q_{OPT} = \sqrt{\frac{2DS}{H}} = \sqrt{\frac{2(\text{Annual Demand})(\text{Order of Set-up Cost})}{\text{Annual Holding Cost}}}$$

$$EOQ = \sqrt{\frac{2(1040)(45)}{15}} = 79 \text{ units}$$

For graphical representation, see Fig. 10.5.

Total cost can be calculated as under:

$$(79/2)(15) + (1040/79)(45) = ₹1187 \ (\text{ Minimum cost})$$

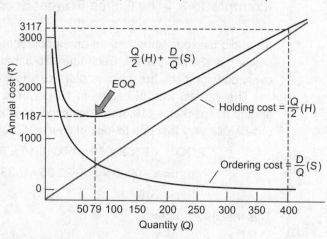

**Fig. 10.5**  Economic order quantity

## Time between orders (TBO)

Sometimes policies are expressed in terms of the time between replenishments.
TBO for a lot size is the elapsed time between receiving orders of Q units.

$$TBO_{EOQ} = Q/D$$
$$TBO_{EOQ} = 79/1040 = 0.076 \text{ year}$$
$$TBO_{EOQ} = (79/1040)(12) = 0.91 \text{ months}$$
$$TBO_{EOQ} = (79/1040)(52) = 3.9 \text{ weeks}$$
$$TBO_{EOQ} = (79/1040)(365) = 27.74 \text{ days}$$

## COST OF ERRORS IN ESTIMATION

One may observe that some of the cost items have to be estimated from a variety of sources, which may not always yield reliable figures. One may say that of all these figures, the costs of storage and obsolescence may sometimes be unreliable. Let us see the damage which a mistake can cost in Example 10.5.

This means that one need not spend too much time and energy to estimate costs for calculating the EOQ.

### Example 10.5  Cost of Errors in Estimation

Let us presume that given the same data as in Example 10.3, the obsolescence may be wrongly estimated as just 18 per cent and cost of storage at ₹9, whereas the correct figures are 20 per cent and ₹10, respectively. Then the calculations of EOQ would be as follows:

$\sqrt{400000}$ × 500/20.55 = $\sqrt{973236}$ = 986, i.e., 20 purchase orders. The total cost of the correct order quantity and the order quantity based on wrong cost estimation, however, appear very close.

Cost with correct order quantity (₹) = 21 × 500 + 948/2 × 22.25 = 21,000 approx.

Cost with wrong order quantity (₹) = 20 × 500 + 987/2 × 22.25 = 21,000 approx.

Cost of error in estimation = ₹0 (21,000 − 21,000)

The bottom of the total cost curve is rounded and for several changes the total cost remains by and large constant. This is due to the square root effect in the formula used.

## RADICAL TRANSFORMATION OF THE COST STRUCTURE

Modern management, particularly Japanese, has radically transformed our perceptions of inventory management by reduction of purchase order costs beyond imagination, with instant communications and fast execution of orders in what is known as the just in time (JIT) systems, which we will discuss later in the chapter. Example 10.6 shows the impact that radical reduction can have on purchase order costs.

### Example 10.6  Impact of Radical Reduction on Purchase Order Costs

If, as has happened in modern Japanese management, purchase order costs are brought down, it will have significant impact on inventory management.

Dramatic drop of purchase order costs in Japan has changed all our perceptions. Thus, from, say, ₹100 the EOQ in Example 10.3 would be as follows:

√ 2 ×20000 ×100/22.25 = √ 179775 = 424, i.e., 47 orders a year, i.e., nearly four orders a month (weekly).

Total cost = 47 × 100 + 424/2 × 22.25 = 9417, a drastic fall from the previous figure of ₹21,000. With frequent orders the chances of obsolescence would also reduce considerably, and the storage costs may even come down further by nearly ₹800.

## COUNTING ON DISCOUNTS FOR BULK PURCHASES

Let us see how we could handle bulk discounts in the exercise. This is done in Example 10.7.

### Example 10.7   Bulk Discounts

Let us assume that bulk discounts of 10 per cent are available in the situation of Example 10.6, where there are purchases of ₹10,000 or more at a time. Since this is a discontinuous function of total costs, we cannot build it into a differential calculus solution. We have to use iterative methods of trial and error. Further, the purchase price will no longer be constant and we will have to modify the total cost equation by including the costs of purchase.

The total relevant costs would then be as shown here:

Variable purchase costs + Variable storage costs + Cost of material
= 9417 (as worked out in Example 10.6) + 20,000 × 35 = ₹7,09,417

For order size of 10,000, i.e., two orders a year,

Total cost = 2 × 10 + 10000/2 × 21.75 (after adjusting for lower prices of cassettes resulting in a lower interest burden on inventory) + 6,30,000 (discounted price) = 7,38,770.

It is, therefore, not worth considering the offer. In particular, the risk of obsolescence increases with heavy stocks which may turn out to be unsaleable.

But at 20 per cent discount prices, the cost will come down further to ₹72,500 (calculation is on the same lines as in the previous calculation) and it may be worth considering the offer.

## WHEN TO BUY AND MANUFACTURE

Let us first assume that the demand and supply time is certain and the pattern is reliable. Let us further assume a situation where the maximum

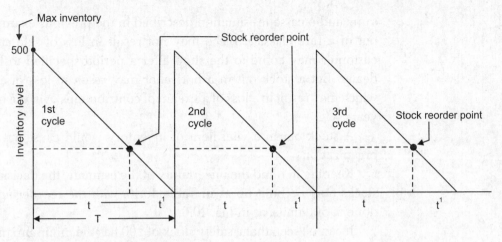

**Fig. 10.6** Ordering pattern in certainty of demand

inventory is fixed at 500 units. We could then follow the pattern of ordering as in Fig. 10.6.

Over a period of time $T$, The entire stock gets exhausted. After a period of time $t\,(t<T)$ when the stocks have depleted by a certain amount, the order for replenishment is given to the vendor (this is indicated by the stock reorder point) who takes a period of time $t'$ (called lead time) to supply the fresh stock. The time period $t$ and $t'$ are fixed in such a way that an order that is placed will result in supply within the prescribed lead time. This whole cycle is then repeated.

## WHEN TO ORDER WITH UNCERTAIN DEMAND AND SUPPLY PATTERN

**Stock out cost**
Cost of stock out is very difficult to forecast even if the probability of stock outs can be worked out reasonably accurately on the basis of past data. But vital items of the inventory call for special attention. A VED analysis is a must.

Since both demand and supply may be uncertain, it is necessary to keep a safety stock so that the contingency of the stocks falling to zero is avoided, or the probability of its happening is very low. The reorder point would have to incorporate the safety stocks.

Costs are the primary consideration for fixing safety stocks.

The basic principle is that due to avoidance of safety stocks, the cost of stock out should be less than the related cost of storage of the relevant level of safety stock.

Unlike the parameters used in the EOQ, the cost of stock out is extremely nebulous and involves subjective judgement (Lipman 1981). At the first level, the stock out cost is the contribution lost by the loss of sale. But the impact of the loss of customer has also to be considered. In the same audio cassettes situation described in the previous example, a stock out of a rare classical piece may not result in loss of sale at all, as the customer may come to the shop after a period specified to him by the dealer. But a stock out in a hot seller may result in loss of a customer, which may result in a loss of a stream of contributions over the next several years.

A stock out in a vital item of inventory would cause a panic in the organization.

Keeping in mind the uncertainty of the estimate, the decision of safety stocks may be built up as in Table 10.10, with the reordering otherwise done at 500 units, as in Fig. 10.6.

It can be seen that a safety stock of 200 has the minimum (marked * in Table 10.10) total cost.

That means the ordering should be done when the stock reaches 700 (500 reorder point plus safety stock of 200).

As the criticality of items of stock increases, the cost of stock out will increase. If, as shown in Column 2 in Table 10.10, the demand in lead time simultaneously increases beyond 800, the safety stocks may have to be increased even if this means further addition to storage costs.

**Table 10.10** Determining safety stocks

| Safety stocks (1) | Demand in lead time (2) | Stock out quantity Col. 2-500 (reorder level) – Col. 1 (3) | Stock probability (4) | Cost per stock out (5) | Total stock out costs 3×4×5 (6) | Storage costs 1×30 (7) | Total stock out costs + storage costs Cols 6+7 (8) |
|---|---|---|---|---|---|---|---|
| 0 | 600 | 100 | 0.30 | 300 | 9000 | 0 | 19,500 |
|   | 700 | 200 | 0.10 | 300 | 6000 |   |   |
|   | 800 | 300 | 0.05 | 300 | 4500 |   |   |
|   |   |   |   |   | 19,500 |   |   |
| 100 | 700 | 100 | 0.10 | 300 | 3000 | 3000 | 9000 |
|   | 800 | 200 | 0.05 | 300 | 3000 |   |   |
|   |   |   |   |   | 6000 |   |   |
| 200 | 800 | 100 | 0.05 | 300 | 1500 | 6000 | 7500* |
| 300 | 800 | 0 |   |   | 0 | 9000 | 9000 |

# ECONOMIC BATCH QUANTITY

**EBQ and EOQ**
The calculation of EBQ is analogous to the calculation of EOQ for purchase.

The issue of EBQ is analogous to that of EOQ except that in the equation batch set-up costs have to be substituted in place of purchase order costs. There can be several components of batch set up costs. Cleaning the mould and fitting it into the machine, and quality testing costs which choose a specified number of samples from each batch are typical costs that need to be considered. Since quality testing may be critical for many products such as computer components, the quality costs can dominate the decision on batch quantities.

Example 10.8 shows the computation of EBQ.

## Example 10.8 The Snacks Shop

The snacks shop makes cakes, biscuits, and snacks of varying flavours, from mild mushroom to pungent garlic. The critical selling feature of the products is that the products should not have even a trace of any flavour other than that on its label. Hence, the baking pans have to be cleaned each time a new product is made. The product is also tested for correct flavour and consistency, which is done on a sample basis. Thus, the set up variable costs are ₹200 inclusive of testing costs. The direct cost of garlic biscuits is ₹100 per kg. The annual demand is for 2000 kg.

Storage cost is ₹15 at the cost of capital at 15 per cent per annum, the storage costs in ₹15 per kg but obsolescence costs are a whopping ₹50 per kg, as the product cannot last more than six months in storage. Thus, the total storage costs are ₹80 per kg.

The EBQ = $\sqrt{2 \times 2000 \times 200/80}$ = $\sqrt{10,000}$ = 100, i.e., there should be twenty batches in a year (2000 ÷ 100), or one batch every three weeks. We are assuming that capacity is not a constraint. If it were so, the opportunity costs of using scarce resources would have to figure in the set up costs.

# PRACTICAL DIFFICULTIES IN ORDERING ONLY AT THE REORDER POINT WITH AN EOQ MODEL

**EOQ model**
The EOQ model becomes redundant with material resource planning with computers, which bypasses the inventory models.

There are several difficulties in applying a simplified system described hitherto in the book. In practice, several modifications have been made.

1. When groups of store items go together in production planning and maintenance plans, material resource planning and purchases are done directly, linking purchases with the production plan and

placing orders (Levin et al. 1982), bypassing the EOQ model. This is aided by fast communications that are possible with the Internet and computers.

2. When the demand goes up and down but groups of items have to be handled for the same vendor, instead of ordering each item separately, a peoriodic review system for a group can be made (Srivastava et al. 1983). In such a case, ordering is done in specified times irrespective of the reorder point, so that the number of purchase orders with the same vendors can be minimized, and costs can be saved. The quantum of orders would be (Vohra 2000):

Q = Target inventory, inventory in hand, previous order not received

The target inventory will be TI, and is the average demand during review period and the average demand during lead time.

In a deterministic model the period is derived by using calculus as follows:

Annual ordering costs = $D/DT \times A = A/T$
Storage costs = $DT/2 \times h = hdt/2$

where, $D$ is annual demand; $T$ is the period as expressed as a fraction of the year; $DT$ is the demand in time $T$ (fraction of the year), which is to be worked out.

A is ordering costs per order; h is the storage costs

$$TC = A/T + hDT/2$$

$$dTC/dT = \sqrt{2A/Dh}$$

We can also handle this togetherness by having a group EOQ (Lipman 1981).

3. Modify the EOQ in units with strong seasonal fluctuations or erratic trends.

## CONVERTING IMPUTED COSTS OF INTEREST TO REAL COST

The interest costs which have been used in the formula would not be explicitly available in financial accounts. Many organizations tackle this problem by internally charging their subordinate managers' interest at their cost of capital in their internal transfers of costs (Horngren et al. 2003). Horngren quotes the practices in Coca-cola and Wal-Mart. Similarly, many Indian companies which have a strong accent on profit centres like L & T, also do so.

## THE BUDGETARY PROCESS AND ITS DIVERGENCE FROM ECONOMIC ORDERING FOR INVENTORIES

We will now deal with this issue of bringing in inventory decisions as worked by the manager in the manner dealt with in this chapter, in congruence with corporate level managers of the organization as has been discussed in Chapter 1.

There could be some conflict in the manner in which budgets for inventories are set as discussed in Chapter 7 and the processes followed in this chapter. The former are conditioned by macro level overall company perceptions, whereas this chapter has a worm's eye view of the processes of balancing the different considerations of inventory management. This has been a subject of academic concern (Hector 1964). At this stage, a manager who handles the micro level issues in this chapter should be able to moderate and modify macro level decisions, which may take a vastly divergent position in the budgets, using across the board figures with no consideration for micro level economic logic. Complete integration of these two methods may prove to be too messy to be solved mathematically, or even logically.

## ABC, XYZ, VED, AND FSN ANALYSIS OF INVENTORY

There are managerial benefits to categorizing inventories into different segments. Each segment has a different economic issue to be considered. Categorizing and subsequently analysing has become considerably easier with the use of computer software, which provide data sorting facilities. The categorization most commonly used is the ABC analysis, which is an acronym for Always Better Control. It has been empirically found that a small proportion of items usually contribute to a large proportion of the value of consumption, whereas a large proportion of items contribute totally to only a small proportion of the value of consumption. Segregating these is called the Pareto analysis, and if applied to consumption value, it is known as ABC (Levin et al. 1982).

How do we perform an ABC analysis?

The data of consumption should be sorted with decreasing value of consumption and the number of items should also be recorded. We can then arrive at the cumulative values and cumulative number of items. We can plot the data with cumulative items in X axis and cumulative value in the Y axis. In most cases, the data would appear as shown in Fig. 10.7.

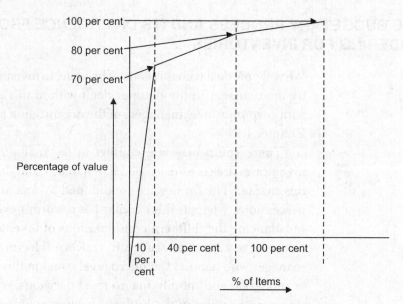

**Fig. 10.7** ABC analysis

We can observe that the graph has first a steep rise in value for a small number of items, followed by less steep curve and then an even flatter curve. The first steep curve covers A items, the second turn is for B items, and the flattest curve is for C items.

If energy and time are focused on A items, the pay off would be much larger than that concentrated on C items.

**A and C items**
A non-moving C item needs to be disposed off quickly and slow moving A items needs reduction of purchase order costs and reduction in lead time.

A items would usually cover raw material. Maintenance spares would usually fall in B and C categories. This distinction is significant, as we will see that it may also be important to monitor some B and C items individually.

The Pareto analysis can also be done for items on the stock of inventory. The shape may be different but it would give an idea of how stocking is done. If there is strong divergence between the results of ABC and XYZ analysis, it would need investigation.

A next type of analysis is the fast moving, slow moving, and non-moving (FSN) store. The data for this would be to record the number of days' consumption that is lying in stock and arrange it in descending order. The non-moving store would show infinity and the fast moving one will have a very low figure. If a C item in the ABC classification is non-moving, it means that the system has broken down and needs immediate attention. If a high value A item is in the slow moving category, storage costs would be enormous, and attempts to reduce purchase order cost, and/or reduction of lead time is important.

The last categorization is the vital, essential, and desirable (VED). This classification is judgemental of the managers and the history of stock outs. V items, even if they are C classification, need close monitoring and constant effort to reduce lead time and lower the purchase order costs. Vital material has to be dealt with by taking the advice of a poet who said the following:

> *For the want of horse a war was lost.*
> *For the want of shoe a horse was lost.*
> *For want of a nail a shoe was lost.*

The cost of stock outs in V items can be abnormally large, whereas in many cases, their value and the cost of storage may be very small.

## Illustration of ABC Analysis

Table 10.11 indicates that item A proportions minimum percentage, that is, 15% only but values the most 74.1%. Item B constitutes 30% and item C proportions 55% but values least i.e 6.8% of the investment only. Thus the tightest control should be exercised on item A in order to maximize the profitability on its investment. On the other hand, for item C simple control will suffice.

**Table 10.11**    Illustration of ABC analysis

| Item | Units | | % of total | Cumulative | Unit price | Total cost | % of total | Cumulative |
|---|---|---|---|---|---|---|---|---|
| 1 | 5000 | A | 5% | 15% | 50 | 2,50,000 | 33.7% | |
| 2 | 10,000 | | 10% | | 30 | 3,00,000 | 40.4% | 74.1% |
| 3 | 17,000 | B | 17% | 45% | 6 | 1,02,000 | 13.7% | |
| 4 | 13,000 | | 13% | 45% | 3 | 39,000 | 5.3% | 93% |
| 5 | 30,000 | C | 30% | | 1.1 | 33,000 | 4.4% | |
| 6 | 10,000 | | 10% | | 1.5 | 15,000 | 2.0% | |
| 7 | 15,000 | | 15% | 100% | 0.2 | 3,000 | 0.4% | 100% |
| | 1,00,000 | | | | | 7,42,000 | | |

## JUST IN TIME CONCEPT

**JIT concept**
JIT has benefits more than just reduction in inventories. It enhances focus on quality control and customer preferred tailor made products.

Just in time (JIT) production and inventory systems are built to get material supplies just in time for production, and production planning just in time for sales. Therefore, it has a lean inventory and most of the methods proposed elsewhere in the chapter would not be relevant.

Obviously, it will work if communications are fast and cheap, and purchase order costs are near zero, as explained in Example 10.3.

Its extension to production systems has other implications.

It may mean decrease in batch size and increase in number of batches. But there are benefits in this, other than reduction of inventory storage costs. It enables production planning to get hooked on to customer preferences. Thus, a customer who needs a car of a particular colour and a particular shape of seat can now have it.

## Accounting Modification to Match JIT

The demands on cost accounting by JIT can be varied. These need to be attended to Durden et al. (1999). If we decide to reduce the batch size, it should not be done without deliberating on the impact of this on the total costs. This would induce effort to reduce set up times and lead times in supplies. Tortuous exercises of allocation of overhead expenses do not add value to the information. On the other hand, a study of the process of manufacture may yield direct benefits. This would commend the short-cut system of accounting, as in back flush costing.

# THROUGHPUT COSTING

Throughput costing of inventories is known as super-variable costing. It considers only direct material as variable costing and inventories as only that part of the costs. Its effect on managerial behaviour has been shown in Example 10.6. Its adherents would generally come from those using JIT.

## Back Flush Costing

This is a ridiculous name for an interesting system. Back flush costing is saddled with an unfortunate name, which has often been used to ridicule it as a crazy idea. Some would, however, say that it is a most appropriate accounting system for a JIT and lean inventory system. Let us see why it is described as a back flush system. The system can be understood only if we follow the several steps it involves.

*Step 1* – The first step is to develop a standard cost for a product, using methods described in Chapter 9. Among other things, this may involve using the data with an ABC approach. It, therefore, stars with an accurate estimate of the standard costs.

*Step 2* – Decide if the pattern of production and purchases would be just in time in relation to purchases, works-in-process, and finished goods. JIT may be chosen for the one without using it for the other.

*Step 3* – Decide which of the following needs to be accurately valued and which can be less casually valued:

1. Raw material
2. Work-in-process
3. Finished goods

*Step 4* – Decide the trigger points (Horngren et al. 2003) that will flush out the costs from an accumulated pool, somewhat similar to the workings of a flush system in a toilet.

Let us see three concrete examples (Examples 10.9, 10.10, and 10.11).

**Example 10.9**  Hasten Slow Company Case for Back Flush Costing

Hasten Slow Company has the following data:

*Material*

Purchase ₹20,00,000 of raw material X with an unfavourable price variance of ₹40,000.

Out of the standard value of the purchase of ₹19,60,000, the standard value consumed for the actual production of 10,000 units of Product A was ₹19,00,000 but standard value of actual usage was ₹19,05,000, i.e., unfavourable material efficiency variance was ₹5000. ₹55,000 standard value of raw material was left in the stock.

Standard conversion cost for 10,000 units was ₹12,00,000. But actual conversion cost was ₹2,60,000. The conversion process is fast and almost nothing lingers on in the work-in-process.

The total standard cost of Product A was ₹19,00,000 (raw material) plus ₹12,00,000 (standard conversion costs). Thus, the total standard cost of actual production of 10,000 was ₹31,00,000.

Of the 10,000 units produced only 9000 were sold. From the company's data, both raw material and finished goods need to be valued but it is not proposed to value work-in-process. We will have to use three triggers for the flush out process; first, at raw material purchase and consumption; second, when finished goods emerge from the work-in-process; and third, when the sale takes place. Conversion costs for each product will not be measured but the variances which will be left after flushing out the standard costs of all products produced, will be flushed out not to finished goods but to cost of goods sold.

The accounting entries for the three trigger points will be as follows:

*Trigger 1: On Purchase*

1. Dr. raw material inventory ₹19,60,000 (at standard price)
   Dr. (cost of goods sold) price variance ₹40,000 (flushed out)

Cr. accounts payable ₹20,00,000
Recording of total conversion cost
2.  Dr. conversion costs ₹12,60,000
    Cr. accounts payable ₹12,60,000

*Trigger 2: On production of 10,000 units*

3.  Dr. finished goods ₹31,00,000
    Dr. material efficiency variance (cost of goods sold) ₹5000
    Cr. raw material inventory ₹19,05,000 (flushed out)
    Cr. conversion costs ₹12,00,000
    (Balance raw material inventory is ₹55,000 at standard prices, finished goods ₹31,00,000 of 10000 units)
    And, conversion cost ₹60,000* being the variance (debit) is to be transferred to cost of goods sold

*Trigger 3: On sale of 9000 units*

4.  Dr. cost of goods sold ₹27,90,000
    Cr. finished goods ₹27,90,000
    (balance finished goods 1000 units for ₹3,10,000)

**Note:** *Would be available only pooled with all conversion cost variances for all the products. Individual product variances would not be available.

## Example 10.10  Speedy Sales Company

Speedy Sales Company's purchase pattern is the same as that of Hasten Slowly Company, but it sells exactly as much as it produces. Thus, it produced 10,000 units and also sold the same quantity. It would, therefore, not be necessary to compute finished goods in stock but have only two triggers, one at purchase and the other at sales. Entries one and two will be the same as in Example 10.9. The balance entries will be as follows:

*Trigger 2: Sales*

3.  Dr. cost of goods sold ₹31,00,000
    Dr. material efficiency variance (cost of goods sold) ₹5000
    Cr. raw material inventory ₹19,05,000 (flushed out)
    Cr. conversion costs ₹12,00,000

Balance raw material will be the same as before but there will be no finished goods, and the conversion cost variance of ₹60,000 will be transferred to cost of goods sold, as in Example 10.9.

In this example there will be no entry number four, as in Example 10.9.

## Example 10.11    Slow Sales Company

In this case, raw material is not kept in the inventory but there will be finished goods. Purchases were made for production of 10,000 units, namely, ₹19,45,000, which included price variance and material efficiency variance. But purchase price variance is ₹40,000 (unfavourable) and material efficiency (usage) variance was the same as before, i.e., ₹5000 (unfavourable). Thus, standard material cost was the same as before, namely, ₹19,00,000 for the production of 10,000 units. Conversion costs were the same as before but sales were only 9000 units, leaving 1000 units in stock. Here, the two triggers have to be at finished goods and sales.

*Trigger 1*

1.  Dr. finished goods ₹31,00,000
    Dr. price variance ₹40,000
    Dr. material efficiency variance (cost of goods sold ₹5000)
    Dr. conversion cost efficiency (cost of goods sold ₹60,000)
    Cr. accounts payable purchase ₹19,45,000
    Cr. accounts payable conversion cost ₹12,60,000
    Total debit equals total credit and is ₹32,05,000

There will not be any raw material inventory but the finished goods inventory will be the same as in Example 10.9. Examples 10.9, 10.10, and 10.11 illustrate the flexibility of the system. There could be other variations. The information available in the three systems may be briefly summarized as in Table 10.12.

**Table 10.12**    Trigger Doli

| Information | Standard cost system | 3 Trigger Purchase production sales | 2 Trigger Purchase sales | 2 Trigger Production sales |
|---|---|---|---|---|
| Raw material inventory | Yes | Yes | Yes | No |
| Work-in-process | Yes | No | No | No |
| Finished goods inventory | Yes | Yes | No | Yes |
| Cost of goods sold (product wise) | Yes | Yes | Yes | Yes |
| Direct product costs | Yes | Yes | Yes | Yes |
| Product wise direct cost variance | Yes | Yes | Yes | Yes |
| Product wise indirect cost variance | Yes | No | No | No |
| Process wise variance | Yes, if we have several conversion cost centres | Yes | Yes | Yes |

Thus, it can be seen that even in considerably decreasing paper and operational work, one may get meaningful information from back flush costing. Conversion costs can be broken into departments or even activity centres but proliferation of activity centres raise their own problems of data collection, as explained in Chapter 6.

## SUPPLY CHAIN MANAGEMENT

Supply chain management goes beyond the problem of inventory within an organization and concerns itself with a chain of actors in a supply chain. If each of them acted on the basis of only limited information that they have on likely demand and the production pattern, there would be a tremendous instability and consequent frustration for all the actors. Therefore, a transparent exchange of information among all, which is quite feasible in the present Internet age, would benefit everyone in terms of cost and effort (Lee et al. 1997).

## MATERIAL RESOURCE PLANNING AS A TOOL

**Material resource planning**
MRP is a major break through in inventory management as it cuts out the guessing game in the EOQ and Reorder and Safety stock game.

The benefits of a direct link up between production and maintenance planning, and purchases, made possible with modern computers and the Internet has obvious advantages. In relation to the material resource planning (MRP) programme this advantage has been explained in the earlier chapter but a brief explanation of its problems may be necessary. MRP requires the inventory records to be updated, and current. Only then can the quantity to be ordered be determined by considering the inventory on hand. If that does not happen, the whole system can go hay wire, as has happened often. Secondly, the push through pressures of the system may result in intermediate production to and from the prior work stations to push it through.

## ECONOMIC RESOURCE PLANNING AS A TOOL

Economic resource planning (ERP) enables intelligent use of resources using computers as tools. It has a tremendous effect of reducing batch sizes as set up costs can be programmed and minimized drastically. Typically, in the book trade, slow moving books can now be printed in small quantities instantaneously, in short runs.

## SUMMARY

Inventory valuation is an effort to match expenses incurred in one account period with the revenues in the succeeding accounting period and has several facets, such as sequencing the flow of values to production costs, inclusion of different items of costs to be charged in the period they are incurred in, and those that need to be inventoried. The accounting policies chosen have their behavioural repercussions. Ordering inventories and setting up batches for production have discrete costs and the total cost in an accounting period increases with the increasing number of orders and batches of production. But, if we reduce them the inventories to be stored would increase. Balancing these two costs are important. If ordering costs are reduced drastically and lead times for supply are reduced, there could be greater saving in storage costs. JIT systems capture this, in addition to enabling customer oriented tailor made products made in shorter production runs. MRP and ERP are computer oriented methods that enable effective links between production planning and purchase, and sales, minimizing costs all round. Back flush costing can considerably reduce the cost of costing with relatively less relevant information.

## KEY POINTS

- Absorption costing incorporates both fixed and variable overheads in inventory and results in steady profits.
- Variable costing includes only variable costing in inventory.
- Indian tax authorities are liberal in allowing both absorption and variable costing.
- Economic order quantity (EOQ) and economic batch quantity (EBQ) balances ordering costs and set up costs with storage costs.
- Reduction in ordering and set up costs will result in considerable reduction in inventories and lowering of costs.
- Stock out costs have to be balanced with storage costs.
- MRP and ERP using computers radically alters inventory management by linking production plans to purchase and sales.
- Back flush costing is a short method which reduces costs of costing.

## CONCEPT REVIEW QUESTIONS

1. How does use of absorption costing for inventory valuation and computation of cost of production affect managerial behaviour?
2. What is the difference between perpetual inventory systems and periodic inventory systems?
3. Distinguish between ABC and XYZ analysis in inventory management?
4. Is it possible for V items in VED analysis to be also non-moving items in an FSN analysis?
5. Why should any person choose to have a periodic review system in inventory ordering?
6. Would you classify an MRP system in the general class of reorder point order systems or periodic review system?
7. Do purchase order costs, batch set up costs, and storage costs used in the EOQ and EBQ formula include fixed costs?
8. Why are stock out costs more vulnerable in case of mistakes in estimation than costs included in the EOQ/EBQ formula?

## NUMERICAL PROBLEMS

1. **Motihari Pump Sets**
   Motihari has a dealership in standard agricultural pump sets, each costing ₹10,000. It takes ₹200 to place orders on the manufacturers. When the sets are received, a qualified engineer has to be employed to test them; he does this on a sample basis and charges ₹300 for the lot. The interest cost is 25 per cent per annum. Storage costs are ₹10 per annum. Pumps have no obsolescence cost. The demand for pumps is 5000 units per annum. What is the EOQ for ordering?

2. **Cost of Error**
   As against the purchase order costs, inspection costs, interest costs, and storage costs shown correctly in Numerical Problem 1, they are estimated wrongly here, as follows:
   Purchase order cost is ₹250. Inspection cost for a lot is ₹350. Interest cost is 20 per cent, and annual storage cost is ₹12 per annum. What is the cost of the error in sum total?

3. **Bulk Discount**
   If in Numerical Problem 1, pump orders of 2000 or more are given a 20 per cent discount, would the EOQ change?

4. **The Goa Cake Shop**

   The annual demand for plum cakes is 1000 kg. Cake making is done in batches and the batch size has to be decided. The set up cost for each batch is ₹150. The direct cost of the cake is ₹120 per kg. Storage costs are 15 per cent per annum. Storage cost is ₹15 per kg. Obsolescence cost is ₹30 per kg per annum. Calculate the economical batch quantity.

5. **Safety Stock of Item V**

   Item V is an important item and a stock in the item will result in total loss of ₹10,000. The item costs only ₹2000.

   Interest cost is 25 per cent per annum and storage costs are 5 per cent of the value per annum. Obsolescence cost is 5 per cent per annum.

   The past data shows the following:

| Stock | Demand in lead time | Stock out in lead time | Probability of stock out |
|---|---|---|---|
| 100 | 150 | 50 | 0.35 |
|  | 200 | 100 | 0.25 |
| 150 | 150 | 0 |  |
|  | 200 | 50 | 0.25 |
| 200 | 0 | 0 | 0 |

   Calculate the Safety stock for item V.

6. **ABC Inventory Control Systems**

   A company has 6 items in the inventory. The following are some data on these items:

| Item number | Average number of units in inventory | Average cost per unit (₹) |
|---|---|---|
| 1 | 31,000 | 30 |
| 2 | 5,000 | 12 |
| 3 | 8,000 | 8 |
| 4 | 10,000 | 18 |
| 5 | 15,000 | 2 |
| 6 | 9,000 | 90 |
| 7 | 6,000 | 100 |
| 8 | 20,000 | 7 |
| 9 | 17,000 | 19 |
| 10 | 11,000 | 22 |

## Question

6.1 Break down the items into A, B, and C classification in order to enable the company to introduce an ABC inventory control systems.

### 7. Global Company

Global Company is a professionally managed company, which has introduced the economic ordering quantity (EOQ) concept of material management. It is a multi-product company. One of its products, Snedlon, requires a chemical Exlon. Every unit of Snedlon needs one unit of Exlon. Monthly demand of Snedlon is 10,000 units

The other details are

| | |
|---|---|
| Price of Exlon | ₹40/ per unit |
| Ordering cost | ₹200/order |
| Holding cost | 10% per annum |

## Question

7.1 Calculate the economic ordering quantity for Exlon.

### 8. Product: ESAI

A company wants to adopt modern material management techniques. It wants to start with one product 'Esai'. The controller of materials has fixed the following limits:

| | |
|---|---|
| Annual Demand | 1600 units |
| EOQ | 320 units |
| Price | ₹20/unit |

The company endorsed the above concept in principle, but during discussions the following points emerged:

1. The price of Esai is traditionally very volatile. In the ensuing accounting year, it is likely to fluctuate between ₹19–₹24 per unit.
2. There is a big order for the finished product expected from Middle-East. If that materializes, the demand for Esai will be about 3000 - 4000 units. The decision is expected soon.
3. Recent hikes in fuel costs have added to the delivery costs of Esai. More hikes are expected.
4. The company has shifted from rented stores to its own storage. Better security and improved storage will reduce 'shrinkages'. The storage costs may witness a reduction of 20%
5. The company is planning to enter into a long term agreement with one single supplier. No supply orders will be required for every fresh purchase. This will reduce ordering costs by 25%

## Question

8.1 Review the impact of each of the above on EOQ, independently.

### 9. LIFO Method

A company adopts LIFO method of inventory pricing. It had the following data:

**Month: June**

| Date | Purchase (Units) | Rate/unit (₹) | Issued (Units) |
|------|------------------|---------------|----------------|
| 2 | 20 | 10 | |
| 5 | 50 | 12 | |
| 11 | | | 55 |
| 16 | 30 | 8 | |
| 19 | | | 25 |
| 25 | | | 15 |

There was no opening stock.

### Questions

9.1 What is the issue price under LIFO?

9.2 If the company shifts to FIFO method what is the impact on profitability.

## PROJECT

Form groups of 4 or 5 students and pick out a sample of four different companies and study their inventory turnover ratios, and suggest what one should look out for.

**CASE STUDY 1**　　　**Orissa Semi Conductors**

Orissa Semi Conductors was a sick company in the field of manufacturing semi conductor chips. Its Chairman, Patnaik, had appointed Radhakanth Rath as the general manager, as he promised he would be able to pull the company through. He said that he would not need a salary but would be satisfied with 10 per cent of the profits before charging cost of capital, which is currently estimated at ₹20,00,000. He wanted a free hand in all the decisions on accounting, inventory, and sales policies. He was allowed this.

1. The inventory of finished goods should be valued at full cost including fixed costs; this would be subject to the usual prudence of valuing at cost or market prices, whichever is lower.

2. He would appoint sole selling agents who would be willing to stock as much as the company wanted them to. They would pay as and when the stocks are sold, and corresponding cash realized.

The company had not kept manufactured chips in stock and had been produced only as much as could be sold. Market research had predicted that the demand for chips in the coming year would be 5,00,000. At that demand, Rath had budgeted that the profit before charging capital charges would be ₹20,00,000, calculated as follows:

Sales @ ₹50 per piece for 5,00,000 units = ₹2,50,00,000
Less variable cost @ ₹20 = ₹1,00,00,000
Contribution @ ₹30 = ₹1,50,000
Less fixed manufacturing costs = ₹90,00,000
Less marketing fixed costs = ₹40,00,000
Net operating income = ₹20,00,000

After charging capital charges of ₹20,00,000, EVA was zero.

His budget was approved by the Board and Chairman Patnaik.

Rath produced 6,00,000 units and shipped 5,00,000 units, putting 1,00,000 units in stock. The variable costs per unit and gross fixed costs, both manufacturing and marketing, were exactly as he had budgeted for, except that production was more. For this achievement he got the appreciation of the chairman.

He showed the sale to stockists as sale. The profits also depended on the valuation of inventories. He proposed to value the 1,00,000 chips in stocks at ₹41.67 per chip, which was less than the market price of ₹50. It was calculated as follows:

Variable cost per chip = ₹20
Fixed cost per chip = ₹21.67 (130,00,000 ₃ 6,00,000)

Total = ₹41.67

The auditors refused to include marketing costs in inventory valuation and reduced the value to ₹35 (i.e., they included only manufacturing fixed costs) provided Rath certified that it would sell above that price. With great show of unwillingness and a sense of being cheated out of a larger bonus package, Rath agreed to the auditor's valuation. The auditors were also happy they had made their point and it was accepted graciously by Rath, and this put them off their guard. They overlooked, in turn, the treatment of sale to stockists, as sale in the accounts of the company. Rath knew that the prices were likely to fall to ₹30 per piece, but the auditors did not.

Meanwhile, he collected his bonus on the basis of the audit certificate and left the company.

## Discussion Questions

1. What was Rath's bonus?
2. Was the remuneration package for Rath correctly designed?
3. How would you have designed the reward system if you were Patnaik?

| CASE STUDY 2 | Sangeeta's *Ustaadon Ka Ustaad*, and *Anu and Seersa* |
|---|---|

Chandra, General Manager, Logistics, of Sangeeta was less fretful when Sangeeta's business shifted from long playing music records to audio cassettes. The batch set up costs for audio cassettes was only a fraction of that for making records. So, it was possible to quickly gear up production and meet any demand. But his worries did not end with this. The marketing people had forecast a sale of one lakh cassettes of the blockbuster movie, *Ustaadon Ka Ustaad*, featuring all the great actors and actresses of India and a great music director. They said they would sell it within one week and thus, beat the pirates. Chandra was ready with one lakh cassettes and stocked wholesalers and retailers in all the remote corners of the country with these. 'Stock out costs can be phenomenally high', the GM Marketing told him. Unfortunately, the film flopped within two days and the sales hardly reached 10,000 units, leaving 90,000 junk cassettes. The dealers and wholesalers were angry at the hype created by Sangeeta for this product. When *Anu and Seersa* was released, not much was expected of it, as the actor and actress were unknown. But every week it picked up added strength. Chandra was again caught napping as he noticed that whereas batch set up costs were very low for cassettes, the inlay to be fitted was printed by an outsider and needed some lead time. Small lots of inlays were charged prohibitively high prices, and large lots were fraught with the danger of becoming junk if the cassettes did not sell. He wished the printer were in online connection with him so that he could quickly place orders on the Internet. Again, the dealers were angry because of the stock outs. A second set of problems Chandra faced was the choice of transport. Cassettes were light and cost less for transport. But when large volumes were involved, it could cut into the wafer thin margins these products had. Chandra had a choice of three modes of transport from Kolkata to the different parts of the country. Typically, the profile of the charge from Kolkata to Mumbai was as follows:

Full truck was 50 paise per cassette if the truck was about 70 per cent full.

Smalls in standard truck runs were 60 paise per cassette. Here, there is a risk of the cassettes being mislaid.

Air transport cost ₹1 per cassette with a minimum booking of 100 cassettes.

Chandra had less of a problem with steady sellers who were selling for the past thirty years. A typical product in this category was the music of M. S. Subbalaxmi. They had some seasonal pattern, but it was never unpredictable. The third logistic problem was regarding audio tapes and plastic granules, which he imported from Singapore. Plastic granules are used to make the cassette covers. Between them they constitute 80 per cent of the cost. There are innumerable spare parts for the machines, the total cost of which was very low, but if they are not available the production could come to a grinding halt.

Chandra had recently been to a seminar on MRP, ERP, supply chain management, and inventory analysis. He wondered if he could use some of these concepts in his work.

## Discussion Questions

1.  What rules can he follow in the choice of mode of transport for different categories of cassettes?
2.  What concepts of MRP, ERP, and inventory analysis can he apply in this situation?

# PART III

## Management Accounting for Decision-making

## CHAPTER 11

# Decision-making and Relevant Costing

**Learning Objectives**

After reading this chapter, you will be able to understand

- the managerial situations where alternative decisions could be feasible
- the cost (financial and non-financial) implications of each of the feasible alternatives, and identify them
- the specific points of difference in the implications in each of these alternatives, which could be labelled as relevant costs and information
- the use of these relevant items in decision-making in an ambience of uncertainty
- the contextual use in the decision-making of

- the concepts of sunk costs, avoidable costs, out-of-pocket costs, opportunity costs, incremental costs, differential costs, imputed costs, historical costs, and future costs
- the theory of constraints
- the difference in the methods used for controls and decision-making
- the difference in the emphasis between ABC analysis and capital investment decisions on the one hand, and relevant costs and theory of constraints on the other

## INTRODUCTION

**Relevant costing**
It focuses on the precise nature of differences between different alternatives and helps us not to miss the wood for the tress.

The topics covered under the rubric of relevant costing are a whole range of concepts, methods and algorithms, which enable one to clearly understand the cost implications of the managerial choice between different alternative decisions generally, having a short and medium-term impact. But long-term issues are also sometimes incorporated under this rubric to highlight the precise source of difference in the financial implications of alternative decisions. It totally shies away from the uses of cost data for control. Everywhere the focus in the rubric of relevant costing is the nature of the differences between alternatives so that adequate critical attention is paid to this. Differences not only need to be correctly identified but also correctly quantified. The point is not to miss the wood for the trees. The subject of relevant costing is also covered by generic descriptions of decision-making in all management. It would be useful to reproduce the advice of Geoffrey Gregory, Professor Emeritus, Loughborough Business School, England, on the steps involved in taking such decisions (Gregory 1988) in points as follows:

1. Make a list of alternative actions to be considered after taking into account (2).
2. List all possible outcomes that can result from action at (1). These will include financial and non-financial outcomes.
3. List the consequence of all feasible combinations of actions and outcomes.
4. Assess the likelihoods of the various outcome possibilities. Some outcomes may be low risk with low uncertainty, and others high risk and high uncertainty. Identify these thoroughly before making a decision.
5. Develop a decision criterion.
6. Decide and implement.

These generic steps should guide our analytical processes for decisions. Further, the outcomes predicted in the decision process may turn out to be different after actual implementation. Therefore, as a supplement to Gregory's decision model we may find it necessary to provide a feedback loop to modify and correct a decision so that it becomes adapted to the realities it attempts to tackle. The eight stage processes may be described by the processes in Fig. 11.1 which is adapted from Horngren (Horgren et al. 2003).

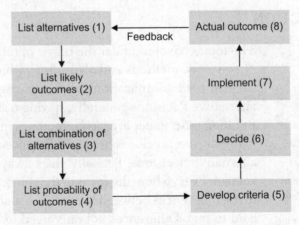

**Fig. 11.1** A feedback decision model

## SPECIAL COST TERMINOLOGY OF RELEVANT COSTS

**Relevant cost analysis**
It is done more meaningfully with gross figures rather than with per unit figures.

Relevant costing has a whole lot of terminology, which are specialized in nature and have not been detailed in Chapter 3 where the terminology of costing was introduced. We will use Table 11.1 as an anchor to detail them. It gives the basic data on a proposal to introduce a new machine to produce more of a product which can be sold at a marginally lower price but at higher volumes than at present. The old machine can be salvaged and sold at a lower price.

The choice is between two alternatives—first, to retain the existing system, and the second, to have a new machine and system.

Let us carefully comment on the figures.

1. Note that whereas item 2, sales prices, is expressed on a unit basis, it is immediately thereafter converted to gross amount in the next item, sales.

   Similarly, even though per unit variable costs are different in the two alternatives, the rest of the items (including variable costs) are all expressed in gross amount and not per unit. Relevant costs of alternatives can be meaningfully used only if gross amounts are used, particularly when the quantities sold in the alternatives are different. The fallacy of the unit cost approach has already been explained in Chapter 3, Example 3.9.

**Table 11.1** The listing of cost data of alternative choices

| | Existing alternative (1) | Proposed alternative (2) | Increment of (2) over (1) | |
|---|---|---|---|---|
| 1. Sale quantity | 10,000 | 18,000 | 8000 | |
| 2. Sales price (₹/unit) | 3 | 2.8 | −0.2 | |
| 3. Sales value (₹) | 30,000 | 50,400 | 20,400 | |
| 4. Variable cost (₹) | 20,000 | 40,000 | 20,000 | |
| 5. Contribution (₹) | 10,000 | 10,400 | 400 | |
| 6. Fixed cost/avoidable costs (₹) | 2000 | 3000 | 1000 | |
| 7. Fixed cost sunk (₹) | 3000 | 3000 | 0 | Irrelevant |
| 8. Salvage value (₹) | 0 | −1000 | −1000 | |
| 9. Net operating income (₹) | 5000 | 5400 | 400 | |
| 10. Opportunity cost (₹) | −5400 | −5000 | | |
| 11. Net of opportunity costs (₹) | −400 | 400 | | |

**Avoidable fixed costs**
These costs can be avoided if the related activity is abandoned or altered radically.

2. The expression 'avoidable fixed costs' distinguish these costs from variable costs which vary instantaneously with the cost driver and the sunk costs which do not vary with even long-term changes in

**Sunk costs**
These costs persist even if the related activity is abandoned. They are irrelevant. Do not cry over spilt milk. Committed costs are a class of sunk costs which on breach of commitment become an avoidable cost.

**Relevant costs**
These costs use future costs but could be based on historical costs used for estimating future costs.

**Opportunity costs**
The concept of opportunity costs would be less trivially used when we deal with allotment of scarce resources to products and services.

the cost driver. Typically, these would include personnel who could be reduced or increased between the alternatives, or even depreciation which can be avoided by selling off the machines. Power agreements provide for alteration of contracted power which can, therefore, increase or decrease between the alternatives. It may be seen that in alternative 2 this cost increases, as would surely happen if a bigger machine is commissioned.

3. Sunk costs are those that cannot be reduced even if one avoids an activity. Examples of these costs are the depreciation costs arising out of, say, installation costs of a machine, arising from earthwork and foundation costs, etc. Employees who cannot be dispensed with or redeployed with change in activity and other irretrievable costs are similarly sunk costs. A bad spouse in social systems where divorce is not allowed would be a case of sunk costs. Committed costs are a sub-set of sunk costs but are distinguishable, as they are avoidable if the commitment can be breached. Typically, a promise of continued employment to a worker, or a contract for taking a minimum amount of power, is sometimes breached.

   Sunk costs are irrelevant except if tax computations allow one to use it as a deduction for calculating taxable income.

4. Salvage value of replaced equipment would go towards reducing the costs of the alternatives which replace old machines. These are relevant for analysis when taking the decisions.

5. The figures in Table 11.1 are all future costs and revenues, and not just past historical costs. Since relevant cost is for making decisions and not for control, they use only future costs and not historical costs. But historical costs are useful for estimating future costs.

6. The concept of opportunity costs in this example is used for a trivial demonstration of the fact that by choosing an alternative, we are losing the opportunity of making a profit of ₹5400 in the alternative proposal. If we deduct this amount from the profit made by retaining the present systems, we end up losing ₹400. However, if alternative 2 is chosen we would lose the opportunity of making a profit of ₹5000 by retaining the present practice. But happily, even if we deduct the costs of this opportunity we will still make a profit.

   The concept of opportunity costs could be extended to non-financial and non-measurable outcomes of choosing an alternative.

   If, for example, alternative 2 may mean that as a manager one may lose leisure and the opportunity of spending more time with the family, this would be shown at step 2 in Fig. 11.1. Sometimes

**Non-financial considerations**
These may sometimes dominate decisions.

**Imputed costs**
These are those items of costs which do not figure in conventional financial books; they are clumsy to estimate.

But they are relevant for decisions. Cost of capital is a typical example.

these non-financial outcomes may dominate the decision for strategic or moral reasons.

7. The incremental costs and revenues are the differences between alternatives 1 and 2. Horngren distinguishes between the differences under each item and the differences in the total, which he labels as differential cost.

8. Table 11.1 has a massive increase in production and sales in alternative 2, over alternative 1. Usually this may mean a sharp increase in raw material, works-in-progress, and finished goods inventories.

This would imply an increase in interest and cost of capital. These costs may or may not be reflected in financial accounts but relevant costs must necessarily incorporate them. These are described as imputed costs; they have not been included in Table 11.1 but in real cases they should be. Figure 11.2 shows the steps involved in the decision-making model.

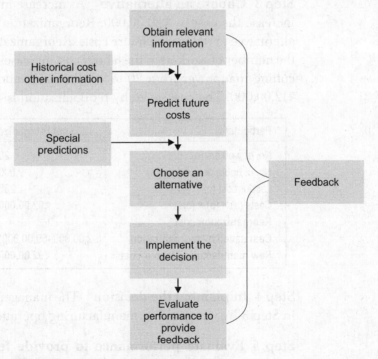

**Fig. 11.2** Decision-making model

Relevant costs are expected future costs that differ among the alternative courses of action being considered. Historical costs are irrelevant because they are past costs and, therefore, cannot differ among alternative future courses of action.

### Step 1  Obtain relevant information

| Relevant cost | ₹/Hour |
|---|---|
| Historical labour costs | 180 |
| Increase in benefits | 50 |
| Future labour cost | 230 |

### Step 2  Predict future cost

| Particulars | Historic cost | Future cost |
|---|---|---|
| No. of workers (a) | 20 | 20 |
| No. of hours per worker (b) | 2000 | 2000 |
| Labour cost (c) | 180 | 230 |
| Costs (a) × (b) × (c) | ₹72,00,000 | ₹92,00,000 |
| Increase in labour cost | | ₹20,00,000 |

### Step 3  Choose an alternative

As increase in labour rate per hour will increase the cost by ₹20,00,000. Reorganization can be considered as an alternative to reduce the future costs. Reorganization is expected to reduce the number of workers as the labour cost increases. The company considers cutting manpower from 20 to 15. Reorganization costs are estimated as ₹12,00,000. The cost saved by reorganization is ₹23,00,000.

| Particulars | Do not reorganize | Reorganize |
|---|---|---|
| No. of workers (a) | 20 | 15 |
| No. of hours per worker (b) | 2,000 | 2,000 |
| Labour cost (c) | 230 | 230 |
| Costs (a) × (b) × (c) | ₹92,00,000 | ₹69,00,000 |
| **Reorganization cost** | | ₹12,00,000 |
| **Cost saved by reorganization** | (92,00,000–69,00,000) | ₹23,00,000 |
| **New manufacturing labour costs** | ₹92,00,000 | ₹81,00,000 |

### Step 4  Implement the decision

The manager implements the decision in Step 3 by reorganizing manufacturing operations.

### Step 5  Evaluate performance to provide feedback

The historical information can help managers take better predictions that allow for more learning time. Manager can improve implementation through employee training and better supervision.

## Determining Relevant Revenues and Relevant Costs for Electric Equipment

The analysis below indicates that reorganizing manufacturing operations will increase the operating income by ₹11,00,000 per year. Note that we get the same conclusion from 'all data' and 'relevant data analysis'. By confining the analysis managers can clear away the clutter of confused irrelevant data and use only relevant costs which have direct effect on the operating income. In the example below the only relevant costs are manufacturing labour cost and reorganizational cost. Understanding which costs are relevant and which are irrelevant plays an important role in decision-making.

| Determining relevant revenues and relevant costs for electric equipment | | | | |
|---|---|---|---|---|
| Units sold | 25,000 | Cost per unit | ₹500 | |
| Price per unit | ₹3,000 | Units | ₹25,000 | |
| Revenues | ₹7,50,00,000 | Direct material | ₹1,25,00,000 | |
| | **All data** | | **Relevant data** | |
| Particulars | Do not reorganize | Reorganize | Do not reorganize | Reorganize |
| Revenues (a) | 7,50,00,000 | 7,50,00,000 | - | - |
| Costs: | | | | |
| Direct material | 1,25,00,000 | 1,25,00,000 | - | - |
| Manufacturing labour | 92,00,000 | 69,00,000 | 92,00,000 | 69,00,000 |
| Manufacturing overhead | 75,00,000 | 75,00,000 | - | - |
| Marketing | 2,00,00,000 | 2,00,00,000 | - | - |
| Reorganizational costs | 0 | 12,00,000 | - | 12,00,000 |
| Total cost (b) | 4,92,00,000 | 4,81,00,000 | 92,00,000 | 81,00,000 |
| Operating income (a – b) | 2,58,00,000 | 2,69,00,000 | 92,00,000 | 81,00,000 |
| Difference | 11,00,000 | | 11,00,000 | |

In this example, manufacturing labour cost is the only relevant cost. Managers can base their decisions on manufacturing labour costs. Identifying relevant costs not only saves time but also gives a much clearer picture to decision-makers and makes them more confident in taking decisions.

## VARIETY OF ALGORITHMS USED IN RELEVANT COST ANALYSIS

The data analysis between the alternative choices can hardly be fitted into stereotyped formats. They have to adapt themselves to the problem definitions. The varieties that are followed are given here.

1. We exhibit the full cost and revenues in alternatives; in large complex problems when there are innumerable inter-connected issues, a more surefooted way is to exhibit the full cost and revenue data to ensure nothing is missed.

2. We extend a column on incremental costs and revenue between the alternatives. This is a necessary step to crystallize the decision process.

3. We exhibit only incremental costs and revenues between the alternatives, and then decide. In simpler problems it may be possible to quickly enumerate the incremental difference between different alternatives and not waste too much time listing out all the costs and revenues.

4. We exhibit only the contribution per unit of scarce resource in the alternatives, and decide. When the identity of a scarce resource is known, it would be time-consuming to list out the innumerable options of allotting the resource for the products and 'search' for the best option. One can shorten the search process by estimating the contribution of the use of resource for a unit of each product. The opportunity gained by using the resource in one product would be the opportunity cost of not using it in another. This would enable one to rank the products in order of preference for allocation of resources. This is an extremely simple way of solving what appears at first sight to be a complex issue.

5. If the number of resource constraints is more numerous and their pattern of consumption of the resources is different for the different products, there would be a conflict between the optimum patterns of allotment of different resources. This involves more complex ways of analysis. We need to use a set of equations. The first one is one to compute the total contribution of all products knowing the unit contribution of each product. Then, a set of equations exhibiting the pattern of consumption of resources by alternate products has to be made. Some deft mathematics would then be needed to solve the problem.

6. We may need to use a combination of cost functions incorporating different segments of the total costs. Thus, in deciding between different alternatives in one purchase order the equation may show carrying costs while in another, it may show ordering costs. Using differential calculus on the sum of the two we can choose the order quantity which will yield the minimum total cost. This has been

detailed in Chapter 10 (Fig. 10.4) and Example 10.3. This is a typical relevant cost analysis.

7. We may use a combination of cost functions, one measuring the carrying costs and another measuring the opportunity costs of loss of sales due to stock out, and develop an algorithm to have optimum safety stock. This has been demonstrated in Chapter 10 (Fig. 10.6 and Table 10.10).

## SPECIAL ONE-TIME ORDERS

The problem of one-time orders has been dealt with in Case Study 1, Gummidupsundi Sintered Products, in Chapter 4. We will discuss it again in greater detail in Chapter 13, when dealing exclusively with pricing and issues revolving around marketing strategy.

In this chapter, we will highlight the fact that special one-time orders could have incremental costs which may yield an average incremental cost for the order, which could be far less than that of normal production. It may include both variable and fixed relevant costs. A typical example is shown in Example 11.1.

### Example 11.1   Ganesh Pens (A)

Ganesh Pens was a well-known manufacturer of ball-point pens. It produced 10,000 pens per month and its cost of production was as follows:

Variable manufacture per pen = ₹2
Fixed manufacture per pen = Re 1
Variable marketing per pen = ₹0.50 (commission to dealers and salesmen)
Fixed marketing per pen = Re 1 (advertisements)
Total = ₹4.50
Sales price per pen = ₹6
Total profit per pen = ₹1.50, but contribution is ₹3.50 (6–0, 50–2).

It received a special order from the government for 5000 pens to be presented to students passing with distinction. They were willing to pay an amount equal to per unit manufacturing costs, i.e., ₹3, plus an amount of ₹3000 as a lump sum.

The accountant estimated that this order will have the same variable manufacturing cost per unit as the normal band but will have no variable marketing cost. There would also not be an increase in fixed manufacturing costs, but it would involve the cost of a new dye for ₹2000.

The pen would not affect normal sales as it would be called Saraswati Award Pen, and would have a different look. Should Ganesh Pens accept the order?

Relevant costs are as follows:

Incremental variable costs @ ₹2 × 5000 = ₹10,000
Incremental fixed costs (dye) = ₹2000
Total incremental costs = ₹12,000
Incremental revenue @ ₹3 × 5000 = ₹15,000
Incremental lump sum revenue = ₹3000
Total incremental revenue = ₹18,000
Total incremental surplus = ₹6000

Thus, the offer should be accepted.

If producing this 5000 reduces the capacity of the existing production, the opportunity cost is the contribution lost in existing sales, which is ₹17,500 (5000 × 3.50 contribution). The offer should not be accepted unless the price is increased by a minimum amount of ₹2.30 (17,500 – 6000)/5000.

**Relevant cost analysis**
Relevant cost analysis for replacement decisions is based on future cash flows, whereas traditional financial books are anchored on historical costs. This conflict needs to be understood and dealt with.

One may note that in this example, it was not necessary to restate the full costs and revenue in the two alternatives. The incremental costs can be identified quite easily. This would be covered by category three of the analytical formats suggested earlier in the chapter.

The alert manager should be able to take quick decisions in similar situations.

## REPLACEMENT OF MACHINES AND DEALING WITH HISTORICAL COSTS

Table 11.1 dealt with replacement of an old machine. The relevant cost analysis enabled us to make the decision to replace. But the same figure transformed into the picture emerging in the financial accounts shown in Table 11.2 could be disconcerting.

Table 11.2 incorporates the financial account entry for the year in which the old machine would be replaced. The book value of the asset less than its salvage value will be adjusted in the financial accounts as what is known in income tax rules, as a terminal depreciation. The amount of current depreciation plus the terminal deprecation, minus the salvage value will yield a result which makes the earlier decision appear to be wrong. And so would it seem to the manager in charge, who may be paid a bonus on the figures appearing in the financial accounts. This would, however, not make the decision wrong. If the value of the old machine is spread over its expected life, even if it had been replaced, the related cost will be the same

**Table 11.2** A modified version of Table 11.1, incorporating financial account entries

| Particulars | Existing alternative (1) | Proposed alternative (2) | Increment of (2) over (1) |
|---|---|---|---|
| 1. Sales quantity | 10,000 | 18,000 | 8000 |
| 2. Sale price (₹/unit) | 3 | 2.8 | –0.2 |
| 3. Sales value (₹) | 30,000 | 50,400 | 20,400 |
| 4. Variable cost (₹) | 20,000 | 40,000 | 20,000 |
| 5. Contribution (₹) | 10,000 | 10,400 | 400 |
| 6. Fixed cost/avoidable costs (₹) | 2000 | 3000 | –1000 |
| 7. Depreciation of the existing machine | 3000 | 13,000 | –10,000 |
| 8. Depreciation of the new machine | 0 | 3000 | –3000 |
| 8. Salvage value (₹) | 0 | –1000 | 1000 |
| 9. Net operating income (₹) | 5000 | –7600 | –12600 |

in both alternatives and would, therefore, become irrelevant for the decision. The whole discussion would highlight that the relevant cost analysis is for future costs, whereas financial accounting would justifiably perforce have to bear the burden of past historical costs.

## TIMING OF INTRODUCTION OF A NEW PRODUCT AND DROPPING OFF OF AN EXISTING PRODUCT

The timing of the dropping off of a product and the introduction of a replacement product needs a sharp understanding of relevant cost analysis which again, as in the previous case of replacement of the old machine, has a dichotomy with traditional financial accounting. It centres around the relevant cost of selling an item in the inventory which is valued in the financial books on the basis of the historical costs of producing that inventory.

We can illustrate this with an example of Ballyco.

### Example 11.2 Ballyco

Ballyco, a computer software company, wished to replace its Bally 200 with a superior Bally 201. Once Bally 201 is introduced, the sale of Bally 200 would undoubtedly be affected. Bally 200 had an enthusiastic and vigorous marketing team headed by Leelavati. They wished to campaign for Bally 200 and hastened the production, and kept all the software packages ready and shrink-wrapped. There were sufficient stocks for three months, from January to March 2006. But unknown to Leelavati, Bally 201 software designers, headed by Anil Patwardhan, after racing against time, had just got to the production stage;

though they had not started production. The production for three months sale could be done in just the last three days. Shivakumar, the MD, learnt of these developments (December 2005). The data of Bally 200 and Bally 201 are as shown in Table 11.3. He made his remarks on the data given to him, which are also shown.

**Table 11.3** Data of Bally 200 and Bally 201

| Particulars | Bally 200 | Bally 201 |
|---|---|---|
| Selling price/unit | ₹1500 | ₹1850 |
| Variable cost after shrink wrapping/unit | ₹200 sunk | ₹250 |
| Development cost amortized over expected sale/unit | ₹650 sunk | ₹950 sunk |
| Marketing and administrative fixed cost charged based on sale value/unit | ₹350 irrelevant as same in both alternatives being fixed in nature | ₹400 irrelevant |
| Total cost per unit | ₹1200 all sunk or fixed | ₹1600 irrelevant except variable costs |
| Operating income per unit | ₹300 irrelevant except contribution of ₹1500 after ignoring sunk costs | ₹250 irrelevant except contribution of ₹1600 |

It is possible to come to definite conclusions by picking out the relevant items by inspection of the data, as was done by the MD, Shivakumar. It would seem that introducing the new product straightaway would be right.

But surely Leelavati would oppose this and the accountant would state that the inventory of Bally 200 would be wasted.

The alternate solution may be to sell Bally 200 to a segment which does not compete with Bally 201 such as, high schools, or exported to a third world country. This may have to be decided after a relevant cost analysis of scrapping the entire stock, or selling it at a discount and recovering at least its variable marketing costs.

## MAKE OR BUY DECISIONS, AND THE ECONOMICS OF OUTSOURCING

The simplest make or buy decisions would revolve around the cost of purchase as compared to variable costs of manufacture. This would, however, be subject to several non-financial considerations, such as the following:

1. The assurance of quality control

2. The assurance of consistency of supply
3. The assurance of protection against stealing of process specifications
4. Protection against supply of component developed by the company to its competitor.

It is possible to take such precautions in all these matters, as is amply evident by the massive growth of outsourcing in US companies in several fields, and more particularly in the IT and automobile sectors. India has been a beneficiary in this process.

The US automobile industry went though a massive phase where a few makers of modular assemblies supplied to the main makers of automobiles, who accommodated their designs to suit these modular assemblies. This gave them a sizable reduction in costs till sometime until the non-financial factor that customers wanted a variety which mass scale modular assembly makers could not provide (Doran 2005 and Sawyer 2005).

The issues of make or buy could be more complex than just a comparison of variable cost of manufacturers' and vendors' prices for a product.

These would revolve around how we propose to use the manufacturing or service capacity freed by outsourcing. Such situations are complex and usually a full exhibition of all the costs and revenues may be necessary to clarify the position.

Example 11.3 describes a further development on Example 11.1 of Ganesh Pens.

**Outsourcing**
Economics of outsourcing is a topic of interest to Indian managers. It uses typically relevant cost analysis.

**Economics of outsourcing**
It depends also on the alternate uses of resources freed by the outsourcing.

## Example 11.3  Ganesh Pens (B)

For ease of reference, the basis data of Ganesh Pens (A) are reproduced.

Ganesh Pens was a well-known manufacturer of ball-point pens. It produced 10,000 pens per month and its cost of production was as follows:

Variable manufacture per pen = ₹2
Fixed manufacture per pen = Re 1
Variable marketing per pen = ₹0.50
Fixed marketing per pen = Re 1
Total = ₹4.50
Sales price per pen = ₹6
Total profit per pen = ₹1.50, but contribution is ₹3.50
(6−0.50−2)

One of Ganesh's ex-employees was willing to take the entire franchising of production and distribution of the basic brand of pens, and was willing to contribute a net royalty of ₹2.00 per pen, provided that Ganesh did the advertising to the value of ₹10,000 every month. Ganesh was willing to consider this only if the franchisee stuck to the price and allowed them to monitor the supplies and quality of production.

Ganesh's corporate planners had determined that if Ganesh outsourced the production of their existing brand of pens, they could produce a new brand called Arjun, where the cost structure would be as follows:

Monthly production and sale, 8000 numbers

Variable cost of manufacture per pen = ₹3

Fixed cost of manufacture where the existing level of fixed manufacturing cost would have to be increased by ₹20,000 per month, which would also contain the monitoring and quality control costs of the basic Ganesh brand that is franchised out.

Variable marketing expenses = 10% of sales

Fixed marketing expenses = ₹15,000 per month

Selling price per pen = ₹9

The problem is quite complicated and it is best to detail it in a comparative chart, as in Table 11.4.

**Table 11.4**   Relevant cost of alternatives

| | Existing | Proposed |
|---|---|---|
| Direct sales (₹) | 60,000 | 72,000 (9 × 8000) |
| Monthly royalty from franchisee (₹) | 0 | 20,000 (2 × 10000) |
| Variable manufacturing expenses (₹) | 20,000 | 24,000 (3 × 8000) |
| Fixed manufacturing expenses (₹) | 10,000 | 20,000 (10,000 + 10,000) |
| Variable marketing expenses (₹) | 5000 | 7200 (10% of 72,000) |
| Fixed marketing expenses (₹) | 10,000 | 15,000 + 10,000 |
| | | (Ad for old product) |
| Net operating income | 15,000 | 15,800 |

The advantage of the new proposal for the Arjun brand is a small sum of ₹8000, as against which a new product with attendant risks is being launched and the risk of franchising out the prime brand has to be borne. As against that, opening up the markets for a vastly superior product may give excellent benefits in the long run. We could take a calculated risk, or we may also use statistical analysis, such as average expectation of profit, the standard deviation, and the coefficient of dispersion.

### Example 11.4  Vivek Mechanics

A company, Vivek Mechanics, has an inventory of 100 assorted parts for motorcycle parts that have been discontinued. The inventory cost is ₹90,000. The parts can either be (a) re-assembled at a total additional cost of ₹50,000 and then sold for ₹40,000 or (b) sold as scrap for ₹5000. Which action is more profitable?

Here, we need to identify the relevant and irrelevant costs in order to make a confident decision. Inventory cost of ₹90,000 is irrelevant regarding the decision to re-assemble or dispose of.

| | Re-assemble | | Dispose of |
|---|---|---|---|
| Future Revenue | ₹50,000 | | ₹5000 |
| Deduct Future Cost | ₹40,000 | | .................... |
| Operating Income | ₹10,000 | | ₹5000 |
| Difference | | ₹5000 | |
| **Decision in favour of Re-Assembling** | | | |

Therefore, decision in favour of re-assembling is taken as it increases the operating income by ₹10,000 which is greater than the disposal revenue of ₹5,000.

### Example 11.5  Sumeet Printers

A printing machine at Sumeet Printers, costing ₹1,00,000 and not insured, breaks down on its first day of use. It can either be disposed of for ₹20,000 and replaced with a similar machine for ₹1,20,000 or repair for ₹85,000 and thus be brand new as far as operating characteristics and looks are concerned. Which action is more profitable?

Cost of ₹1,00,000 is irrelevant regarding the decision to replace or repair.

| | Replace | | Repair |
|---|---|---|---|
| New printing machine | ₹1,20,000 | | ₹85,000 |
| Deduct current disposal price of old machine | ₹20,000 | | |
| **Operating income** | **₹1,00,000** | | **₹85,000** |
| **Decision in favour of replacing** | | ₹15,000 | |

Therefore, decision in favour of replacing should be taken as it increases the operating income by ₹15,000 which is greater than the revenue of ₹85,000 by repaired machine.

## PRODUCT MIX AND ALLOTMENT OF PRODUCT TO SCARCE RESOURCES

Allotment of products to resources usually gives rise to a plethora of options along a spectrum. As mentioned earlier, the concept of opportunity costs could be effectively used to simplify the calculations. One has to assume that every product has a contribution per unit (say C) and a consumption of unit of the single scarce resource (say R). This scarce resource is usually referred to as the 'limiting factor' (Lucey 2002), before the modern days of linear programming. The opportunity cost of not producing a product is equal to R/C. In the choice of allocation, a product with the highest R/C should get the first preference till its demand is met, and thereafter the products must be chosen in descending order until no more resources are available for allotment.

This is explained in Example 11.6.

### Example 11.6 Tomato Industries

Tomato Industries can make four products, namely, ketchup, jam, juice, and raw tomato. All of these use the same raw material, namely, raw tomatoes. Since the industry is in a remote area where transport is not available, it has to accept that they can only use the tomatoes available in every harvest. In the current harvest it has 10,000 kgs. It was, therefore, a scarce resource that has to be cautiously distributed between the products.

The products use different plants and they have abundant capacity, but it is not the policy to switch the plants on and off. They will continue to remain there, awaiting changes in product prices and tomato availability. It is not stipulated that all the products will be necessarily made in the year if it is not economically desirable. The present product cost and sales price is given in Table 11.5.

Table 11.5 Cost–volume data

| Products | Ketchup | Jam | Juice | Raw tomato |
|---|---|---|---|---|
| Sale value of product made out of 1 kg tomato (₹) | 20 | 40 | 30 | 5 |
| Variable cost of product made out of 1 kg tomato** (₹) | 5 | 10 | 8 | 0 |
| Fixed cost of product as in 1 and 2*/kg tomato used (₹) | 5 | 8 | 10 | 0 |
| Market demand of product as expressed in kg of tomato used (kgs) | 3000 | 5000 | 3000 | 20,000 |

* Calculated on the assumption that the plant will be fully utilized.
** Excludes cost of tomato.

The cost of producing tomatoes is Re 1 per kg.

Following the text, the contribution per kg of tomato, which is a scarce resource, is ₹30 for jam which is the highest, followed by ₹22 for juice, and ₹15 for ketchup.

Fixed costs are irrelevant as it is common across the products and so is the variable cost of producing the tomato, as this too is common across the products.

Therefore, we must use 5000 kg for jam, 3000 kg for juice, and the balance 2000 kg for ketchup, and raw tomato should not be sold.

If non-financial considerations could be pressed home, one might have held that at least 1000 kg should be used for every product to make sure of its presence in the market, etc. But such a consideration should figure only after a hard-headed relevant cost analysis is done and one should not confuse the first-cut decision. It has, therefore, been stipulated in the example that this need not affect the decision.

## CLOSING DOWN AND OPENING SEGMENTS OF AN ORGANIZATION

Very often organizations are confronted with a figure from the accounts department indicating that a particular segment is losing money and should be closed down. This could be, say, the vegetarian section of a composite restaurant, or a particular branch from a chain of branches. In such decisions, it is necessary to see the positive and negative cash flows of alternative decisions and abstract the relevant costs for comparison. Typical items which could figure in the analysis would be those shown in Table 11.6.

**Table 11.6**  Typical items to be considered in closing a segment of a business

| Item | How it will figure |
|---|---|
| 1. Floor space saved | Sale of space would be a positive cash flow.<br>Opportunity cost of alternate use can be measured by contribution gained.<br>Alternative use can give further intangible benefit, say, a sense of space. |
| 2. Sales decrease | Opportunity cost of contribution is lost. |
| 3. Manpower saved | Recruitment avoided in another segment is positive cash flow; retirement benefits will be a negative cash flow. |
| 4. Equipment and machinery sold | Salvage value. |
| 5. Raw material inventory | If sold at a discount the amount of sales is a positive cash flow. If the future purchases avoided gain can be higher, then even the contribution which can arise if the material is used in production in the organization can be high. |

## DROPPING OFF AND ADDING A CLASS OF CUSTOMERS

Chapter 6 on activity-based costing (ABC) discussed the methods of using that technique for customer-wise profitability. Example 6.3 on Bansal stores compared two classes of customers, the rich and the modern, and the poorer and the older ones. If the two sets had a common set of services and manufacturing facilities, it would not always be obvious that one class of customers should be discarded and a new set introduced. An analysis of the alternatives would be somewhat as shown in Table 11.7.

If we are told that if we discard Mallya we can rent out the space released for ₹40,000, it would be worth doing this. On the other hand, if discarding Mallya gets the company a bad name for its inability to develop a long standing customer relationship, one has to reconsider the decision.

**Table 11.7**  Analysis of yearly financial implications of discarding and adding customers

| Item | Discarding Mallya | Adding Kamath |
|---|---|---|
| Revenue yearly (₹) | (4,00,000) | 6,00,000 |
| Cost of goods sold (₹) | 3,30,000 | (5,00,000) |
| Transportation costs (₹) | 30,000 | (40,000) |
| Rent (₹) | 0 | 0 |
| Market support (₹) | 10,000 | (10,000) |
| Salvage value of equipment (₹) | 5000 | |
| Administrative overheads (₹) | 0 | 0 |
| Corporate overheads (₹) | 0 | 0 |
| Net (₹) | (30,000) | 45,000 |

## THEORY OF CONSTRAINTS

The theory of constraints (TOC) is an important management philosophy, which explains the limiting factor or factors that prevent an organization from achieving its goal fully. It finds application in Dr Eliyahu M. Goldratt's 1984 book titled *The Goal*. Organizations face a variety of constraints in the functional areas and departments. Some of them could be

- availability of raw material
- technical manpower
- capacity of some equipments, having limited capacity
- market based limitations

Thus, it may be internal or external to the organization. In the latter case, it may be driven by market, legal, environmental, or other forces. It is a *limiting factor* or *bottleneck* which forces organizations to restrict their output. Let us take the example of a dairy company. The constraints and its impact are shown in the following table (Table 11.8).

**Table 11.8**  Analysis of constraints and their impact

| Sl No. | Constraint | Impact |
|---|---|---|
| 1. | Availability of raw milk | Output and product-mix restricted to available milk supply |
| 2. | Processing capacity | Limits the extent of milk products that could be processed |
| 3. | Cold storage | Limits the extent of butter that could be stored |
| 4. | Transport | Decides how much can be moved—both for raw milk and finished products |

This is not an exhaustive list but a suggestive one. Obviously, a constraint is that segment having the lowest capacity in a chain of activities. If this can be expanded, it can increase the overall capacity until a stage is reached when a new constraint takes over. This is relevant in cost accounting studies in determining the correct product-mix and in pricing decisions.

Let us take the example of a cafeteria in a crowded city. There is good patronage during lunchtime and it is not able to satisfy all the customers due to the limited seating capacity. It can therefore cater only to the extent of the chairs available at a point of time. The theory of constraints applies in this case. Improvements made elsewhere cannot enhance the sales unless the constraint is removed. For example, the cafeteria may improve the quality of the items, add variety to the menu, or reduce the price. These can attract more customers but many of them will return dissatisfied due to lack of space. This can encourage a competitor to start a new cafeteria which may rob the organization of future clientele. Hence, the seating capacity (the constraint) limits turnover and has to be addressed.

The theory of constraints can be studied by applying the concept of contribution analysis (Example 11.7).

## Example 11.7  Contribution Analysis of Vogue and Vista

Stringent Co. Ltd makes 2 products, Vogue and Vista, which are very popular in the market. The costs associated with them are as follows:

| | Vogue (₹) | Vista (₹) |
|---|---|---|
| Unit selling price | 50 | 60 |
| Variable cost per unit | 20 | 36 |
| Unit contribution margin | 30 | 24 |

The unit contribution margin for Vogue at ₹30 is higher, and the CM ratio comes to 60 per cent. It is certainly preferable to Vista whose margin is only ₹24 and the CM ratio is 40 per cent.

Let us assume that the restricting factor in the entity is a special welding machine which has limited capacity and thus constitutes the constraint. The capacity of the welding machine cannot be enhanced in the short run, due to fund limitations. Due to this constraint the company has to turn down number of orders for both these products. There is no other constraint except for the welding machine for the given demand for both the products.

Let us further assume that Vogue takes 10 minutes of welding time and Vista takes 5 minutes. Since the welding machine constitutes the 'bottleneck', we should calculate the contribution margin per unit of the limiting factor in order to understand the relative contributions of Vogue and Vista in relation to the optimum utilization of the constrained resource.

**Vogue:**

| | |
|---|---|
| Contribution margin/unit | ₹30 |
| Welding time required | 10 minutes |
| Contribution margin/minute | ₹3 |

**Vista:**

| | |
|---|---|
| Contribution margin/unit | ₹24 |
| Welding time required | 5 minutes |
| Contribution margin/minute | ₹4.8 |

While in the earlier calculations, Vogue has a higher contribution of ₹30 per unit, when compared to Vista's contribution of ₹24 per unit, the impact of the constrained resource adds a further dimension to the contribution analysis. This shows that Vista has a higher contribution of ₹4.8 per minute as compared to Vogue's contribution of ₹3 per minute.

In order to assess the total contribution for each of the product by applying the above calculations, we can assume that an additional day is available to the welding machine (a day consisting of 8 hours of production). This works out to 480 minutes. During this period, the number of additional units that can be produced is as follows:

**Vogue**: 480 ÷ 10 = 48 units
**Vista**: 480 ÷ 5 = 96 units

The total contribution of each of the product comes to the following:

**Vogue**: 48 x 30 = ₹1440
**Vista**: 96 x 24 = ₹2304

This would help the management to produce more of Vista till the constraint (availability of welding time) is removed. This, however, is subject to other factors such as retaining customers and other long-term impacts.

## Ambushing the Constraints

Once the management has the aforementioned data, it can take steps to develop the optimum product mix of Vista and Vogue. If the situation warrants it, they should go to the next step in the ladder, which is removing the limiting factor or else mitigating its impact. They may use the welding machine for a second shift, if it is otherwise profitable. The welding activity may be an operation somewhere in the middle of the entire process cycle in which case they have to engage the other equipments and its operators also for the next shift. This may bring in additional costs, and may warrant revised cost estimates. After all, the costs that are provided for the revised product mix should bring in sufficient profits to support the decision for working extra shift.

Instead, the management may choose other options. It may outsource some of the welding job if the logistics support such a move. They may install an additional welding machine after calculating the return on the investment. Thus the management has several options to choose from once the impact of the constraints is clearly understood.

In real life business situations, usually the organizations face more than one constraint. In the above case, in addition to the welding time there may be constraints due to limited availability of raw material, transportation, storage capacity or packing material. In the earlier case of the dairy industry the constraints have been explained. There can be individual constraints for the various dairy products (cocoa beans for chocolates, packing material for yogurt, etc.) in addition to the limited availability of raw milk, which is a constraint common to all the products. The management may have to adopt geometrical methods to calculate the best product mix.

As described in Chapter 6, the proponents of ABC had perceived that ABC was a more powerful tool for decision-making than the earlier methods of costing. But even they conceded that it is important to supplement the ABC approach with proactive insights for short-term decisions that could sometimes radically improve profitability. They hold that often some 'bottleneck' maybe holding back the production and one needs to discover such constraints and find a quick remedy for them (Atkinson et al. 2004). The decision would revolve around increasing contribution, i.e., sales minus variable costs, multiplied by increased quantity sold after de-bottlenecking, and deducting from it the increase in fixed costs for de-bottlenecking. This has been illustrated in Example 11.8.

### Example 11.8   Lalmati Mines (Sekhar 2005)

Chandra, the director of a coal company, went underground on a visit to Lalmati Mines and found that the coal loaders were idle while waiting for the tubs to arrive. Lalmati Mines otherwise had excellent control over its costs of explosive, timber, and other items. But the overall profits were not increasing as the production was not rising above 15,000 tonnes per month. Moreover, it was a mine with prime cooking coal which was being imported at exorbitant costs. Chandra now knew the reason for the idleness. The tub shortage was the bottleneck. He immediately ordered the required 2000 tubs. 'Let the tubs wait for men, and not vice versa', he said. He did the relevant cost exercise on his scratch pad:

*Extra monthly costs of ammortization of cost of coal tubs (4,00,000 ÷ 24) = ₹1.67 lakh*
*Monthly increase in the contribution (10,000 × 80) = ₹8 lakh*
*Monthly surplus = ₹6.33 lakh*

The next year he visited the mines and found that the tubs were now waiting not for the men but for a place in the skip which went up and down the shaft and transported the coal to the surface. He realized the bottleneck was the size of the shaft and the capacity of the skip and its motor. If one widened the shaft all this could be done smoothly. Some heavy costs would be involved, but in the end the production could go up to 50,000 tonnes per month. Chandra could not do this cost analysis on a scratch pad, which is quite normal in most relevant cost situations. His corporate planning team came out with the numbers which were as follows:

*A detailed project was prepared and the investment came to a crore. The monthly surplus from a 25,000 tonne increase in production was ₹20 lakh. This meant that the pay-back period for the investment was also just five months, again a dramatic figure.*

### SUMMARY

Relevant costing focuses on the differences in the outcomes (both financial and non-financial) between alternative decisions. It is a part of the generic theory of managerial decisions. Its greater focus is in short- and medium-term decisions and, therefore, does not go along with the assumptions in ABC analysis that all costs are ultimately variable. The format of the analysis ranges from the simple to the complex and mathematical, and includes linear programming, non-linear programming, and differential calculus. A variety of terminologies and concepts, specific to relevant cost analysis, are used. The application of the analysis are varied and include pricing for special orders, product mix, replacement of machinery, change in processes, and adding or abandoning customers and segments of an organization. Relevant cost analysis focuses on future costs but uses historical costs to estimate these.

## KEY POINTS

- Relevant costs are those which vary between differing alternative decisions.
- Clarifying the contours of alternative decisions clearly is the first step in relevant cost analysis.
- Avoidable fixed costs are those fixed costs which vary in alternative decisions.
- Sunk costs are those which cannot be avoided and do not vary in alternative choices. They arise from historical costs such as the cost of spilt milk; one just has to live with it.
- Committed costs are a class of sunk costs which become avoidable only if the commitment is breached.
- Incremental cost and revenue is the difference between alternatives.
- Imputed costs are costs that exist and are relevant for decisions but which are not incorporated in financial accounting, e.g., cost of capital.
- Relevant cost analyses usually presume linear cost functions to simplify decisions.
- Traditional financial accounting reports may show an outcome of a decision that is different from relevant cost analysis, as the former is anchored on historical costs, whereas the latter is based on future costs.
- Relevant cost analysis can use complex mathematical methods which have however become commonplace and routine, and are available to the daily decision-making of managers due to computerized software.

## CONCEPT REVIEW QUESTIONS

1. What is the eight step process in a feedback decision model?
2. Are historical costs irrelevant for managerial decisions?
3. Fixed costs are always irrelevant in relevant cost analysis. True or false?
4. A component should always be purchased if its total cost of manufacture is more than the vendor price. True or false?

5. Depreciation of equipment being replaced is not relevant for any decision. True or false?
6. An error in estimation of a contribution function would invariably result in wrong product mix decisions. True or false?
7. Linear programming uses fixed costs in its computations. True or false?
8. Explain a class of problems in which relevant cost analysis can use differential calculus?
9. Explain the process of use of relevant cost analysis to decide safety stock in an inventory model.

## NUMERICAL PROBLEMS

1. **Scrap Disposal**

A company has an inventory of ₹8,00,000, of various rejects. It has the following alternatives: (i) Do some work on them by spending ₹10,000, and re-use them in production, in place of purchases required to the value of ₹50,000, for which we have to spend ₹5000 as purchasing costs, (ii) Use a scrap dealer who can sell it for ₹30,000 but will charge a 10 per cent commission on sales.

**Question**

1.1 Recommend the correct decision.

2. **The Dropped Video Camera**

Sonali was a favourite executive assistant to Sunil Kulkarni, the managing director, even though she was known to be impulsive. When she rashly carried the heavy professional video equipment and walked down the stairs in her stiletto heels, she tripped and fell, along with the equipment which crashed into shattered pieces. There was no hope of repairing it. It had cost the company ₹2 lakh.

Sunil rushed to the spot, accompanied by Raghavan, the accountant. 'I hope it has been fully depreciated,' asked Sunil. When Raghavan assured him that it had zero value in the account books as it had been fully depreciated, Sunil was relieved.

**Question**

2.1 Was Raghavan's response correct?

3. **Coimbatore Butta Saris**

The Coimbatore Handloom Cooperative has 130 weaver members, all of whom are old. Each of them owned a loom which was kept in the cooperative shed. Young weavers are all employed in other vocations and earn handsomely. These weavers can only work 8 hours a day for 25 days a month.

A weaver at work cannot work beyond these hours as he gets exhausted.

They have a monthly order from Co-optex, the Handloom Marketing Federation of Tamil Nadu, for 10,000 plain cotton saris, and 5000 saris which have an embroidered design and are called butta saris.

Co-optex offers ₹150 for plain saris and ₹230 for the butta saris. Both the saris need 250 gms of yarn, costing ₹50 (₹200 per kilogram). Thus, plain saris give a contribution of ₹100 each (150 – 50) and the butta sari, ₹180 (230 – 50).

The weavers can weave a plain sari in two days and the butta sari in four days. Yarn is not in short supply.

In addition to these costs, the cooperative has a fixed monthly cost of ₹10,000. At the end of the month, the weavers calculate the contribution from the production, and after deducting the fixed cost, distribute the net surplus equally among the members.

## Questions

3.1  How many plain saris and butta saris should they supply to Co-optex?
3.2  If there is a shortage of yarn and only 3000 kg of yarn is available, would the answer be different? (Hint: Examine, in turn, the corners of the feasible area of production of plain and *butta* saris with the constraints and pitch in on the maximum contribution by trial and error, or else use a computer with an LP programme.)
3.3  If the organization was not a cooperative and could hire 130 looms at ₹3 per day from the130 weavers, import workers who were paid ₹75 per plain sari and ₹90 per butta sari, and there was a restriction on yarn, would the answer be the same?
3.4  If the organization was indeed a cooperative controlled by weaver members and could have taken a decision as applicable to sub-question (4) only in consultation with the members, how would they come to a decision taking into consideration financial and non-financial factors? (Hint: Calculate the per member weaver earning in all alternatives.)

### 4.  Kalimatha Printers

Kalimatha Printers operates a printing press with a monthly capacity of 2000 machine hours. It had two main customers, namely, Ramdas Corporation and Seeta Corporation. Data on each of these customers for January 2006 is shown in Table P4.

**Table P4** January 2006 cost data

| | Ramdas | Seeta | Total |
|---|---|---|---|
| Revenues (₹) | 1,20,000 | 80,000 | 2,00,000 |
| Variable costs (₹) | 42,000 | 48,000 | 90,000 |
| Contribution (₹) | 78,000 | 32,000 | 1,10,000 |
| Fixed cost allocated (₹) | 60,000 | 40,000 | 1,00,000 |
| Operating income (₹) | 18,000 | (8,000) | 10,000 |
| Machine hours (hrs) | 1500 | 500 | 2000 |

The data of Seeta indicated that it wanted to place more orders worth ₹80,000 for printing jobs during February 2006, i.e., it could order ₹1,60,000 worth of jobs in February. These jobs were identical to the ones done by Kalimatha for Seeta in January 2006 in terms of variable costs and use of machine hours, etc. Ramdas would also be willing to give Kalimatha more jobs than in January. Kalimatha can accept as much work as they can perform in 2000 machine hours.

## Question

4.1 How much work should Kalimatha take on from Ramdas and Seeta?

5. **Howrah Engineering Works**

Howrah Engineering Works manufactures small motors which are fitted to agricultural pumps. It has recently received an offer from Gowri Engineering, that has its workshop across the street, to supply the starter assembly at ₹40 per piece.

The assemblies were hitherto manufactured in-house. The cost accountant has provided the annual cost of the assembly section as shown in Table P5.

**Table P5** Costs of the starter assembly for 2009

| Direct materials | = ₹20,00,000 |
|---|---|
| Direct manufacturing labour | = ₹15,00,000 |
| Manufacturing overhead charged | = ₹40,00,000 |
| Total | = ₹75,00,000 |

Since they manufactured 1,50,000 assemblies, the cost per assembly was ₹50 (75,00,000 ÷ 1,50,000).

Of the manufacturing overhead, 25 per cent was considered variable, i.e., ₹10,00,000. Of the fixed overhead of ₹30,00,000, 50 per cent, i.e., ₹15,00,000, is the general overhead which will not change if the starter assembly work is outsourced. ₹10,00,000 can be avoided. This leaves

₹5,00,000, which is the divisional manager's salary. If the starter assembly department is closed down, he will be accommodated in another division at the same salary, but will enable Howrah Engineering a saving of ₹4,00,000 salary for a new appointee in that division.

## Questions

5.1 Should Howrah Engineering outsource the starter assembly? What are the non-financial considerations that could matter in this case? (Hint: If there is a surge in the requirement of starter assemblies next year, would the decision cause problems?)

5.2 If the space vacated by the starter assembly results in avoidance of ₹5,00,000 for outside storage charges, would it change the decision?

## 6. Munnar Hill-side Restaurant

Munnar Hill-side is a small restaurant nestling in the mountains. It has a small refrigerator and has to ration its space. It provides four drinks that have characteristics as described in Table P6.

Table P6    Munnar Hill-side

|  | Buttermilk | Lemonade | Coconut drink | Munnar special |
|---|---|---|---|---|
| Selling rice per case (₹) | 180 | 192 | 264 | 384 |
| Variable cost per case (₹) | 135 | 152 | 201 | 302 |
| Cases sold per foot of shelf space per day (No.) | 25 | 24 | 4 | 5 |

Munnar has a shelf space of 12 feet to accommodate four drinks. They want to keep a minimum of one foot of space for every drink, and a maximum of six feet for any drink.

## Questions

6.1 Compute the contribution per case for every drink.

6.2 An accountant advises that the ranking should go by contribution per case. What is your recommendation for the allocation? Give reasons.

## 7. SAE Company

The SAE Company produces a single product X which has a very good market. It produces 90,000 units of X each year. The current selling price is ₹30 per unit and the company's cost sheets are as follows:

|  | (₹) |
|---|---|
| Direct material | 11.50 |
| Direct labour | 3.00 |

| Manufacturing overhead—variable | 2.50 |
|---|---|
| Selling expenses—variable | 1.00 |
| Manufacturing overhead—fixed | 4.50 |
| Selling expenses—fixed | 4.00 |

The overheads are calculated for an output of 90,000 units. Hence, the total annual fixed overheads come to the following:

| Manufacturing overhead | 4,05,000 |
|---|---|
| Selling overheads | 3,60,000 |

During October the SAE Company's main supplier had a serious breakdown in its operations. They informed SAE Company that their supplies will be resumed only after 2 months. The CEO of SAE Company convened an urgent meeting to discuss the situation. It transpired they would be having adequate material in hand to operate a 30 per cent capacity during the 2 month period when their supplies will be stopped. The CEO asked the cost accountant to calculate the financial position if the operations are closed down entirely for the two months. The calculations revealed that the fixed manufacturing overheads would be reduced to 50 per cent of the usual levels during the 2 months of closure. There will not be much saving in the fixed selling expenses though, where the savings will be only up to the tune of 20 per cent of the normal levels. The marketing head, however, seriously objected to the idea of closing down the factory. 'Our customers will surely migrate to the competitor's products,' he said.

### Questions

7.1 Calculate the impact of the decision of closing the factory for the two month period upon the profitability of the company.

7.2 Besides profitability, what are the other considerations to be taken into account?

## PROJECT

Form groups of four students. Pick a company with some diversification. Analyse its annual report containing segment-wise costs and profits, and develop a cost function for the segment with sales in the X-axis and costs on the Y-axis. Before using this, deflate it with an inflation index, either using internal data, external consumer price, or industrial price indices. Analyse the consequence of closing any segment on the overall profitability.

## Saving on Naval Training Costs

The Indian navy had two training colleges, one on the west coast and the other on the east coast. The Government of India was keen to reduce its defence budget without jeopardizing its defence preparedness, and wished to close down one of them and enhance the capabilities of the other, reducing the overall costs. The respective states in the East and West were, however, very keen that the training school in their state should not be closed. The scenario is as follows:

1. The training base on the west coast was built at a cost of ₹1 crore. Its yearly operating costs are ₹4 crore. The land on which it is built belongs to the Navy and can be sold for ₹5 crore if the training school is closed.

2. The training base on the east coast was built at a cost of ₹1.50 crore, on land that is leased on a permanent lease payment of ₹0.3 crore per annum. If a fund of ₹6 crore is invested in government securities at 5 per cent annual interest, it can finance the lease amount of ₹0.3 crore per annum. If the base is closed, the land will revert to the owner. The operational cost for the base without lease payment is ₹3 crore per annum.

3. If the west coast base is closed down, the Navy will transfer some of the staff to the east coast. As a result, the yearly operating costs will increase by ₹1 crore. If the east coast base is closed down, no extra cost will be incurred by the west coast base.

    The west coast politicians argue that their institute has an advantage as (i) it could result in a saving of ₹1 crore in the east coast; (ii) it would save ₹0.30 crore for the lease money for the east coast (Recall that the West has no lease cost as the land is owned by the Navy).

### Discussion Question

1. Do the relevant cost analysis for the decision in any of the formats chosen by you from among those suggested earlier in the chapter.

## Bharat Chemicals

Bharat Chemicals of Pune made specialized chemicals which were well-known for their purity. The quality of the chemicals was maintained because they were packed in excellent containers that withstood not only the transport, but also subsequent storage very well. Kasturirangan, the Chief Accountant, had just attended a training workshop which discussed strategic planning and he returned with the idea that every company should concentrate on its core competence. In his perception, Bharat's competence was in making chemicals and not in making the containers for these chemicals. He, therefore, took the initiative to explore outsourcing opportunities for container manufacture. He found Pune Packagers were willing to supply the containers required for ₹25 lakh per annum. In addition, they were willing to do all the repair jobs on the containers whenever the need arose for ₹7,50,000. Katurirangan showed the Managing Director, Marathe, the cost sheet of the container department which showed ₹37,80,000 as annual expenditure, as against the expenditure of ₹32,50,000, which Pune Packages would charge. He suggested that they close down the container division.

He showed him the data as in Table CS 2.

**Table CS 2**  Yearly expense of the container division

| Items | Expense (₹) |
| --- | --- |
| Material polymer coating material (PCM) | 4,00,000 |
| Other material | 10,00,000 |
| **Total material** | **14,00,000** |
| Labour | 10,00,000 |
| Overheads: | |
| Manager | 1,60,000 |
| Rent | 90,000 |
| **Total** | **2,50,000** |
| Depreciation machinery | 3,00,000 |
| Maintenance of machinery | 72,000 |
| Other expenses | 3,15,00 |
| General administration | 4,50,000 |
| Total | 37,87,000 |

Marathe felt it was proper to consult Harbans Singh, the General Manager of the container division. He assured Harbans that he should respond without being concerned about his own future as he said he would be protected anyway.

Harbans Singh said he would need a day to think it over and the next day he said, 'You will be throwing the old machinery away for, say, just ₹ 4,00,000, whereas it is good for at least four years, and we bought it at ₹24,00,000, four years ago. Then, we have a stock of polymers worth ₹20,00,000, that can last us for four years more. So Kasturirangan's cost, which includes this cost, is really at zero now.'

We bought it for ₹10,000 per tonne and today it costs ₹12,000 per tonne. However, if we sell it, it will not fetch more than ₹8000 per tonne.'

Marathe said that he was also worried about the workmen who would become redundant as he was doubtful about Pune Packages taking any of them. He was also concerned about Lalu and Mani, the two oldest hands, who had been with them ever since he could remember. Their contract provided for a life pension of ₹30,000 per annum on retirement.

Harbans Singh then questioned the overheads, 'Surely we cannot save any overheads if we close down the container department'.

Marathe asked Harbans if they could at least contract out the maintenance portion of the work to Pune Packages.

Harbans was not sure but he said, 'If we give the job to Pune Packages, I could dispense with a foreman and we could save ₹60,000 per year. We could also save some workmen, say, for ₹2,00,000; some materials, say, ₹2,00,000; and some other expenses, say, ₹1,30,000; but no space will be saved.'

Marathe wondered what he should do now.

## Discussion Question

1. What is your recommendation?

## CHAPTER 12

# Capturing the Complex
# Behaviour of Costs

**Learning Objectives**

After reading this chapter, you will be able to understand

- the patterns of cost behaviour which cannot be captured only by the simpler concepts of fixed costs with reference to a limited range, and linear variable costs
- managerial situations which require one to use the more complex behaviour of costs
- the methods of analysing empirical cost data to deduce the patterns that will help in future prediction and control of costs
- the relation between physical processes to

- enable one to build a plausible hypothesis for the cause and effect relationship between an activity base and the corresponding costs
- the use of statistical tools such as regression and multiple regression in conjunction with computer packages to predict costs as driven by a chosen cost driver
- how to cope up with imperfect data
- the methods to rectify faulty data and prepare them for proper use for analysis

## INTRODUCTION

The use of cost behaviour patterns for managerial control and decisions has been dealt with in several earlier chapters. The first concepts and its applications were introduced in Chapter 3. Chapter 4 had a full exposition of the managerial applications of the concepts of fixed and variable costs. Chapter 5 on job costing and Chapter 6 on ABC analysis described the identification of cost drivers to apply overheads to the cost objects, which basically required identification of the patterns of cost behaviour. Chapter 8 explained the use of the patterns to prepare budgets and also to flex them. In Chapter 9 the use of regression analysis to establish a pattern for fixing standards has been explained. We also saw in Chapter 9 the interesting feature of cost behaviour patterns following a learning curve, which is a typical non-linear cost curve.

This chapter will focus on using, what is known as, 'the deductive method of analysis', which is the process of collecting data and figuring out the patterns by a deductive process of analysis, and fitting it to the 'model' that one may have in mind through an inductive process of reasoning. The two processes of analysis would together provide management with a powerful instrument for decision-making and control.

## BASIC OBJECTIVE OF DEVELOPING COST FUNCTIONS

**Simple or complex cost functions**
Cost functions can be simple or complex, based on one cost driver or multiple cost drivers, used for management within organizations or to suggest public policy.

The basic objective of making a cost function in management is to develop models which are understandable and can be related to physical processes in the organization. It is, however, possible that by careful 'transformation' of the data in the X and Y axis of a graph, we may discover a logic in the related cost function.

We will show the process of discovering understandable patterns of relationships between cost drivers which we will plot on the X axis, and costs which will be plotted on the Y axis.

We will illustrate this with six examples (Examples 12.1–12.6) which are commonplace in business. We will show the cost functions as definite values of Y predicted with a known value of X.

This is represented by sharp lines. The actual values we would see in real life situations may be scattered around these sharp lines and we will explain this.

### Example 12.1   A White-washing Contract

Let us have a simple contract with a contractor for white-washing the walls of your buildings. We may have a preferred colour scheme but all the pigments are more or less the same price, and the contractors do the work at a standard rate, say, ₹5 per square foot. The contract may also provide that some parts of the wall may have to be patched up after inspection of the related portion, just before the white wash. The contractor may give you a mini estimate which you approve on the spot. No two patch jobs are alike. The total number of patch jobs is unpredictable but luckily, the amounts involved are very small compared to the overall costs. The cost function for the work would be as follows:

$$Y = bX$$

where $Y$ is cost in rupees, $X$ is the square feet of the wall, and $b$ is ₹5.

The graph would appear as in Fig. 12.1.

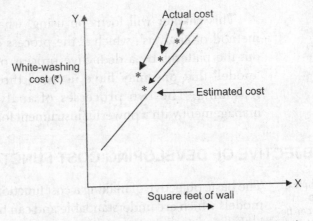

**Fig. 12.1** Cost function for white-washing contract

The actual data when plotted would show a scatter around the sharp line because of the irregular patch jobs but the overall estimates based on this cost function would be a reasonable basis for estimating and budgeting, as also decisions to award the contract for white washing.

**Example 12.2** Flat Tariff Based on Horse Power of Agricultural Pumps

Several states in India have a policy of encouraging agricultural productivity by supporting the use of agricultural pump sets run on power. They have great problems organizing the measurement of the consumption of power for charging the farmers. It is too expensive. Many Indian states, therefore, have a flat tariff with fixed monthly charges calculated on the connected load of agricultural pump sets. Usually a 5-horse power pump would be charged, say, ₹500 per month. If there is a prolonged power shut down, some rebate could be allowed for the shut down days. If the charges have to be represented by an equation, it would be as follows:

$Y = 500 + b \times X$ the hours of running of the pump set, where $Y$ is the total cost, and $b = 0$.

This can be represented by Fig. 12.2.

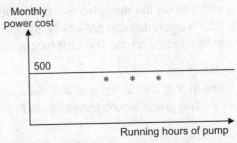

**Fig. 12.2** Flat tariff for agricultural pump sets

One may notice the odd plot of *. This could be caused by a long break-down when rebate was given to the farmers as a relief. But the solid line is good enough for forecasting and provisioning the budgets.

## Example 12.3  Expenses of a Transport Company

A bus transport company with a fleet of fifty buses has a monthly fixed cost of about ₹1.60 crore, and variable costs of, say, ₹6.50 per bus kilometre. Of this ₹1.60 crore, ₹0.30 crore is for maintenance, and of the ₹6.50 variable costs, about 50 paise is spent on maintenance costs, which is incurred precisely in the periods when the bus has less heavy load and a large number of them are in preventive maintenance schedules. If, therefore, monthly and yearly total expenses would follow the cost function, we get the following:

$$Y = 1.30 \text{ crore} + b \times \text{bus kilometres}$$

where $Y$ is total monthly cost, excluding maintenance costs, and $b = 6$.

And,
$$Y^1 = 19.20 \text{ crore } (1.60 \times 12) + b^1 \times \text{bus kilometres}$$

where $Y^1$ is yearly cost and $b^1$ is 6.50 (6 + 0.50).

The second cost function accommodates the physical fact that in a cycle of one year there will be time enough to do maintenance. The cost function will appear as in Fig. 12.3.

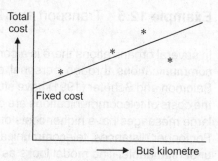

**Fig. 12.3**  Transport company costs

The scatter around the sharp line is due to variations caused by the quality of engine maintenance, road conditions, and driver care in driving within a permitted range of speed. We must recollect the use of this cost function for construction of budgets which was discussed in Chapter 8.

## Example 12.4  Energy Expenses for Sterilizing Milk in a Dairy

Milk has to be sterilized thoroughly before it is sold to customers. Dairies use boilers to prepare hot water to sterilize the milk. The boilers usually use fuel oil. The heating required is more in winter months than in the summer. But the energy required to start a boiler in summer and winter is not vastly different.

Based on this, the cost of fuel oil used in the boilers would follow two equations:

$$Y = a + b \times X$$

where $Y$ is total cost during summer months, $a$ is a constant, and $b$ is the variable costs in summer months, and $X$ is the quantity of milk sterilized.

$$Y^1 = a^1 + b^1 \times X$$

where $Y^1$ is total cost during winter months, $a^1$ is a constant, and $b^1$ is the variable costs in winter months, and $X$ is the quantity of milk processed.

The cost function will appear as shown in Fig. 12.4.

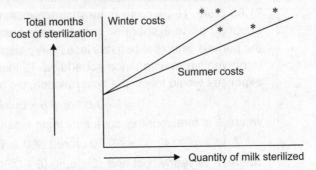

**Fig. 12.4**  Cost of sterilization of milk

The scatter of actual cost around the sharp line shows variations in efficiency.

## Example 12.5  Transport and Telecommunication Costs

In several organizations there is a continuous dialogue regarding the choice of communications through personal contact or through telecommunications. Salomon and Schofer (1991) have studied the models in Israel and shown how the costs of telecommunications are complicated by costs of congestion. Thus, large messages have higher costs due to the decongestion required for them. For longer distances, telecommunications are cheaper. This is quite intuitively understandable. The model looks as shown in Fig. 12.5.

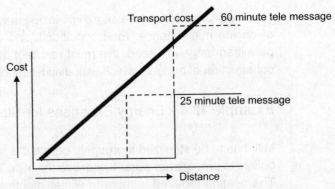

**Fig. 12.5**  Transportation and telecommunication costs

The study has many policy implications for setting up decongesting strategies and tariffs for telecommunications.

## Example 12.6    Average Cost of Indian Insurance Companies

This example is from the paper of D.V.S. Sastry (2006), the Director General of the Insurance Regulation Authority of India. Sastry studied 36 Indian insurance companies and showed that the percentage of expenses incurred by an insurance company as a proportion of premium collected by it is governed by the following formula:

$$AC = 0.476 + 349259\ (1/P) - 0.355\ (D) + 0.107\ (I/P) - 0.784\ (Gp/P) + 0.034\ (NP\ ration)$$

where AC = total expense/premium collected; P is premium collected; D is equal to 1 if the premium is above a critical annual amount and 0 if it is below that critical amount; Lp is premium collected from individual policies; Gp is the premium collected on group policies; and NP ratio is the ratio of new premiums to the total premium collected. The analysis by Sastry broadly concludes that AC falls steeply with size and then remains somewhat constant at 18 per cent. Thus, insurance companies with a low level of premium would be deep in loss and are public hazards as they are not financially viable. This should influence licensing policies. The AC ratio falls steeply when the threshold of premium level is reached. If the proportion of group premium increases, costs fall drastically. New premiums entail more expenses to procure new business. These are quite plausible explanations of cost behaviour.

Through the data analysis in Fig. 12.6, Sastry shows that the empirical data closely touches the solid line indicted in the graph.

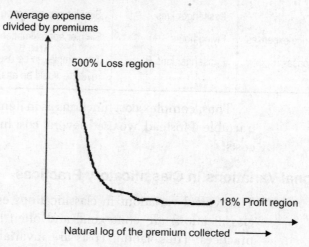

**Fig. 12.6**    Expenses as a proportion of premiums in Indian insurance companies

# COST CLASSIFICATION

**Cost classifications** These have often to be made simpler and more tractable in day-to-day management functioning.

While complex costs have been described in the earlier section, in this section attention will be given to the simplification of such complex functions so that they become more tractable in day-to-day managerial functioning. This needs to be kept in mind for practical work.

## Choice of Cost Objects and Related Cost/Revenue Drivers

The criterion for choosing and constructing a cost object, and cost and revenue drivers have been discussed in Chapters 3, 5, and 6.

There are several models that would come to mind. One needs to choose the simpler functions and discard the more complex ones. Table 12.1 shows a typical range of choices.

**Table 12.1**   Cost functions in the aviation industry

| Cost object | Cost driver | Nature of function |
|---|---|---|
| 1.  Fuel and lubricants | Distance flown | Complex and will have to consider air speed, altitude, air temperature, etc. |
| 2.  Fuel and lubricants | Flying hours | Simpler approximation |
| 3.  Depreciation | Flying hours | Simple and rugged and recognizes physical wear and tear |
| 4.  Catering costs | Passenger kms | Complex |
| 5.  Catering costs | Passenger meal count | Simpler approximation. Short trips will have less meal counts for same number of passengers |
| 6.  Revenue | Passenger kms | Simpler approximation |
| 7.  Maintenance expenses | Flying hours | Simpler approximation |
| 8.  Total expenses | Passenger kms | Too complex to be used directly even though comparison with revenue would be easier if we used passenger kms |

Thus, complex cost functions as in item 8 would become managerially tractable if instead, we used several cost functions to break down the total costs.

## International Variations in Classificatory Practices

The typical variations in classifications evident in Table 12.1 show how classifications are contextual and often have differing perceptions and practices. Thus, labour costs are invariably treated as variable costs in construction companies where labour policy is hire and fire, whereas in large steep plants or in oil refineries they are highly skilled and cannot be

**Table 12.2** International comparison of cost classifications

| | US companies | | | Japanese companies | | | Australian companies | | |
|---|---|---|---|---|---|---|---|---|---|
| | Variable % | Mixed % | Fixed % | Variable % | Mixed % | Fixed % | Variable % | Mixed % | Fixed % |
| Production labour | 86 | 6 | 8 | 52 | 5 | 43 | 70 | 20 | 10 |
| Set up labour | 60 | 25 | 15 | 44 | 6 | 50 | 45 | 33 | 22 |
| Quality control labour | 34 | 36 | 30 | 13 | 12 | 75 | 21 | 27 | 5 |
| Tooling | 32 | 35 | 33 | 31 | 26 | 43 | 25 | 28 | 47 |
| Energy | 26 | 45 | 29 | 42 | 31 | 27 | - | - | - |
| Depreciation | 1 | 7 | 92 | 0 | 0 | 100 | - | - | - |

hired and fired; they are treated as fixed costs. Joye and Blayney in 2005 (Horngren et al. 2003) have done the international analysis as shown in Table 12.2.

## Time Horizon

Cost functions may get unduly complicated by the choice of inappropriate time horizons.

Thus, Example 12.3 on the costs of a transport company, shows that if we choose the time horizon as a month, the relationship between bus kilometres run and the maintenance costs may show an inverse relationship—the higher the running of the buses, the lower are the maintenance costs. This is an absurd implausible inference, made due to inappropriate choice of time horizons. The correct plausible relationships would emerge if the time horizon is increased into a series of years. Months of heavy work of the buses would leave little time for maintenance. Nevertheless, the consequent impact on costs would come up after a time-lag when the time for maintenance is available.

So too would be the case of relationships between sales and advertisement. Advertisements would usually be quickened when sales are down. But its impact will appear in the succeeding months, as we gradually reduce the scale of advertisements after the product has caught on.

Example 12.4 from a dairy would show that the time horizon should be split into winter and summer months in order to reveal the correct pattern of costs in these seasons and which are very different in different dairies.

Horngren et al. (2003) show how in the Boeing Company inspection hours would seem not to be related to inspection costs if the analysis is done for the short run, because the inspectors are not turned on and off like a tap. The relationship would be established in the longer time horizon.

## Relevant Range

Figure 12.7 shows how, with higher production, the wage costs could gradually increase in its share of overtime. Many cost curves which would be concave in shape can be conveniently broken to smaller ranges which approximate to linear costs. This can be seen in Fig. 12.7.

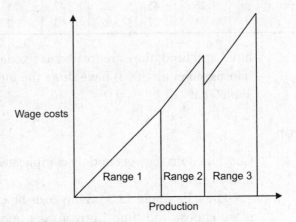

**Fig. 12.7**   Adjusting a relevant range

## COST ESTIMATION METHODS

There are four methods of cost estimation. These are as follows:

1. Industrial engineering method
2. The conference method
3. Accounts analysis method
4. Quantitative analysis method

Industrial engineering methods are painstaking, and measure work and identify the element of material labour time using time and motion studies, etc. and use engineering knowledge of the processes to estimate the cost functions. It is similar to the methods of building up standards described in Chapter 9. Needless to add, this is very time-consuming even if it is the most scientific of all methods.

The conference method would press home opinions and judgements of those who are familiar with the related work. Thus, a manager in a restaurant may be aware of the diurnal variation in the flow of customers.

He can adjust his shift workmen in such a manner that the element of idle labour as fixed costs is minimized, and most of the costs are variable, harmonizing with the ebb and flow of the customers.

The accounts analysis method uses the account information of cumulated data on costs which are already a priori classified as fixed, variable, and semi variable. Obviously, such a prior classification would inhibit fresh appraisal to discover cost patterns and will often beg the question.

The use of quantitative analysis is often the most convenient alternative.

## Six Steps of Building Cost Function Using Quantitative Methods

Cost estimations are intended to project future costs. But these costs cannot be produced out of a magical hat. They are a result of patient and sometimes ingenious efforts to use past historical data.

This involves six steps. They are as follows:

### Step 1: Choosing the dependent variable

This is the process of fixing a cost object we are seeking and has been discussed in Chapter 5 (Job costing) and Chapter 6 (activity-based costing). The element of costs which we seek to ascertain for a cost object is a dependent variable. It is obvious that these variables should be capable of being measured.

### Step 2: Identifying the independent variable, namely, the cost driver

1. This must have a plausible physical relationship with the dependent variable. For example, when machines work longer they use more power and increase power costs.
2. It embodies a contractual arrangement which enforces the relationship in a definite pattern. For example, if we pay the contractor for a length of road built, the length of the road would inevitably drive the road costs.
3. It has embedded a logic of the knowledge of operations. Thus, if ordering costs obviously increase with the number of parts ordered, an equipment with more parts would drive the costs to a higher level than an equipment with fewer parts.

One must be warned against using a cost driver only because it has a high correlation with the dependent variable. This correlation must be backed by an understanding of a cause and effect relationship. Only then can the cost driver be reliable in the long run.

In Bernard Shaw's famous play *A Doctor's Dilemma* (1946)[*], a doctor found a high negative correlation between wearers of top hats and the incidence of tuberculosis, and somewhat foolishly prescribed wearing of top hats to the poor of England as a cure for tuberculosis. This was nonsense as only the rich wear top hats, and they were free of tuberculosis only because they could afford better nutrition than the poor. Top hats are inappropriate drivers for the cure of tuberculosis.

### Step 3: Collect data

Data can be collected from the accounts books or production units, or from marketing and sales departments, depending on the nature of the data.

### Step 4: Plot or enter the data in the computer

The data can be either plotted on a graph sheet (choosing the scales carefully, so that they are framed properly within a page) or entered on a spreadsheet in computer programmes. Typically the plots could appear as in Fig. 12.8.

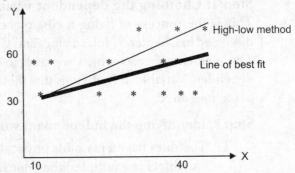

**Fig. 12.8** Plotted data

### Step 5: Estimate the cost function

In the simplest alternative one can use the high-low method, wherein one can connect the $Y$ for the highest value of $X$ with the $Y$ of the lowest value of $X$.

Reading from the graph in Fig. 12.8, one can surmize that if we fit the data in the equation $Y = mX + C$

$$30 = 10\ m + C \tag{1}$$

$$60 = 40\ m + C \tag{2}$$

---

[*] Shaw, G.B. (1946), *A Doctor's Dilemma*, Penguin reproduction says, '...it is easy to prove that the wearing of tall hats and the carrying of umbrellas enlarges the chest, prolongs life, and confers comparative immunity from disease; for the statistics show that the classes which use these articles are bigger, healthier, and live longer than the class which never dreams of possessing such things.'

(2) minus (1) would yield $30 = 30 \, m$

Therefore, $m = 1$. Substituting in Eq (1), $C = 20$.

The cost function is $Y = X + 20$, and is represented by the thin line.

This conclusion totally ignores all the information available in the graph in preference to two observations. It is a waste of valuable information.

To remedy this, one can draw a line of best fit which attempts to have as many points south of the line as there are north of the line. This would be the thick dark line and would be somewhat as follows:

$$Y = 0.75 \, X, + 15$$

which means it will be less steep.

If we try to use the thin line for forecasting, we may land up in seriously wrong decisions.

Or else, one can use a computer package to draw the line of best fit and spell out the cost function.

The theory behind such regression equations are discussed in Annexure 12.1.

## EVALUATING COST DRIVERS

The essentials of the process of the decision on the cost driver are as follows:

1.  Economic plausibility
2.  Goodness of fit

The goodness of the fit will be judged on how accurately one can predict the dependent variable if we have the independent variable. Sometimes the goodness of fit is obvious. In Fig. 12.9 it is obvious that the cost driver in Graph A is a better fit than the one in Graph B.

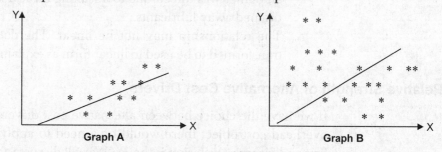

**Fig. 12.9**   Visual appreciation of the goodness of fit

It is possible to use quantitative rather than visual methods to assess the goodness of fit. This would calculate the error in the estimation as being the distance of the star marks from the solid line. This is also computed by correlation coefficient between $X$ and $Y$. If $Y$ moves in sympathy with $X$ in a similar pattern over the range of observations of $X$, it is correlated. The appendix to this chapter shows that if the observations of $X$ and $Y$ move exactly in the opposite direction, $R = -1$ and in exact unison, it will be $+1$. The square of $R$ described as $R^2$ will naturally always be positive.

If $R^2$ is high, say, above 0.80, it is very likely but certainly not definite that $Y$ is causally related to $X$. The cost driver with a high $R^2$ is acceptable only if the causal relationship is proven.

If the causal relationship is high but $R^2$ is low it could be due to any of the following reasons:

1. There are more than one cost drivers, and these need to be explored and firmed up. The appendix explains how multiple regression can be used and how the cost function can take the follwing form:

$$Y = C + aX + bZ$$

   where, $X$ and $Z$ are two cost drivers and, $a$ and $b$ are coefficients. As in the case of one cost driver, one can calculate the $R^2$ of the resultant $Y$ based on the known values of $X$ and $Z$, and the coefficients $a$ and $b$. The error in the estimates will determine the value of $R^2$. The mathematics of this will be discussed in Annexure 12.1.

2. The managerial efficiency waxes and wanes due to several factors which need attention. This would feature in having budgetary control mechanisms.

3. There are some odd figures which are described as outliers. An examination of these would yield important information on why it happens. Thus, in Atherkara Mines in Coal India (western coalfield) an outlier was traced due to a leaking oil seal in a machine which drained away lubricants.

4. The relationship may not be linear. The data may have to be transformed to be used in linear form as explained in the annexure.

## Relative Strength of Alternative Cost Drivers

If we have the choice between alternative cost drivers for estimating the overhead cost object there would be a need to apply clear criteria. The first and foremost criterion is the $R^2$. We will discuss this in Annexure 12.1. Some texts mistakenly mention that the slope should determine the criteria of choice. Undoubtedly, the higher the coefficient the higher is the slope, but the slope will be governed also by the scale of measurement of $X$ and $Y$. If $X$ (machine time) is measured in minutes, it will have a lower coefficient and lower slope than if it is measured in hours. In the same way, if cost is measured in units of hundred rupees, it will have a higher slope than if it is measured in lakh rupees.

If the graph is to be made scale neutral it needs to be plotted as $\Delta Y/Y$ (changes of $Y$ as a proportion of the base $Y$ value) and $\Delta X/X$ (changes in activity as a proportion of the base activity), or alternatively, for every percentage change in $X$ what is the percentage change in $Y$? This will measure the magnitude of the impact of the cost driver. The cost driver with the higher figure could be chosen provided it also has a high $R^2$. That is, we will have to see both its predictive power as well as its impact on the costs.

In multiple regression analysis, it is possible to see which of the variables are more reliable and influential, even if all the variables together have a high reliability, as evidenced by a high $R^2$. This will also be discussed in the more technical part of the annexure.

## COST DRIVERS, ABC, AND ESTIMATES OF OVERHEADS

The discussions so far have dealt with the estimation of overheads via the information on the activities of a chosen cost driver. In Chapter 6 we saw that overheads could be conveniently broken down to segments arising in different activities. The chapter also dealt with the great problems of ascertaining the overheads pertaining to each activity. We will deal with easier solutions to the problem of ascertaining the costs of each activity. This can be done without actually measuring these activity expenses but by treating these activities as cost drivers by themselves, and measuring only the cost of overheads in which they are included. These are available from accounting data quite conveniently. Let us illustrate this in Example 12.7, in the case of a bakery.

### Example 12.7  Pondicherry Delight

In Chapter 6 on activity-based costing, Pondicherry Delight had introduced a great range of baked snacks in several flavours. These flavours were strong as in the garlic-based snacks, or delicate as in the spinach-based ones. Every product had varying durations for baking, but every batch had to be loaded into the oven using special pans which needed thorough cleaning, and preparation of the dough for each variety so that the old smells do not linger in the pans and get transferred to other products. This involved labour costs, material costs, and inspection costs from time-to-time. The higher the number of batches, the higher is the inspection cost. Each variety had its direct material costs which could be computed based on the weight of the dough and the ingredients added to it. The activity-based batch preparation costs have no separate identity in the data. The overheads included gas used for firing and other fixed costs, and maintenance costs, as well as batch preparation costs without a separate identity.

The management had an option to calculate the cost of every batch and total the batch preparation costs, and compute the total activity costs and apply it to the product. But they felt it was tedious. On the other hand, it was not difficult to calculate the total overhead costs. They could be charged to the product on the basis of baking hours as it is economically plausible that baking hours will consume more gas and should, therefore, be charged more. Alternatively, they could charge the products based on the number of batches it uses. However, they tried to simplify matters by attempting to build a cost model on sound cause and effect principles, and use quantitative methods of regression equations to firm up the pattern.

Two models were developed—one based on the number of batches, and the other on oven hours.

The equations were as follows:

$$Y = a + bX$$

where $Y$ is the overhead cost and $X$ is the number of batches (cost function 1).

$$Y' = a^1 + cZ,$$

where $Y'$ is the overhead cost and $Z$ is the oven hours (cost function 2).

The data was as shown in Table 12.3.

**Table 12.3** Pondicherry Delight overhead cost and activity data

| Months | Overhead (₹) | Oven hours | Number of batches |
|---|---|---|---|
| January | 84,000 | 2250 | 309 |
| February | 41,000 | 2400 | 128 |
| March | 63,000 | 2850 | 249 |
| April | 44,000 | 2700 | 159 |
| May | 44,000 | 2700 | 216 |
| June | 48,000 | 2250 | 174 |
| July | 66,000 | 3800 | 264 |
| August | 48,000 | 3600 | 162 |
| September | 33,000 | 1850 | 147 |
| October | 66,000 | 3300 | 219 |
| November | 81,000 | 3750 | 303 |
| December | 57,000 | 2000 | 106 |
| Total | 6,73,000 | 32,850 | 2436 |

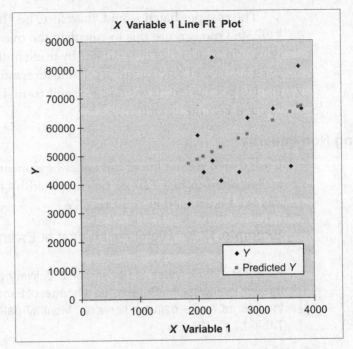

**Fig. 12.10**  Oven hours (cost function 2) R²0.20

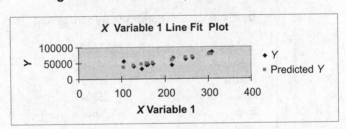

**Fig. 12.11**  Cost function 1 R²0.68

It may be seen that whereas both variables–oven hours and batch numbers–are economically plausible, batch numbers are more strongly correlated, have a much higher $R^2$, and should be accepted. One can see that Fig. 12.10 with oven hours has a much higher slope than Fig. 12.11 representing batch numbers. Nevertheless, batch numbers ought to be chosen. The related equation as thrown up by the computer programme which fitted the data looked like the following:

|  | Coefficients |
| --- | --- |
| Intercept | 16030.87 |
| X Variable 1 | 197.3028 |

The cost per batch would, therefore, be ₹16,031/number of batches + ₹197.30. One can use this to calculate the overhead cost of product. One can perhaps improve the estimate by using multiple regression, using both oven hours and batch numbers. If one forecasted the number of batches in the budget period, it would be useful to make the overhead budget by fitting it into the equation.

## Handling Non-linearity

Costs which are not linear can either be truncated into the different ranges as described in Fig. 12.7 or be converted by transforming the variables; this will be detailed in Annexure 12.1.

### Example 12.8  High Low Method of Estimating Cost Function

Excellent Gift Services Ltd does home delivery service for any order placed through their website. Suresh, the manager of Excellent Gift Services examines the cost of home delivery services. Monthly data for year 2010 is shown in Table 12.4.

Table 12.4  Monthly data of Excellent Gift Services Ltd

| Month | Home delivery service cost | Number of home deliveries |
|---|---|---|
| January | 27,690 | 402 |
| February | 41248 | 414 |
| March | 25882 | 244 |
| April | 36904 | 772 |
| May | 29686 | 548 |
| June | 43780 | 872 |
| July | 33662 | 642 |
| August | 42858 | 656 |
| September | 36534 | 486 |
| October | 33664 | 322 |
| November | 33708 | 468 |
| December | 30486 | 686 |

Answer the following questions:
1. Plot the relationship between the home delivery service cost and the number of home deliveries done (cost driver).
2. Compute the cost function using high low, relating delivery service costs to the number of home delivery reports.

Here are the answers:
1. The following graph (Fig. 12.12) shows the relationship between the home delivery service cost and the number of home deliveries done (cost driver).

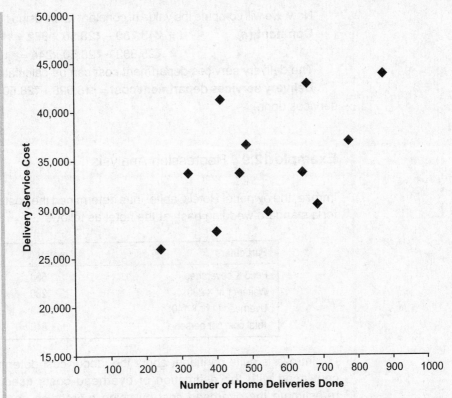

**Fig. 12.12**  Relationship between number of service reports (a cost driver) and customer service department costs

The home delivery service cost and the number of home deliveries (cost driver) show a positive correlation, which means that the home delivery service costs are bound to rise with the increase in the number of home deliveries. Hence, this relationship is economically plausible.

2.  The following table shows the highest and the lowest observations of cost driver:

| | | |
|---|---|---|
| Highest observation of cost driver | ₹43,780 | 872 |
| Lowest observation of cost driver | ₹25,882 | 244 |
| Difference | **₹17,898** | **628** |

Home delivery service department costs = $a + b$ (number of delivery services done)

where slope coefficient ($b$) can be calculated as under:

$$\textbf{Slope coefficient (}b\textbf{)} \quad = \quad \frac{₹17,898}{628}$$

$$= ₹28.50 \text{ per delivery service}$$

Now, we will compute the value of constant (*a*) by using the following method:

**Constant (*a*)**      = ₹43,780 − ₹28.50 × 872 = ₹18,928

                 = ₹25,882 − ₹28.50 ×244 = ₹18,928

The delivery services department cost can be calculated as follows:

**Delivery services department cost** = ₹18,928 + ₹28.50 (number of delivery services done)

## Example 12.9    Regression Analysis

Imroze, the owner of Hotel Capitol, has determined the cost of catering services for a standard wedding bash at the hotel as follows:

| Particulars | Amount (₹) |
|---|---|
| Food & beverages | 500 |
| Waiter (1 hr × 200) | 200 |
| Overhead (1 hr × 140) | 140 |
| Total cost per person | 840 |

Imroze is quite confident about the labour cost determined but he is not convinced with the estimation of overhead costs used. Imroze wants to re-estimate the overhead cost by using regression analysis based on the monthly data shown in Table 12.5.

**Table 12.5**   Monthly Database

| Months | Labour hours | Overhead costs (₹) |
|---|---|---|
| January | 5000 | 11,00,000 |
| February | 5400 | 11,80,000 |
| March | 6000 | 12,00,000 |
| April | 8400 | 12,80,000 |
| May | 15,000 | 15,40,000 |
| June | 11,000 | 14,20,000 |
| July | 13,000 | 14,80,000 |
| August | 9000 | 13,40,000 |
| September | 14,000 | 15,00,000 |
| October | 9000 | 13,60,000 |
| November | 6200 | 12,40,000 |
| December | 13,000 | 14,60,000 |
| | 1,15,000 | 1,61,00,000 |

The calculation of overhead costs is shown as under:

$$\text{Overhead cost} = \frac{\text{Total cost}}{\text{Total labour hours}} = \frac{₹1,61,00,000}{1,15,000}$$

Overhead cost = ₹140

The regression analysis shows that overhead costs vary with labour hours used. The relationship between overhead cost and labour hours is as follows:

$$Y = 39.261X + 965412$$

Overhead cost = 39.261 (Labour cost) + 965412

where overhead cost is the dependent variable and labour hours is the independent variable.

1. Plot the regression line and evaluate using economic plausibility, goodness of fit, and slope of regression line.
2. Determine the variable cost per person using regression analysis.
3. Imroze has received a wedding bash booking order for 300 persons next month. What should be the minimum bidding offer that Imroze must make in order to recoup the variable cost?

Here are the answers:

1. The following graph (Fig. 12.13) shows the relationship between labour hours and overhead costs, and the regression line.

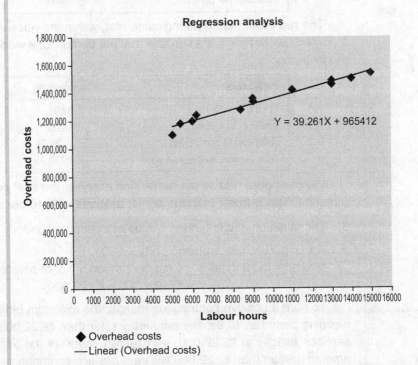

**Regression analysis**

$$Y = 39.261X + 965412$$

Labour hours

◆ Overhead costs
—Linear (Overhead costs)

**Fig. 12.13** Relationship between labour hours and overhead costs of Hotel Capitol

Regression line equation is given as under:

Overhead cost = 39.261 (Labour hour) + 965412

Here, overhead cost is the dependent variable and labour hour is the independent variable.

**Economic plausibility** For a catering company, labour hours represent an economically plausible driver of overhead costs.

**Goodness of fit** It is evident that the difference between actual and estimated costs is quite small. This implies a very good fit, which signifies a positive correlation between labour hours and overhead costs.

**Slope of regression line** The regression line has a reasonably steep slope from left to right. The positive slope of regression line signifies the positive correlation between overhead costs and labour hours. This indicates that on an average, overhead costs are bound to rise with increase in the labour hours.

2. The total cost per person without using regression analysis is given as under:

| Particulars | Amount (₹) |
|---|---|
| Food & beverages | 500 |
| Waiter (1 hr × 200) | 200 |
| Overhead (1 hr × 140) | 140 |
| Total cost per person | 840 |

The regression analysis indicates that, within the relevant range of 5,000 to 15,000 labour hours, the variable cost per person for a wedding party equals the following:

| Particulars | Amount (₹) |
|---|---|
| Food & beverages | 500 |
| Waiter (1 hr × 200) | 200 |
| Overhead (1 hr × 39.261) | 39.26 |
| Total variable cost per person | 739.26 |

We can notice that as per regression analysis, the cost per person is ₹740 (approx.). This is lower than the earlier estimate of ₹840 per person.

3. The minimum bidding price can be calculated as under:

No. of persons for wedding party = 300

Minimum bidding price = Cost per person × No. of persons

= ₹740 × 300 = ₹2,22,000

To earn a positive contribution margin, the minimum bid for a 300-person wedding party has to be any amount greater than ₹2,22,000. By offering his services exactly at ₹2,22,000, Imroze can cover all the variable costs. Any amount greater than ₹2,22,000 will earn positive contribution margin, which in turn will help in paying the fixed costs.

# USE OF ACTUAL COST DATA TO DECIDE PARAMETERS OF LEARNING CURVE

The cost functions which govern learning curves have been detailed in Chapter 9. This fitting can be done either manually or by using computers.

## Data Collection

Data would usually be available in accounting, production, and marketing records. Some typical problems would be as follows:

1.  Accounting records would show consumption of material when it is issued to the works. But if it is lying as material at site without consumption, it could cause serious problems. Thus, diesel issued in a month shown in Example 12.4, should properly be adjusted for consumption.

2.  Production is often shown in a given month to indicate high achievements, but intended to be covered by the following month's production, would typically vitiate the analysis.

3.  Special quantity discounts would distort the cost in the month in which heavy purchases are made and would vitiate the analysis. This can be remedied if only standard prices are used, and price variances are adjusted immediately on receipt of the goods.

4.  Some organizations having transfer prices from one department to another may pass off their fixed costs which will be wrongly perceived as a variable cost by the receiving department. Thus, the power department may charge the user department a per kilo watt hour charge, whereas it ought to show fixed and variable costs separately.

5.  Sometimes misplaced decimal points would vitiate the analysis.

6.  Cost functions dynamically change. Thus, change in catalysts may dramatically change process recovery. One needs to keep the cost forecasts up-to-date to catch up with technological changes.

7.  Inflation would vitiate the costs. This is resolved by using appropriate deflators and is particularly important when time horizons are large.

8.  While we are forewarned by improper use of a range, we must also make sure that there are enough variations in the data on $X$, so that its reflection on the dependent variable $Y$ can be studied with some confidence.

Efforts taken to clean up the data would avoid much wasteful effort and wrong conclusions after analysis.

## Understanding Macro-level and Public Policy Implications of Cost Behaviour

Many cost behaviour studies done across organizations and using the analytical methods explained in this chapter are used for policy decisions. Some elementary examples have been explained as in Examples 12.5 and 12.6.

## COPING UP WITH IMPERFECT DATA

In real life one often comes across situations where the cost data is not reliable or is based on imperfect assumptions. If managements rely on such data for making major decisions, it could lead to disastrous consequences. In the area of cost behaviour studies particularly, such errors frequently occur due to imperfect understanding of the cost structure. The following is a case involving the use of cost data for taking major decisions.

### Case of Decision Dilemma at Hearty Foods Ltd

Mr Ramesh reached for his cigar, which was a sure signal that he was agitated. He had good reasons to do so. As the managing director of Hearty Foods Ltd, he had to closely watch the performance of his four regional offices at Mumbai, Chennai, Delhi, and Kolkata. His business is competitive and the entry barriers are few. It was a low-tech food-processing chain where brand loyalties were few and feeble. He was waiting for his accountant, Ms Fernandes, a cost accountant with a record for fastidious details and good common sense.

'Good morning, Sir,' said a measured voice. 'You called?'

'Come in,' said Mr Ramesh without any delay and took out a sheet of paper with a lot of figures on it. It read as follows (Table 12.6):

**Table 12.6**  Cost Sheet for the Quarter October–December 2008

(in ₹ lakh)

|  | Mumbai | Chennai | Delhi | Kolkata | Total |
|---|---|---|---|---|---|
| Sales | 20.00 | 16.00 | 12.00 | 24.00 | 72.00 |
| Less: variable costs | 12.00 | 9.60 | 8.40 | 11.50 | 41. 50 |
| **Contribution** | **8.00** | **6.40** | **3.60** | **12.50** | **30.50** |
| Less: fixed costs | 4.00 | 4.00 | 2.80 | 12.00 | 22.00 |
| **Profit before depreciation and tax** | **4.00** | **2.40** | **0.80** | **0.50** | **8.50** |

'I don't understand this,' he said. 'The sales are good; for the previous quarter we achieved 65 lakh, indicating a jump of more than 10 per cent.

But the profits are more than 10 per cent lower. I do not understand it. Another thing; Vikram from Mumbai informs me that either McDonald's or Wimpy's has purchased the corner building that is 100 yards from our cafeteria. We may have a tough time if they open up an outlet there.'

'But also tell me what is wrong with our Kolkata establishment. It accounts for a third of our sales, but the profit is almost zero. I put in ₹5 lakh in October for a complete re-fit of the furniture and showroom. The sales are satisfactory, but where is the return?'

Ms Fernandes who had prepared the statement knew that there was something wrong in it. She had introduced a uniform code of accounts with detailed instructions. She personally went to the Mumbai and Chennai offices to ensure that it was implemented. However, the Delhi office had staff problems and the competent regional accountant had left a few months ago for a better opportunity elsewhere. In Kolkata, they were busy shifting the office and the regional accountant was put in-charge of the administrative arrangements. Even otherwise, with a diploma in management from an obscure business school, he had no taste for accounting. Ms Fernandes suspected that he was related in some way to the regional manager and never bothered about HO. She was, therefore, not very sure about the figures from Delhi and Kolkata.

'I am in a fix,' continued Ramesh. 'I want to launch the "Cola Chips" from next month. It will sell well in the east and we may be able to push through some in the North. I expect additional sales of ₹8 lakh in the East alone. My all–India promotion cost for the initial launch is an additional ₹6 lakh, but I see no profits. So, tell me how I can achieve this with this sort of performance. My fixed cost is exactly the same in all the regions, but this paper tells a different story.'

Suddenly, Ms Fernandes saw some light. 'The costs, both variable and fixed, do not look right to me. You see Sir, I have been asking for a proper accountant in the Kolkata office for some time. The Delhi office too does not have one since Mr Gupta left for Muscat.'

'I can give you somebody at Delhi as their fixed costs are low, but not at Kolkata where they are so high. In fact, I have half a mind to accept the offer from Home-foods. Madan says he will pay ₹5 lakh goodwill and take all the assets at book value for the Kolkata office and our east zone business. I would rather invest the 5 lakh to improve the Mumbai office.

Ms Fernandes said, 'Sir, please wait till I re-do the costings. Give me just 2 days.' 'Go ahead,' said Ramesh, but there is something else I wanted to tell you. I am going to refuse that export offer for Dubai from Mumbai. It is just for 4 lakh and the net return is the same as in the Mumbai zone, and it involves a lot of paper work. And another thing; Chandran from

Chennai is willing to sell his products through us. His sale is about 15 per cent that of our Chennai sales and will cost us 10 per cent more in direct costs; but he is will no longer be a competitor if we accept his offer.

### Solution:

The above case illustrates real life situations in a hypothetical organization. The CEO is planning to take certain decisions based on the cost sheet prepared by his organization. His proposals look prima facie logical, based on the data available. But, a careful study of the conversation between the CEO and his cost accountant reveal certain serious loopholes in the cost accounting.

The accounting system in the Mumbai and Chennai offices were set right by the cost accountant, whereas in Delhi and Kolkata there were staff problems. Hence, it is safe to presume that the first two offices have a more dependable cost data than the latter. A look at the contribution statement confirms this presumption. The variable costs at Mumbai and Chennai have a uniform rate of 60 per cent of the sales, whereas at Delhi and Kolkata no such pattern is evident. This situation is further collaborated by the facts of the case, which state that Ms Fernandes was 'not very sure of the figures of Delhi and Kolkata'. Hence, there is room for some doubt about the accuracy of these figures.

The fixed costs again show a skewed picture for the four locations. According to the CEO, 'My fixed cost is exactly the same in all the regions, but this paper tells a different story.' Hence, there seems to be scope for reviewing the fixed costs shown in the cost sheet. This is particularly high in Kolkata, which has a correspondingly low figure of variable costs of below 50 per cent of the sales figure. In all the other locations the variable costs are 60 per cent or more of the sales figure.

With the above broad information, the cost sheet can be redrawn with the following assumptions:

1. The variable costs are 60 per cent of the sales. This assumption is based on the figures of Mumbai and Chennai offices which have reliable accounting systems.
2. The fixed costs are ₹4 lakh for each of the four locations. This is again based on the figures from the Mumbai and Chennai offices and the CEO's statement that fixed costs are the same throughout.
3. It is apparent that there is some overlap between the various cost components in the Delhi and Kolkata offices.
4. In the absence of information to the contrary, it is assumed that the sales figures are correctly arrived at.

**Table 12.7**  Revised Cost Sheet for the Quarter October–December 2008

(₹ in lakh)

|  | Mumbai | Chennai | Delhi | Kolkata | Total |
|---|---|---|---|---|---|
| Sales | 20.00 | 16.00 | 12.00 | 24.00 | 72.00 |
| Less: variable costs | 12.00 | 9.60 | 7.20 | 14.40 | 43.20 |
| **Contribution** | **8.00** | **6.40** | **4.80** | **9.60** | **28.80** |
| Less: fixed costs | 4.00 | 4.00 | 4.00 | 4.00 | 16.00 |
| Profit before depreciation and tax | 4.00 | 2.40 | 0.80 | 5.60 | 12.80 |

From the above revised cost sheet (Table 12.7) it is evident that there are mistakes in the identification of variable and fixed costs at the Delhi and Kolkata offices. At the Delhi office some fixed costs have been wrongly shown as variable cost, due to which the contribution figure was less. After the corrections it has shown an increase. However, the profit figures remain the same. But wrong allocation can vitiate the contribution margin which is an important indicator for decision-making.

The case of Kolkata office is even worse. Here, the profits were highly understated. Apparently the amount of ₹5 lakh spent in October for capital expenditure has been shown as revenue expenditure. Besides, some of the variable costs have been shifted to a fixed cost component. When the adjustments are made, it reveals a healthy profit.

Based on the above revised cost sheet, the CEO must take the following decisions:

1.  *Staffing:* He must immediately provide competent staff for both Delhi and Kolkata offices. His contention that the fixed costs are low at Delhi and high at Kolkata is not substantiated.

2.  *Madan's bid for Kolkata office:* The 5 lakh goodwill is a throw away offer. Kolkata provides a healthy contribution of ₹9.60 lakh, and is the most profitable unit of the company. The revised costing proves the futility of accepting this offer.

3.  *Profitability:* The revised cost sheet reveals a profit of 12.80 lakh as against 8.50 lakh shown in the original cost sheet. This is a healthier picture and should encourage the CEO to launch more products. He may invest ₹6 lakh as promotion cost for launching 'Cola Chips' and treat it as deferred revenue expenditure to be written off over a period of 4–5 years.

4. *Export offer to Dubai:* The 4 lakh export offer to Dubai from Mumbai constitutes 20 per cent of the current sales. Since this is a competitive business, the offer should be accepted even though the profit margins are not very high. There is no indication of additional fixed expenditure for affecting the exports, and hence it is assumed that this is negligible. Hence, the contribution increases by ₹1.6 lakh (40% of 4 lakh) with no additional fixed costs. This also opens up new markets and hence is advised.

5. *Selling Chandran's products at Chennai office:* The costing for this activity is as under:

| | |
|---|---|
| Sales (15% of ₹16 lakh) | = 2.40 lakh |
| Variable cost [60% + (10% of 60%) = 66%] | = 0.58 lakh |
| **Contribution** | **= 0.82 lakh** |

Hence, the proposal brings in additional contribution and is therefore welcome. Besides, it has the advantage of reducing competition. Hence, Hearty Foods should grab it.

The above case throws light on the need for a proper understanding of the behaviour of costs. Many of the earlier decisions of the CEO are proved to be wrong when the cost sheet is properly constituted. A good cost accounting revision can be a great asset in the decision-making process. This case also highlights the close links between the various functions of an organization, such as finance, marketing, HR, and corporate planning. The role of leadership also comes out diligently, and the need for data-based decision-making and participative approaches is highlighted.

## SUMMARY

Cost functions may relate to a single or multiple cost drivers to predict the cost of the cost object. The cost functions are built on the bedrock of plausible economic relationships, but confirmed only by the empirical test of being able to make reasonably accurate predictions. The predictability is assessed by the term $R^2$, the coefficient of determination. Cost functions are efficiently developed by using computer software which is available in wide variety. The reliability of the individual coefficients in a cost function is also thrown up by computer software, in terms of standard errors which have to be tested by their ratio to the related coefficients. A $t$ test is applied using standard statistical tables to see if the coefficients are significant.

## KEY POINTS

- Regression equations enable estimation of the dependent variables based on the values of independent variables, using linear and non-linear equations with an error term that throws up a scatter spread all over the predicted line.
- A cost function is a typical regression equation.
- No relationship between dependent and independent variables are to be valued unless a plausible economic relationship is shown to exist between them.
- The coefficient of every variable can be tested using standard error and the $t$ ratio and tested against the table of $t$ statistics available in any standard statistical text book.
- One of the practical ways to estimate the activity-based costs without it explicitly being available in the accounts ledgers is to use a cost function derived through regression equations that are constructed using the least square method.
- The least square method attempts to minimize the square of the vertical difference between the observed value of $Y$ and the estimated value of $Y$ in the regression equation.
- The coefficient of activity bases (say, batch) is the variable element of activity costs.
- Multiple variables may be used to increase the $R^2$ to an acceptable level.
- Non-linear cost functions can be transformed into linear functions by using several techniques.

## CONCEPT REVIEW QUESTIONS

1. What are the two basic criteria used for using a cost driver in a cost function?
2. High correlation between two variables means that one is the cause and the other is the effect. Do you agree?
3. Name the four approaches to cost functions.
4. Indicate a typical example when the 'range' is a critical factor in a cost function.
5. Indicate a typical example when the 'time horizon' is a critical factor in a cost function.
6. Large insurance companies have a cost advantage not available to small insurance companies. True or false. Give reasons.
7. Indicate methods to transform non-linear functions to linear functions.

8. Comparing two cost functions, one in which the slope of the curve of Y values plotted against X values are higher are to be preferred as they show greater impact of the cost driver on costs. True or false.

9. Indicate three typical situations where the data used for forecasting and cost functions may get distorted or become inaccurate? Suggest remedies for these situations.

## NUMERICAL PROBLEMS

### 1. Understanding Patterns

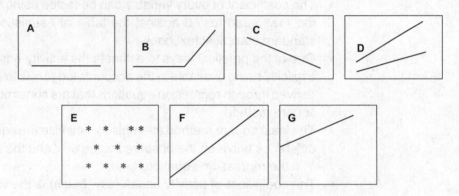

**Fig. P1** Different patterns

Indicate against each of the following the appropriate graphical pattern marking it as A, B, C, D, E, F, G, or none of the above, along with brief reasons:

1. The X axis indicates the machine hours, and the Y axis represents maintenance expenses each month; maintenance is done usually in the slack months when the machines are not being used.

2. The X axis is the machine hours in the month while the Y axis is the depreciation charged on usage, i.e., machine hours in the month.

3. The X axis is the quantity of milk sterilized each month in a dairy and the Y axis is the fuel cost of the boiler producing the water for sterilization in the months from January–December. Winter months need greater fuel.

4. The X axis shows the quantity of goods stored in a leased godown in a month and the Y axis represents the lease rent for the month. There is only one godown and the lease is not adjusted upward or downward for space actually used.

5. The X axis is the production in a month, while the Y axis is the labour costs. Labour is time rated and employed on overtime in months where the production is high.
6. The X axis is the number of students attending class on a day and the Y axis is the canteen revenue for the day; the propensity of the students to eat at the canteen or the amount they eat is unpredictable.
7. On the X axis is the monthly number of babies born in a hospital and on the Y axis is the variable cost of the incubator used to warm them. Winter months need greater use of heating devices.
8. On the X axis are the monthly plots of the hours for which an electric pump is used on an agricultural farm and on the Y axis is the power cost for that month. The power charge is flat and is based on the installed capacity of pumps, and this has not changed in the months considered.
9. The X axis is the number of kilometres that a taxi used in long distance travel between crowded towns runs for. The Y axis is the total cost of the taxi including depreciation, driver, fuel and lubricants, and repair. Depreciation is heavy and is time-based, not usage-based.

2. **Prems's Fast Reaction**

Prem had just started an engineering firm and had enthusiastically registered for a course on cost accounting. He was excited by the concept of using regression equations for estimating costs. He asked Geeta, his accountant, who was struggling to get a basis for forecasting maintenance costs. He produced the following data for the two months of April and May 2008. They are shown in Table P2.

**Table P2**  Data for April–May 2008

| Month | Machine hours | Maintenance costs (₹) |
|---|---|---|
| April | 4000 | 3000 |
| May | 7000 | 3900 |

Prem felt that was good enough. There were two equations and two unknowns, namely, fixed costs (F) and variable costs (V). He solved the equation on his scratch pad and handed it over to Geeta for making the budget.

## Questions

2.1 What are the estimates of fixed costs and variable costs that Prem must have given to Geeta?
2.2 Give two reasons why Prem's suggestion to Geeta is absurd.

### 3. Ravi Kukreja's Control Over Customer Service Costs

Ravi Kukreja was a brilliant electronics engineer and in a short period of two years since he had started his company, he had introduced a hundred electronic products of various types. He had provided a six-month warranty for all his products with free repair and replacement of defectives. He was, however, concerned about his increasing customer service costs. They included materials and labour. It was quite impossible for him to keep track of the customer care costs for each of the products; the least he could do was to make sure there was no leakage of money. He roughly estimated that there would be a correlation between the number of customer complaints which were accepted and resulted in a customer service report, and the related customer service departmental costs.

His accountant gave the data as in Table P3.

Table P3   Kukreja's Customer Service Costs

| Week | Customer service costs (₹) | Number of service reports |
|------|---------------------------|---------------------------|
| 1 | 1,38,450 | 201 |
| 2 | 2,06,240 | 276 |
| 3 | 1,29,410 | 122 |
| 4 | 1,84,520 | 386 |
| 5 | 1,48,430 | 274 |
| 6 | 2,18,900 | 436 |
| 7 | 1,68,310 | 321 |
| 8 | 2,14290 | 328 |
| 9 | 1,82,670 | 243 |
| 10 | 1,68,320 | 161 |

### Questions

3.1  Plot the relationship between the number of service reports and the customer service department costs on a graph. Comment.

3.2  Is the relationship between these two variables economically plausible?

3.3  Use a high and low method to build the cost function.

3.4  What variables other than customer service reports are likely to improve the goodness of fit?

### 4. Badami Institute Overhead Costs

Badami Institute of Management was concerned about its rising costs. The students were demanding a variety of options and an increase in the number of academic programmes. The institute knew that the costs depended both on the number of students it enrolled and the number of courses it offered. They had the following data for 12 years, suitably deflated for the inflation factor. The data is in Table P4.

**Table P4**  Data for 12 Years

| Year | Costs in ₹ thousand | Number of programmes | Number of enrolled students |
|---|---|---|---|
| 1 | 13,500 | 29 | 3400 |
| 2 | 19,200 | 36 | 5000 |
| 3 | 16,800 | 49 | 2600 |
| 4 | 20,100 | 53 | 4700 |
| 5 | 19,500 | 54 | 3900 |
| 6 | 23,100 | 58 | 4900 |
| 7 | 23,700 | 88 | 5700 |
| 8 | 20,100 | 72 | 3900 |
| 9 | 22,800 | 83 | 3500 |
| 10 | 29,700 | 73 | 3700 |
| 11 | 31,200 | 101 | 5600 |
| 12 | 38,100 | 103 | 7600 |

With the use of computers they derived three cost functions:

1. $Y = a + bX$, where $X$ is the number of programmes which had an $R^2$ of 0.72.
2. $Y = a + cZ$, where $Z$ is the number of students which had an $R^2$ of 0.55.
3. $Y = a + dX + eZ$, which is multivariate and had an $R^2$ of 0.81.

The coefficients and their standard errors were as follows (again, available in a computer printout).

**Equation 1 $R^2$ 0.72**

| Variable (1) | Coefficient (2) | Standard error (3) | T ratio 2 ÷ 3 |
|---|---|---|---|
| Constant | 7127.75 | 335.34 | 2.14 |
| Number of academic programmes | 240.64 | 47.33 | 5.08 |

**Equation 2 $R^2$ 0.55**

| Variable (1) | Coefficient (2) | Standard error (3) | T ratio 2 ÷ 3 |
|---|---|---|---|
| Constant | 5991.75 | 5067.88 | 1.18 |
| Number of students | 3.78 | 1.07 | 3.53 |

### Equation 3 Multivariate $R^2$ 0.81

| Variable (1) | Coefficient (2) | Standard error (3) | T ratio 2 ÷ 3 |
|---|---|---|---|
| Constant | 2779.62 | 3620.05 | 0.77 |
| Number of academic programmes | 178.37 | 5154 | 3.46 |
| Number of students | 1.87 | 0.92 | 2.03 |

## Questions

4.1 Which of the equations should Badami Institute choose and why?

4.2 Suggest ideas for the fee structure for the basic courses and diversified optional course which would inevitably increase the number of academic programmes.

5. **Segosts Corporation**

Segosts Corporation uses a sophisticated technology for making two products Kee and Zee, which are used in the chemical industry. There is good demand for these products. The cost data per unit for the products is:

| Head | Kee (₹) | Zee (₹) |
|---|---|---|
| Direct materials | 12 | 6 |
| Direct labour | 9 | 10 |
| Variable overhead | 9 | 12 |
| Sale price | 50 | 60 |

The company is facing a problem in getting a critical raw material used for making both the above products. Kee needs one litre of the limited raw material whereas Zee needs two litres. Looking at the cost situation the company decides to concentrate on the manufacture of Zee which gives a higher contribution as compared to Kee. The shortage situation will continue for some time.

## Questions

5.1 Review the decision of the management from the cost data available

5.2 What other factors need to be considered?]

6. **Vague Corp.**

Vague Corp. does not have a professionally managed accounting system. The company's new CEO wants to know the fixed and variable costs separately to enable a data-based decision making philosophy. His accountant (who has limited exposure to book-keeping) produces the following data of production and costs for the first five months.

| Month | Output | Total Cost (₹) |
|---|---|---|
| April | 2000 | 6,00,000 |
| May | 2500 | 7.50,000 |
| June | 3200 | 10,00,000 |
| July | 4000 | 9,00,000 |
| August | 3600 | 10,20,000 |

The CEO was stunned to see the haphazard cost figures. So he called for an analysis of the costs which revealed some information, given as under:

(a) The company's fixed costs come to ₹2,00,000 per month
(b) A capital expenditure of ₹1,60,000 was incurred in June
(c) The July salaries were paid in August and were accounted in that month.
(d) In May advances to staff were paid for the education of children
(e) There were negligible semi variable expenses

## Question

6.1 Based on the given information arrive at the correct cost figures for each month and explain the differences.

## 7. Jayes Corp.

Jayes Corp. has employed a new cost accountant with the mandate to analyse the costs behaviour and arrive at a unit cost system. The following data is available:

| | Quarter I | Quarter II | Quarter III |
|---|---|---|---|
| Production (units) | 15000 | 18000 | 21,000 |
| Expenses (₹) | | | |
| Prime cost | 75,000 | 90,000 | 105,000 |
| Factory overheads | 40,000 | 46,000 | 52,000 |
| Admin overheads | 55,000 | 55,000 | 55,000 |
| Selling commission | 15,000 | 18,000 | 21,000 |
| Marketing overheads | 20,000 | 23,000 | 26,000 |
| Advertisement | 35,000 | 35,000 | 35,000 |

## Questions

7.1 Calculate the unit variable cost.
7.2 Calculate the total fixed cost per quarter.

## PROJECT

Form groups of four or five students, select a company, and study the cost and profit structure spread over, say, ten years. Using deflators for inflation, suggest a cost function which relates costs to a chosen cost driver, say, sales or production.

 **CASE STUDY 1**                     **A Puzzling Hypothesis**

Pradeep Kashyap, an engineer fresh from a B school was asked by his managing director to prepare an acceptable budget for advertisement and maintenance expenses. Pradeep felt that he could use his knowledge of regression analysis to forecast the budgets. He hypothesized that

1. sales increased with advertising; and
2. maintenance expenses had a base level and above this it increased in a linear fashion with machine hours used.

He wished to confirm his hypothesis quantitatively. He prepared a table of data for every month on advertisement expenses, maintenance expenses, sales, and machine hours. He entered the data in a spreadsheet on MS Excel and was delighted to note that the $R^2$ of the two relationships was very high. He showed his results to his M.D. who pointed out that this was a nonsensical relationship as it did not confirm his hypothesis, and the coefficients of the numbers were negative. His equations were as follows:

$$S = 10,00,000 - 0.05 \times A$$

where $S$ is sales and $A$ is the advertising expenses for the month in ₹

$$E = 20,00,000 - 0.05 \times M$$

where $E$ is maintenance expenses for the month in ₹ and $M$ is the number of machine hours.

The M.D. called the finance manager, the marketing manager, and the production manager to see if there was something wrong with the data. After checking, they confirmed that the data was correct.

### Discussion Questions

1. How do you explain this set of puzzling regression equations?

2. How would you suggest Pradeep to reframe the hypothesis for empirical checking with the data?

| CASE STUDY 2 | Bulandsher Packaging |

Bulandsher Packaging was a company started with a view to service a thriving ayurvedic and *unani* pharmaceutical industry in the district of Bulandsher in Uttar Pradesh, India.

Dharmveer, its owner, had a novel arrangement wherein he had a set of machines which could make plastic bottles of various shapes and sizes, fill them with the liquid medicines, and seal and package them in cartons supplied by the manufacturers.

Dharmveer, a first class entrepreneur was, however, impatient with rigid systems of costing and wished to quote his rates to the manufacturers on intuition.

Things changed when he attended a course where he learnt to use cost functions to cost the products using regression equations with less paperwork.

He appointed Sangeeta as his accountant. She told him that it would be pointless to use sophisticated methods such as regression equations when the basic data was hopelessly imperfect.

Very naively he suggested that he could maintain his accounts on the palm of his hand as he bought material once in three months and paid part of it in cash and part of it with a three-month credit.

He advised her that she should take whatever was paid in cash as the cost, since the figure left no doubts of accuracy. He said these could be related to the machine hours in a regression equation. Sangeeta prepared the data as desired.

The cost had two elements—wages and materials. She used this data to construct a regression equation.

Knowing the whole exercise was futile, she rummaged the data and obtained the information on the actual cost of consumption material, irrespective of its time of arrival in the factory or its time of payment. She did not find any need to correct wage expenses as accrued costs and cash costs coincided quite easily.

Her corrected data and the original data are shown in Table CS 2.

**Table CS 2**   Data of Bulandsher Packaging in the Year 2005

| Month (1) | Labour cost (in ₹ thousand) (2) | Matrerial cost reported (in ₹ thousand) (3) | Material cost restated (in ₹ thousand) (4) | Total reported costs reported (in ₹ thousand) (5) 2+3 | Total revised costs (in ₹ thousand) (6) 2+4 | Machine hours (7) |
|---|---|---|---|---|---|---|
| March | 347 | 847 | 182 | 1194 | 529 | 30 |
| April | 521 | 0 | 311 | 521 | 932 | 63 |
| May | 398 | 0 | 268 | 398 | 666 | 49 |
| June | 355 | 961 | 228 | 1316 | 583 | 38 |
| July | 473 | 0 | 348 | 473 | 82 | 57 |
| August | 617 | 0 | 349 | 617 | 966 | 57 |
| September | 245 | 821 | 125 | 1066 | 370 | 19 |
| October | 487 | 0 | 364 | 487 | 851 | 19 |
| November | 431 | 0 | 290 | 431 | 721 | 42 |

Sangeeta also ran a regression with the revised data. The results of the two regressions were as follows:

**Equation 1 with reported data  $Y$ (costs reported) = $a + bX$ (machine hours) $R^2$ 0.43**

| Variable (1) | Coefficient (2) | Standard error (3) | T ratio (4) 2 ÷ 3 |
|---|---|---|---|
| Constant | 1393.20 | 305.68 | 4.56 |
| Machine hours | −14.23 | 6.15 | −2.31 |

**Equation 2 with corrected data  $Y$ (corrected costs) = $a + bX$ (machine hours) $R^2$ 0.94**

| Variable (1) | Coefficient (2) | Standard error (3) | T ratio (4) 2 ÷ 3 |
|---|---|---|---|
| Constant | 176.38 | 53.99 | 3.27 |
| Machine hours | 11.44 | 1.08 | 10.59 |

## Discussion Questions

1. Plot the data in two separate graphs, one for equation 1 and a second for equation 2. Comment.
2. What should Sangeeta advise Dharmveer?
3. What are the practical problems that may arise if equation 2 has to be adopted in the future?

# ANNEXURE

## Annexure 12.1

### Regression Analysis

There are extensive references throughout this chapter to this technical annexure. A reading of this annexure would no doubt improve an intelligent understanding of the scope of applying statistical techniques to the development of cost functions. The concept of regression analysis is that given the data of a dependent variable, say $Y$, and an independent variable, say $X$, it is always possible to build the linear relationship between the two as follows:

$$Y = a + bX + E,$$

where $Y$ is the dependent variable, $a$ is a constant which is the intercept in the graph against the $Y$ axis, $X$ is the value of the independent variable, $b$ is a coefficient, and $E$ is what is known as an error term which results in the scatter of the values of $Y$ with reference to the line provided by the equation. $E$ is a value which varies and the assumption is that its distribution is normal over its mean.

Let us illustrate this with a contractor's daily costs of road repair contained in Table A 12.1 (a). The contractor's task is to repair the potholes in the road and he is paid by the public works department on the basis of the number of potholes repaired. Some potholes are close to his headquarters and some are further away. The skills of his labourers vary from day to day.

**Table A 12.1 (a)**   Data of a Petty Road Repair Contractor

| Day number | Labour costs (₹) | Number of potholes repaired in the road |
|---|---|---|
| 1 | 1190 | 68 |
| 2 | 1211 | 88 |
| 3 | 1004 | 62 |
| 4 | 917 | 72 |
| 5 | 770 | 60 |
| 6 | 1456 | 96 |
| 7 | 1180 | 78 |
| 8 | 710 | 46 |
| 9 | 1316 | 82 |
| 10 | 1032 | 94 |
| 11 | 752 | 68 |
| 12 | 963 | 48 |

The mathematical approach to drawing the regression line is what is known as the least square technique. This means that the vertical difference between the actual value of $Y$ from the data and the predicted value based on the value of $X$ fed into the equation, should be minimized. Since the difference could be both positive and negative, it would be best if the differences are squared, i.e., $\Sigma (Y - y)^2$ is minimized, where $Y$ is the actual value of $Y$ and $y$ is the predicted cost of $Y$.

It can be shown by simple algebra that this would happen if

$$a = (\Sigma\ Y)\ (\Sigma\ X^2) - (\Sigma\ X)\ (\Sigma\ XY)/[n\ (\Sigma\ X^2) - (\Sigma\ X)\ (\Sigma\ X)]$$

and,
$$b = n\ (\Sigma\ XY) - (\Sigma\ X)\ (\Sigma\ Y)/[n\ (\Sigma\ X^2) - (\Sigma\ X)\ (\Sigma\ X)]$$

The value of $a$ and $b$ for the data we provided in Table A 12.1 would yield

$a = 300.98^*$, $b = 10.31$ which means that there is a daily fixed cost of ₹300.98 and variable cost per pothole of ₹10.31.

### Goodness of Fit

A regression equation can always be fitted between any two variables irrespective of whether the relationship is reliable or not. The reliability can be established only after computing the extent of the difference labelled as coefficient of determination $R^2$. This is computed by the following formula:

$$R^2 = 1 - \frac{\text{Unexplained variation}}{\text{Total variation}} = 1 - \left[\frac{(\Sigma Y - y)^2}{(\Sigma Y - \tilde{Y})^2}\right]$$

Where, $Y$ is the actual value of $Y$, $y$ is the predicted value of $Y$ and $\tilde{Y}$ is the average value of $Y$ in the 12 observations.

Applying this to the data, we get

$$R^2 = 1 - 290.824^{**}/607.699 = 0.52$$

It is clear that estimation is not absolutely perfect though the relationship is economically plausible but does not take into account the size of the potholes or the distance from the headquarters, the skill level of the workers, and the number of gangs employed. If we now try to use what is known as multiple regression or modify the independent variable to the area and depth of the potholes, and classify them as small, medium, and large sized portholes, and the distance travelled, or the number of gangs employed, one may improve the coefficient of determination. But the number of observations would have to be increased as the number of variables have increased. This brings us to the topic of the significance of the coefficients individually.

### Significance of the Coefficient of Independent Variables

This brings us to the subject described as $t$ values. The attempt is to be absolutely satisfied that the coefficients are certainly different from zero. This way of putting it is known by statisticians as null hypothesis that coefficient $b = 0$. It is possible through an algebraic exercise (Hildebrandt and Ott

---

\* $a = (12501)(64900) - (862)\ (928.716)/12(64900) - (862)^2 = 300.98$

And, $b = 12(928.716) - (862)(12501)/12(64900) - (862)^2 = 10.31$

\*\* $\Sigma X = 862\ \Sigma X^2 = 64900\ \Sigma Y = 12501\ \Sigma XY = 928716\ \Sigma Y = 12500\ \tilde{Y}$ average $= 1041.75$

1998) done very quickly and elegantly on a computer to see the 'standard error in both the constant figure and the coefficient'. This is automatically available in any computer statistical programme. Depending on the number of observations and the number of variables one can read a $t$ statistic table in any standard statistics book to see if the standard error has exceeded the limit with reference to the value of the coefficient. If the ratio of the coefficient and the standard error is higher than the prescribed $t$ value, it means that the variations are not so high as to make us accept the null hypothesis that the coefficient is likely to be equal to zero. The statistical tables would also show the probability of the coefficient being zero.

The data was as shown in Table A 12.1 (b)

**Table A 12.1 (b)**   Result of Regression Equation of Total Cost of a Petty Road Contractor

| Variable | Coefficient | Standard error | *t* value |
|---|---|---|---|
| Constant | 300.98 | 229.75 | 1.31 |
| Independent variable (number of potholes) | 10.31 | 3.12 | 3.30 |

One can see the cut off $t$ value as 2.28 in a statistical table. This means that whereas the coefficients showing the variable costs are reliable being above the cut off point of 2.28, the estimates of the constant are not. It may be recalled that the overall $R^2$ (0.52) was not high and the whole exercise is not absolutely reliable, even though economic plausibility was recognized and the total costs should obviously be relatable to the number of potholes repaired.

### Some Assumptions

Before we use the results of the regression equation, statistical theory requires one to make some assumptions which need to be verified:

1. Linearity within the range chosen—It is suggested that before we do the analysis on the computer one needs to plot the data on the graph sheet. Such a procedure is always recommended (Horngren et al. 2003). Non-linearity would come out clearly.

2. The second verification would be to see if the errors in the residuals have a tendency to crowd around some areas. Typically, the scatter graph in Fig. A 12.1 would show such a tendency of what is known as heteroscedasticity.

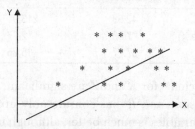

**Fig. A 12.1**   A case of heteroscedasticity

Heteroscedasticity will affect the precision with which inferences can be drawn.

3. It is assumed that residuals are normally distributed along the central line.

## Multiple Regression

We had mentioned earlier that the $R^2$ could possibly be improved by adding one more independent variable. Let us have a look at the additional data as in Table A 12.1 (c) The new data is regarding the number of gangs deployed.

**Table A 12.1 (c)**  Data of a Petty Road Repair Contractor

| Day number | Labour costs (₹) | Number of potholes repaired on the road | Number of gangs deployed |
|:---:|:---:|:---:|:---:|
| 1 | 1190 | 68 | 12 |
| 2 | 1211 | 88 | 15 |
| 3 | 1004 | 62 | 13 |
| 4 | 917 | 72 | 11 |
| 5 | 770 | 60 | 10 |
| 6 | 1456 | 96 | 12 |
| 7 | 1180 | 78 | 17 |
| 8 | 710 | 46 | 7 |
| 9 | 1316 | 82 | 14 |
| 10 | 1032 | 94 | 12 |
| 11 | 752 | 68 | 7 |
| 12 | 963 | 48 | 14 |

If we feed the data into a software programme on multiple linear regression, we would get a formula:

$$Y = 42.58 + 7.60\ X + 37.77\ Z$$

where $Y$ is total costs, $X$ is the number of potholes, and $Z$ is the number of gangs. $R^2$ is 0.72, a much more satisfactory result with two variables than the earlier one of 0.52 with one variable. Both variables have an economic plausibility, and cause and effect relationship. The $t$ test for the coefficients is as shown in Table A 12.1 (d).

**Table A 12.1 (d)**  Result of Regression Equation of Total Cost of a Petty Road Contractor with Number of Gangs Added to the Data

| Variable | Coefficient | Standard error | t value |
|:---|:---:|:---:|:---:|
| Constant C | 42.58 | 213.91 | 1.31 |
| Independent variable number of potholes (Variable X) | 7.60 | 2.77 | 2.74 |
| Number of gangs (Variable Z) | 37.77 | 15.25 | 2.48 |

One may notice that both the coefficients for $X$ and $Z$ are significant, being above the cut off point 2.28. Both are economically plausible and $R^2$ has considerably improved. Therefore, this second multivariate equation with two variables is much better, although unfortunately, the figure of the constant is still not reliable as its $t$ value is too low. The constant may as well be treated as zero.

## *Multicollinearity*

One may also have to see if the two variables are both features of the same phenomenon. If we draw a correlation coefficient between the number of potholes and the number of gangs, you would get a coefficient correlation of 0.4, i.e., that the two are also related to some extent but not too much. This means that both variables together would largely include the features not common between the two variables. If the correlation were high, say 0.70, it would affect the coefficients in the equation but would not affect the overall estimate of $Y$ in the equation.

## *Transforming Non-linear Equations into Linear Equations*

Software for non-linear regression equations exist in abundance. But one must be aware of the fact that many non-linear forms can also be transformed into linear equations. The advice of Hildebrandt and Ott (1998) is as follows:

1. If the plot indicates a relation that is increasing but at a decreasing rate, and if the variability around the curve is roughly constant, transform $X$ using square root, logarithm, or inverse transformation, i.e., $(1/X$ or $1/Y)$.

2. If the plot indicates that a relation is increasing at an increasing rate and variability is constant, use both $X$ and $X^2$ as predictors. This would involve multiple regressions, as there are two variables.

3. If the plot increases and then decreases, and the variability is constant, use $X$ and $X^2$, and the curve is like a sine curve.

4. If the plot indicates increasing at a decreasing rate and the curve increases as the value of $Y$ increases, use $Y^2$.

5. If the relationship increases at an increasing rate and variability around the curve increases, try ln $Y$ (logarithmic function). One can also use ln $X$ (logarithmic function) as has been done in Example 12.6 and Fig. 12.6 earlier in the chapter.

CHAPTER **13**

# Costing for Pricing Decisions

## Learning Objectives

After reading this chapter, you will be able to understand

- the economic origins of market prices
- the economic and production and pricing logic of individual firms
- the relevance of short-term and long-term costs for pricing
- the contours of the overall logic of costing and pricing, and its relation to the myriad pricing strategies which firms actually deploy

- the life cycle costs and pricing strategies
- the practice of yield management pricing emerging all over the world including in the Indian Railways
- the relevance of cost-volume-profit, relevant costing, and ABC to pricing strategies
- the laws and government regulations which hem in the choices in strategic pricing

## INTRODUCTION

Pricing is one of the critical functions of a marketing executive and its relationship to cost data is fundamental, whatever the strategy of pricing may be. As observed by Philip Kotler (2003), the doyen among professors of marketing at the Kellogg School of Management, pricing is one of the most flexible and easier tools for adapting a product to any situation; easier than the other attributes which need modification of the product design and production process. This chapter will explore the several ways in which pricing strategies use costing data. Care has been taken not to trivialize this relationship, as pricing is otherwise a subject which intricately and expertly combines economics, social and behavioural psychology, operations management, and cost accounting. No two pricing situations are alike.

Pricing issues have implicitly come up in the earlier chapters. But the more explicit treatment has been provided on negotiated administered prices in Chapter 5, on target pricing in Chapter 9, and short-term and special order pricing in Chapter 11 on relevant costing. These topics will be fitted into broader frameworks in this chapter.

Readers who want a more detailed account of pricing strategies will benefit by reading Chapter 16 of Kotler's (2003) book on marketing management.

## MODERATING ADAM SMITH'S INVISIBLE HAND

It is often said that pricing is not done by deliberate effort and that it is a result of the forces of supply and demand, which Adam Smith, the great economist of eighteenth-century Scotland, described colourfully as the 'invisible hand' (Samuelson and Nordhaus 1992). An old apocryphal story, i.e., a story whose veracity is not confirmed, adapted to Indian audiences, is as follows:

> Murugan, a fierce admirer of Valluvar, the Tamil author of Thirukural and a great calligrapher, decided that he would engrave the entire one thousand three hundred and thirty verses of the Thirukuaral on the head of a button. It took him ten years to do this. One could read his writing using a large microscope. He estimated that this had cost him ₹10 lakh. He offered it for sale but the most he could get for it was ₹10,000 simply because it was a novelty. The result was: cost ₹10 lakh, price ₹10,000.
>
> On the other hand, Muniandi and his wife Ramayi were huddled together in their hut on a terribly stormy night. When they awoke the morning, they found there had been a rainfall of gold in their vegetable kitchen garden. They gathered the gold in a big sack and took it to a goldsmith who said he could give them ₹10 lakh for it.
>
> The result was: cost zero, price ₹10 lakh. The economic moral is that price does not depend upon cost but on the pattern of supply and demand.

The contemporary modern problems in pricing are more complex and are not savagely inclined to the two extremes of the story—of rushing to massive costs without any thought of the market, or passively hoping that the market will reward those who make little or no effort. We will first get a simple overall economic logic of the entire mechanism of the formation of prices in the market, starting from Adam Smith. The later paragraphs will have the variegated patterns from real life.

**Adam Smith's invisible hand**
We need to moderate the invisible hand of Adam Smith with variable costing, relevant costing, ABC, and target costing.

The economic chain of causes for the formation of market prices will be brought out in four figures, namely Figs 13.1(a)–(d).

Let us explain the four figures. They attempt to integrate the seminal ideas of Adam Smith with the several instruments of cost analysis which we developed in Chapter 3 (variable costs), Chapter 6 (ABC), Chapter 9

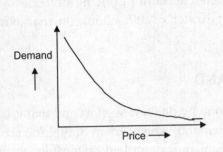

Fig. 13.1(a)   Demand curve

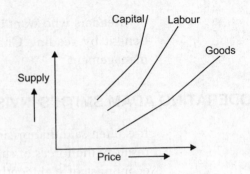

Fig. 13.1(b)   Supply curve

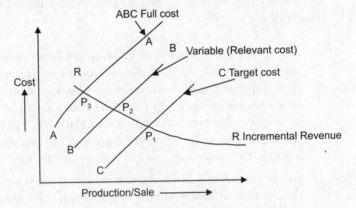

Fig. 13.1(c)   Optimum allocation of resources by supplier (producer)

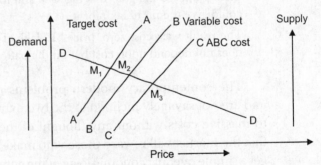

Fig. 13.1(d)   Market mechanism for price formation

(target costing), and Chapter 11 (relevant costing). The steps in the arguments are as follows:

1. Everybody has utility preferences among various goods and services including the choice between leisure and work, and supplying their own labour.

2. This preference can be expressed quantitatively as: X units of A is equal to Y units of B, etc.
3. If we convert the preference into a common unit of money, it can be called the price one is willing to pay.
4. This would indicate the quantities one would be willing to exchange at different prices.
5. Aggregating all the individual preferences as in points 1 to 4 into an aggregate for collection of human beings, one obtains the graphs as in Figs 13.1(a) and 13.1(b). These can be reliably tested by empirical experiments.
6. In Fig. 13.1(c) the analysis is for the collective, i.e., a collection of producers/sellers and buyers of goods and services.

The line RR shows that as the sale/production increases, the last unit will earn a lower amount than the average. Incremental revenue is reduced as society gets satiated with the product. The line BB indicates that the producers and suppliers of goods have some idle capacity and would be prepared to supply as long as the variable costs are equal to or more than the incremental revenue (Chapter 11 on relevant costs).

The line AA represents producers who have collectively come to the understanding that all costs are variable in the long run, and would pull out the product if the revenue is too little compared to their costs. They would do an accurate costing using ABC (Chapter 6) and come to a decision that ABC full cost needs to be covered in their prices. Note that they are pulling back on production moving westward, and not rushing in the way they do in line BB to the east of AA.

Good and positive entrepreneurs would, however, be looking for a technological breakthrough or cost reduction measure and will try to reduce their product costs working towards a target cost (Chapter 9). This may be accompanied by further investment and the average long-term costs would fall. The result would be line CC. The production is increased as the line CC is to the east of BB, and further away east from the line AA or the earlier unreduced ABC costs.

The phenomenon of the average long-term costs sometimes being lower than short-term variable costs is observed as an economic reality. As Hirshleifer (1985) puts it, 'The firm would rationally accept an increase in fixed costs, precisely because doing so is less costly (involves a more economical mix or proportion of various factors) than to expand output by increasing variable costs alone.'

7. The seventh step is arriving at Fig. 13.1(d). As prices in the X axis increase, the quantity demanded on Y axis will come down as a consequence of the behavioural phenomenon described in the earlier graphs. That is the line DD which is sloping downwards.

If the relevant costing and short-term consideration rules the mind (Chapter 11), the quantity will traverse along the lines BB, following the behaviour described in Fig. 13.1(c) (resign to our fate and cut down losses!).

But the moment the mindset becomes long-term and the rationality is that of ABC (Chapter 5), the trajectory will be the line CC (we cannot lose all the time!). Volumes will come down.

The third approach is one of aggressive cost reduction and target costing; the trajectory will shift to AA (we will conquer the world!).

In these three different behavioural patterns, the place where the demand line cuts the supply line is different. The points where they cut the incremental revenue line are the three market prices, $M_1$, $M_2$, and $M_3$.

$M_3 > M_2 > M_1$, i.e., the aggressive target costing approach typically of the Japanese (Horngren et al. 2003) can dramatically reduce the price ($M_1$) from the panicky reaction, typically in the US, using arguments of relevant costing ($M_2$) not to speak of an extreme passive approach born out of punctilious ABC system ($M_3$). The dramatic demonstration of this phenomenon was the fall in the price of computers and IT, and telephonic services all over the world. The discussion so far is on how market prices are determined collectively by the players in a free market without any of the players consciously making an effort. This is the magical invisible hand described earlier in the chapter.

This section on the social psychology (behavioural features) of collective decisions must be treated as a general description of trends. As we go along in the chapter, we will see that there could be several deviations from these trends which the practice of pricing needs to contend with, making it more contextual rather than merely normative.

## THREE C'S OF PRICING

An understanding of the collective consequences described in the previous paragraph should enable us, at this stage, to change gears and see how individual decisions on pricing need to be taken by individual firms. Before we get into specifics of strategies, we must recapitulate the bottom line of each firm's pricing strategy as described by Gerard Tellis (1986), the young professor from Iowa University, as 'a reasoned choice from a set of alternative choices (or price schedules) that aim at profit maximization within a planning period in response to alternate scenarios'.

To suggest a quick overall point of view, pricing by individual firms involves adequate consideration to the three C's of pricing (Kotler 2003):

1. Customer
2. Competition
3. Costs

The customers' behaviour are represented by the demand line typically as at Fig. 13.1(a) (Kotler 2003). This line for individual firms can be estimated by market research; there are several market research organizations that can do this work competently. But more than the final outcome as a graph, market research attempts to use qualitative information on what the customer needs and desires. Among the attributes would also be prices and the elasticity of demand towards prices as can be seen in Fig. 13.1(a). That is the change in demand $(D)$ with change in price $(P)$, i.e., $\Delta D \div \Delta P$.

The other important feature of the customer is to 'segment' them into homogeneous groups and broadly identify them into strategic categories which the famous Professor Porter of Harvard (Porter 1996) describes as an overall cost leadership strategy when the customer will be looking for standard products which are available at low costs. The differentiated strategies, on the other hand, will look for high quality premium priced products.

The process of further disaggregated homogenization of the customers will be dealt with later in this chapter. The taxonomy will be as developed by Tellis (1986). Customer value analysis (CVA) can be done as coming out of a formula:

Customer value = Customer benefits – Customer costs

Ford looked into this aspect in providing higher prices for their automobiles (Horngren 2003), which may have cost the customer higher initially, but would ultimately be cheaper as operation and maintenance costs would be lower.

Competitors, the second C, is to be studied as five forces described in another of Porter's (1985) well-known writings. They are as follows:

1. Threat of intense segment rivalry
2. Threat of new entrants
3. Threat of substitute products

**J&J**
Johnson and Johnson hopelessly failed in its strategy for pricing its stents for heart surgery as it failed to keep a tab on competitor's prices.

4. Threat of the buyer's growing bargaining power
5. Threat of one's own suppliers growing bargaining power

Competitors can be analysed in terms of their strategies, objectives, strengths and weaknesses, and reaction patterns.

Competitive intelligence systems, without its becoming industrial espionage attracting penal provisions of law covering the right to privacy, should be devised which could collect data that could be analysed in several ways, including customer value as described earlier.

Competition must be understood as strong versus weak, close versus distant, or good versus bad.

**Costs**
The varied concepts of costs used in product pricing are variable costs, ABC, target costs, lock-in costs, life cycle costs, etc.

One of the classic cases of a disaster was that of Johnson and Johnson, a well-known company which failed to keep track of the pricing strategy of the competitor for stents which are devices for heart surgery (Winslow 1998). A stent is a tiny scaffold used to prop the obstructed heart vessel. In just 37 months after introduction of this breakthrough device J&J tallied more than $1 billion sales, with more than 90 per cent of the market. In 1997 another company introduced a substitute and with a shrewd pricing strategy captured almost overnight 70 per cent of the market. The concern of the US health administration to keep medical costs low was reflected in their pricing strategy. Very soon J&J's share plummeted down to 8 per cent. It was a collapse of both the product design and the pricing strategy.

**Application of overheads**
Application of overheads to products for purpose of pricing strategies becomes reliable with increase in the number of overhead cost pools, each of which is homogeneous with respect to its chosen cost driver.

The last of the three C's, namely costs, have been dealt with earlier in the chapter as also in earlier chapters. We have shown the use of short-term variable and relevant costs, ABC for long-term costs, and the springboard it can provide for target costs. We have described the constraints on cost reduction potential due to a large part of the costs getting locked in at the time of design, and the need for being careful at the design stage. Later in the chapter we will describe the concept of life cycle costs of a product which may require a pricing strategy that could cater to the varying demand for the product over its life cycle.

Product cost data became richer and more accurate and reliable only with the application of overheads accumulated in several homogeneous cost pools.

## PRICING OBJECTIVES

The discussion so far has been on the prices which emerge collectively in an economy and the considerations of the three C's—consumer, competitor, and costs. An important parameter not discussed so far is that the nature

**Pricing objectives**
They may be sur-
vival, current profits,
market share, market
skimming, product
quality leadership,
and several other
objectives for non-
profit organizations
and public
institutions.

and situation of an organization, namely internally set objectives, would also play a part in it. Kotler (2003) suggests that business organizations 'pursue any of the five major pricing objectives through pricing: survival, maximum current profits, maximum market share, maximum market skimming, or product quality leadership'. The strategic choice may not just be an outcome of the autonomously evolved philosophy of the organization, but may also be determined by the situation of the business environment.

Survival may be critical if there is a strong possibility of organizational collapse.

Current profits may be important if there is a strong cash crunch. Market share may be important if the competitor is aggressively pursuing a policy of cornering the market.

Product quality leadership may be critical in industries where product quality is critical, say, for example, in surgical instruments, or aviation, or the space industry, etc.

As we will see later in this chapter, even business organizations may be subject to state regulations or straightforward price controls.

Apart from business and non-business, organizations may have different objectives. Educational institutions may have social objectives in addition to minimizing the need for external donations or government grants. Hospitals may like to support the poor and charge richer patients who could subsidize the poor. Public utilities and state run organizations may have social objectives in addition to ensuring that their customers are not made to bear the costs of inefficiency.

## WHO DECIDES THE PRICES?

**Cost plus mark-up**
It is the traditional
pricing strategy but is
still extensively used.

In most Indian organizations pricing is usually a decision of the top boss. Kotler (2003) says that this is the general practice all over the world. Even if there is delegation, prices are usually approved and endorsed ultimately by top level managers. In large companies with several products, a pricing department usually assists them, and reports to the marketing and finance departments. Others who influence the pricing decision are the production managers, finance managers, and accountants. In summary, pricing is done after consulting multi-disciplinary groups.

## ROLE OF THE THREE C'S IN VARIED PRICING STRATEGIES

In the following paragraphs we will get to see the role of the 3 C's in varied pricing strategies.

### Cost plus mark-up

The starting point of a pricing exercise is ranked number one in the US as against the Japanese practice of ranking market price as a starting point.

The costs could be variable manufacturing costs, variable costs, manufacturing costs, or full cost of the product. The mark-up is decided by an estimate of the investment for the product. Product-wise investment is often very difficult to get as many products use common assets. The mark-up also is adjusted depending on the costs included at the starting point. The pattern of mark-up could be as shown in Table 13.1.

**Table 13.1** Patterns of mark-up

| Cost base | Mark-up percentage (%) |
| --- | --- |
| Variable manufacturing costs | 65 |
| Variable costs | 45 |
| Manufacturing costs | 50 |
| Full cost of the product | 12 |

As demonstrated by Horngren (2003) varying mark-up percentages usually converge into similar end results, as the starting points are different.

Cost plus pricing is the traditional pricing strategy but however much it is repugnant to rationality, it is still largely followed. Many people may feel that cost plus pricing is fairer to both the buyer and the seller, and if all producers of goods and services use it, there is likely to be more stability in the markets (Kotler 2003).

### Negotiated or administrated prices and cost plus contracts

These are quite common in India as purchases by the government usually adopt this method which was pioneered by Muhammed Shoaib while he was in India. He later became the Finance Minister of Pakistan. This has been discussed in Chapter 1. All the prices are governed by agreed norms of costs.

### Price controls

Price controls, to a lesser or larger degree, exist all over the world, both in socialist and capitalist countries. All prices in price controls are generally cost plus-based decisions. According to the US Economic Intelligence Unit (*Wall Street Journal* 2006) price controls apply to some regulated monopolies in the US (utilities and the postal service), and certain states and localities control residential rents. Hawaii imposes caps on gasoline prices. The government also influences prices through subsidies, particularly for the agricultural sector, dairy products, and some forms of transportation. The federal government imposes a minimum wage. Canada has price controls on several commodities and more particularly on drugs. Drugs in Canada are therefore much cheaper than in the US (Francis 2005). India has extensive legislation for imposing price controls, such as the Essential Commodities Act, the Patents Act, the Industries Development and Regulation Act, etc. These will be dealt with in a later section covering legal controls on prices.

## Two-part tariffs of public utilities

Indian utilities, such as producers of electricity and suppliers of water, have a two-part tariff. One part is based on the assessment of facilities provided, and a second on the actual usage. Thus, power bills will have a fixed portion for the connected load and a second variable portion on the kilowatt hours (kWh) used. Sometimes the kWh use will have a minimum guarantee calculated on the connected load. This system enables the producers and users to optimize methods to plan loads and usage. The two parts are related to the cost structure of the producer, the fixed costs being related to the fixed charges and the variable costs to the variable charges.

## Differential pricing

Differential pricing means that the same product is priced differentially for different segments. Differential pricing must guard itself with a very sure cost logic which justifies the differentiation. Otherwise it will be caught in the web of law.

## Quantity discount

Differentiation on the basis of quantity is a way of pricing differentially for different segments. Thus, small lots of purchases are usually made by the poor while richer customers buy in bulk. Long distance passengers are usually rich, whereas short distance passengers have a higher proportion of the poor. Quantity discounts and telescopic rates used by the railways as a discount for long distance passengers is an income discriminator. But it could be justified in law if there is a corresponding cost advantage for the producer of the goods. Judicial pronouncements will be dealt with later in the chapter.

### Skimming

A skimming strategy is a strategy to increase prices when there is no competition for a new product and gradually bring it down as competition increases. This is again dealt with in life cycle pricing later in this chapter.

### Second market discounting

Generics (non-branded medicines), a secondary demographic segment, and some foreign markets provide opportunities. Often pioneering drug manufacturers are faced with competition from identical, much lower priced generics after the expiry of the patent. Such firms can sell generics at a heavy discount with benefits all around.

### Periodic discounting

This is extensively used in India, with the discounting taking place usually during festival seasons. Intuition suggests that even if the demand for the product is not exactly known, a strategy for pricing high and systematically discounting with time is likely to ensure that the firm covers up costs and makes a reasonable profit, but this may give it a bad image.

### Random discounting

We find random discounting when discounts come randomly. A firm should adopt a strategy of random discounts if the increased profit from new, informed customers who buy at discounted prices, exceeds the cost of informed buying plus the cost of administering the discount.

### Penetration pricing

Penetration pricing is a strategy to penetrate the market when there is competition. It is relevant only when the average cost does not exceed the minimum average selling price. The strategy can come to grief if it is legally shown to be predatory pricing, which will be discussed in the section on legal provisions, which hem in pricing options.

### Price signalling

Price is used as a signalling device, for example, as a proxy for quality. Here, it is presumed that the knowledge of the consumer is otherwise inadequate on quality. The purchase of any inferior quality brands at very high prices are regularly reported in consumer research journals (Tellis 1986).

**Geographical pricing**
Locations such as Silvassa with lower tax rates have a *de facto* potential for geographical pricing.

## Geographical pricing

Prices are different for different geographical reasons. If done within one country, one may get embroiled in a legal battle on discriminatory pricing. We will discuss this in another section of the chapter. But the greater problem is one of arbitrage and the resale of goods from one region to another. Such cross-selling happens profusely in India, as taxes and duties vary from state to state.

Organizations provide a sales point in states with lower tax rates as a feature of *de facto* geographical pricing. Silvassa, an enclave in Maharashtra, was a well-known haven for low taxes.

## Product line pricing

Products in the same line need to have a correlation in pricing as a marketing strategy.

## Price bundling

Bundling of complementary products could enhance consumer value and increase profit. But it must be carefully distinguished from tie-in arrangements which are illegal. This will be dealt with in another section.

## Premium pricing

Premium pricing strategy exploits consumer heterogeneity. Premium pricing applies to a large number of products in the market today. It follows the logic of differentiated products propounded by Porter (1996).

It is used in pricing durable goods, typically appliances for which multiple versions, each differing in prices, are marketed. A similar strategy is used for pricing of alternate service plans such as terms in insurance policies. A firm using premium strategy uses joint economies of scale and this enables it to jointly reap the benefits simultaneously, from the higher volumes enabled by the premium, as well as the ordinary brands.

Both premium pricing and price bundling may use joint economies of scale, but they are different because the former applies to substitutes and the latter to complements.

## Image pricing

By image pricing a firm brings out an identical version of its current product. The intention is to signal quality. The strategy is between price signalling and premium pricing. The demand patterns are similar in all the three strategies.

### Captive pricing

Captive pricing is seen where buying one item would make the consumer captive to a future stream of products. These cover razors and blades, cameras and film, autos and spares, sound and video systems, and compact video and audio discs, etc.

### Two-part pricing

If we buy a piece of equipment, there would be the possibility of a following maintenance contract. This is not the same as two-part tariff described earlier, for public utilities. Here, one part follows the other. The Trade Practices Act prohibits forcing the customer to the second leg of this pricing strategy. Thus, a customer must have the option to choose the maintenance contractor, independent of the original seller. This will also be dealt with in the section on law.

## LIFE CYCLE COSTING

Traditional costing techniques provide detailed cost data on a short term perspective, but the information provided is not adequate when the product development as well as the usage extend over a number of years. For example, a software company like Infosys may take a number of years to develop a product which may have a long life span. The costing techniques have to consider this longer time span to provide cost data in a proper perspective. Similarly, an automobile manufacturer like Maruti, Hyundai, or Tata Motors will have to make reasonable forecast of the amounts to be spent from the conception and design stage until the time the production is stopped, and after sales service is concluded. The pricing strategy has to be based on these details.

### Definition

Life cycle costing is the method of calculating costs incurred over the entire period of the product's life cycle. It has two sides namely the manufacturer's perspective and the customer's perspective. Hence it is sometimes referred to as the cost of ownership.

Let us consider the example of an engineering company which wants to introduce a new equipment for the Indian market. It expects that the R&D stage will take 18 months. The model will need a processing period of 6 months. The product launch and marketing will take another 6 months and the equipment can be marketed with minor modifications for 5 years. The projected costs are given in Table 13.2.

**Table 13.2**  Projected Cost (Figures in ₹ crore)

| Costs | Year 1 | Year 2 | Year 3 | Year 4 | Year 5 | Year 6 | Year 7 | Total |
|---|---|---|---|---|---|---|---|---|
| Research | 10 | 10 | | | | | | 20 |
| Development | 5 | 20 | | | | | | 25 |
| Concept design | | 5 | 10 | | | | | 15 |
| Manufacturing costs | | | 50 | 100 | 125 | 150 | 175 | 600 |
| Selling and marketing | | | 30 | 30 | 20 | 10 | 10 | 100 |
| After-sales service | | | | 10 | 10 | 15 | 15 | 50 |
| Profits | | | | | | | | 190 |
| Revenues | | | | | | | | 1000 |

The expected sales are 10,000 units of the Model I described above. At current prices the company expects to price it at ₹10 lakh. With some added features Model II can be priced at ₹15 lakhs, but only 8000 units can be sold at this price. The comparative analysis of the two models is given in Table 13.3.

**Table 13.3**  Comparative Analysis (Figures in ₹ crore)

| | Life cycle sales (units) | Life cycle costs | Life cycle revenue | Life cycle profits |
|---|---|---|---|---|
| Model I | 10,000 | 810 | 1,000 | 190 |
| Model II* | 8,000 | 1050 | 1,200 | 150 |

*Additional costs are involved for design and manufacturing

It could be seen that selling 10,000 units at ₹10 lakh is more profitable. However this is a tentative schedule of costs. As the time span is roughly 8 years it cannot be very accurate at the beginning. The figures need suitable improvisation at every subsequent stage.

**Need for discount**  In the above example, the figures are shown at current prices. Over a period of time the money value declines. There are standard discounting ratios which can be suitably applied.

**Customer life cycle costs**  The above example deals with life cycle costing from the manufacturer's perspective. The rule applies *mutatis mutandis* to customers also. Purchase of equipment, vehicles and all such items having medium to long term utility, require adoption of life cycle costing technique. A buyer of a car will have to not only consider the initial costs of investment in the car, but will have to look at various associated costs over the life time of the vehicle. This includes fuel costs, maintenance costs and spare parts. The Japanese cars could overtake the American models globally because of the higher fuel efficiency of their cars. At the time of growing petrol costs the buyers get concerned about the fuel economy and their purchase decisions are hence influenced by the 'mileage per litre' consideration. Thus the buyer would look at costs from two perspectives as under:

(a) Capital costs: Cost of equipment, initial installation training, and transportation

(b) Recurring costs: Periodic training of staff, maintenance costs, spare parts, loss due to production stoppages, and disposal (resale) costs

It is seen that the recurring costs can exceed the capital costs by a factor of 10 and above in the case of major equipment. In spite of this fact, overriding importance is attached to initial costs rather than the life time costs. The bureaucratic tendency of separating the buyer department and the user departments is a major factor responsible for this approach.

## Limitations

It is however, not easy to apply life cycle costing due to the following reasons:

1. Ascertainment of long term costs is often found to be very difficult. Many costs cannot be accurately forecast, while some future cost may not be even known

2. Technological defects cannot be planned adequately in advance.

3. The effective life cycle of a project depends upon marketing conditions and development of newer products by the competitors

4. Externalities: Legal stipulations can increase costs in chemical products; emission controls may require additional cost for introducing suitable changes; drugs undergo changes/withdrawals due to global regulations.

5. Political developments, trade restrictions, foreign exchange fluctuations can invalidate earlier cost calculations.

Both the product life cycle and customer life cycle are taken into consideration by the manufacturers. A typical example is the popularity of the fuel efficient cases in India. Many of the new buyers are those who are shifting from the two wheeler segment. This segment of buyers are used to lower fuel costs and hence prefer models which do not leak too much of money towards fuel costs. With vehicle loans becoming popular, the initial costs are not the sole consideration. The life cycle costs have become more relevant. This preference is further reinforced by the lack of adequate parking facilities in cities. Hence, the global automobile manufacturers are developing exclusive small car models for catering to the booming Indian market.

At the other end is the personal computer model, where the maintenance costs are relatively less hence the buyer is more influenced by the initial costs and the benefits offered in a particular model as compared to the rest.

## TARGET COSTING, LOCKED-IN COSTS, AND PRICING REVISITED

The concept of target costing, similar to that of life cycle costing, has to be long-term oriented. Since it is also vitally connected with setting cost standards and cost reductions, it has been dealt with in the chapter dealing with standards (Chapter 9). The additional emphasis on locked-in costing is intended to show that even a large part of the variable costs in Table 13.2 are already predetermined by the design chosen.

## YIELD MANAGEMENT—A NEW CONCEPT IN PRICING NON-INVENTORIABLE PRODUCTS

To quote Anjos, Cheng, and Curie (2005) of the Operations Research Group School of Mathematics, University of Southampton, 'In many industrial settings, managers face the problem of establishing pricing policy that maximizes the revenue from selling a given inventory of items by a fixed deadline, with the full inventory of items being available for sale from the beginning of the sale period. The problem arises in a variety of industries, including the sale of fashion garments, flight seats, and hotel rooms. These pricing functions are particularly well-suited for application in the context of an increasing role of the Internet as a means to market goods and services.'

Netessine of the Wharton School, and Shumsky of the University of Rochester (2002), focus on the 'yield' part of the subject title. The bottom line is that the pricing strategy 'ultimately optimizes the "yield" from a given investment in perishable goods or in service industries which cannot "store" and is therefore typical of many service industries.'

Kimes of Cornell University and Wirtz of the National University of Singapore (2003) call this entire concept one of revenue management, and summarize it very succinctly as 'setting prices according to predicted demand levels so that price sensitive customers who are willing to purchase at off-peak times will be able to do so, whereas price insensitive customers who want to consume at peak hours will also be able to do so.'

Netessine and Shumsky (2002) have spelt out five characteristics of business environments when yield management (YM) would be appropriate:

1. It is expensive or impossible to store excess resource (we cannot store tonight's room for use by tomorrow night's guest).
2. Commitments need to be made when future demand is uncertain (we must set aside rooms for business customers, i.e., 'protect' them from low-priced leisure travellers, before we know how many business customers will arrive).
3. The firm can differentiate among customer segments, and each segment has a different demand curve (purchase restrictions and refund ability requirements help to segment the market for leisure and business).
4. The same unit of capacity can be used to deliver many different products or services (rooms are essentially the same, whether used by business or leisure).
5. Producers are profit-oriented and have broad freedom for action (in the hotel industry withholding rooms from current customers for future profit is neither illegal nor immoral. On the other hand, such behaviour would be wrong when allocating organs for transplants).

Applying the above characteristics, there have been major applications in varied expanding fields in recent times.

The applications have been in the aviation, hotels, fruit and vegetables, railways, garments, and television industries. East Japan Railways dramatically increased their earnings using YM. European and British Railways extensively use YM and have increased their earnings tremendously. Lalu Prasad Yadav, the former Minister for Indian Railways, dramatically announced that wait-listed passengers could get vacant, higher accommodation without any increased charge. It saved the railways the cost of refund and did not increase their relevant costs in anyway. The American Airlines report an increase in earnings of $500 million, and the Delta Airlines of $300 million per year. The television industry uses it for reserving slots for unplanned television advertisements rushed in at the last minute. The way it is all done is by using probability statistics.

The crux of the treatment is prices, which discriminates between those who cannot wait and those who can. Thus, vegetables bought late in the evening can be sold at dirt cheap prices to save storage and waste disposal costs. Garments getting out of fashion can be sold at ridiculously low prices at the end of the season. Restaurants can have exclusive tables which are reserved for the elite and which can be allotted 'at the last minute' at ordinary

**Applications of yield management** The dramatic announcement of a Republic Day (2006) gift by Lalu Yadav of automatic allotment of vacancies in higher class to lower class wait-list ticket holders without extra charge is a typical yield management decision, hugely beneficial both to the railways and the customers.

**YM strategy**
Overbooking by airlines is a typical YM strategy but like many other YM strategies may cause customer wrath.

rates when the elite, willing to pay high charges, do not turn up in required numbers at the right time.

Airlines can overbook passengers with confirmed tickets, taking a risk that if they do not turn up, the aircraft can accommodate those who do. However, if they all turn up, they will have to pay penalty to passengers for not providing a seat and incur customer wrath.

But does all this sound unprofessional, opportunistic, and manipulatory? Kimes and Wirtz (2003) based on their customer surveys in Singapore say that not all such acts result in customer dissatisfaction although some definitely do.

## APPLICATION OF YIELD ALGORITHM IN HOTEL INDUSTRY

The yield algorithms can be explained in relation to a hotel and a vegetable vendor shop. A hotel having 210 rooms can sell out all its rooms to leisure travellers at a daily charge of ₹1050. This can be done even a long time before the day of occupation. But it could reserve some rooms for the business class and charge them ₹1590. However, this class arrives unexpectedly and if one has to get the benefit of this higher charge, one will have to 'protect' some rooms from the leisure class for this purpose. The quality of service is the same in both categories. If we protect too many rooms we will lose out on the revenues from the leisure class residents, but if we protect too little, we may lose on account of not getting the higher tariff from the business class. How do we decide on how much to protect? The statistically optimum number will be when the opportunity costs lost by the reservation is exactly equal to the probability of increased revenue by accommodating the leisure class (Belobaba 1989).

Let us examine the empirical data in demand for rooms by the business class in Table 13.4.

As a generalized description, let $Q$ be the accommodation demanded. This is a random variable whose cumulative frequency is $F(Q)$. If $Q^*$ is the optimum reservation, the revenue lost by reservation is that which would have come in the frequency $[1 - F(Q)]$. The revenue gained would be the same frequency.

$$1 - F(Q) \, (1590) \leq 1050$$
$$F(Q) = (1590 - 1050) = 0.339$$

**Table 13.4** Historical Demand for Rooms

| Demand for rooms (Q) | Days with that demand | Cumulative probability frequency F (Q) |
|---|---|---|
| 0–70 | 12 | 0.098 |
| 71 | 3 | 0.122 |
| 72 | 3 | 0.146 |
| 73 | 2 | 0.163 |
| 74 | 0 | 0.163 |
| 75 | 4 | 0.195 |
| 76 | 4 | 0.228 |
| 77 | 5 | 0.268 |
| 78 | 2 | 0.285 |
| **79*** | **7** | **0.341** |
| 80 | 4 | 0.374 |
| 81 | 10 | 0.445 |
| 82 | 13 | 0.561 |
| 83 | 12 | 0.659 |
| 84 | 4 | 0.691 |
| 85 | 9 | 0.764 |
| 86 | 10 | 0.846 |
| Above 86 | 19 | 1.00 |
| **Total** | **123** | **1.00** |

Table 13.4 shows that $Q^*$ is 79 rooms and corresponds to the cumulative frequency 0.341. That is, if we protect 79 rooms we can provide $210 - 79 = 131$ rooms for the leisure class. This will be the optimum reservation.

But imagine a situation when, on a particular day 79 rooms were protected, but we had one unoccupied room, as the business class person did not arrive. If our judgement is that she will not arrive, we can discard our statistical data and decide to give the room to the leisure class even at the lower rate.

Suppose we are still not sure if the business class guest would come, but if a leisure class person is willing to pay the higher rate, our decision will depend upon our concern for customer relationship with the business class who are the richer clients. More importantly, whatever be our standing rule that the reservation of 79 rooms till the cut off time would continue to be statistically valid, a decision taken on the event of one day cannot change the statistical prediction. In future, if the frequency mentioned in the data is changed due to further arrival of data, we would have to change our strategy.

And lastly, the risk associated with the use of the data also depends on the standard deviation of the number of days and the coefficient of dispersion being standard deviation/mean. The higher the coefficient of dispersion, the greater is the risk of using the data.

## Application to Airlines

The same logic would be applicable for business class reservations in airlines vis a vis economy class.

A variation of the algorithm could be easily adapted if Internet data of last minute prices from other competing airlines are available. Using the same logic used in the analysis but substituting the new rates of lower fare, we can rework our strategy. This can be done easily using computer software.

Another application to the airline is the decision to overbook. Netessine and Shumsky (2002) have shown that typically if the airline has 210 seats and the average drop out of confirmed passengers is 20, the standard deviation is 10, $B$ is the opportunity cost of running an empty seat, and $C$ is the penalty of not providing accommodation for a confirmed seat, the critical ratio is as follows:

$$B/(B + C) = 105/(300 + 105) = 0.2592$$

Taking the standard deviation into account, the overbooking which may be permitted is the following:

$$20 - (0.645^* \times 10) = 13.5 \text{ or } 14$$

That is, the airlines can book 224 (210 + 14) seats and may be able to sail through without severe damage.

## Application to Mother Dairy Vegetable and Fruit Shop

Lastly, let us see the adaptation of the algorithm to a vegetable booth, typically run by Mother Dairy in India. Let us take a situation where tomatoes are bulk purchased by Mother Dairy and sold at ₹10 per kg from the morning till, say, 8.30 pm, when regular customers start dwindling. But the poor slum dwellers wait for the prices to be lowered. At ₹5 per kg the entire stock can be sold out in five minutes. But unfortunately some odd customer who is willing to pay ₹10 per kilo may turn up after 9 pm. If one does keep some stock for such a customer and she does not turn up, the balance left has to be thrown away as the slum dwellers would not also return to the booth. How many kgs of tomato should be reserved for the upper classes?

Note: *The figure 0.645 can be obtained by seeing the statistical tables for normal distribution against the figure of 0.2592.

The first step is to construct a frequency table of sales after 8.30 pm as shown in Table 13.5.

**Table 13.5** Frequency Table of Upper Class Customers in a Mother Dairy Booth after 8.30 pm

| Demand in kgs | Number of days | Cumulative frequency |
|---|---|---|
| 0–5 kg | 10 | 0.192 |
| 6 | 10 | 0.38 |
| **7 Q*** | **6** | **0.50** |
| 8 | 10 | 0.69 |
| 9 | 5 | 0.79 |
| 10 | 5 | 0.88 |
| 11 | 3 | 0.94 |
| 12 | 1 | 0.96 |
| 13 and above | 2 | 1.00 |
| **Total** | **52** | **1.00** |

By applying the logic developed earlier, we should keep 7 kgs as reserved for the upper classes, which corresponds to a cumulative frequency of 0.5, computed as (10 – 5)/10. If the discount price is reduced, the reserve stock for upper classes will go up (say, (10 – 3)/10 – 070, which means 8 kgs). Similarly, if the number of days' demand for higher weights go up, we will keep larger stocks to meet the demand of the richer classes, as the cut off point 0.50 will get marked at a higher reserve stock. If on the other hand, the demand for the upper classes had been very low even before 8.30 pm, it may be possible for the manager to rework the demand pattern likely after 8.30 and the stocks to be kept. This can also be worked out in a computer programme.

## LAWS AND GOVERNMENT REGULATIONS THAT HEM PRICING OPTIONS

We have noted that many pricing strategies may not be countenanced by law if they are taken to the extreme of customer manipulation or snuffing out competition. We must also have seen that several governments in the world do not like a total free play of market forces, and total freedom to the producers in fixing prices. They also sometimes take the proactive step of having price controls.

This section is a brief resume of these, in respect of India, with some allusions to international situations (www.taxguru.in).

The MRTP Act in India has been annulled and is replaced by the Competition Act 2002, with effect from September 1, 2009. This was notified by The Ministry of Corporate Affairs, Government of India by a notification dated 28 August 2009.

The most important laws which empower the government to control prices are the Essential Commodities Act (Section 3), Industries (development and regulation) Act (Section 18g), the Patents Act (Section 84), and the Electricity Act (Section 178).

We will get the reader to savour the legal environment by providing extracts from two of the legislations, namely, the Competition Act and the Essential Commodities Act, and describe cases from the Competition Act, with a description of the processes followed to establish drug prices under the Essential Commodities Act. A fuller understanding of the subject would need a more detailed perusal of texts and cases in the related laws.

Here are the extracts from the Competition Act.

## CHAPTER II of Competition Act 2002*
## Prohibition of Certain Agreements, Abuse of Dominant Position and Regulation of Combinations

### 3. Anti-competitive Agreements

(1) No enterprise or association of enterprises, or person or association of persons, shall enter into any agreement in respect of production, supply, distribution, storage, acquisition, or control of goods or provision of services, which causes or is likely to cause, an appreciable adverse effect on competition within India.

(2) Any agreement entered into in contravention of the provisions contained in sub-section (7) shall be void.

(3) Any agreement entered into between enterprises or associations of enterprises, or persons or associations of persons, or between any person and enterprise or practice carried on, or decision taken by any association of enterprises or association of persons, including cartels, engaged in identical or similar trade of goods or provision of services, which:

    (a) directly or indirectly determines purchase or sale prices

    (b) limits or controls production, supply, markets, technical development, investment, or provision of services

    (c) shares the market, or source of production, or provision of services by way of allocation of geographical area of market, or type of

---

* Adapted from http://www.netlawman.co.in/acts/competition-act.php

goods or services, or number of customers in the market, or any other similar way

(d) directly or indirectly results in bid rigging or collusive bidding, shall be presumed to have an appreciable adverse effect on competition:

Provided that nothing contained in this sub-section shall apply to any agreement entered into by way of joint ventures if such agreement increases efficiency in production, supply, distribution, storage, acquisition, or control of goods or provision of services. Explanation: For the purposes of this sub-section, 'bid rigging' means any agreement between enterprises or persons referred to in sub-section (3), engaged in identical or similar production, or trading of goods or provision of services, which has the effect of eliminating or reducing competition for bids, or adversely affecting or manipulating the process for bidding.

(4) Any agreement amongst enterprises or persons at different stages or levels of the production chain in different markets, in respect of production, supply, distribution, storage, sale or price of, or trade in goods or provision of services, including:

(a) tie-in arrangement

(b) exclusive supply agreement

(c) exclusive distribution agreement

(d) refusal to deal

(e) resale price maintenance,

shall be an agreement in contravention of sub-section (1) if such agreement causes or is likely to cause an appreciable adverse effect on competition in India. Explanation: For the purposes of this sub-section,

(a) 'tie-in arrangement' includes any agreement requiring a purchaser of goods, as a condition of such purchase, to purchase some other goods

(b) 'exclusive supply agreement' includes any agreement restricting in any manner the purchaser in the course of his trade from acquiring or otherwise dealing in any goods other than those of the seller or any other person

(c) 'exclusive distribution agreement' includes any agreement to limit, restrict, or withhold the output or supply of any goods, or allocate any area or market for the disposal or sale of the goods

(d) 'refusal to deal' includes any agreement which restricts, or is likely to restrict, by any method, the persons or classes of persons to whom goods are sold, or from whom goods are bought

(e) 'resale price maintenance' includes any agreement to sell goods on condition that the prices to be charged on the resale by the purchaser shall be the prices stipulated by the seller unless it is clearly stated that prices lower than those prices may be charged.

(5) Nothing contained in this section shall restrict:

(i) the right of any person to restrain any infringement of, or to impose reasonable conditions, as may be necessary for protecting any of his rights which have been or may be conferred upon him under:

(a) the Copyright Act, 1957 (14 of 1957)

(b) the Patents Act, 1970 (39 of 1970)

(c) the Trade and Merchandise Marks Act, 1958 (43 of 1958), or the Trade Marks Act, 1999 (47 of 1999)

(d) the Geographical Indications of Goods (Registration and Protection) Act, 1999 (48 of 1999)

(e) the Designs Act, 2000 (16 of 2000)

(f) the Semi-conductor Integrated Circuits Layout-Design Act, 2000 (37 of 2000)

(ii) the right of any person to export goods from India to the extent to which the agreement relates exclusively to the production, supply, distribution, or control of goods or provision of services for such export.

## 4. Abuse of dominant position

(1) No enterprise shall abuse its dominant position.

(2) There shall be an abuse of dominant position under sub-section (1) if an enterprise:

(a) directly or indirectly, imposes unfair or discriminatory–

(i) conditions in purchase or sale of goods or service; or

(ii) price in purchase or sale (including predatory price) of goods or service.

*Explanation:* For the purposes of this clause, the unfair or discriminatory condition in purchase or sale of goods or service referred to in sub-clause (i) and unfair or discriminatory price in purchase or sale of goods (including predatory price) or service, referred to in sub-clause (ii), shall not include such discriminatory condition or price which may be adopted to meet the competition; or

(b) limits or restricts–

(i) production of goods or provision of services or market there for; or

(ii) technical or scientific development relating to goods or services to the prejudice of consumers; or

(c) indulges in practice or practices resulting in denial of market access; or

(d) makes conclusion of contracts subject to acceptance by other parties of supplementary obligations which, by their nature or according to commercial usage, have no connection with the subject of such contracts; or

(e) uses its dominant position in one relevant market to enter into, or protect, another relevant market.

*Explanation:* For the purposes of this section, the expression:

(a) 'dominant position' means a position of strength enjoyed by an enterprise in the relevant market in India, which enables it to—

    (i) operate independently of competitive forces prevailing in the relevant market; or

    (ii) affects its competitors or consumers, or the relevant market in its favour;

(b) 'predatory price' means the sale of goods or provision of services, at a price which is below the cost, as may be determined by regulations, of production of the goods or provision of services, with a view to reduce competition or eliminate the competitors.

*The Essential Commodities Act, 1955*

The following is an extract from Section 2 of the Essential Commodities Act.

(a) 'essential commodity' means any of the following classes of commodities:

    (i) cattle fodder, including oilcakes and other concentrates

    (ii) coal, including coke and other derivatives

    (iii) component parts and accessories of automobiles

    (iv) cotton and woollen textiles

(iva) drugs

*Explanation:* In this sub-clause, 'drugs' has the meaning assigned to it in clause (b) of section 3 of the Drugs and Cosmetics Act, 1940 (23 of 1940).

    (v) foodstuffs, including edible oilseeds and oils

    (vi) iron and steel, including manufactured products of iron and steel

    (vii) paper, including newsprint, paperboard, and straw board

    (viii) petroleum and petroleum products

    (ix) raw cotton, whether ginned or unginned, and cotton seed

       (x) raw jute

      (xi) any other class of commodity which the central government may, by notified order, declare to be an essential commodity for the purposes of this Act, being a commodity with respect to which Parliament has power to make laws by virtue of entry 33 in list 111 in the seventh schedule to the Constitution.

(b) 'Food crops' include crops of sugarcane.

## The Essence Emerging from These Extracts of Law

The essential purpose of the Commodities Act is to encourage competition unlike the MRTP Act which it supersedes. One of the most critical differences is that the Commodities Act has no provision for curbing 'monopolistic prices' which give the producers super profits. But the MRTP Act had one. Thereby, it hopes to ultimately support the consumer. The MRTP Act, on the other hand, emphasized controlling the competitor and directly encouraging consumer protection.

The Essential Commodities Act would directly provide consumer protection by controlling the prices. Thus, drug price control is a part of public policy, as it is in many countries of the world, excluding the US.

We will understand the nuances of the law if we get acquainted with some decided cases under the captions available in the Competition Act. We had referred to these provisions earlier in the text when dealing with strategies.

### Tie-in Arrangement (Section 4a of the Competition Act)

A tie-in arrangement is one in which a purchaser of goods is required as a condition of the purchase to buy some other good or service. It seems dangerously close to some of the strategies we have described earlier in the text. These have been extensively struck down in Indian and foreign law. One typical case is that of Voltas (RTPE 84 of 1975), whose condition that the guarantee for a refrigerator would be available only if maintenance was done with the authorized dealer was struck down.

Similarly, *The Statesman* (RTPE 53 of 1975) was directed to desist from forcing an advertiser to advertise in all their editions, and was required to have separate advertisements for its individual editions. But the judicial decisions sometimes accepted this combined advertising as in the case of Bennett Coleman (RTPE 57 of 1975) for their *Indrajal* comics. The acid test applied was if competition was affected. As would be obvious, the judgment in this is quite intricate and a broad brush view would not work.

### Collusive Bidding (Section 4d of the Competition Act)

Collusion happens when different producers, traders of identical or similar goods, or provision of services collude to eliminate competition.

Kasturi & Sons and *The Indian Express,* Madurai (RTPE 47 of 1975), *The Statesman,* and *Ananda Bazar Patrika* and *Amrit Bazar Patrika* (RTPE 49 of 1975), and Bennett Coleman/Indian National Press/*The Indian Express* (RTPE 46 of 1975) were restrained from acting in concert.

### Resale Price Maintenance (Section 4e of the Competition Act)

The condition of resale price maintenance is the most frequent legal hassle. If a producer sells his/her goods to his/her dealer and tells him he/she cannot sell it for less than the list price, it would be illegal, as it interferes with competition. He/she is well within his legal rights to have a ceiling on the price, but not a floor. We had mentioned that one of the pricing strategies was to signal quality through prices. This will be the consequence of such a strategy. However, the law comes down heavily on this. There are extensive cases of this; two such instances were American Universal Electric (RTPE 7 of 972) and the dealers of Ambassador cars at Delhi (RTPE 2 of 1975).

### Predatory Practice (Explanation (ii)b under Section 4 of the Competition Act)

Predatory pricing is selling at below costs in order to eliminate competition. Distinguishing between competitive pricing and predatory pricing has been a continuous problem. In India, the judiciary is inclined to reject such accusations (Venkatesh 2004). The former helps competition, whereas the latter is intended to destroy it. As Calvani (1999) observes, from earlier knee jerk reactions the US judiciary has now acquired a balance and maturity. In India, the judiciary has been chary of admitting any case of predatory pricing. In two cases, Johnson and Johnson (RTPE 59 1985) and All-India Float Glass Manufacturer's Association versus Haridas Exports (SC 1739 2002), courts took the view that the case was in the description of competitive pricing rather than predatory pricing.

### Discriminatory Price (Explanation under Section 4 of the Competition Act)

The meaning of this is quite clear and there are cases galore in India. These are too numerous to be listed here. They have revolved around indiscriminate discounts and bulk discounts and the judiciary has been severe on this. Typical was the case of Grindwell Norton (RTPE 29 of 1974) who gave a four slab quantity discount to its customers, but they could not reconcile it with its cost advantages. Discounts just to capture markets are not permitted though the strategies we have described in the text may strike one as appropriate. It was struck down.

### Monopolistic Trade Practices—Fixation of too High a Price Making Super Profits

The issue is soon to become irrelevant. As mentioned earlier, the Competition Act does not cover monopolistic prices. Even earlier, when the MRTP Act provided an opening for this situation, the judiciary was unwilling to penalize super profits. Thus, even though Cadbury, Colgate, and Coca Cola were shown to be making nearly 45 per cent profit on cost of sales and nearly 50 per cent on capital employed, the Delhi High Court refused to entertain any complaint against them (Reference No. 2 of 974 and Delhi High Court order dated 13 December 1979).

### The Drug Control Act

Considering the extensive impact of drug prices on health administration on the one hand, and the economics and healthy growth of drug industry on the other, the processes of fixing drug prices are as elaborate as they try to be transparent. The National Pharmaceutical Pricing Authority (NPPA) provides a detailed exercise to fix drug prices. It includes a 22 per cent return on capital employed or 14 per cent on net worth. It provides a formula which includes
(a) Material costs
(b) Conversion cost
(c) Packing costs
(d) Excise duty
(e) Other quality costs
The Act empowers special power to exempt any manufacturer from the operation of the above provisions. Exports are not covered by these orders.

Judicial pronouncements emphasize the need for transparency in the processes. This was made explicit in the case of the Secretary, Ministry of Chemicals and Fertilizers, Government of India versus Messrs Cipla Ltd (SC 570 2003).

---

### Example 13.1  Costing for Profit Calculation

---

Dhoot Ltd sold 1000 vacuum cleaners in 2009 at a price of ₹1500 each. The cost structure of vacuum cleaners is as follows:

| | |
|---|---|
| Materials | ₹500 |
| Labour | ₹200 |
| Variable cost | ₹150 |
| Marginal cost | ₹850 |
| Factory overhead (fixed) | ₹300 |
| Total cost | ₹1150 |
| Profit | ₹350 |
| Price | ₹1500 |

Due to heavy competition in 2010, price has to be reduced to ₹1400 for the coming year. Assuming no change in costs, what should be the number of vacuum cleaners that would have to be sold at the new price to ensure the same amount of profit as that of 2009?

Here,

Fixed cost for 1000 vacuum cleaners = ₹300 x 1000 = ₹3,00,000

| | | |
|---|---|---|
| Profit on the sales of 1000 vacuum cleaners | ₹3,50,000 | ₹350 x 1000 |
| New reduced sales price (a) | | ₹1400 |
| Less material | ₹500 ⎫ | |
| Less labour | ₹200 ⎬ ₹850 | |
| Variable cost | ₹150 ⎭ | |
| Marginal cost (b) | | ₹850 |
| Contribution per unit (a – b) | | ₹550 |

No. of units to be sold in order to earn same profit as that of year 2009 can be calculated as follows:

$$\text{No. of units sold} = \frac{\text{Profit on the sales} + \text{Fixed cost}}{\text{Contribution per unit}}$$

$$= \frac{₹3,50,000 + ₹3,00,000}{₹550} = 1182 \text{ vacuum cleaners}$$

Verification:

Profit on sales = Sales – Marginal cost – Fixed cost
= (1182 x 1400) – (550 x 1182) – (300 x 1000)
= ₹3,50,000

## Example 13.2 Costing for Pricing Decisions

An electric appliance company decides to manufacture 1,00,000 electric irons in 2010. In a meeting, the marketing manager makes a proposal of using full cost method in fixing the selling price for each electric iron. He also suggests a profit margin of 25% of total cost.

| | |
|---|---|
| Variable cost per iron | ₹1000 |
| **Fixed cost** | **60,00,000** |
| **Profit margin** | **25%** |

The finance manager disagrees with the proposal made by the marketing manager. He presents the following information depicting the elasticity of price which portrays that iron is an elastic product. With increase in price, the quantity demanded for iron decreases. Demand elasticity of iron is shown in Fig. 13.2.

| Price per unit (₹) | Demand (units) |
|---|---|
| 1800 | 8000 |
| 2000 | 7000 |
| 2200 | 6000 |
| 2400 | 5000 |
| **2600** | **4000** |

Which proposal is useful for the company?

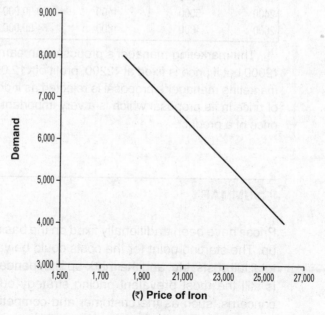

**Fig. 13.2** Demand elasticity of iron

1. Marketing Manager Proposal A

| | |
|---|---|
| Variable cost per unit (a) | ₹1,000 |
| Fixed cost per unit (b) | ₹600 |
| Total (a + b) = c | ₹1,600 |
| Profit margin (d) | ₹400 |
| Selling price (c + d) | ₹2,000 |
| No. of units to be sold at ₹2,000 | 7000 |
| Total contribution | ₹70,00,000 |
| Less fixed cost | ₹60, 00,000 |
| **Net profit** | **₹10,00,000** |

Net profit = ₹10,00,000

2. Finance Manager Proposal B

Profitability statement at different selling prices:

| Selling price (a) (₹) | Units demanded (b) (₹) | Contribution (selling price – variable cost 1,000) (c) (₹) | Total contribution (b) × (c) = (d) (₹) | Fixed cost (e) (₹) | Net profit (d) – (e) (₹) |
|---|---|---|---|---|---|
| 1800 | 8000 | 800 | 64,00,000 | 60,00,000 | 4,00,000 |
| 2000 | 7000 | 1000 | 70,00,000 | 60,00,000 | 10,00,000 |
| 2200 | 6000 | 1200 | 72,00,000 | 60,00,000 | 12,00,000 |
| 2400 | 5000 | 1400 | 70,00,000 | 60,00,000 | 10,00,000 |
| 2600 | 4000 | 1600 | 64,00,000 | 60,00,000 | 4,00,000 |

The marketing manager's proposal can earn profit of ₹10,00,000 at price ₹2000 but if price is fixed at ₹2200, profit of ₹12,00,000 can be earned. So, the marketing manager's proposal is rejected as it does not consider the elasticity of price in its proposal which is a very important factor while fixing the selling price of a product.

## SUMMARY

Prices have been traditionally fixed on the basis of costs plus desired mark-up. The starting point for the costs could be variable, fixed manufacturing, total full costs, etc. and the mark-up is dependent on this. Cost plus strategy is still the most prevalent pricing strategy but there is a variety of other concerns, such as the customer and competition. These, therefore, form myriad sub-strategies. At the core of all strategies is customer segmentation and addressing the strategies to a specific homogeneous customer population, and in the process benefiting both the buyer and the seller. The most dramatic recent developments in pricing strategies are those that could be covered by the term yield management which uses statistical tools to have discriminate pricing between those who cannot wait and those who can. The hemming in of all pricing strategies by law, which on the one hand protects customers and on the other, encourages competition, is a more recent development in India. Price controls exist for socially critical commodities all over the world and are more widely prevalent in India.

## KEY POINTS

- Pricing is one of the most flexible tools to adapt a product to a customer.
- Market prices are determined by the point where the demand curve cuts the supply curve.
- Pricing strategy is a reasoned choice of a set of alternative choices that aim at profit maximization within a planning period in response to alternative scenarios.
- Strategies attempt to segment customers and address the task of mutual satisfaction of the seller and the buyer. These strategies use cost analysis of the producer as also customer value.
- Customer value = Customer benefits – Customer costs.
- Strategies can range from premium prices to large discounts over the life cycle of the product.
- When the customer is veiled with an information haze, price can signal quality but often only deceptively.
- Yield management (YM) is a statistical technique to decide the price discrimination between different classes of customers who consume perishable goods that cannot be inventoried.
- YM is sometimes perceived as manipulatory and undesirable.
- There are extensive laws in India and abroad, which hem in pricing strategies to ensure competition and customer protection.

## CONCEPT REVIEW QUESTIONS

1. What are the three C's in a pricing decision?
2. Why are prices based on cost plus desired mark-up the most prevalent pricing strategy?
3. What are the factors that influence the mark-up in the prices?
4. Give two examples of pricing with a short-term focus.

5. How is ABC analysis used for pricing?
6. What is the nature of target costs and target prices?
7. Explain locked-in costs.
8. Explain life cycle costs and prices.
9. What is skimming strategy in pricing?
10. Indicate the status of law on predatory pricing in India.
11. Is making super profit prohibited under Indian law?
12. What does the Indian judiciary consider the most important feature of fixing controlled prices?
13. Competition, and not the competitor, is the current focus of Indian law. True or false?
14. Indicate two situations where yield management would destroy a good customer relationship.

## NUMERICAL PROBLEMS

### 1. Cannanore Brand Shoes

The Cannanore brand of sports shoes (CBS) was designed by a graduate of the National School of Design, and had caught the imagination of the Indian public. They produce 10,000 shoes per year. Their variable cost per shoe is as follows:

| | | |
|---|---|---|
| Direct material | = | ₹150 |
| Direct manufacturing labour | = | ₹80 |
| Variable manufacturing labour | = | ₹70 |
| Fixed manufacturing overhead | = | ₹100 |
| Total | = | ₹400 |

CBS is sold at ₹500 per shoe. Of this a commission of 5 per cent is paid (i.e., ₹25 per shoe). An amount of ₹6,50,000 is spent each year on fixed marketing costs.

CBS is approached by the defence ministry for purchase of 1000 shoes but they have considered alternate suppliers and said they could not pay more than ₹380 per shoe.

CBS has spare capacity. The defence ministry says that after their sportsman try this out, they can suggest to the authorities that they should be willing to pay the market price.

No marketing costs are involved in this sale.

## Question

1.1  What are the considerations that CBS should consider before agreeing to this one-time offer?

## 2. Susruta Surgicals—Target Pricing

Susruta Surgicals manufactures well-regarded surgical equipment. It has one direct cost category (direct material) and three indirect cost categories. But there are pressures on the company to reduce its costs and prices. In early 2005, it took steps to reduce its costs by 10 per cent. Its indirect costs in 2004 and 2005 are shown in Table P2(a), and its direct costs and other manufacturing details in P2(b).

**Table P2(a)**  Indirect Costs (2004–05)

| | 2004 | 2005 |
|---|---|---|
| Set up production order and materials handling cost per batch | ₹80,000 | ₹75,000 |
| Total manufacturing costs per machine hour | ₹550 | ₹500 |
| Cost per engineering change | ₹1,20,000 | ₹1,00,000 |

**Table P2(b)**  Direct Costs (2004–05)

| | 2004 | 2005 |
|---|---|---|
| Units produced | 3500 | 4000 |
| Direct material cost per unit | ₹12,000 | ₹11,000 |
| Number of batches for production | 70 | 80 |
| Machine hours used | 21,000 | 22,000 |
| Number of engineering changes | 14 | 10 |

## Questions

2.1  Calculate the manufacturing cost of the product in 2004.
2.2  Calculate the manufacturing cost of the product in 2005.
2.3  Did Susruta achieve its targets in 2005?
2.4  State how the reduction could be explained.

## 3. Lalit Musical Clock—Life Cycle Costs

Gadisthan of Chandigarh in India designed an electronic musical clock which had a charming musical chime and woke one up to the classical raga of one's choice. The most popular raga which it projected was the classical morning raga, Lalit.

Its estimate of the life cycle costs were as follows:
Life cycle units produced and sold  =  4,00,000
Selling price per clock  =  ₹400
Life cycle costs:

| R&D and design | = | ₹1,00,00,000 |
|---|---|---|

Manufacturing:

| Variable cost per clock | = | ₹150 |
|---|---|---|
| Variable cost per batch | = | ₹6000 |
| Watches per batch | = | ₹500 |
| Fixed costs | = | ₹1,80,00,000 |

Marketing:

| Variable cost per watch | = | ₹32 |
|---|---|---|
| Fixed costs | = | ₹1,00,00,000 |

Distribution:

| Variable cost per batch | = | ₹2800 |
|---|---|---|
| Watches per batch | = | ₹160 |
| Fixed costs | = | ₹70,20,000 |
| Customer service per watch | = | ₹15 |

## Questions

3.1 What is the budgeted operational cycle income?

3.2 What percentage of the total cost will be incurred by the end of the R & D period?

3.3 It is estimated that 80 per cent of the budgeted total product life cycle is locked-in by the end of the R & D phase. What are its implications?

1. It is estimated that if we decrease the sale price by ₹30, unit of life cycle sales in quantity will increase by 10 per cent. The increased production can be managed by increasing the batch size all the way by 10 per cent. Should they reduce the price by ₹30 as suggested?

## 4. Gorakhpur Labour Agency

Gorakhpur Labour Agency (GLA) was a well-known concern in Eastern UP which supplied labour for contract jobs. GLA planned to supply 80,000 hours of labour. Its variable cost was ₹12 per hour and its fixed cost was ₹2,40,000. Pappoo Yadav, the manager, has proposed that they should follow a cost plus model of pricing with a mark-up of 20 per cent.

## Questions

4.1 What should be their quotation per labour hour?

4.2 What should Pappoo Yadav do if they decide that they should follow the market and assess that the demand will be greater with a reduction in the quotation as in Table P4.

**Table P4**  Assessment of Demand

| Price per hour | Demand hours |
|---|---|
| ₹16 | 1,20,000 |
| ₹17 | 1,00,000 |
| ₹18 | 80,000 |
| ₹19 | 70,000 |
| ₹20 | 60,000 |

## 5. Karvalli Hotel

Karvalli Hotel on the west coast was a 220-room hotel. It has an active business class clientele who are charged ₹1000 per day for the room. They usually come announced. They also have a thriving tourist traffic whom they charge ₹500 per day. At that rate their rooms will always be fully occupied. Vasanth Kinni, a student of the Badami Institute of Management, was given the task of calculating the number of rooms they should reserve for the business class. Kinni saw the past statistics of demand for the rooms and presented the data as in Table P5.

**Table P5**  Historical Demand for Rooms

| Demand for rooms (Q) | Days with that demand |
|---|---|
| 0–70 | 12 |
| 71 | 3 |
| 72 | 3 |
| 73 | 2 |
| 74 | 0 |
| 75 | 4 |
| 76 | 4 |
| 77 | 5 |
| 78 | 2 |
| 79 | 7 |
| 80 | 4 |
| 81 | 10 |
| 82 | 13 |
| 83 | 12 |
| 84 | 4 |
| 85 | 9 |
| 86 | 10 |
| Above 86 | 19 |
| Total | 123 |

## Question

5.1  What are the numbers of rooms that Kinni must recommend for reservation for the business class?

### 6.  Smart Products

Smart Products produce utility baggage trolleys and suit cases. Their latest product is USK SOFT which is a popular overnight box. It is priced at ₹500 and sells 20,000 units annually. The variable costs are ₹350 per unit. The fixed costs for USK box is ₹15,00,000.

The management was concerned with the rather limited returns of USK boxes and instituted a market study. It revealed that

(a)  USK box is in a price sensitive market
(b)  every drop in price by ₹20 will increase the sales by 5000 units
(c)  around ₹400, it has no competitor, and hence at ₹400 it can sell 50,000 units
(d)  beyond this further reductions may not fetch more sales
(e)  there will be a saving of ₹25 in material costs if the company sells more than 35,000 units

The company feels that there will be no change in the fixed costs under any of the above options.

## Question

6.1  Find out the best pricing policy in terms of profitability.

### 7.  Semuri Enterprise

Semuri Enterprise makes a popular brand of cream biscuits which it sells at ₹20 per packet. The variable costs come to ₹12. The present sales are 1,00,000 packets and the company makes a profit of ₹3,00,000.

The company's management has set a target profit of ₹5,00,000 as the current capacity utilization is only 50%. The company has the following options:

(a)  Reduce the price by ₹1 and invest ₹1,50,000 in advertisement. Expected sales are 1,50,000 packets.
(b)  Add a pen as a free gift, which will cost the company ₹4 per unit. The price may be increased to ₹25.  Sales will jump to the same level as (a) above.
(c)  Reduce the price to ₹18. The company can operate at full capacity.

## Questions

7.1  Which option gives the best results?

7.2  What additional facts are to be considered? (Cream biscuits market is highly competitive and price sensitive).

### 8. Videsi Products

Videsi Products makes CVX, which is an intermediary chemical product. It can be sold in wholesale and retail. The wholesale price is ₹100 per tin and it accounts for 60% of the sales. The retail which accounts for 40% commands a price of ₹120. CVX currently sells 50,000 tins under both the segments put together. The cost structure of CVX is

|                   | ₹/tin |
|-------------------|-------|
| Direct material   | 40    |
| Direct labour     | 20    |
| Variable overheads| 10    |

The company's fixed overheads is ₹10,00,000 and is related to a capacity of 50,000 tins. Beyond that it jumps to ₹15,00,000. 50,000 additional tins can be produced at this level. Retail sales involve additional variable selling costs of ₹10 per unit.

Due to inflation, the company expects higher costs in the coming year. The expected costs are:

- Direct material costs will go up by 20%
- Direct labour and variable overheads will register a 10% jump
- Retail selling overheads will go up by 20%

The company can sell the entire 1,00,000 tins in the same ratio of retail and wholesale. The wholesale prices will remain the same.

## Questions

8.1  If the company wants to make the same profits in the coming year, what should be the retail price per tin?

8.2  The company wants to discontinue retail marketing, and focus only on the wholesale operations constituting 60% of the sales. What would be your advice?

## PROJECT

Form groups of four students and choose five establishments of varied businesses, ascertain the pricing practices, and draw some conclusions.

## The Cost Accountant's Dilemma

Bangalore Autos had a thriving spare parts business in automobiles. Ajit Chopra was, however, keen that they should expand their business further. Ajit felt that his board of directors had cramped his style by saying that the pricing must be done only after clearance by the cost analyst Swaminathan. The board had laid down the rule that prices must be at full costs plus a mark-up of 10 per cent. Ajit had a proposal to capture a new automobile entrant, and asked Swaminathan for the cost data for the quantity he wished to sell to the new concern. The data was as shown in Table CS1.

**Table CS1** Cost Data for New Automobile Entrant

| Direct material | | = ₹4,00,000 |
|---|---|---|
| Direct labour | | = ₹1,00,000 |
| Overheads: | | |
| | Design and parts administration | = ₹40,000 |
| | Product order | = ₹50,000 |
| | Set up costs | = ₹55,000 |
| | Material handling costs | = ₹65,000 |
| | General administration | = ₹90,000 |
| **Total** | | = **₹8,00,000** |

Ajit felt that the overhead was overestimated. Swaminathan, however, was satisfied as it was just 30 per cent of the direct costs which is the usual pattern. Ajit said, 'Surely you do not mean that overheads will increase with the new order. I just do not agree.' Swaminathan was uncomfortable with Ajit's aggressive posture. He felt that Ajit was eager to get the order as he would earn a bonus on the extra profits of the company. While he too would also get a similar bonus, he did not want to flout the policy order of the board for pricing for that reason.

## Discussion Questions

1. What are the options Swaminathan now has?
2. Should he look for a genuine increase in profitability or the literal application of the board policy?
3. Are there some things he should bring to the attention of Ajit?

| CASE STUDY 2 | **Budhijivi Housing Building Society** |

Budhijivi House Building Society (BHBS) of Delhi had 200 flats. The residents were among the intellectual elite of the city, though not all of them were financially well off. Somewhat disgusted with power cuts, they decided to install a generator set in their society. The issue now was, how to charge the residents for its costs?

The residents had varying connected loads; the average was 8 kw. The common services, such as the lifts and an auditorium, had another 100 kw. The total connected load was therefore 1700 kw. Each resident had direct connections with the BSES, Yamuna Power Ltd., and had individual meters which measured their consumption. BSES charged them ₹10 per kw per month and the usage was charged on slab rates ranging from ₹2.40 per kw to ₹4.60. The second meter inside the house could measure the total current consumed which included both external as well as internal supply. The generator sets would cost a monthly fixed cost of ₹50,000 and a variable cost of ₹8 per kw. Ten residents did not wish to be connected to the internal power grid. But they would use the lifts and in case of a power break-down they would partake in the benefits. The same would apply to the auditorium. The auditorium could also be rented out to outside parties.

## Discussion Questions

1. Suggest a way for charging the residents.
2. Would it be worthwhile to give the ten residents who are not opting for the generator some concessions so that the overall burden could be reduced?

| CASE STUDY 3 | **Loni Fruits and Vegetables Cooperative** |

Loni Fruits and Vegetables Cooperative was 100 kilometres away from Delhi. It has a rich soil and has a tradition of growing vegetables. Ruchita Singh was a management graduate who was keen on rural development and during one of her field visits to Loni she found that the farmers grew an extremely delicious species of spinach.

She interviewed the farmers and found that the life cycle of each set of plants would yield spinach at a cost of ₹2 per kg. She found that local traders bought it from the farmers at ₹2.50 and sold it in Delhi at ₹15 per kg after spending about fifty paise for transport, and incurring an overhead of another fifty paise. She proposed that the farmers form a cooperative and she would handle their sales in Delhi through the Mother Dairy booths. She had the cooperative deliver five hundred kgs early in the morning each day during the season. She priced it at ₹15 per kg and neatly packed it for sale.

Often she had some stocks left over at 8.30 pm, by which time the elite customers started to dwindle.

However, the poor slum dwellers were waiting for the prices to be lowered. At ₹5 per kg the entire stock could be sold out in five minutes. But, the odd customer who is willing to pay ₹15 per kg could turn up after 9 pm. If some stock is kept aside for this customer and she does not turn up, it has to be thrown away as the slum dwellers would not also return to the booth. How much of the spinach should be reserved for the upper classes? A frequency table of sales after 8.30 pm is shown in Table CS3.

**Table CS3**  Frequency Table of Upper Class Customers at a Mother Dairy Booth after 8.30 pm

| Demand in kgs | Number of days |
|---|---|
| 0–5 | 10 |
| 6 | 15 |
| 7 | 20 |
| 8 | 20 |
| 9 | 5 |
| 10 | 5 |
| 11 | 3 |
| 12 | 1 |
| 13 and above | 2 |

## Discussion Question

1. How many kgs would Ruchi be advised to reserve for the elite?

# Professional Ethics and Behavioural Issues

## INTRODUCTION

The *Oxford English Dictionary* defines ethics as a 'science of morals and principles'. Professional ethics are a code of conduct adopted by professionals belonging to a particular profession on the basis of moral considerations applicable to their field of specialization. In many professions and trades, the professionals themselves enforce these internally by forming groups and associations which include members of the same occupation. These associations circulate a memorandum of code of conduct among its members to preserve the integrity of their profession. Not only clients, but the professionals also benefit from following ethics, as it instils confidence in the society regarding them and their profession. The discipline enforced by the code of conduct helps practitioners to maintain a standard level of ethicality in their profession, thus making a framework where the professionals use their knowledge for the welfare of society.

Business scandals which are a regular highlight of the commercial world today underscore the need for business ethics. The old adage 'the business of business is business' no longer holds water in these revised circumstances. This chapter studies the impact of ethics and behavioural issues in the realm of management in general, and the accounting profession in particular.

Professions involve people, and people involve sentiments and morals. As specialist knowledge surfaces and becomes the need of the hour, their delivery as services involves moral issues. It is the specialized knowledge that differentiates a lay person from a professional. Hence, their use of knowledge should be governed by ethical standards while providing a service to people. The professional expertise adds moral accountability to their basket of responsibilities. Accountability and authority are two sides of the same coin. People trust professionals and hand over their problems to them with a belief that they will provide the required solution. Sometimes situations arise where professionals exploit people with their specialized knowledge. Clients who are not aware of the technicalities involved are easy bait for unnecessary expenditures which are easily avoidable but yield financial gains to the professional involved. For example, a lawyer may elongate the number of appearances in court by taking future dates at every hearing for a case, in order to earn more income. A doctor who recommends various kinds of physical tests which are actually not needed for a particular surgery can bring additional revenue to his private multi-specialty hospital. This is why it is necessary to have an ethical code of conduct for every profession. Example 14.1 shows ethics in a supermarket.

### Example 14.1 Ethics in a Supermarket

When we go shopping at a super-bazaar or a mall, the billing line is sometimes very long. In such situations, customers just want to get their commodities billed and escape from the congestion. If taking advantage of this, the cashier by suitable nuances puts an extra amount in the bill, the customers will be easily duped. In the hurry to go out they may not have the patience to check the total bill amount. Though the act might earn some extra money for the supermarket, it is ethically wrong. If customers find out about this, they will lose their confidence in the outlet and this can be injurious to its reputation. There is a thin line between what is ethical and what is unethical. A single attempt to earn a little extra can mar the hard-earned reputation of an organization.

Apart from the direct impact, the cheated customers may also begin to doubt the supermarket in other areas, such as quality of the products, the weighing scales used, etc. In a competitive market, unfavourable customer response can spell doom for the unethical entity.

# INTEGRITY IN A COMPETITIVE WORLD

Profits are an ever-alluring driving force in the business world. In today's world of numbers and digits, profit figures which are released every quarter are the determinants of the financial health of any company. External circumstances may cause serious damage to the bottom-line. Hence, the role of the accountants who formulate the financial statements becomes crucial. If there had been a sudden loss, the reputation of the company may decline in the eyes of investors and shareholders. Thus, bringing the facts to light directly can sometimes prove to be dangerous to the long-built reputation of the company. Due to all these implications, the official in-charge of making the financial statements may sometimes modify the numbers due to fear of losing his income or job, or under pressure from his seniors. Inflating the figures may solve the troubles on the face of it, but internally the problem goes on eating at the financial front of the company like a termite. Apart from this, the approach is also not ethically correct. The trust of the people associated with the company is artificially maintained and once the reality is out everything is destroyed forever.

Once the company's real situation comes to light, it can have a severe impact on the group and associated entities. The damage also spreads to other interested segments of society, such as the employees, bankers, and principle suppliers. Hence, the need for ethical controls is felt.

Professional ethics is a not merely a text to be read, learnt, and forgotten. It is to be followed and remembered while taking every crucial decision in one's professional commitments. It is a constant process of reviewing one's behaviour against constantly changing circumstances and standards.

Accountancy is a specialized field of knowledge and only trained professionals can undertake to do it. Professionals working as cost and management accountants are bound by the code of ethics that are commonly agreed upon by the members of the Cost Accountant's Association operating in a particular country. The codes are exclusively framed for a particular nation depending on the system of accounting practised in the domestic arena. Global standards, however, are gaining currency.

The standards that are expected consist of certain dos and don'ts from the technical, professional, and behavioural/ethical angles.

## Technical Standards

These relate to areas of work of the management accountants involving technical competency.

1. Opinions expressed on any financial statement should be unbiased and explain all the facets of the same to the client without any hidden intention.
2. Knowledge in the technical and related areas should be constantly updated.
3. The members (accountants) shall not mislead the clients and make no departures from the generally accepted accounting practices and principles.
4. Only those projects that he/she is confident of handling and guiding on the basis of his/her competence should be accepted.

## Professional Standards

These are certain yardsticks of standards vis-à-vis the dignity of the profession and that of the members. They do overlap into the arena of technical standards but emphasis is more on the preferred decorum rather than the technical aspects. Following are the professional standards accountants should abide by:

1. Sovereignty of thought and action.
2. The accountant will try and establish a clear and concise understanding to the client regarding the steps that he/she recommends to be taken.
3. He/she should refrain from getting involved in malicious and illegal acts that may bring down the fame of self and the profession.
4. The client should be informed about all the relevant business information connected with the statement on which opinion of the account has been requested.
5. An estimate of the expenditures involved in the consultation and in exercising the opinion provided by the consultant should be furnished.
6. Assignments that include reviewing the work of other accountants should not be accepted without their knowledge except where the situation involves termination of services of one accountant and the project is transferred to another officially. Hence, the rule is: 'do not practise professional back-stabbing'.

## Behavioural/Ethical Standards

These relate to the moral and ethical bias expected of the members of a professional body and provide the basis for deciding the professional misconduct of the members.

1. The confidential financial information and details of their statements should not be disclosed to any outside party unless it involves a legal probe or enquiry, with an order from a court of law.
2. The accountant shall not take any monetary benefit without the knowledge of the employer or client.
3. He/she should be courteous to other members of the same profession and not indulge in unhealthy rivalry.
4. The accountant should not get involved in commission business to secure management accounting work.

These guidelines mentioned above are to help the accountants to maintain a high decorum in their profession, and meet high standards of professionalism and performance. The basic objectives involved are as follows:

1. Maintaining uniformly high professionalism
2. Dissemination of information which meets the letter and spirit of the various legal pronouncements and can stand scrutiny at a later stage.
3. Performance that commands respect from all the stakeholders (employers, regulators, statutory authorities, clients, and society).
4. Uniformly high standards in the discharge of work.

# THE INDIAN CODE OF ETHICS FOR COST ACCOUNTANTS

The Institute of Cost and Works Accountants of India (ICWAI) is the duly constituted governing body to issue guidelines in the form of an elaborate code of ethics for the cost and management accountants working across the country.

It has set the following standards for a code of ethics to be followed:

## Integrity

An accountant is expected to be straightforward and honest in performing his services.

## Objectivity

The cost accountant should not entertain any kind of prejudice or bias while giving his opinion.

### Competence

He/she should not undertake any task or assignment that he/she may not be competent to perform. Once a commitment is made, he/she should ensure that justice is done to it with the highest standards of work.

### Confidentiality

Disclosure of information regarding the financial details of his/her client should be protected from superfluous exposure unless a legal authoritative warrant enquiring this is produced.

### Professional behaviour

A cost accountant should maintain the decorum of the profession and conduct in a respectable manner in the society.

Apart from the above guiding principles, every cost accountant needs to think before he/she acts or takes decisions to ensure that the work does not tarnish the reputation of the profession in the society. It should, on the other hand, enhance the profession's fame in the optimum possible manner.

## ETHICS AND SOCIAL RESPONSIBILITY

Externalities are a known feature of the manufacturing sector. In some industries, the negative externalities overweigh the positive ones. Leather tanning is one such sector. The environmental consequences are one of the exogenous factors involved here. Disposal of water used in chemical, leather and manufacturing units is a boiling issue. Some units discharge this water directly into nearby water sources, inviting the wrath of environmentalists. Pollution control boards have a regulation that the liquid being disposed of should be purified and the toxic chemicals it contains should be neutralized. The purification process involves expenditure and directly affects the finances of the company. The management of many manufacturing units try to avoid these costs as it affects their profit numbers. The management accountant who formulates the budget is often instructed to allocate lower funds than is actually required for the purification process. He/she cannot overrule the management's decision to neglect the regulation. This gives rise to an ethical dilemma for the accountant. He/she has to choose between the roles of a citizen who knows the harmful effects of water pollution, and an obedient accountant who does what his management asks him/her to. Though ethically wrong, a promise of higher increments and promotion by being in the 'good books' of the management is certainly an alluring result. Thus, the ethical conflict tears him/her into two different personalities who rebel against each other.

# INSTITUTE OF MANAGEMENT ACCOUNTANTS (IMA) OF THE US

Cost accountants around the world have their associations or institutes as a monitoring agency to enforce a code of professional ethics. The American Institute of Cost Accountants is called the Institute of Management Accountants (IMA). Situated at Montvale, New Jersey, it is dedicated to providing higher standards of accounting practices to the citizens of America.

The IMA gives practical guidelines to its members to be implemented in their work spheres. The posting of the institute begins with a powerful sentence that all the members of the IMA shall behave ethically. Its overarching principles include honesty, fairness, objectivity, and responsibility. It encourages all its members and various organizations to adhere to these highly esteemed principles.

The IMA strictly states that any member's negligence in maintaining the standards will be met with disciplinary action. The four pillar-stones of the American code of ethics for management accountants are as follows:

## Competence

Being the premier monitoring body for cost and management accountants in America, the institute expects its members to maintain professional expertise by constantly updating their knowledge of the ever-changing business situations. The minimum expectation from the members is to provide opinions abiding by the laws and regulations of the land, maintaining the technical standards. Providing accurate and timely advice to the clients is also covered under the same principle of competency. Apart from this the accountants can provide effective professional and unbiased communication to this clients, and can successfully guide them through the issues they are consulted on.

## Confidentiality

Financial details are one of the most crucial statements and accountants who deal with these, have access to some of the most confidential details of revenue on the assignments they deal with. The institute instructs its members to keep the information held by them regarding the assignments they handle confidential and not 'spill the beans' in public, unless it is demanded with a legal warrant or summoned by a court of law for its legal procedures.

## Integrity

Veracity is the foundation of a management accountant's profession. The clients reveal various intricate details of their finances to explain their case. The help of the management accountant is usually sought to reduce the troubles involved in the revenue calculation and management. Neutralizing the conflicts involved in the financial matters on which the accountant's opinion is sought upon is the basic responsibility that the IMA bestows upon its members. It is also recommended that the cost accountant refrain from engaging in any activity that is illegal or unethical (Example 14.2).

### Example 14.2 Suppressing Liability

An apprentice accountant of an engineering firm has ordered for some materials in the month of March which are required only by mid-April. The invoice for payment has arrived but the management is not too happy to see a fairly huge liability at the end of the financial year. There is a temptation on the part of the management to ignore the invoice and push the liability to the next year. This defeats the concept of *true and fair* accounting.

### Questionable accounting practices

Unethical accounting practices have led to the downfall of MNCs, such as Enron, WorldCom, etc. Once an unethical practice is started, it becomes a habit and a precedent. It is repeated in the subsequent years until the big crash happens. Once a mistake is made, corrective measures do not come easy. Hence it is said, 'Prevention is better than cure.' Example 14.3 shows the importance of ethics in dealing with customers in an automobile service centre.

## Credibility

Gaining the trust of people is possible if the professionals involved in the occupation maintain their credibility. Every member of the cost accountant's institute should abide by communicating the information clearly and concisely to the parties involved. They are required to make sure the client understands the details and technicalities of the assignment on which the opinion is asked. Shortcomings and delays if any are to be revealed and the reason should clearly be explained to the client.

**Example 14.3** Faith should Run along with the Car

Not everyone can fit spare parts in a bike or a car! The automobile servicing industry is a specialization based work arena. Customers accept a mechanic's advice without much debate and pay for the changes to be made without a thought, as they trust that the mechanic knows their vehicle best. Ask an automobile enthusiast and he would happily confess that the service guys are his vehicle's foster parents. In such a backdrop, if some day the ace driver learns that the same person who takes care of his vehicle like a baby is taking advantage of his love for the automobile and charging him extra at every visit and pushing unnecessary fancy spares, he would definitely feel he was being duped. This is the result of an unethical policy adopted by the automobile service centre. Once the customer feels cheated, it is almost impossible to get him to come back through the same door again. In an era where an alternative choice is available on every street for every other product, losing a customer's trust can prove suicidal for the business. Thus, good ethics play a marketing role in turning customers into the famous adage—diamonds are forever.

## MANAGING CONFLICT

Applying ethics to the profession has led to conflicts at times. Personal ambitions always make a person go 'weak at the knees' when huge amounts of money are involved. Thus, the IMA understands the need to support its members in times of need. If a conflict arises in the process of applying the ethical conduct to professional practice, the IMA gives certain guidelines to solve them. These are as follows:

1. In case of conflict the first remedy suggested by the IMA is to discuss the issue with the immediate supervisor, if he/she is not involved in the dilemma. The best way out is to discuss the problem with the level of management that can handle the issue. Discussion with outside parties is discouraged at this stage.

2. There is a provision to discuss the issue with a duly constituted body (audit committee, vigilance authorities, board of trustees, etc.). This is an important option in case the supervisor himself is suspected to be involved in the issue.

3. The IMA also provides for specialized help. Clarification of the ethical concern with an IMA ethical counsellor or any unbiased advisor is the second method of troubleshooting. The need for

professional help comes as a leash of fresh air in difficult times and can put many issues straight. The problem is visibly clearer to a third person who is not directly involved and can lead to a workable solution.

4. The last option left is to seek guidance from legal experts and confide the details of the problem to them. Some of the complications may involve legal implications and certain intricacies may appear clearer from a legal angle. Thus, the conflict could be resolved with this insight.

5. If all the above options fail, then the best thing would be to resign from the position and seek redressal elsewhere. This, however, involves other personal issues, such as income, employment opportunities, etc.

The IMA leaves no stone unturned in acting as a mentoring body to the management accountants practising in the US and has emerged as a role model for the governing institutes of various other countries. By fostering ethical and professional conduct among its members, it has contributed in making the work of a management accountant respectable in all circles of society.

## BEHAVIOURAL ISSUES AND THE MANAGEMENT ACCOUNTANT

All ethical issues have a significant behavioural attribute. Besides, there are a few apparently ethical issues which have negative behavioural impact as well. Ethics cannot be imposed by a set of rules and regulations alone. It is a mindset and the organizational culture must support an ethical conduct. It is interesting to note that Kautilya's *Arthashastra* (written by about 320 BC) has insisted upon a series of ethical and behavioural issues at the various functional areas of the rulers.

Financial accountants, who report to the external stakeholders, are covered by a clear set of enactments (such as the Companies Act, Income Tax Act, SEBI Regulations, etc.). Management accountants, on the other hand, primarily provide data for the internal management, and are hence constantly exposed to the dilemmas of ethical and behavioural issues.

## BEHAVIOURAL ISSUES AND EMPLOYEE MORALE

An organization is built with the support of its employees. Each member has a role to play in its progress and advancement. As the employees have a sense of commitment and involvement towards the organization, they expect the management and top officials to endow some responsibilities to them, and seek their opinion in the decisive areas of production and allocation. Budgeting is an important part of the annual planning process for the allocation of financial resources. Each department has its own plans for expansion for each financial year. They would expect to be consulted and be taken into confidence before a final statement of budget is drawn and forwarded to them. A participatory budget is essential for the smooth functioning of a company. It instils confidence in the employees and makes it easier for them to adjust to the changes occurring on the financial side. On the contrary, if a budget is autocratically imposed, the employees feel suffocated within the boundaries to which they are limited. A lot of energy is wasted in adjusting to the allocated limit and dissatisfaction emerges in their mind about the workplace. This can largely affect the productivity and can cause migration of human resource in search of free horizons or, in other words, a more conducive work environment where the employee's opinion matters.

Budgeting is an area where serious behavioural issues creep in. Except in very small organizations, budgets are prepared based on the inputs from various departments. But, top managements often make the annual budget without consulting the units/divisions under them. This becomes a top-down approach and will have the following behavioural impacts:

1. A realistic position will not be taken into account in the absence of inputs from the field staff.
2. Individual employees will have no ownership of the budget figures since they were not a party to it.
3. The top-down budgets tend to be either too tough or too easy to achieve.
4. This defeats the whole purpose of budgeting, which is supposed to be a participative exercise.
5. Resource allocation is unrealistic in top-down budgets; either there will be excess allocation of resources or a shortfall in the genuine requirements. This lopsided allocation could harm the company.
6. Performance measurement will be ineffective in such circumstances, as the 'doers' are different from the 'planners'.
7. The major shortfall is a lack of synergy and teamwork in the entire organization.

## NOT A 'SWEET' DILEMMA

Imagine the case of a confectionery company with branches all over India. It has tight budget controls and had been successful in the past. In order to increase the return on investments (ROI), the chief budget officer has recommended an across the board reduction of 20 per cent of all expenditure. He has mandated the production managers to 'somehow cut the costs and give me profits'.

This kind of control could trigger a variety of negative behavioural patterns:

1. It could lead to creative accounting practices which deflate expenses.
2. Quality controls can be relaxed which can allow sub-standard food products to reach the customers, which could damage the brand image.
3. Another way of short-circuiting the control mechanism is by invoicing returned defective products to other, less complaining regions/customers.
4. Another option is to sell expired products, may be at a discount. Yet another method is to refuse responding to complaints from customers for replacing the spoiled/defective goods.

The above behaviour (which is seen under competitive circumstances in a few companies) has many ethical downstream effects. From a management accountant's perspective the ethical issues are related to integrity and professional behaviour. He/she must ensure that the commercial and ethical fallouts of the above budgetary systems are brought to the top management's attention. Besides there are the serious behavioural issues which could harm the fair image of the company.

## SUMMARY

Professional ethics are codes of conduct adopted by the professionals of a particular discipline on the basis of certain moral considerations applicable to their specialized field. The accountancy profession also needs a set of ethics to make them accountable to the stakeholders. Such ethical codes help both the professionals and the stakeholders who benefit from their services. The members are bound by the code of ethics that are commonly agreed upon by the profession. The codes are usually nation-specific and are dependent on the prevailing systems and practices.

The codes are basically a set of standards, and for the profession of management accounting, fall under three major categories. The technical standards are the expected technical competency levels required to discharge their functions effectively. The members must constantly update their knowledge and be unbiased, and make no departure from the accepted practices and principles. The next is a set of professional standards, which are related to the dignity of the profession and the expected levels of decorum. These standards provide a bridge between the levels of technical and professional competencies expected of them. The next is a set of behavioural and ethical standards. They constitute the moral and ethical bias expected of the management accountants, and generally fix the milestones for deciding the professional conduct levels.

The Institute of Cost and Works Accountants of India (ICWAI) has issued an elaborate code of ethics for management accountants in this country. They come under five broad categories, namely, integrity, objectivity, competence, confidentiality, and professional behaviour. The Institute of Management Accountants (IMA) USA, has a code of ethics based on the four pillars of competence, integrity, confidentiality, and credibility. It also provides a hierarchical structure and edifice to mitigate conflicts.

Since ethical issues have behavioural impacts, they cannot be imposed by a set of rules alone. Behavioural issues affect employee morale significantly. Certain areas of management accounting, such as budgets and the resultant control measures, have a major impact on employee behaviour.

## KEY POINTS

- Ethics is the art and science of morals and principles.
- Professional ethics are codes of conduct adopted by members of a particular profession.
- Technical standards refer to the area of work involving technical competency.
- Professional standards are yardsticks of standards vis-à-vis the dignity of the profession and that of its members.
- Behavioural/ethical standards relate to the moral and ethical bias expected of the members of a profession.

- Managing conflict in the context of professional ethics refers to a systematic approach to handling conflicts in an organization.
- *Arthashastra* is a book on administration and finance written by Kautilya around 320 BC.
- SEBI regulation is a set of rules issued by the Securities and Exchange Board of India, for regulating certain aspects of corporate governance.

## CONCEPT REVIEW QUESTIONS

1. Define ethics.
2. Why do professionals need ethics?
3. Discuss the role of integrity in a competitive world.
4. Discuss the technical standards applicable to management accountants.
5. What are the professional standards specifically required for management accountants?
6. Do management accountants need behavioural/ethical standards?
7. What are the standards set for the code of ethics for Indian cost accountants?
8. Explain the pillar-stones of the American code of ethics for management accountants.
9. What are the courses of action specified for managing conflicts by the Institute of Management Accountants (IMA) US?
10. Explain the behavioural issues that arise in the budgeting area.

## CASE STUDY 1 — Ethics and Overheads Recovery

Mr Patel, CEO of Western Enterprises, has evolved a system of rewarding the twelve divisions under his control on the basis of the cost reports submitted by them. He was happy that he had selected this approach rather than the traditional method of rewarding units on the basis of the profit figures at year end. 'This way I reward my people based on the plans we have made in advance,' he used to tell the board members.

The household utilities division had shown good results ever since the new Divisional Manager, Mr Sitaram, took over the reins six years ago and he had consequently earned huge bonuses. He wanted to ensure that his unit continues to bring him the bonuses in spite of some slowdown in the economy. However, in order to avoid any possible hiccup, he told his accountant to have a re-look at the projections for the next year.

Western Enterprises had a system of recovering overheads based on machine hour rate. The statement which Sitaram saw had provided for 2,40,000 machine hours, and the overhead rate was accordingly arrived at. He told his accountant to reduce it to 2,20,000 hours so that the results showed an over recovery by the end of March when the bonus calculations are made.

The accountant was not very sure whether this was an ethical approach since the production department had accurately calculated the machine hours. Sitaram explained that they were not going to show fictitious profits or anything of that sort. 'Look, these costing figures are not subject to any audit; you are, after all, making an estimate. Do as I say and you will get a nice bounty when the bonus is declared.'

The accountant thought that his boss was probably correct, but was not very sure.

## Discussion Questions

1. Why did Sitaram ask the accountant to show lower machine hours?
2. Are there any ethical issue involved in this case?
3. What will be the consequence to the company if this practice continues all over the organization?

 **CASE STUDY 2**        **Ethics and Inventory**

A company wanted to achieve certain pre-set profit estimates. By the year end it became clear that it would fall short of the expected range of profits by a margin of around 10 per cent. Some executives felt that increasing the inventory would make it possible to absorb more of the overheads during the current period. Additional costs would certainly be involved but the year end profits would look better.

## Discussion Questions

1. Does the above approach enhance the profitability?
2. From the code of conduct prescribed for the management accountants, can any infringement or in contrast any specific adherence be noticed?
3. What could be the impact of the above practice if the market is robust and the demand is high in the next year?
4. During a period of recession, what could be the impact in the subsequent year?

| CASE STUDY 3 | Ethics and Behavioural Issues |

Tight Fit is an acknowledged name in the branded menswear market. They mainly cater to the medium-priced market segment. There are some popular brand names under the Tight Fit umbrella, such as *7 pm*, *The Mach Man,* and *Dinner Shirt*. The competition has been increasing and the management desperately wants to do something. A new CEO was hired to ensure growth of both the top and the bottom line with full power. Within months after the initiative, there were several complaints followed by a spate of resignations at the top and middle levels. The chief of HR, Mr Ramesh Gupta, was asked by the board of directors to look at the position and submit a report. He made the following report after three weeks of closed interviews with various executives.

**A Report on Some Behavioural Issues (Confidential)**

To,

The Board,
Tight Fit Company
New Delhi

Dear Sir,

As per your direction, I made a discreet study of the prevailing situation in our company. I have the following comments:

1.  Mr Premchand, who has been hired from our consultant's office to lead the organization as the CEO, has been holding the post for the last 9 months. He has taken several steps to improve the performance. While some of them were highly beneficial, the overall impact of his efforts, I am sorry to report, is negative. He has given a challenging budget to all our brand managers but they all complain that there are no incentives attached for good performance. Instead, when the monthly target was attained, the next month's target for sales went up by 10 per cent. This has acted as a disincentive. The manager of '7 pm' brand has already quit. The sales manager of 'The Mach Man' has been ill for sometime and is reportedly suffering from a nervous breakdown.

2.  Last October, Mr Premchand introduced a new scheme to stitch uniforms for hotels and schools. These do not come under the regular brands and were arbitrarily given to any of the brand managers without proper consultation. These were not included for the sales target figures and often had to be completed at short notice. The brand managers are frustrated at this

arbitrariness, as it created avoidable problems in achieving the targets, fixed for them.

3. No provision is made for repairs to equipment and maintenance expenses. The wear and tear has been higher due to extended hours of work. In the absence of provision for repairs, our equipment is depreciating at a faster pace. Mr Premchand, however, blames poor workmanship.

4. In the last plant committee meeting he seems to have made some sarcastic remark about the aging managers and said, 'Go and relax with your grandchildren if you cannot meet the targets.' This was not well received by some of our senior executives.

5. Mr Premchand is reported to have an 'I am right, you are wrong' attitude while dealing with people. He is often supercilious, bossy, and irritable. He is hard-working and energetic, but much of his energy is lost in finding fault with others rather than in developing team spirit.

6. The accountant-in-charge of budgets is not a qualified person. He seems to be supporting all Mr Premchand's moves in order to safeguard his position.

These are the major observations and I request that immediate action be taken to rescue our organization from these man-made errors.

Mr Ramesh Gupta
(Chief HR)

## Dicsussion Questions

1. What are the ethical and behavioural issues in the whole case?
2. Suggest ways to improve the company's budgetary systems.
3. What could be the role of a managerial accountant in such a situation?

# PART IV

## Management Control Systems

# Management Control Systems

## INTRODUCTION

Management control systems refer to a series of actions taken by the management in order to achieve its purpose. However, the term has not been uniformly understood and there is some disagreement about its precise scope amongst authors who have written on this topic (Maciariello and Kirby 1999). The leading book on the subject by Robert N. Anthony and Vijay Govindarajan defines the focus of this topic as strategy implementation. It puts all the managerial activities under three broad categories, namely, strategy formulation, management controls, and task control. Hence, the control systems help to convert the policies and goals of the organization to their final implementation. However, the performance of individual tasks at various levels is covered under the final basket, namely, task control (Anthony and Govindarajan 2007).

However, there are other definitions of this topic, which vary from each other in some degrees. Maciariello and Kirby (1999) give it a wider scope covering both the control of strategy and the control of operations. Other authors have viewed control as a basic managerial activity along with planning, organizing, and leading. There is a broad commonality among all these definitions, and the differences are mainly in terms of the degree of control and the focus. As R. C. Sekhar (2006) succinctly states, 'The purpose of all management control systems (MCS) is to achieve the goals and objectives of an organization with ease and at least cost. At the outset, this book discards the earlier notion that MCS should "control" persons; the ultimate purpose of any system is that it should be "in control" instead of controlling people.'

All organizations tend to have control mechanisms which are developed over a period of time. The traditional tools of control were predominantly financial in nature. This consisted of accounting controls, and to some extent the disclosure requirements of various legal measures played a part. This consisted of built-in checks called internal controls. For example,

1. One section places the purchase order, another inspects the goods, and a third section receives them. Thus, there is division of work and fraud can be reduced.
2. The preparation of the payment voucher, approval of the payment, and preparation of cheques are all carried out by different authorities. This prevents wrong and unauthorized payments unless there is collusion among all these authorities.

The examples shown are simple control systems to prevent frauds and embezzlements. As organizations became bigger the need for such controls became more important. This has taken a different dimension due to computerization. Under the current systems, an entry made through the computerized system is automatically repeated in the other records. This has led to greater control and accessibility to the data, thereby facilitating MIS. However, like all good things this has a flip side too; it has led to a new branch of crimes whereby crooks have found ways to misuse the data and embezzle huge amounts of money.

## SINGLE FOCUS AND DUAL FOCUS

Control systems have close links to the organizational culture; they can be dictated by an elitist at the top of the organization. Under the single focus approach, a single individual or group makes the strategies and also implements them. This is the standard pattern in small organizations. This has an influence even in medium-sized family-owned organizations, where the patriarch holds complete control over the entire organization.

The dual focus control systems envisage participative controls, whereby the operating entities exercise the control by coordination and interaction. Under this system strategic shifts are required, and are also permissible. The strategic control groups work in coordination.

# HUMAN IMPACT ON CONTROL

The control systems are designed by human beings, which influence people at work, and their success is eventually measured by another set of human beings. Hence, people ultimately decide the outcome of the control systems. Two important aspects of human beings need to be considered in this context.

## Rationality Issue

While people externally appear to be rational and logical, more recent studies have seen them drifting away from the logical pedestals erected by Adam Smith and others. H. Simon, who won a Noble Prize in Economics in 1978, discovered after a series of studies that human beings come within the parenthesis of, what he calls, *bounded rationality*. This means that the average individual is neither fully rational nor is totally irrational. Extending this theory, Kahneman discovered that the Smithonian man is a laid back individual who tries to work within the limited range of information available to him while making decisions. He shared the Nobel Prize (again for Economics) in 2002, which indicates the impact of his findings. Taken together, these economists provide the edifice for a practical approach to management controls.

## Ethical Issue

While human beings have a basic tendency towards the ethical side of behaviour, there are often cases of unethical conduct in all entities. Studies have proved that the average individual will try to misuse the organization's assets to his personal advantage, unless there are preventive checks.

Based on the above two influences on human behaviour an *outcome improvement model* can be developed (Table 15.1).

Table 15.1 highlights the need for a humane approach to MCS. The following are the preferred routes for installing a control system:

1.  Study the organization and the work culture before installing control systems.

**Table 15.1** Outcome improvement model

| Issues | Assumptions | MCS focus |
|---|---|---|
| Rationality | People are basically rational. | Enhance rationality through structured systems and constant monitoring. |
| Management | It is competent and is willing to improve the performance of the organization. | Provide a supporting system consisting of formal and informal controls appropriate to the nature of the entity. |
| Ethics | Human beings have a basic tendency towards ethical conduct. | Strengthen the ethical instincts by influencing behaviour by a set of systems supported by a carrot and stick approach. |
| Creativity | Most people have a creative urge and a desire to use it. | Within the organizational context, build on the creative mechanism. This changes significantly from entity to entity. |
| Systems | Entities have basic control systems. All organizational cultures can absorb more systems. | Top-down drive to install appropriate systems. |
| Controls | Human beings have an inherent dislike towards all controls, and unless there are checks and balances they will try to break the rules. | Shift the mindset from controlling people to ensure that systems are in control. Build systems on a participative approach and enhance the urge for commitment to the new systems. |

2. Communicate the proposed systems and obtain a feedback.
3. The ultimate controls should fit in with the environment of the entity.
4. Build in margins for human and systems failures while developing the performance measurements.
5. Appropriate flexibility in the design is a must in order to make the MCS effective.
6. Avoid the *silos syndrome* and leave enough room to tap the creativity of the individuals.

## ORGANIZATIONAL TENSIONS

Control systems have gained significance in the second half of the last century when entities began to face tensions between different forces that pull them apart. The primary source is due to the conflict between the tripod of profit, growth, and control. This is explained in Fig. 15.1.

Profits are the single most important parameter by which shareholders and potential investors evaluate an organization. This is usually based on the annual accounts and hence, has a short-term focus. In spite of well-

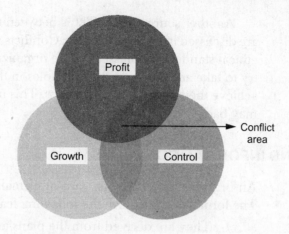

**Fig. 15.1** Tripod of profit, growth, and control

recognized standards of accounting, entities sometimes take recourse to *window dressing* by adopting creative accounting techniques.

## Self-defeating Controls

An automobile company has a strict target to meet before the end of the year. The company usually invoices heavily during the last week of the year. In order to meet the target, salesmen sometimes invoice cars to dealers in amounts higher than what the dealers are willing to pay. These excess cars are often returned by the dealers at the beginning of the next year. The process has thus shown higher sales in the current year by artificially invoicing more cars. This defeats the philosophy of effective controls.

Growth is a desirable feature for all organizations in the long run. This makes organizations sustainable and hence, the strategies have to support the growth plan. This is reflected by an increase in turnover, higher market share, and increase in output. Often, this may have to be achieved by offering attractive discounts and other special features which increase the cost. These two approaches contribute to increasing the growth but can have a negative impact on the profits. Similarly, growth involves greater investments in research and development, and advertising, etc. which involve huge outlays. These expenditures may impact the profits of the year. Hence, there is a conflict between the profit focus on the one hand, and the growth focus on the other. The control systems have to address both the mentioned plans of the top management.

Another source of conflict is between tight and loose controls. These are discussed later in the chapter. Conflicts can also arise due to the desired ethical standards professed by the organization. Some organizations may try to take advantage of the loopholes in the law and administration, and achieve their ends by unfair means. This may bring short-term gains, but may back-fire in the long-term.

## FORMAL AND INFORMAL CONTROLS

An organization is an amalgam of formal and informal control systems. The formal systems have the following features:

1. They are derived from the plans and strategies of the entity.
2. They are debated and emerge out of conscious plan to develop a control system.
3. They are driven by the top management.
4. They are documented in the form of manuals, rules, circulars, office orders, etc.
5. They follow a structured approach with monitoring systems, rewards, and punishments.

The formal systems are visible and are practised in all organizations. They have a close relationship to the leadership styles. In family-owned organizations they may be loosely structured, whereas in a government organization they will be very tight and procedure-based.

The hierarchical structure of formal controls is shown in Fig. 15.2.

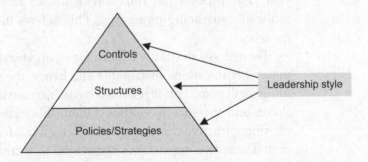

**Fig. 15.2** Hierarchy of formal controls

Formal controls are driven by the strategies of the entity and its overall policies. It has a regular platform, usually followed by a rigid structure and is heavily impacted by the leadership styles, both at the time of the conception and implementation of the control mechanism. Success, however, depends upon the extent of its adoptability into the organizational culture. The formal controls are enforced through various instruments such as the following:

- Accounting manuals which give the details of the method of accounting, internal controls, and financial controls
- Budgetary controls
- Organization charts and delegation of control
- Formal reporting systems
- Physical controls, such as logs, passwords, ID calls, etc.
- Stock verification and stock controls
- System safeguards, data backup
- Poka-yoke or fool proofing method of control.

Formal controls are very effective in established organizations, particularly during the periods of stability and less uncertainty. These organizations tend to be hierarchical and relatively less flexible. Many MNCs, offering unique brands which have a long-established clientele, adopt formal controls for both domestic and foreign operations. Even organizations which are not too rigid on the documentation of formal controls adopt certain aspects of formal control.

Informal controls are the less visible side of the MCS structure. They arise due to the interactions between people, the specific needs or defects of any group of people, and also due to real or perceived threats. These are closely aligned to the specific culture of the organization or its sub-groups. In Japanese organizations, the relationship between the supervisor and the workers is very intense and as a result, the control systems tend to become less formal. There is also a great emphasis on self introspection through relentless reflection (called *Hansei*). This makes the control mechanisms have greater ownership amongst the staff. Thus, the informal controls co-exist along with formal controls.

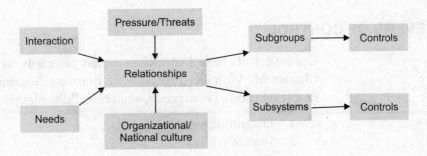

**Fig. 15.3**  Mechanism of informal controls

Figure 15.3 shows the origin and flow of informal controls. These are predominantly behavioural in nature and are driven by constraints such as emotional or professional inadequacies, and a need for protection or betterment. Such control systems exist in all types of organizations and at times work for better enforcement of the formal controls. These are seen as spontaneous controls which emerge due to a mismatch between the formal controls and the organizational culture. As they are supplementary glue to the MCS in force, they can benefit the organization. But, if they function tangentially with formal measures, it can lead to frictions and conflicts. The latter happens due to merger of entities with widely differing environment and cultures. If the management tries to force the control systems of one of the merging entities, this can create the conflict of acceptability in the other units who find it difficult to embrace the new set of control measures.

**Table 15.2** Difference between formal and informal controls

|  | **Formal controls** | **Informal controls** |
|---|---|---|
| Nature | Structured | Unstructured |
| Focus | Sustaining the organization | Managing uncertainty |
| Approach | Planned approach | Interactions |
| Base | Structure | Trust |
| Time span | Long | Sporadic |
| Measurement | Rewards and punishments | Satisfaction of specific issue or threat |

A progressive organization must be aware of the informal control systems that exist in it, or is part of it. As long as they supplement the formal controls, it can discretely encourage such controls. But if they are harmful or have undesirable outcomes, the management needs to review the two forms of control, and modify the formal systems to overcome any gap or excess in the prevailing system. Table 15.2 shows the difference between formal and informal controls.

## LEVERS OF CONTROL

The levers of control owe their origin primarily to Robert Simons, the Charles M. Williams Professor of Business Administration at Harvard Business School. He suggests, what he calls, the levers of control as follows:

1. Diagnostic systems
2. Interactive systems
3. Boundary systems
4. Belief systems

## Diagnostic Systems

This is the most popular system of control which is adopted in varying degrees in almost all organizations. It is simple and easy to understand and has the following ingredients.

1. Set up goals and objectives.
2. Develop performance measures to achieve the goals.
3. Collect active data.
4. Identify deviations from the above measures.
5. Take remedial actions.

The above system is widely practised. It manifests itself in the form of budgets, internal checks, controls, and audits. It has both financial and non-financial parameters. Under financial parameters we have budgets, standard costs, target revenue, profit plans, investments, and various accounting ratios. The non-financial parameters include tools like PERT and CPM, time overrun calculations, quality controls, etc. Modern tools such as balanced score cards and six sigma are increasingly used under this category.

### Benefits of diagnostic systems

The following list shows the benefits of diagnostic systems.

1. It provides a quantitative basis to measure performance.
2. It is easy to understand and is well accepted.
3. It has close links to the achievement of the organizational goals.
4. It enables proper allocation of scarce resources.
5. It provides for an objective method for corrective actions.
6. It is a fair measure of providing rewards.

### Setting up of objective standards

In order to succeed, the organization must be able to set up objective standards. The data on the actual performance must be collected properly, and it must be reliable and possess credibility. A reasonable flexibility must be built into the system to assess performance under dynamic conditions. There must be a good communication system within the organization. However, on the flip side it must be noted that it is very difficult to set up objective standards. The conditions in real life are rarely static and pre-set standards must be flexible enough during times of uncertainty to enable revision. Otherwise they will lose their credibility and employees will view the performance measure with suspicion.

### Factors for successful use of diagnostics controls

The diagnostic control system will be effective if the following conditions are fulfilled.

**Goal clarity**  The entity has a clear goal, supported by suitable strategies which are communicated down the line.

**Targets/performance measures**  Realistic and objective standards such as budgets, standard cost, and quality standards are the next important step to establish good diagnostic controls. Very tight or lax standards will have a negative impact on the performance of the organization.

**Monitoring performance**  The entity should have a method of collecting the actual performance within a short time so that comparisons with targets are possible. Uniform measures of quality, accounting codes, and clear identification of the performance measures in the standard pattern must be used by all the units of the entity. Usually, manuals are prepared in large organizations describing the codes and methods of evaluating the performance measures.

**Follow up actions**  The variances thrown out in the monitoring process must be acted upon swiftly. This includes incentives and rewards for good performance, review of adverse variances, and also taking actions to correct the deficiencies. Figure 15.4 explains the relationships.

Figure 15.4 shows the interrelationship among the mentioned steps. The culmination lies in reviewing the performance measure after the monitoring and follow-up stages. This is a learning process and helps the entity to constantly review the standards in the light of actual performance.

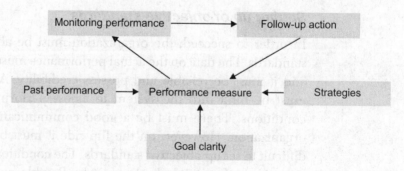

**Fig. 15.4**  Diagnostic system flow chart

## *Limitations of diagnostic controls*

The success of the diagnostic control measures depends upon the proper use of the various steps described earlier. The shortcomings of this system that managements should guard against are the following:

**Setting wrong standards**  Standards can be a deterrent to good performance if set wrongly. This can be due to procedural or system based errors, or it can be deliberate. The former refers to errors arising out of wrong data or incorrect approach to budgeting and standard setting. These can be eliminated by the learning process mentioned earlier. The deliberate errors are those created by smart managers to set easily achievable targets for their units. This is more difficult to trace, particularly if the top management is not involved in the standard setting exercise.

**Defects in the data collections**  The actual data collected must be objective and timely. Lack of uniformity across the organization and long delays in correcting actual performance will defeat the control system.

**Monitoring and follow-up**  The monitoring team should have the authority to take corrective actions. If it is relegated to junior level executives, or there is no specified authority to act on the variances, the whole exercise will become a paper tiger and a ritualistic exercise.

**Ineffective reward system**  If good performance is not recognized and rewarded adequately along with punishments for sub-standard performance, the control system will fail as a motivating mechanism.

Diagnostic control systems are the most popular and time-tested methods used by almost all organizations. If the organization can guard against the shortcomings, this control system can be very effective.

# Interactive Control Systems

The diagnostic control works effectively during periods of certainty and static conditions. But business uncertainties and growing competition make strategies obsolete and short lived. Often, while the basic strategy may remain valid over a period of time, the procedures of execution change from time to time. This dynamic nature of business conditions underscores the need for better and continuous interaction among the different layers of management. Besides, interaction with interested parties outside the organizations also becomes a great imperative.

### Interactive controls in a dairy company

In dairy industries, interactive controls become very important due to various reasons. The demand for the products depends upon factors such as weather, which cannot be predicted accurately. Ice-cream sales are heavily dependent on weather conditions, as well as celebrations such as a victory in a sports event. Usually, the marketing department follows up the developments very closely and ensures that supplies are positioned to meet the demand adequately.

### Interactive controls in snacks outlets

A small company making snacks and bakery products has several outlets in a city. The customers prefer crisp and fresh products. The sales manager at the head office constantly monitors the turnover of each item in each shop. If an item is moving slowly in one outlet, but has demand elsewhere, they take prompt steps to transport it to the outlet where there is demand. They keep constant touch with the shops through telephone, and ensure that the outlets have crisp and fresh products under each category.

A new dimension has been added to the interactive controls by the innovations in information technology. The collection of data has become easier and knowledge management has taken a quantum leap in the last quarter of the 20th century. Communication has been rendered cheaper and quicker. As a result, interactive controls have been made easier.

The following is a list showing how an interactive control system works in an entity.

1. Standards are set by managers after close deliberations.
2. Subordinates are involved in decision-making processes.
3. Uncertainties and emergencies are quickly communicated, and the concerned employees meet and discuss to arrive at the corrective actions.
4. Senior managers encourage suggestions for improvements.
5. Inter-disciplinary teams work to enhance efficiency.
6. Actual performance is collected on a real time basis and corrective actions communicated on the spot.
7. The standards and assumptions are constantly challenged.
8. Resource allocation and de-bottlenecking are constantly addressed.
9. Interactive control measures are constantly applied with suppliers and customers.

Obviously, interactive control measures are becoming more and more significant in a globalized economy where competition is high and uncertainty is the only predictable business phenomenon. This system is widely applied in all types of businesses and is equally relevant in an MNC, as it is to a small family-owned business.

### *Limitations of interactive controls*

Interactive control measures can be successfully employed along with diagnostic and other forms of control. If, however, they become the predominant measure of control, performance measurement can tend to become more subjective. Informal groups may start dominating the organization, and powerful individuals or groups will become highly influential. This will work against professionalism and management controls will start to lose credibility.

In highly centralized organizations, where very few powers are delegated down the line, interactive controls cannot be effective. Similarly, such controls may not find application in strict bureaucratic structures. However, with expansion of businesses beyond national boundaries where flexibility rather than rigidity becomes the rule, human and system interaction become inevitable.

## Boundary Control Systems

All organizations have rules and procedures to prevent unethical and unlawful activities. However, in practice, entities have different dimensions of the correct behaviour. The dos and don'ts are more related to the culture of the organizations, rather than the written rules and regulations. While unlawful activities can have clearer demarcation, the ethical boundaries are not that obvious. The leadership styles and the organizational culture ultimately decide the real boundary system. Example 15.1 shows the boundary control system followed in an organization.

An entity can have a list of prohibited activities or areas of behaviour, along with the punishments for indulging in such acts or behaviour. The list could include actions such as the following:

1. Making false claims
2. Theft, misappropriation, and fraud, involving money or the stock in trade
3. Misbehaviour with colleagues, including sexual harassment and assault

**Example 15.1** Boundary Control System

A marketing organization has clearly written travel guidelines for its sales persons on official tours. They are entitled to travel by air-conditioned coaches while on duty. Many sales persons travelled by ordinary second class, but claimed air-conditioned coach fares. The company permitted such claims on the grounds that the salesmen often have to make some 'extra payments' in the course of their normal work which could not be claimed. However, when the company discovered that a member of staff claimed the fare for a journey he never made, he was promptly dismissed. This was the boundary line prescribed by the organization.

4. Breaking the law of the country—whether they are caught or not
5. Marketing goods below prescribed standards, thereby showing higher profits for the unit
6. Indulging in corruption and such other actions even though the intention may be to benefit the organization

From time to time cases such as Enron, WorldCom, etc. have come to light, indicating a breach of the boundary limits. Organizations constantly face the dilemma when senior managerial personnel indulge in breaches of conduct, overtly or covertly. At times, such behaviour may involve no personal gain, and is done for the interest of the corporation. In such cases, organizations have difficulty in enforcing discipline.

The boundary system can be enforced by the following approaches:

1. Prescribing an explicit set of rules and punishments
2. Communicating these so that the employees are aware of it
3. Establishing machinery for enforcing the rules regarding breach of behaviour
4. Ensuring a sense of credibility in the system and transparency in the approach enforcing this lever of control
5. Being sensitive to the external environment, particularly in the case of global corporations

## Belief Control Systems

Unlike the other levers of control, belief systems are concerned more with the organizational culture rather than written rules. All organizations have a set of beliefs and values which are usually the outcome of the leadership's vision. These issues distinguish world-class companies such as Infosys and

Tata Steel from the rest. They may have explicit codes of conduct for their employees, which are developed by voluntary consent. The top management has a big role to play in ensuring that these codes are followed, not only in letter but by the spirit in which they were meant.

The belief system has a big role to play in developing the diagnostic and boundary controls. If there are strong values and a sound belief system is in place, then the diagnostic control becomes less rigorous. This will reduce the scope for *opportunistic behaviour* by the employees. Some organizations conduct periodic surveys to assess the effectiveness of the belief system.

## Traditional Controls

The traditional controls usually consist of three categories, namely, physical controls, financial controls, and internal controls. These are adopted in varying forms and degrees in all organizations.

### Physical controls

This consists of constraints that limit access to the assets or to information. Locks for cash boxes, electronic ID cards, passwords for computers, etc. are some of the physical constraints usually adopted by individuals and organizations. The unfolding knowledge era has underscored the need for restricting access to sensitive data.

### Financial controls

These represent limits on expenditure and manifest themselves in various forms such as budgetary controls, signing of cheques, passing cheques, passing bills for payments, and financial limits on sanctioning capital expenditure. These forms of control exist in all organizations and tend to be stronger in family-owned entities, highly authoritative and centralized organizations, as well as in organizations with weak cultures. The success of financial controls depends upon their relevance to the needs of the organization.

As a part of financial controls, organizations develop certain cost controls which supplement the other controls. These include various tools such as allocation of overheads, flexible budgeting, and standard costing. Certain new areas such as activity-based costing, target costing, value-chain analysis, and life cycle costing are emerging in this field. Several measures for inventory control—just-in-time (JIT), EOQ re-order levels, etc.—are but a few techniques adopted in this area.

### *Internal controls*

This is a process by which the work done by one individual is automatically checked or complimented by another. To a large extent, this system prevents frauds and embezzlement. Examples are the following:

**Purchase procedure** One department places the purchase order, the stores receiving section receives the goods, the quality control staff check the quality, and the accounts department makes the payment.

**Cheque issue procedure** The accounts clerk makes the payment vouchers, the accounts manager approves them, the cashier's office prepares the cheques, the specified authorities sign them, and the dispatch section dispatches them.

While the internal control system effectively prohibits unwarranted behaviour on the part of the staff, it also at times leads to excessive control causing avoidable delays. This is witnessed in many government departments. Hence, the system of internal control has to be judiciously applied in order to avoid delays in carrying out the normal transactions.

These traditional controls are also called *procedural controls*. They have been developed over a period of time when commercial enterprises and business activities started to grow. Some of the controls in the information technology sector have started to grow in recent years. The financial controls in most countries have resulted in certain disclosure norms in order to ensure that the stakeholders get adequate information about the organizations. In India, the Companies Act, 1956, has made elaborate provision for disclosure. Besides, many organizations both in the government and commercial sector have elaborate *accounting manuals* to properly book the expenditure.

The Companies Act has also made it mandatory for limited liability companies to have an external audit carried out by chartered accountants who will certify whether the accounts represent a *true and fair* view of the accounts for the period. There are specific accounting standards issued by the Institute of Chartered Accountants of India (ICAI) which are mandatory to guide the auditors in the presentation of the accounts.

The concept of *delegation of authority* is closely associated with financial controls. This states the powers enjoyed by the managers at various levels within the organization. This could be in relation to sanctioning expenditure, investment, cheque signing, and purchasing powers and also covers non-financial areas, such as recruitments, punishments, production, marketing, and others.

## Cultural and Ethical Controls

These controls are related to the norms and behaviour exerted by societies which impact the behaviour of employees. These can be specific to a particular country or territory, or even to a tribe or sub-section. The Japanese work culture has been widely discussed and has been well-documented. There the employees prefer to stay in the same organization (called lifetime employment) and believe in high levels of commitment to the organization. This means that the control system can be less formal. These societal norms dictate to a considerable extent the control system in such enterprises. The basic culture and the control norms thus derived remain rigid over a period of time, even when the external pressures change the plans and strategies of the entity. Going back to Simon's four levers of control, the interactive and belief controls are mainly derived from the cultural ethos of the organization. The countries following the British colonial system generally follow a very strong diagnostic control system. Even today, the government in India has a lengthy set of rules and regulations which are very elaborate and contain several provisions regarding the public service. Even in the private sector, the impact of the government system is seen to a considerable extent. In a global context, the control measures for enforcing contractual obligations seem to have the long shadows of cultural impact. It is stated that in parts of the developing world the written terms of contracts are taken as broad indicators rather than as binding obligations.

The globalization era which started in the last decade of the 20$^{th}$ century has added horizontal dimensions to the impact of culture in the control context. There is a fusion of various cultures as many MNCs have started operations in various parts of the globe. There is a fresh wave of cultural winds enveloping the existing cultures, which has changed the working pattern of organizations. There are more interactive controls, thanks to the western cultures entering India. The Japanese culture has brought in more informal controls and the hierarchical boundaries are crumbling to give way to more personal interaction. However, there is a flip side, as certain cultural aspects which are incompatible with the domestic culture may create conflict situations. Example 15.2 shows the codes of conduct followed in the corporate sector.

**Example 15.2** Corporate Codes of Conduct

Certain large companies in India and elsewhere have developed specific codes of conduct. The Mitsubishi Code of Conduct is acknowledged as a highly value-based set of conduct rules. In India, the Tata Iron and Steel Company (TISCO) has an admirable code which is mutually respected by the employer and the employee. Obviously, such codes lead to greater efficiency in enforcing management controls, particularly when the employees are willing to own them and voluntarily come forward to follow such rules.

## Effective and Efficient Controls

Management controls have two dimensions in terms of the ultimate deliverables (Fig. 15.5). They have the micro purpose of meeting the aspirations of its immediate stakeholders; at the same time they have to meet the larger perspective in the economic and social context.

Table 15.3 highlights the respective roles of effective and efficient controls.

**Table 15.3** Roles of effective and efficient controls

| Type | Focus | Target | Measurement | Range |
|---|---|---|---|---|
| Effective | Overall purpose | Social needs | Macro (socio-economic) viability | Long-term (however, harmful effects can manifest in the short run as well) |
| Efficient | Constituent purpose | Stakeholder needs | Profits/EPS/ROI | Short- and medium-term |

The efficiency perspective dominates the day-to-day affairs of the business and the control measures filter down to the lowest rungs of the hierarchy. These controls manifest through a *pressure dynamics* due to the immediacy of the outcome of these controls. The effectiveness perspective is driven more by the external compulsions and is the main prerogative of the top management. Ignoring the environmental and labour issues, for example, can bring pressure from activist groups and trade unions which can tarnish the image of the organization.

The MCS should have a holistic mechanism to combine both the type of controls. In most of the cases, the control measures overlap between the two mentioned perspectives, but occasionally there can be conflicts between the two leading to organizational tensions. A typical example is ignoring pollution controls which may benefit the organization by reducing costs, but can lead to serious problems in the long run.

**Fig. 15.5**   Effective and efficient controls

## SHIFTS IN CONTROL SYSTEMS

Several factors have contributed to the change of control systems. They can be broadly grouped as external factors and internal factors.

### External Factors

These are basically economic and business related developments that impact the entity. These factors include

1. increase/decline in competition
2. consumer preferences
3. technological advancement
4. industry growth
5. global trends
6. legal and regulatory matters
7. environmental and political pressures

These factors create a need for the organization to respond to the external developments. In these circumstances, the existing control mechanisms will have to yield to the threats and opportunities created by the above forces. This situation leads to informal controls.

### Internal Factors

Pressures and conflicts can also arise due to internal factors. These can be grouped under managerial, technological, and cultural factors.

#### Managerial factors

This heading includes changes in the top management which lead to a different management style. Such changes may happen due to mergers and acquisition, a new CEO taking over, or a significant shift in the managerial philosophy due to some external pressure. The control systems can shift from diagnostic and boundary concept to interactive and belief concept. Formal controls may yield to informal controls. Perfect controls may be replaced by good controls. Such changes happen frequently in the corporate world.

### Technological factors

Changes in the product mix, production technologies, and logistical tools can all lead to a different approach to controls. The impact may not be very significant in the short run, but there can be significant differences due to advance technology in the long term.

### Cultural factors

Cultural issues sufrace when there are mergers, joint ventures, or overseas expansions. When employees of varying cultural backgrounds come together, existing control systems may not function smoothly. Such situations also arise due to nationalization/denationalization, where the organization may have to shift to a newer management model. Suitable adjustments may be needed to overcome control weaknesses emerging under such circumstances. Many a time, the problems may not be visible for some time, and the weaknesses may only surface during a crisis.

## DEGREE OF CONTROLS

Control may vary between the two ends, namely, highly focused controls and highly diffused controls. Centralized, highly controlled entities show case focused controls. Decentralized, risk-sharing (insurance, franchising, outsourcing) organizations tend to have diffused controls.

Entities adopt varying degrees of controls that suit their requirements. The degree of control is highest in a centralized structure where all activities are under the control of a few managers at the headquarters. This can be partly diluted by decentralizing the activities to branches or departments. Another way of reducing the degree of control is by taking an insurance policy. There is scope for sharing the span of control by franchising or outsourcing some of the activities. The ultimate step in eliminating controls is by closing down an operation. Obviously, this is not a planned reduction in the control spectrum but is dictated by economic reasons such as losses, etc. Such a closure may relate to some of the products or services alone. Besides, certain activities may be eliminated by technological improvements or better process controls.

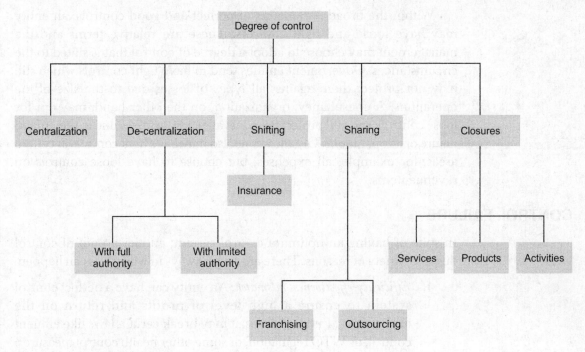

**Fig. 15.6**   Degree of controls

Figure 15.6 explains the degree of control which is the maximum at the left hand corner, and gets diluted as it goes towards the right.

## CONTROL OPTIMIZATION

An entity might aim at having a *perfect control system* which provides for all types of risks and ensures that no undesirable activity occurs. This is possible under circumstances of certainty and predictability, and in small and medium entities with a single unit of operation. The competition and technological innovations must be predictable to have such a control system.

In real life situations, perfect control is not always feasible due to competition, globalization, and the need to be innovative. Software companies and other service providers often have to look for products that satisfy the demanding global customers. Creativity and dynamism are the prerequisites in such situations. Hence, organizations aim to have *good control systems* which protect them against normal levels of uncertainties. These controls are more flexible and aim at acceptable levels of prevention against improper actions.

Within the broad parameters of perfect and good controls, an entity may have loose and tight controls. These are relative terms and the management may choose to adopt a degree of control that is suited to the circumstances. Government entities tend to have tight controls which still may not protect them against all types of losses due to the size of the operations. A consultancy, organization, on the other hand, may opt for loose controls and still protect it against all possible losses due to the limited nature of its operations. Organizations also may have tight controls in certain areas, for example, all expenses, but choose to have loose controls on revenue items.

## CONTROL FAILURE

In spite of having an optimum control system, entities go out of control due to a variety of reasons. There are several ways in which this can happen.

1. *Efficiency-effectiveness mismatch:* An entity can have a perfect control system to ensure a high level of profits and return on the investments. In this process, it may break certain laws like effluent control, or WTO regulation, or some other health control measures. This could lead to avoidable problems with the concerned authorities and may even lead to its closure.

2. *Behavioural problems:* All controls are exercised by human beings. Even the best of control systems are no proof against fraud. The Enron and WorldCom cases highlighted manipulations by the top management which led to the collapse of these mighty empires. The agency theory explains certain reasons for the behaviour-based problems in the context of controls.

3. *System failure:* An organization may suffer due to the failure of the system established within or outside. Loss of computer data is a typical example of an internal system failure. External failures can happen due to problems at an agent's level. A BPO operation may collapse due to staff problems and this could lead to control failures.

4. *External factors:* This includes a whole gamut of issues beyond an entity's control. The financial crisis arising out of the US sub-prime led economic problems has affected several entities across the globe. Natural calamities such as tsunami, floods, etc. can play havoc. Similarly, other political and social issues have given rise to control failures beyond the realm of the organization.

The following flow chart in Fig. 15.7 explains the hierarchy of the control mechanism which leads to the success or the failure of the MCS.

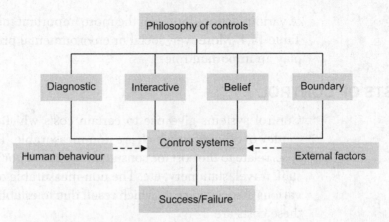

**Fig. 15.7**  Control hierarchy

Figure 15.7 provides the links between the generic control systems of Simon with the environmental factors. Human behaviour can ensure the success or failure of the control systems based on the levers. Factors beyond the realm of control of the organization (called externalities in economics) can impact the outcome of the established systems. Hence, the former is called the internal factor and the latter the external factor.

## Performance Measures

Human behaviour (the internal factor) needs some feedback on performance. Control measures require a set of measures to assess the outcome

**Table 15.4**  Financial and non-financial measures

| Financial measures | | Non-financial measures | |
|---|---|---|---|
| **Measures** | **Role** | **Measures** | **Role** |
| Gross profits | Relationship between revenue and direct costs | Market share | Indicator of successful marketing |
| Net profits | Profitability | Differentiation, uniquences | Patents, product leadership |
| Dividends | Shareholder satisfaction | Order book | Medium-term viability |
| Return on investment | Financial measure on investment | Inventory | Turnover of goods |
| Accounting ratios | Relationship measure between two parameters for liquidity, profitability, etc. | Human resources | Attrition, key staff, output |
| | | Licensers/franchisers | Risk |
| | | Balanced scorecard | Integrated and coordinated control measures across various activities |

of various actions. Some of the more important measures are explained in Table 15.4. Moreover, social or environmental pressures or reactions also play an important role.

## COSTS OF CONTROL

Control systems give rise to certain costs which are measurable, and a motley of other costs which are non-measurable. The measurable or direct costs relate to the cost for consultants recruited for introducing MCS, audit staff, travel, stationery, etc. The non-measurable or indirect costs relate to various associated costs which result due to establishing controls. Some of these costs are

1. employee time for implementing controls and ensure compliance,
2. lack of focus or commitment arising out of a tight control system,
3. manipulation or 'window dressing' performance indicators to show better results, and
4. excessive deployment of resources to achieve the standard set.

**Example 15.3** Misplaced Controls

An organization had a control system under which the cost of replacing a lock was treated as a capital cost that needed approval from the zonal offices. The cost of replacing a door (along with the lock) was treated as a revenue expenditure which required approval by a lower authority. Hence, the department preferred to change the entire door when the key was lost, in order to avoid the delay of approaching the zonal office. Thus, there was a huge indirect cost arising out of defective controls.

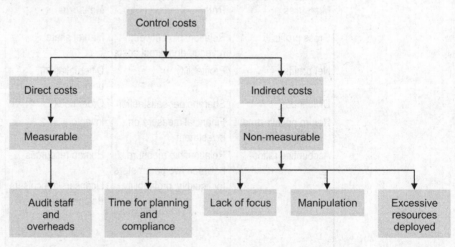

**Fig. 15.8** Costs of control

Many of the above indirect costs cannot be measured and even the impact may not be felt.

Figure 15.8 highlights the costs of control.

## MYTHS OF ACCOUNTABILITY AND CONTROLS

Control measures often lead to misinterpretations due to certain myths. Some of the more common myths and the reasons for the same are given in Table 15.5.

**Table 15.5**   Myths of control

| Myth | Reason |
| --- | --- |
| Budgets control expenditure. | Budgets only give the details of the expenditure which is incurred by the concerned executives. |
| Cost control is done by cost accountants. | Cost control is exercised by all staff. |
| Profits are earned by turnover. | Profits are the difference between revenue and expenditure. |
| Reduction in costs means more profits. | Reduction of costs may also lead to reduction in efficiency. |
| Computerization leads to cost controls | Computerization shifts a part of the manual controls into the computer systems. |

## SUMMARY

The term 'management control system' is not understood uniformly and has been interpreted in different ways by various authors. It broadly represents various actions taken by the management to achieve its goal. It may follow the single focus approach or dual focus approach, depending upon the extent of organizational participation in determining the control mechanism. Since control systems are designed by human beings, aspects such as rationality, ethics, creativity, etc. become major issues. Besides, the controls are also affected by various organizational tensions such as the conflict between growth, profit, and the desired levers of control.

Organizations are a fusion of formal and informal control systems. Formal systems are visible controls evolved by design and are driven by the strategies of the entity. Informal controls are a product of human interactions and are less visible. Further, controls may be grouped under the four levers developed by Robert Simons of the Harvard Business School. The first is the diagnostic system where performance is measured against specific targets. The second lever is called the interactive system which focuses on continuous interactions within and outside the organization. The boundary system constitutes the third lever and is based on rules and procedures to prevent unethical and unlawful activities. The fourth lever is the belief system which is determined by the entity's beliefs and values.

The traditional controls fall into three categories, namely, physical, financial, and internal controls. Further, there are cultural and ethical controls which are exerted by the societies and communities, which in turn are influenced by the national work culture. Effective controls address the overall purpose of the entity and target the long-term macro viability. The efficient controls are directed at satisfying stakeholder needs and are measured by short-term results, such as net profits, return on investments, etc. Together effective and efficient controls lead to sustainable growth. Besides, control systems may change due to a variety of external, internal, and technological factors.

Entities have varying degrees of control between the two walls of highly focused controls and highly diffused controls. This requires control optimization, which swings between perfect and good control systems on the one side, and control failure on the other, which can happen due to a variety of reasons. Entities may also choose between loose and tight control measures for specific activities. It is important to develop an appropriate blend of performance measures and balance the costs of control with its benefits.

## KEY POINTS

- Management control systems are a set of actions taken by the management of an entity to achieve its goal.
- Single focus control approach consists of a single or small number of individuals who plan the strategies and control measures.
- Dual focus control approach involves entities exercising control through participative and interactive approach.
- Organizational tension arises due to various forces that pull an entity in different directions.
- Formal control systems are visible systems which are planned and structured by the management.
- Informal control systems are less visible and come into place due to interactions between people, to address specific needs or threats.

- Levers of control are the broad divisions of control developed by Robert Simons, which are not mutually exclusive.
- Diagnostic systems are methods by which actual performance is measured against predetermined standards.
- Interactive systems arise due to human interaction between different layers of management and with interested parties outside the organization.
- Boundary systems are the limits of the correct behaviour within an organization.
- Belief system is a set of beliefs and values of an organization which arise due to the passage of time, leadership styles, and its value systems.
- Traditional controls are the commonly practised control measures over a long period of time.
- Physical controls are constraints that limit access to the assets or information of an entity.
- Financial controls generally represent limits on expenditure and include cost controls.
- Internal control is a process by which the work done by one individual is automatically checked by other individual(s).
- Cultural and ethical controls are norms and behaviour influenced by the national or societal culture.
- Effective controls are long-term controls to achieve the overall purpose of the entity.
- Efficient controls are short-term in nature and are focused on specific stakeholder needs.
- Degree of controls is the extent of control exercised by an entity and ranges between highly focused controls and highly diffused controls.
- Control optimization is the extent of perfection desired by a company from its control systems.
- Perfect control system provides for all types of risks and ensures that all activities are totally under control.
- Good control systems aim at acceptable degrees of control and levels of prevention against improper actions.
- Control failure occurs when entities go out of control in spite of having a good control system.
- Control hierarchy is the flow of controls embracing a combination of the control methods available.
- Costs of control consist of measurable or direct costs arising out of enforcing a control system as well as several indirect costs related to the control system.

## CONCEPT REVIEW QUESTIONS

1. What is meant by the term "management control systems"?
2. Explain single focus and dual focus methods of control.
3. What are the issues in relation to human behaviour vis-à-vis controls?
4. What is the role of organizational tensions in designing the control system?
5. Explain formal and informal controls.
6. What are the levers of control?
7. Explain diagnostic control systems.
8. Why are interactive control systems important?
9. Describe belief control systems.
10. Explain boundary control systems.
11. Describe the components of traditional control methods.
12. Elaborate the impact of cultural and ethical forces in the context of management controls.
13. Differentiate between effective and efficient control methods.
14. What do you understand by the term 'control optimization'?
15. What are the causes that lead to control failure?
16. Explain the structure of control hierarchy.
17. Give examples of some financial and non-financial performance measures.
18. What constitute the costs of control?
19. Explain certain myths of accountability and control.

## NUMERICAL PROBLEMS

1. **Suggest appropriate control measure(s) in the following cases.**

   (i) Seetha refused to pass the bills of the marketing department for the amounts claimed for paying bribes to pass their trucks ahead of others at check posts to avoid delays.

   (ii) Sriram of Chandigarh office earned promotion above his colleagues, for meeting all the standards set by the H.O. Not all agree that he deserves it.

   (iii) Sale of defective products of Subha biscuits has been now stopped. Earlier broken biscuits were sold at cheaper prices.

   (iv) During the monthly meetings at BLK Ltd, branch managers debate all the issues at length and arrive at the work programme of the subsequent month.

   (v) A company operates simple budgets for all departments. For production units only, standard costing systems are used.

(vi) Sarkar was happy when he signed the dismissal letter of Soman, their brightest sales executive, for misbehaving with the female receptionist.

(vii) Sarvottam Enterprises has recently dispensed with expenditure controls. All executives are expected to be reasonable in spending.

(viii) Sidhharth has developed a computerized control system by which the time taken for each process can be monitored with the results of the 'Time & Motion Study'.

(ix) Breaking News: Seniors Ltd's Board has sacked Mr Greames, the expatriate MD for drinking alcohol in Gujarat, knowing that it is a dry state. He pleaded in vain that he was not caught.

(x) Bret Lara was happy that his team has voluntarily agreed to share the proceeds of the 'Best Cricketer' awards given annually amongst them.

(xi) Competition in toy industry has changed the approach of Kapoor. He now starts his annual plans after consulting all his managers.

(xii) Cooperative dairy sector encourages best treatment for milk producers (the poor farmers). Invariably, they get their payments first. Some shopkeepers who sell milk wonder why it should be so.

(xiii) Mr Shetty, the MD of Olives Inc, is worried that the profit targets, which are the main control function in Olives, may not be achieved in January 2007 in his unit.

(xiv) Mr Sule, the Marketing Manager of Forit Ltd, believes in making personal calls to the company's 4 zones every week to ensure that the targets are achieved.

(xv) Kala Niketan has no prescribed fee for dance classes. They expect students to pay the prevailing market rates.

(xvi) The policy statement of Bonda Inc. provides for marketing staff to enquire about defects in their new model. Even non-sales staff seem to do it.

(xvii) Milk packed in sachets has a short shelf life. Govind Pandey talks on phone to the retailers before sending the required quantities.

2. **What is the single most appropriate control device relevant in the following contexts?**

(i) The staff of a company complain of too many checks on their travel bills. They cannot produce vouchers for tips given, etc.

(ii) The Ethics Control Manager uses his office car for the club visits of his wife.

(iii) There are too many variances between the actuals and budgets. The company wants to give up budgetary controls.

(iv) The financial standards are met but the company finds a lack of coordination between its various departments.

(v) The customers of a retail supermarket complained that there is too much delay at the cash counter.

(vi) Too much of milk was getting spoilt at the retail outlets. The main reason is inability to get a quick feedback of the sales on a real time basis. As a result, some shops go out of stock, while others have excess milk which is spoilt.

(vii) Ram, the Sales Manager, feels let down. He has lived within the budgets and obeyed all rules. 'The company wants me to do miracles,' he complained to his wife.

(viii) The software company believes in recruiting excessive number of engineers to face future rush of work.

(ix) Krishna Rao was charged with negligence in performing his duties as the head of the security department. He alleges that he is not responsible for the activities of his staff.

(x) The Novel Tannery Company has made excellent profits. There are however complaints that it has not cared for the community and the harmful effluence are allowed to mix with the drinking water system. There are some threats from the environmental groups recently to stop work at the tannery if corrective measures are not taken.

(xi) India Groceries is a supermarket. They are lenient with the first time embezzlements by their staff, but the subsequent offence is dealt with termination of service.

(xii) The new energy company is functioning very well without a formal administration and finance manual.

(xiii) There were too many problems in transporting the finished goods. The company wants to outsource the entire activity.

(xiv) The bonuses are given to all mangers on an ad hoc basis. There is a feeling that there must be a way of assessing the profits of each functional area.

(xv) Guha and Co. has dispensed with checking the accuracy of the medical claims submitted by the employees. Experience has taught them that they normally do not cheat.

3. **State if the following are TRUE or FALSE.**

(i) Computerization helps management controls in a multi-location entity.

(ii) A control system developed in one organization can easily be implemented in all other organizations.

(iii) Centrally controlled entities can impose control systems and obtain better results.

(iv) Budgetory control system produces excellent results when there are uncertainties in the industry.

(v) Diagnostic systems are suitable for measuring the performance of software groups addressing the needs of various clients.

(vi) Removal of punishments of all sorts will improve the performance of workers.

(vii) If a firm makes sufficient profits, it need now worry about control systems.

(viii) All controls need not be reduced to writing supported by formal orders.

(ix) Punishments are a part of MCS.

(x) Human beings are not always very rational or logical.

## CASE STUDY 1   Apna Ghar Retail Store

Sipping milk from his long stainless steel *lota*, Ram Nivas told his friends, '*Dekho yaar,* I am not widely read, but I can give my friends at Harvard a few good tips as to how to run a decentralized business.' His success endorsed his statement.

Ram Nivas founded the Apna Ghar retail store concept in 1960. He was a pioneer in the concept of mini-super markets at that time. Soon he started seven such stores in the state of Paschim Pradesh. His focus was to meet the entire needs of middle class families in that area under one roof. He believed in developing strong rapport with the families of the farming community in the neighborhood and serve all their household as well as agricultural requirements. He appointed a number of persons from his home district for the various locations during the start and they proved to be loyal to him always. Though he delegated wide powers to all his field units, he made personal visits at least once a month to all of them and supervised the operations. He got monthly profit and loss statements from all the units and ensured that they ran in profits.

He died a happy man in July 2006. His son Pritam, an MBA from a reputed institute known for its strong marketing focus with high value systems, took over his father's empire. Within the first 6 months, he felt that the organization lacked proper control measures. His efforts to introduce a budgetary control system met with opposition—at times fierce—from his unit heads. He noticed that while the profits were good, the entity was running into heavy overdrafts. The units often seemed to have cash balances, but were not transferring the same to the H.O. because these were claimed to be needed for local purchase of some items in high demand.

Confused by these anomalies, Pritam appointed PKS Consultancy to review its working. After a quick 3 week study of the 7 units, the following report was given:

---

**PKS Consultants Ltd.**

**Confidential**

**2nd January 2007**

**Mr Pritam,**
**M.D., Apna Ghar**

Dear Sir,

As per your oral request our teams visited the seven locations of Apna Ghar during the period 5th December to 26th December 2006. This period is insufficient to cover all aspects of the operations, but our quick report is submitted herewith.

I. All the seven units are managed by the friends of Late Mr Ram Nivas. They have wide experience and have been with the group for the last 30 plus years. (Age group 55–70)

II. Reporting system consists of a monthly P & L a/c. No bank reconciliations or stock verifications are conducted.

III. The Heads have fierce loyalty to Late Mr Ram Nivas. They are touchy about changes and resist even suggestions of inter-group transfers.

IV. No internal audit system is prevalent.

V. Originally all the purchases were centralized. Gradually, the units started purchasing urgent items and over a period of time the local purchases started exceeding the central purchases.

VI. The 7 locations sell about a third of sales through cash payments. No invoices are made for sales below Rs 1000 and sales to regular customers. This seems to be a local practice though.

VII. The Heads are very hospitable and enjoy high standards of living.

VIII. Majority of the staff are related to the Unit Heads; this helped an informal work culture.

IX. Re-cash sales one Head said, 'Every time Mr Ram Nivas visited my place he collected the money from cash sales as per my oral declaration. No sales tax was paid in these sales. Who will pay all the taxes? *Saheb* knew how to run the business. Please tell *Chota Saheb* not to change anything.'

X. The stores had close personal links with the local communities and made home deliveries. There is some decline in sales due to the newly started super markets but the Heads felt that they enjoy strong client loyalties.

XI. Five out of the seven units are located in semi-urban areas where IT industry is growing fast. The traditional agrarian complexion is rapidly changing.

Thanking you,

(Deshmukh)
**PKS Consultants Ltd**
P.S. Our invoice is enclosed

**Discussion Questions**

1. Identify the major weaknesses in the control system of the Apna Ghar Group.
2. Suggest a system of change over to better control systems ensuring a smooth change process.

| CASE STUDY 2 | The Consultant's Dilemma |
| --- | --- |

Inspite of a long stay at New Delhi, Bhimsena Rao has not got out of the one habit he picked up in his home town, Vijayawada. This is to stretch out for a cup of strong filtered coffee whenever he is preoccupied. Today he has good reasons to reach for his third cup for he is worried. The proposal from Central India Fresh Juices (CIFJ) company is a good case for a consultancy firm of his size. The fee will be good. But he is not sure how to go about it.

The facts before him tell a fairy tale. The company has plants at Nagpur and Hyderabad, where it has enormous processing capacity. It makes orange juice at Nagpur plant and grape juice at Hyderabad. The brand name 'Fruitable' is not widely known, but its users have a strong brand loyalty, which is mainly due to its distinct sour taste. It commands a strong support amongst user groups between 25–40 years of age. More advertising, based on proper customer feedback could enhance the sales substantially. The turnover was ₹17 crore at Nagpur and ₹14 crore at Hyderabad for the last financial year (2007–08). But the company has been in losses for the past 3 years after five consecutive years of profits. From the information available, Mr Rao could get the following facts:

- The plants are operating roughly at 40 per cent capacity, mainly due to the seasonal nature of the harvest of fruits. It reached a peak of 75 per cent in 2001, but since then has been declining, partly due to lower wages offered to workers who are in demand during the peak season.
- The board consists of 6 members all of whom are influential farmers from A.P. and Maharashtra.
- There is a financier with immense funds willing to invest in new business but prefers the equity route.
- With minor modifications the plants can handle other fruits, such as guava, mango, pineapple, tomato, etc.
- The company has an excellent team of technical staff. But there is patent labour discontentment due to lack of increments and bonuses. A strong labour union has regular battles with the management.

- The marketing function is weak. No strategic decisions are ever made in pricing, market research. and customer feedback.
- They have good retail networking in western and southern India.
- Attempts to branch off into dairying (milk, lassi, and ghee) were made two years back, but they all ended up as flops contributing to only losses.

Mr Rao also noticed a curious attitude amongst the six departmental heads. They could agree on nothing at any point of time. They all were well-qualified persons with strong commitments to the company's growth, but took rigid stands when it came to decision making.

## Discussion Questions

Refer to the enclosed 'proceedings of a recent meeting' and answer the following questions.

1. What is wrong within control systems in the Company?
2. Suggest a good management control system for the company?
   (Hint: Certain behavioral issues come out from the proceedings of the meeting. These give a hint to the approach of the members. Study them in relation to the other facts and relate them to your suggestions.)

| | |
|---|---|
| Proceedings of a recent meeting of the departmental heads as made by Mr Rao (strictly for his own use) | |
| Date | : 12-8-07 |
| Venue | : Small meeting hall (Amrut Hall) |
| Present | : |
| Ms Shanta Apte (MD) | |
| Mr Krodhit Singh (Chief—Production) | |
| Mr Jolly Jogaunnath (Chief—Marketing) | |
| Mr Dukkalal Sokaram (Chief—Finance) | |
| Ms Nutan Adhikari (Chief—Planning) | |
| Ms Lilywhite (Chief—HR & Admin) | |
| Shanta | : Welcome all of you. Let me introduce Mr Bhimesena Rao, our consultant to look into our management control systems and suggest improvements |
| Dukkalal | : We are doing fine. Do we need a consultant? |
| Shanta | : We are in red for the last 3 years. Something has to be done, isn't it? |
| Nutan | : I like it. Let us go ahead. |
| Rao | : Thank you. I would like to have some feedback on what went wrong, or let me say this way–what did not go right. |

| Nutan | : | Let me chip in Mr Rao. I think we are not very clear about our goals at times. At the beginning we focused on the high quality of our products and return on investments. It worked. We were making profits for 5 years. Then we shifted to this new idea—market share—whatever it means at any cost. We offered too many discounts, gave extended credits, and landed up in this mess. |
| --- | --- | --- |
| Jogaunnath | : | Well, it was my idea. It is very sound even now. It failed because we never followed up collections, and my idea for computerizing the whole process was refused. So, the finance guys never knew who owed what. And then suddenly the whole plan was dropped in October 2005. No discounts….no credit sales. Dealers shifted to the competitors. India Juices took away all the sales. |
| Shanta | : | We also lost heavily on the sachets. |
| Krodhit | : | O God! Don't mention the name. It is nauseating. The planning and marketing guys messed up everything, and I got all the blame. The plastic material stuff we got was so flimsy. Half of them leaked and who in his senses will buy stuff like that. Purchase Department made another mess, wish I could kill them. The whole project cost was…… |
| Dukkalal | : | A colossal 20 lakhs. Do not forget Krodhit-ji, it was you who wanted the dairy business in. Nutan supported as well. Another flop. Here, Mr Rao, I tell you nothing works. People with all wrong ideas are liked by our MD….and when the accounts are finalized, who gets the blame….the finance guy. |
| Ms Lilywhite | : | There are other problems too. We have 75 permanent staff and something around 600 temporary workers. Some of them work regularly, but were never made permanent. Now, they have formed a union. No bonuses or increments for the last 2 years. The finance people say our manpower cost is 17 per cent of the turnover, and is increasing…. |
| Shanta | : | Oh! don't go into that again. Mr Rao, she is so good in figures. She must have been in finance. May be Dukkalal may shift places. He is becoming so negative these days. By the way, nobody blamed finance for the losses, only we expressed concern. |

## CHAPTER 16

# Balanced Scorecard

## Learning Objectives

After reading this chapter, you will be able to understand

- the limitations of lag indicators for performance measurement
- the need for an integrated and coordinated set of performance measurement tools
- the role of balanced scorecards as an effective tool of planning and control
- the need for balancing the activities to convert the strategic plan into realistic action plan
- the cause and effect relationships between various performance measurement tools

- the various perspectives of an organization's balanced scorecard
- the individual indicators to assign relative weightage to each of them to realize the organization's strategy
- the various issues that impact the preparation and execution of the scorecards
- how organizations benefit by adopting the balanced scorecard technique and act upon them

## INTRODUCTION

Studies in business management have repeatedly highlighted the limitations of financial measures to assess the performance of organizations. From the management's point of view it is easier to understand a simple parameter such as return on investment or net profits, as a target for assessing performance. But from a control point of view, it is prudent to have an integrated system of measurement rather than a single yardstick. Besides, financial tools are often seen as *lag indicators* of past performance. In this context, balanced scorecard (BSC) provides an integrated control system which tries to focus on overall improvement as its bottom line. This helps the management accountant to measure and control the performance of the various activities of the entity more effectively. BSC is closely associated with the other costing tools, such as activity-based costing (ABC), target costing, value-chain analysis, and standard costing.

In recent years, the BSC has emerged as an important enabler for performance measurement of commercial as well as not-for-profit organizations. It provides an edifice for linking the lag and lead indicators, and comes out with an elite map for achieving the strategy of the organization. It provides futuristic directions and enhances accountability and responsibility. Its importance can be understood from the fact that more than 50 per cent of Fortune 1000 companies and 40 per cent of the major European companies use this approach.

Peter Drucker (1993) underscores the need for a combination of lead and lag indicators based on the economists' model. According to him, in a competitive world lead indicators become significant as they facilitate an effective decision-making process, which gives rise to desirable future outcomes. This is basically an integrated planning and control exercise adopted for achieving the long-term perspectives of the company. Kaplan and Norton (2001) vote for a balanced scorecard with a judicious mix of outcomes and performance drivers.

The BSC provides the logical link between the lead and lag indicators based on a cause–effect rationale. It provides a chain of indicators which highlight the smooth flow of actions, deriving its source from the vision and strategies.

In commercial organizations, profits are the ultimate goal and are driven by the shareholder perspective. But in order to achieve this, the activities have to harmoniously flow between the various measures in order to achieve the ultimate goal. Empirical evidence is more important in cost–effect relations. It is better to express them as an if–then statement to highlight the measures and the drivers (Kaplan and Norton 2001).

## STRATEGY

Strategy is the basic platform on which an entity's operations are planned. This is derived from the entity's vision and is the core ideology to create value for all its stakeholders. It is specific to organizations and cannot be standardized. Once it is formulated, the detailed planning process starts. The BSC is the most comprehensive tool of management control to achieve its strategic plans.

In a majority of cases, the real problem was not one of failed strategies, but was more due to bad execution. Nearer home, Kautilya in his *Arthashastra* emphasizes the need for various resources in a project management plan which resembles the BSC approach.

### Strategy Maps

A strategy is an abstract and brief statement of the entity's broad approach derived from its vision and mission to convert them into the desired outcomes. Strategy maps are additional layers of information which facilitate the preparation of the BSC. This adds clarity and granularity to the task of preparation of the final scorecards. This process is called strategy mapping and facilitates the preparation of practical and efficient BSCs.

'The strategy map provides the missing link between strategy formation and execution,' opine Kaplan and Norton (2004).

This is an inter-disciplinary exercise and establishes the primary cause–benefit flows which lead to the eventual preparation of the BSC. This is an inevitable process in converting the strategy into an action path depicted in the form of the scorecards.

Balanced scorecards enable organizations to support the implementation of their strategy. An entity in the food processing sector may have a basic strategy of ensuring good prices for the producers (farmers) in order to ensure committed supply of the raw materials. The company is still interested in ensuring adequate returns for the shareholders, enhancing market share, etc. and hence, it must develop a coordinated approach to integrate procurement, production, marketing, finance, and HR functions, to meet its strategy and also run the company successfully. Its strategy to pay higher prices to farmers is to ensure a loyal set of producers who are committed to ensure the company's procurement of raw material. This also enhances their ability to adopt more sophisticated farm-related technology. The company must develop a set of scorecards for its major activities in order to remain profitable. Balanced scorecard enables the organization to do it exactly.

This concept was popularized by Robert S. Kaplan and David P. Norton (1992) who have published a number of articles in this area. They have basically suggested four scorecards. These are as follows:

a. Financial perspective
b. Internal business processes perspective
c. Customer perspective
d. Learning and growth perspective

Kaplan and Norton have, however, indicated that the above measures are not necessarily sacrosanct and suggest that entities may choose other appropriate measures for meeting their specific requirements. However, the above perspectives are widely used and the authors have proved by virtue of various consultancy assignments that the balanced scorecard approach helps entities to implement their strategies.

# RELEVANCE OF SCORECARDS

The financial performance measures are usually kept at the top of the scorecard as entities are ultimately judged by the financial returns accruing to the shareholders. But this is the result of the cumulative performance of all the functions of the entity. Hence, there is a need to *balance* the performance of all the functional areas. This implies that the measures should flow from the company's strategy, and must be consistent and understandable. They should have the following basic elements if the balanced scorecard approach is to yield the desired benefits.

1. The company should have a well adopted strategy. If the strategies are vague and keep changing any performance measure will prove to be ineffective.
2. The internal communication system should be effective and the strategies must be well understood and internalized by all the employees.
3. There must be an effective reporting system with consistent parameters.
4. The work culture of the entity should allow transparency in performance evaluation; otherwise there will be distrust and lack of commitment.
5. Other control measures such as budgeting, standard costing, performance targets, etc. should be tuned to the balanced scorecard approach.
6. Performance measures should be largely controllable by the unit and must be well understood; otherwise this will turn out to be a theoretical exercise.
7. There should not be too many performance measures under any of these scorecards. If the number of measures is too high it could render the exercise more complicated and less effective.

Besides the overall company scorecard, the individual departments can develop their own scorecards that are more specific in nature.

# CHARACTERISTICS OF SCORECARDS

Scorecard consists of a number of performance measures which have a cause–and–effect relationship. It means that improvement in one measure will have an impact on other measures. If a measure does not have such an association, it is not included. Most of the measures will have an impact on the finished results. This is the unique nature of BSC.

## Internal Business Processes Perspective

This scorecard consists of a number of measures which the company takes to produce goods and provide services that satisfy the customers. It differs from company to company and becomes very relevant in a competitive environment. It could include a number of measures, such as set up time, quality costs, timely delivery, defective units, number of complaints received, time to settle customer claims, favourable and unfavourable cost variances, age of inventory, timely introduction of new products, market share, etc.

Basically, the above measures fall into two categories:

*Efficiency of production or service provision:* This consists of various measures pertaining to timely completion, quality, and costs.

*New products/services:* This consists of number of such products introduced, rate of introduction per quarter, sales of new products, number of units sold, and feedback.

It can be seen that some of the parameters show an upward trend and others show a downward trend in realizing the goal of *overall improvement* towards achieving the strategic goals. Usually, they are denoted by the symbol + for upward trend and – for the downward trend. Under the above perspective, measures such as the number of new products will show a + sign, meaning that it should grow higher; whereas the number of complaints should show a – sign. To explain this further, the following items must show a + sign:

1. Timely delivery
2. Favourable variances
3. Timely introduction of new products
4. Market share

All these indicators should show growth in quantitative terms.
The following items shall show a – sign:

1. Set up time
2. Quality costs
3. Defective units
4. Number of complaints received
5. Time to settle customer claims
6. Unfavourable cost variance
7. Age of inventory

A decline in quantitative terms is desirable.

## Customer Perspective

The success of an enterprise depends on the satisfaction derived by the customers using its products and services. There are several ways of measuring this. Just as for the internal business process perspective, there are positive (+) and negative (−) indicators. The + sign can relate to the following:

1. New customers added
2. Customers retained from earlier periods
3. Product sales
4. Market share

The + sign refers to a positive trend in the particular perspective. The − sign relates to:

1. Customer complaints
2. Product returns
3. Percentage of customers lost from the previous period

The − sign denotes areas where there is deterioration in the marketing area. It may be noted that the + and − signs are *directional* in nature and not quantitative. Hence, they have to be supported by the appropriate figures to evaluate performance. Usually, these details are obtained by internal and external approaches. The internal approach consists of statistics relating to the number of customers retained, new customers, the number of new orders, etc. which can be obtained from the company's records. It may have to conduct market surveys, often with help from opinion survey agencies, in order to get reliable data in areas, such as customer satisfaction, customer perception of order taking, and the overall satisfaction results.

## Learning and Growth Perspective

This is also referred to as the *learning and innovation* perspective. Many companies in competitive environments consider this as the base of the pyramid for the growth of the organization. It is obvious that both internal processes and customer perspectives depend upon the quality of products and services along with the quality of the executives and employees. In the current knowledge-based economy, this perspective drives performance to a considerable extent and organizations are placing greater importance on acquiring the right type of processes and human resources. It is somewhat difficult to arrive at very precise performance indicators that can be quantified, for this perspective. However, a number of positive (+) indicators can be used as shown here:

1. Training costs per employee
2. Suggestions per employee
3. Number of patents registered
4. Number of new processes developed
5. Value added per employee
6. Number of training man hours

Similarly negative (−) indicators are as follows:

1. Employee turnover
2. Reductions in training budget
3. Extension of probation

The relevance of this performance perspective is very high also in the service sector. Companies in the information technology, ITES, and BPO sectors are vying with each other to acquire the right quality personnel. In the pharmaceutical sector, higher budgets are provided for the R&D activity. Intellectual property has become a hotly debated topic and at times is an issue of contention between various nations.

## Financial Perspective

This has been the most popular performance measure for a long time. In the commercial world, entities have to deliver value to the owners and therefore, the financial numbers become the widely used indicators of good and bad performance. Even in the case of not-for-profit organizations, such as NGOs, government departments, and charitable organizations, some type of financial indicators are always used. Here also, the positive (+) and negative (−) indicators are applicable. The usual measures are as follows:

1. Net profit
2. Sales growth
3. Gross margin
4. Operating profits
5. Financial ratios
6. Cost variances
7. Earning per share

The popularity of this perspective is also due to the fact that it is precisely quantifiable. There are also legal obligations which make it mandatory to prepare financial statements for the stakeholders, showing the mentioned figures. It also enables inter-organizational comparisons.

# MODEL SCORECARD

Based on the knowledge regarding scorecards, we can now attempt to compile a BSC for a dairy company. Let us assume that the company is in a very competitive business atmosphere and a new MD has been appointed and he has convened a meeting of all the departments to discuss the important issues confronting the company. After a month of detailed debates and meetings he has arrived at the following major issues which need to be addressed.

1. The shareholders were not happy with the return on their investments.
2. The main reason for inadequate returns was the relatively low revenue generation compared to other units of the same nature.
3. Customer satisfaction with the regularity of supplies was poor as the products were often not available.
4. Customer satisfaction with the range of products of the company left much to be desired.
5. The main reason for the inadequate supplies was the shortage of milk, particularly during summer months.
6. The percentage of spoiled milk due to storage conditions was higher than the industry average.
7. The market demands new flavours of ice-cream and yogurt, which competitors are offering.
8. The dairy should offer new products more frequently to stay in the market.
9. The solution for increasing milk supply is to educate local farmers to form cooperatives and develop refrigerated chilling centres.
10. Training the young technical staff in dairy technology at company's cost will improve their competence.

The above indicators can be classified under two broad heads, namely, increasing milk supply, and improving the technological aspects. With the given information, a balanced scorecard can be prepared (Fig. 16.1). The plus and minus indicators show the desired directions of growth of the performance measure.

## Number of Scorecards

Kaplan and Norton recommended the above four perspectives in their scorecard model, but they also mentioned that the number and the titles of the perspectives are suggestive, and entities may develop scorecards to suit their specific requirements. However, it is seen that most of the

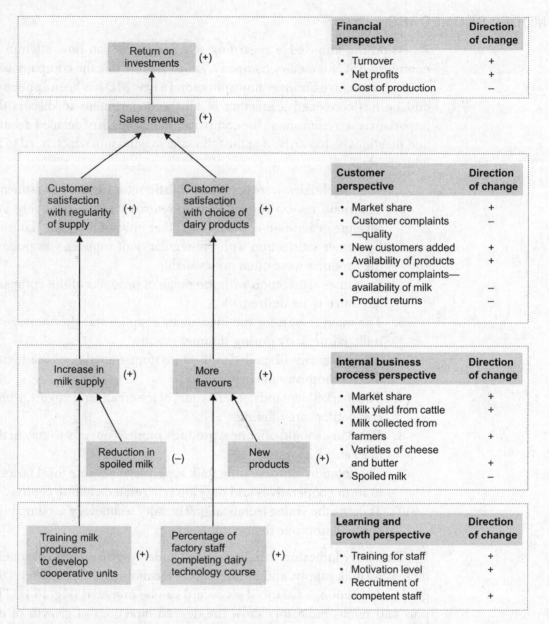

**Fig. 16.1** Balanced scorecard in a dairy company

organizations have adopted the above perspectives, at times with slightly different titles.

A study conducted in south-east Asia by James Creelman and Naresh Makhijani (2005) suggests that 66 per cent of the reviewed organizations have four perspectives, while 25 per cent adopted five perspectives.

A few organizations chose only three perspectives and dropped the financial perspective. The argument for this approach was that the financial targets by themselves may not trigger a chain of actions, particularly in creative organizations which are driven by other motivators. Similarly, in not-for-profit and government entities financial perspectives are not considered as significant. Besides, some entities adopt peculiar perspectives which are relevant to their nature of business. Examples are as follows:

Pharmaceutical companies   :   New medicines developed
Mining companies              :   Safety
Community organizations    :   New members enrolled
FMCG                              :   Brand promotion

It could be seen that the basic imperative of the balanced scorecard is to develop a vibrant measuring system. The individual scorecards are organization-specific and must be developed in relation to its unique characteristics.

## Weightage of Scorecards

All the items in the scorecard may not be of equal importance for the overall purpose of achieving the strategy. Hence, organizations may assign appropriate weightages to the different perspectives and the actions there under. The following (Fig. 16.2) may be the weightages allocated by the dairy company for its perspectives under the scorecard.

It may be seen that the company has attached the maximum weightage to the customer and to internal processes. Under the customer perspective, importance is given to capturing new markets (35%) since the company is in a competitive business. This is supported by the emphasis on service quality (25%). These indicators are also supported by the other scorecards. For example, under internal processes, the highest priority is given for milk procurement (40%) in order to ensure greater scope to meet the increasing demand. The company's desire for capturing new markets is also supported by the emphasis on training (20%) and recruitment of competent staff (20%). The correspondingly lower emphasis on new processes (20%) and technology development (15%) indicate the strategy to continue a more or less *status quo* approach as far as new products are concerned. This is also supported by the emphasis on asset utilization (30%) and lower cost (20%) indicators. Thus, the various scorecards are linked by a cause–and–effect relationship.

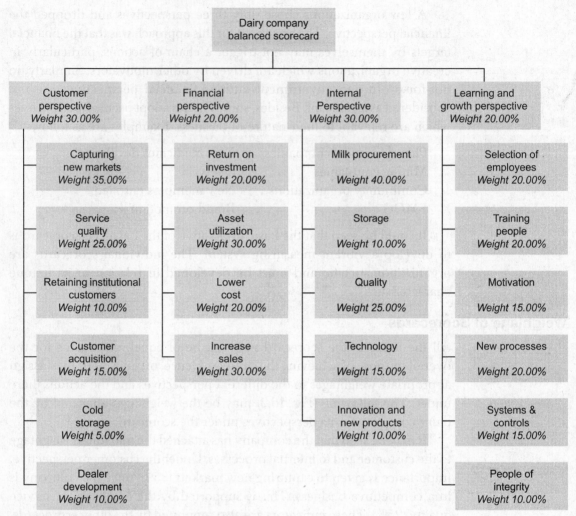

**Fig. 16.2**   Balanced scorecard with weightages

## Balancing the Balanced Scorecard

The balanced scorecard integrates the financial and non-financial measures of performance and provides a holistic set of measures to assess all the areas of performance across the different functions. In its absence, managers were assessed only on the basis of financial performance, such as quarterly or annual net profits or ROI. This has a few drawbacks. The emphasis becomes short-term and the financial figures can be tailored to show the desired level of performance called 'window dressing'. The firm's performance as revealed by the financial accounting is the result of integrating and coordinating all the short-term functions. Certain long-term measures such as product innovation and customer satisfaction may not be adequately reflected by the rupee or dollar figures of the earnings. But by using a number of scorecards, the firm can balance the different functions and focus on the weak links to enhance overall performance. This is also a learning process for executives to understand the inter-dependence of each function. Thus, a healthy integration of lag and lead performance measures is achieved.

### Issues in balancing

The concept of balancing the individual scorecards poses a few issues. It is obvious that each scorecard would require adequate resources to achieve the targets. Besides, all the parameters may not be amenable to the cost-and-effect relationships. Most of these issues can be sorted out by careful planning and interaction between the departments. The concerned executives must be aware of certain inherent issues in balancing the scorecards. They are as follows:

**Conflict between qualitative and quantitative parameters** Certain activities such as research and development, advertising, etc. may not reveal quantifiable results in a linear fashion. This may create certain issues in drafting a BSC, where some of the participants may like to see benefits flowing out in the short run.

**Balancing financial and non-financial parameters** This is inherent in the BSC structure itself. Each indicator, though related to others, may not be amenable to an expression in financial terms. Careful strategy mapping, however, ensures that these indicators are drawn up with measurable relationships.

**Impact of external environmental factors** One of the problems associated with budgeting and other project planning exercises is the unpredictable nature of external forces. This has increased considerably with globalization and growth. To a considerable extent, the concept of flexible budgeting has addressed this problem. Similarly, in the case of BSC, a certain measure of flexibility has to be introduced. This implies that the indicators can affect and also be affected by changes in the other indicators. Besides, due to the competitiveness of the markets certain new indicators may have to be adopted and certain changes in the existing nature of the indicators, and their relative weightages will become imperative. These are however associated with all the planning exercises of organizations in the competitive world.

Besides, the balancing test may be difficult in the early years of adoption of BSC. Achieving the ideal cause-and-effect relationship requires certain familiarity with the BSC concept. Hence, the balancing act may face rough weather in the early years of BSC systems and may tempt organizations to give up the approach altogether. Usually, the help of an external consultant is taken to overcome this problem. A study reviews that 35 per cent of organizations built their enterprise BSCs within 6 months, while 60 per cent took more than a year. Example 16.1 shows the success story of a company's BSC.

### Example 16.1 A BSC Success Story

The example of the diary industry can be used to illustrate the relevance of the balanced scorecard. Let us assume that North Bound Dairies (NBD), an imaginary company, is a state-of–the-art diary with a variety of products. We can examine the above four perspectives with reference to NBD. This illustrates the progress made by NBD with the help of a BSC framework at all levels of its activities.

First is the learning and growth perspective. The company has a team of efficient engineers with required skills. It has developed sophisticated processes, particularly in products such as cheese and yogurt, and enjoys technological superiority over its competitors. It has in place a good information system and all the processes, both in the factory and in the offices, are fully computerized. NBD emphasizes regular training for all technical staff. A performance-based reward system is in place and it has lower attrition levels than the rest of the industry.

Second is the internal business process perspective. NBD's thrust in this perspective is two-fold. One is the innovative steps under which it aims to create a niche product differentiation in terms of taste, longevity of shelf life, etc. It constantly strives to make the product more suitable to the climatic, social, and economic conditions of its market segments. The second is the cost focus. NBD has a well-internalized benchmarking system vis-à-vis the best producers globally, and constant endeavours to reduce cost.

Third is the customer perspective. Since NBD is in a very competitive market, it has to be very alert to market clues. It depends on first hand information from its teams of field sales representatives and conducts periodical market surveys to understand customer preferences. Through its real time computer network it is able to monitor the customer profile. It has a clear-cut policy which empowers field staff to immediately address all quality issues.

The fourth is the financial perspective. The ultimate profitability of the firm is measured by this perspective. NBD has taken steps to be a cost leader, and constantly uses the benchmarking technique to monitor costs and reduce them wherever possible. The emphasis on market share supported by good quality products ensures attractive sales. Thus, NBD's strategic initiative helps to ensure a satisfactory return for the shareholders.

## The Cause–and–effect Relationships

Now, one can appreciate the interrelationship between the scorecards. The learning and growth scorecard provides the foundation upon which the firm's other activities are based. For NBD, it provides the technical base for its manufacturing and marketing activities. This leads to better internal processes and enables a company to produce good quality products, and also to make innovations to outsmart competitors. This, in turn, leads to better customer relationship through successful marketing initiatives. The combined result of good internal processes and customer scorecards result in good financial performance. This again enables the firm to strengthen its learning and growth perspective. Hence, it is a cycle whereby each scorecard contributes to the other, leading to synergy and integration.

## Barriers to Success

There are many recorded instances of the successful implementation of balanced scorecards. However, the implementation path is not strewn with rose petals. A good knowledge of the barriers will help to a large extent (Table 16.1).

**Table 16.1**  Barriers to implementing scorecards

| Barrier | Nature |
|---|---|
| Lack of clarity on strategy | Many entities do not have clearly defined strategies. Some of the well-worded strategy statements remain merely management jargons; others are well-articulated desires, unsupported by actions. A BSC cannot translate a vaguely conceived strategy. |
| Lack of cause–and–effect relationship | A BSC's success depends upon a clearly laid down chain of related flow of actions. Drawing up this relationship comes with experience. This requires some skill in drafting a BSC and during the early years, the help of consultants will be of relevance. |
| Communication barrier | BSC involves an elite level of coordination between the staff in different departments. This requires a well-developed communication channel. It is stated that less than 5 per cent of the workforce understand the strategy. Even at top levels, conceptual clarity is sometimes missing. Hence, the communication systems have to be strengthened. |
| Work culture | The organizational culture should provide for a healthy and transparent system. This is essential for the success of the BSC. Professionally managed entities find it easier to implement scorecards than autocratic or traditional entities. |
| Resource barrier | Various resources such as technology, manpower, funds, equipments, etc. are required for the implementation of the scorecards. If there is any significant shortage then the activity flow will be seriously hampered. |
| Incentive system | Usually the BSC is used as a performance measurement tool to motivate the workforce. If the incentives are absent (or worse still, are defectively implemented), then the system will collapse. |

*(Contd.)*

**Table 16.1**   (*Contd*)

| Barrier | Nature |
|---|---|
| Monitoring and feedback | This is often considered as the biggest barrier for BSC implementation. Regular feedback mechanism helps effective monitoring. With the progress in information technology, availability of real time information is made easy. |
| Top management support | The top management in many organizations starts enthusiastically with the BSC concepts, but somewhere down the line they lose their interest. The absence of sustained support from management can seriously harm the success of this endeavour. |

## Cost of Implementing Balanced Scorecard

The costs of implementing BSC are usually not shown as a specific expenditure head. However, in a few cases, attempts are made to show it as a cost item. The scorecard implementation requires certain resources which are mostly in the form of employee time. This consists of the BSC team which may be involved on a full-time basis. These teams may consist of membership ranging from 2 to 20 people. Besides this, there are other costs involved. Many entities prefer to appoint a team of consultants who will naturally charge a fee for their services. This is a good investment, as a competent consultancy team can bring them huge benefits.

Apart from these visible expenditure heads, there will be other costs as well. Employees will be required to attend meetings and programmes in this connection. This will be an invisible cost. Some entities book the hours the employees spend and charge it to the separate BSC account. Certain costs will be incurred towards training, which can include training materials, infrastructure and related charges, logistics expenditure in the form of travelling, lodging and boarding, etc. Niven (2003) is in favour of offsite programmes to train the staff without interruption. Example 16.2 shows the example of a company venturing into the BSC technique to sort out its problems.

### Example 16.2   West Coast Dairies

West Coast Dairies (WCD) has been in business for the last 15 years, mainly in southern and western India. It deals with a number of reasonably popular dairy products such as pasteurized milk, butter, cheese, and yogurt. It has its own cattle farm in Maharashtra, but depends on the local farmers to supply milk to the extent of 70 per cent of its requirements. It has a dairy situated within 50 kilometres of the cattle farm.

Mr Ramesh, MD of WCD, was reviewing the financial performance of the company for the financial year just concluded. The results were not encouraging.

Sales had declined by 10 per cent; but what worried the MD more was a steep decline of 18 per cent in the net profits. Suresh, his GM (finance), was explaining the reason for the decline in profits thus:

Suresh: 'There are a number of reasons for the decline in profits. Look at the purchase prices we are paying to the farmers. It has gone up by 25 per cent in the summer months, when the milk production is low. Again, we are forced to buy from farmers at distant places and this has added to the cost of transportation, along with the higher prices paid.'

Ramesh: 'One moment please. What is the reason for buying from these far-off places?'

Suresh: 'We took a policy decision 2 years ago not to buy the excess milk, which the farmers produce in winter months when the milk output is more. This has led some of the farmers to shift to our competitors who are willing to buy the entire milk they produce. Besides, our own milk yields are decreasing. Perhaps Mukesh (the GM for production) can tell you more about it.'

Mukesh: 'I am pretty concerned about the milk procurement. The yield of our own cattle farm is declining. The veterinary expert, Ramkumar, informs me that we are not buying high quality nutritious cattle feed. You decided against buying this from the regular suppliers two years ago and suggested that we depend upon the grass available in our own farm. Besides, Ramkumar also says that a few cattle died due to lack of medical facilities.'

Ramesh: 'Yes, I know I had abolished the post of the veterinary doctor when I joined. This was done as part of various measures I introduced to reduce the overhead cost. Now, I think we should sort out the issue once and for all with the marketing and HR guys also.'

(Kamlesh, GM (Marketing) and Rakesh, GM (Human Resources development) join the meeting).

Ramesh: 'Tell me Kamlesh, what is the reason for the drop in sales?'

Kamlesh: 'There are a number of reasons. Our milk sales have dropped steadily because the customers do not get the supplies regularly in the summer months. They have shifted to other brands. There is also a drop in the yogurt sales; we are offering only two varieties but our competitors have come out with new flavours, such as mango, strawberry, and mixed fruit varieties. In the case of cheese too, it is the same problem; the complaint is that there is no variety. Our brand is not visible.'

Ramesh: 'Why are we not shifting to these new flavours? What is the problem?'

Kamlesh: 'I think I will pass on this problem to Rakesh.'

Rakesh:  'Yes sir. This is an HR related problem. You see, last year both Keshav and Menon left us because they felt that they were not getting promotions. This left blanks in the cheese and yogurt sections. Nobody else has been trained in these areas so far. Either we should recruit new people with the necessary qualifications or train some of our young staff.'

Mukesh:  'This, Sir, is the exact problem. I cannot produce a variety of yogurt for which there is a ready market only because I do not have competent staff.'

Kamlesh:  'I also want to repeat my request for two extra hands in the computer section. I have been insisting on a good database of our customers. Without this support, I am unable to plan new markets or new products. Already some of the good sales staff have resigned due to the poor image of our brand.'

**Solution:**

Ramesh made copious notes of the entire discussion and told his colleagues that he would convene a meeting with his friend Raghav, who is a well-known consultant for turning around sick companies. He discussed the problems in detail with Raghav who suggested that a balanced scorecard be adopted for the company as a whole. He told Ramesh that he could not try to improve performance only by looking at one department as there were problems in a number of areas and they were all interrelated.

Raghav had detailed meetings with all the departments and prepared the BSC within a period of 3 months and using this he stepped up his actions. He recruited staff as suggested in the meeting and addressed the veterinary issues. This created a chain of actions and enabled WCD to produce more varieties of yoghurt and cheese. With improved data on customers, the marketing activities geared up within a period of 15 months and the sales revenue showed a healthy increase of 22 per cent.

# GOVERNMENT AND NON-PROFIT ORGANIZATIONS

There is a significant rise in the number of non-profit organizations across the globe, which are active in various socio-economic activities. According to Niven (2002), these organizations represent a significant 8 per cent of US GDP and 7 per cent of employment. According to this source, the annual payroll generated by this sector exceeds $480 billion. In India too, the contribution of the non-profit sector is significant.

Measurement issues in such entities are derived from their missions. Thus, the major function becomes financial accountability. This requires a detailed set of controls and documentation. The other relevant parameters are as follows:

1. *Programmes/projects:* These entities usually have several programmes funded by government, donors, the public, etc. Hence, they make detailed project reports supported by budgets. These are linked to the activities.
2. *Performance indicators:* Key performance indicators (KPI) are developed to measure both financial and other targets.
3. *Progress monitoring:* This is a crucial area where prudent oversight is required to overcome cost and time overruns.
4. *Deliverables:* The projects have many benefits, often based on non-economic considerations. The success of the entity depends upon how well the projects are executed and client satisfaction reported.

Many non-profit organizations are adopting the BSC method to improve the integration and coordination of their activities. The financial perspective is often not considered, as it is not a motivating indicator for these organizations. However, some entities use them for controlling cash flows, particularly where the fund flows are uncertain, and hence become critical. Recently, an NGO which was working towards an ambitious educational project for which multiple-donor funding is planned had adopted the BSC approach to monitor the various perspectives. This, they considered as a superior version than the traditional budgetary approach. The following example (Example 16.3) shows the application of BSC in the case of the administration of a city.

The above example proves that government and not-for-profit entities can successfully adopt the BSC model to convert its strategy into laudable achievements.

## Example 16.3 The BSC of the City of Charlotte

A successful case of introduction of BSC was by the city of Charlotte, North Carolina, US. This has been widely acclaimed and in 2002 it made an entry into the Balanced Scorecard Collaborative's Hall of Fame. It has the following four perspectives:

1. *Develop employees:* This is equivalent to the learning and growth perspective and broadly considers the HR areas of skill development, work satisfaction, and the learning culture. It boasts of achieving a positive employee climate as the bottom line.

2. *Manage resources:* This broadly coincides with the finance perspective, and addresses topics of enhancing revenues and investments in infrastructure. It also has interesting goals such as maintaining 'AAA' rating to enhance its image. Another indicator is to deliver competitive services for the welfare of the citizens.

3. *Run the businesses:* This has a close similarity to the internal process perspective and addresses the two major areas of concern to a city administration, namely, technological enhancements and improved customer service. An interesting indicator is to *develop collaborative solutions*, which is a positive directional approach for a progressive entity.

4. *Serve the customer:* The customer perspective is related to citizen welfare areas such as transportation, environment, safety, crime reduction, etc. Besides, it addresses promoting economic opportunities and strengthening neighbourhoods.

These provide the strategy map for the city and shows that it has planned meticulously to reach its lofty vision of *community of choice for living, working, and leisure*. It has the target of 10 per cent increase in tax valuation with a less than 5 per cent increase of staff turnover.

## THE TEN COMMANDMENTS FOR SUCCESSFUL IMPLEMENTATION OF BSC

The BSC is developing as a popular measurement tool, but it requires a planned approach to achieve the desired fruits. In many organizations, the BSC has produced highly satisfactory results due to a scientific and systematic approach. Based on the experience of various successful case studies adopting BSC, the following 10 principles for achieving success can be derived.

1. **Vision, mission, and strategy:** An organization should have a vision–mission statement which is owned and accepted by the entire organization. Based on these pillars, the strategies are formed and communicated down the line. A BSC cannot be finalized without a proper strategy and if attempted, it will be a collection of unrelated indicators. There will be no integration and the exercise is bound to fail.

2. **Stakeholders' support:** A strong commitment to the BSC implementation is required from the top management. Besides, the external stakeholders such as the shareholders or other governing bodies should also staunchly support this endeavour. It must be cascaded down the line and employees at all levels must own the initiative. The biggest issue is often the decline in the excitement level after the enthusiastic start.

3. **Need for change:** BSC is adopted by progressive entities that have an urge for change. This may be provided by the factors of competition, globalization, and growth. But even in government and not-for-profit organizations, the BSC approach can be used for improving service delivery and quality enhancement criteria.

4. **The cause–and–effect relationship:** The indicators should be linked *inter se* by strong relationships and should not be stand-alone actions. In the initial stages of BSC adoption, entities may fail to develop this relationship model and cascade it down the line. As a result, the BSC may remain a blueprint and will not be translated into actions. But the learning curve teaches the relationship angle and as the learning improves, the BSC gets firmed up.

5. **The BSC team:** Successful implementation depends upon a full-time team which is well-versed in the BSC techniques. This team may be supported by external consultants during the early stages of implementation. These people act as the *change agents* for ushering in transformation to the BSC philosophy. Supported by a fully committed CEO, this team can ensure the success of the BSC. It is important that the members are not frequently changed and that there is good synergy between the team members, who are usually drawn from different departments.

6. **Communication:** In large organizations, with a wide geographic spread, the need for communication becomes very important. Since the success of BSC depends upon the performance of all the departments and units, a clear understanding of the goals as well as the process of BSC is critical for success. This is difficult to achieve in organizations where there is no uniform work culture. Communication channels vary and often informal channels work as effectively as formal channels. The BSC team will have a big role to play in this area.

7. **Resources:** The direct costs of BSC implementation may not be huge, but resources in the form of employee time, CEO commitment, a fully dedicated team, and authority for ushering in the changes are other non-financial resources that will be required for this exercise. However, cost for training programmes and consultant fees shall be provided for. Besides, a shift to sophisticated information technology may call for additional resources in terms of software and hardware.

8. **Data/information:** A BSC is not an activity that can be performed in isolation and envelops all functions of the entity. Data inputs are needed from the various departments to identify the major indicators of performance and to draw up the cause–and–effect diagram. Besides, the measurement function also requires real time information. These have become easier due to the spread of IT and many entities have computerized all their data in the last decade when feverish activities were witnessed in this field. But data external to the organization such as changes in demand, new technologies, etc. will have to be sourced professionally.

9. **Incentives and rewards:** The balance scorecard provides a new way of measuring performance. It must be supported by rewards for good performance and acknowledgement of merit. The objectivity of measurement lends credibility to this mechanism but incentives are double-edged swords, and if the measurement tool is either defective or is inadequately communicated, it will lead to the lowering of morale among employees. However, in all cases of successful BSC implementation, it is noticed that it has created an open ambience of performance-linked incentives based on a system which is well-understood by the entity as a whole. It is often seen that non-financial incentives work better at the higher levels of hierarchy than financial incentives.

10. **Professional management:** The nine commandments stated above clearly indicate the need for a competent team of executives who can bring the desired levels of transformation through balanced scorecards. This underscores the need for professional managers at the major levels of strategy execution. Here, the term *professional* does not mean the academic qualification alone; but more importantly, it underscores a work culture which focuses on objectivity and change. An open and transparent management can develop a positive work culture which can have a stabilizing influence in planting a dynamic BSC platform.

These ten principles can provide the beacon of light for BSC implementation in an organized and sustainable way to achieve the desired result. But an equally important activity, which is common to all new programmes, is a series of processes coming under the head of *management of change*. This may be called an invisible hand, or even the eleventh commandment. The sustainability of BSC depends entirely on how well the entity as a whole is geared up for the change management process.

## BUDGETS AND THE BALANCED SCORECARD

Budgets are the most significant financial instrument of measurement in all corporations as well as in government and not-for-profit entities. This acts both as a planning as well as control tool, and integrates all functions of the organization. In some entities, the physical targets are incorporated along with the financial targets, thereby providing a basis for an integrated business plan. Since BSC maps all the indicators of performance, there is scope for combining BSC and the traditional budgets. Figure 16.3 explains the relationship between the two.

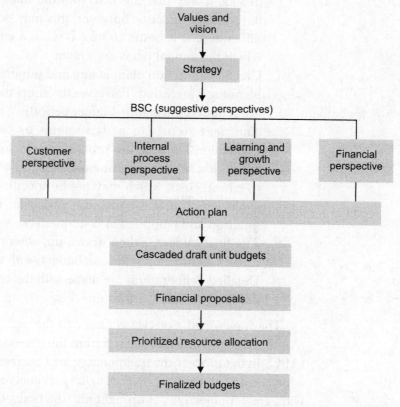

**Fig. 16.3**   Budgets and the balanced scorecard

The relationships between the top line activities (vision and strategy) and the detailed action plans can be visually understood through Fig. 16.3. The various scorecards are based on the strategy of the organization. Now, the resources have to be allocated to the various actions through the budget mechanism. It may be noted that while the budgets are usually annual plans, the BSC is a continuous activity. This however poses no problem, as the strategy driven BSC provides the policy inputs upon which the annual budgets can be prepared. The steps in brief are as follows:

1. Develop the scorecards based on the vision and strategy, and ensure that it is communicated to all the units.
2. Break the individual indicators into detailed action plans, both at the corporate level and unit level. This is a parallel activity along with the scorecard mapping exercise and needs the involvement of all the units.
3. The targets for the budget period are now derived. It can be made in such a way that the BSC and the budgets are both made co-terminus. In practice however, this may pose certain operational difficulties. It is better to take BSC as a continuous activity from where the annual plans are drawn.
4. Cascade the action plans at unit and subunit level so that the micro planning is activated. This gives the entity the various actions which are required during the budget period.
5. The next step is to assign values to each activity based on calculations. During this process certain common overheads such as salaries, service department costs, and administrative and other overhead costs, which may not be specific to any activity, will be evaluated so that the financial proposals from each unit can be finalized and compiled at headquarters.
6. The final budget is then drawn up, where some panel beating is usually done to adjust the unit budgets with the resource constraints. Detailed deliberations are made with the various departments and the final budget is drawn up.

The mentioned exercise is closer to the activity-based management (ABM) principle which is derived from the tenets of activity-based costing (ABC). In this process, the traditional style of 'incremental budgeting', which adds a certain percentage increase to the previous years' actuals, is dispensed with, greater objectivity is brought into the budget-making process, and it also has the advantage of 'ownership' by all the units and departments. Strategy execution is well-entrenched in this process, and the budgets themselves become a holistic management control rather than merely a tool of financial control.

# SUMMARY

Balanced scorecard (BSC) provides an integrated system to coordinate the various performance measures in order to achieve overall organizational goals. It is an excellent edifice to link the lag and lead indicators. This is basically an integrated planning and control exercise to reach the medium- and long-term goals of the company. This concept was developed by Kaplan and Norton during the 1990s.

The BSC is basically derived from the strategies of the organization. It is the most comprehensive tool of management control to achieve the entity's strategic plans. Before preparing the BSC it is desirable to have a strategy map which provides the missing links between the strategy formation and its execution.

The BSC can have a number of perspectives depending upon the specific requirements of the entity. Kaplan and Norton recommend 4 perspectives which most organizations generally follow. These are financial perspective, internal business processes perspective, customer perspective, and learning and growth perspective. The financial perspective is usually kept at the top of the scorecard since entities are judged by the financial returns they provide. Internal business processes constitute a number of measures taken to produce goods and to provide services of the desired quality. The customer perspective denotes the satisfaction derived by customers who use the products and services. The learning and growth perspective measures the ability of the entity and its employees to provide the type of goods and services which create a sustained demand for them. This perspective has become the basis for the growth of the organization. Each of these perspectives consists of a number of performance measures. Besides the overall organizational BSC, there can be individual BSCs for the various departments and units. It may be noted that some of the parameters should move upwards and others should move downwards in order to achieve the strategic goals.

Organizations, however, adopt scorecards suited to their own requirements. Some adopt three scorecards and others may adopt five or more. Besides, all the measures may not be of equal importance in a given context. Entities assign suitable weightages to the different perspectives depending upon their relative role for the overall purpose of achieving the goal.

The balanced scorecard is constructed on a cause–and–effect relationship wherein each scorecard is closely integrated with another, so that a change in one performance measure has an impact on another measure. Hence, it is a cycle whereby each scorecard contributes to the other, leading to synergy and integration. Thus, there is the inevitable balancing of the various measures on the basis of cause–and–effect relationship. This concept is becoming widely popular in both commercial and not-for-profit organizations. It may be difficult to construct and successfully adopt the BSC structure in the early years, but once it is internalized by the departments it proves to be a valuable tool. There is also ample scope for combining the BSC and the budgeting process.

## KEY POINTS

- Integrated system of measurement refers to multiple inter-connected measures of performance.
- Lag indicators are based on past performance.
- Lead Indicators are futuristic.
- Strategy is an abstract and brief statement of the entity's broad approach derived from its vision and mission, to convert them into the desired outcomes.
- Strategy map provides the missing link between strategy formulation and its execution. This is an additional layer of information which facilitates the preparation of the balanced scorecards.
- Balanced scorecard is a system of integrating and coordinating the performance measures of the various functional areas and striking a balance based on a cause–and–effect relationship.
- Financial perspective consists of financial performance measures, such as profits, return on investments, etc.
- Internal business process perspective consists of a number of measures taken to produce goods and to provide services at satisfactory levels.
- Customer perspective refers to a variety of measures to enhance customer satisfaction, market share, and related marketing activities.
- Learning and growth perspective stands for the various measures taken to enhance the knowledge levels and skills available to boost the intellectual capital of the entities.
- Number of scorecards indicates the constituent functional areas considered for a balanced scorecard by an organization.
- Weightages of the scorecards refer to the importance assigned to the different perspectives and the actions there under.

## CONCEPT REVIEW QUESTIONS

1. Explain the need for balanced scorecards.
2. What are lag and lead indicators?
3. Describe the role of strategy in the formation of balanced scorecards.
4. What is a strategy map?
5. Who originated the concept of balanced scorecards?
6. What are the usual perspectives used in balanced scorecards?
7. Explain the basic elements of a balanced scorecard.
8. Describe internal business process perspective.
9. What is the relevance of plus (+) and minus (–) signs in a balanced scorecard?
10. Describe the components of the customer perspective.
11. What is the importance of learning and growth perspective?
12. Give examples of the important measures under financial perspective.
13. Why do companies adopt varying numbers of scorecards?
14. Why are different weightages given for performance measures and scorecards?
15. Elaborate the main issues in balancing the different scorecards.
16. Explain the cause–and–effect relationship in a balanced scorecard.
17. Narrate the barriers to implementing scorecards.
18. Specify the costs of implementing the balanced scorecard concept.
19. Is the concept of balanced scorecard relevant in not-for-profit organizations?
20. Narrate the important principles for the successful implementation of the balanced scorecard.
21. State the relationship between budget and the balanced scorecard.

## CASE DISCUSSIONS

### 1. Balanced Scorecard

The balanced scorecard is built on the assumption that there must be a cause–and–effect relationship between the various indicators. For example, a lower price should attract more customers. Similarly, training enhances performance.

### Questions

1.1 Highlight a few cases of cause–and–effect related performance measures.

1.2 Can there be instances where such a relationship planned originally is not realized in the end due to certain hypothesis going haywire?

## 2. A Pharmaceutical Company

A pharmaceutical company facing a reduction in turnover is planning to introduce a number of branded medicines in the near future. It plans to fix the time taken for developing each medicine as the performance indicator for its research department.

### Questions

2.1 Is this approach a correct measure for the company as a whole?

2.2 What are the pitfalls associated with the method?

## 3. Fast Print

Fast print is a company with reputation for high quality printing. It has developed the following performance measures for its various functions:

1. Number of paper purchase orders successfully placed
2. Number of people served in the canteen
3. Number of printing orders executed in time
4. Number of complaints received on poor quality of finished products
5. Number of mistakes located and identified by the customer post delivery
6. Amount of salary paid to staff to assess employee costs

### Questions

3.1 Review the above measures and suggest alternatives wherever necessary.

3.2 State the scorecard under which the above perspectives can be associated.

## 4. Jal Mahal Palace

Jal Mahal Palace (JMP) Resort was a family owned concern in the once princely state of Bikaner. It served as a holiday resort to travellers and desert safari campers. Due to some internal squabble in the family, Mr Jai Singh has recently taken over as the CEO of the group. An MBA from a reputed business school, the new MD has ideas to upgrade the resort to a star hotel in order to attract more foreign as well as Indian tourists. In this plan, the new MD would like to bring in major changes in the quality of service to upgrade it to international levels. Apart from this he wants to upgrade the quality of Jal Amrith, the lake restaurant. The menu at the hotel is very limited comprising only traditional Rajasthani food. Situated in the remote desert area, the previous management had faced little competition. This became the reason for their laid-back attitude towards the development of the restaurant.

The new CEO had extensive discussions with the resort staff. His uncle Mr Vir Singh, the erstwhile MD, had made it clear to his nephew that no staff should be thrown out of employment and recruitments in future should be from the local area. Otherwise, he gave Jai Singh full freedom to manage the resort. The CEO realized that the local staff had difficulty in speaking English and other foreign languages. A standing complaint was on the limitation of choice of food. Based on the discussions and the limitations of the resort, the CEO listed the following core activities for the resort:

### Management Activities
- Selection of the menu
- Recruitments
- Taking care of daily operations
- Procurement

### Restaurant Activities
- Preparation of food
- Cleanliness of premises
- Taking orders
- Serving the food
- Table arrangements and bookings

In order to have a planned growth Jai Singh suggested a strategy of creating a balanced scorecard for the resort. He developed the following performance measures in consultation with the staff:

1. Number of cuisines offered in the menu
2. Number of cooks who hail from local area (they will have expertise in Rajasthani cuisine.)
3. Estimated time taken to prepare an order
4. Cleanliness and maintenance to be supervised based on feedback from the customers as per international standards
5. Satisfaction regarding service to be estimated by feedbacks and surveys
6. Estimated time taken to place an order
7. Weekly sales
8. Weekly costs
9. Number of staff that have undergone formal hospitality training
10. Number of complaints received from customers regarding food
11. Number of corporate customers enrolled
12. Number of employees who can speak a foreign language
13. Number of complaints on service quality
14. Number of new items added on a quarterly basis

### Questions

4.1 Prepare a balanced scorecard based on the above information.

4.2 Explain the assumptions underlying the above performance measures and explain their significance.

## 5. Snacks Company

A company manufacturing and distributing a popular brand of snacks wants to allot weightages to its various indicators under its internal processes perspective. Its major activities and main focus areas under each activity are given as follows:

| Sl No. | Activity | Focus area |
|---|---|---|
| 1. | Procurement of raw materials for its snacks items | i) High quality: There are regular suppliers of repute.<br>ii) Price is a burning problem.<br>iii) Time and supply is crucial for some items (wheat) which are seasonal. |
| 2. | Inventory control | Avoid wastage of raw material. |
| 3. | Processing time | Within industry norms |
| 4. | Technology | The market is competitive and hence innovations are needed. |
| 5. | Quality controls | i) The snacks have to be crispy.<br>ii) There are some complaints that in humid conditions its products are not fresh. |
| 6. | Innovations | The packages are not very attractive. There are no new flavours added in the last 15 months. |

### Question

What shall be the relative weightage of these measures? (The total weightage of internal process in the balanced scorecard is 40 per cent.)

## 6. Quick and Fast Couriers

Quick and Fast (Q&F) is a courier service situated in the heart of the city. While it had good business for many years, now it is facing stiff competition from multinational couriers which are growing in number. Recently, however the city culture has been undergoing tremendous changes in preference for courier services over traditional postal service. Mr Omkar, the MD, appointed 'Veehelp', a firm of consultants to assess the situation and prepare a report.

Veehelp came out with the following report:

To,
Mr Omkar Sharma,
MD, Q & F Couriers,

Dear Sir,

We have made a detailed study of your company and are pleased to make the following report:

*Situation analysis:*
The company's services enjoy a fair reputation as the quality standards are good. It is sensitive to customer needs and is prompt in delivery.
The company has two types of customers, namely cash and credit.

The credit facilities are available for the 45 big customers who regularly use those services. They are billed regularly and payments are to be made within 3 weeks of billing. The credit customers constitute nearly 70 per cent of the entire revenue.

A good advertising agency has been retained by Q&F couriers. The advertisement agents have spent a lot of money on TV ads.

*The pain areas:*
1. In the last 2 years there is a declining trend of net profits to sales.
2. The bad debts as a percentage of sales have gone up significantly.
3. The 3 weeks credit period has been exceeded by debtors in 28 per cent of the cases.
4. The collection department's costs have gone up by 30 per cent. This includes additional recruitment and travel.
5. There has been an increase in advertising costs by 20 per cent.
6. The number of complaints for wrong delivery is on the increase.

*Recommendations:*
The customers who come to the shop are usually from local area. Hence, the TV advertisements may be replaced by hoardings which will reduce costs by around 35 per cent.

The credit scheme has to be reviewed. A bulk deposit may be taken and the periodic bills may be adjusted against them. The delays are mainly due to the errors in calculations which lead to disputes. There is an increase in the number of employees leaving services due to good demand elsewhere.

To settle all these issues we recommend the balanced scorecard approach. We are willing to assist you in this.

Yours truly,

For Veehelp Consultants,
Vinayak

Mr Omkar felt that this approach could help and therefore, convened a meeting of the senior staff. The following performance measures were agreed upon after consultation with Mr Vinayak.

1. Percentage of bills containing calculation errors
2. Percentage of trained accountants working at the store
3. Profit per staff
4. Customer satisfaction timeliness of service
5. Total sales revenue
6. Number of suppliers making prompt deliveries
7. Bad debts as percentage of total sales
8. Total profit
9. The total advertising costs
10. Customer complaints for wrong delivery
11. Attrition rate

The store hopes that its improvements will bring its hay-days of high profits back to its pedestal.

## Questions

1. Construct a balanced scorecard based on the above measures of performance.
2. What are the assumptions on which the scorecard is built?
3. Can you think of any additional measure which could be added to the above list of indicators?

# PART V

## Appendices

1. E-budgeting
2. Cost Audit
3. Cost Accounting Standards
4. Costing in Government and Not-for-profit Organizations

# E-budgeting

The growth of Internet and electronic communication has touched the business environment in various ways. Two significant features of this revolution are the speed of communication and the quality and timeliness of the information systems. An emerging manifestation of this phenomenon in the commercial world is the e-budgeting concept. Budgeting is the routine process of estimation and calculation of revenues and expenditures that is followed by all organizations. Traditionally, budgeting has gained the reputation of being a cumbersome task. A typical budgeting scenario is always picturized as financial officers and management accountants spending sleepless nights over collaborating and merging numerous spreadsheets, which display a wide array of data emerging from operations in the various departments of the respective organizations. Apart from this, the fright of approaching deadlines engulfs their peace and composure.

But this is no longer the picture and the credit for this goes to new technology and innovations. The impact of computers and software has touched the realms of budgeting too. With the electronic methods of preparing budgets, life has just become easier for people who work on budgets and e-budgeting is the toast of most financial departments today.

The 'e' in the term e-budgeting stands for the electronic medium involved in the budgeting process. It is an avant-garde mechanism, a corporate service application that supports an organization's business and competence with enterprise-wide planning over the Internet, and helps in guesswork and disparity free planning for the future of the company. With the help of this web-based technology, budgeting becomes an 'anywhere, anytime' activity. It offers the management a real time control over the expenditure and activities of the organization.

Managers in present day organizations do not like to spend a great deal of time in the calculation process as there are many other tasks they need to concentrate on simultaneously. Organizations are growing at a rapid pace and in such a situation they cannot afford any planning and budgeting error, as in such crucial tasks mistakes can prove fatal for their future plans. Thus, e-budgeting comes as a breather from such fallacies which are common worries in manual compilations.

## How E-budgeting Works

An e-budgeting solution is a complete package of automation for the company's budget and forecast. The contributors can make their entries from any part of the world and any time. An Internet connection and simple logging-in procedure connects the employees to the budgetary process of the organization. As the process is centrally monitored and administered it has lesser chances of being manipulated.

In the first phase, the accounts section requests information from the concerned departments and thus the people relevant are involved in the formulation process. It is set in motion from corporate managers to frontline employees. They enter the required information and authorize it. This liberates the finance department and enables it to focus on more important issues such as budget modelling and fiscal strategy formations, rather than wasting time on data entry and verification. The finance department needs to determine the budget key-factor and the various parameters to be used. Once this is done, the application does the processing on its own, thus providing hassle free results. Further, if there is any change that needs to be made, such as the percentages of allocations, the finance personnel just needs to feed in the change in the allotted frame and the entire budget gets recalculated and updated.

It provides maximum flexibility for present day organizations to handle their multi-faceted tasks and expand the efficiency of their staff to the ultimate extent. The accessibility and transparency generated by the system instils confidence in the employees regarding the entire mechanism and their participation in the process of budgeting.

The most favourable feature of e-budgeting is the possibility of constant monitoring of the variances by the concerned department. This is particularly relevant in MNCs in competitive business segments, where the availability of real time information and remedial actions play a vital role in ensuring organizational effectiveness.

## Benefits of E-budgeting

There are numerous benefits of using the e-budgeting application in an organization. Some of these are listed as follows.

1. **Reduction in accounting stress:** As e-budgeting is a computer application, it makes assimilation of numbers from different spreadsheets easy and a hands-on task. Entering data, reconciliation, and uploading tasks are cut down to a considerable extent.

2. **Convenience:** The anywhere, anytime accessibility makes e-budgeting a tool of convenience. As managers and executives are short on time, they can make their entries from anywhere in the world, say, during their waiting hours for a connecting flight at an airport. All that is required is Internet accessibility and their domain names.

3. **Adjustability:** The e-budgeting application provides a very adjustable base for the employees to work on. The changes required to be made can be incorporated very easily and the updating takes place automatically. This allows the organization to include even last minute changes and decisions very easily in the working budgetary model. Examples for this could be the decisions of the board to change resource allocations with effect from immediate periods.

4. **Safety:** As e-budgeting is an electronic medium it has very high security measures. Check-in and check-out is protected by passwords and authorization measures. Any change or modification is immediately communicated to the authorities with built-in systems. Budgets are of a highly confidential nature and an organization needs extreme safeguards in this regard. Thus, even though the user base is highly distributed, it helps maintain the security of the sensitive data.

5. **User-friendly:** E-budgeting caters to various ranges of people involved in the organization's operations, both from financial as well as non-financial departments. Their accounting knowledge may be minimal but the tool helps all users to use and understand the mechanism through easy user-friendly menus and generalized techniques.

6. **Planning tool:** The e-budgeting application emerges as a significant planning aid. It helps the company to estimate and account the budgets with easy methods. It helps to build differential budgets for different departments and collate them into a final sheet. It not only facilitates the calculation but also the estimation with availability of 'what if' type of capabilities. This helps to make estimations regarding the changes and effect on total budget if the allocation to any one department or task is reduced or increased.

7. **Flexible budgeting:** This concept facilitates the budgets to be related to the levels of activity actually attained vis-à-vis the planned

levels. The programming can relate the variable components of budgets to be tuned on to the activity levels, so that the budgets indicate the revised targets with reference to the activity levels.

8. **Revisions due to environmental factors:** The budgets which were prepared at the beginning of the financial year may become unrealistic due to external environmental factors, such as the following:

    (i) Escalation in global commodity prices
    (ii) Advancements in technology
    (iii) War and other political developments
    (iv) Recession, inflation, and similar economic reasons
    (v) Legal and trade issues, such as IPR, WTO, etc.

    In such cases e-budgeting enables quicker revisions to the original budgets.

9. **Advanced management techniques:** Tools such as activity-based costing (ABC), value engineering, etc. call for detailed calculations based on a variety of data from different sources. Electronic systems can handle these better than the manual operations.

10. **Multiple uses:** Data collected under e-budgeting can be used for a number of MIS reports, such as segment-wise profitability statements, incentive fixations, cost control statements, etc.

Thus, e-budgeting helps the organization to make strategies and plan its course of revenue and expenditure allocation to sustain its business and earn required profits. Apart from these, the e-budgeting mechanism is also cost effective and boosts the efficiency of employees by reducing the fatigue factor.

E-budgeting mainly helps to overcome the gridlocks of traditional accounting methods. The number of people who devote their time to the cumbersome task of budget calculations gets considerably reduced. The time factor involved is the most crucial beneficiary. The amount of time committed to the task is reduced and the employees of the financial section can concentrate on the implications of the budgets rather than spending too much time on calculating them.

The dramatic reduction in the amount of administrative resources engaged can help the company harness higher levels of task-orientation from its employees.

## Shortcomings of E-budgeting

There are, of course, some shortcomings of the e-budgeting tool and it is important to consider these for a total evaluation of the same.

Some of the possible shortcomings are as follows:

1. The information obtained through Internet should have restricted accessibility. Usually this is possible with password controls, but leakages are not uncommon. Hence, the secrecy of data is a concern in e-budgeting.

2. In global corporations, the success of e-budgeting depends on the knowledge levels of the employees in various locations in handling the e-budgeting process. The computer literacy levels in parts of the developing world may be inadequate to handle the software and hardware problems. Proper de-bottlenecking support can overcome this problem.

3. Technical pitfalls, such as power failures or telecommunication problems, can hamper the process.

4. The concerned authorities not logging-in for a long period of time due to unavailability of Internet access on a travel regime is another problem.

5. When the data is fed from several locations, the possibility of data manipulation cannot be ruled out. Some units may resort to this in order to paint a rosy picture and show themselves in a favourable light.

6. The single biggest disadvantage of e-budgeting is the possibility of data loss and data corruption due to software and hardware issues. This, however, can be overcome by proper data backup arrangements and security measures.

7. The e-budgets, even though accurate, sometimes have limited applications and usability.

# Cost Audit

India has been the first country to introduce the concept of compulsory cost audit through a proper legal process. This unique feature has some economic and historical background. It can be traced back to the world war period, when, in the absence of other measures for awarding contracts, a number of these were given to contractors on a *cost plus* basis. This necessitated the requirement for some uniform cost data among the contractors, which could be verified by the government authorities. Professional competence in cost accounting as a special division of knowledge was called for and this led to the birth of the Institute of Cost and Works Accountants of India (ICWAI) during the Second World War period.

Post-independence the Institute of Chartered Accountants of India (ICAI) was constituted under an act of parliament in 1949, and exactly a decade after that the Cost and Works Accountants Act (1959) was passed.

## Landmarks in the Development of Cost Audit

- The passing of the Companies Act in 1956 was the first step towards the formal development of regulatory forces, and oversight of accounting and finance data. Section 209 (1) of the Act insisted on mandatory information on certain predominantly financial accounting data, such as cash transactions, sales, and purchases as well as the assets and liabilities of the company. There was a requirement for statutory audit of companies by chartered accountants.
- Recommendations of certain specific commissions which assisted the growth of cost audit, namely
  
  (a) Vivian Bose Commission
  
  (b) Dutta Commission
  
  (c) Shastry Committee

- Amendments to the Indian Companies Act in 1965, which formally gave the sanction for the cost audit.

The subsequent developments led to a number of industries coming under cost audits. This has also led to the setting up of the Cost Accounting Standards Board (CASB) which has already come out with seven standards. The CASB has been very active from the turn of the millennium, and proposes to cover some 39 areas, with more under review, such as the services sector.

## Legal Provisions

Sections 209 (1) (d), Section 224, and Section 233-B of the Indian Companies Act, 1956, contain provisions regarding cost audit. Under this Act the government makes rules and regulations for the conduct of cost audit that are contained in the Cost Audit (Report) Rules, 1968, which has been periodically amended.

## Definition

The ICWAI has defined cost audit predominantly as a system of audit under the instructions of the government of India 'for the review, examination, and appraisal of the cost accounting records, and added information required to be maintained by specified industries'. This adds more functional details and depth of coverage compared to the earlier definitions which limited its scope to the 'adherence to the cost accounting plan'.

Hence, it can be seen that the intention of the authorities goes beyond the review of merely the cost accounting records, and extends to other information. Its focus is on the efficiency of the operations of the specified industry rather than restricting it to a mere 'voucher audit'. This also extends to the propriety of the various actions taken by the industry and the ultimate benefits thus occurring. This can be readily seen in the provisions of the Cost Audit (Report) Rules whereby the cost auditor has to report on the capacity utilization details of the industry, consumption of major raw materials alongside the standards set, and the standard consumption data. Besides, the auditor has to comment upon power and fuel consumption per unit along with the applicable norms. There are requirements on direct labour vis-à-vis the past data for two years, overhead expenditure for two years, and also a report on various financial ratios. Hence, the efficiency functions are effectively addressed.

## Expanding the Scope

In an era of globalization, there are no borders to trade. Free trade agreements (FTAs) are the toast of the century. In a situation of heightened economic activity, the government needs to have the cost audit data to estimate the amount of transactions that take place in the economy on the basis of free trade. Cost audit has been made mandatory in a list of companies in order to identify the new threshold levels. The ministry of corporate affairs has constituted an internal committee to check and review the schedule of companies to be assessed in the mandatory cost audit norms. There are 44 sectors listed in this list, mainly the ones with higher profit margins. Many more are likely to be added in the future.

A cost audit process assesses the cost effectiveness of the various processes involved in the manufacturing segment. In most listed companies there is already an audit in the areas of raw material consumption, production, sales, and marketing. But with recent developments, the government is also likely to take criteria such as the turnover, capital stature, level of public stake holding, and debt exposure, under the wing of cost audit.

## Rationale for Cost Audit

The *economic rationale* of cost audit is derived from the canons of welfare economics. Governments provide infrastructure and other facilities for industries at various levels. Certain concessions are given in indirect taxes. Now there is a need to know whether these facilities have been used effectively for the benefit of the consumers, who become the stakeholders in an economic sense. The citizens have a right to know how the industries use the facilities provided out of the taxpayer's money.

The *financial rationale* consists of the financial inputs provided by the government in the form of concessional loans, subsidized power, reductions in excise and customs, tax holidays, etc. The government is entitled to know how the industries perform after utilizing these favours, and bestow welfare measures to the nation.

The *pricing rationale* requires governments to control and be aware of the cost of products for which prices are fixed by them.

Besides, there is an emerging force which may be termed as the *global commercial rationale*. With an increase in global trade, and thanks to the more sophisticated communication network, the national boundaries are shrinking. This requires some financial oversight to prevent unethical commercial practices such as dumping, etc. The World Trade Organization (WTO) has provided for some pricing mechanism to prevent such commercial activities, and cost monitoring becomes an important ingredient. In this process, cost audit helps regulate authorities to monitor trade related disputes.

## Healthy Cost

Cost audit is also helpful to estimate the margins applied by the manufacturers on various products. The pharmaceutical sector is a multi-variant manufacturing zone. The National Pharmaceutical Pricing Authority (NPPA) takes the cost audit appropriations of all companies with a turnover of more than ₹10 crore to estimate the profit margins imposed on each of their products. This step is taken to check overpricing of drugs. The NPPA identifies drugs with high trade margins, and attempts to put a ceiling limit on the amount of margin that can be earned by the companies on a certain component. For example, some anti-inflammatory pills and anti-allergy drugs once had a trade margin of over 1000 per cent.

The audit covers all areas involved in the manufacturing, such as research and development, royalty payments, cost of raw materials, quality maintenance, and export obligations. The cost auditing data helps to reveal the actual amounts of profits that the companies can earn. Thus, it helps to ensure fair pricing to all concerned.

## Scope of Cost Audit

Basically, cost audit evolves around two issues which may be broadly termed as *external* and *internal* in terms of their relevance to the organization.

1. The external scope involves legal compliance. The Companies Act, 1956, has prescribed Cost Audit (Report) Rules which mention the scope of the audit and the company is expected to adhere to these rules. This is a report which goes to the prescribed authorities and is mandatory. Thus, the primary scope of cost audit is legal compliance.
2. The internal or managerial perspective ensures that the audit assesses the cost accounting systems and organizational efficiency which enable the management to improve its existing performance. This is a secondary result of the cost audit.

It may be noted that the second perspective is not independent and the basic scope is primarily concerned with the legal compliance. The managerial perspective is a down stream offshoot, but in the spirit of the cost audit it benefits the management to enhance its performance. (The Cost Audit Report (Amendment) Rules, 2006, is enclosed as Annexure 1)

Thus, the cost audit is quite different from the financial audit conducted by chartered accountants. The latter is applicable to all companies coming under the provisions of the Indian Companies Act, 1956. The cost audit, on the other hand, is restricted to those companies for which such an order has been issued by the government. Even there, it is restricted to the products which are covered by the governmental order, and the other activities of the entity are excluded.

Moreover, the statutory financial auditors are appointed at the annual general meeting by the shareholders and the audit report is placed before them. In the case of the cost audit, the auditor is appointed by the board of directors and the report is sent to the central government, and a copy is given to the company. It does not go to the shareholders due to reasons of confidentiality.

## Costing in Essential Services

As the subsidies given for some of the social sectors such as health, education, and basic infrastructure, etc. are reducing or are getting privatized, there is an increasing demand for mandatory cost audit in these sectors. The rationale for this call is that the free pricing mechanism will necessitate monitoring of the cost structure. Back in 2004, such a demand was made by a parliamentary committee attached to the finance ministry. While there are significant benefits accruing to the nation, the doyens of industry utterly muted complaints about the high cost of compliance of this statutory requirement.

## The Cost Auditor

The cost auditor is appointed under the provisions of Section 233-B and Section 224 of the Companies Act. The cost auditor must be a cost accountant as per the Cost and Works Accountants Act, 1959, and a firm of cost accountants can be appointed as cost auditors. However, even if all the members are cost accountants, a corporate body cannot function as cost auditor. Similarly, a person holding a full-time appointment cannot function as a cost auditor. The logic is apparent, as one may not be able to spare adequate time for the cost audit. There are restrictions on the number of cost audits which a cost auditor can take. A person appointed as the financial auditor under Section 224 of the Companies Act cannot function as the cost auditor. This ensures functional independence. There are also prohibitions on persons having financial dealings and thereby being indebted to the company beyond certain limits from holding the post of cost auditor.

## ANNEXURE

### Annexure 1 The Cost Audit Report (Amendment) Rules, 2006

**G.S.R.148(E).**–In exercise of the powers conferred by sub-section (4) of section 233B read with sub-section (1) of section 227 and clause (b) of sub-section (1) of section 642 and section 610A of the Companies Act, 1956 (1 of 1956), the Central Government hereby makes the following rules further to amend the Cost Audit Report Rules, 2001, namely:

1. (1) These rules may be called the Cost Audit Report (Amendment) Rules, 2006.

    (2) They shall come into force on the date of their publication, in the Official Gazette.

2. In the Cost Audit Report Rules, 2001,

    (i) After sub-rule 2 of rule 4, the following sub-rules shall be inserted, namely: -

    "3. The Forms prescribed in these rules may be filed through electronic media or through any other computer readable media as referred under section 610A of the Companies Act, 1956 (1 of 1956).

    (4) The electronic form shall be authenticated by the authorized signatories using digital signatures, as defined under the Information Technology Act, 2000 (21 of 2000).

    (5) The forms prescribed in these rules, when filed in physical form, may be authenticated by authorized signatory by affixing his signature manually."

    (ii) In the form for the heading "FORM OF THE COST AUDIT REPORT", "FORM II - THE COST AUDIT REPORT" shall be substituted;

    (iii) Before the existing form, the following form shall be inserted, namely:

### FORM I

### Form for filing cost audit report and other documents with the Central Government

**[Pursuant to section 233B(4),600(3)(b) of the Companies Act, 1956 and rule 2(c) and rule 4 of the Cost Audit (Report) Rules, 2001]**

**Note: All fields marked in * are to be mandatorily filled.**

### I. General information of the company

1. (a). *Corporate identity number (CIN) or foreign company registration number of the company

    [                    ]          Pre-fill

    (b). Global location number (GLN) of company

    [                    ]

2. (a). Name of the company

   (b). Address of the registered office or of the
        principal place of business in India of
        the company

3. Cost audit report (CAR) pertains to:

   (a) Name of the industry

   (b) *Product or activities

   (c) Central excise tariff chapter heading

   (d) *Name and location of the unit

   (e) *State where unit is located

   *Financial year    From [          ] (DD/MM/YYY) To [          ] (DD/MM/YYY)

4. *Location of other sites manufacturing or producing or processing or mining the product or carrying out the activity under reference (refer CAR annexure 1 .5)

5. (a) *Income-tax permanent account
       number of cost auditor

   (b) *Name of the cost auditor

   (c) *Membership number of cost auditor

6. *Cost audit order number [          ] dated [          ] (DD/MM/YYY)

7. *Service request number (SRN)
   of relevant Form 23C seeking
   approval of appointment of the
   cost auditor [          ] dated [          ] (DD/MM/YYY)

8. *Whether the cost audit report has been qualified          ○ Yes          ○ No
   or contains adverse remarks

   *Whether there is any transaction with the related parties
   during the period to which the cost audit report pertains          ○ Yes          ○ No

## II. *Quantitative information (for the product or activity under reference)

Unit of measurement (UoM)

| S. No. | Particulars | CAR annexure reference | Current year | Previous year |
|---|---|---|---|---|
| 1. | Total available capacity | 4.3 | | |
| 2. | Total production quality | 4.5 | | |
| 3. | Capacity utilisation percentage | 4.7 | | |
| 4. | Total available quantity | 4.9 | | |
| 5. | Quantity captively consumed | 4.10 | | |
| 6. | Quantity sold (domestic) | 4.11(a+b) | | |
| 7. | Quantity sold (exports) | 4.11(c+d+e) | | |
| 8. | Closing stock (finished goods) | 4.12 | | |

## III. Export commitments (amount in ₹thousands) [As per cost auditor's certificate-para3(g)]

A. Export commitments

B. Actual export towards export commitments

## IV. *Standard and actual consumption per unit (for the product or activity under reference)

| S. No. | Particulars | Unit (specify) | Standard (Quantity/unit) | Actuals (quantity/unit) | |
|---|---|---|---|---|---|
| | | | | Current year | Previous year |
| | Consumption of input materials per unit [Annexure 5(B)] - specify details of major input materials, components | | | | |
| 1. | | | | | |
| 2. | | | | | |
| 3. | | | | | |
| 4. | | | | | |
| 5. | | | | | |

| | Consumption of power, fuel and utilities per unit [Annexure 7(B)] | | | | |
|---|---|---|---|---|---|
| 1. | | | | | |
| 2. | | | | | |
| 3. | | | | | |
| 4. | | | | | |
| 5. | | | | | |

## V.  *Key information from Cost Audit Report (for the product or activity under reference)

| S. No. | Particulars | CAR annexure reference | Unit (specify) | Current year | Previous year |
|---|---|---|---|---|---|
| 1. | Total employee costs | 8B.6 | ₹in thousands | | |
| 2. | Total repairs and maintenance | 9.5 | ₹in thousands | | |
| 3. | Depreciation absorbed | 10.5 | ₹in thousands | | |
| 4. | Total overheads | 12(1 to 4) | ₹ in thousands | | |
| 5. | Total research and development expenses | 13.5 | ₹ in thousands | | |
| 6. | Total royalty and technical know how charges | 14.5 | ₹in thousands | | |
| 7. | Total quality control expenses | 15.6 | ₹in thousands | | |
| 8. | Total pollution control expenses | 16,6 | ₹in thousands | | |
| 9. | Total abnormal non-recurring costs | 17 | ₹in thousands | | |
| 10. | Total closing stock | 18.(A).e2 | ₹in thousands | | |
| 11. | Total value of non-moving stock | 18.(A).e3 | ₹in thousands | | |
| 12. | Non-moving stock to closing stock | 18.(A).e4 | Percentage | | |

| 13. | Total written off stock | 18.(B)5 | ₹in thousands | | |
|---|---|---|---|---|---|
| 14. | Total value of inventory as per cost accounts | 19.(A).10 | ₹in thousands | | |
| 15. | Total value of inventory as per financial accounts | 19.(A).11 | ₹in thousands | | |
| 16. | Estimated demand of the product in the country | 22.2 | | | |
| 17. | Total production in the country | 22.3 | | | |
| 18. | Quantities imported in the country | 22.4 | | | |
| 19. | Percentage share of the company in total inland production | 22.6 | Percentage | | |
| 20. | Net sales (excluding excise duty) | 23.3 | ₹in thousands | | |
| 21. | Adjustments in stocks | 23.4 | ₹in thousands | | |
| 22. | Cost of bought out materials and services | 23.5 | ₹in thousands | | |
| 23. | Value added | 23.6 | ₹in thousands | | |
| 24. | Capital employed (for the product) | 24.1 | ₹in thousands | | |
| 25. | Net worth (for the product) | 24.2 | ₹in thousands | | I |
| 26. | Profit or loss for the product | 24.3 | ₹in thousands | | |
| 27. | Operating expenses as a percentage of net sales (for the product) | | | | |
| (a). | Material cost | 24.5a | Percentage | | |
| (b). | Factory overheads | 24.5b | Percentage | | |

(*Contd.*)

(*Contd.*)

| | | | | | |
|---|---|---|---|---|---|
| (c). | Royalty on production | 24.5c | Percentage | | |
| (d). | Salaries and wages | 24.5d | Percentage | | |
| (e). | Research and development expenses | 24.5e | Percentage | | |
| (f). | Quality control | 24.5f | Percentage | | |
| (g). | Administrative overheads | 24.5g | Percentage | | |
| (h). | Selling and distribution | 24.5h | Percentage | | |
| (i). | Interest | 24.5i | Percentage | | |
| 28. | Profit or loss as a percentage of capital employed | 24.6 | Percentage | | |
| 29. | Profit or loss as a percentage of net worth | 24.7 | Percentage | | |
| 30. | Profit or loss as a percentage of net sales | 24.8 | Percentage | | |
| 31. | Value addition as a percentage of net sale | 24.10 | Percentage | | |
| 32. | Excise duty (ED) payable | 27.D.1 | ₹in thousands | | |
| 33. | ED paid through cenvat - inputs | 27.D.2.3 | ₹in thousands | | |
| 34. | ED paid though cenvat - capital goods | 27.D.2.b | ₹in thousands | | |
| 35. | Personal Ledger Account (PLA) | 27.D.2.C | ₹in thousands | | |
| 36. | Total | 27.D.2 | ₹in thousands | | |

**VI. *Margin per unit of output (for the product or activity under reference) Annexure 21**

| S. No. | Particulars | Current Year | | | Previous Year | | |
|---|---|---|---|---|---|---|---|
| | | Cost of sales (₹/unit) | Sales realisation (₹/unit) | Margin (₹/unit) | Cost of sales (₹/unit) | Sales realization (₹/unit) | Margin (₹/unit) |
| | Purchase ○ Year ○ No If yes, specify details of major products | | | | | | |
| 1. | | | | | | | |
| 2. | | | | | | | |
| | Loan license basis ○ Year ○ No If yes, specify details of major products | | | | | | |
| 1. | | | | | | | |
| 2. | | | | | | | |
| | Own manufactured ○ Year ○ No If yes, specify details of major products | | | | | | |
| 1. | | | | | | | |
| 2. | | | | | | | |
| 3. | | | | | | | |
| 4. | | | | | | | |
| 5. | | | | | | | |

**Attachments**

List of attachments

1. *Cost audit report as per the Cost Audit (Report) Rules, 2001    [Attach]
2. Optional attachment(s) - if any    [Attach]

[Remove attachment]

**Declaration**

To the best of my knowledge and belief, the information given in this application and its attachments is correct and complete

We have been authorised by the board of directors' resolution dated to sign and submit this form.    [_____] (DD/MM/YYYY)

**To be digitally signed by**

Managing director or director or manager or secretary (in case of an Indian company) or an authorised representative (in case of a foreign company)    [_____]

Director of the company

Cost auditor

| Modify | Check Form | Prescrutiny | Submit |

**For office signed by**

This e-Form is hereby rejected

**Digital signature of the authorizing officer**          Submit to Bo

# Cost Accounting Standards

Cost Accounting Standards (CAS) are a set of cost accounting practices formulated to achieve standardization amongst all the constituents in terms of consistency in the cost measurement techniques and also uniformity in the allocation of costs. Along with the standards for financial accounting, CAS are becoming increasingly popular. Various countries have established different bodies to develop CAS. In India, the role is entrusted with the Institute of Cost and Works Accountants of India (ICWAI), which was created by an Act of Parliament in 1959. In the US, it is done by the Cost Accounting Standards Board (CASB).

## Preparation of CAS

The standards are country-specific and are prepared based on prevailing cost accounting practices generally followed in the trade and industry. The procedures followed are as follows:

1. Members of the profession as well as other industry related bodies and government agencies are consulted.
2. Reference is made to the current practices in other countries.
3. Prevailing literature on the topic is studied.
4. An exposure draft is then made on a standard format and circulated to members of the profession and other experts.
5. The comments received are reviewed and adopted suitably.
6. The final CAS is released with the effective date it comes into effect.

The standards are kept simple and functional. They allow flexibility as warranted by the profession. They have a standard format and the actual standard is highlighted.

### The American Standards

In the US, the cost accounting standards came out as a result of certain pricing issues between the government and defence contractors in ensuring consistency in cost accounting practices. Its genesis goes back to 1968 when in response to the request of Congress, the General Accounting Office

(GAO) studied and recommended the creation of the Cost Accounting Standards Board (CASB). This body was made responsible for preparing the standards. CASB became an independent and permanent board in 1988 under the Office of Management and Budget (OMB).

### Constitution of the US CASB

1. It will have a 5-member board.
2. The OFPP administrator will be the chairman.
3. It will have one representative each from the department of defence and general services administration.
4. One member will be from industry and commerce.
5. A cost accounting expert from the private sector will constitute the fifth member.

CASB has the final authority in the measurement and allocation of costs, and no contravening provisions are applicable.

A list of the US standards is given in Annexure 1. It is not the mere compliance with the letter of the standards, but more importantly with its spirit that matters. Hence, the disclosure statements must describe the costing practices adopted and explain how it complies with the applicable standards.

### *Indian CASB*

**Constitution:** The CASB will have a chairman and other members appointed and nominated by the council of the institute. The director (technical) of ICWAI will be the secretary of the CASB.

**Objectives:** CASB will develop cost accounting standards on important issues/topics relating to cost and management accounting with the following objectives. The objectives as given in the website under CAS 1 are reproduced.

- To equip the profession with better guidelines on standard cost accounting practices.
- To assist the cost accountants in preparation of uniform cost statements.
- To provide guidelines to cost accountants to make a standard approach towards maintenance of cost accounting record rules and undertaking cost audit under Section 209 (1) (d) and Section 233B of Companies Law respectively, and various other acts, such as Income Tax Act, Central Excise Act, Customs Act, Sales Tax Act, etc.

- To assist the management to follow the standard cost accounting practices in the matter of compliance of statutory obligations.
- To help Indian industry and the government towards better cost management.

**Approach:** The CASB has developed a standardized pattern for the CAS and a suitable methodology. This has evolved over a period of time and tows the line of international accounting bodies who have formulated similar standards.

The approach to the preparation of CAS should be principle based. It is capable of further amplification to provide clarity. It must avoid complicated semantics and confusing methodology. The standards should deal with the principle of costing and provide guidance to members in the matter of attestation of cost statements.

**Operating Procedure:** The Institute has adopted an elaborate and participative approach for developing standards. The data is collected from various sources and an 'exposure draft' is first drawn. This is circulated to the members of the Institute for their comments within a specified time. Besides accounting institutes of standing, industry associations such as chambers of commerce and government bodies are also invited to comment. Due weightage is given to all the above before they are pronounced as standards, and the effective date is mentioned.

The CAS consists of an explanatory part which covers its scope, topic covered, and the need for standardization. It will discuss the methodology adopted and will be in the nature of a prelude to the standard and recommendatory in tone. The actual standard is given in the operative part which will be precise in nature and provide specific directions. A reading of the standards explains the depth into which the CASB has gone to provide the standards.

**Contents of the Indian CAS:** The CAS has a specific structure to facilitate easy reading. It also provides for uniformity and is as follows:

1. **Introduction:** Consists of brief details about the topic and its role in the cost statements.
2. **Objectives:** Provides the basic objective which has necessitated framing of the standard.
3. **Scope:** Details the scope of the standard.
4. **Definitions:** Explains the terminology used.
5. **Principles:** Elaborates the principles applicable for the various components.

6. **Assignment of costs and revenue:** Highlights the basis of assignment of costs and the relevant cost accounting principles behind such assignment.

7. **Presentation:** Contains the main standard which is generally followed for certification purposes.

8. **Disclosure:** Discusses the detail disclosures which are required to add objectivity in the use of the standard.

9. **Application guidance** (including formats/records to facilitate computation of costs): This is a general portion dealing with the optional methods that may be followed and contains explanations on the terms used in the standard.

**Coverage:** The ICWAI proposes to come out with 39 standards under the following two categories:

(a) Components of cost

(b) Cost accounting methodology and procedures

The detailed list of these is given in Annexure 2. The services sector is emerging as a distinct component of the Indian economy. Hence, developing cost accounting standards for the services sector becomes an important responsibility. However, as this is an emerging area, the CASB proposes to prepare a conceptual document for the services sector giving the basic architecture for framing cost accounting standards in this sector.

The current status of the various CAS issued and exposure drafts circulated is as shown in Table A.

**Table A**   Cost Accounting Standards

| Cost Accounting Standards | | | |
|---|---|---|---|
| **CAS No.** | **Title** | **Objective** | **Useful for** |
| CAS1(Final) | Classification of cost | For preparation of cost statements | Assessment of excise duty and other taxes, anti-dumping measures, transfer pricing, etc. |
| CAS2(Final) | Capacity determination | For determination of capacity | Proper allocation, apportionment, and absorption of cost |
| CAS3(Final) | Overheads | For collection, allocation, apportionment, and absorption of overheads | Determining cost of products, services, or activities |
| CAS4(Final) | Cost of production for captive consumption | To determine the assessable value of excisable goods used for captive consumption. | Determining cost of products, services, or activities |

*(Contd.)*

| CAS5(Final) | Average (equalized) cost of transportation | To determine averaged/ equalized transportation cost | Calculating the amount of deduction from assessable value of excisable goods, freight subsidy, insurance claim valuation, etc |
|---|---|---|---|
| CAS6(Draft) | Arm's length price | For computation of arm's length price | Determining arm's length price for transactions between related parties |
| CAS7(Final) | Material cost | To bring uniformity and consistency in the principles and methods of determining the material cost with reasonable accuracy in an economically feasible manner | Applicable to all cost statements which require measurement, assignment, classification, and presentation of material costs. To be followed in all cost statements requiring assurance including attestation |
| CAS8(Draft) | Employee cost | To bring uniformity and consistency in the principles & methods of determining the employee cost with reasonable accuracy | Applicable to cost statements which require classification, measurement, assignment, presentation, and disclosure of employee cost, including those requiring attestation |
| CAS9(Draft) | Cost of utilities | To bring uniformity and consistency in the principles & methods of determining the cost of utilities with reasonable accuracy | Applicable to cost statements which require classification, measurement, assignment, presentation, and disclosure of cost of utilities, including those requiring attestation |
| CAS11(Draft) | Direct expenses | To bring uniformity and consistency in the principles and methods of determining the direct expenses with reasonable accuracy | Applicable to cost statements which require classification, measurement, assignment, presentation and disclosure of direct expenses, including those requiring attestation |
| CAS12(Draft) | Packing material cost | To bring uniformity and consistency in the principles and methods of determining the packing material cost with reasonable accuracy | Applicable to cost statements which require classification, measurement, assignment, presentation, and disclosure of packing material cost, including those requiring attestation |

*Source:* www.icwai.org

## ANNEXURES

### Annexure 1  Operating Procedure for Preparation of Standards

The ICWAI's CAS1 provides the procedure for preparation of standards.

They are quoted from the Institute's website and are as follows:

• Organizing and initiating discussion and deliberation at the national level to identify the areas/topics in respect of which needs for standards are felt.

• Generating information on all alternative cost accounting practices in respect of selected practices.

• Preparation of drafts on standard cost accounting practices in respect of chosen areas/topics in cost accounting and circulate it to the members of the Institute, national accounting institutes, and other end user bodies, such as industry associations, chambers of commerce and industry, government bodies, etc.

• Allowing sufficient time for consideration and comments on the exposure draft.

• Pronouncement of the exposure draft as 'standard' after giving due consideration to the suggestions and modifications generated on the circulated exposure drafts from such individuals and agencies.

• Fixing a date for the standard to be effective.

• Propagating and generating acceptance and commitment to follow the 'standards' prescribed by CASB.

• Revising the 'standards' once issued, if dictated by the environment, government, legal authority, and other situations.

### Annexure 2  Proposed Indian Cost Accounting Standards

The CASB of the ICWAI proposes to come out with 39 standards.

**A. Components of cost**

1. Materials
2. Salaries and wages
3. Direct expenses
4. Transportation costs
5. Utilities
6. Service department expenses
7. Repairs and maintenance
8. Costs of packing—primary and secondary
9. Production/operation overheads

10. Pollution control expenses
11. Administrative overheads
12. Head/corporate office overheads
13. Selling overheads
14. Distribution overheads
15. Depreciation
16. Amortization
17. Royalty, technical know-how, and intellectual property charges
18. Research and development expenses
19. Quality control expenses
20. Interest and borrowing costs
21. Treatment of revenue for cost statements
    (including treatment of government grants, subsidies, and incentives in cost accounts)

## B. Cost accounting methodology and procedures

22. Classification of cost
23. Presentation of the cost statements
24. Identification and recognition of cost centres
25. Capacity determination
26. Valuation of captive consumption
27. Stock valuation
28. Cost variances
29. Costs of conversion
30. Determination of arm's length price
31. Joint product and by-product costs
32. Determination of average transportation cost
33. Reconciliation of cost and financial statements
34. Shared services costs, including outsourcing
35. Profit centres and reportable segments under cost reporting
36. Return on capital employed
37. Predatory pricing
38. Non-cost income and expenses
39. Capital assets manufactured in-house

*Acknowledgements*

Assistance and guidance by Mr M. Gopalakrishnan, Chairman, Cost Accounting Standard Board of ICWAI-2008-09.

# Costing in Government and Not-for-profit Organizations

The accounting and costing functions in the government and the not-for-profit sectors differ from those in commercial organizations due to the difference in their focus of operations. These entities are interested in welfare activities and hence their bottom line is not profits as such.

However, accounting functions which deal with recording transactions, keeping financial and costing records, analysing the information, and applying it in a systematic manner for decision-making continue to be important for measuring the performance in the above sectors. Hence, organizations have to keep proper records to track their transactions. It helps to access the information regarding the entity's performance and the measures to be taken for betterment and improving performance.

## Costing in Government

Governments are welfare-oriented institutions. Spending is their primary action. Hence, public expenditure management (PEM) becomes a major concern in the governmental system. They need costing data for the following purposes:

1. To determine the cost of services provided to the public, for example, health, education, etc.
2. To levy user charges for amenities provided. This includes various civic amenities, such as water supply, electricity, health services, etc. While profit may not be the motive, user charges are calculated for cost recovery. Within this overall principle, differential rates can be charged for specific usage. Usually, concessions are given for agriculture and to the poorer sections of society. Hence, the entities should know the cost of the services.
3. Privatization is the accepted economic policy of many governments in the post-globalization. This requires knowledge of the cost of various activities which are transferred from the public sector.

Governments take the role of regulatory authorities for privatized services, such as banking, insurance, telecom, roads, ports, and other infrastructural and utility services. These agencies can be effective only if they have a good knowledge of the cost of the services provided.

4. Governments undertake new projects at various levels, often involving the latest technology. The projects have to be meticulously budgeted so that funds can be allocated appropriately. This requires a good grasp of capital budgeting. Other modern tools, such as target costing, activity-based costing, and similar tools come into the picture while making estimates.

5. Liberalization has gained momentum in the twentieth century. Foreign direct investments (FDIs) are allowed in a number of sectors. Governments, however, carefully monitor such investments in order to support local institutions. They need a good knowledge of the internal and external 'value-chain analyses' to arrive at the right decisions.

6. There are quite a few products under 'administered pricing', both in the industrial and agricultural sectors. The prices of these commodities are fixed by the government in the public interest. Hence, a good grasp of cost accounting would be needed for price fixation.

7. Government agencies in production areas (e.g., defence production, electricity, housing for the poor, etc.) do keep detailed cost records for various activities. They are also adopting evolving tools and techniques to modernize the cost data.

The government sector today is under increasing pressure to improve its governance measures under the welfare state concept. Public platforms are created to discuss how the government funds are spent. In advanced countries, performance measurement techniques are rigidly applied. The balanced scorecard is a tool by which the performance measures of the various functional departments are integrated. The use of this is becoming increasingly popular in the third world countries. Singapore has developed scorecards for some of its departments, such as prison services and subordinate courts. In the latter case, three basic goals, namely, community, organizational, and employee perspectives with various performance measures under each scorecard have been developed (Niven 2003).

The New Zealand government has been the forerunner in developing various managerial accounting initiatives. While analysing a proposal, governments generally look at the investment in terms of the projected results. While this is simpler, it denies the opportunity for looking at the options. The existing costing tools provide sound bases for comparing a proposal vis-à-vis the existing state of affairs, as well as reviewing the various options available.

It adopts the method of cost-benefit analyses to estimate the uses of its projects to the citizens and society. In this method, the expenditures and benefits are assigned costs and values in monetary units. Extensive costing techniques are used to make future forecasts of the benefits of various projects in relation to the expenditure incurred on them.

The various steps adopted by governments are shown as a flowchart in Fig. A.

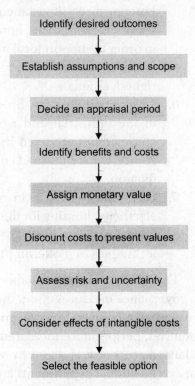

**Fig. A**   Cost-benefit analysis

In the above process three major cost/financial activities are performed:

(a) All costs and benefits are quantified by adopting acceptable norms.
(b) The cost and benefits are then expressed in monetary terms.
(c) The monetary values are discounted to the present values by adopting standard norms.

Investments by governments are huge and the benefits are often social in nature. Hence, quantification is not a very easy process and certain assumptions are required. Sunk costs are avoided in such processes. Current government practices often err by considering sunk costs which can vitiate proper comparisons.

The New Zealand government has developed the marginal costing techniques in budgeting. This is relevant while calculating the economic benefits. For example, an over-bridge could result in significant savings in the marginal operating costs of maintaining alternative routes. In such cases average operating costs are not very relevant.

In US, cost accounting is used fairly extensively and some costing standards have been developed. This enables the government to estimate programme costs with a fine degree of precision. The opportunity cost concept is adopted and the costs of alternative methods are calculated.

The public expenditure management has a very high focus on disclosing the costs of various activities and welfare measures, not only in absolute but also in relative terms. The budgetary process also adopts various costing techniques and tools to decide the allocations under various heads of account.

## Cost Accounting in Not-for-profit Organizations

Not-for-profit organizations are created for specific welfare activities, and vary in size and geographic span. Their accounting details are fairly simple and consist of revenue and expenditure transactions. Records are maintained mainly for budget creation which is the planning activity for balancing the monetary resources for them. Proper showcasing of the flow of funds instils confidence in the working of the institution (Granof 2007).

In not-for-profit organizations the accounting and budgeting are independent of changes in the financial scenario of other companies and institutions, as they are autonomous and have no worries of beating competition. Unlike in business entities, profits are never held as a determining head (Table A). The costs of operation of schemes and activities are taken as the criteria to determine the expenditures without any profit margins. The generation of surplus is less important as most of their activities are done without expectation of returns. The social cost and advantage are more definable parameters to determine the extent of channelization of funds and the benefits derived from per unit of expenditure made for social utilization.

**Table A** Difference between Accounting in Business Firms and Not-for-Profit Organizations

| Sl. No. | Business firms | Not-for-profit firms |
|---------|----------------|----------------------|
| 1. | Profit focus | Welfare focus |
| 2. | Market-oriented | No concern of competition |
| 3. | Revenue drives expenditure | Expenditure drives revenue |
| 4. | Economic targets | Social objectives |
| 5. | Owners equity-based | No distinct ownership interests |

The participants in not-for-profit organizations take note of the principles on which the budget is prepared to establish the credibility of the operations of the organization. Accounting details help them to decide whether the funds sufficiently meet their operations.

It also provides a basis for the annual auditing norms and helps access the lawful progression of money issues in the internal records of the organization.

In not-for-profit organizations, there are no demand and supply relations between the revenue generated and the expenditure incurred. Fluctuations in revenues are not directly connected to the services and their operations. Thus, the conventional information regarding revenues and expenditure cannot help decipher the underlying relations of demand and supply.

Another notable feature is that of capital assets. The investments in assets neither produce revenue nor reduce expenditure for the entity. Thus, they have significant bearings on the accounting heads, not from a commercial but from a social point of view. The concept of return on investments (ROI) does not hold good in this context.

## Need for Cost Accounting in Not-for-profit Organizations

The need for accounting and financial reporting in any not-for-profit organization arises due to the following reasons:

1. **To check adherence with law:** The participants want proof that the funds flowing in and out of the organization are not being misappropriated. This instils confidence in the operations of the organization.
2. **To measure efficiency:** The ability of the firm to meet its goals and targets measures its efficiency. The more efficient a firm is, the better will be its services.
3. **To facilitate comparison:** The participants and members need assurance that the budgets are being appropriated in accordance with the needs of the organization. Keeping accounts helps to

develop records which enable comparisons between the proposed budgetary norms, and the ones implemented.

4. **Estimate of finances:** Members need to analyse the financial condition of the organization to undertake its proceedings and determine the future course of actions. The fiscal conditions help foresee the changes in the near future.

5. **To levy charges for goods and services:** Some not-for-profit organizations make rural handicrafts and agricultural produce, and even market them. In such cases, the costing records become inevitable.

6. **Funded projects:** Donors who fund specific projects may ask for details of the cost of activities. This involves using the tools of capital budgeting, etc. Sometimes specific activity-wise cost sheets are required.

It can thus be seen that costing and managerial accounting are needed under different circumstances for the not-for-profit entities.

# References

## Chapter 1

Asquer, Albert 2003, 'In for a Penne', *Financial Management*, March.

Atkinson, Anthony A., Robert S. Kaplan, and S. Mark Young 2004, *Management Accounting*, Pearson Education, Delhi, p. 3.

Clinton, B. Douglas and Sally Webber 2004, 'RCA at Clopay', *Strategic Finance*, pp. 21–26, October.

Hiromoto, T. 1988, 'Another Hidden Edge: Japanese Management Accounting', *Harvard Business Review*, pp. 22–25, July–August.

Hopper, Trevor et al. 2003, 'The State They are in', *Financial Management*, pp. 14–19, June.

Horngren, C.T., Srikant M. Datar, and George Foster 2003, *Cost Accounting: A Managerial Emphasis*, 11th edition, Pearson Education Pvt. Ltd, New Delhi, p. 8.

Ijiri, Yuri 1975, *Theory of Accounting Measurement*, American Accounting Association, Sarasota and Ijiri, Yuri 1983, 'On the Accountability Based Concepts in Finance and Accounting', *Journal of Accounting and Public Policy*, Vol. 2, No. 2.

Jackson, Paul, David Tinius, and William White 1990, *Luca Paciolli: Unsung Hero of Renaissance*, South West Publishing, Cincinnati.

Krumwiede, Kip R. 2005, 'Rewards and Realities of German Cost Accounting,' *Strategic Finance*, Vol. 86, Issue 10, p. 27, April.

Larson, Robert K. and Sara York Kenny 1995, 'An Empirical Analysis of International Accounting Standards, Equity Markets, Economic Growth in Developing Countries', *Journal of International Financial Management and Accounting*, Vol. 6, No. 2.

Mattessich, Richard 2000, *The Legacy of Accountancy and Accounting Thought of Ancient Period in the Middle East (800 BC–200 BC) and Ancient Hindu India (300 BC)*, Garland Publishing Inc. New York.

May, Robert G. and Gary Sudem 1995, 'Research in Accounting Policy', in Bloom, Robert and Peter Elgers (eds), *Foundations of Accounting Theory and Policy*, The Dryden Press, Fort Worth, p. 19 and Mwita, John Isac 2000, 'Performance Management Model', *International Journal of Public Administration*, Vol. 13, No.1, pp. 19–37.

Rajan, Raghuram G. and Luigi Zingales 2000, 'Which Capitalism? Lessons from the East Asian Crisis', in Stern, Joel M. and Donald Chew Jr (eds), *The Revolution in Corporate Finance*, 4th edition, Blackwell Publishing House, London.

Saxena, V.K. and C.D. Vashist 2000, *Cost Audit and Management Audit*, Revised edition, Sultan Ahmed, Delhi.

Sekhar, R.C. 2002, *Ethical Choices in Business*, 2nd edition, Sage, New Delhi, p. 128.

Todman, J.C. 1922, 'The Necessity for Scientific Costing', *Cost Accountant*, 1-179-183 quoted in Boyns, Trevor, Mark Mathews, and John Richard Edwards 2004, 'The Development of Costing in the British Chemical Industry', c1870–c1940, *Accounting and Business Research*, Vol. 34, No. 1, pp. 3–24.

http://www.icai.org/rsource/C_state_audit_accou.html

## Chapter 2

Altman, Edward I 1993, *Corporate Financial Disaster and Bankruptcy*, 2nd edition, John Wiley and Sons, New York.

Hindustan Unilever Limited Report 2004, p. 12.

Hindustan Unilever Limited Report on 'Accounts', 2004, p. F 42.

International Labour Organization, 1991, *How to Read a Balance Sheet*, 2nd revised edition, Geneva.

May, Robert G. and Gary Sudem 1995, 'Research in Accounting Policy', in Bloom, Robert and Peter Elgers (eds), *Foundations of Accounting Theory and Policy*, The Dryden Press, Fort Worth, p. 19 and Mwita, John Isac 2000, 'Performance Management Model', *International Journal of Public Administration*, Vol. 13, No.1, pp. 19–37.

Sverige, Chris 2004, 'The Parmalat Scandal; Europe's Ten-billion Euro Black Hole', World Socialist website accessed on 6 January 2004.

Vasudevan, S. 2005, 'Gaps in the Cash Flow', *Business Line*, 4 April.

## Chapter 3

Anshen, Melville 1965, 'The Programme Budget in Operation, in Novak, David (ed.) *Program Analysis and Federal Government*, Harvard University Press, Boston, p. 358.

Atkinson, Anthony A., Robert S. Kaplan, and S. Mark Young 2004, *Management Accounting*, Pearson Education, Delhi, p. 64.

Horngren, C.T., Srikant M. Datar, and George Foster 2003, *Cost Accounting: A Managerial Emphasis*, 11th edition, Pearson Education Pvt. Ltd, New Delhi, p. 34.

Lucey T. 2002, *Costing*, ELST Publishers, London, p. 11.

Nadani, K.K. 2000, *Implementing Tally 5.4*, BBP Publishers, New Delhi, p. 107.

Shillinglaw, Gordon 1971, *Cost Accounting Analysis and Control*, D.B. Tarporewalla (republished from Richard Irwin and Co.), Mumbai, p. 26.

## Chapter 4

Horngren, C.T., Srikant M. Datar, and George Foster 2003, *Cost Accounting: A Managerial Emphasis*, 11th edition, Pearson Education Pvt. Ltd, New Delhi.

## Chapter 5

Horngren, C.T., Srikant M. Datar, and George Foster 2003, *Cost Accounting: A Managerial Emphasis*, 11th edition, Pearson Education Pvt. Ltd, New Delhi, pp. 96–97.

Owler, L.W.J. and J.L. Brown 1978, *Wheldon's Cost Accounting and Costing Methods*, 14th edition, English Language Book Society, p. 332.

## Chapter 6

Atkinson, Anthony A., Robert S. Kaplan, and S. Mark Young 2004, *Management Accounting*, Pearson Education, Delhi.

Blankley, Alan I. 2000, 'Hyperion Activity-based Management Software: A Tool for Analysing Cost and Operational Processes', *CPA Journal*, Vol. 70, Issue 5, May.

Clinton, Douglas and Sally Webber 2004, 'RCA at Clopay', *Strategic Finance*, October.

Compton, Ted R. 1996, 'Implementing Activity-based Costing', *CPA Journal*, Vol. 66, Issue 3.

Dhavale, Dileep 1989, 'Product Costing in Flexible Manufacturing Systems', *Journal of Management Accounting Research*, pp. 66–89, Fall.

Failing, R.G., J. Janzen, and L. Blevins 1988, 'Improving Productivity through Work Measurements: A Co-operative Approach', American Institute of Certified Public Accountants (AICPA), New York.

Horngren, C.T., Srikant M. Datar, and George Foster 2003, *Cost Accounting: A Managerial Emphasis*, 11th edition, Pearson Education Pvt. Ltd, New Delhi, p. 137.

Kaplan, Robert S. 1983, 'Measuring Manufacturing Performance: A New Challenge for Managerial Accounting Research', *The Accounting Review*, pp. 686–705, October.

Kaplan, Robert S. and Steven R. Anderson 2004, 'Time-driven Activity-based Costing', *Harvard Business Review*, pp. 131–137, November.

Krumwiede, Kip R. 2005, 'Rewards and Realities of German Costing', *Strategic Finance*, April.

Shields, Michael, Chee N. Chew, Yushido Kato, and Ya Nakagama 1991, 'Management Accounting Patterns in US and Japan: Comparative Survey', *Journal of International Financial Management and Accounting*, Vol. 3, Issue 1, pp. 62–77.

Smith, Carl S. 2005, 'Going for GPK', *Strategic Finance*, April.

Stammerjohan, William W. 2001, 'Marriage of ABC and Traditional Costing Techniques', *Management Accounting Quarterly*, Fall.

## Chapter 7

Anthony, Robert and Vijay Govindrajan 2003, *Management Control Systems*, 10th edition, Tata McGraw-Hill, New Delhi, p. 374.

Atkinson, Anthony A., Robert S. Kaplan, and S. Mark Young 2003, *Management Accounting*, 3rd edition, Pearson Education, Delhi, p. 472.

Ginsburg, Sigmund G. 1981, 'Navigating Budgets, Games People Play', pp. 89–91, September, quoted by Atkinson et al. 2003, pp. 478–479.

Hansen, Don R. and Maryanne, M. Mowen, *Cost Management*, 4th edition, Thomson Asia Ltd, Singapore, p. 356.

Hopwood, A.G. 1972, 'An Empirical Study of the Role of Accounting in Performance', *Journal of Accounting Research*, Vol. 10, pp. 156–182.

Horngren, C.T., Srikant M. Datar, and George Foster 2003, *Cost Accounting: A Managerial Emphasis*, 11th edition, Pearson Education Pvt. Ltd, New Delhi.

Mintzberg, Henry, Bruce Ahlstrand, and Joseph Lampal 1998, *Strategy Safari*, Free Press.

Otley, David 1978, 'Budget Use and Managerial Performance', *Journal of Accounting Research*, Vol. 16, Issue 1, p. 122, Spring.

Owler, L.W.J. and J.L. Brown 1978, *Wheldon's Cost Accounting and Costing Methods*, 14th edition, English Language Book Society, pp. 485, 521, 668.

Report of a speech by Jack Welch in *Chicago Business Line*, 10 November 2005.

Robert, Simons 2000, *Performance Measurement and Control Systems for Implementing Strategy*, Prentice Hall, New Jersey.

Sekhar, R.C. 2005, *Management Control Systems: Text and Cases*, Tata McGraw-Hill, New Delhi.

Smith, Vernon 2003, 'Constructivist and Ecological Rationality', *American Economic Review*, Vol. 93, No. III, pp. 485–508, June.

Williamson, Oliver 1975, *Markets and Hierarchies*, Free Press, New York.

## Chapter 8

Chartered Institute of Management Accountants (CIMA) 2000, *Terminology of Costing*, 10th edition.

Cheatham, Carole B. and Leo R. Cheatham 1996, 'Redesigning Cost System: Is Standard Costing Obsolete?' *Accounting Horizons*, Vol. 10, No. 4, pp. 23–31, December.

Horngren, C.T., Srikant M. Datar, and George Foster 2003, *Cost Accounting: A Managerial Emphasis*, 11th edition, Pearson Education Pvt. Ltd, New Delhi, pp. 228–230.

Kroll, Karen M. 2004, 'The Lowdown on Lean Accounting', *Journal of Accountancy*, Vol. 198, Issue 1, pp. 63–67, July.

Lucey, T. 2002, *Costing*, 6th edition, Educational Low Priced Sponsored Texts, pp. 417–418, 422, and 469.

## Chapter 9

Bureau of Mines, 1993, *A Cost Comparison of Selected Mines from Australia, South Africa and United States of America*, Special publication.

Chartered Institute of Management 2000, *Terminology of Management Accounting*.

Cook, Sarah 1995, *Practical Benchmarking–A Manager's Guide to Creating Competitive Advantage*, Kogan Page, London.

Cooper, Robert, Scot Edgettt, and Elko Kleinschmidt 2000, 'Best Marking Best PPD Practices', and Iabocuci, Dawn and Christie Nordhelm, 'Creative Benchmarking', *Harvard Business Review*, November–December.

Denrell, Jerker 2005, 'Selection Bias and the Perils of Benchmarking', *Harvard Business Review*, April.

Govindarajan, Vijay and Chris Trimble 2005, '10 Rules for Strategic Innovators from Idea to Execution', Harvard Business School Press.

Harrington, H.J. and J.H. Harrington 1995, *High Performance Benchmarking–20 Steps to Success*, McGraw-Hill, New York, p. 37.

Horngren, C.T., Srikant M. Datar, and George Foster 2003, *Cost Accounting: A Managerial Emphasis*, 11th edition, Pearson Education Pvt. Ltd, New Delhi, p. 418.

Lenin, V.I. 1965, *Collected Works*, Vol. 39, Progress Publishers, Moscow, p. 152.

Lucey, T. 2002, *Costing*, 6th edition, Educational Low Priced Sponsored Texts.

Mishra, R.K. and K. Nadagopal 1991, 'Effieciency through Organisational Innovation in Passenger Road Transport: The Case of Tamil Nadu Transport Undertaking', *Management Review*, Vol. 16, No. 1, pp. 3–32, January–December.

Report in Coal International Mining and Quary World, May/June 2001.

Sakurai, M. 1989, 'Target Costing and How to Use It, *Journal of Cost Management for the Manufacturing Industries*, Vol. III, No. 2, and Ansari, S. and J. Bell 1996, *Target Costing—The Next Frontier in Strategic Management*, Homewood Ill, Irwin.

Schwaber, B. and Mauryl Wright, 'Standard Procedures—Telecommunications', EDN, 11 November 2004, Supplement 2, Vol. 49, pp. 19–26.

Sekhar, R.C. 1979, 'Manpower Wastage and Control in Industry—New Thoughts and Statistical Methods', *Management Accountant*.

Singh, Sanjay Kumar, 'Technical Characteristics of and Efficiency of the Indian State Road Transport Undertakings', *Indian Journal of Transport Management*, Vol. 24, Issue 8, pp. 533–543.

Sowman, Collin 2005, 'Buy the Kit', *Plant Managers Journal*, Vol. 32, June.

*The Hindu*, 11 August 2003.

Tucker, Frances Gaither, Seymour Zivan, and Robert Camp 1987, 'How to Measure Yourself against the Best, *Harvard Business Review*, January–February.

http://mizopwd.nic.n, accessed on 4 March 2006.

## Chapter 10

Burton, Lipman 1981, How to Control and Reduce Inventory, Prentice Hall.

Chris, Durden, L.G. Hassel, and David Upton 1999, 'Cost Accounting and Performance Measurement in

Just-in-time Production Environment', *Asia Pacific Journal of Management*, Vol. 16, pp. 11–125.

Hector, Anton 1964, *The Budgetary Process and Management Control* in Bonini, Charles P., R. Jaedicke, and Harvey Wagner, *Management Control: New Directions in Research*, McGraw-Hill, New York.

Horngren, C.T., Srikant M. Datar, and George Foster 2003, *Cost Accounting: A Managerial Emphasis*, 11th edition, Pearson Education Pvt. Ltd, New Delhi.

*International Accounting Standards: A Practical Guide*, 2nd edition, The World Bank, 2001.

Lee, H., V. Padmanabhan, and S. Whang 1997, 'The Bullwhip Effect in Supply Chains', *Sloan Management Review*, Spring.

Levin, Richard R., Chares Kirpatrick, and David Rubin 1982, *Quantitative Approaches to Management*, 5th edition, McGraw-Hill, New Delhi.

Srivastava, U.K., G.V. Shenoy, and S.C. Sharma 1983, *Quantitative Techniques for Managerial Decisions*, Wiley Eastern, p. 614.

*Taxmans Master Guide to Income Tax*, 1996, Taxman Publications, New Delhi, p. 4.264.

The Institute of Chartered Accountant of India, *Compendium of Statement of Standards of Accounting Including International Accounting Standards*, 3rd edition, New Delhi.

US Internal Revenue Code 1-471-11.

Vohra, N.D. 2000, *Qauntitative Techiniques in Management*, Tata McGraw-Hill, pp. 414–416.

Williams, Jan R. 1997, *GAAP Guide*, Harcourt Brace, New York.

## Chapter 11

Atkinson, Anthony A., Robert S. Kaplan, and S. Mark Young 2004, *Management Accounting*, 4th edition, Pearson Education, Delhi, p. 191.

Dantzig, George B. 1963, *Linear Programming*, Princeton University Press.

Doran, Desmond 2005, 'Automobile Industry and Trade', *International Journal Physical Distribution and Logistics Management*, Vol. 35, Issue 9, pp. 64–663 and Sawyer, Christopher 2005, Yesterday Today Tomorrow AD&P, December available at www.auofielfguide.com

Gregory, Geoffrey 1988, *Decision Analysis*, Pitman Publishing, London, pp. 3–4.

Horngren, C.T., Srikant M. Datar, and George Foster 2003, *Cost Accounting: A Managerial Emphasis*, 11th edition, Pearson Education Pvt. Ltd, New Delhi.

Lucey, T. 2002, *Costing*, 6th edition, Educational Low Priced Sponsored Texts, p. 314.

Sekhar, R.C. 2005, *Management Control Systems: Text and Cases*, Tata McGraw-Hill, New Delhi, pp. 76–77.

## Chapter 12

Hildebrandt, David H. and R. Lyman Ott 1998, *Statistical Thinking for Managers*, International Thomson, Singapore, p. 502.

Horngren, C.T., Srikant M. Datar, and George Foster 2003, *Cost Accounting: A Managerial Emphasis*, 11th edition, Pearson Education Pvt. Ltd, New Delhi.

Joye, M. and P. Blayney 1991, 'Cost Accounting and Management Practices in Australian Manufacturing Companies—Survey Results', Accounting Research Centre, University of Sydney, cited in Horngren, C.T., Srikant M. Datar, and George Foster 2003, *Cost Accounting: A Managerial Emphasis*, 11th edition, Pearson Education Pvt. Ltd, New Delhi, p. 328.

Salomon, Ban and Joseph Schofer 1991, 'Transportation and Telecommujications Costs–Some Implications of Geographical Scale', *The Annals of Regional Science*, 25:19-29, Springer Verlag.

Sastry, D.V.S. 2006, 'Life Insurance Expenses–An Economic Analysis Proceedings of 8th Global Conference of Actuaries', Mumbai, 10–11 March 2006.

## Chapter 13

Anjol, Miguel F., Russel C. Cheng, and Christine S.M. Curie 2005, 'Optimal Pricing of Perishable Products', *European Journal of Operation Research*, Vol. 166, Issue 1, pp. 246–254, October.

Calvani, Terry 1989, 'Predatory Pricing: An Analysis', Competition Bureau Canada, March.

Hirshleifer, Jack 1985, *Price Theory and Application*, Prentice Hall, New Delhi, p. 191.

Horngren, C.T., Srikant M. Datar, and George Foster 2003, *Cost Accounting: A Managerial Emphasis*, 11th edition, Pearson Education Pvt. Ltd, New Delhi, p. 424.

Kimes, Sheryl E. and Jochen Wirtz 2003, 'Has Revenue Management Become Acceptable?' *Journal of Service Research*, Vol. 6, No. 2, pp. 125–135, November.

Kotler, Philip 2003, *Marketing Management*, 11th edition, Prentice Hall, New Delhi.

Porter, Michael 1985, *Competitive Advantage: Creating Superior Performance*, Free Press, Simon and Schuster.

Porter, Michael E. 1996, 'What is Strategy?' *Harvard Business Review*, November–December.

Samuelson, P.A. and W.D. Nordhaus 1992, *Economics*, McGraw-Hill, New York.

Tellis, Gerard J. 1986, 'Beyond the Many Faces of Price: An Integration of Pricing Strategies, *Journal of Marketing*, Vol. 50, October, pp. 146–160.

US Economic Intelligence Report, Index of Economic Freedom 2006, Heritage Foundation, *Wall Street Journal*.

Venkatesh, M.R. 2004, 'Predatory Pricing: Lessons for India Inc', *Business Line*, 20 October.

## Chapter 15

Anthony, Robert and Vijay Govindrajan 2007, *Management Control Systems*, Tata McGraw-Hill, New Delhi, pp. 1–7.

Creelman, James and Naresh Makhijani 2005, *Mastering Business in Asia*, John Wiley & Sons Inc, New Jersey, p. 37.

Drucker, Peter 1993, *Managing in a Time of Great Change*, TT Dutton, New York, p. 118.

Kaplan, Robert S. and David Norton 1996, *The Balanced Scorecard: Translating Strategy into Action*, Harvard Business School Press, pp. 32, 149.

Kaplan, Robert S. and David Norton 2000, *The Strategy Focused Organization: How Balanced Scorecard Companies Thrive in the New Business Environment*, Harvard Business School Press, 2001. pp. 1–5.

Kaplan, Robert S. and David Norton 2004, *Strategy Maps: Converting Intangible Assets into Tangible Outcomes*, Harvard Business School Press.

Kaplan, Robert S. and David Norton 2006, *Alignment: Using the Balanced Scorecard to Create Corporate Synergies*, Harvard Business School Press.

Maciariello, J.A. and C.J. Kirby 1999, *Management Control Systems*, Prentice-Hall of India Private Limited, New Delhi, p. 2.

Niven, Paul R. 2002, *Balanced Scorecard Step by Step: Maximizing Performance and Maintaining Results*, John Wiley & Sons Inc, New Jersey, p. 51.

Niven, Paul R. 2003, *Balanced Scorecard Step by Step for Government and Not for Profit Agencies*, John Wiley & Sons Inc, New Jersey, p. 29.

Sekhar, R.C. 2006, *Management Control Systems: Text and Cases*, Tata McGraw-Hill, New Delhi, p. 3.

## Appendices

Gopalakrishanan, M., 'Framework of Cost Accounting Standards–the Revised Approach', *Management Accountant Journal*.

Granof, H. Michael 2007, *Government and Not-for-profit Accounting: Concepts and Principles*, John Wiley & Sons Inc, New Jersey, USA.

Niven, Paul R. 2003, *Balanced Scorecard Step by Step for Government and Not for Profit Agencies*, John Wiley & Sons Inc, New Jersey.

http://fast.faa.gov/archive/v1198/pguide/98-30C14.htm, accessed on 5 December 2009.

http://www.icwai.org/icwai/docs/CASB/icwaicas1.pdf, accessed on 6 March 2009.

http://www.icwai.org/icwai/docs/CASB/icwaicas1.pdf, accessed on 6 March 2009.

http://www.treasury.govt.nz/publications/guidance/costbenefitanalyses/primer/cba-primer-v, accessed on 6 March 2009.

# Index

# Related Titles

## DERIVATIVES AND RISK MANAGEMENT
### [9780198064343]

**Rajiv Srivastava**, *Indian Institute of Foreign Trade, New Delhi*

*Derivatives and Risk Management* is a comprehensive textbook designed for management students specializing in finance. Besides providing extensive coverage of the core concepts of the subject, it includes numerous solved examples and worked-out Excel sheets to provide students with a practical orientation towards financial derivatives.

### Key Features

- Discusses recent additions in the Indian derivative market such as currency futures and interest rate futures
- Discusses the latest Accounting Standard AS 30 along with suitable examples to highlight accounting for derivatives under different circumstances

## MERGERS AND ACQUISITIONS
### [9780198064510]

**Rajinder S. Arora**, *Future Innoversity, Mumbai;* **Kavita Shetty**, *Management Consultant;* **Sharad R. Kale**, *Director, CKP Co-operative Bank Ltd, Mumbai*

*Mergers and Acquisitions* is a comprehensive textbook designed for students of postgraduate management programmes. It explores the core concepts of M&As and the challenges encountered in implementing them.

### Key Features

- Discusses numerous types of takeover strategies and over 30 takeover defences
- Provides plenty of solved numerical problems, examples, case studies, and exhibits

## PROJECT MANAGEMENT AND APPRAISAL
### [9780198066903]

**Sitangshu Khatua**, *Jyotirmoy School of Business, Kolkata*

*Project Management and Appraisal* is a comprehensive textbook specially designed to meet the requirements of postgraduate management students specializing in finance and operations. It aims to familiarize the readers with the core concepts of project management, including its planning, execution, control, and appraisal.

### Key Features

- Explains the concept of financial appraisal in project scanning and selection including the fundamentals of capital budgeting decisions comprehensively
- Includes recent examples such as the Tata Nano, Delhi Metro, and Nayachar chemical hub projects

## Other Related Titles

- 9780198072072  *Financial Management 2/e,* Srivastava and Misra
- 9780195695250  *Management Accounting,* Shah